EXODUS FROM THE ALAMO

Exodus
from the
Alamo
THE ANATOMY OF THE
LAST STAND MYTH

By
PHILLIP THOMAS TUCKER

CASEMATE
Philadelphia & Newbury

Published in the United States of America and Great Britain in 2009 by
CASEMATE PUBLISHERS
908 Darby Road, Havertown, PA 19083
and
17 Cheap Street, Newbury RG14 5DD

Copyright 2010 © Phillip Thomas Tucker

ISBN 978-1-932033-93-9

Cataloging-in-publication data is available from the Library of Congress
and the British Library.

10 9 8 7 6 5 4 3 2 1

Printed and bound in the United States of America.

For a complete list of Casemate titles please contact:

CASEMATE PUBLISHERS (US)
Telephone (610) 853-9131, Fax (610) 853-9146
E-mail: casemate@casematepublishing.com

CASEMATE PUBLISHERS (UK)
Telephone (01635) 231091, Fax (01635) 41619
E-mail: casemate-uk@casematepublishing.co.uk

Contents

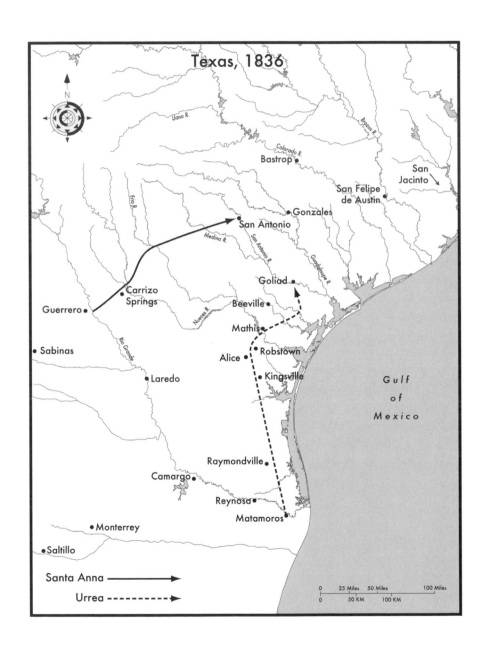

Texas, 1836

Llano R.

Colorado R.

Bastrop

San Jacinto

San Felipe
de Austin

Frio R.

Gonzales

San Antonio

Medina R.

Carrizo
Springs

Goliad

San Antonio R.

Guadalupe R.

Guerrero

Beeville

Nueces R.

Mathis

Sabinas

Alice

Robstown

Rio Grande

Laredo

Kingsville

Gulf
of
Mexico

Raymondville

Camargo

Reynosa

Matamoros

Monterrey

Saltillo

Santa Anna ⟶

Urrea ⤏

0   25 Miles   50 Miles   100 Miles
0   50 KM   100 KM

Preface

Almost everything Americans have been taught, or think they know, about the Alamo is not only wrong, it is nearly the antithesis of what really occurred on the early morning of March 6, 1836. The battle that was fought has been embellished over many decades through story, song, and cinema, resulting in a mythical Alamo and an enduring romantic legend based upon a simplistic morality of play of good versus evil. This myth is founded on the notion of a heroic "last stand," which allegedly resulted in the deaths of hundreds of attackers as every defender of the garrison fought at his post, dying to the last man in a deliberate act of self-sacrifice. New documents, especially Mexican and Tejano, and careful historical research definitively prove that the real truth is far more complex, and that this traditional heart of the Alamo story is largely false, based on fantasy rather than historical fact.

The cornerstone of the Alamo myth has been so powerful that it has never been seriously investigated. Moreover, no historian has ever asked a relatively simple, elementary question: If all of the defenders were killed, then how do we really know what happened at the Alamo? Even more importantly, was there actually a heroic last stand? And how can we know what in fact happened, since the fighting inside the Alamo took place in predawn darkness? This unusual twin handicap—the lack of garrison survivors and a struggle that occurred in blackness—has made it unusually difficult to ascertain tactical developments and the course of the fighting, leaving historians and writers guessing at the details.

A fresh, unbiased perspective on the Alamo is especially long overdue, given that current stereotypes and myths about the battle were created by writers and journalists long before professional historians explored the subject. Serious investigation requires us to cut through multiple layers of romantic fantasy and literally start from scratch. Almost everything that we know about the Alamo has been based on third-hand, inaccurate, and biased accounts from highly questionable sources; moreover, these tell the story from primarily one side—the side that possessed a vested interest in laying the foundation for the mythical last stand. Most importantly, it is necessary to understand and reconstruct the struggle realistically, in its setting of predawn darkness, yet previous books on the subject have portrayed the contest as a set-piece battle fought in broad daylight.

Nor was the Alamo an epic clash of strategic importance, as it is so commonly portrayed. One undeniable truth about the events came directly from Mexico's top military commander. The commander-in-chief of the Army of Operations, General Antonio Lopez de Santa Anna, baldly, almost nonchalantly, described the struggle to possess the Alamo as "but a small affair." American historians have nevertheless ignored such views because they contradict the romantic lore surrounding the Alamo, and especially call into question the fabled last stand.

One of the great iconic, though widely misunderstood, stories of American history, the Alamo has been distinguished by a seemingly endless number of enduring mysteries. Few concrete facts, including even the exact number of Alamo defenders, can be verified with a degree of certainty. The Alamo myth is firmly entrenched as a piece of national folklore, while ironically, the true story of what actually occurred lies hidden in newly found or previously overlooked accounts by forgotten Mexican soldiers and officers. Other better known accounts by Santa Anna's men, including those that magnified the resistance and the defenders' heroism to reflect favorably upon themselves and to portray events as a battle rather than a massacre, have proven less reliable.

In truth, the Alamo was a surprisingly brief clash of arms. Only later did admiring generations of Americans invent the myth of a great heroic battle in order to obscure a host of ugly, embarrassing realities. These included the fact that consecutive commanders of the Alamo needlessly lost the tiny garrison instead of withdrawing earlier to fight another day. The ensuing disaster was reinvented as a noble self-sacrifice in the cause to save Texas, ignoring the obvious fact that those leaders foolishly chose to fight and die at a place of no strategic importance and for no gain.

Rather than mounting a climactic last stand with a well-organized, tenacious defense, a totally unprepared Alamo garrison was caught in its sleep by a well-conceived night attack that took the men completely by surprise. The garrison consisted of citizen-soldiers with little of the military training or experience of their well-honed Mexican opponents, whose attack left them so stunned that they never recovered from the shock. This initial tactical success ensured that hundreds of veteran Mexican troops had already reached the Alamo's walls *before* garrison members were aroused from their sleeping quarters, negating any chance of an organized, effective, or sustained defense.

More of a rout and a slaughter than a battle in the traditional sense, the struggle for the Alamo lasted only about twenty minutes, making it one of the shortest armed clashes in American military history for an iconic battle. Winning one of his easiest victories, Santa Anna's success was ensured when his troops swiftly breached the walls. This tactical success directly contradicts the portrayal of the event as an epic conventional battle, as envisioned by generations of historians and writers, Hollywood filmmakers, painters and artists. Common depictions show the entire garrison aligned in their assigned defensive positions along the walls, manning their blazing artillery, offering organized resistance, and inflicting terrible damage on the attackers under daylight conditions. However, new evidence from the most reliable sources shows that even the heroic last stand immediately in front of the Alamo church and its famous facade is a romantic embellishment. Instead, a large percentage—perhaps the majority—of the garrison fled in multiple attempts to escape the slaughter, trying to quit the compound before the battle inside had ended. No unified, solid defense took place along the walls that dark, early morning. In fact, the defense of the perimeter was so relatively weak that some of the hardest fighting very likely occurred outside the garrison walls, resulting in the deaths of more defenders outside than inside the Alamo.

Given that the Alamo was a fortified position possessing a formidable arsenal of around twenty artillery pieces, the Alamo's defense was surprisingly weak, if not feeble. Had there been a tenacious last stand, Mexican casualties would have been far greater. They were, in fact, less than three hundred—and a very high percentage, perhaps even a majority, of these resulted from fratricide, or what we now call "friendly fire." Contrary to legend, the greatest advantage for Santa Anna's attackers was not their numbers, which American and Texas historians have endlessly inflated, just as they have inflated Mexican casualties, but the stealthy, surprise attack that worked exceedingly well under the cover of the late winter night.

The truth of this "skirmish," as one Mexican participant called it, not only differs from the myth, it directly contradicts it. Fought in a remote location more than a hundred miles from the United States border, the struggle at the Alamo was both unnecessary and pointless in overall strategic terms. The Mexican Army had only to bypass the Alamo to reach the east Texas settlements, or march north up the coast of the Gulf of Mexico to outflank the frontier outpost at San Antonio. Alternatively, Santa Anna could have conducted a lengthier siege to reap a victory over the tiny garrison, making an assault entirely unnecessary.

Why were Mexican casualties in a frontal assault on a fortified position so relatively low? Why have generations of historians failed to recognize or acknowledge the truth about the Alamo, refusing to face obvious facts? Why have so many reliable Mexican primary accounts, which coincide with official Mexican Army reports, been overlooked and ignored for so long? Investigation of such key questions not only requires us to strip away the long-accepted romantic mythology of the Alamo, but to re-examine the deeply ingrained racial and cultural stereotypes on which it has been founded.

First and foremost, Texas and American historians, writers, and journalists have conveniently overlooked the best Mexican sources contemporary to the battle. These are more reliable, accurate, and authentic than the controversial Jose Enrique de la Pena diary-turned-memoir, which contains post-1836 Alamo-related material—including the story of David Crockett's execution—from a host of other published sources, including Mexican and United States newspapers. In addition to being romantic and melodramatic, de la Pena's work is largely a post-war political document whose notorious anti-Santa Anna sentiments make some of its descriptions and conclusions highly suspect. These include an exaggeration of both casualties and resistance, in order to demonstrate Santa Anna's folly in launching an assault.

Problems with the de la Pena memoir, which essentially appeared out of nowhere in Mexico City in 1955, exemplify the need to carefully re-evaluate primary documents to separate fact from fiction by comparing them with more reliable accounts. Unfortunately, many Anglo and Mexican accounts have been equally biased and self-serving. Comparative readings are especially necessary for Anglo accounts, but they are also essential for other questionable Mexican sources in addition to de la Pena. My own attempt to separate fact from fiction has sometimes meant that I have accepted parts of accounts that previous historians have dismissed, while I have sometimes discounted elements of others that were formerly considered as definitive.

For the most part, American and Texas nationalist historians have casually dismissed the truth of the Alamo because the legend has always shored up a sense of Anglo-Celtic superiority over a mixed-race people of Catholic faith. The romantic mythology of the heroic last stand has long provided a comforting sense of cultural, racial, and national self-satisfaction for many Americans. Over time, the sacrifice of the Alamo garrison has popularly come to represent the inevitable price of national expansion, progress, and the spread of civilization. Generations of Americans have thus viewed the garrison's slaughter as not only a necessary, but also an understandable sacrifice for a greater good.

In an ironic twist of historical memory, latecoming interlopers, primarily from the United States, of the Mexican province of Texas were transformed into the righteous defenders of a white bastion of Anglo-Celtic civilization, while Mexican troops, who were defending their republic's home soil in a struggle that was but one chapter of a larger Mexican civil war, were tarnished as godless invaders and barbarians. This mythical Alamo justified a sense of moral supremacy and righteous entitlement to Texas at the expense of the Indian, Tejano, and Mexican people. The mythical last stand, in which a relatively small band of white heroes defy the mixed-race horde, demonstrated the moral, racial, and cultural superiority over Latino brown people needed to justify and rationalize one of the greatest land grabs in American history.

The military incompetence and glaring failures at every level of the Texas political and military leadership that doomed the Alamo garrison to unnecessary slaughter have been largely dismissed. Instead, "history" has given us a hallowed trio of Alamo leaders—David Crockett, William Barret Travis, and James Bowie—transformed into immortal figures. Meanwhile, mythmakers have turned a relatively minor military action and first-rate fiasco, stemming from folly and a long list of mistakes, into a great *moral* victory which supposedly bought the time for General Sam Houston to rally Texas and defeat Santa Anna at San Jacinto, thereby winning Texas independence.

The myth of a tenacious last stand against overwhelming odds has hidden the truth of a mass exodus of defenders from the Alamo, obscuring the facts to create larger-than-life heroes in a "glorious cause." However, xenophobic feeling ran extremely high on both sides of the old Spanish mission's walls: the Texas Revolution was very much a religious war, pitting Catholicism against Protestantism. It was also very much a racial war, pitting Anglo-Celts against a mixed-race people of color. For those in the Alamo, too, the struggle was as much about the right to retain and purchase slaves as the right to an independent republic, because Mexico had long before abolished slavery. This belief in white "superiority" caused the defenders to underestimate the combat prowess and motivations of Mexican leaders of all ranks, as well as the high quality of the common Mexican *soldado*; in parallel, the overconfidence of the Alamo leadership fueled a host of fatal delusions, including a gross overestimation of the garrison's combat capabilities and the Alamo's defensive strength.

Handicapped by military inexperience and a lack of training and discipline, the Anglo-Celts, especially the leadership in San Antonio, failed to win the Tejano population—the garrison's principal source of manpower—over to their side because of prevailing cultural prejudice and racial arrogance. And yet the defenders are still commonly portrayed as fighting from enlightened, egalitarian principles alone, in a confrontation between democracy and dictatorship, or good versus evil. For historical, military, and cultural reasons, it is high time to re-examine this crucial chapter in Texan and American history in an effort to discern the facts and expose the prejudices and stereotypes behind the persistent myth of the Alamo's last stand.

The author is indebted to many people who made invaluable contributions to this work, and I thank them all for kind assistance. Most of all, I would like to thank the good people at Casemate Publishing, including Tara Lichterman and especially Steven Smith, who contributed so much.

Dr. Phillip Thomas Tucker
Washington, D.C.
January 2010

Foreword

By Antonio "Tony" Zavaleta, Ph.D.

The book you are about to read is a critically important and timely contribution to our understanding of the Texan identity, its formation, and Texans in general. Dr. Phillip Thomas Tucker's *Exodus from the Alamo* courageously re-examines what happened in March 1836 at the battle for the famous mission turned-fort. The Alamo is the national metaphor of Texas and defines not only the state but Texans themselves, yet this identity has been clouded for over 170 years by historical jingoism. Uncovering the truth about the defenders' "last stand" is critical to understanding who we are; making the truth available for popular consumption and educational purposes, we address the even more important need to unite our diverse population.

Over at least the course of the last 30 years, our knowledge and understanding of the facts surrounding one of the most famous battles in our nation's history has come into question. *Exodus from the Alamo* gives us the freshest look at the whys and wherefores of what really happened in the run-up to the battle, and the most thought-provoking analysis of the conflict to date. Dr. Tucker revisits all of the important personalities high and low in an exceptionally well-documented and informative discussion that allows us for the first time to view new information and interpretation through the eyes of Mexican combatants and community eyewitnesses.

Why is this important? A new generation of Texans is being educated in the state's public school system with textbooks that continue to omit and obfuscate the facts. Today's young Texans will face societal and economic challenges like no other generation. In order to prevail in the global economy, the next generation of Texans must forge a personal and societal identity that unites them through a mutual and

xiii

respected history. The prosperity of our state lies in our ability to merge the diverse ethnic tapestry of today into the Texas of tomorrow.

Reared in south Texas in the second half of the 20th century, I was taught historical reality as it was forged by our Texas founders. The original history of Texas was written by historical giants whose legacy and importance lives on. Their accounts of what happened at the Alamo in 1836, and in that great swath of land between San Antonio and the Rio Grande River, literally shaped south Texas and influenced the outcome of national politics. In the nine years between 1836 and 1845, Texas become a republic and the American army invaded the nation of Mexico. Three years later, in 1848, the national boundary was established at the Rio Grande and Mexico lost half of her landmass. Today, 163 years later, the United States government seeks to build a wall along the country's southern border, failing to place this ill-conceived act in historical perspective and to realize its future implications.

The Republic of Texas was followed by statehood; its legacy provided my generation, born in the 1950s, with both a national and a cultural identity, a road map that leads us through life in Texas today. We were taught that Anglo Texans were heroes and nation builders; but our Mexican ancestors were no less capable as nation builders when in 1840 they founded the Republic of Rio Grande, carved out of the three northeastern-most Mexican states. The cultural and historical realities of Texans and Mexicans have underpinnings on both sides of the Rio Grande. So who are we: Texans, Mexicans, Americans, Mexican-Americans, or simply Tejanos?

Raised by a mother from California, I took years to feel comfortable in my cultural skin, to understand and come to terms with my mixed and confused identity. My father's parents heralded from prominent Spanish land grant families that traced their heritage across the Spanish province of Coahuila y Tejas long before there was a State of Texas. Even today, the family stretches out along the Camino Real from Saltillo, the capital of Coahuila, to Ciudad Mier on the Rio Grande, northward through the brush country to San Antonio de Bejar and southward to Matamoros on the Gulf Coast. As a kid of "mixed blood," I was at the same time neither Mexican nor American. Torn between historical realities, I made a conscious decision to embrace both as compatible, and Texas-Mexican history supported this decision.

As I was growing up in the 1950s, my hometown of Brownsville was widely divided along racial and ethnic lines that had to be carefully navigated. Coming from a well-known family was good, but not speaking Spanish was bad. We grew to become Texans molded by the stereotypes and misrepresentations of a one-sided historical drama in which there were only two clear sides, winners and losers. As a schoolboy I learned that the Alamo was important and my father took me to see it. We were descended from the side that carried the field of battle in 1836, but had lost in almost every way since then. I had family who served in the Matamoros Battalion at the Alamo, but I was told I shouldn't talk about it because people wouldn't understand. Santa Anna was a family friend of my ancestors, but I was told I shouldn't be proud of that either.

Dr. Tucker's work helps to explain something my grandfather once told me: *Diles quien eres*—tell them who you are. It took forty years for me to truly understand what he meant. His advice was an essential requirement in his day, but was it still so in mine? It was. People have long been identified by their lineage. Do you come from people who ride horses, a *caballero*, or are you a person who walks, a *peon*? Your status and the opportunities that life can bring are often determined by personal history.

This is why Dr. Tucker's book is so important. An entire generation of young Texans is searching for meaning in their lives, just as I did. They are looking for their cultural and historical roots. They want to know where they fit. The sensible choice is to recognize and honor both Mexican and Texas history as "the history of Texas." Throughout my life, and for reasons I do not totally understand, I have revered history with all its intrigue and failings. I comprehend how things that happened in the past affect people's lives in the present. History must be constantly called into question and it must be constantly corrected. Dr. Tucker corrects history, and that is serious business in Texas.

This is all the more true because the books used in Texas classrooms continue to limit the contributions of our Hispanic and African-American heroes. When I first learned about the Battle of the Alamo, I believed the account that I read to be true. I was taught that the cowardly Mexican army slaughtered the heroic Texans. But from my perspective, I asked, what had the Mexican army and their leader done wrong in protecting their nation? The response was always the same: the Mexicans were responsible for the deaths of Texas heroes. Must the Texas Hispanic population of the twenty-first century still be held responsible for the deaths of Texas heroes in the nineteenth?

Simply stated, I don't want children today to experience the conflict that I experienced. While I do not believe that racism and classism are now actively taught and practiced in Texas classrooms, the icon of the Alamo nevertheless continues as our most important symbol of modern Texas. Its very definition divides us into good and bad, Anglos and Mexicans. Texas mythology is in fact the present and future of Texas. Texans of Mexican descent continue to be stereotyped as treacherous, as cheaters, and as back stabbers, while the heroes of the Alamo are revered as exemplars. What message does this send to our youth?

Early Texas historians spun their historical narrative of the events of March 1836 for purposes of the past that have no place in the future. We are taught that the evil despot Santa Anna with a huge professional army marched across south Texas, arriving in San Antonio to stage a bloody siege of the old Spanish mission and its defenders. It was there that the valiant and righteous Texans made their last stand in defense of the rights of Texas and its citizens. Bowie, Travis, and the gentleman from Tennessee, Congressman Crockett, defended the Alamo to the death for the glory of Texas. Cry, "Remember the Alamo."

But what exactly are we supposed to remember? What really happened? The new information validated and analyzed in Dr. Tucker's work means we can no longer "remember" or believe what we were told by earlier generations. I exonerate early Texas historians from any mistakes in their original descriptions of the siege and the deaths of the defenders. These early chronicles served the important purpose of building symbols for modern Texas and Texans' identity. But *Exodus from the Alamo* breaks new ground and supports a new history of Texas that began to emerge decades ago, and remarkably includes the contributions of Latinos, African-Americans, Native Americans, and others.

Dr. Tucker examines the real story behind the premier symbol of Texas, a symbol that defines who we are and who we are not, providing us with new information and a fresh way of interpreting the Battle of the Alamo. Additional information most certainly will continue to emerge, the merits of which we must closely examine if we are to continue the task of correcting the historical record for the benefit of future generations. As courageous as it is insightful, *Exodus from the Alamo* is a major contribution to the goal of teaching us about the value of inclusion, as opposed to the divisions of exclusion.

Introduction:
From Fact to Fantasy

The defenders' ghastly deaths at the Alamo were anything but glorious. Yet the events that took place at that rundown Spanish mission have evolved into an heroic legend, becoming an enduring feature of the American imagination and national memory quite unlike any other historical event. Even though America always loves a winner, the Alamo is a rare example of an American love affair with a loser, an affair that is largely based on the romantic appeal of the mythical last stand.

The Western world has long embraced the ancient Battle of Thermopylae as one of its primary example of heroism, honoring the small band of free men who stood up to Persian hordes who possessed no democratic political tradition. So, too, Americans have long viewed the Alamo as a great symbolic showdown between liberty and slavery, freedom-loving men versus a tyrant, and republicanism versus dictatorship. But what if such traditional interpretations of the Alamo were in fact false, making a mockery of the Spartan heroes of Thermopylae?

The Spartans' last stand served as the model for the Alamo legend, transforming an instance of relatively weak resistance and massacre into a classic New World myth of an epic battle that represented the epitome of self-sacrifice. Not long after the fighting on March 6, 1836 concluded, the nickname "The Thermopylae of Texas" was bestowed upon the Alamo by those who knew relatively little, or nothing, of the actual facts of the struggle. From their readings in ancient history, enthusiastic mythmakers actually understood far more about the battle of Thermopylae in 480 B.C. than they knew about what transpired at the Alamo. Americans, then and today, have identified with the heroism of King Leonidas' band of 300 Spartans, who fought to the bitter end

1

against Xerxes' Persian warriors, defending the key Pass of Thermopylae armed with iron discipline, bronze shields, light armor, and long spears. Here, the king's forces, including Leonidas himself, died to the last man in a legitimate, heroic stand against the odds in the hope of saving Greece. All perished beside their comrades in the Spartan sacrificial tradition—an ancient cultural value not shared, or even imaginable, by the ragtag members of the Alamo garrison.

How did the last stand myth begin in the first place? On the one hand, it sprung from the overactive imaginations of a good many journalists across the United States. On the other, it grew in large part out of a popular work, published almost immediately after the fall of the Alamo, which quickly reached all corners of the country: *Colonel Crockett's Exploits and Adventures in Texas* by Richard Penn Smith. This well-received book was supposedly based on David Crockett's "authentic diary," which a Mexican officer was said to have taken after Crockett's death. Needless to say, Crockett had nothing whatsoever to do with its authorship.

The first book to recount the story of the Alamo, this immensely popular work appeared only eight weeks after the fort fell; most recently, it was republished in 2003 to capitalize on the release of the Disney Company's major film, "The Alamo."

The spring 1836 publication of *Crockett's Exploits* was calculated to sensationalize the Alamo tragedy that had just occurred. The book was an entirely bogus account, written as Smith sat comfortably in his Philadelphia home more than 1,000 miles northeast of San Antonio. One of the most important fictions of Smith's hyperbolic efforts is the claim that Lt. Col. William Barret Travis exhorted the Alamo garrison that "in case the enemy should carry the fort," they should "fight to the last gasp, and render their victory even more serious to them than to us." Travis' words as imagined by Smith provided an early, though completely unsubstantiated, foundation for the last stand legend, despite many contemporary newspaper accounts to the contrary. Unfortunately, Smith's work of fiction (and a bad one at that) has long been treated as an authentic document, broadening the emotional and psychological appeal of the heroic last stand concept.

But no one was more responsible for the creation of the myth than early Alamo "historian" William P. Zuber. To counter rumors that some defenders, including Crockett, had surrendered, while others hid instead of fighting to the bitter end, he solidified the central notion that not a single garrison member "escaped or surrendered, or tried to do so; but every man of them died fighting." Smith's and Zuber's unsubstantiated accounts were later picked up and further embellished by Hollywood scriptwriters, distorting reality out of all proportion. More surprisingly, the scholarly and academic community nevertheless still faithfully adheres to the core tenants of the Alamo myth that arose from these early fictionalized renditions.

By contrast, the account written by General Antonio Lopez de Santa Anna, who had a penchant for embellishment second to none when it came to his own military successes, shows he was sorely disappointed by the brief, inconsequential fighting. Fully realizing that the Alamo was strategically unimportant, he desired to reap a victory for political effect, and to sow the seeds of terror into remaining Texas forces while impressing his own public in Mexico City. Instead, according to his own account, his minor victory at the Alamo deprived him of glory.

This lack of glory also explains why there have never been any paintings or romantic illustrations of the last stand from the Mexican side. Had the Mexicans encountered resistance on an epic scale, they certainly would have celebrated their great victory in dramatic visual form to display their own heroism against such gallant opposition. Instead, and initially like the Texans themselves, the Republic of Mexico and its people, including the *soldados* who fought there, simply forgot about the Alamo, as if it was an insignificant footnote to history.

A close look at the sources, both old and newly discovered, and especially the most reliable accounts of Mexican officers and men, reveals a mass exodus by the Alamo garrison. Taken alone, a single Mexican account of an exodus from the Alamo would be highly suspect, but more than half a dozen reliable Mexican accounts exist. Almost all mutually support and reinforce each other, and assert that a large percentage of the Alamo garrison attempted to escape.

General Vincente Filisola, Santa Anna's second in command, summarized the pervasive sense of disillusionment among the victors: "In our opinion [the engagement at the Alamo] was useless." And, while historians have grossly inflated the number of Mexican losses, the Filisola document shows that most of the attackers' losses were due to fratricide. In truth, the Mexicans lost far fewer men than traditional accounts have claimed: in all, less than three hundred casualties. The large percentage of fraticidal casualties means that the entire Alamo garrison may have killed or wounded barely a hundred of their opponents during Santa Anna's assault. Nor were there ever three distinct attacks; as Santa Anna lamented to Captain Fernando Urriza, his young, competent aide-de-camp: "It was but a small affair."

Most defenders were neither rugged frontiersmen nor seasoned veterans, thus largely incapable of a tenacious defense, especially when caught in their sleep by a surprise attack. Most of them died at the hands of pursuing Mexican cavalry and lancers on the open prairie outside the walls while fleeing the deathtrap. Quite simply, for the young men and boys at the Alamo, there was no glory on the early morning of March 6, 1836. Unfortunately, none were left to tell the tale of their bitter defeat in military reports, diaries, letters, or memoirs.

Today, *A Time to Stand* by Walter Lord continues to be considered the best work about the Alamo, even though it was published more than forty years ago. The dismal scholarly track record of Alamo historiography perhaps can be best explained by the continued acceptance of the 1931 doctoral dissertation by Amelia W. Williams, *A Critical Study of the Siege of The Alamo and of the Personnel and Its Defenders*, written almost a century after the event. Not surprisingly, this dissertation merely reflected the ultra-conservative and traditional rural, cultural, and racial biases prevalent in nineteenth century Texas, and more generally across America. In a bizarre historical paradox, the Alamo's reputation has been created by the losers, while the victors' versions—the accounts by eyewitness survivors, including those written shortly after the battle—have remained largely occulted.

The private journal of Colonel Juan Nepomuceno Almonte, which describes in detail what he witnessed at the Alamo, is another excellent case in point. Almonte was an erudite man educated in the United States, whose journal was discovered after his capture at the Battle of San Jacinto in April 1836. This was then translated and published in the *New York Herald* the following June. As the *Herald*'s editors candidly admitted in the introduction of the journal's fourth installment on June 27, 1836, "Almonte's account differs very differently from what we received at the time through the Texas papers." Almonte's journal states: "The enemy attempted in vain to fly [from the Alamo], but they were overtaken and put to the sword," by Mexican cavalry positioned outside the walls.

Almonte personally witnessed only a single flight of Alamo defenders. Other eyewitness accounts testify to the flight of several large groups as well as individuals, whose numbers taken together comprise the *majority* of the defenders. This exodus of so many soldiers doomed the relatively few men still fighting inside the walls, especially in the Long Barracks, the infirmary, and the church, sealing their fate and hastening the Alamo's fall. Another excellent source of information is a rare battle report by General Joaquin Ramirez y Sesma, which was discovered in the Secretaria de la Defensa, Archivo Historico, Militar, in Mexico City. Sesma's report, written on March 11, 1836, only five days after the fall of the Alamo, corroborates other Mexican sources. It describes multiple escape attempts by a large number of defenders, around 120 men in primarily three separate groups.

In an ironic twist, the mass exodus of so many Alamo defenders now actually places David Crockett's alleged death by execution on Santa Anna's orders—the most heated Alamo controversy—in a much more heroic light. If, indeed, the de la Pena account and other sources are correct in this regard, the fact that Crockett was among the minority of soldiers who remained inside the fort speaks for itself.

The flight of so many Alamo defenders does not disparage their characters or courage, although it does erode the heroic romance of their deaths. The Alamo garrison had little chance to resist in any organized manner during the predawn attack that literally caught them asleep. Mexicans began pouring over the top and through a small gate at the north wall "like sheep" in the early morning darkness. Fleeing the deathtrap was not only the instinctive response of ill-fated soldiers; it was also tactically sound and the only realistic alternative under the circumstances.

Mostly boys and young men in the prime of life, these citizen-soldiers possessed promising futures and looked forward to claiming thousands of prime Texas acres. The last thing these men—mostly volunteers from the United States—desired was to throw it all away for the largely apathetic Texians who had failed to reinforce the Alamo, or to give their lives for a factionalized Texas government that had abandoned them. Fleeing in an attempt to survive and fight another day under more favorable circumstances was a much more rational choice. And we should also not forget that once the Mexicans had breached the walls, further resistance inside the Alamo could not have been sustained and made no tactical sense.

The distortion of the Alamo story is in many ways comparable to the way Custer's Last Stand was distorted for the occasion of the United States Centennial on June 25, 1876. America needed heroes and especially martyrs to glorify. For generations, the white, or Anglo, version of the death of Custer and his men was the only received account. Once again, a first-rate military disaster was turned into a moral victory in terms of a myth of self-sacrifice.

Both the Alamo and the Little Big Horn fiascos were almost incomprehensible to white America, for they shook entrenched racial and cultural assumptions about a God-given superiority over other peoples. Accounts of the struggle at the Little Big Horn in the Montana Territory, which took place forty years after the Alamo fell, repeated the romanticized story of a valiant last stand of white troops heroically battling a darker, "inferior" race against impossible odds. In both cases, American illustrators and painters, in the notable absence of either Indian or Mexican pictorial representations, left an enduring dramatic imprint on the American popular consciousness. Fantasies replaced mundane facts because no white soldiers of either contest survived to describe what actually occurred.

Much like the story of the Alamo, the Anglo version of Custer's Last Stand was readily received, even though it ran directly contrary to eyewitness accounts of Native Americans. Again, too, the words of Little Big Horn's victors were conveniently overlooked, because they challenged the idealized heroics that immortalized the defenders' courage and demonstrated racial and cultural superiority, despite the fact that they had lost the battle.

Corroborating a good many Native American eyewitness and oral accounts, recent archeological studies of the Little Big Horn battlefield have shed light on what really happened that hot June day in Montana, including the fact that white troopers offered relatively little resistance and sometimes panicked, paving the way to annihilation. New research derived from archeological evidence taken from the battlefield has proven that the romantic account of Custer's last stand was in fact false: moreover, Native American losses, like those among Mexicans at the Alamo, were surprisingly low.

Many contemporaries viewed the fall of the Alamo as the most shameful episode of the entire Texas Revolution. Sickened by what he saw as a complete waste of life on March 6, one angry Texas newspaperman caught the representative mood. Writing with disgust that the Alamo garrison was needlessly "sacrificed by the cold neglect" of the Texians, he cast "shame" on "the hundreds and thousands that might have gone up to the rescue—but they would not." If a parallel between real life events is to be made, the drama of the Alamo—both inside and outside its walls—was grotesque and hideous, comparable not to Thermopylae but to the sad slaughter of the Southern Cheyenne at Wounded Knee, South Dakota, in late December 1890.

Soldiers on both sides at the Alamo fought and died for what they believed to be right, but these motivations deserve fresh reassessment and closer scrutiny, especially in regard to the complexities of slavery. While the Alamo defenders struggled for possession of a bountiful land yet owned by another people, the Mexicans fought on behalf of a far more equitable republic than the United States. Most Texans were either slave-owners or aspired to become so in order to fully exploit the promises of the land. These sentiments were certainly common to both the pantheon of Alamo leaders such as Travis and Bowie and the rank-and-file soldiers.

Today we can no longer afford to ignore that the Alamo defenders were on the wrong side of the slavery issue, while the Mexicans were in the right. Mexico, unlike the United States, had abolished slavery in 1829, more than half a decade before the Alamo battle. One of the crucial reasons why the Texans revolted against Mexico in 1835 was to maintain the constitutional safeguards of the Mexican Constitution of 1824, which protected slavery, as did the United States Constitution on which it was modeled.

Given the United States' current wars in Afghanistan and Iraq, it all the more behooves us to better understand our past and present military involvements, especially in foreign lands. We must endeavor to strip away as many myths and prejudices as possible in order to more correctly see ourselves, as well as the opposing viewpoints of other lands, cultures, and ethnic groups, especially those of our enemies. Any nation that indulges in the self-serving process of sentimentalizing and glorifying military disasters to bolster cultural and racial fantasies only makes itself more vulnerable to folly in the future. Even today, a host of fresh, practical lessons can yet be glimpsed from the Alamo disaster, if we can only understand the timeless factors that led to the debacle.

In 1836, as today, the greatest military sin of all is hubris: to thoroughly underestimate an enemy, while overestimating one's own capabilities, righteousness, and combat prowess. History has proven that such misperceptions often stem from erroneous beliefs rooted in fantasies of racial and cultural superiority. Dismissal or ignorance of the intelligence, determination, organizational skill, cultural pride, sense of personal and national honor, and war capabilities of a foreign opponent in his own homeland has long been a guaranteed formula for inevitable military disasters like the Alamo. Today, as in March 1836, truth is often the first casualty of war, and history's lessons linger.

I

Golden Prizes:
Land and Slaves

Emphasizing the moral importance of the mythical last stand, the traditional view of the Alamo defenders maintained that they were the highest minded of freedom fighters who died in defense of liberty, republican government, and democratic principles in their struggle against a tyrannical, abusive Mexico. In order to uphold the time-honored stereotype of freedom fighters, historians have minimized the fact that many soldiers of 1835–36 were either slave-owners, defenders of the right to maintain slavery, or aspired to own slaves one day. This historical situation is especially ironic in light of today's politically correct environment in the United States. Confederate soldiers who fought for the same republican principles as guaranteed by the United States Constitution, including the right to own slaves, have been condemned as politically incorrect, if not immoral, while the Alamo defenders have been transformed into revered saints deserving of endless hero worship.

Paradoxically, in rewriting history, the victors of the Civil War gained the luxury of tainting the Confederacy's bid for independence because of slavery, while San Jacinto's winners benefited from the fact that the importance of slavery to their cause was forgotten. In Alamo and Texas Revolution historiography, therefore, the importance of slavery has been virtually a non-factor. In most books and films about the Alamo, the issue has been noticeably absent, almost as if the institution did not exist in Texas at the time. Texas historians and textbooks have long overlooked slavery, especially in regard to the Alamo, leaving its history relatively free of the excessive "burden of Southern history."[1]

Instead of developing a "lost cause" mythology, which partially allowed white Southerners to psychologically compensate for their bitter defeat, white Texans developed an Alamo mythology. The romanticism of the Alamo and its heroes—primarily Travis, Crockett, and Bowie—obscured an ugly reality: that so many of the men who fought for Texas liberty were slave-owners at one time or another, and fought and died in part for the "peculiar institution's" defense.

From the beginning, the institution of slavery played a vital role in the earliest settlement of Anglo-Celtic Texas. No one realized slavery's importance to Texas' future prosperity more than Stephen F. Austin, the "Father of Texas." Barely ten years after the visionary from Missouri, a slave state, established the first Anglo-Celtic colony in 1821 in east Texas, with the blessing of Mexico City, he emphasized: "Texas must be a slave country [because] circumstances and unavoidable necessity compels it [and] it is the wish of the people there."[2]

Austin explained, "My object and ambition was to succeed with the enterprise and lay a foundation for the fortune of thousands." And his vast "fortune" could only be retrieved from the rich Texas soil with the assistance of thousands of men, women, and children of African descent in lifetime servitude, especially after the invention of the cotton gin and the power loom. As articulated in 1833, Austin's unshakeable pro-slavery views represented the opinions of the vast majority of Anglo-Celtic colonists in Texas. Such entrenched attitudes of settlers, mostly from the South, ensured that no single issue more separated the Mexican people and government from the colonists than slavery. The "peculiar institution" was the permanent fissure that divided the two peoples, transcending issues of economics, class, religion, race, and culture. After all, the Mexicans were a mixed-race people of Spanish and Indian blood—the *Mestizo*—including some African blood as well.

Anglo-Celtic Texas, therefore, early feared that the more racially egalitarian Mexican republic threatened slavery's vibrancy and future. Unlike United States citizens, the people of Mexico, with Indios, or Indians, in the majority, embraced an entirely different perspective of race relations. The mere concept of holding people in slavery was revolting to the people of Mexico.

Texas in the early and mid-1830s, like the South in the antebellum period, was threatened by the new realities of a changing world, including the rise of liberalism, abolitionism, and humanism, especially in Europe. Thanks to the industrial revolution and humanitarian enlightenment, slavery was a dying institution around the world, with British abolitionists leading the way in the 1830s, followed by New Englanders. But as the first Americans to settle west of Missouri, in a vast land ruled by other powers—first Spain and then Mexico—the Anglo-Celts who migrated to Texas brought no such enlightened thought with them across the Sabine, because slavery was part of Southern Anglo-Celtic culture, law, and everyday life.

Texas was an unexploited land, and in need of dramatic transformation after centuries of government neglect, Indian threats, and the lack of successful colonization by both Spain and Mexico that resulted in a low population. As a warm Mediterranean people without a forest-to-farm heritage like the American colonists, the Spanish, from the arid, mountainous lands of the Iberian Peninsula, had brought their Roman-influenced civilization with them to Mexico's arid northern frontier. Like ancient Rome, Spain's historic pattern of settlement called for establishing towns centered around churches and protected by military outposts for security against hostile native peoples.

Even though an anachronism by this time, a vibrant system of slavery was absolutely necessary for the successful economic development of Texas. Consequently, Anglo-Celtic settlers looked with apprehension south at Mexico, when the young republic officially abolished slavery, unleashing a "bolt from the sky." On September 15, 1829, President Vicente Guerrero, a successful former general during the war of independence against Spain, and in office barely six months before a coup overthrew him and ordered his execution, abolished slavery throughout Mexico. Texas would later be exempted, however. He ensured that the Mexican Constitution allowed all Mexicans—white, black, or Indian—the opportunity to hold office. Mexico's first president possessed a blend of African, Indian, and Spanish heritage.

Most significantly, Mexico's emancipation proclamation was issued more than thirty years before President Abraham Lincoln's, and not for pressing wartime reasons, unlike in the United States. The Republic of Mexico, although tarnished by a caste system, consequently possessed a proud heritage of liberty for all people, regardless of color. Slavery's death-stroke in Mexico ensured that a great chasm would be opened between Mexico and the Anglo-Celtic settlers, even though they were already considerably divided by race, culture, and politics. President Guerrero's "decree was seen in Texas by Austin and all his people, and by members of the several colonies scattered to the east, as a mortal blow to their existence; for the economy of the settlements rested upon slave labor, and ever since their foundation they had had to resist

Mexican attempts to abolish slavery by law."[3]

In late January 1830, a prophetic Captain Henry Austin wrote to his cousin from Mataromos, Mexico on the Rio Grande's south bank near the river's mouth, summarizing how Mexico's anti-slavery stance sowed the seeds of rebellion: "We have many rumors here of a revolutionary disposition in the people of Texas on account of the decree freeing all slaves in the Republic."[4] But this was not "rumor." Concerned about the "property" that formed the basis of their agricultural wealth and future prosperity, Anglo-Celtic settlers were literally up in arms against the emerging threat to slavery. Even the ever-prudent Austin, himself a slave-owner, "sternly resolved to fight for the right to hold slaves."[5]

Slavery had to be defended because few colonists doubted the undeniable truth: as voiced by the political head of San Antonio in response to the 1829 decree from Mexico City, the end of slavery would mean the inevitable destruction of Texas prosperity. After all, the economy was based primarily on cotton culture, which depended on "the aid of the robust and almost indefatigable arms of that race of the human species which is called negroes."[6]

Long before the transplanted Americans brought cotton culture from the Deep South to Texas with the Austin Colony's birth, African American slaves in and around the Tejano town of San Antonio were nothing new. The first official census of San Antonio in 1783 revealed that of the 1,248 residents of both the town of Villa de San Fernando de Béxar, the future San Antonio, and the adjacent presidio, the Presidio de San Antonio de Béxar, more than 20, both men and women, were slaves. From the earliest dates, many northern frontier communities of New Spain consisted of a racial mixture of "Spaniards, Mestizos, and Mulattos."[7]

Widespread race mixing in San Antonio was commonplace from the earliest date. By the middle of the 1700s, the three distinct classes of European-born Spaniards, Indian peasants, and black slaves had been long intermingling and procreating, both inside and outside marriage, gradually becoming one people at San Antonio. Larger numbers of mulattos from the union of Spaniards and black slaves, Mestizos from the union of Spaniards and Indians, and other "mixed- race" people were accepted as equal citizens of San Antonio with fluid upward mobility—an impossibility in the race-conscious United States.

By 1821, most of Tejano Texas was a Mestizo land. San Antonio provided a rare example of relative racial harmony as part of a Mediterranean-based way of life and vibrant Tejano culture that thrived in Mexico's north. A successful national liberation effort by a mixed-race people, Mexico's independence from Spain had naturally bestowed even greater equality on these "new" people along the northern frontier.[8] To the American colonists, even San Antonio's Tejanos therefore represented a threat to a racially restrictive Anglo-Celtic culture and social values based upon artificial barriers of color and race. The ample visible proof throughout both San Antonio and Texas of how easily widespread racial intermixing could result in a unified people from divergent races shocked newly-arrived Americans, especially migrants from the Deep South.

The obsessive fear of an abolitionist Mexico played on the historic Southern-based paranoia of the Texas colonists to a much greater extent than historians have recognized. The issues and divisions over slavery served as a primary cause of the Texas Revolution, without which there would have been no struggle for the Alamo. In analyzing the internal dynamics of that revolution, American historians have further overlooked the importance of slavery as a catalyst because of the power of the Alamo myth. Instead of focusing on slavery, most writers on the period have portrayed the Texas Revolution as a righteous struggle for freedom, emphasizing simplistic explanations.

A much more accurate view was written by Mexican historian José María Roa Bárcena, who concluded with considerable insight that "the rebellion of Texas [was] more due to the emancipation of the slaves in Mexico than to the fall of the federalist constitution of 1824."[9] Of course, this conviction—in part for which the Alamo garrison died—of the right of one race to keep another in servitude ran directly contrary to the mythical Alamo.[10] Acknowledging the fact that slavery served as a leading cause of the Texas Revolution would have diminished the lofty status of the Alamo's heroes.

First and foremost, the traditional explanations that the Alamo defenders fought and died for liberty have been much too simplistic, Anglo-centric, and one-dimensional. By far, the greatest ambition of the vast majority of Alamo's defenders was to acquire vast amounts of land. Land hunger was like a raging fever that motivated an entire generation of Americans in the 1820s and 1830s. Heady dreams of acquiring a quick fortune by easily acquiring thousands of acres of rich Texas land served as a powerful motivation. And that burning ambition of mostly lower-class men, including many who had never owned land before, went hand in hand with the institution of slavery because development of the land—cutting down trees, plowing fields, building fences, planting and harvesting crops, and so forth—was essential for successful agricultural enterprises. From the beginning, the sheer vastness of the untamed land and the seemingly boundless fertility of the soil guaranteed the critical importance of slavery in serving as the central foundation of Anglo-Celtic civilization in Texas.

North Texas and the area around San Antonio was part of the southern end of the Great Plains. Around San Antonio, this fertile region was part of a vast sea of prairie grasslands, the central plains of Texas. Beginning mostly south of the Colorado River, the sprawling prairie extended farther south, reaching almost to the Nueces River. South of the Nueces, the land became less rolling and fertile and more arid. East Texas looked much like the Deep South's lands of the Mississippi River Valley, covered in a thick, green blanket of pine forests, with fertile soil and wetlands. Blessed with abundant sunshine and a mild climate, this well-watered region west of the Sabine River, the natural dividing line between Texas and Louisiana, was an ideal cotton country eagerly sought by Southerners.

To the delight of land-hungry Americans who desired virgin lands of incomparable fertility, this majestic land of Texas was a paradise, a dream come true. Its broad meadows of bluebonnets, prairies, pine forests, dense cane-breaks often higher than a horse's head, and gently rolling hills seemed endless. Moreover, despite hundreds of years of Hispanic rule, Texas was yet undeveloped: an agricultural empire could not be created without a robust population, even if it consisted primarily of chattel labor.

Ever since the first organized Anglo-Celtic settlement sanctioned by the Mexican government in Texas, the Austin Colony settlers quite correctly "considered slavery vital to their future." Along with the terror unleashed by the raiding Apache and Comanche who had kept Hispanic migrants away from the northern frontier for generations, the absence of slavery was one key factor to explain why both Spain and Mexico had largely failed to colonize Texas, or Tejas, as it was known. For decades, Texas had merely served as a defensive buffer protecting the northern Mexico borderland as well as cosmopolitan Mexico City and the luxurious, fertile heart of the sprawling Mexican nation, the great valley of central Mexico.

The first American settlers of Austin's Colony—Mexico's initial experiment with Anglo-Celtic settlement—brought with them the most distinctive feature of southern Anglo-Celtic culture: slavery.[11] At stake was the rejuvenation of a stale economic system of the feudal world of Spanish antecedents. For the American settlers, this virtually uninhabited virgin land, distinguished by little agricultural exploitation and only modest cattle ranching and sheep herding by local Tejanos, represented a great opportunity. After three centuries of settlement, the vast expanse of Texas had a population of barely 3,000 people in the 1820s. The antiquated economic and agricultural system based upon the feudal European model was transformed by colonists bringing thousands of slaves to turn this backward region into a wealthy, productive land dominated by extensive cotton and sugar plantations.[12]

The young men and boys of the Alamo garrison were also consumed by this vision. They had recently migrated to Texas from the United States as part of the most recent wave of Anglo-Celtic settlers moving ever-farther west. Led by the restless Scotch Irish since before the American Revolution, each new generation of Americans was motivated by the dream of acquiring more land to generate wealth for a better life for themselves and their families. And this ambition of the common man of relatively little means was always the same: continue pushing west, crossing rivers, primeval forests, Indian country, and mountains, and take the inevitable risks in settling a new land. Consumed with the ever-contagious "Texas Fever," ambitious American settlers crossing the Sabine River only continued the drive ever-westward, or southwest in this case, in an historic migration, which also transformed Texas into the western frontier of slavery.

The men of the Alamo—almost wholly recent volunteers from the United States and not native Texans from the east Texas settlements—fought primarily to ensure that they would eventually take possession of thousands of acres for their military service. In October 1835, the Headquarters of the Department of Nacogdoches, the historic Tejano gateway located about halfway between San Antonio and the Louisiana line (just west of the Sabine): "Volunteers are invited to our standard. Liberal bounties of land will be given to all who will join our ranks with a good rifle and one hundred rounds of ammunition."[13]

The ambitious brother of a mountain man who roamed the Rocky Mountains in search of fur and fortune, young Charles Ferris of Buffalo, New York, was one such idealistic volunteer. He was so anxious "to be

rewarded with land in Texas" for military service that he left his pregnant wife behind in a rage of fortune-seeking fever not seen again
among Americans until the Gold Rush of 1849. A relative wrote how
Charles fled New York in haste in order to "harvest laurels (I mean
land)" in Texas. Ferris fortunately resisted his early desire to proceed to
San Antonio after reaching Texas soil, and thus, unlike the Alamo's
defenders, the native New Yorker eventually won his gamble: he survived his military service to eventually lay claim to 5,400 acres.[14]

For citizens all across the United States, the initial outbreak of open
warfare between the Texas colonists and Mexico in early October 1835
was viewed as the opportunity of a lifetime. The conflict—only part of
a larger civil war on Mexican soil—opened the doors to a flood of zealous volunteers from the United States. In the words of Tennessee-born
John Salmon Ford, of Scotch-Irish descent, one of the eager volunteers
who raced to Texas, the initial fighting of the Texas Revolution "caused
many men in the United States to turn longing eyes towards the new
land of promise."[15] But first the Alamo defenders would be forced to
fight to make good and validate their claims. If the Mexican Army was
victorious and Texas was successfully reclaimed by the mother country
during the campaign of 1836, then these optimistic young men from the
United States and Europe would gain nothing except an early grave in
a strange land—a calculated gamble lost by the Alamo garrison.

The newcomers could reap the reward of thousands of Texas acres
without ever risking their lives in battle, if Mexico City only decided not
to attempt to reclaim Texas by force. By January 1836, ironically, most
Alamo garrison members believed that the war was already over. They
were convinced that the decisive victory already won in the 1835 campaign had decided the issue once and for all, or so they hoped. During
the winter of 1835–36, consequently, these men looked forward to
claiming the land that was due them for Texas military service. They
elected to stay in San Antonio to focus on securing land claims instead
of returning to the U.S., once the "old Texian" soldiers had returned
home after the town had been captured in December 1835. Ironically,
to the soldiers stationed at the remote, frontier outpost at San Antonio,
the future never looked brighter—or so it appeared at the time.

During the winter of 1835–36, these men served in San Antonio primarily to make their ambitious dreams come true. The chance of a lifetime beckoned: two distinct economic factors—hard economic times at
home and plentiful available land in Texas—combined to prompt men

and boys from all across the United States to risk their lives in Texas military service. An agricultural decline, a reduction of exports, an influx of currency from state banks (and hence inflation), and wild land speculation (including Texas speculation in 1835), had created an economic depression in the United States.[16] Even prosperous New Orleans was shaken by the economic shock waves. Inflation soared to new heights, leading eventually to financial panic and crisis. The old economic model was on the verge of collapse and the financial fallout hit the United States especially hard in 1836. Epidemics of fatal disease, yellow fever and cholera, that swept New Orleans in 1832 and 1833 also sent thousands of migrants to the windswept plains of Texas on ships that departed the Crescent City every five days.[17]

Representing the fulfillment of the American dream during these hard times, Texas offered the most bountiful opportunity for Americans to reap the greatest natural rewards, in terms of total acreage and fertility of the soil, anywhere on the North American continent. Combining with the economic crisis in the United States, the incentive to migrate to Texas to carve out a large slice of this rich land was further promoted by official Texas policy.

Sam Houston was a former United States regular army soldier who had been wounded during General Andrew Jackson's victory over the militant Red Stick Creeks at Horseshoe Bend, Alabama. He was also a former governor of Tennessee. In early October 1835, he offered the best opportunity in North America to swiftly gain wealth when he penned an appeal at the outset of the Texas Revolution: "If volunteers from the United States will join their brethren in this section, they will receive liberal bounties of land. We have millions of acres of our best lands unchosen and unappropriated."[18] Appeals directly to United States citizens were later published in scores of leading American newspapers, such as the *New York Herald*, calling for volunteers: "The people of Texas, a small number of men [now] need your assistance. We present to you one of the most delightful countries on the face of the globe; we offer you the most liberal remuneration in land."[19]

This almost unbelievable bonanza in land in the midst of a severe economic depression especially beckoned members of the lower and middle classes across the west and south. Another alluring appeal appeared in a March 1836 issue of the same newspaper, promising that "all volunteers shall be entitled to one mile square, or 640 acres of land, to be selected out of the public domain of Texas."[20] This large amount of land especially impressed War of 1812 veterans who, as opposed to their Revolutionary forebears, had received only a paltry number of acres for their military service. When the young American nation had been on the verge of its second war with Great Britain in less than thirty years, Congress had authorized an increase in the number of regular troops, sweetening the pot of patriotism with the promise of 160 acres for wartime service.[21]

The almost unheard-of amounts of prime acreage being offered to those who signed up to fight for Texas seemed nearly unbelievable to the average American. As one United States citizen wrote with amazement: "I was offered by Texas 50,000 acres of land on going there" to serve.[22] The Texas General Council requested additional volunteers from the United States: "We invite you to our country—we have land in abundance, and it shall be liberally bestowed on you [and] every volunteer in our cause shall not only justly but generously be rewarded."[23] A journalist of a leading newspaper proclaimed, "Now is the moment for all young men, who want to create a name, and make a fortune, to bestir themselves. Go to Texas. Enroll yourselves in the brave army of [Texas] . . . A splendid country is before you. You will fight for a soil that will become your own [because Texas is] a territory equal to that of France—a soil far superior—a climate as healthy as any in the world [and all can be gained] If men will avail themselves of the tide now setting in for fame and fortune."[24] Even Tejanos could not resist the lure. As a "Texas soldier," Gregorio Esparza "was promised much land" for his service, recalled his son, who lost his father at the Alamo.[25]

The life of David Crockett, who had once been an indentured servant like so many other Scotch-Irish in early America, provides one of the best examples of the real motivations of Alamo garrison members, from top leaders to the lowest soldier in the ranks. Crockett had a lengthy track record of alternate success and failure in business and politics, and had been unable to fulfill his lofty dream of transforming himself from a hardscrabble west Tennessee farmer into a gentleman planter. He sought a quick renewal of personal fortunes by gaining large amounts of Texas land. This was the magical formula for success and almost unimaginable prosperity that was otherwise unattainable for lower and middle class Americans in the United States at this time.

Like his Scotch-Irish forefathers who had steadily pushed toward the setting sun, Crockett most of all traveled southwest to Texas in the hope of acquiring vast acreage for a new start on the Texas frontier for himself and his hard-pressed Tennessee family. Crockett was motivated by the hope of restoring his sagging personal and financial fortunes—combined with his budding political ambitions in a new Texas republic—by "staking out a very large ranch in Texas."[26] Little short of an act of desperation, his decision to "go to the wilds of Texas," as he put it in a letter at age 49, had little, if anything, to do with a struggle for liberty. Disgusted by United States partisan politics and the sudden demise of his once bright political career, he embarked on a hunting foray and scouting expedition in the autumn of 1835 to "explore" and discover east Texas and to start life anew.[27]

Like most Americans who migrated to Texas, Crockett made his decision primarily on economic grounds. He sought to escape long-existing debts and the prospect of impoverished status for the rest of his life after the abrupt end of his Congressional career. Contrary to the popular stereotype, he had gone forth with no initial intention of joining the struggle for Texas independence. With harsh economic realities continuing to hound him, Crockett decided to go to Texas much as a gambler bets on his last roll of dice—it was "the culmination of his efforts to get out of debt [because] he needed a big break and was looking for a homestead in a new country."[28]

Texas more than fulfilled Crockett's expectations. Exploring the lush woodlands, broad meadows, and grassy prairies of east Texas, he viewed a pristine, primeval wilderness. A luxurious bayou country that was well watered and heavily forested, the region around the Red River's headwaters was little short of a natural paradise, full of game, fine timber, and clear waters. Most of all, Crockett's mind was consumed with the prospect of securing a "league of land." He excitedly penned a letter to his family: "I expect in all probability to settle on the Border of the Chactaw [Choctaw] Bro [Bayou] of Red River that I have no doubt is the richest country in the world."[29]

After exploring the Red River country that left him breathless, a gleeful Crockett wrote with unbounded optimism in what would be his last letter—written on January 9, 1836 from San Augustine, barely two months before his death at the Alamo—to his oldest daughter, Margaret: "What I have seen of Texas, it is the garden spot of the world, the best land & prospects to any man to come here, and I do believe it is a fortune to any man to come here; there is a world of country to settle, it is not required to pay down for your league of land; every man is entitled to his headright of 4438 A[cres] and they may make the money to pay for it off the land."[30] Even the most impoverished American citizen or recent immigrant from the urban squalor of Europe without a penny in his pocket could own thousands of prime acres of rich Texas land. After viewing the available opportunities, Crockett enthusiastically told his family in the same letter: "I am in great hopes of making a fortune for myself and family" in Texas "by way of large land-holdings."[31]

Another incredulous Alamo defender who could hardly believe he could own so much fertile land was 27-year-old surveyor David P. Cummings of Lewistown, Pennsylvania. Writing to his father, a wealthy "canal man" and a friend of Sam Houston, Cummings sent a letter from Gonzales, Texas, just east of San Antonio, on January 20, 1836: "I have the satisfaction of beholding one of the finest countries in the world and have fully determined to locate myself in Texas."[32] The golden, once-in-a-lifetime opportunity to acquire such large amounts of Texas land was almost like winning the lottery for lower-class Americans. Clearly, U.S. citizens from Crockett to Cummings were primarily on Texas soil because of their "intention of acquiring headright certificates and of becoming the owner of a princely domain."[33] Later, from San Antonio, Cummings ecstatically penned on February 14, 1836: "I believe no country offers such strong inducements to Emigration [sic], affording all the convenieces [sic] of life that man can devise."[34]

Born in South Carolina, James Butler Bonham, a young lawyer from Montgomery, Alabama, was a founder of the volunteer military unit known as the Mobile Greys, and a friend of Travis. Bonham, too, was convinced by his friend to migrate to Texas primarily because it was "a place to build a fortune."[35] This great opportunity to "build a fortune" and live a long, healthy life was more probable in Texas, thanks to the healthy, mild climate. The long growing season only reinforced the seemingly limitless agricultural possibilities.

On a journey from New Orleans to San Antonio, George Wilkins Kendall, the founder of the New Orleans *Picayune*, was amazed by the sheer natural beauty in the rolling prairie lands just east of San Antonio. He favorably compared the milder, dryer climate, in contrast to the disease-ridden lowlands around New Orleans and even east Texas: the fertile grasslands of the Texan central plains were free from "the bilious fevers and debilitating agues so prevalent upon the Colorado, the Brazos and other muddy and sluggish rivers of Eastern Texas . . . no finer or more healthy openings exist in America."[36] Kendall's words of praise were no exaggeration. In describing the success of the prosperous Austin Colony, the editor of the *Connecticut Herald* wrote in the September 22, 1829 issue: "The rivers running through the colony are the Brazos and the Colorado, besides many large creeks. The soil of the margins of the Colorado and Brazos are in general alluvial [which] the planters considered equal to any soil in the world."[37]

Incredibly, even though they knew that Santa Anna's Army was about to push north to San Antonio to initiate the 1836 Texas campaign, Cummings and ten other Alamo garrison members yet planned to take the time to stake out their headright claims, so obsessed were they about securing rich Texas lands, instead of working hard to make the Alamo's defenses stronger. One of these was Micajah Autry, a 42-year-old slave-owner from Tennessee who was destined to die at the Alamo as a member of the Tennessee Mounted Volunteers. Somewhat of a Renaissance man, he benefited from a fine education as a son from a leading North Carolina family, and was a die-hard romantic who wrote poetry and "played the violin beautifully" on summer nights. He also sketched both nature and people with skill, although his drawings failed to depict the slaves that he or his family owned. After his overly ambitious literary plans met frustration, the young man was forced to become more realistic about life's expectations. Texas then became his new passion, supplementing youthful fantasies and unrealistic visions.

On January 13, 1836, the optimistic Autry wrote a letter to his wife, whom he was planning to bring to Texas once the conflict with Mexico ended, that emphasized a far brighter future than offered in Jackson, Tennessee. He wrote: "From what I have seen and learned from others there is not so fair a portion of the earth's service warmed by the sun [than Texas]. Be of good cheer Martha, I will provide you a sweet home. I shall be entitled to 640 acres of land for my services in the army and 4,444 acres upon condition of settling my family here. For a trifle here, (one) may procure a possession of land that will make a fortune for himself, his children and his children's children of its own increase in value and such a cotton country is not under the sun."[38] For Autry and other Alamo garrison members, such sentiments were not hyperbole. With their gangs of slaves laboring in vast cotton fields and reaping a fortune for their owners with hard work, Texas planters produced the highest quality cotton that ever existed in the cotton market in New Orleans.[39]

Autry wasn't the only newly arrived American who linked boundless prosperity with vast Texas acreage and cotton cultivation. Daniel

William Cloud, a 24-year-old Kentuckian who had failed to find meaningful work as a lawyer in St. Louis, was then unable to secure sufficient farming land, and who was likewise to be killed at the Alamo, served Texas as a lowly enlisted man. But the young man from the Kentucky Bluegrass region already felt fabulously wealthy with the knowledge that, as he penned in a letter, "If we succeed, the country is ours. It is immense in extent, and fertile in its soil, and will amply reward all our toil."[40]

The liberal land bounties only grew larger as the Texas Revolution lengthened, ensuring that the irresistible appeal to serve Texas consumed citizens all across the United States. Originally, each volunteer in the People's Army of Texas was entitled to 640 acres. But after March 2, 1836, unknown to the Alamo defenders, this amount was increased. After that date, each Texas soldier would gain an entire league of land, or 4,428 acres and one labor, or 177 acres, if he settled his family in Texas. Even a single man was entitled to 1,476 acres.[41]

Clearly, the powerful lust for land was a principal, if not the most dominant, motivation for United States citizens to cast their fates with the Texas Revolutionary Army. Having placed their high-stakes bet, and having made the gamble with their lives, Alamo garrison members served in large part because they possessed such a sizeable stake in one of the richest natural empires on the North American continent. In an agrarian society where status, wealth, and class were linked directly to the acreage one owned, such easy availability to thousands of prime Texas acres could not only mean a fortune for the Alamo men and their families, but also for future generations to come. Never before in the nation's history had Americans been offered such vast land-holdings for military service, even as a lowly private.

But the gamble made by these ambitious young men was that they might well die at obscure places with Hispanic names hundreds of miles from home. One such remote location had been bestowed the Spanish name for a thick stand of cottonwood trees, nourished by the warm rivers of the San Antonio River, that grew beside the old Spanish mission at San Antonio—the Alamo. Overall, strange twists of fate, fortunes, and tangled destinies brought most of the men who would die at the Alamo to Texas. Losing a hardscrabble Kentucky, Virginia, or Missouri farm for failure to pay debts or taxes; repeated crop failures due to bad weather; poor yields because of infertile, badly eroded soil; the collapse of crop prices; and an overall declining market for the average yeoman farmer during the American nation's first great depression motivated the United States volunteers to risk their lives at the Alamo.[42]

From the beginning to end, the real bone of contention in the Texas Revolution was about possession of the land. The territory consisted of more than 267,000 square miles. Ironically, the recent volunteers from the United States felt a greater sense of entitlement to all of Texas than the "Old Texian" colonists, who had been granted only a limited number of acres in east Texas. American citizens who joined the Texas Revolution, including many of the Alamo defenders, already sincerely believed that Texas, Mexico's northeastern frontier, was already part of the United States.

A common view existed across the United States that Thomas Jefferson's 1803 Louisiana Purchase from Napoleon included Texas, all the way south to the Rio Grande River. Because the southwest boundaries of the Louisiana territory was "vague," to say the least, ever-expansionist minded Jefferson had long insisted that the Rio Grande was its true southern boundary, while Spain claimed the Sabine River, or Louisiana's western border. John Quincy Adams, however, agreed to Spain's claim as a trade-off for its 1819 cession of Florida to the United States, and for Spain's claim to the Oregon territory. But the average American citizen believed that Texas, all the way to the Rio Grande, rightfully belonged to the United States. The many settlers in Texas, especially the late U.S. arrivals, felt that they possessed both a natural and a moral right to Mexico's fertile lands.[43]

With Spanish and then Mexican approval, the dream of hard-luck Missourian Moses Austin, father of Stephen Austin, who took over the ambitious colonization project after Moses' death, had become a reality by the early 1830s. Austin's ambition was to establish an immense empire in Spanish Texas, comparable in prosperity to nearby Louisiana. In the beginning, the elder Austin had planned to lay out a new town at the mouth of the Colorado River, which he hoped would eventually rival bustling New Orleans.

As in Louisiana, the new western empire envisioned by Austin called for thousands of slaves. Texas could best prosper from the development of agricultural estates comparable to the vast cotton and sugar cane plantations of Louisiana, which had been modeled after the highly profitable plantations on the French islands of the Caribbean. The most prosperous of all the French islands in the West Indies during most of the 18th century had been St. Domingue, or today's Haiti—minus the massive 1791 slave revolt that brought an end to French dominion, it provided a proven formula for Texas, but with cotton replacing sugar cane.

From the beginning, Austin's colony offered a rare opportunity for Americans to bring large numbers of slaves to cheap virgin lands. At this time, acreage in the United States, for sale privately or by the government, was simply too expensive for the average man, especially the lower classes. In stark contrast, before Mexico won its independence from Spain in 1821, the Spanish government simply "gave away rather than selling its open land to settlers acceptable to it."[44]

Left both undeveloped and under-populated by first Spain and then Mexico, Texas land seemed endless, boundless, and with unlimited potential. No one had seen anything as expansive yet empty as Texas, unless it was the ocean itself. Not only fertile and virgin, the land was also breathtakingly beautiful. More than a dozen rivers, smaller than those east of the Mississippi Valley, ran roughly parallel from northwest to southeast, flowing toward the Gulf of Mexico. The rolling hills of east Texas, the rich, low-lying coastal plain, and the relatively light flow of river water meant little erosion and flooding. The best soils hence were not washed away as they were along the Mississippi, making Texas river valleys ideal for agricultural production. Consequently, the river bottomlands remained amazingly fertile; combined with an ideal climate and sufficient labor, the situation fairly beckoned large-scale cultivation.

The fertile gulf coastal plain, the heartland of Tejano settlement with its dominant ranching economy, lay to the east and south. This land became more arid farther south toward the Rio Grande (or the Rio del Norte to the Spanish), and was more like northern Mexico than east Texas. The most prominent east Texas rivers were the Brazos (the largest in the state), the Trinity, Red, Colorado, Rio Grande, and Sabine Rivers. The generally flat or gently rolling land, carpets of virgin hardwood forests, and soil fertility of the gulf coastal plain was comparable to Louisiana and Mississippi, where the cotton culture dominated.

Of the major Texas rivers flowing gently into the gulf's warm waters, the Rio Grande was the southernmost. This river spawned from the snow-capped mountains around the Continental Divide in southern Colorado, and at 2,000 miles was the longest watercourse in Texas. Three distinct and vibrant civilizations—Native American, Spanish, and Mexican—had developed along this historic river and mixed into one people, although in the process they had often fought each other and died for possession of the land they loved.[45]

A prophetic Stephen Austin early predicted an undeniable truth: "Nature seems to have formed Texas for a great agricultural, grazing, manufacturing, and commercial country."[46] Dr. John Sibley at Natchitoches, Louisiana, just east of the Sabine, agreed with Austin's heady vision of future possibilities. Marveling at what he had seen in Texas, Dr. Sibley wrote with passion: "The Country is Larger than all France & has a finer Climate & the soil is as rich as any & can support a great population."[47] As reported in the *New-Orleans Mercantile Advertiser*, the prosperity of the Austin Colony and east Texas was based upon the "rivers running through the colony [and] the soil of the margins of the Colorado and Brazos is generally alluvial, and covered with timber . . . and is to the planters considered equal to any soil in the world for the cultivation of cotton and sugar."[48]

For the men of the Alamo, possession of this land was well worth risking one's life, regardless of its rightful ownership by the Republic of Mexico. More than any other crop, cotton was ideal for the thick soils of the fertile Blackland Prairie, where the annual rainfall and the hot summers were especially similar to the Black Belt of Alabama.[49] Another incredibly fertile region of east Texas was in the area just west of the Sabine River around Nacogdoches and San Augustine. This area was known was the Red Lands, named after the region's lush red soil, which was ideal for high crop yields. Anglo-Celtic settlers of this distinct area were known as the "Red Landers," a name they embraced with provincial pride.[50]

By the early 1830s, Texas had caught the imagination of an entire generation of Americans. For thousands of young men and their families, this promise of regeneration and the prospect of future fortunes made severing ties with the United States relatively easy. The lure of obtaining wealth in Texas was stronger than the ancestral bonds to old family farms carved out of the Kentucky, Tennessee, and North Carolina wilderness by ancestors who had fought at Cowpens and Kings Mountain—like David Crockett's namesake grandfather—during the American Revolution. Land had always been the great catalyst that pushed restless Americans westward; migrating much like their forefathers, those who went to Texas posted notes or carved the letters G.T.T.—Gone to Texas—on cabin doors throughout the 1820s and early 1830s.

To understand why so many Texas revolutionaries fought on behalf of the Mexican Constitution of 1824, it is first necessary to examine the complex dynamics of both land and slavery and their intertwined relationship and synergies. The Constitution of 1824 was established only three years after Mexico achieved its hard-won independence from Spain after an 11-year struggle, breaking from its Spanish centralist past. But why were so many American volunteers in Texas willing to fight for the Mexican Constitution instead of independence, if they were in fact battling for the principles of liberty and freedom during the Texas Revolution as so commonly believed?

For the most part, to the average American and Texas volunteer in the ranks, this conflict was primarily about land ownership, but it was also about the right to possess slaves. Modeled after the United States Constitution, the Mexican Constitution of 1824 safeguarded both land ownership and slavery. After winning its independence, Mexico naturally looked to the United States, not to Spain, as the best example of representative government. For the nationalists, Mexico's future lay in the promise of New World liberalism, not the feudal Old World past.[51]

Within the context of slavery, the violent beginning of the Texas Revolution was not at Gonzales, Texas, during the "Lexington of the Texas Revolution" in early October 1835; instead the first battle line was drawn in the fight led by William Barret Travis years earlier against Colonel Juan (or John) Davis Bradburn, an abolitionist serving Mexico. Bradburn was an enlightened liberal, having fought in the wars for Mexican independence from Spain. Ironically, the native Kentuckian was an active abolitionist in the service of an anti-slave nation in a Texas dominated by slavery.

Fueling the worst Anglo-Celt fears, he correctly informed Texas slaves that Mexico, rather than the United States, now "knew no slavery" and was the true land of the free. Therefore, he allowed two escaped slaves, who appeared in August 1831 seeking asylum, to join his Anáhuac military garrison, after having recently established both the town and fort on Galveston Bay. Here in east Texas, near the future site of the city of Houston, men of African descent became soldiers for the Republic of Mexico. Bradburn, who with his troops founded Anáhuac to stop slave smuggling along the coast, engendered the early wrath of the American colonists, stirring up this most sensitive issue and guaranteeing that open revolt was only a matter of time. Of this Bradburn was well aware. The Texas colonists, he wrote, "have only observed

Anglo-American laws" and not those of Mexico.[52]

To this day in Alamo and Texas Revolution mythology, Bradburn has been portrayed as an arch-villain second only to Santa Anna. Bradburn served in the Louisiana Militia during the War of 1812 and was present at the battle of New Orleans, and then commanded the "American Division" of filibusters who invaded the Mexican coast to be defeated by the Spanish, but he has since been viewed as a traitor in the tradition of Benedict Arnold. In truth, Bradburn, born in Richmond, Virginia in 1787, was not unlike one of the heroes of America's War of 1812, William Hull, who as Governor of the Michigan Territory, refused to return slaves who had fled Canadian owners. Hull furthermore viewed men and women of African descent as United States citizens, just as Bradburn considered runaways deserving of freedom.[53]

DEEP CELTIC-GAELIC ROOTS

The Texas Revolution was about the clash of different races—Mexican, Tejano, African American, and Anglo-Celtic—as much as it was about land. The settlement of Texas and the Texas Revolution had deep Celtic-Gaelic, or Irish, antecedents, in terms of both the ancestry of its principle migrants and its dominant culture. The Mexican republican government had in part allowed the establishment of the Austin Colony to serve as a buffer against the greatest menace to the development of Texas for three hundred years, marauding Indians. Now confronting this threat, most new settlers who migrated to Texas were Scotch-Irish, the latest wave in the western Scotch-Irish migration that had begun before the American Revolution.

Two primarily Catholic Irish colonies, one at San Patricio and the other at Refugio, were established by Mexico to contain the ever-growing Anglo-Celtic threat by way of "countercolonizing." Once again Irish Catholics were pitted against Protestant Scotch-Irish, at least potentially, as they had been for hundreds of years in northern Ireland. Ironically, in this regard, Mexico merely repeated what the English government had done in establishing the Ulster Plantation system of lowland Scottish settlers—the Scotch-Irish—to counter the Irish Catholic, or native, influence in the seventeenth century.

Mexico City's timely development of a strategic plan based upon the fighting prowess of the always-cantankerous Scotch-Irish was not only nothing new, it was a familiar remedy. Born near Belfast in northern

Ireland, James Logan had deliberately settled the western Pennsylvania frontier during the colonial period with hardy Scotch-Irish, his "brave fellow countrymen," because he knew how tenaciously they had fought the native Irish people, or Catholics, in northern Ireland to claim the land of Ulster Province as their own. Ever-combative, the Scotch-Irish were specifically chosen to serve as the best protective buffer to ensure that Philadelphia and other Pennsylvania communities farther east would be secure from the Indian threat.[54] In much the same way, Mexico City and also the Tejanos understood that Anglo-Celtic settlers were simply the "most efficient, quick, and economical means to destroy the Indians," the ancient enemy of both the Mexican and Tejano people.[55]

In the words of Pulitzer Prize winning historian Paul Horgan, the wrong-headed government decision to settle Texas with immigrants from the United States "released forces that must clash in always increasing energy until in the end they would meet in bloody battle," during both the Texas Revolution and the Mexican-American War. Most of all, the conflict between Mexico and Texas was inevitable because the Anglo-Celtics brought to Texas the cultural baggage that was most guaranteed to lead to open warfare: the institution of slavery.[56] This process began once the Appalachian barrier was breached, and settlers pouring from the eastern seaboard encountered no more huge natural obstacles to further movement westward. Emphasizing the impact of the historic Anglo-Celtic migration, historian T. R. Fehrenbach concluded that when Kentucky became a state in 1792, "the doom of Hispanic empire on the continent [including the fate of Texas] was sealed."[57]

Ironically, the initial success of Austin's colonizing enterprise only caused Mexico to issue additional land grants for colonization along the same liberal lines as the Austin grant. Land was free for settlers of the Austin colony; he waived the cost of around 6 cents per acre, while public lands in the United States cost around $1.25 per acre. This offer came at a time when many common people in the South could barely make a living especially in North Carolina and Virginia, where the soil had become infertile and eroded due to over-extensive tobacco cultivation.[58] By 1829, thanks to the prosperity enjoyed by the Austin Colony, the price of land had gone up, but it was still incredibly cheap.

Aside from official land grants issued by Mexico, the heavy flow of illegal migration from the United States to Texas made conflict all but inevitable. An influx of thousands of illegal aliens from the United States took possession of Texas lands as squatters without paying a cent and without Mexico's consent. Free Texas land for squatters was available at a time when land along the Mississippi River's rich alluvium plain were selling for around $35.00–$40.00 per acre.[59] The disparity between the costs per acre of prime farming land versus uncleared forested land was wide, but American citizens securing Texas land were attracted by the fact that large land-holds for both settlement and military service, at least in theory, included a good many prime acres along creeks or rivers. This meant that a settler could obtain not only a large number of acres that he could not afford in the United States, but also some of the most fertile acres, which were too expensive for the average man east of the Sabine.

A new Texas colonist who headed a family or intended to raise livestock was promised by the government—both Spanish and Mexican—a total of 4,429 acres, or a square league of land. Best of all for Southerners, Anglo-Celtic settlers who migrated to Texas with capital assets, including slaves, were granted additional leagues of land, promoting the rapid growth of slavery and hence more extensive and quicker development.[60]

THE PECULIAR INSTITUTION

While slavery played a leading role in the antagonism between the slave-owning Anglo-Celts in Texas and the political and military leaders of the abolitionist Republic of Mexico, it was also the most decisive factor in laying the foundation for both "the drive for personal independence" and regional independence. In the estimation of historians James S. Olson and Randy Roberts, "nothing loomed larger than slavery" in the dispute between Texians and Mexico. As in other English-speaking slave regimes in the New World, especially in the thirteen colonies, and even as in Jamaica, slavery fueled a bent toward independence, self-sufficiency, and assertive defiance toward centralized authority, and paved the way for breaking away from government rules and regulations.

The importance of slavery in the American Revolution has been overlooked because it failed to fit the simplistic view of colonists as righteous underdogs and the British as oppressors, rather than the liberators of American slaves. Historians' negligence on this subject has led to misconceptions and misleading stereotypes about the Anglo-Celts and some of their deepest motivations, including those of the Alamo garrison and principal Texas Revolutionary leaders. Just as slavery played a vital role in fueling colonial resistance to the British, especially in the South, during the American Revolution, so the selective silencing of this complex aspect of Texas' past occurred because it had no place in the romance of the mythical Alamo.

The supreme importance of slavery can be partly understood by examining the relationship to the peculiar institution of the primary leaders of the Texas Revolution and the Alamo. All of the primary Alamo leaders, James Clinton Neill, James Bowie, David Crockett, and William Barret Travis, were current or former slave-owners. Colonel Neill, who was proud of his family's Southern plantation "heritage," even "dabbled in the slave market" to reap dividends, and then raised cotton that was picked by his own slaves. Crockett was the smallest slave-owner, who "owned [only] a few slaves" in his lifetime. The first member of his hardscrabble Tennessee family ever to own slaves, he was in fact far more anti-slavery in sentiments and actions than Neill, Bowie, or Travis. By far, the wheeling-dealing Bowie possessed the deepest roots and ties to slavery.

As a relatively young slave-owner, Travis fell between Crockett and Bowie in the legendary Alamo triumvirate. Seeking a badly needed fresh start in early 1831, he left a failed marriage with Rosanna E. Cato, as well as a son and unborn daughter, never to return. Departing the little town of Claiborne, Monroe County, located amid the gently rolling lands and "cane country" of southwest Alabama, twenty-one-year-old Travis headed for Texas in a big hurry. Like so many other United States migrants, he was determined to make "a splendid fortune." Travis then became a lawyer in San Felipe de Austin and Anáhuac, a distinctive Aztec name that held an important place in Mexican culture. Thereafter, he looked to purchase choice east Texas lands for speculation, when not engaged in his legal practice.

In going to Texas, Travis was following the tradition of his South Carolina family, which was largely rooted in the booming cotton culture and slavery in the 18th century. The fertile "cane country" of southwest Alabama, especially along the brown-hued Alabama River, was better for cotton-growing than South Carolina. Here the Travis family had moved and thrived, and the prodigal son was determined to apply the same magical formula for success in Texas.

Travis was fully accustomed to being around African American slaves. He crossed the Sabine with a twenty-year-old male slave by his side, Joe, who served beside him at the Alamo. His own personal household at the little southwest Alabama town of Claiborne had included three slaves. At Anáhuac, one of Travis' first legal cases was to represent a Louisiana slave-owner seeking the return of two slaves who had fled to Texas and ended up with the Mexican garrison at Anáhuac. Travis was hired to return them to their owner.

Primarily because of deep-seated issues over slavery between Texas and Mexico, Travis emerged as a war hawk and pro-slavery advocate by 1832. He early clashed with Colonel Bradburn, who refused to return the two runaway slaves because they now served as soldiers in his garrison, and had requested Mexican citizenship or freedom. Bradburn also violated traditional "property rights," as the settlers saw it, impressing the slaves of nearby planters for labor on the Anáhuac fort. But worst of all, Texians feared that Bradburn had indoctrinated African Americans with the ideals of liberation and equality. The early clash over slavery between Travis and Bradburn therefore, in many ways, represented the Texas Revolution in microcosm; it also gave a foretaste of his later showdown with Santa Anna at the Alamo.

As he gained more income from his legal practice, Travis continued to acquire more Texas land. These included property along Buffalo Bayou as early as 1832, and later land holdings in the Ben Milam grant, besides his claims to acreage as a colonist's right in 1835. The dream of becoming a large landowner and gentleman planter was never far from his mind. To Travis and so many other migrants from the Deep South, Texas was the ideal place to transform themselves into respected members of the planter class.[61]

Year after year, Travis continued to profit from slavery in many ways. As an ambitious young lawyer, he pocketed a tidy fee when he oversaw the purchase of twenty-three slaves for a client. He even earned revenue from clients as far away as New Orleans and San Antonio for lucrative slave transactions. In addition, Travis owned both male and female slaves himself, whom he hired out to ensure himself a steady income. One of his last large purchases was for a slave couple. Like so many Anglo-Celts in Texas by the early 1830s, much of Travis' total assets was based upon sanctioned slavery, while other enterprising Americans in Texas profited immensely from the illegal slave trade.[62]

Jim Bowie possessed a lengthy record as one of the largest slave smugglers and also one of the greatest land speculators in Texas history, activities that went hand-in-hand. Just as in the Travis clan, slave-owning was a Bowie family tradition. His family owned slaves in the 1790s, and throughout its migrations from Tennessee and then across the Mississippi to Louisiana. Bowie's farsighted father had even jump-started the independent adulthood of both of his sons in Louisiana by giving them each ten slaves.

By 1829, Bowie owned plantations in both Louisiana and Mississippi, both worked by gangs of slaves. James and his brother sold property in LaFourche Parish in February 1831, which was paid for partly by their acquisition of sixty-five slaves from the buyer. But he reaped his greatest financial boon when he smuggled into the United States and then sold large numbers of slaves, or "black ivory," reaping a lavish return. The unfortunate Africans were transported in Jean Laffite's ships from leading slave-trading ports like Havana. Because the transatlantic slave trade had been outlawed in the United States since 1808, transporting slaves illegally from Texas into chattel-hungry Louisiana made Bowie a lavish fortune.

The fantastic amount of money reaped from selling slaves allowed Bowie to purchase even more land. He thrived as a land speculator on both sides of the Mississippi. After selling thirty-four slaves to raise money in early 1830 to permanently settle in Texas, Bowie developed an ambitious speculative plan to secure three-quarters of a million acres in Mexican lands. Like Travis, Bowie brought slaves into Texas from the beginning; when Bowie first applied for a league of land under Mexican law, he possessed 109 slaves, and their labor remained a large part of his long-term plans for acquiring a fortune in Mexico. He established, for instance, one of the early cotton mills at Saltillo in the state of Coahuila, Mexico, after securing the required approval from the Mexican government.[63]

Sam Houston grew up in a Scotch-Irish family in Rockbridge County in western Virginia. But like so many other Scotch-Irish, the family migrated west over the mountains to east Tennessee. Here, at the little town of Maryville located in the foothills of the Great Smokey Mountains, life was made easier for young Houston and his male siblings by a number of hard-working slaves, who cut down trees and cleared the land for farming.[64]

Another especially enterprising slave-trader who reaped fantastic profits in Texas was James W. Fannin, Jr. Ultimately proving to be a better slave-dealer than a military commander, Fannin forsook a military career, squandering a fine West Point education and a promising future, to make money by smuggling. He illegally brought 153 slaves from the Spanish island of Cuba into Texas in 1833.

In fact, Fannin originally migrated to Texas primarily "to perpetuate his trafficking in African slaves" after the direct importation of slaves from Africa became illegal in the United States. Fannin and other Texas slave traders reaped vast rewards from slave smuggling. Like Bowie, Fannin brought slaves illegally from Cuba to the United States, and later transported gangs of them from Texas for sale in nearby Louisiana. By mid-January 1836, he owned a good many slaves with a value of $17,000. But Fannin was only doing what came natural to a Southerner of sound business mind. He had grown up on a Georgia cotton plantation with plenty of slaves. In Texas, he himself raised crops of cotton, continuing the family tradition of living well as a member of the aristocratic planter class: a privileged existence that he would defend with his life.[65]

The primary leaders of the Alamo and the Texas Revolution were not alone in owning slaves or engaging in slave smuggling to reap astronomical profits. The majority of the average soldiers, the lowly privates of the Alamo, were either small slave-owners or had visions of one day acquiring them. Slavery was deeply ingrained in Southern Anglo-Celtic culture and society as well as in the legal system—an inheritance from England, which gained its legal legacy from ancient Rome, whose imperial legions had long occupied the island. In fact, slavery had been "America's original sin," stemming from the founding fathers' failure to abolish the institution in the effort to create a union of confederated states.

Typical of the average soldiers found at the Alamo, brothers William and Mial Scurlock departed Tennessee for the express purpose of acquiring as much Texas acreage as possible. They headed for the east Texas area just west of the Louisiana border around San Augustine, bringing one male and a female slave with her four-year-old son. Acquiring 640 acres, the Scurlock brothers and their slaves cleared the land and built a log cabin. Both brothers joined in the attack that resulted in San Antonio's capture during the 1835 Campaign. While William rode south on the ill-fated Matamoros Expedition that departed San Antonio at the end of 1835, Mial stayed behind with the tiny garrison in San Antonio, where he met his maker at the Alamo.[66]

Even a strong religious faith failed to alter or diminish the passion for slave-owning across Texas. Protestants and Catholics owned slaves in Texas with equal relish, exploiting them against God's word in the name of bestowing Christianity upon "heathens." Jewish Alamo defender Abraham (Anthony) Wolfe, from the Galveston area just south of Anáhuac, was considered "the black sheep" of his family; he assisted Jean Laffite in smuggling slaves from Texas to Louisiana to sell to rich planters and aristocrats in and around New Orleans. An English Jew, he migrated from London to settle in Nacogdoches, Texas in 1835 after the death of his wife, Sarah. One of the few Jews to serve at the Alamo, Wolfe was destined to die with the garrison along with his two sons, Michael and Benjamin.[67]

Named in honor for the incomparable founding father from Philadelphia, Benjamin Franklin Smith won widespread "notoriety as a trader in African slaves."He wrote to the Convention on November 8, 1835, proposing an amazing offer: "At the present time our Country is involved in war, & without means to carry it out—It may become necessary that individuals should contribute to the public fund—I therefore take pleasure in communicating to you that I have eleven leagues of land which I desire [now] to place at the disposition of my country."[68]

In November 1835, Fannin, no longer a slave trader but a prosperous cotton planter near the port town of Velasco on the gulf coast, offered the Texas government a deal it could not refuse: authorization to sell his personal property, consisting mostly of the monetary value of 36 of his slaves, for the purchase of munitions to sustain the fledgling Texas war effort.[69] Fannin made this decision because he knew that when Santa Anna invaded Texas, he would liberate Africans in bondage. Like other Texas slave-owners, Fannin realized that slave "property . . . will not be worth owning, if we do not succeed" in winning the Texas Revolution. He was fated to be executed by Santa Anna's troops with hundreds of his command at Goliad on Palm Sunday, 1836.[70]

Fannin's motivation was shared by the men of the Alamo as well. Yet despite the extreme importance of slavery, the Texas Revolution and especially the Alamo are primarily viewed as part of western history, rather than part of mainstream southern history. Nevertheless, examining the all-important role of slavery is fundamental to understanding both the Texas revolutionaries and what occurred at the Alamo. Slavery was key to the successful development of Texas and the exploitation of its natural riches, just as it had been key to developing the eastern seaboard in states like Virginia and Maryland. If Santa Anna's Army emerged victorious, slavery would be illegal in Texas, causing it to revert back to a land of impoverished shepherds and their flocks.[71]

However, slavery served as a central foundation of Anglo-Celtic settlement. Austin first proposed that Spanish officials grant slave owners an additional 50 acres per slave, and later this was increased to 80 acres for each slave. This bonus for bringing slaves to Texas not only encouraged large planters but also yeoman farmers: by 1825, one quarter, or more than 440, of the Austin Colony consisted of slaves. Indeed, almost one in four of Austin's colonists owned slaves, making them better off than their middle class peers in the United States. Like his fellow transplanted countrymen, Austin realized that the abolishment of slavery in Texas would ensure that "we [would be] ruined forever."[72]

In regard to chattel labor, the world of the Anglo-Celts in Texas and that of the Mexicans, a mixed-race people, could not have been more diametrically opposed. Austin traveled to Mexico City in a desperate 1823 effort to convince Mexico's enlightened leaders, who wanted slavery abolished in Texas and all slaves to be freed in ten years, to modify their position. Representing prevalent Anglo-Celtic sentiments, Austin advocated life-long slavery for existing Africans in bondage. His only compromise was to suggest that emancipation be allowed for slave children upon reaching adulthood. As during the antebellum period in the United States, compromises over the issue of slavery in Texas only delayed the inevitable conflict to come concerning the highly combustible matters of race and economics.[73]

When the Mexican government abolished slavery in Mexico in 1829, the freeing of Mexico's slaves that September 15 caused great consternation among the American colonists, who realized that "immediate, total abolition would destroy at one blow the population, property, and agriculture of an important part of the state."[74] Perhaps no one in Texas was more upset by such anti-slavery developments than Jared E. Groce, aged thirty-nine, from Alabama. A member of one of the original 300 Austin Colony families, he was "one of the first pioneers of Texas, having emigrated here in [January] 1822."[75]

Groce reaped considerable financial success from his sprawling cotton plantation, Bernardo, thanks to the hundred slaves that he transported from the Deep South in early 1822. Carving out his own cotton kingdom in the wilderness, he became the lord of "Groce's Retreat," adding to his original 44,000 acres to become the largest cotton grower in Texas. By 1825, Groce had built his own cotton gin, the first in

Texas, for the New Orleans market. Four years later, Texas could boast of seven operating cotton gins in the Austin Colony, with a cotton crop estimated at 1,000 bales.

Nothing proved more profitable in all Texas than the combination of slavery and cotton culture. A single crop of cotton from a small farmer could reap a fabulous profit of $10,000. When General Manuel de Mier y Teran visited the Groce plantation, he was amazed to discover that the planter already had 30,000 pounds of cotton ready for shipment to New Orleans. Reflecting class differences in the Texas Revolution, no member of the Groce family served in the army's ranks; however, Groce, who was raised in Virginia, provided supplies to the Texas Army in early April 1836, less than a month after the Alamo's fall.

In 1833, Texas' rich, dark soil, especially along the creek and river bottoms, produced 4,000 bales of cotton, each weighing around 2,000 pounds. The following year, 10,000 cotton bales were produced. Aside from smuggling slaves, raising cotton in Texas was the quickest and easiest way to get rich. A single young male slave could pick more than 150 pounds of cotton from sunup to sundown. Not coincidentally, the colonists at Gonzales who sparked the beginning of the Texas Revolution in 1835 did so in early October, after the cotton had already been picked and baled at summer's end. Cotton in Texas was white gold, going hand-in-hand with the amassing of black gold, or slaves[76]

Shock waves echoed across the United States with Mexico's September 1829 decision to abolish slavery. The almost unbelievable prosperity of cotton culture across Texas was threatened overnight. Alarmed journalists across the South decried the act, raising a "howl of protest," as even the South itself seemed threatened by Mexico's example. And across Texas, talk of separation from Mexico became deadly serious: revolutionary seeds had been planted. Then, the Mexican Congress, based on the 1829 recommendations of General Teran, decided on April 6, 1830, that slaves were no longer allowed to be brought into Texas by United States citizens—a possible first step, it was feared, toward general emancipation of Texas slaves.[77]

Like Southerners who later viewed slavery's abolition as inevitable when President Lincoln was elected in the winter of 1860, and thus determined to secede from the Union, so Texans viewed abolition in Mexico as catastrophic. In 1829, just one year before Mexico outlawed the import of slaves into Texas, one Southern journalist, with the "lessons of St. Domingue" in mind, summarized what the abolitionist threat entailed for Texians: "An attempt by the General Government to emancipate our slaves . . . would not only threaten to deprive us of a large part of our property, it would also produce immediate danger of the massacre of our families, and of a horrid servile war."[78]

It could no longer be denied that Mexico's enlightened philosophies and humanitarian principles posed a serious long-term threat to the Texans' way of life. When Mexico declared independence from Spain, Mexico's leaders, ironically motivated by the same ideals that had sparked the American Revolution in 1775, promised equality for Mexicans of all castes, colors, and classes. Far more egalitarian than anything in the United States, these enlightened principles for mixed-race peoples and people of African descent, all of whom were denied equality in the United States, astounded white Americans. Mexico's position posed a serious threat to the firmly entrenched racial, economic, political, and social norms that held the fragile fabric of society together.[79]

After much protest, Texas received an exemption from Mexico's president, because the original 1822 grant from the Mexican government to Austin had placed no restrictions on slavery. However, Mexico's leaders and people yet desired gradual emancipation for slaves in Texas. The clock was therefore ticking away from an early date, and everyone knew it. Austin admitted as early as 1822 what lay at the heart of the differences between the new republic of Mexico and the Anglo-Celtic settlers: "the principal difficulty is slavery."[80]

Other than armed might, only legal restrictions from Mexico City on what Anglo-Celts believed to be slavery's natural extension could slow the flood of Americans migrating to Texas. Austin knew that "ruin would befall the colony if the original three hundred families could no longer rely on their slaves."[81] Yet Mexico, committed to gradual emancipation, declared that all African American children in bondage would be freed once they reached the age of fourteen, ending the cycle of generations of men and women in permanent bondage. In response, Austin, heading a committee to buy time, advocated a key concession: he proposed a revision of abolitionist laws and regulations to provide a legal guarantee that "the slaves and their descendants of the [original] 300 families [of the Austin Colony] shall be slaves for life."[82]

In addition to laws emanating from faraway Mexico City, decisions passed by the legislature of Texas and Coahuila likewise threatened slavery. Unrest spread through Anglo-Celtic settlements when rumors began that the legislature was considering abolishing slavery in its juris-diction. Constitutional restrictions on slavery were indeed enacted and issued in the March 1827 Constitution of the State of Coahuila and Texas. These decisions included mandating the freedom of slaves at birth and prohibiting the arrival of new slaves six months after the law's passage. Employing a loophole in Mexican law, however, Texas settlers continued to bring slaves into Texas under the guise of indentured ser-vants, or slaves for life.[83]

Nevertheless, legal restrictions allowing only for the entry of slaves with contracts as indentured servants were seen as a threat, given the common view that slavery in Texas—not to mention the booming econ-omy based on cotton—was no longer safe as a long-term investment. At any time and upon a whim, faraway Mexican politicians, whether hon-est or bribed, might pass a law to abolish slavery in Texas altogether, and the settlers could do nothing to stop it.

After a revealing pre-Texas Revolution inspection of Texas, an alarmed Teran, who advocated anti-slavery laws, reported to President Guadalupe Victoria: "If these laws [prohibiting slavery] were repealed—which God forbid—in a few years Texas would be a powerful state which could compete with Louisiana."[84] In 1830, confirming the anti-slavery measures passed by the legislature of Coahuila and Texas, the Mexican Congress was adamant that no additional slaves should be brought to Texas. Texas, whose slave population had swollen nearly to the size of the Tejano population by the end of the 1820s, was now threatened with certain "economic ruin."[85]

With recurring threats to slavery after 1824 by Mexico's efforts to undo the "salutary neglect" long enjoyed by the Anglo-Celtic settlers, Texans began to view the liberal Constitution of 1824 as a guarantee for future prosperity, because it was modeled after the United States Constitution, which possessed ample safeguards to protect slavery. As long as the 1824 Constitution was in place, the "peculiar institution" in Texas would endure. Support for the 1824 Constitution became stronger after the 1827 prohibitions of slaves to Texas by the state con-stitutions of Coahuila and Texas, and by the Mexican federal govern-ment degree of 1830. It grew further and became especially important in 1832, when the loophole allowing for indentured servants was tight-ened, limiting service by contract to no more than ten years. [86]

Without question, by the time of the Texas Revolution cotton was king, especially in east Texas. Cotton production boomed in the Austin

Colony, which contained the best "soil in the world for the cultivation of cotton and sugar," as a New England newspaper proclaimed in September 1829, and where production had grown from 600 bales in 1827 to 2,000 bales in 1833. The same editor wrote: "The prospects of the crops [in July 1829] were very flattering and it was estimated that 1,000 bales of cotton . . . would be made" by the Austin Colony's farmers. Amid the fertile lands located just west of the Sabine, the Nacogdoches District of east Texas alone grew 2,000 bales in 1834. Most cotton was shipped to New Orleans for markets in the north and Europe, but hundreds of cotton bales were sent to Mexican ports, such as Matamoros, Vera Cruz, and Tampico.[87]

The lines between Mexicans and Texans were being drawn fundamentally over the contentious issue of slavery, which was the core element of the desire for greater autonomy and independence. The Texans held conventions in April 1830 and October 1832, requesting repeals of the slavery prohibitions and the establishment of a separate state government for Texas, independent of Coahuila. When Santa Anna assumed dictatorial powers as president in April 1833 to overthrow federalism for centralism, Texans saw him as a threat both to their aspiration for separate statehood for Texas and to their maintenance of slavery. Austin wrote from Matamoros at the end of May 1833 on his mission to Mexico City to emphasize that, above all else, Texas had to be "a slave country."[88]

At the time, a good many voices, both Anglo-Celtic and Mexican, blamed the beginning of the Texas Revolution on the curse of slavery. In the words of José María Tornel, the Secretary of War: "The land speculators of Texas have tried to convert it into a mart of human flesh where the slaves of the south might be sold and others from Africa might be introduced, since it is not possible to do it directly through the United States."[89] Benjamin Lundy wrote in 1837 that "the immediate cause and leading object of the contest originated in a settled design, among the slaveholders of this country (with land speculators and slave traders) to wrest the large and valuable territory of Texas from the Mexican Republic, in order to reestablish the SYSTEM OF SLAVERY; to open a vast and profitable SLAVE-MARKET therein."[90] Clearly, the battle on behalf of the Constitution of 1824, which emphasized states rights as opposed to centralized authority, and which protected slavery in Texas, was a principal motivation for Texas Revolutionaries, including those at the Alamo, especially at the opening of the war.[91]

Colonel Francis White Johnson, a key player who nevertheless did not know of the New Orleans Greys' flag at the Alamo, explained in a November 27, 1836 letter that "if any flag was used [at the Alamo] it was the Mexican, as Col. Travis had not been informed of the declaration of independence, which was made on the 2d March" 1836.[92] Ironically, the men of the Alamo fought not only for their own freedom, but also for the freedom to keep men, women, and children in bondage. "One of the freedoms cherished by the American colonists in Texas was the freedom to maintain slavery."[93] In his classic *Santa Anna of Mexico*, historian Will Fowler correctly identified the central paradox of the Texas Revolution: "The fact that the imposition of a centralist state would result in the abolition of slavery in Texas remains one of the main, yet often downplayed, reasons why the Texans rose up in arms."[94]

Indeed, fearful Texans finally resorted to open revolution because of Santa Anna's ascent to the presidency and his consolidation of centralized power, which now meant that the abolition law of 1829 could be enforced to the letter, and they were convinced that General Cós' troops sent by Santa Anna into Texas in 1835 were determined "to liberate your slaves."[95] In October 1835, the Matagorda, Texas committee of safety and correspondence declared that Mexican troops under General Cós were determined "to give liberty to our slaves [so as] to let loose the blood hounds of savage war upon us."[96] This all-consuming fear was confirmed by General Cós himself, who undiplomatically declared in no uncertain terms that "the inevitable consequences of war will bear upon [all revolutionaries] and their property."[97] This, of course, meant the slaves would be liberated.

The Texas Revolution was not triggered over the ownership of the little "Come and Take It" cannon at Gonzales in early October 1835; it was brought on by the fear of Texas slave-owners that Cós and his Mexican troops, as Robert McAlpin Williamson warned at a protest meeting in San Felipe de Austin, would "compel you to liberate your slaves."[98] Such warnings also played into the deep-seated fear of a possible slave revolt, which was felt throughout the South, and had helped to galvanize support for the patriot cause there as early as the American Revolution. Paradoxically, the fear of slave revolt also brought such overriding concern during General Cós' occupation of San Antonio, that calls for peaceful reconciliation were raised in Texas.[99]

This Anglo-Celtic obsession was well founded. Across Texas, an historical analogy was made between Texas and St. Domingue, where a slave revolt that sent the great sugar plantations of the island's northern plains up in flames during the summer of 1791 erupted into a fiery revolution, transforming the island into a hell on earth. Inspired by the ideals of the French Revolution, "Liberty, Equality, and Fraternity," the success of the Black Jacobins led to the establishment of the first black republic in the New World in 1804, after more than a dozen years of bloody warfare. Americans read about the slave revolt and resulting massacres in newspaper articles, and heard of its horrors from thousands of French refugees, including not only whites but many free blacks of the mulatto class, who poured into the Deep South and especially into New Orleans. The lesson learned was that slave revolts could unleash the nightmare of a savage race war to threaten the South's political, social, and economic foundations, including those of Texas.[100]

The fear of repeating the events at St. Domingue was no less of a major catalyst for the Texas Revolution than it was for the Civil War. Fortunate to have escaped the hellish Caribbean island with their lives, St. Domingue refugees in New Orleans were nearby visible examples for the Texans, who feared how liberal French revolutionary concepts would also inspire their own slaves to revolt. Indeed, slaves across the South had already been influenced; the thousands of slaves who had risen up just north of New Orleans in January 1811 in America's largest, yet quickly crushed, slave insurrection had been inspired by events on St. Domingue.

St. Domingue was a powerful moral symbol for black regeneration and "Avengers of the New World." A good many heads of black Louisiana rebels were planted on poles for slaves to see as a warning, yet concern among whites about future revolt remained high. Remembering the most radical political, racial, and social revolution in the "Age of Revolution," Stephen Austin warned of impending doom as early as 1831, expressing great concern that not only Texas, but the South as a whole, would "be Santa [sic] Domingonized" in the future.[101]

Austin was so consumed by this fear of slave insurrection that he, unlike most colonists, became anti-slavery, because he believed that slaves were potential enemies who would rise up one day in a war of revenge. Austin was also concerned that the increase in the slave population would lead to the worst of all horrors in the minds of white Southerners: miscegenation. He was obsessed by the "horrible fate" that would befall "a long-cherished, beloved wife, a number of daughters, granddaughters, and great granddaughters" and the "overwhelming ruin" that he believed miscegenation would bring if slaves were freed.[102]

Fully realizing the deadly potential of his Faustian bargain—great wealth reaped at the risk of slave revolt—Austin further revealed in a June 1830 letter the deep psychological impact of his concern: "The idea of seeing such a country [Texas] as this overrun by a slave population almost makes men weep—It is in vain to tell a North American that the white population will be destroyed some fifty or eighty years hence by the negroes, and that his daughters will be violated and butchered by them."[103] Paranoia about possible slave revolts was rampant across the South. Making the analogy with the black revolutionary Jacobins, who rose up in righteous rage against their French masters on St. Domingue, one Southerner declared: "Let it never be forgotten; that our Negroes are freely the JACOBINS of the country [and] the COMMON ENEMY OF CIVILIZED SOCIETY, and the BARBARIANS WHO WOULD, IF THEY COULD, BECOME THE DESTROYERS OF OUR RACE."[104] On the other side, abolitionist William Wells Brown, the son of a white plantation owner and black slave, eagerly awaited a slave revolt. "The day is not far distant when the revolution of St. Domingo will be reenacted in South Carolina and Louisiana," he grimly warned.[105]

The genesis of Stephen Austin's fear was ironic, as it stemmed from the consequences of the original idealistic vision of his father, Moses Austin. It had been Austin's dream to establish a great cotton and sugar cane empire, based upon slavery in Texas. The vast sugar cane plantations of Louisiana were based upon the St. Domingue model, after thousands of St. Domingue refugees, including sugar cane planters, resettled there. In this sense, the analogy with the most successful and largest slave revolt in modern history was most appropriate.[106]

The fear of "another St. Domingo" and the rise of some charismatic "black Spartacus" was omnipresent west of the Sabine. This was because more native Africans—always the most revolutionary of slaves, as opposed to American-born blacks—existed in Texas, as a direct consequence of the widespread smuggling that took place there after the United States ended the slave trade and barred native Africans from entering the country. The slave trade was ended as a direct response to St. Domingue, where Africans from the Congo had spearheaded the massive uprising; the United States desired to halt both refugees and "French negroes" from spreading the seeds of revolution from the Caribbean island. Even at the time of the Texas Revolution, many slaves in Texas yet bore tribal margins on their faces from the traditions of their West African tribes, and could neither speak English nor communicate with other slaves from different tribes and areas of Africa.[107]

In addition, Texas also came to be viewed as necessary to the expansion of slavery to act as a "safety valve" for the future salvation of the Deep South as abolition activity increased in the northern U.S. and in Europe, especially England during the early 1830s. An entire generation of Tennesseans, including men like Crockett and others at the Alamo and in the Texas Revolution, found wisdom in the analysis of the delegates of the Tennessee Constitutional Convention of 1834, who stated, "It is expedient, both for the benefit of the slave and the free man, that the slaves should be distributed over as large a territory as possible."[108] Such concerns about slavery sparked early 19th century filibuster activities, primarily of U.S. Southerners in Texas.

A wide variety of diverse factors—the expansion of slavery, self preservation, reaping vast profits, quest for land, and especially the unforgettable lessons of St. Domingue's holocaust—combined to lay a firm foundation for the eventual fateful break with Mexico.[109] Because of General Cós' own words, and because he was notably leading hundreds of "colored hirelings," in John W. Hall's words, of the Mexican Army to Texas, revolution was inevitable. It was believed that the intention of Cós' men was to liberate the slaves. As William H. Wharton wrote, Mexico's abolitionist ambitions were to "emancipate [the slaves] and induce them to turn their arms against their masters."[110]

Subsequent events demonstrated that the fear of "another San Domingo" in Texas was not unfounded or unwarranted paranoia. In 1833–34, Colonel Juan Nepomuceno Almonte was dispatched by the Mexican government on a top secret mission to spread the news to slaves in Texas that a day of liberation lay ahead for them: freedom and even land ownership in the Republic of Mexico.[111] Complicating the situation was the fact that Texas slaves were more prone to insurrection because many of them were aware that slavery was illegal in Mexico. Mexico was a nearby land of the free and a magnet for escapees.

When the Texas Revolution erupted in the early autumn of 1835, nearly a hundred slaves rose up in revolt among the east Texas settlements along the Brazos River, which flowed between the Trinity River to the north and the Colorado River to the south. This desperate bid for freedom was sparked by rumors of an approaching Mexican Army. Bringing immediate retaliation from whites, the budding revolt was put down swiftly before it could escalate into something more serious.[112]

For the Anglo-Celts, this premature slave insurrection demonstrated that if a large Mexican Army invaded Texas, slaves would be more than ready to turn on their masters in a bid for freedom. If so, then the rustic Texas revolutionaries would face two foes at once: Santa Anna's invading army and a homegrown army of enraged slaves in their midst—a guaranteed no-win situation. Indeed, the outnumbered Texians would have no chance at simultaneously defeating opponents on two fronts, front and rear.

Dark-haired Ben Milam was killed during the attack on San Antonio in December 1835 and buried near La Villita, or the "Little Village," a collection of Tejano huts (*jacales*) that stood several hundred yards beyond the Alamo's south wall. Before his death, he presented a stern warning to Colonel Frank White Johnson. Milam had been granted a large segment of land to establish his own colony, which was annulled in 1832 because of lack of process. He emphasized that the Mexicans' overall strategic plan was to subdue the Texans not only with Indian allies, but worst of all, "if possible to get the slaves to revolt." Such a combined threat would leave "a wilderness of Texas, and beggars of its inhabitants."[113] In 1836, even Austin, in a desperate appeal for United States aid, emphasized that Santa Anna was determined to conquer Texas and inhabit "that country with Indians and negroes."[114]

Nor was this much-feared alliance between slaves and Native Americans an idle threat. In late 1835, the diminutive United States Army engaged in a bitter guerrilla conflict, a virtually unwinnable war of attrition, in the morass of the Florida wilderness. Seminoles and their black allies—Black Seminoles from distinctive African American villages hidden deep in the Florida swamps, and ex-slaves—rose up as one to devastate the vast sugar plantations and liberate gangs of slaves along the St. John's River in Florida during the Christmas season of 1835. It seemed to be an eerie repeat of the St. Domingue insurrection of 1793. In both cases, the rebellious slaves sought not only to destroy the whites, but also to deliver a crippling blow to the hated institution of slavery.

At that time, Brevet Major Francis Langhorne Dade, of King George County, Virginia, and his command of United States regulars, including many Irish immigrants, were ambushed on a grey, overcast winter day. Amid a semi-tropical forest of tall grass, ancient oaks dripping with lengthy strands of Spanish moss, dense stands of pines and palmettos, the Seminoles struck back with a fury. More than a hundred regulars were wiped out on a bloody Monday, December 28, 1835. The event, which occurred barely two months before the Alamo's fall, caught the attention of America, sparking the Second Seminole War. Nearly fifty Black Seminoles and former slaves extinguished what little life remained among the piles of wounded white soldiers, hacking away at them with axes and knives in a grim celebration of the one-sided victory.

In this vicious Florida conflict, the combined might of Indian Seminoles, Black Seminoles, and ex-slaves proved more than a match in combat for the best U.S. regular troops and their West Point-trained officers. The Second Seminole War provided a painful lesson that reminded Anglo-Celtic settlers of Texas about the potential enemy in their midst, who already possessed a natural ally in the Plains Indians.[115] Even the Mexican Secretary of War warned the United States of its perpetual Achilles heel: "Is the success of your whole Army, and all your veteran generals, and all your militia calls, and all your mutinous volunteers against a miserable band of five or six hundred invisible Seminole Indians, in your late campaign, an earnest of the energy and vigor [necessary to win a] far otherwise formidable and complicated war? . . . Your Seminole War is already spreading to the Creeks, and, in their march of desolation, they sweep along with them your negro slaves, and put arms into their hands to make common cause with them against you; and how far will it spread, sir, should a Mexican invader, with the torch of liberty in his hand, and the standard of freedom floating over his head, proclaiming emancipation to the slave and revenge to the native Indian, as he goes, invade your soil?"[116]

Mexico's insightful secretary of war indeed had threatened the United States with the nightmare of "a Mexican, an Indian, and a negro war."[117] Fears were fanned among the Texas settlements when Horatio Allsbery, who visited Mexico, proclaimed a grim warning to the people of Texas in a public letter. Relying on the worst possible interpretation of events, he stated how the Mexicans were determined to march into Texas to "put your slaves free and then loose upon your families."[118] It is no wonder that the arrival of Santa Anna's Army on Texas soil sent shock waves across the South. As reported in the pages of the New York *Herald* in spring 1836: "Santa Anna has proclaimed the emancipation of the slaves in Texas and called the Indians to his aid. This is one of the most alarming aspects for the safety, peace, and happiness of the south and west . . . Santa Anna not only wars against the colonists of Texas, but he has unfurled the flag against the domestic institutions of the South and West."[119]

Sharing the historic fears of the Southern planter class from which he hailed, Sam Houston accused Santa Anna of desiring to arm Texas slaves "for the purpose of creating in the midst of us a servile war."[120] In February 1836, just before he launched his invasion of Texas, Santa Anna wrote to the Minister of War and Marine in Mexico City of his intentions: "There is a considerable number of slaves in Texas. . . . Shall we permit those wretches to moan in chains any longer in a country whose kind laws granted the liberty of man without distinction of cast[e] or color?"[121]

On Texas soil in 1836, Santa Anna was destined to play the role of enlightened liberator to those held in chains during his campaign north of the Rio Grande. In Texas, he did not plan to act as an abolitionist fanatic, but was determined to uphold the anti-slavery laws and principles of the republic by liberating the slaves. Clearly, Santa Anna was in step with the day's most enlightened thought, and especially with humanitarian thinking in Great Britain. In late 1835, as Santa Anna was laying his well-conceived plans to invade Texas, Frenchman Gustave de Beaumont, the grandson of Marquis de Lafayette of American and French Revolutionary fame, published a harsh critique of American slavery. He denounced the nation's hypocrisy as a betrayal of its fundamental republican principles that victimized millions of African Americans across the South.[122]

The alarmed editor of the New York *Herald* warned, "Santa Anna has proclaimed the emancipation of the slaves in Texas. . . . Taking this movement in connection [then] we should not be surprised to see the whole South and West pour en masse [to Texas because] Santa Anna not only wars against the colonists of Texas, but he has unfurled the flag against the domestic institutions [slavery] of the South and the West— he throws out menaces upon their safety, which as far exceed the puny efforts of the northern abolitionists as it is possible to conceive . . . Santa Anna has declared war against the inhabitants of the south."[123] Although the editor was a northerner, he concluded: "If Santa Anna and the Mexicans are allowed to possess Texas, they will cause negro insurrections in the south, and thus become one of the most dangerous neighbors to the Union that ever appeared on our borders."[124]

Texas settlers were also incensed by rumors that Mexican agents were stirring up the Indians, an ancient foe in Texas, seeking their assistance in wiping out a white enemy. A September 14, 1835 letter from Nacogdoches, Texas, told of how "the people of Texas are in a great state of anxiety, in consequence of the despot Santa Anna having excited the Indian tribes to war against the settlers."[125] A good many tribes, especially the Creeks, or the Muskogee people, had old scores to settle with whites after the slaughters in Alabama, especially at the battle of Horseshoe Bend during the Creek War. A letter in the *Philadelphia Gazette* published during the early stage of the Texas Revolution expressed the opinion that the Texians were most concerned not about native Texas tribes, but the Creeks because of the cruel legacy of the War of 1812: "The people of Texas have written to President [Andrew] Jackson to arrest the emigration of the Creeks, 3,000 of whom were soon expected, and who, it was feared might be induced to join the other Indians" of Texas in a holy war against the Texians.[126]

The hard-fighting General Andrew Jackson, a Scotch-Irishman who had learned of war's cruelties as a South Carolina teenager in the American Revolution, was most responsible for the conquest of the Creeks, who made the fatal mistake of allying with the British and standing up to Jackson during the War of 1812. In distinctly Celtic-Gaelic fashion, the Irish-born Jackson had taken the war aggressively to the Creeks, or Redsticks, striking deep into their Alabama heartland. The Creeks however only rose up in a "sacred revolt" in 1813–14, when the encroaching whites threatened to forever destroy their way of life and culture. In his typical no-nonsense style, General Jackson unleashed a frontal assault on a strong defensive position to decisively break the back of Creek resistance at the battle of Horseshoe Bend, in a loop of the Tallapoosa River in late March 1814.

There at Tohopeka, Jackson's troops, including United States regulars and their Indian allies, took more lives of Native Americans, who refused to give up, than in any other battle of the Indian Wars. Indeed, "the butchery was continued for hours [and] None asked for quarter." Tragically for the Creeks, their ancestral homeland of Alabama, which was admitted to the Union in 1819, became part of a vast cotton kingdom. At the time of the Texas Revolution, the Creeks yet nursed deep grievances against the whites in Texas, including soldiers like Houston who had served under Jackson as a regular, and David Crockett who had served as a volunteer.[127]

Not surprisingly, Indian trouble in Texas reached new heights in 1835, and further escalated shortly after October, when the Revolution broke out. "The war with the Indians began in 1835," wrote frontier ranger George Bernard Erath, who had seen many horrors of Indian warfare. Isolated cabins of Texas settlers and parties of surveyors and migrants were attacked throughout the fall.[128] As in Florida during the Second Seminole War, Indian uprisings sparked slave revolts, with Native Americans and African Americans forming a formidable alliance. One Alamo garrison member destined to die on March 6 had just returned from battling the Seminoles: Ohio-born Robert Mussel-man, age 31 and a former sergeant of the New Orleans Greys. One indi-cation of exactly how close an Indian and Mexican alliance came to forming in Texas was the headdress of a Comanche chief who met Houston wearing "a Mexican officer's hat, of which he was quite proud."[129]

Historians have not bothered to look beyond the freedom of a rela-tive handful of men at the Alamo to understand the larger issue of free-dom for all people in Texas. While the Texans and United States volun-teers at the Alamo in part defended slavery, "Mexican leaders indicated that slavery would be one of the casualties in their conquest of the rebels."[130] A sense of outrage, if not incredulousness, rose among Texians at the sight of an invading Mexican army that included black soldiers in neat uniforms, dressed in both the Napoleonic style of the regulars and the much plainer militia garb of the conscripts. Although such a sight was almost unbelievable to the average Texian, the tradi-tion of Africans, including slaves, serving faithfully in the military ranks in Latin America, the Caribbean, Spanish Florida, and Louisiana, and of course in Spain was as lengthy as it was distinguished, existing long before the American Revolution.

In contrast to America's historic reluctance, including that of George Washington, to use soldiers of African descent, Mexico contin-ued the tradition of European nations, particularly Spain in Latin America, of employing black troops. Not surprisingly, then, a number of blacks served as soldados of the Morelos Battalion, which marched under General Cós. Significantly, these men proved to be the most reluc-tant of any command to surrender in December 1835. The battalion's members were considered by some Anglo-Celts as "the best soldiers in the [Mexican] Republic" in Texas in 1835 and for good reason.[131]

Ironically, what these Anglo-Celts, who were familiar with slavery and generally comfortable around it, could hardly realize that as early as the 1720s, half a century before the American Revolution and at a time when many of their own ancestors lived in squalor in Europe, a black soldier, Juan Blanco, in the service of New Spain was killed by

Apaches just northeast of the Alamo. And conveniently, they also forgot about the vital role played by the free black battalion—composed of young men from St. Domingue—at the battle of New Orleans, where white riflemen from Tennessee and Kentucky gained almost sole credit for the success over Wellington's British veterans, who had just defeated the French in Spain.[132]

Even more unsettling for the Anglo-Celts in Texas was the easy, effortless intermixture of diverse peoples of a wide variety of colors and hues. Unlike the English, the Spanish had always been more open-minded and tolerant toward different races, including intermixing. The mixed-race Mexican of part Indian and part Spanish blood, the *Mestizo*, was a horror to the Anglo-Celts, despite the fact that whites often fathered children with their slaves. To the Anglo-Celtic mind, slavery ensured that a free mixed-race people, children of slave women and whites, remained slaves; the increasing numbers of these "new people" were meant to be forever in bondage. Consequently, the mere threat of a successful slave revolt sparked by a Mexican invasion was seen as a prelude to racial intermixing on a grand scale. In general, those of Anglo-Celtic descent rarely mixed with any other people, be they French, Spanish, Indian, or black. Although both the Anglo-Celts and the Spanish had existed on the North American continent for more than 250 years, intermixing between them was still rare.

Just as Mexicans were outraged by whites who owned slaves, Anglo-Celts were shocked by the racial background of Tejanos like Rafael Morales of San Antonio. The blood of the Comanche, the ancient enemy of the Texas settlers, flowed in Morales' veins, inherited from both sides of his family. His great-grandfather Ramon Balderas, a Spanish Army Captain, had married a Comanche woman out of love, while stationed on the untamed northern Texas frontier of New Spain. When Santa Anna's Army invaded Texas and employed some of "the ways of the Comanche," Morales served as a scout, providing intelligence about the lack of preparedness at the Alamo.[133]

As in Rafael Morales' case, the Tejano people of San Antonio and other parts of Texas consisted of a mixture of Spanish and a variety of Native American peoples: Comanche, Tlaxcalan, and Coahuilatecan. This race mixing had been a regular feature of life in Mexico for nearly three hundred years by the time of the Texas Revolution. The Coahuilatecans were a native people indigenous to both Texas and Coahuila. Tlazcalen warriors, who had allied themselves with Hernando Cortes to defeat the Aztecs, had accompanied Spanish soldiers and missionaries north to Texas to settle along the northern frontier. A mixture of Tlaxcalans, Spanish, and Coahuilatecans, with a lesser blending of African and sprinkling of Aztec, had produced the Tejano people.[134]

Anglo-Celts generally looked down upon the Mexican and Tejano people, denouncing the Mexican people simply as a "despicable race" of mulattoes. Long accustomed to the slave regime of Virginia, William Fairfax Gray, who migrated Texas to locate land for opportunistic United States investors, wrote with disgust how the Mexicans were "swarthy, dirty looking people, much resembling . . . mulattoes, but having straight hair."[135] By 1836, whites in Texas viewed the Texas Revolution almost purely in racial terms as a battle against a "mongrel Spanish-Indian and negro race."[136] Most galling, if not unbelievable, to Texans was the fact that both blacks and mixed race people enjoyed the status of free citizens in the Republic of Mexico. Such an ideology threatened the entire social order that Texans had been taught since birth.[137]

A distinguished African heritage, both slave and free, went all the way back to the beginning of New Spain, or colonial Mexico. In fact, colonial Mexico contained more free blacks than anywhere else in the New World. Slipping away from Spanish masters soon after arrival from Africa, escaped slaves established maroon communities in the remote mountains and swamps of Mexico. By 1810, the number of free blacks, 624,000, equated to ten percent of Mexico's total population, most of whom were concentrated around Mexico City. Compared to the United States, where color rather than religion mattered the most, a greater acceptance of blacks by both the Church and the Crown was in part a cultural, societal, and military legacy of the wars against the Moors. For centuries, Christian blacks fought beside white Spaniards against Islamic warriors, with religion superseding race.

Along with more liberal attitudes toward race and sex than the British of North America, this greater acceptance of Africans resulted from wider race mixing. Across the breadth of Mexico, Spanish, African, and Indian people mixed as one on a scale unlike anything seen in the United States. This development led to the mulatto class of blacks—the largest free class of African descent in all of the Western Hemisphere. Clearly, for African Americans, Mexico and not the United States was the land of freedom and equality.[138] The one exception to the rule was the Mexican province of Texas.

Conversely, like the Spanish (especially the pure bloods, or peninsulars), the Mexican people expressed a xenophobia toward the Anglo-Celts that was deeply ingrained in their Mediterranean-based culture. To them, these non-refined Protestants, Methodists, Baptists, Episcopalians, and Presbyterians, mostly Scotch-Irish from the north, were heretical *northamericano* barbarians who threatened civilization.[139]

The fact that the Anglo-Celts held darker-skinned people in contempt caused widespread underestimation of Mexican fighting men, which helped set the stage for the Alamo fiasco. Unlike the Christians of Spain, the Anglo-Celts of Texas had never learned of the ferocity of the Muslim warriors who had conquered Spain in the name of Islam and successfully defended it for hundreds of years. The fact that so many Moors who had invaded Spain and southern Europe were black created the popular European name for this dark-skinned Islamic people from North Africa, "Blackamoor."[140]

Yet another factor that fueled the Anglo-Celtic revolt against Mexico City was a little-known scheme favored by the Mexican government to establish a free black colony in Texas. Planned by a white Quaker abolitionist, Benjamin Lundy, and a former Mexican Army officer, who was a mulatto, this colony was to be composed of free blacks from the United States.[141] To the Anglo-Celtic mind, free blacks would further threaten the stability of slavery in Texas, and possibly incite a slave revolt.

Texans, like most Southerners, most of all detested abolitionists, especially if they were dressed in Mexican Army uniforms and armed to the teeth. Clearly, in all forms, the issue of slavery and the abolitionist views of Mexican political and military leaders, became "a major source of discontent."[142] The "battle" of the Alamo would never have been fought without the unbridgeable gulf in the way the issue was perceived by Anglo-Celts and the Mexican people. Anglo-Celts viewed Mexicans as a natural, almost inevitable enemy because of their race, just as Native Americans had been for generations, and as African Americans would be if they rose up in revolt. In their eyes, they therefore faced a potential triple threat if these three groups united against them. Clearly, the outnumbered Texians could never successfully resist the combined might of Mexicans, Native Americans, and Africans.[143]

Symbolically, Santa Anna's Army of Operations soon would march into Texas after crossing the Rio Grande River at the little river town of Guerrero, southwest of San Antonio, where he established headquarters after emerging from the depths of northern Mexico. Amid the deserts of rocky hills, a few mesquite trees, and patches of prickly pears, this quaint little community had been named in honor of the president of part-African blood who had freed Mexico's slaves in 1829. It was an ominous warning for the people of Texas for more than one reason.[144]

MATTERS OF CLASS

The Texas Revolution was also very much a rich man's war and a poor man's fight. This was nothing new, and had been largely the case in America since its first struggle for liberty. During the War of 1812, a Scotch-Irishman, Samuel McKee of Kentucky, correctly predicted how it would be the burden of the hardy "yeomanry of the country," which was largely Scotch-Irish of lower and middle-class origins, to fight "an ignoble war" against Great Britain, and to pay the high cost of an unprepared young nation's headlong rush into war.[145] Although historians have portrayed the 1835–36 conflict largely as a classless struggle with Texians united as one, class was very much a factor in the Texas Revolution, and played an essential role in the Alamo disaster.

The Texas Revolution and the struggle with Mexico were also about big business. Sizeable loans from United States banks were contingent upon a declaration of independence in Texas, which would ensure a dramatic rise in land values and hence guarantee repayment of the loans in timely fashion, once victory over Mexico was secured. Average United States volunteers in the Texas Army likewise realized that the promises made to them of hundreds and thousands of Texas acres, "vast amounts of land," could only become reality with ultimate victory.[146]

Mostly the poor, especially the squatters, migrated to Texas to create a new world for themselves by acquiring large amounts of land. Along with the lower classes, middle class men like Bowie and Travis also aspired to rise higher by fulfilling their Texas dream.[147] James Atkins Shackford perhaps made an appropriate tribute to Crockett, focusing on the key aspect of class without the usual romanticism: "A poor man who had long known the devastating consequences of poverty and who all his life had fought a dedicated life for the right of the dispossessed to a new opportunity, he died defending a poor and insecure people" in Texas.[148] Indeed, the "greatest ambition" that fueled Crockett's migration to Texas was the desire to do what no one in his family had been able to accomplish since arriving in the New World from Ireland: move up the social ladder to become a large, landholding gentleman. Like no other place on earth, Texas possessed the potential to fulfill such dreams that had eluded generations of lower and middle class citizens across America for so long.[149]

It was largely the poor who fought and died in the Texas Revolution, and especially at the Alamo. The wealthy cotton planters and other members of the upper class remained largely absent from the Texas Army's diminutive ranks. Commanding United States volunteers, Thomas J. Green was appalled by the inequitable situation that caused so many poor soldiers to die like sacrificial lambs. In disgust that could not be disguised, he wrote how the common soldiers in the field fought and died in the "defense of the poor men, women & children in this country," while the rich were nowhere to be seen. "In God's name," he wrote, "where are the larger land holders? Why are they not fighting for their freedoms? . . . Is our blood to be split defending their immense estates?"[150]

While Alamo defenders risked their lives in the hope of gaining their relatively small piece of the Texas dream, those longer-resident colonists who had already fulfilled that dream—the majority of "Old Texians," wealthy merchants, large landowners, and politicians—were indeed noticeably absent from the army's ranks at the time of the Alamo's fall.[151] The assumption that the Texas Revolution was inspired by the common man of Texas, much like the lower and middle-class Minutemen of Lexington and Concord, has become a staple of the myth of the Alamo. One editor of a major eastern newspaper, the *Baltimore Gazette*, for example, denounced the Texas Revolution as a vast covert conspiracy by "secret agents," lamenting that lower class American citizens in Texas fought and died only to "enrich a few land speculators, robbers, and brokers" from Wall Street.[152] Modern scholarship has verified this claim. The historian Will Fowler wrote: "Of the rebels who defended the Alamo, only a handful had been born in Texas. The great majority were settlers of U.S.-European extraction, backed financially by the Galveston Bay and Texas Land Company and other land speculators based in New York and New Orleans."[153]

The flow into Texas of both colonists and squatters was largely a product of a convulsive economic event east of the Sabine: the Panic of 1819. With deflation racking the financial markets, fear spread across America. Thousands of common people across the United States lost their land, experiencing soaring debt, defaults, and mortgage foreclosures that resulted from the bursting of a great land bubble, itself based on ever-rising prices, which deeply affected the entire national economy. Additionally, cotton prices plunged to new lows, although previously the ever-increasing price of cotton had been the key catalyst not only for new settlement of the southwest, but also for the spread of the institution of slavery.[154]

The migrant population was clearly in search of both cheaper and better lands; and these existed for the taking in Texas more abundantly than in any other place on the continent. So many squatters illegally flooded across the Sabine's brown waters that Mexico overlooked the longtime threat the Indians had posed to its existence, and redirected this omnipresent menace toward the increasing numbers of Anglo-Celtic newcomers. Mexico's leaders now viewed the thousands of newly arriving Americans as the greatest potential threat to Texas' future, because Anglo-Celts were beginning to dominate the Tejano land.[155]

On March 4, 1836, just two days before the Alamo's fall, a Mexican government official, Pedro Sánchez, wrote: "There is no question that the rebel colonists of Texas are striving to dismember the Republic of its most rich and fertile part of its territory." On the same day he also penned: "It is not the Constitution of 1824 which they have hypocritically invoked as their intention to support . . . Their only object is to take those fertile regions of the Mexican territory."[156] James Clinton Neill, the man who was most responsible for the decision to defend the Alamo, reinforced the opinions of Mexico's leaders. In a letter written on January 14, 1836, the very day he ordered the San Antonio garrison of only 75 men to take up position inside the Alamo, he almost inadvertently and in nonchalant fashion explained the real reason behind his decision. This was the "wish to preserve those lands she [Texas in 1835] had acquired in the infant stage of her campaign," which consisted of all of Texas south to the Rio Grande.[157]

THE FORGOTTEN TEXAS REVOLUTIONARIES: THE IRISH

The widespread participation of the lowly Irish in the Texas Revolution Alamo is perhaps an even better example of how this was essentially a poor man's fight. Because the Irish, especially those of the lower class, were without land or capital to acquire extensive amounts of acreage in either Ireland or the United States, the lure of Texas was especially strong for them.

Even before the American Revolution, the Irish were the only major group of immigrants in America to largely avoid urban areas. Their tendency instead was to push ever-farther west where land was cheap. The Irish almost always seemed to instinctively migrate as far away from societal rules, governments, and upper classes as possible in order to live life as they pleased on the remote western frontier. For the Irish, both Protestant and Catholic, and the Scotch-Irish Presbyterians, Texas represented only the most recent western frontier as part of a great and (importantly) "armed" migration that primarily had begun in the port of Philadelphia. Pushing across the Appalachian Mountains to what is today east Tennessee, mostly Scotch-Irish settlers, including members of Crockett's family, established America's first independent community, the Watuaga Association, in 1774. Here, David Crockett, the grandfather, and William Crockett, signed the historic Watuaga Association petition of 1776.[158]

The largest numbers of Alamo defenders were of largely Scotch-Irish descent, from the states of Tennessee and Virginia, respectively. The Irish presence at the Alamo was the third highest, consisting of at least fifteen Irish-born soldiers, and a good many more Scotch-Irish who could claim Irish roots. Their presence in early 1836 also had a symbolic cast: a Dubliner in the service of Spain, Hugh O'Connor, had established the defensive line of presidios across the northern frontier of New Spain; and visionary Irish-born filibusters Philip Nolan and Augustus Magee led respective expeditions to free Texas of Spanish rule. Hugo O'Connor, as he was known to the Spanish, had first journeyed to San Antonio in the summer 1768, in large part to improve the defense of the town against Comanche raids. Becoming a lieutenant colonel and commandant inspector of presidios along the entire northern frontier, the versatile Irishman played an early role in strengthening the Alamo.

Unlike the United States volunteers, the Irish hailed from an almost feudal society that had been dominated for centuries by England. Most Irish immigrants had been landless peasants of Catholic faith who were discriminated against by the English and Anglo-Irish who ruled Ireland with an iron hand, partly because they were not members of the Anglican Church. For such landless Irish, the lure of hundreds and even thousands of acres in Texas was made even stronger by the fact that it predominantly was a Catholic land. At the beginning of the Texas Revolution, some Irish Catholics were initially even more in favor of the pro-1824 Constitution than were the largely Protestant volunteers from the United States. But in the end, the majority of Irish allied themselves against Mexico. These included the more militant, independent-minded Refugio Irish, who wholeheartedly supported the revolution, as well as the residents of San Patricio, or St. Patrick, an Irish colony named for Ireland's patron saint, which consisted mostly of settlers who had migrated from County Wexford in 1834.

The Emerald Islanders from Refugio, especially Irish-born Nicholas Fagan, were among the earliest and most fiery Texas revolutionaries. These forgotten Irish (who were mostly Scotch-Irish) played leading roles in raising the first flag of Texas independence at Goliad in late 1835, declaring independence months before the official declaration of independence by the Texas government in early March 1836. That these Irish were considered "foreigners" and Catholics, like the Mexican people, ensured that historians and the people of Texas would forget the role they played, once the Texas Revolution had been won.

Precisely because of their Catholicism, the San Patricio Irish had been granted south Texas lands by the Mexican government in the hope that their presence would negate the more radical Protestantism of the colonists. On the broad gulf coastal plain of flowing grasslands southeast of San Antonio, the sons of Erin, including some indentured servants from Ireland, made their dreams come true after a six-week, 4,000-mile journey across the Atlantic. Advancing from poverty to independence by acquiring more than 4,428 acres, these Emerald Isle immigrants created a largely Irish community in a Tejano land.[159]

The Irish, however, had been present in Texas even before the settlements of Refugio and San Patricio were established as part of Mexico's colonization schemes. For instance, Ireland-born John J. Linn, who early migrated to what he called this "terrestrial paradise," signed the Texas Declaration of Independence and served in the Texas Revolution. Another early Irishman who settled in Texas was Edward Gallaher. Born in Belfast, Ireland, the adventurous young man had run away from home at fourteen, and then cast his fortunes with Austin's Second Colony.[160] An Irishman from Brazoria County, Walter Lambert, age thirty-four, served in the 1835 campaign. Thirty-nine-year-old John Forbes, who had migrated from Ireland in 1817, came to Nacogdoches in 1835 and served as a reliable aide-de-camp to General Houston during the San Jacinto campaign.[161]

In total, fifteen confirmed Irishmen fought and died at the Alamo, including the following: Samuel E. Burns (age 26); Andrew Duvalt (17, from Gonzales); Robert Evans (36); Joseph Mark Hawkins (37); Burke Trammel (26); William Daniel Jackson (29, a former sailor); William B. Ward (30); Stephen Dennison (24, who had left Galway for New Orleans); Thomas Jackson (from Gonzales); James McGee; Robert McKinney; John Mormon; Jackson J. Rusk; John Spratt and Edward McCafferty (ages unknown). Hawkins spoke for the entire group when he described the Texas revolutionaries as "the sons of Washington and St. Patrick." With typical Celtic-Gaelic pride, he called himself a true "son of Erin and a friend to Texan independence."[162]

From the urban squalor of New York City by way of New Orleans, Major Evans, in charge of ordnance, was the highest-ranking Irish-born soldier at the Alamo. Cheerful and optimistic, Evans was also known for his high Gaelic-Celtic spirits and dedication to duty, which made him an inspirational leader at the Alamo. The Irishman, dark-haired and blue-eyed, was an imposing physical presence—large, muscular, and standing nearly six-feet tall. His responsibilities included the care and maintenance of the Alamo's artillery arsenal, a critical chore. Embodying typical Celtic-Gaelic ways, Evans was "always merry," seeing the bright side of life.[163]

In addition to the many Scotch-Irish and Irish-born soldiers, other Alamo defenders possessed distinct Irish roots. For instance, 22-year-old Christopher Adams Parker was a proud descendant of the Sparrow family, which had been persecuted for their religious beliefs as Quaker dissenters and fled England, migrating to Ireland. During Robert Emmet's abortive 1803 revolt, Samuel Sparrow followed the revolutionary flag of green and nationalist visions of an independent Ireland. With the crushing of yet another Irish insurrection, he was forced to depart the Green Isle forever. He fled for America, another historic haven for Irish rebels and political exiles who hated England's imperialism with a Celtic-Gaelic passion. Although his grandfather had served in Washington's Continental Army during the American Revolution, Parker was more proud of his father's role under General Jackson at the battle of New Orleans in early January 1815.[164]

James Clinton Neill, the Alamo's first commander after the departure of the Matamoros Expedition, was also of Scotch-Irish descent, and raised on the tales of a family history filled with rebels and revolutionaries who fought against the British in both Ireland and America.[165] That Irish contributions to the Texas Revolution came so early stemmed in part from this lengthy tradition of revolutionary struggles, though in vain, against the British. Even the legendary "Come and Take It" flag that flew in the warm breeze sweeping off the Guadalupe River during the battle of Gonzales—the Lexington of the Texas Revolution—was sown from the white satin wedding dress of a young Irish bride.[166]

Typical among the early Irish colonists in Texas were Robert Henry and his wife, Elizabeth, who departed northern Ireland in 1820 and settled in South Carolina where they raised cotton in the Scotch-Irish community known as the Waxhaws in the Piedmont, where Andrew Jackson grew up as a young man on the frontier. They then moved across the Sabine to Brazos County, Texas, in 1829. Four years later, more industrious Scotch-Irish immigrants of the Presbyterian faith from northern Ireland joined them to create a distinctively Scotch-Irish community known as "Little Ulster."[167]

In contrast to these Presbyterian Irish, the Catholic Irish settled primarily along the gulf coastal plain of Texas. This is where the previously mentioned, mostly Irish colonies of the empresarios James Power and James Hewetson were established at Refugio and at San Patricio under John McMullen and James McGloin. In addition, Irishman John J. Linn became a respected leader of the Martin De Leon colony, even though this was primarily a Mexican colony. A Green Isle immigrant, Linn was nevertheless imbued with the spirit of Manifest Destiny; he wrote with considerable pride that the "Americans had gained a footing on Texan soil which they were destined never more to relinquish."[168]

Some Texas Irishmen had escaped the Irish ghettoes of major Atlantic port cities in the northeast like New York, Boston, and Philadelphia, where large numbers of immigrant Irish had landed since the colonial period. Other Alamo Irish hailed from New Orleans, where the immigrants found many other Celtic-Gaelic people in the largest, busiest city on the Mississippi. New Orleans became the home of the largest Irish community in the South, in part because it was the port to which fares from Ireland were the cheapest.[169]

A number of Alamo Irishmen were members of the New Orleans Greys. These men remained behind in San Antonio and at the Alamo after most of their comrades proceeded south on the Matamoros Expedition at the end of December 1835. One such Irish-born soldier was Thomas William Ward. A devout Catholic, who embraced his Irish heritage as much as his newfound love of Texas, he had migrated to New Orleans from the French city of Quebec, Canada, desiring to remain close to Catholicism and the blessings of a parish priest. At the

Crescent City curving along the Mississippi's banks, this young Irish intellectual devoted himself to the study of engineering and the art of writing.

Privates James McGee, John Mormon, and John Spratt were likewise members of the crack New Orleans Greys, who "had in [their] imaginations already conquered Mexico" before departing from New Orleans for what they believed would be a great adventure. Instead, a tragic reality awaited these naive New Orleans Irish, who were destined to meet untimely deaths on March 6, 1836. On a bloody Palm Sunday of that gruesome year in Texas, other New Orleans Greys Irishmen were executed, under Santa Anna's express orders, at Goliad, including Privates James Noland, Dennis Mahoney, and William Harpen.[170]

For the Irish in Texas, the confrontation between Texas and Mexico was eerily comparable to other conflicts in the tortured course of Ireland's history. The natural beauty of Ireland and Texas both, green as the emerald sea, picturesque, and well watered, masked the horror of the endless saga of human tragedy. That both Ireland and Texas were lands worth fighting and dying for ironically provided the motivation of countless young men from the United States, Ireland, and Mexico by early 1836.[171]

Further confounding the simplistic stereotype of the defenders as western frontiersmen, other exiles from foreign-dominated homelands also fought at the Alamo. Like the Irish, the Scots possessed a distinguished revolutionary heritage of fighting British rule, and four of them died at the Alamo: Robert W. Ballentine, John McGregor, Isaac Robinson, and David L. Wilson. Scotland-born Ballentine viewed the struggle through the lens of Scottish history, comparing the plight of the Texians under Mexico City "to that of our forefathers, who labored under tyrannical oppression" emanating from London.[172] He and the other Scots might have seen some irony in the fact that one of the Alamo's artillery pieces, the little carronade naval gun, was manufactured in the 1770s in Carron, Scotland.

The most colorful Scotsman among the Alamo garrison was red-haired Sergeant John McGregor. He brought his Scottish bagpipes to the Alamo, lifting the garrison's spirits throughout the siege, after leaving a 4,000-head cattle ranch near Nacogdoches. Like so many Irish and Scots in America since the colonial period, the McGregor family possessed deep revolutionary Jacobite roots. Exiled from their native homeland, the McGregors preferred to leave Scotland rather than change their Celtic name as their English rulers dictated. The British had been longtime masters of Scotland by 1836, having decimated the Highland clans, which were always the most rebellious, at Culloden in 1746.[173]

James Bowie proudly claimed Scottish Jacobite roots. One ancestor forced to flee Scotland for his revolutionary activities in 1715–16, migrated to Maryland. Another Bowie Jacobite "rebel" was John Bowie, who somehow survived the slaughter of Scots at Culloden and was "sold [as an indentured servant] in Maryland in 1747."[174]

Other Celtic warriors, both Irish and Scots, served under the Scotland-born Texas revolutionary leader, Dr. James Grant, who led the Matamoros Expedition on its ill-fated attempt to conquer the Mexican city near the Rio Grande's mouth. The colorful, erudite Grant possessed abundant military experience as a proud officer in one of the famed Highlander regiments so respected in the British Army, but he sabotaged any chance for San Antonio and the Alamo to be successfully defended because he convinced the majority of the garrison to join him on his quixotic expedition.[175]

While many Texas soldiers and United States volunteers drew inspiration from the analogy between the Texas Revolution and the struggle of their American Revolutionary forefathers, the Irish and the Scots possessed a longer memory of far more revolts against a centralized government, and a pantheon of heroes and martyrs that spanned generations. Nearly all the migrants who came to Texas were hence bound together by both the lust for land and a lengthy revolutionary tradition against centralized authority.

2

Napoleonic Influences

Few figures in history have been more vilified by Americans than Santa Anna. Yet he perhaps is even more hated by Mexicans, who have historically blamed him for the loss of Texas, and castigated him as the exclusive cause of "all of Mexico's misfortunes." This attitude remains largely prevalent today, as the 2002 biography by Robert L. Scheina, titled *Santa Anna, A Curse upon Mexico*, suggests. Nevertheless, Santa Anna was a bold, dynamic, and imaginative military leader, whose qualities came to the fore at the Alamo, although the fortunes of war finally turned against him at San Jacinto.[1]

While Santa Anna has long been the military leader Mexicans and Americans all "love to hate," some modern historians on both sides of the border have begun to challenge the stereotype. One Mexican historian, for instance, has emphasized that "there is no proof that Santa Anna gave orders that the defenders were to be slaughtered without mercy"; instead, he writes, "Mexican politicians who were enemies of Santa Anna" as well as "American patriots" initially promulgated this view. After San Jacinto, hating Santa Anna became a national pastime not just in the United States but in Mexico, where he was viewed as a traitor and became a scapegoat for the country's many woes. This negative reputation is a primary factor in the Alamo myth that transformed the defenders, after the fact, into a band of heroes pitted against the epitome of evil.[2]

Santa Anna was also endlessly mocked because of his self-styled title as the "Napoleon of the West," and the "Napoleon of the South." Nevertheless, he performed brilliantly in catching his opponents by surprise, swiftly eliminating opposition as he did at the Alamo, and winning repeated victories during the late winter of the 1836 campaign. But like an over-confident, impatient Napoleon, who had been led deep into Russia only to meet disaster in 1812, Santa Anna was made vulnerable precisely because the Alamo's defense had been so feeble, and his initial victory in the campaign was so relatively easy.[3]

Contrary to the Texan stereotype, Santa Anna was not motivated by simple bloodlust, but by a sincere desire to "save" the Republic of Mexico, which of course meant the re-conquest of Texas. And like Napoleon, who refused to stay safely in Paris and personally fought on both ends of Europe, from Spain to Russia, Santa Anna volunteered to lead his army into Texas, temporarily handing over presidential duties. In his own words, he "preferred the hazards of war to the seductive" life amid the comforts and luxuries of Mexico City. Most of all, he was a masterful politician who made his career by adroitly exploiting opportunities. Even the destruction of the Alamo garrison was more important as a political than a military act. His victory sent a powerful, much-needed message to Mexico City, ensuring continued support, and simultaneously was meant to cow the rebels on the Texas frontier, be they Tejanos or Anglo-Celts.

Santa Anna believed that his mission was to save not only Texas, but also the territorial integrity of the Republic of Mexico. Waging war to keep Mexico intact, he explained his primary objective in simple terms: "Our country found itself invaded not by an established nation . . . nor by Mexicans. The invaders were all men who wished to take possession of that vast territory extending from Béxar to the Sabine belonging to Mexico. All existing laws . . . marked them as pirates and outlaws."[4]

A handsome Creole from a middle class family, and one of seven children, Santa Anna was a member of the privileged Criollo class of Vera Cruz on the Gulf of Mexico. Of pure Spanish descent, or "white" in terms of social status and appearance, the ambitious Santa Anna rose to power amid the turmoil of the ideological struggle among Mexico's ruling elites. Mexico's conservatives—pro-church centralists and pro-monarchical—were aligned against the enlightened, anti-church Mexican liberals, who desired a republic based on the United States model. This internal conflict made the young republic vulnerable to outside interference and aggression. After winning independence from Spain in 1821, Mexico (unlike the United States) never completely severed the umbilical cord of the monarchical system, and therefore never thoroughly adapted to become a true constitutional republic.

This deep schism, where issues of religion caused fissures among the ruling class, ensured the existence of two "warring camps" in Mexico. As always, Mexico's military strongmen dominated the ranks of the nation's leadership, because in that yet immature country politics and religion had long been one and the same. Santa Anna rose to become Mexico's supreme leader after overturning the conservative federal government in 1832. The following year, even though he had fought against the revolutionary priests Miguel Hidalgo and José María Morales, who had led the masses in revolt against Spanish rule, Santa Anna was elected president. He enjoyed the powerful backing of the Catholic Church and the Mexican people, especially in Vera Cruz, where he was viewed as a hero for repelling the 1829 Spanish invasion. Perhaps one Mexican officer said it best, when he described Santa Anna as "the pampered son of fortune." In this, too, Santa Anna was much like Napoleon until his fatal invasions of Spain and Russia.[5]

More adept at rhetoric than he was at forging war plans, the Mexican Secretary of War, José María Tornel y Mendívil, referred to Napoleon to explain the situation in Texas, condemning America's obsession to acquire "the greater part of the territory that formerly belonged to Spain." Mendovil continued: "It has been neither an Alexander nor a Napoleon, desirous of conquest in order to extend his dominions or add to his glory, who has inspired the proud Anglo-Saxon race in its desire, its frenzy to usurp and gain control of that which rightfully belongs to its neighbors; rather it has been the nation itself which, possessed of that roving spirit that moved the barbarous hordes of a former age in a far remote north, has swept away whatever has stood in the way of its aggrandizement."[6]

The Mexican Secretary of War also compared the feisty Anglo-Celts of Texas to the Goths who descended on Rome from the depths of the dense evergreen forests north of the Danube River. Mexicans held these transplanted Americans in utter contempt, viewing them as little different from the barbarians who sacked imperial Rome. In this view, too, the Anglo-Celts were primitive forest dwellers from the north who sought to vanquish a culturally superior Mediterranean people to the south.[7]

By referring to Napoleon, Mexico's politically astute but largely incompetent Secretary of War was in part pandering to Santa Anna's obsession. Historians have only made occasional references to Napoleon and his impact on the Texas Revolutionary generation, yet no other military figure more significantly molded the military mentality of both Americans and Mexicans during this time. Four Alamo defenders, including thirty-two-year-old Napoleon B. Mitchell, born in 1804, carried Napoleon's name with them to their graves. This was the same number as those named for the Marquis de Lafayette, and twice the number named for James Madison and Christopher Columbus. Only the six defenders named after Thomas Jefferson surpassed the number named in Napoleon's honor.

The story of the Alamo, in fact, begins with Napoleon and his dramatic impact on world history. Quite possibly there would have been no Texas Revolution or struggle for the Alamo without him. To extend his continental blockade to the Iberian Peninsula and to fulfill his own limitless ambitions, Napoleon invaded Spain in 1808, took possession of Madrid, and deposed the King of Spain. Beginning with the revolt led by Father Miguel Hidalgo in 1810, the collapse of the Spanish government opened the door for the Mexican people to rise up and break away from Spanish rule in 1821. Thus it happened that an independent Mexico, established on the premise that all men were created equal, became subject to turmoil between liberals and conservatives, including the horrors of civil war. The Texas Revolution was only one part of this larger struggle.[8]

The Mexican civil war north of the Rio Grande ended in disaster at San Jacinto. On April 21, 1836, General Sam Houston awoke late; the weather was already as hot as a summer's day on the humid gulf coastal plain. Although Santa Anna, fresh from his Alamo victory, had pursued the remaining Texan forces toward the Louisiana border for weeks, Houston proclaimed that morning: "The sun of Austerlitz has risen again."[9] Houston was of course referring to Napoleon's greatest victory—the bloody December 2, 1804 battle at Austerlitz against combined Russian and Austrian forces that allowed him and his Grande Armée to reach their zenith. Santa Anna could very likely have embraced identical thoughts on the morning of March 6, 1836.[10]

Perhaps the destinies of Santa Anna and Houston were linked from the beginning. Some Americans were convinced that "Houston was to have gone into Texas, and kindled the fire of rebellion, whilst Santa Anna fired his friends in Mexico with the same spirit." In a battle won more by accident than design, Houston, not Santa Anna, gained immorality on April 21, 1836, linking his name forever to Napoleon when he won his own Austerlitz along Buffalo Bayou and the muddy San Jacinto River.[11] Although Santa Anna had conducted a brilliant campaign, won a string of victories, and even threatened the United States border in one of the most audacious military campaigns in Mexican history, he has gone down in history not for his successes, but for his defeat at San Jacinto and the loss of Texas.[12]

Rather than the glorious Austerlitz he so confidently anticipated, the Texas campaign of 1836 resulted in Santa Anna's Waterloo. He nevertheless performed in a manner reminiscent of Napoleon. Exhibiting the "boundless energy for which he became famous," he conducted an aggressive campaign marked by boldness, tactical innovativeness and flexibility, and distinguished by a swift, unexpected approach that caught opponents completely by surprise.[13] From the beginning of the campaign, Santa Anna emphasized classic Napoleonic axioms in his orders to General Sesma, who was to lead the army's advance into Texas on December 7, 1835. If Santa Anna's suggested maneuvers, instead of frontal assault, could not force the Texans from an advantageous defensive position on good terrain, then the forces were to "use the artillery, before anything else." Most importantly, he advocated delivering a crushing blow at exactly the right moment: "Upon noticing the slightest disorder or indecision with the enemy ranks, a bayonet charge will be rapidly unleashed," he ordered.[14]

In the end, Santa Anna became a victim of his own success, much like Napoleon, who gambled against fate once too often when he marched deep into Russia in the belief that he possessed a special destiny impervious to defeat. Both the Russian and San Jacinto campaigns were classic examples of an overly ambitious drive to glory that led ultimately to destruction far from home.[15] Santa Anna long basked in his fame as the "Napoleon of the West," after employing aggressive tactics to repulse the forces of Spain, emerging "as the vindicator of the republic and the savior of the revolution." However, his sobriquet was appropriate only up to his rendezvous with disaster when he was caught with only a small portion of his army on the San Jacinto River.[16]

At no phase of the 1836 Texas campaign did Santa Anna act more like Napoleon than at the Alamo, were he showed a penchant to do the unexpected, both tactically and strategically. He had learned his lessons well in studying Napoleon's campaigns across Europe—these emphasized adhering to the tactical offensive and striking an unprepared enemy when he was least expecting an attack. Napoleon's victory at

Austerlitz was set up by a swift, unexpected march from the English Channel, which thrust deep into the enemy's heartland to catch his allied Russian and Austrian opponents completely by surprise. In much the same way, nothing more distinguished Santa Anna than his decision to conduct a lengthy but rapid march into Texas when his opponents least expected it.

Everyone, especially the Texans, thought a winter campaign to be impossible. Following the conventional wisdom of the day, the Alamo leaders believed that an invading Mexican army marching north, pulling wagons and artillery caissons, would be unable to travel the long distance from northern Mexico deep into Texas in the wintertime before the deluge of spring rain. Therefore, Texas (or so the leaders of the Alamo believed) would be safe from invasion until April or even May, when spring grasses dotted the land. As it turned out, this was a fatal miscalculation.[17]

Defying conventional military wisdom, Santa Anna refused to wait for the brown prairie grasses to turn lush and green from rainfall and warmer temperatures. He had learned the Corsican's axioms well, understanding that swift advances, a skill in which Napoleon's armies excelled, had been key to their amazing successes across Europe. His army moved faster and more lightly than its opponents, and struck more quickly and unexpectedly. So, too, Santa Anna defied the conventional—relying on his keen understanding of both the geography and the vegetation of the land through which he would march, he launched a winter campaign, striking hard when least expected.[18]

No single influence was greater—not even the 1492 *Reconquesta* by the Christians of Spain in expelling the Islamic Moors from the Iberian Peninsula—on Santa Anna than the career of Bonaparte. He had devoured one Napoleon biography after another ever since becoming a cadet; as if to conceal his middle-class upbringing in Vera Cruz, he even attempted to look, dress, pose, and act like his cherished idol. In his early forties by 1836, Santa Anna even combed his hair forward in the style of his idol and rode white horses, just like the French emperor. To inspire the ranks so far from home, he also employed one of Napoleon's favorite means of lifting morale among common French soldiers: badges of honor. For the Texas campaign, Santa Anna created the Legion of Honor, which Napoleon had originally created in 1802 to honor heroic French soldiers. His goal in so doing was "to foster ambitions."

The legacy of Napoleon hovered over Santa Anna's Army of

Operations from the beginning to the end of the 1836 Texas campaign. The General had spent much time, effort, and money in collecting all things related to Napoleon, and in time, a sprawling collection of Napoleonana "fill[ed] Santa Anna's estate." The walls of his magnificent hacienda, located just outside Vera Cruz on the road to Xalapa, Manga de Clavo, were decorated with scenes of Napoleonic history and portraits. Pretty women dressed in the latest Paris fashions especially caught the eye of this ardent ladies' man, who was smitten with French culture as well.

Not surprisingly, in the Texas campaign the Mexican troops were clothed in colorful Napoleonic uniforms, carried similar weapons, and were trained in Napoleonic tactics, perpetuating Santa Anna's fantasies.[19] According to General Vincente Filisola, who rode with him to the Alamo, the single-minded Santa Anna would "listen to nothing which was not in accord with ideas" espoused by Napoleon.[20]

Also like Napoleon, Santa Anna was a gambler, both in his personal life and on the battlefield, proving himself as impulsive and bold as his predecessor—which usually paid dividends in the bedroom as well as in war. Just as Napoleon fell prey to the charms of his beautiful Polish mistress, Marie Walewska, Santa Anna had a weakness for beautiful women, marrying a fourteen-year-old beauty at the age of thirty-one. On the battlefield, the penchant for risk-taking that led to disaster at San Jacinto nevertheless paid him early dividends, leading to promotions and acclaim as a daring young cavalry commander, when he often staked everything on one throw of the dice.[21]

Santa Anna understood the urgent necessity of crushing a revolt as soon as possible, before it gained momentum and wider support, and his love affair with the tactical offense and the element of surprise reaped success at the Alamo. By late 1835, after the Texans captured San Antonio, time was of the essence. Delay meant that the Texans would grow stronger from the steady flow of money, supplies, manpower, and munitions from the United States. And his personal and political enemies in Mexico, the ever-opportunistic liberals, would likewise become emboldened if he did not unleash a vigorous response. In addition to Napoleon's own formula for success across Europe, past Anglo-Celtic filibuster incursions into Texas also told Santa Anna that it was urgent to smash the revolutionaries as soon as possible.

Historians have long treated the Alamo as something almost wholly unique, as if it were a landmark event of epic proportions isolated in time and space. But the story of the Alamo was just a single chapter, and a small one at that, in the much longer saga of aggressive Anglo-Celtic filibuster activities and open revolution in Texas sparked by Americans and widely supported by U.S. interests during the first third of the 19th century. The only thing new about it was that the Texas Revolution was directed against Mexico, whereas earlier struggles for independence were waged against Spain. Both Mexico and Texas possessed a lengthy history of slaughter; the Mexican Army had perfected the massacre of American troops begun by the Spanish, turning it into an art form by 1836. One of the greatest benefactors of the cruel lessons about how to effectively crush revolutionary movements—Anglo-Celtic or Tejano—in Texas was Santa Anna himself.

Santa Anna's estate, located amid the high, cool breezes at nearly 5,000 feet above sea level, was a peaceful haven far away from the horrors of war. It was nestled in the Sierra Madre Oriental Mountains northwest of the port of Vera Cruz, where his father, Don Antonio, had established a family with Doña Manuela Pérez de Lebrón, and made a modest living far from the center of power in Mexico City. Santa Anna took considerable pride in his Manga de Clavo hacienda, which he preferred to the national palace in Mexico City. Purchasing the estate in 1825, he had grown his holdings to seventy square miles by 1842. Vast orchards of fruit trees bearing oranges, bananas, and mangoes lined the hillsides, along with coffee trees that thrived in high, cool elevations. The estate also boasted "an abundance of beef cattle and horses."

Like Napoleon, who had risen despite the fact that he was a Corsican outsider, the ambitious Santa Anna remained an outsider in Mexico City, in part because he was from Vera Cruz. He felt that he had much to prove, both to himself and to others. He had been born into a world where Spaniards of pure blood, born in Spain—the privileged peninsulars—were Mexico's aristocracy and the top political and military leaders. Hailing from a family of modest means from the Creole gentry class, Santa Anna had occupied a lower rung on the social ladder. With a provincial middle class background, he had relatively little education, unlike the aristocratic peninsulars; a military career therefore offered him the best possibility to move up the social ladder.

Much like the Anglo-Celts in Texas, Santa Anna felt little empathy for the lower-class Mexican people, who were mixtures of Spanish, Indian, and black. Most of all, he identified with Major General José Joaquin Arredondo, a ruthless Spanish officer of considerable military

ability. His early experiences with native peoples were marked by vio-
lence, contempt, and ruthlessness, not unlike the experiences of many
settlers in Texas from the United States. As a young cadet, he fought the
Chichimeca Indians, suffering an ugly wound in his left arm in 1811
near San Lusi Potosi. A 19-year-old of promise, he earned the rank of
second lieutenant and the praise of his commander, Arredondo.

But by far, Santa Anna learned his most important and bloodiest
lessons at the nightmarish battle of Medina, during the Anglo-Celtic and
Tejano revolution sparked by Father Miguel y Costilla Hidalgo and his
revolutionary "Army of America," when Texas attempted to break
away from Spain's New World Empire. Dominated by large numbers of
United States volunteers, and financed by bankers and investments in
New Orleans, the Gutierrez-Magee Expedition of 1812–13 entered
Texas and declared independence. In response, a powerful Spanish army
under General Arredondo, Santa Anna's mentor and idol after
Napoleon, was dispatched north into Texas. Battle-hardened Spanish
soldiers were determined to purge Texas of revolutionaries, just as their
forefathers had swept the Moors out of Spain.

Just south of San Antonio, the battle of Medina was fought on
August 18, 1813, barely three years after Santa Anna had been com-
missioned as a "gentleman cadet" of the Permanent Infantry Regiment
of Vera Cruz in the Spanish Army. But the lessons Santa Anna learned
as a teenager were antithetical to the gentlemanly conduct and conventional rules of early nineteenth century warfare, especially the European
model during the Age of Napoleon. Mexico's proud cavalrymen exceeded all others in slaughtering Anglo-Celts, Mexicans, Europeans, and
Tejanos—anyone who opposed Spain—with business-like efficiency. At
the time he first distinguished himself on the battlefield, the young Santa
Anna gained a deeply ingrained contempt for American fighting men,
whom the hard-riding dragoons and lancers so easily dispatched in the
sweltering, mesquite-covered lowlands of the Medina River. What happened to so many ill-fated Anglo-Celts at Medina—"the bloodiest battle ever fought in Texas"—was something he would never forget, and
served as a lesson to be put to good use at the Alamo.[22]

The crushing defeat of the rebels at the battle of Medina was hardly unprecedented: the history of American filibusters in Texas was as
lengthy as it was bloody. The first such expedition to cross the Sabine
was led by Irishman Philip Nolan, who entered Texas with an armed
party of filibusters in October 1800. Nolan's expedition included slaves,

in a portent of the future source of troubles between Anglo-Celtic colonists and Mexico City. Spanish officials were convinced that Nolan planned to start a "revolution" in Texas against the Spanish, and Spanish troops crushed the filibusters, killing Nolan in a clash in east Texas.

Then, in late spring 1819, Dr. James Long (a veteran of the battle of New Orleans) and his Anglo-Celtic filibuster expedition, organized and recruited in Natchez, Mississippi, marched boldly into Spanish Texas; more boldly yet, Long issued a Declaration of Independence for the Republic of Texas at Nacogdoches. This quixotic expedition ended in disaster, overwhelmed by Spanish Royalist forces. Later, Long was shot and killed while a prisoner.

A third confrontation and another American defeat occurred in December 1826, less than a decade before the start of the Texas Revolution, when independence-minded settlers of the Benjamin Edwards Colony near Nacogdoches created the east Texas republic of Fredonia. Setting a pattern that would be repeated, Edwards' colonists settled on land owned by Tejanos. When the Mexican government aided the Tejanos and revoked Edwards' contract, Edwards and a handful of Anglo-Celtic colonists established a new republic. Within a month, Mexican troops crushed the movement.[23]

Mexico was born of the violent revolution against Spain, and Santa Anna knew the nature of revolts far more intimately than did Texans. Most of all, he knew that the potent swelling of revolution had to be stopped as soon as possible. If it were not, the new Mexican republic, ripped apart by escalating political divisions, economic problems, and civil war, would die an early death. Meanwhile, Mexico's conservatives looked with apprehension at the United States and its seemingly dangerous experiments in democracy. To the ruling elite in Mexico City, the image of the Anglo-Celtic revolutionaries from the United States, who had earlier defeated the armies of a powerful European monarchy on the other side of the Atlantic, was a consummate fear.[24]

Throughout the 19th century, no city in the United States was more consistently a thorn in Mexico's side than New Orleans, the economically thriving city from which all Anglo-Celtic filibustering incursions, including the Texas Revolution and the recent invasion attempt at Tampico in 1835, had been organized.[25] Economic ties between the powerful merchant class of New Orleans and Texas settlers were tight: thousands of cotton bales produced by Texas slaves filled the New Orleans cotton market, reaping the highest prices because of their high quality. Ample capital, transport connections, and a common culture all tied the future prosperity of Texas more closely to New Orleans than to Matamoros, and the even more distant Mexico City.[26]

Mexico City officials suspected a deep-seated Anglo-Celtic conspiracy on both sides of the Sabine, designed to steal Texas away for the financial benefit of the United States, and especially for New Orleans. New Orleans provided ample manpower, including organized military companies raised expressly for service in Texas. Symbolically, one of the first and most prominent United States volunteer companies to serve in Texas was the New Orleans Greys, which evolved into "the premier Texas military unit" of the Texas Revolution. These young soldiers, neatly clothed in the grey uniforms that gave the company its name, became the first United States volunteer unit to join the Texas Army in mid-October 1835.

The Crescent City volunteers added a measure of professionalism to the rustic Texas rookies in rebellion, infusing new vigor and providing much-needed stability to Stephen Austin's ragtag revolutionary army of 1835. Playing a leading role in San Antonio's capture, they were "in the forefront of the fighting" from beginning to end.[27] Disgusted with Texas politics and the endless bickering among military and government leaders, many disillusioned New Orleans Greys eventually returned to the United States after the 1835 campaign, refusing to fight any longer to "enrich a few land speculators," including principal Texas revolutionary leaders like Houston and Bowie.[28]

THE RAPE OF ZACATECAS

Before Texas once again erupted in revolt, the most recent example of revolution in Mexico had occurred in Zacatecas. Like Texas and Zacatecas, secession movements had long flared up in the rebellious north, far away from the grip of Mexico City. After Santa Anna took power as a liberal, newly elected president in 1833, he ordered the drastic reduction of the state militias, although they were guaranteed by the Constitution of 1824. The militia act had emboldened state autonomy, running contrary to the centralized interests of Mexico City. He also desired to strengthen the regular army. This astute plan for eliminating potential future threats caused liberal states like Zacatecas to rise up in revolt, after the sentiments that had led them to vote Santa Anna into office had been betrayed.

Backed by the church, business interests, and large landowners, Santa Anna planned to quell the rising of revolution in both Coahuila and Zacatecas before dealing with the rebellious Anglo-Celts in Texas. Zacatecas posed the most serious threat. Here the Mexican people had taken up arms to repel the centralist "assault on our liberty," refusing to disband their sizeable militia. In this, it was backed by its independent-minded legislature, on the premise that Santa Anna was overthrowing the 1824 Constitution. Zacatecas boasted the largest militia force in all Mexico. As in the later Texas Revolution, this confrontation between Mexican citizens of differing political philosophies was a classic civil war, with the forces of centralized power taking action to crush state autonomy and secession-minded liberal republicans.

To defend the republican government of Zacatecas, Governor Francisco Garcia organized a militia of 4,000 men, which rivaled the size of Mexico's national army. Without formal training, however, these young militiamen never had a chance. With republican banners flying in the bright spring sunshine, Garcia made his stand against Santa Anna's approaching army at the little village of Guadalupe, near the town of Zacatacas.

More politician than military commander, Garcia was no match for the energetic, forty-one-year-old Santa Anna, who had conceived a tactical plan for total victory over the neophyte militiamen. In the early morning darkness of May 11, 1834, Santa Anna maneuvered and then attacked swiftly, using tactics that later became his trademark, to catch his opponents by surprise. The Zacatecas militia, though bolstered by a dozen artillery pieces, was easily crushed by Santa Anna's tactical skill, which took "a page out of Napoleon's book . . . surprising the city's defenders with a surreptitious attack from the rear."[29]

The fiercely xenophobic Santa Anna was well aware that liberal Anglos had played a key role in the Zacatecas revolution. One noted example was German-born Edward Harcourt, who commanded the Zacatecas artillery and tried to take charge of the hapless militia upon its collapse. Believing, as did leaders in Mexico City, that the revolt was largely Anglo-inspired, an enraged Santa Anna ordered the execution of every foreign fighter, especially any Americans, found among the militia's ranks or in Zacatecas. Then, to set a bloody example for other revolt-minded liberals throughout Mexico, including any potential revolutionaries in Texas, he unleashed his troops in an orgy of rape, pillage, plunder, and murder. As one foreign official wrote, surviving Americans became special targets, with men executed on sight and women stripped and "run through the streets."[30]

Less than two years later, having earned renown as the "Hero of the Fatherland," Santa Anna determined to wipe out the Anglo-Celtic presence in Texas, just as he had in Zacatecas, when the "once fair city was [left] a burning, screaming shambles."[31] The slaughter of the Alamo garrison would send a bloody message throughout Texas and the United States. Confident after his victory at Zacatecas, Santa Anna dissolved the Mexican Congress, and dismantled the liberal Constitution of 1824. With the death of republicanism, he became Mexico's dictator. And in seizing absolute power, it was again as if Santa Anna were following Napoleon's script.

For Santa Anna, it was all the more crucial to crush revolutionary resistance as soon as possible because Texas was on the United States border. He therefore dispatched his brother-in-law, General Perfecto de Cós, to maintain order and quell unrest among the unruly Texians, sending five hundred Mexican troops into the last bastion of liberalism and final "Federalist stronghold" in Mexico.[32] But the people of Texas rose up as one and descended on Cós, who was far from Mexico City and reinforcements: ironically, this would be the future predicament of the Alamo garrison only a few months later. General Cós surrendered San Antonio to besieging Texas forces on December 11, 1835, leaving Santa Anna determined to avenge both the stain to his family name and Mexico's national honor—a potent motivational mixture. Thus he began to prepare a mighty expedition to punish and reclaim Texas.

Launching a large-scale expedition overland to reclaim a wayward Texas was a daunting task for Mexico, especially in regard to logistics and securing sufficient manpower for the ambitious push north of the Rio Grande. As a poor agrarian nation long wracked by internal strife, and severely handicapped by a lack of industry and manufacturing, Mexico had a pathetically small treasury. Budgets were all the more strained because of the great expense of suppressing revolts over a vast arid, mountainous, and tropical land that stretched from the Pacific to the Gulf of Mexico. Mexico had only a small army, which combined with the size and difficulty of the terrain made it extremely difficult to wage an aggressive war, especially a lengthy one, located far from the army's base of operations.

In addition to securing established, or regular, units—the disciplined, well-trained *permanentes*—for the 1836 campaign, Santa Anna also relied upon impressments, largely drawing from the Indian and Mestizo population to gain recruits for a new force, the Army of Operations. Thinned ranks were "filled by recruits snatched away from the crafts and from agriculture, by heads of families, who usually do not make good soldiers," lamented de la Pena. He also complained that the army consisted of too many young and overaged soldiers. In derogatory fashion, the Texians derided these fighting men of Mexico as "colored hirelings," fusing issues of race with revolution.

Arriving in early December some 600 miles below San Antonio, Santa Anna began the formidable task of assembling an army at San Luís Potosí, designated as his headquarters, with his customary energy. It was here that the Army of Operations was born. Ironically, while Santa Anna sought to redeem his brother-in-law's tainted military reputation for the defeat at San Antonio, yet another brother-in-law, Colonel Ricardo Dromundo, who was the army's commissary general and married to Santa Anna's sister Francisca, either squandered or stole the already limited funds allocated by the government to properly clothe and uniform the approximately two thousand new recruits. A third brother-in-law, Gabriel Nuñez, who would be captured at San Jacinto, stayed out of trouble, much to Santa Anna's relief.[33]

In the process of forming an army from units yet arriving, Santa Anna relocated at Saltillo, founded in 1577 and the oldest colonial city in northern Mexico, in early January. Located just over 360 miles southwest of San Antonio amid the arid mountains of northeast Mexico, Saltillo served as the launching point for the march into Texas. The capital of the state of Coahuila, Saltillo was an important staging point both logistically and politically. Both regular units (*permanentes*) and the active militias (*activos*) from across Mexico now marched toward northern Mexico to join Santa Anna. These included General Sesma, who received his orders in Zacatecas, where he had been placed in command to organize the newly designated "Vanguard Division of Operations." Sesma originally had moved north to reinforce Cós in Texas, but San Antonio's fall aborted the movement.

Another command destined to join the Army of Operations was the disciplined Tres Villas Active Battalion garrisoned at San Carlos at old Fort Perote, which dated from the previous century. The battalion departed the state of Vera Cruz on December 9, 1835, in an early indication of the extent of Santa Anna's frantic preparations for the Texas campaign prior to Cós' defeat. As a proud Veracruzano, Santa Anna especially desired these troops from his native state.

Battalion commander Colonel Agustín Alcerreca, like his men (of whom less than one-third were recruits), was inspired to defend "the sacred rights of our Fatherland." Dusty and weary from their lengthy march, the *soldados* of the Tres Villas Active Battalion joined the army at Saltillo, ready for the challenge of the Texas campaign. It was a good command that would serve as the Second Brigade's rear guard during the push north.

Hundreds of troops drilled at Saltillo in the early winter weather, made even chillier by the high altitude, as the sun shone brightly through the thin mountain air, reflecting off muskets, buttons, and belt buckles. Among them was the Active Battalion of San Luís Potosí, commanded by Colonel Juan Morales, along with the Jimenez and Matamoros Battalions and the Dolores Cavalry Regiment. Together, Morales wrote, these units "formed the 1st Brigade who took the vanguard of the army [when] we marched into Texas."[34]

As demonstrated in the past, and especially when he vanquished the Spanish invader at Tampico, Santa Anna was a genius at improvisation. This was never truer than when he could count on little government assistance or support, as was the case in early 1836. At the time of Cós' defeat, Mexico had been unable to respond to the Texian uprising because the troubled republic had been caught without a standing army. Always fearful of a coup, anti-standing army liberal politicians had committed the folly of defanging and dispersing the regular army. And now Santa Anna was busily creating one almost from scratch.

Santa Anna was confident of success, despite the host of obstacles he encountered as he prepared for the invasion. He knew full well that San Antonio's garrison was weak—more than five hundred men, including artillery and cavalry, had departed with the Matamoros Expedition near the end of December. He also knew that the remaining Alamo garrison, lacking cavalry to perform scouting missions, could be surprised by a quick strike. As reported in the *New York Herald*, "From Saltillo where [Santa Anna] was encamped on the first of February, he had written to a gentleman in Mexico, that he would conquer and that he could easily vanquish the Texians [in a war] which the Mexican Congress had declared to be a national contest against insurgents."[35] As Santa Anna himself wrote in a report to the Secretary of the War and Navy on February 1, 1836: "The last Brigade of Cavalry and other sections have left from this city (Saltillo) and already the whole army is marching for the Capital of San Antonio de Béxar whose plaza I will occupy precisely before the end of the month. Today it begins, despite the fact that the distance from here is almost 600 miles."[36]

To successfully crush the latest filibuster attempt to wrest Texas from Mexico, an attempt that was also the first serious challenge to the republic's territorial integrity, Santa Anna once again relied upon Napoleon's example. His timing could not have been better—the smug overconfidence, complete disorganization, and non-vigilance of the Texas revolutionaries was at its peak in early 1836. Texas victories of 1835 had been too easy and relatively bloodless, creating hubris among the rustic victors.

The successful Texas Army of 1835 dissolved and faded away once General Cós and his paroled soldiers marched south, heading for Laredo, where he would link with Sesma's advance leading the way for Santa Anna's army into Texas. Convinced that the war was over and that the Mexicans would never return, native Texans went back to their homes and families and placed their muskets above their fireplaces. There was much work to do on ranches and farms, for the men had been absent during the later summer, fall, and early winter of the 1835 campaign. The handful of soldiers who remained garrisoned at San Antonio were there by default—especially the Irish and other young immigrants from Europe who had nowhere else to go.

While Santa Anna worked overtime to mold a formidable invasion force, the Texas military thus remained disorganized, chaotic, and much too democratic for its own good, becoming weaker with each passing day. By early 1836, the tiny force of volunteers and handful of regulars were least able to successfully defend San Antonio at the exact time they were to face their greatest challenge.[37]

Santa Anna's knowledge of his opponent's vulnerabilities allowed him all the better to formulate his strategy. This was two-fold: he would rely on the element of surprise by advancing swiftly in the dead of winter, and also take the least expected route. Rather than advancing through Laredo, to which Cós had withdrawn, Santa Anna decided to take a circuitous route, going by way of Guerrero. Although the way through Laredo, on the Rio Grande almost directly south of San Antonio, was the most direct, it also included the harshest terrain—the deserts and mountains of northern Mexico. Going by way of Guerrero, which was up the Rio Grande and more directly west of San Antonio, increased the chances of victory through surprise, and perhaps even without a struggle, by striking from where least expected.

Meanwhile, some at the Alamo believed that Santa Anna would advance northward by way of Matamoros. Downriver from Laredo and slightly southeast of San Antonio, this well-traveled route ran through the mesquite flatlands of south Texas, hugging the coastline. Amateur military thinkers were convinced that Santa Anna would favor this route in order to supply his army from Mexican ships plying the Gulf of Mexico. Others thought the Mexican Navy might stage an amphibious landing, and launch a seaborne invasion from the Gulf. Much like United States volunteers who had landed on the east coast of the Gulf from New Orleans and then marched inland to San Antonio, so Santa Anna's Army could land north of Matamoros along the lengthy coast for a direct march westward to San Antonio to take the city from the flank or rear.

While Santa Anna closely embraced his Napoleonic lessons, young William Travis failed to do so, although he likewise possessed a lively interest in Napoleon. The aspiring gentleman-planter from the Alabama River country devoured an 1831 book, *Court and Camp of Bonaparte*, studying Napoleonic warfare and learning about the qualities necessary to become a great commander. Santa Anna knew that speed, above all, was essential, regardless of which route he chose, in order to achieve surprise. Napoleon marched rapidly from the French coast and across central Europe to catch the Russians and Austrians off guard at Austerlitz; so, too, Santa Anna planned to strike the Alamo rapidly and by surprise before additional volunteers, cannon, and supplies from the United States could arrive. His concerns were valid and his decision was wise—in a classic Napoleonic division of force, he planned to advance his right wing to occupy the strategic city of Matamoros before he pushed north up the Gulf Coast of Texas and toward the east Texas settlements. He would thus thwart efforts from New Orleans, preventing any shiploads of guns, munitions, and volunteers from reaching San Antonio.[38]

3

The Ultimate Folly: Defense of the Alamo

Perhaps the most timeless aspect of the Alamo is its continued relevancy in providing valuable military lessons. For the most part, the real story of the Alamo is not about romantic heroics or an alleged, deliberate self-sacrifice, but concerns the consequences of sheer folly. A fatal mixture of overconfidence, unpreparedness, and miscalculation ensured that an easily avoidable mistake—deciding to remain in San Antonio, or Béxar (as it was long known by the local Tejanos) to defend the Alamo—made Santa Anna's job much easier than he imagined.

Much more than the flawed strategic vision, the lack of tactical and strategic insight on the part of the Alamo's leaders—James Clinton Neill, James Bowie, and William Barret Travis—brought Santa Anna a relatively easy victory. Revealing their collective inexperience and lack of military training, all three Alamo leaders possessed a poor grasp of strategic realities. Combined with little tactical insight, and aggravated by personal ambitions and priorities, the failure of command judgment doomed the Alamo garrison to a tragic fate.

A forgotten San Antonio commander, Colonel Francis White Johnson, also played a key role in setting the stage for the disaster in two ways. Johnson led the Matamoros Expedition south from San Antonio after its members stripped the diminutive garrison of provisions, munitions, and supplies. Johnson wrote on January 3, 1836 to inform the Council that before departing San Antonio for Matamoros on December 30, 1835, he "ordered all the guns from the town into the Alamo."[1] The recipe for disaster was already set firmly in place.

The longest lasting misconception that ultimately doomed the Alamo was the widespread belief across Texas that the war with Mexico was already over after the successful 1835 campaign. Even before the war had begun in early October, Texans had believed that victory was inevitable, in large part because they counted on so much support from the United States, especially in manpower. In October 1835, for instance, George Fisher confidently wrote to Austin of the flood of U.S. volunteers headed for Texas: "You see you will have plenty of men . . . and in a short time you will have more fighting people in Texas than necessary."[2]

Captain William R. Carey, of Austin's Colony, viewed the mission of the volunteers at San Antonio and the Alamo as only temporary. As he saw it on January 12, 1836, he and the other handful of volunteers had only decided to "maintain the post until [the] Texas government could make some provision to keep the Standing army here."[3] By early 1836, this band of men at San Antonio consisted of fragmentary remnants of Austin's ad hoc "Army of the People," which had captured San Antonio, and recent volunteers from the United States. Laying out plans for the defense of Texas in late 1835, after San Antonio's capture and in preparation for the upcoming spring 1836 campaign, General Sam Houston initially wanted to defend this remote "station" on the southwestern frontier. He thus appointed James Clinton Neill, second in command of Fannin's regiment, to take command and fortify the "Post of Béxar." He even appointed Green B. Jameson, an engineer, to assist Neill in "fortifying the place."

But Houston rethought the situation after learning from Neill of the garrison's "alarming weakness." The lack of supplies among the volunteers in San Antonio made garrisoning of the remote outpost impractical. The troops of the Matamoros Expedition, which picked up 200 men from the San Antonio garrison who had been infected by "Matamoros fever," and who had enlisted against Neill's protests and orders, swept through the town in late December 1835 like a plague of locusts. Merely a token force sent by Houston—Bowie and a small relief party of mounted men—rode toward San Antonio in a classic case of too little, too late. Bowie reached San Antonio on January 19, possessed with Houston's authority—if the governor gave final approval—to abandon the exposed and isolated position.

Like Neill, Bowie was simply "the wrong person" for this key assignment because of his personal, financial, and emotional ties to San Antonio and the Tejano people. After having realized that a mighty Mexican Army was about to invade Texas, Houston dispatched only

Bowie, who was too alcoholic and unhealthy for active command re-sponsibilities. Having tried to resign not once but twice, after the 1835 Texas Campaign, he had lost his "old fire" for offensive operations.

Eventually, Governor Henry Smith was influenced by the defense-minded Neill, despite some initial apprehension because of the garri-son's size. He was also persuaded by the newly converted Bowie, who likewise embraced Neill's strategic viewpoint, to disregard Houston's advice and instead bolster the tiny garrison. Seemingly everyone, includ-ing the Council, which had by then been influenced by the governor, had eventually all come around to Neill's way of thinking for defending the Alamo. But the fatal decision to maintain a remote garrison in an inde-fensible place, in a distant land that belonged to another republic, whose population far exceeded that of Texas, began with Neill, who was much worse than simply a "second-rater."

The governor subsequently ordered Lieutenant Colonel William Barret Travis and his small party of regular Texas horse soldiers to the Alamo. In a disastrous chain reaction, Neill had influenced Bowie, and Bowie had influenced the governor, selling the folly that the Alamo could and should be defended at all costs. Neill might also have been unduly swayed by the inexperienced Captain Carey, one of the few Alamo officers to carry a sword and whose judgment Neill respected, even though the young captain believed that "a small number of us can whip an army of Mexicans." This was a dangerous illusion at a time when realistic thinking was needed.

Although their forces were "very small," Bowie felt misguided enthusiasm, heavily influenced by Colonel Neill, who had become the Alamo's first commander after Johnson's departure, to defend San Antonio to the bitter end. By February, Bowie had been transformed into a passionate convert to the growing faith of holding San Antonio and the Alamo. Even Travis, who hesitated to take the San Antonio assignment and seemed to sense a monumental disaster in the making, was eventually seduced. Despite initial objections to the concept of defending the place, which served as little more than an isolated, early-warning outpost for the east Texas settlements, the leading officers had been converted to the defensive-stand faith by San Antonio's seductive, if not mysterious, appeal. Among the converts, Travis can perhaps be excused because he lacked combat experience and maturity; he was also a product of a later generation, as compared to Neill, Bowie, Crockett, and Houston, and knew even less than them about the art of war.

As much as anything else, the Alamo's story was more about the mistakes and misjudgments of leadership, both military and civilian, that doomed the band of defenders as much as the overwhelming might of Santa Anna's Army. Now the key players in the unfolding disaster, hallowed Texas revolutionary leaders—albeit men who were more land speculators than conventional military leaders like Neill, Bowie, Johnson, Grant, and Fannin— recklessly, if not foolishly, gambled with their men's lives.[4]

Ironically, before Neill's and Bowie's arguments—proffered by Governor Smith—turned him into a blind believer, a radical who shunned any idea of uniting with Mexican liberals had advised on January 22 against the folly of attempting to defend San Antonio and the dilapidated Alamo: "The siege of Béxar [and General Cós' December 1835 surrender] ought to be sufficient to teach us a lesson. That fortress . . . is now stripped [by members of the Matamoros Expedition], and left with only seventy naked men, destitute of clothing, provisions, ammunition, and every comfort, threatened by a large invading Mexican army, who, hearing of the weakened situation of that garrison, ha[s] determined to re-take it."[5]

Even worse, the Texas government still thought mainly in terms of remaining within the Mexican Republic under the Constitution of 1824. In early 1836, the rebellious Texans did not therefore declare independence, in the hope that Santa Anna and Mexico would not retaliate for General Cós' defeat by sending an army north to reconquer Texas. Once again, the Anglo-Celts had badly miscalculated, underestimating the resolve of a proud Mexican nation and her leaders, both military and political. Santa Anna's Army now included General Cós and more than eight hundred soldados who simply ignored their paroles.[6]

In evaluating the decision to defend the Alamo, which only repeated General Cós' earlier fatal mistake of his "drastic withdrawal," into the entrapment of the Alamo's confines, Colonel Robert I. Chester declared in no uncertain terms: "The fight at the Alamo was a blunder. What did a man [Neill, Bowie, and Travis] shut himself up in a fort, and allow Santa Anna to surround him for? It was downright folly!"[7] Clearly, it was foolish to attempt to defend the Alamo given the state of the Texans' preparations. Quite simply, as Houston had warned, the overly confident Texans in October 1835 had plunged into a "bloody struggle with Mexico, before she was prepared for it."[8] However, now it would be different as the Mexicans resolved to strike back.

The Texans were pressing their luck. Texas had been most fortunate in winning the 1835 campaign, when Mexico had been unready for the challenge posed by the rise of revolutionaries on her northern frontier. But at that time, few installations in all of Texas were more ill-suited for a defensive stand than the Alamo. Across the river from San Antonio, the fort was located just east of a big looping bend in the San Antonio River. Situated at almost the lowest point of the San Antonio River valley amid an otherwise flat, grassy landscape of sprawling prairie, the Alamo had adobe walls as high as twelve feet at some point, consisting of a mixture of relatively soft limestone and even softer sandstone. It was not located in a geographically advantageous position to thwart an enemy army's march through the surrounding terrain or along a vital road. Instead, the compound merely defended under three acres of strategically unimportant ground.

The sturdiest building was the Alamo's limestone church, or chapel, which served as the defensive anchor at the compound's southeast corner. This had likely been quarried by missionary Indians under Spanish supervision from deposits in the hill country to the northwest, or at some rocky point along the San Antonio River. Regardless of the height of its formidable-looking walls, the Alamo was indefensible. Enrique Esparza described the edifice as "old and gray and tumbling." Only months before the Alamo fell, a keen observer, Captain John Duncan of Mobile, Alabama, writing in the *New Orleans Bulletin*, evoked the serious disadvantages of defending the Alamo, which was located in "a valley upon the banks of a river [San Antonio] commanded by the hills on both sides," and he stated that it was "therefore ... indefensible."[9] The captain was also was convinced that "Goliad is of vastly more importance in a military point of view than Béxar."[10]

Explaining Houston's own strategic views, which called for abandoning the Alamo, historian H.W. Brands correctly stated: "San Antonio wasn't essential to the Texan cause. It was too far from the American settlements, too close to the rest of Mexico, too hard to defend. The war would never be won at San Antonio, but it might be lost there."[11] Consequently, Houston, the newly appointed major general of the Texas Regular Army that still existed mostly on paper, considered Gonzales, around seventy-five miles to the east, as "the most important interior key to Texas (proper)." In a letter to Wylie Martin, he advocated making a defensive stand at Goliad as early as November 24, 1835.

Unfortunately for the Alamo garrison, Bowie and Neill thought otherwise, relying on their instincts rather than military realities. Even though both Houston and Johnson had advised the government to destroy the fortifications because the garrison was insufficient and an isolated frontier "post" was of no strategic consequence, Neill was more responsible than any other single leader for making the fatal decision to defend the delapidated "ancient Mexican fort," and "very old building," as Captain Carey penned in a January 12, 1836 letter. This error was later compounded by his the promotion of the idea to Bowie and others, including the governor.

Neill, a low-ranking Tennessee and Alabama militiaman and Indian fighter with an undistinguished record but an overly inflated military reputation, not only ignored Johnson's advice but also Houston's orders to abandon San Antonio and withdraw to the east to better defend the east Texas settlements. Born in 1778 in North Carolina, Neill was a slave-owner who passionately embraced the folly that a small band of men could successfully defend the Alamo, despite having witnessed the slaughter of hundreds of Creeks who attempted to defend a fortified point within the confines of Horseshoe Bend. Neill, "unmilitary-like . . . ignored the order of his commander-in-chief Sam Houston to abandon the fortification at San Antonio and retreat to Gonzales." Compounding this mistake, he was the most influential leader to think that the Alamo could be successfully defended, and also held "to the last" man: "If I have only 100 men, I will fight 1,000 as long as I can and then not surrender," he wrote.[12]

Odds never concerned Neill. He and 17 other nondescript citizen-soldiers of Gonzales had driven off a hundred finely uniformed Mexican dragoons of Cós' command on Ezekiel Williams' ranch along the banks of the Guadalupe River, just outside Gonzales, on October 2, 1835. He thus had the ear of a good many people, especially Bowie, who listened to his glowing words praising the possibilities of a successful defense of the Alamo. Neill's opinion also may have commanded respect because he knew something about artillery when few others in Texas did. Perhaps he believed that with all the Alamo's cannons, he could simply scare the enemy— regardless of their numbers—with a few shots, as he had done at Gonzales in October.

The first shot of nails and cut-up horseshoes from the tiny "Come and Take It" cannon initiated the war, echoing over the brown-hued Guadalupe River. The cannon was forged in Mexico, and was the only one loaned to the Anglo-Celtic colonists for protection against Indian raids; Mexico's demand for its return soon became a bone of contention. Neill had easily driven off Mexican cavalry sent from San Antonio to retrieve the gun during the "Lexington of the Texas Revolution," and he could never forget that glorious day when he became, along with Bowie, the first hero of this rustic revolution of amateurs. Since he had proved that he knew what he was doing at Gonzales, or so it seemed to others, then it might have been logical to assume Neill also knew what he was talking about in strategic terms. This, however, was not the case.

For the most part, these frontier leaders failed to see the serious defensive liabilities of the Alamo. There was no systematic arrangement of firing platforms, nor were there parapets for riflemen along the perimeter, or even mutually supporting strongpoints like bastions, ravelines, or interior "redoubts." Part of this negligence stemmed from historical and cultural bias—nothing more influenced the tactical thinking of an entire generation of American military men than General Jackson's defensive stand, bolstered by cannon, that resulted in victory at the battle of New Orleans, or "the good old Orleans plan," in the words of the history-minded editor of the *New Orleans Advertiser.*

But most of all, overestimation of the defenders' own military abilities, combined with a serious underestimation of their opponents', led to the disastrous decision to make a defensive stand at San Antonio.

Located almost 150 miles west of the gulf, and looming on the far southwestern frontier "in the midst of a prairie wilderness" that spanned to the horizon, San Antonio was as remote as it was isolated. The Tejano town, at a distance of two weeks travel by land from New Orleans, was situated in the middle of nowhere. Located amid an expanse of chaparral, mesquite thickets, and rolling prairie, this obscure frontier location disguised the fact that San Antonio had long served as the Spanish colonial capital of Texas, situated in an ever-volatile border region between Spanish and French territory.

San Antonio was a small town in 1836, consisting of clusters of one-story abode buildings. This isolated vestige of Tejano civilization was lost amid a vast expanse of grasslands, which mirrored the town's lack of strategic importance. Nevertheless, San Antonio was now the largest Mexican community north of the Rio Grande—a status that belied the unsavory spectacle of endless dust, flies, and skinny dogs that filled its narrow streets, and the single-story abode houses of which the town largely consisted. An unimpressed Frenchman who maintained a diplomatic tone in his evaluation, Jean-Louis Berlandier, wrote that Béxar "resembles a large village more than the municipal seat of a department" of the Republic of Mexico.

Strategic and military priorities had dominated San Antonio's history from the beginning. Issued in September 1772, only three years before the American Revolution, a Spanish royal order provided for the establishment of a defensive cordon to protect the northern frontier of New Spain, consisting of a string of fifteen far-flung presidios, or forts, stretching from the Pacific Ocean to nearly the Gulf of Mexico. This decision stemmed from the international, strategic chess game between Spain and France over possession of the vast expanse between Pensacola, Florida, and the Rio Grande River.

As part of an ambitious plan, presidios were established to protect Spain's claim to Texas against French encroachment from the east. One was located along the San Antonio River at the future site of San Antonio, and another at La Bahia, later known as Goliad. As if to make a point about the fate of future foreign encroachments in Texas, now claimed by Spain, La Bahia was built upon the site of an old, evacuated French settlement.

This string of presidios was also created to protect the Mexican settlers, or Tejanos, against the wrath of the native people, the "Chichimecs" whom Santa Anna had once fought as a young cavalryman. Unlike in central Mexico, these native Texas tribes could not be subdued by the Spanish military methods that had conquered the Aztec. The presidios were a direct response to a tough native people, skilled in waging war on horseback across the northern frontier, and whom the Spanish could not defeat despite their best efforts.

Father Antonio de San Buenaventura y Olivares established what became known as the Mission San Antonio de Valero—the Alamo—as soon as he reached the San Antonio River on May 1, 1718. Founded in early July 1731 by the families that lived in and around the presidio, and migrants of Spanish ancestry from the Canary Islands who had arrived in March 1731, the nearby civilian community of Villa de San Fernando de Béxar lay close to the newly christened Presidio San Antonio de Béxar. This presidio had been established only four days after the creation of the Mission San Antonio de Valero, and was located about a mile north of the chapel and mission.[13]

The Alamo was only one of five Spanish missions in the immediate area. The Alamo's antecedents predated Father Olivares' arrival on the San Antonio River, and can be traced back to the Mission San Francisco Solano, founded on March 1, 1700, which was moved north from the Rio Grande region to the Villa de San Fernando de Béxar. At this new location, near the future site of San Antonio, the mission was renamed San Antonio de Valero before acquiring the name Alamo. According to local legend, the Alamo was named for the large stands of cottonwood trees growing nearby along the sluggish waters of the river.[14]

Ironically, like the village of San Antonio itself, the old Spanish mission was isolated even from nearby San Antonio, separated by the San Antonio River that flowed to the west. After the mission was secularized in 1793, the Alamo existed as an independent community, the self-governing Pueblo of Valero, which operated free of San Antonio's control. Just to the Alamo's south along the Gonzales Road, the La Villita, or little village, grew in independent fashion near the river's east bank until its merger with San Antonio in 1809.[15]

Symbolizing the so-called "civilizing influence" of New Spain, the other Spanish missions in the San Antonio area were located farther down the San Antonio River from the Alamo. Both the mission and the presidio systems were key ingredients of Spain's strategic plan to develop and defend its vulnerable northern frontier region against French encroachments. However, Spain's longtime efforts to tame the land and its native people seemed lost amid a sea of grasslands and rolling plains better suited to immense herds of bison, prairie dogs, and rattlesnakes than to a relatively few cultivators of the soil. To many with strategic insights, San Antonio seemed like the least likely place for a dramatic military showdown of any kind in early 1836. To note only one example, the lack of military and strategic importance of the Alamo prompted Lieutenant Colonel Jose Enrique de la Pena to describe it as a "holding . . . unimportant either politically or militarily."[16]

This sound viewpoint by one of Santa Anna's most promising young officers was neither new nor an isolated opinion, as the judgment that San Antonio lacked importance had been pervasive for some time. After inspecting the northern frontier of Texas for the government of New Spain, Marques de Rubi, for instance, presented "bold" proposals in his 1768 report to Mexico City: much like the entire Spanish defensive arrangement to protect the lengthy northern frontier, San Antonio was vulnerable, weak, and indefensible, because it was located too far north, above Rubi's ideal or natural line of defense—the Rio Grande—and its isolation disrupted the geometric logic of his protective cordon to protect the northern frontier. The presidio at San Antonio and the town obviously presented a logistical and military nightmare for New Spain if threatened by outside forces, because it was almost impossible to supply and adequately garrison with troops. Ironically, these same liabilities later plagued the Texas government and military, except that for them the Alamo was situated too far south and west.[17]

From the beginning of the Texas Revolution, Texans themselves had realized the vulnerability of the Alamo. After the capture of San Antonio in December 1835, and the return of victorious Texas warriors to their farms and ranches—falsely believing that the war was over— San Antonio continued to be garrisoned by a diminutive force. Because the Texas Army had dissolved quickly after capturing San Antonio, this isolated forward position was only held as an advance warning post, through which the small garrison could obtain intelligence to warn the East Texas settlements of an impending invasion from Mexico. By late 1835, no one of sound tactical and strategic insight had dreamed of defending it if an entire Mexican army advanced from the south.

In overall strategic terms, San Antonio therefore should not have been garrisoned in the first place. Anglo-Celtic soldiers were stationed in San Antonio in early 1836 only because they had captured the Tejano town in December 1835, remaining in place simply because it was newly won. Captain Carey explained the rationale for the garrison soldiers in a January 12, 1836 letter: "After we took this place . . . it was thought requisite for some to remain to protect it, [therefore] volunteers [were] called for to enlist [sic] for four months."[18]

As if ordained by an ill-fated destiny, the Alamo garrison was also waiting for the formation of a Texas regular, or "standing army," to relieve the untrained, ill-disciplined volunteers who had decided to stay in San Antonio. The quarrelsome Texas government dissolved in early 1836, and the concept of a regular army remained more fantasy than reality. Consequently, the Alamo defenders remained at San Antonio awaiting relief from sizeable numbers of regular troops who would never come.

Clinging to twin illusions, Alamo soldiers gambled with their lives in regard to the belated effort of the Texas government to form a regular army, and the hope that Texas settlements would rally to their assistance if they were threatened. If a Mexican Army crossed the Rio Grande, they hoped to be reinforced not only by the "Old Texians" of east Texas, but also by the newly enlisted troops of the Texas regular army. This, however, was a dual no-win gamble. First, even if they had attempted to assist the Alamo, those living in the "Cane Brake" and the "Red Lands" country of east Texas were too distant to be quickly galvanized; second, it would take months for Texas to create a real regular army.

The Alamo garrison failed to grasp these undeniable realities. Ample manpower did exist in the "Red Lands," with its twin towns of San Augustine and Nacogdoches, known as the "Gateway to Texas." But compared to the rich Brazos, Trinity, Red, and Colorado River Valleys, the vulnerabilities of the remote southwest frontier around San Antonio were only distant concerns at best for the "Old Texians" by early 1836.

Unfortunately, hundreds of potential Texas soldiers who were hardened veterans of the frontier, Indian warfare, and the 1835 campaign, now believed that the war was over. By early 1836, these men were back on their farmsteads and plantations, and there they remained until it was too late for the Alamo garrison. Much work had had to be done in their absence during the fall of 1835. Fences had to be mended, cattle and sheep slaughtered and the meat cured for winter, virgin oaks and pines had to be cut down, and more land had to be cleared for future pastures and fields to get an ambitious farming enterprise into full operation once again. These middle and lower class volunteers, especially those without slaves, had suffered economic losses, failing to get much of the 1835 cotton harvest crop out while they were away defeating General Cós' troops.

Many Texans were now busily planting crops for spring, ensuring that they would remain absent from military service during the initial stages of the 1836 campaign. One of these primary crops was wheat, which thrived on the central plains. Spanning endlessly across rolling hills to the horizon, these flowing wheat pastures provided ideal winter grazing for cattle. Unfortunately for the Alamo garrison, a large percentage of the men of military age in the fertile "Red Lands" of east Texas were more interested in their own personal lives, future crops, and private lands than they were in military service.[19]

The interim governor, James W. Robinson, realized that it would be an all but impossible task to rouse Texan farmers to take up arms for the 1836 campaign: "I regret to make [this request of] you at this season of the year, when the case of your domestic concerns, claims all your attention," he wrote.[20] Indeed, "many of the substantial men in the Redlands, which saw Americans settling there even before the establishment of the Austin Colony, failed to respond to Houston's desperate call for reinforcements in the spring of 1836, either delaying military service or evading it altogether."[21] This general apathy among such a large percentage of the east Texas population helped to seal the Alamo's doom.

By early December 1835, even *before* the capture of San Antonio, "the Texas revolution had been [already largely] abandoned by the Texans and was being revived and carried on and principally officered by citizens of the United States," and this included the Alamo garrison. In fact, only the timely arrival of the U.S. volunteers of the New Orleans Greys had "prevent[ed] the collapse of [Austin's] army and, therefore, the revolution itself," while ensuring the capture of San Antonio.[22]

Ironically, one reason the "Old Texians" abandoned the Alamo defenders was the same as that which led Mexicans and Anglo-Celts to war in October 1835: possession of the most fertile land in Texas and its boundless potential wealth. "Old Texians," including Austin and the "Austin faction," were concerned that all the lavish land bounties promised to the flood of United States volunteers might usurp the older land grants that the Mexican government had issued to the empresarios. If Texas broke away from Mexico, the victors—leaders and soldiers from the United States, and mostly recent arrivals to Texas—would have a more legitimate claim to this rich land than the "Old Texians," especially those that were hedging their bets by remaining neutral or non-supportive of the United States volunteers. The mere prospect of independence posed a threat to existing land claims sanctioned and honored by the Republic of Mexico; a war to preserve the Mexican 1824 Constitution, not independence, would preserve the land grants already officially issued to the east Texas colonists.[23]

Therefore, not surprisingly the United States volunteers in Texas were angered and "resented the fact that the resident Texans had all but disappeared when the fighting had begun" at the Alamo. They did not realize that they were in fact the natural opponents of the older settlers for the possession of rich lands.[24] In addition, the U.S. volunteers, including most Alamo garrison members, were concerned that they might well fight and die for the interests of the land speculators, who would then scoop up the tens of thousands of acres that would go to soldiers who survived the war. The concern that land speculators "would carry off the spoils" became a nagging fear among the young men and boys now serving in Texas. Approximately 700,000 acres would be due to the Alamo defenders if they won and survived the war; if they did not survive, the land would go to other Texans, including those who remained at home and land speculators.[25]

Even after Houston's victory at San Jacinto, a strong feeling was rumored to exist among those in power in Texas, including the infant republic's president, that it was preferable for the victorious Texans to return "Texas to the Mexicans [rather than] turning it over to U.S. volunteers."[26] Most symbolic of this deep split between newly arrived United States volunteers and the old Texas colonists were the sentiments of the Alamo's first commander. Neill's loyalty, in the end, seemed more with his fellow "Old Texians," than with the U.S. citizens and recent volunteers who made up the vast majority of his command. Barely more than half a dozen men at the Alamo were Texians, and by early February 1836, Neill began to have reservations about remaining in command of so many recent volunteers from the United States.[27]

The considerable differences among the Anglo-Celts themselves grew greater with each passing day. Many United States volunteers had grown seriously disillusioned with the Texas Revolution by early 1836. These soldiers had had enough of apathetic Texans. Some were merely homesick and returned to the United States; large numbers of others were disgusted to discover that the lands they had gained for 1835 military service were not as promising as they had originally expected. Much to their dismay, they found that the old settlers, land speculators, politicians, and men of wealth had already acquired the most desired Texas lands. Consequently, a growing number of disillusioned volunteers who had fought in 1835 returned to the United States. They had also ascertained that the very people on whose behalf they were fighting possessed no interest in risking their lives to assist them.

An editor of the *Baltimore Gazette* explained the exodus of United States fighters thus: "Volunteers are returning from Texas. Many that have returned from that country speak of the land as being rich and productive. But of its inhabitants they give a miserable account. They are said to be very poor, and care not a fig under what government they live [and that for] the majority of Texians that fight is [for only] plunder and pillage. The country is now free of Mexican troops, but Santa Anna is expected in the spring with a powerful force. The Texians are said to be indolent, and quite contented [to remain civilians, not soldiers]. The only lands that can be given to volunteers are upon the head-waters of the streams, and back in the interior, the fine lands on the navigable streams being included in the grants to companies by the government."[28]

Cashing in before it was too late, some "Old Texians" panicked and sold their lands when the war caused the Texas economy to crash, bringing about a sharp fall in prices. They sold headrights of thousands of acres at bargain prices to savvy American investors and land speculators who knew that land prices would eventually rise once again. This development placed many "honest but generally poor families in the hands of the [land] speculators," while denying large numbers of Texans any "inducement to fight" during the 1836 campaign.[29]

With a powerful Mexican Army on its way north in early 1836, "Old Texians" in military service also naturally worried that the Indians and the slaves would rise up to settle old scores. Military service for the Texians of the eastern settlements therefore presented the fearsome prospect of leaving families behind and at risk to dual threats that seemed more dire, at least in their minds, than Santa Anna's army. The families of the United States volunteers were secure and far away, and so these volunteers did not suffer the same fears as the people of Texas, whose general "indifference . . . to the cause of Texas," helped to seal the Alamo's fate.[30] Consequently, from the beginning to the end, the "actual dying and fighting in the Texas Revolution was done by a very small group—fewer than two thousand people, out of a population of thirty-five thousand."[31]

The thinking, political outlook, and overall priorities of the more conservative "Old Texians" were thus at odds with those of the more radical United States volunteers, ensuring that they would be less likely to serve beside or even assist the pro-independence Alamo garrison in its hour of need. Incredibly, even at the beginning of the 1836 campaign, the U.S. volunteers in Texas were themselves deeply divided about what they hoped to achieve in the war against Mexico. Perhaps Texas revolutionary Noah Smith best described the divided state of mind of these ill-prepared amateurs in rebellion, whose animosity against each other was almost as intense as their animosity toward Mexican troops: "Some were for independence, some were for the Constitution of 1824, and some were for anything, just so long as it was a row."[32]

Meantime, Captain Carey was shocked by San Antonio's forlorn isolation amid the open prairie. The young captain, who was originally from the bustling port city of Baltimore, Maryland, wrote: "This place is so far in the interior that it takes some time for news to go and supplies to come. The Savage Camancha [sic] Indians is [sic] near at hand [and] we expect soon to have a fight with them."[33]

Carey's concern was not ill founded. Comanche warriors had dominated the high plains and central plateaus of Texas since 1724, when they first arrived with their horses and fierce dispositions, not unlike the surging nomadic tide of Genghis Khan. Known as the Snake People, the resourceful Comanches were the finest light cavalry in the world. The horse completely dominated Comanche culture, making them among the most nomadic of native people in America. They had adopted this widely roaming life after receiving the horse as a "gift" from the Spanish, who themselves had become expert horsemen through centuries of battle with mounted Moors.[34]

The lack of development in both San Antonio and, more generally, in Texas, was partly due to Comanche domination. The Comanche referred to themselves as "the People," but among other Native American tribes, Comanche meant those "who want to fight me all the time." Population levels remained low on the northern frontier because neither the Spanish nor the Mexican government could ever solve its Indian problem. Confident warriors even boasted that Texas towns existed only so their inhabitants could raise an endless supply of horses for them to steal.[35]

Likewise, the Lipan Apache—the Comanches' ancient foes—had terrorized Spanish settlers ever since San Antonio was established. Just west of the Alamo flowed the appropriately named Apache Creek. Coming from the hill country of Edwards Plateau just north of San Antonio, Apache raiders continued to strike at the vulnerable town throughout the 1730s, killing settlers and soldiers and stealing horses, sheep, and cattle. Punitive Spanish expeditions met with little success, and fear ran so high that many families departed San Antonio never to return. The back of Apache resistance, which came from both the Lipans and Mescaleros, was not broken until 1790.[36]

Although some Alamo garrison members had served under Andrew Jackson during the Creek War in Alabama, relatively few of them possessed experience in fighting Indians, which had been a feature of life from the beginning of Anglo-Celtic settlement in Texas, just as it had been in colonial times farther east. The first Texas Rangers were born out of necessity in the spring of 1835, when Indian raids became more frequent. These organized militia companies took the offensive by mounting expeditions deep into the heart of Comanche country.

James Clinton Neill, who commanded at the Alamo in early 1836, was an experienced Ranger leader who had fought under Jackson at Horseshoe Bend, and also at the battle of New Orleans. He had served as the adjutant of Colonel John Henry Moore's Ranger command, the original Ranger battalion, during its 1835 Indian campaign into the north Texas plains. Two Alamo defenders from Gonzales, Almeron Dickerson, a Kentucky-born settler, and Kentucky-born Jacob C. Darst, had previously served as scouts for Captain Bartlett D. McClure's company, a mounted frontier command that aggressively took the war to the Comanche in April 1835. Both men hailed from Gonzales, the capital of the Green De Witt Colony. Returning from their Indian campaign in the north, Moore's volunteers were among the revolutionaries who confronted Mexican troops at Gonzales during the "Lexington of the Texas Revolution." Foremost among these units was the Ranger company of thirty-two men that included the forty-two-year-old Darst. These hard-riding troopers of the Gonzales Ranging Company were the last men to reinforce the Alamo.[37]

But experience in fighting Indians on the frontier paid no dividends for the soldiers at the Alamo, who confronted a conventional army that was trained in European ways of waging modern warfare and was commanded by a skilled general. Alamo commanders should have learned a tactical lesson from the hit-and-run warfare of the Comanche, ensuring that they would never allow themselves to be trapped in a weakly fortified position. But as Jameson lamented in a letter, the Alamo garrison suffered from the "lack of horses," after the Matamoros Expedition had stripped the town and entire area of mounts. This glaring deficiency meant that "all the patrol duty [has] to be done by the officers [and] has to be done on foot," making the Alamo vulnerable to surprise.[38]

In a January 12, 1836 letter that revealed his disillusionment, Captain Carey wrote that the "Town [is] divided by a small river [the San Antonio] which emanates [sic] from Springs. The town has two Squares [or plazas] and the [San Fernando] church in the centre, one a military and the other a government square. The Alamo or the fort as we call it, is a very old building, built for the purpose of protecting the citizens from hostile Indians."[39] Clearly, this was not much of a place to fight or die for, but Captain Carey and the other young Alamo men stayed anyway, hoping for the best.

First and foremost, the Alamo was never conceived or built to serve as a defensive bastion. No one knew this better than Jameson, who met with endless frustration in his attempts to fortify the place. Despite sound defensive improvements by General Cós' engineers in 1835, Jameson felt contempt toward the old mission-turned-fortress, writing to Houston on January 18, 1836: "You can plainly see that the Alamo never was built by a military people for a fortress."[40]

Much too large to defend with such a small garrison, the sprawling Alamo compound consisted of a large rectangle, some 250 feet in length on each side. The defensive perimeter, some 440 yards, was nearly a quarter mile in length. A ring of adobe buildings, almost all single story except at the long barracks on the east side, surrounded the huge open plaza, forming a compound of nearly three acres. "Although its walls were wonderfully thick—usually two or three feet—they had no embrasures, portholes, or barbettes for firing either cannon or rifles. They were mostly twelve feet high, yet there were no parapets. Worst of all, the place was too big," wrote Walter Lord, pinpointing the Alamo's greatest defensive liability—its sheer size.[41] Enrique Esparza heard garrison members say that the Alamo "was too big [and] they did not have enough men to hold it."[42]

The inherent defects of the Alamo as a fortress stemmed largely from the facts of its original design and function. Created by Franciscan priests, the Alamo followed the same basic design as missions across the southwest frontier of New Spain. The largest, sturdiest structure in the compound was the stone chapel, or church; the next largest building was the so-called "long barracks," which was the original convento, or personal quarters, for the Spanish missionary priests who converted Indians to Catholicism and often paid for the privilege with their lives.[43] The men of God who ventured into the New World wilderness to spread the Catholic faith were not trained in military arts; they promoted brotherly love, not war. The old Spanish compound was hence more of a community of buildings than a fortress. Linked by walls in places where no building existed, it evolved to form the rectangle over the years, and much of its weakness originated in this ad hoc construction.

Even worse in overall defensive terms, the small Anglo-Celtic garrison was attempting to defend not only the Alamo but San Antonio, a feat that would have been a virtual impossibility, even for thousands of well-trained troops. As Captain Carey explained: "The forces here is [sic] commanded by Lieut. Col. J. C. Neill who has his quarters in the Town which is called the left wing of the forces and your brother

William has the command of the Alamo which is called the right wing."[44] Historians have largely forgotten that the Anglo-Celts were also in San Antonio to defend the town itself, a task made all the more impossible for the tiny garrison because the Alamo and the town were separated by a distance of nearly 1,000 yards and the San Antonio River.[45]

LOGISTICAL NIGHTMARE

Logistical realities also made the Alamo a bad place to support a garrison for any extended length of time. Nature herself discouraged farming around San Antonio: the topsoil was much better suited for the growth of small, twisted mesquite trees than for raising corn or wheat. Even in the best of seasons blessed by heavy rains, foodstuffs were far from plentiful. Any garrison stationed at the Alamo for lengthy occupation thus risked starvation, especially in the winter.[46]

Even more importantly for logistics, San Antonio was located more than a hundred miles from the Gulf coast. Copano, southeast of Goliad, near the mouth of the San Antonio River, had served as a port for supplies, volunteers, and arms in 1835, which were primarily shipped from New Orleans. The nearest port to San Antonio was located at Dimmitt's Landing on Lavaca Bay, northeast of Copano, which was linked to the Gulf of Mexico. Supplies from New Orleans also landed at this key logistical point.

Because the San Antonio River was too small to navigate, supplies and munitions destined for San Antonio had to be hauled by wagon or oxcart overland. This was a time-consuming process over dusty summer and muddy spring roads. This, combined with the fact that the United States and its Gulf ports were more than a hundred miles away, made a lengthy defensive stand at the southern end of the Great Plains logistically untenable to support.

In early 1836, manpower from the United States had yet to flood into Texas. Any volunteers, almost all without horses, who landed on the coast had to march inland to San Antonio over a route that a relative handful of Mexican troops, especially cavalry, could easily block. As east Texas settlements were so far to the northeast near the Louisiana border, newly arriving United States volunteers were too far away from San Antonio. Moreover, the "Old Texians" naturally preferred to defend their east Texas settlements than the frontier so far forward.[47]

INTERNAL WEAKNESSES

Perhaps the greatest defensive liability that doomed the Alamo was the fact that, by eary 1836, Alamo garrison members were mostly novices at war. Like the majority of the fort's young officers, Captain Carey, who was Colonel Neill's top lieutenant, attempted to learn the ways of war on the job, but not enough time remained. As he penned in a letter: "As I have not been a graduate of West Point, I must study military affairs now for I am rejoiced at the opportunity to do something for myself."[48]

However, Neill, Bowie, and then Travis remained overly optimistic. All expected ample Tejano support if Santa Anna's army arrived. In a letter to Houston, Neill wrote on January 14 how they could expect "great aid from the citizens of this town," if Santa Anna marched on San Antonio. The many Tejano volunteers who fought against General Cós in 1835 only reinforced this widespread idea of Tejano support for the small Alamo garrison until it was far too late. But unlike in early 1836, the common people of San Antonio had not been in jeopardy or at risk in late 1835, as they would be if Santa Anna arrived with vengeance on his mind.[49]

Béxar citizens who fought beside General Cós's troops included members of the local San Antonio Tejano militia, Presidial Cavalry Company of Béxar. Francisco Esparza was one of these Tejano militiamen. After General Cós' surrender, they were allowed to leave with his force, after signing paroles. Ironically, however, the local Tejano militia of San Antonio was allowed to disperse and return to their Béxar homes, despite having battled against the Texans. The victors' benevolence would come back to haunt them. When Santa Anna reached San Antonio, this militia unit would be reactivated to join his army.[50]

Clearly, Bowie's and Neill's decision to defend San Antonio was also folly because of the realities of dual demographics. After all, San Antonio was the heart and center of Hispanic Texas, while the Anglo-Celtic settlements—and hence the potential reservoir of reinforcements—were far away in east Texas. While Texas had become more than three-quarters Anglo-Celtic by 1830, garrison members now found themselves the only Americans in the town, except for two residents. The majority of the Tejano population would remain either neutral or covertly anti-American, providing support, including invaluable intelligence, to Santa Anna. The intelligence was crucial, revealing the considerable weaknesses of both the undersized garrison and the Alamo as a defensive structure. Jameson, a perceptive and increasingly cynical engineer—who suspected that the garrison would be abandoned by most Tejanos in San Antonio—realized as much. As he penned to Governor Smith on January 18, 1836: "I believe they know our situation as well as we do ourselves."[51]

In addition, another forgotten factor that contributed to the garrison's weakness, especially in terms of discipline, was the well-known seductive lure of the pretty Tejano women and young girls with their dark beauty and exotic good looks. Unlike in Nacogdoches, where the Tejano population and the Anglo-Celts remained segregated in largely separate worlds with "no social intercourse," wrote a surprised William F. Gray, who had recently arrived in Texas, San Antonio was the exact opposite. Perhaps the isolated frontier setting played a role in fueling greater interaction between the two people. But for whatever reason, San Antonio was the place where Anglo-Celts and Tejanos openly and freely mixed on a scale unseen elsewhere in Texas.

Of course, what was ultimately most exciting for the Alamo's soldiers, these graceful Tejano women acted, danced, and flirted in a more open manner than the straight-laced, Bible-reading Anglo-Celtic women the soldiers had left behind in the United States, where the Puritan ethic dominated. What was most intoxicating for these young soldiers so far from home were "the seductive fandango, a style of dance more provocative than the American volunteers would have been accustomed to [and] They were riveted by the pulsing beat, the foot stomping, and swirling dresses of the exotic women," of the finest Tejano families of San Antonio.[52]

Naturally, as young men, some Alamo defenders were motivated by simple lust or more calculating ambitions relating to the opposite sex. The more dashing Anglo-Celtics, especially the ladies' men, desired to emulate Bowie's social and financial success in marrying a teenage, blonde-haired beauty from one of San Antonio's leading Tejano families distinguished by elegance, wealth, and aristocratic tastes. Bowie's father-in-law, Don Juan Martin de Veramendi, was the tax collector and mayor of Béxar. He also served as the governor of the combined state of Coahuila-Texas in 1832. Fluent in Spanish, enamored with Tejano culture, and fully accepted by the leading Tejano families, Bowie married the young Ursula in April 1831. He had easily adjusted to Tejano life in San Antonio, little realizing that he had little time to live, fated to die in the town he loved so much.[53]

One Alamo defender who came to Texas with the hopes of marrying a woman of wealth was Dolphin Ward Floyd of Gonzales. As revealed in a letter, ever since leaving his North Carolina home in November 1825, Floyd had always "intended Marrying some old Rich widow that she might Die directly & then he would be independent" for the rest of his days. However, the ambitions of this young North "Carolina farm boy" would be unfulfilled because, even though he had succeeded in marrying a Gonzales widow, Ester Berry House, who he married in Gonzales in late April 1832, Floyd himself met a premature end at the Alamo.[54]

But a garrison member could also have a "young Mexican girl" as a mistress without marriage. Instead of busily preparing for war, life in San Antonio for the garrison was little more than one big party for fun-loving, hard-drinking young men like Irishman William Malone, a rowdy teenager, and Henry Warnell, red-haired and freckle-faced (an unusual, appealing look to some Tejanos), who were both artillery privates of Captain Carey's "Invincibles." Week after week during the late winter of 1836, beautiful Tejano women took away—easily surrendered of course—the energies, focus, and priorities of these young men, who were lonely when far from their native homelands and families. Relaxed social interaction and romance was much more fun than strengthening an old Spanish mission, especially if Santa Anna marched up the Gulf coast and bypassed San Antonio. Along with much alcohol, mescal, and tequila, the music-filled fandangos—fiestas and dances with their historic cultural roots in peasant festivals of medieval Spain—brought out lingering inhibitions among the American boys far from home.

One young officer smitten by the abundant charms of the local Tejano women was thirty-year-old Captain Carey. With little concern about class, cultural, or racial distinctions, he fell in love with his Tejano housekeeper. Following Bowie's example, the captain from Baltimore wanted to marry her without question, but ran into unexpected resistance that caught him by surprise. Carey wrote in a letter, in regard to Tejano women, how "in time of peace the ladies would gladly embrace the offer or accept the hand of an officer, but in these war times they would too soon become a widow."[55]

Already knowing that a large Mexican Army was about to march on San Antonio with the intention of killing every Anglo-Celtic soldier present, these Tejano ladies naturally knew it would be unwise to marry a garrison member. Harsh reprisals would almost certainly be forthcoming when Santa Anna arrived. In addition, bachelor Americans making love to Tejano daughters and sisters was an unsettling prospect to their devoutly religious fathers, mothers, and brothers, who embraced traditional Catholic family values. Young Protestant soldiers of fortune, especially those who were worldly, on the make, or with relatively little means, were not a Tejano father's fondest desire for his daughters, especially if young and innocent.

Therefore, the escalating social and sexual activity became an increasing source of tension between the Anglo-Celtic soldiers and Tejano males of San Antonio, from whom the Alamo defenders expected assistance when Santa Anna struck. Many Tejano males, such as Francisco Esparza, and especially those among the lower classes without economic ties to the Anglo-Celtic community, worried about the corruption of traditional Tejano values. Expressing traces of xenophobia that flourished like a cancer in Texas, seemingly among everyone, they believed in the cultural-racial-nationalist creed that was gaining popularity in Texas by early 1836: "Mexico for the Mexicans."[56]

Week after week, a host of illusions continued to linger over the muddled thinking of the men stationed at San Antonio. Ironically, the Alamo garrison, including Travis, continued to be overconfident because they believed that the Tejano people of San Antonio would fully rally to their support. Thoroughly deluded, Jameson wrote in a letter on January 18: "We can rely on aid from the citizens of this town in the case of a siege." But on March 3 on the siege's tenth day, Travis would reveal the bitter truth of the untapped manpower source that was heavily counted upon to ensure the garrison's survival: "The citizens of this municipality are all our enemies except those who have joined us."[57]

Yet Colonel Neill had believed that the garrison could depend upon hundreds of Tejano fighting men from San Antonio, even though at this time the town only had a population of around 2,000. Bowie was also guilty of overestimating possible Tejano assistance, seeing more supporters than potential enemies or neutrals. Revealing that he was out of touch with reality, Neill expected that the garrison could count on the timely assistance of fully 80 percent of the Tejano male population. Ironically, not only was Neill completely wrong about future Tejano support, but he would be long gone from San Antonio by the time Santa Anna struck, almost as if having suddenly realized how his miscalculations spelled the end of the Alamo garrison's existence.

Ample evidence that some Tejanos had assisted General Cós in the

Alamo's defense by firing on the attacking Americans, even killing Ben Milam it was thought by some Texans, was conveniently overlooked. Ironically, the Anglo-Celts naively placed their lives in the faith of two distinct people—both the settlers of east Texas and the Tejanos, both of whom were destined to fail them in the end. However, the Tejanos would remain mostly neutral because they were caught between opposing factions in a civil war. The only exceptions were the handful who either served in the Alamo garrison and those who provided intelligence to Santa Anna.[58]

One key indication of which way the majority of Tejanos would go was early evident in the anti-Anglo-Celtic sentiment of their priest, Manuel Menchaca. In the tradition of Father Hidalgo, he was a warrior-priest who had led foraging raids on the ranches of pro-American Tejanos, including Juan Sequín. This nationalist priest might have been troubled by Protestants expressing disdain toward Catholicism, and certainly by the corruption of the good Catholic Tejano girls, who may have become pregnant, of his flock.[59]

By the early weeks of 1836, a good many Alamo garrison members had not only been seduced by the expansive beauty of this land that could make them a quick fortune, but also by the alluring Tejano women, the comforting promise of Tejano male assistance, and a vibrant, fun-loving Tejano culture. Like Bowie, many single Alamo garrison members were thoroughly charmed, not only by the ladies but by the richness of Tejano culture. As never before, the young Anglo-Celtic men and boys basked in the greater openness, friendlessness, and courtesies of Tejano life. Already smitten, Virginia-born John William Smith had married pretty María de Jesús Curbelo, and had long made San Antonio his home.

Month after month, Alamo garrison members spent their time drinking, dancing at fandangos, courting, and attempting to romance both the aristocratic Tejano women dressed in the latest styles of New Orleans (and, hence, Paris) styles, and lower class Tejano girls in peasant garb, while enjoying exotic Tejano dishes of corn tamales and enchiladas filled with beans, spices, and corn. Older Tejano women, including the mother of Gregorio and Enrique Esparza, "sold many tamales and beans" to garrison members. The men also basked in the relatively warm winter weather, with plenty of bright sunshine. Such developments played a role in reducing the overall vigilance, while fueling complacency that steadily eroded what little morale remained among largely inexperience men in arms.[60]

Not surprisingly, discipline among the Anglo-Celtic garrison in San Antonio had broken down by early 1836. No longer were soldiers drilling or training, sharpening their skills to meet the enemy. A frustrated Jameson could only lament in a January letter: "The officers of every department do more work than the men and also stand guard, and act as patrol every night." And with a classic understatement, a diplomatic Jameson, as if not to blemish the reputations of his fellow officers, merely commented with sullen resignation: "We have had loose discipline."[61]

Meantime, if the garrison were relying on the strength of the Alamo as a fort, they were mistaken. Santa Anna's second in command, aristocratic General Don Vicente Filisola, openly mocked the concept that the Alamo fit the definition as a "fortress." Santa Anna's personal secretary, Cuba-born Ramón Martinez Caro, who would be captured at San Jacinto, also ridiculed the place, referring to "the so-called fortress of the Alamo." Not long after the Alamo's fall, he criticized General Urrea for even referring to the Alamo as a fortress: "Does he call the battered and crumbling walls of the mission of Refugio, the fort of Goliad, and the defenses [sic] of the Alamo fortresses?"[62]

General Filisola, a seasoned veteran with more than thirty years of military service, including in the Napoleonic wars, easily ascertained the extensive weaknesses and liabilities of the Alamo as a defensive structure. A well-educated Italian who had joined the Spanish army as a teenager, Filisola migrated to Mexico in 1811. Possessing considerable tactical and strategic insight, he was Santa Anna's most trusted lieutenant during the 1836 campaign. In no uncertain terms, he all but laughed at the Alamo's lack of strength, realizing that defensively the antiquated structure was utterly "useless at all times and under any circumstances."[63]

Of course, no one in the Army of Operations was more aware of the Alamo's considerable defensive liabilities than General Cós. After all, he had been overwhelmed by the Texians at the Alamo in December 1835. Indeed, the Alamo's feeble defenses had sealed the doom of his own force, compelling him to surrender only a few months before. Despite extensive preparations made by his engineers and troops to enhance the Alamo's defensive capabilities, General Cós, who lamented the "circumstances in which I found myself [which were] extreme," and his Mexican soldiers had learned the hard way that the Alamo compound simply could not be adequately defended. Therefore, throughout the siege, educated Mexican leaders viewed the Alamo as little more than a large cattle pen. Along with General Juan José Andrade, one of these men was Santa Anna's respected, well-educated personal secretary, Ramón Martínez Caro. He described the Alamo as a "mere corral and nothing more."

Indeed, and contrary to the mighty "fortress" of myth, this was a common Mexican view of the Alamo. In defensive terms, they realized that the Alamo was already compromised by its large interior space and lengthy perimeter, before the 1836 campaign's first shot was fired in anger. For such reasons, all of Santa Anna's senior officers believed that Goliad was not only far more strategically important than San Antonio, but also more defensible. Indeed, the Alamo's interior space of nearly three acres was so extensive that it had served as a corral for cattle or horses in the past. Here, deep in the heart of Tejano cattle country, such old Spanish missions, now obsolete reminders of Spain's imperial past greatness, were often utilized as corrals. For instance, Mission Concepcion, located just south of the Alamo, was used as a horse and cattle corral for the vast ranchos that bordered both sides of the river that flowed southeast between San Antonio and Goliad.[64]

In time, the old Spanish mission that had begun as little more than a church grew so large that new buildings were constructed to form a defensive perimeter. Mission Indians lived in the rows of buildings that now formed the lengthy, rectangular perimeter: the Alamo's walls. While the presidios were created by military men for defensive purposes, the mission enclosures, like the Alamo, were not created with defense against a conventional opponent in mind. Instead, they were built deliberately large so that large numbers of cattle, sheep, goats, and horses could graze in the interior's vastness for protection, even as local people took shelter from slashing Indian raids. The walls, such as they existed, were suitable against arrows or musketry, and also limited the mounted tactics of marauding Indians, but they had not been constructed to withstand artillery and a conventional army.[65]

Therefore, in a strange paradox that doomed the garrison, the Alamo presented an inviting illusion to the Alamo's leaders that simply could not be resisted, especially by inexperienced commanders. Bowie and Neill failed to appreciate that this massive complex had not been built by military men or trained engineers. The Alamo garrison could not defend its hundreds of yards of perimeter spanning nearly a quarter of a mile, regardless of the number of artillery pieces. Instead the young men and boys of the Alamo were themselves corralled.

Even the thick-walled Alamo chapel was compromised as a defensive bastion because of its proximity to the weakest point in the compound—a low, wooden palisade. Here, at the southeast corner of the Alamo chapel, the Spanish missionaries, thinking more of God than sound defensive arrangements, had not thought of erecting a protective wall. In addition, a small spring that released a trickle of water to make wet, soft ground precluded the erection of a sturdy wall at this point. Consequently, by early 1836, the wooden palisade erected by Cós' troops was the weakest defensive point along the perimeter.

Extending around 100 feet in length and standing about seven feet high, this wooden palisade—compared to sections of the adobe and limestone walls as high as twelve feet—consisted of two rows of upright cedar logs separated by about six feet and filled with earth. An outside ditch—not as deep as it should have been to impede attackers—and a relatively slight network of abates—cut and sharpened, interlacing tree limbs that pointed toward assaulting force—bolstered the position. Dwarfed by the church's towering south side to its left and the buildings of the low barracks along the southern perimeter on its right, this wooden palisade extended from the Alamo's southeast corner to the east end of the south wall.[66]

Not surprisingly, the educated, military-trained Mexican officers, especially the elite engineers, looked upon the Alamo quite differently from not only the opposing leadership, but also modern historians. Indeed, the various earthen defensive emplacements, or "forts,"—such as the small lunette protecting the Alamo's main gate on the south side—were created by General Cós' engineers to better protect the north, west, and south sides of the Alamo. The Mexicans saw the Alamo as not a single fortress but merely a series of fortified bastions of earth positioned along the perimeter. Because they knew that the Alamo had been a Spanish mission and used extensively as a corral, the lunettes on both the west and south side of the Alamo were seen as the true forts, each getting a distinctive name after being constructed by Mexico's highly trained engineers.

The creation of these distinct "mini-forts" along the Alamo's perimeter on the south and west side were necessary in tactical terms, because the Alamo's greatest liability was that its walls could not be adequately defended by infantrymen, or even artillerymen to a lesser degree, regardless of their numbers. General Filisola concluded after a close examination of the Alamo, and after witnessing the feeble defense, wrote how "our losses should have been greater than they were if the [artillery] pieces of the enemy had [sic] could have been placed in the wall or enclosure. But the rooms of the latter of the inner part would not permit it, and those that were in the right location could fire only to the front."[67]

It has been estimated that at least a thousand men, perhaps more, were necessary to defend the mission-turned-fort. But in fact, a thousand defenders would have made little difference because of the Alamo's seemingly endless defensive liabilities and vulnerabilities. As it stood, the Alamo's total defensive perimeter of nearly 450 yards, or the length of more than four football fields, was to be protected by less than 200 defenders—a recipe not only for a weak defense but for certain disaster.[68]

For such sound reasons, Houston had been against making a defensive stand at the Alamo. Nevertheless, he left the final decision to Bowie, who was convinced by Neill, almost as if washing his hands of the matter. Houston was certain that "Our forces must not be shut up in forts, where they can neither be supplied with men or provisions. Long aware of this fact I directed, on the 16th of January last, that the artillery should be removed, and the Alamo blown up; but this was prevented by the expedition upon Matamoros."[69]

So with memories of Horseshoe Bend yet strong, Houston had wanted to abandon the Alamo in preference for the establishment of a defensive line farther east and closer to the Gulf ports, which received supplies and volunteers from the United States. But compared to the expansive prairie lands around San Antonio, and from where threats would come, the old Spanish mission, almost having a hypnotic affect, seemed to beckon the Anglo-Celtic soldiers. The walls and the church itself offered an unwarranted sense of security. The Alamo seemed to offer a warm, sheltering womb that could keep these young men and boys from harm, or so it seemed to these innocents in the art of war.

At first glance and to the untrained eye, the Alamo appeared to be strong, even formidable. This was not only a mirage but also a fatal illusion. General Cós' engineers had improved the Alamo's defensive qualities, but only to a limited degree. Defensive enhancements were principally only in regard to the Alamo's greatest strength, its plentiful amount of artillery. This heavy arsenal resulted in construction—by

Mexican soldiers—of artillery platforms, especially along the north wall, the lunette on the southern perimeter, and at the southwestern corner, where the 18-pounder stood. These defensive improvements by the Mexicans also included "planting cannon on the top of the church, cutting down trees" to form an abatis, as revealed in the *Maryland Gazette* of November 26, 1835.

Cós and his men had focused on maximizing the Alamo's greatest strength—artillery, in the Napoleonic tradition—at the expense of the Mexican rifleman. Consequently, the engineers had failed to create firing platforms or catwalks for riflemen atop the walls. Additionally, no rifle slots or portholes were cut into the walls for firing. John Sutherland lamented about "There being no portholes in the [north] wall." Even the Red Stick Creeks at Horseshoe Bend had cut both lower and upper ranges of portholes for rifles in their wooden breastwork. And no parapet was built to protect soldiers firing from near the top of the walls.

Basically, the Mexican engineers had ample reason for favoring artillery emplacements over positions for infantrymen because Mexican soldiers were largely untrained in marksmanship. Without a cultural heritage of firearm use like American settlers, Mexican troops, who were mostly of Indian descent, were armed with inferior weapons, such as old smoothbore muskets, which were unlike the rifles of the Americans. The standard firearm of the Mexican soldier was the .753 caliber British India Pattern Brown Bess musket. Aging flintlocks, the same Brown Bess that English troops used in battling the colonists during the American Revolution, had been purchased from England by Mexico. Also used by the British Army that had fought Napoleon from the late 1790s to 1815, these smoothbore muskets, now largely obsolete, were notoriously inaccurate and only effective at extreme, short-range distance.

Ironically, the fact that General Cós' men had focused on strengthening the Alamo's defensive positions for artillery and not riflemen—a fact not lost on Santa Anna—now served to undermine one of the Anglo-Celt's best defensive assets: skilled riflemen. Incredibly, Neill and Bowie chose to make a defensive stand from which a heavy and sustained musketry fire could not be leveled against attackers, especially if they struck all sides of the Alamo at once. In this way, one of the few strengths of the Alamo garrison—its small arms range and accuracy—was already negated long before the two forces met.

Why no Alamo commander—not Neill, Bowie, and later Travis—

embarked upon any type of construction project to build a catwalk, erect lengthy firing platforms, create a network of loopholes in the walls, cut embrasures for cannon, or create a parapet atop the walls for riflemen is almost inexplicable. Under Cós' command, Mexican engineers had done far more to strengthen the Alamo, demonstrating innovativeness and problem-solving skills, than the more complacent Anglo-Celtics accomplished for months. Incredibly, the Alamo commanders believed that the plentiful amount of artillery would be entirely sufficient to defend the massive compound, especially since there were too few riflemen to adequately defend the walls.

Nevertheless, while Neill possessed a blind faith in artillery, Bowie's faith resided mainly in the Long Rifle. Bowie realized that past victories—though more skirmishes than battles—had been won by this relatively accurate, long-range weapon. After all, Texas riflemen had unleashed impressive firepower from the cover of a bank in the San Antonio River during the October 28, 1835 battle of Concepcion, and on the open prairie during the so-called November 26, 1835 "Grass Fight." About a mile south of town along Alazán Creek, this fight resulted in the capture one of General Cós' foraging details, with Bowie thinking it was reinforcements for the besieged Cós. But these early Texan victories that instilled so much over-confidence were more flukes than authentic military successes. The Texas riflemen won primarily by fighting from the cover of a riverbank, and then from behind the cover of an arroyo, further fueling a dangerous contempt for their opponent and overreliance upon what the Long Rifle could accomplish against soldados.

But in truth, the Texans had yet to engage the elite of the Mexican Army, especially its cavalry. Clearly, Anglo-Celtic soldiers were at home fighting from natural cover in the eastern woodlands as opposed to the grassy plains of the sprawling Rio Grande flats, while Mexican horse soldiers dominated the land south of the Colorado River.[70]

For this generation of Americans, two opposing military examples provided a rationale to both those advocating a defense of the Alamo and those who wished to abandon it. Houston's reasoning for not wanting to defend the Alamo stemmed from the lessons of Andrew Jackson's March 1814 victory at Horseshoe Bend, while the pro-Alamo defense advocates cited the lessons of Jackson's January 1815 victory at the battle of New Orleans. Not coincidentally, Bowie's own brother, Rezin, who spoke both French and Spanish, had served as a Louisiana militia private during the showdown at New Orleans. Veterans of that battle were scattered across Texas, including among the Alamo garrison.

No single military event dominated the thinking of the generation of Americans in Texas and at the Alamo than Jackson's overwhelming victory on the open plains of Chalmette. There, a ragtag force of Americans had defeated battle-hardened English regulars, who had recently vanquished Napoleon's finest troops in Spain. Jackson's defensive stand along an earthen work (not a cotton-bale breastwork as so commonly believed) resulted in the slaughter of Major General Sir Edward Pakenham's attacking British columns in systematic fashion. But the ends of Jackson's lengthy defensive line were protected on the right by the Mississippi and on the left by a waterlogged cypress swamp, while the Alamo could be hit from all sides simultaneously, making the analogy inappropriate.

Nevertheless, the influence of the New Orleans victory and the hero of that success, General Jackson, upon this generation can partly be seen in the name of Alamo defender Andrew Jackson Sowell, a native of Tennessee from Gonzales. Also destined to meet his maker at the Alamo was Tennessee-born Private Andrew Jackson Harrison, age twenty-seven, yet another young man who had been named after the Scotch-Irish general.

On the other hand, Horseshoe Bend had demonstrated how even carefully prepared works could easily be surmounted by a superior army, in this case Jackson's force overcoming the Red Stick Creeks. Houston, as a young Virginia-born regular officer of the 39th United States Infantry, had been severely wounded during Jackson's headlong attack against the fortified Indian position in a bend of the Tallapoosa River. The strong breastwork at Horseshoe Bend had been stormed in typical Andy Jackson style: a hard-hitting frontal assault. Nearly 1,000 Creek warriors were slaughtered against a cost of 51 Americans, resulting in a decisive American victory over the pro-British Red Stick faction and sending the Creek Nation on the road to oblivion.[71]

In regard to his ill-fated decision to defend the Alamo, Colonel Neill should have known better; after all, he was a veteran of Horseshoe Bend. There he had manned one of General Jackson's two artillery pieces, a little 3-pounder and a 6-pounder. Facing an opponent who could not respond in kind, these guns had opened the battle, but had no effect on the formidable, log defensive work, thanks in part to green timber. Ironically, even though Neill had made his decision to hold the

Alamo largely because of its ample armament of guns, the old artillery-man overlooked the folly of defending a static position against a superior, better-trained conventional opponent.[72]

But it was the influence of Jackson's defensive victory over the British, not the Indian battle, that most influenced—if not inspired—the defense of the Alamo. In fact, twenty-one years after the battle, two veterans of New Orleans were present in the fort. One was Isaac Millsaps, who had served in the east Tennessee militia as a teenager. He was now the proud owner of a league of land in Jackson County, Texas.[73] A zealous volunteer named Sampson Connell, from the little community of Bastrop, was also a New Orleans veteran.

Also from Bastrop, northeast of San Antonio, was the second oldest man of the Alamo garrison, Corporal Gordon C. Jennings. He had been born in Windham, Connecticut as the son of a Revolutionary War veteran. This roaming New Englander possessed a restless spirit, seemingly always moving on toward the setting sun. He first migrated across the Mississippi to find a home in Troy, Missouri. But in 1833, he and his brother packed up and headed for the southwest frontier. The Jennings boys then settled in Bastrop, Texas.

Gordon enlisted in a volunteer company in late July 1835. Then he joined the small regular Texas cavalry command led by Travis, venturing into the Alamo from which there was no return. Here, the mature Corporal Jennings held responsibility befitting his age, serving as the wagon master. He would never see his daughter, Catherine, again, while another Jennings family member was destined to be executed by Mexican troops at Goliad not long thereafter.[74]

Unfortunately, for the Alamo defenders, they had brought to Texas not only their idealistic concepts of republican government, and their families and slaves to work the land, but also an obsolete means of waging war in a land that was utterly strange to them. Defeating the Creeks in the tangled woodlands of Alabama and whipping the British on the narrow plain of the plantation, named Chalmette south of New Orleans, brought a host of tactical lessons that were useless for the Alamo garrison.[75]

FATAL ARTILLERY SEDUCTION

In the end, what was most seductive about the Alamo was not its rectangle of limestone and masonry walls and adobe buildings, but its considerable arsenal of artillery and, ironically, the recently constructed defensive improvements, including artillery platforms, made by Cós' troops. As early as December 7, 1835, even Santa Anna was concerned about the artillery situation, issuing orders "to ascertain" the "number of cannon" in San Antonio and the Alamo.

As a former artilleryman of the Alabama militia, this fact was appreciated most thoroughly by Colonel Neill. He simply could not bring himself to abandon the artillery at the Alamo—there were not enough horses or oxen to haul off the guns—and retire east. Quite simply and on his own, he had decided "to stay with his guns," thereby dooming the garrison in the process. He believed that only the combination of a fortified defensive position, bolstered by large numbers of artillery, could negate the vast superiority of the Mexican cavalry, not to mention infantry. A fatal lure, "the Alamo's twenty fine guns [were] probably the strongest collection [of artillery] between Mexico City and New Orleans," and north of the Rio Grande.[76]

Therefore, after Colonel Johnson had ordered that all artillery was to be removed from San Antonio and placed in the Alamo, Colonel Neill, despite lamenting in mid-January 1836 that the garrison was "easy prey" if not reinforced, then "determined that the defense—if it became necessary—would have to be made from the Alamo."[77]

Yet in truth, this sizeable arsenal was not an asset but in fact the Alamo's greatest liability. Quite simply, not enough soldiers were available to both serve as gun crews for the cannon and to defend the place as riflemen. Even worse, most of the artillery pieces were situated to fire over the top of the walls instead of through embrasures. This serious liability ensured that the cannon could not be sufficiently depressed if the attackers reached the walls. And the so-called artillerymen assigned to the cannon seriously lacked in skill, experience, and training. A better defense would have come from the entire Alamo garrison defending the walls with rifles and muskets—if only firing platforms had been constructed—rather than dispersing so many men in isolated pockets at spread-out artillery pieces along the perimeter, ensuring neither a concentrated fire nor solid defense, even if everyone was ready and awaiting an attack.[78]

A great source of pride, the largest gun at the Alamo was the 18-pounder from New Orleans. It is not known, but this cannon might have been present at the Battle of New Orleans—one 18- pounder was situated to bolster Jackson's weak left flank along the cypress swamp at

Battery Number 5, and another was in Battery Number 7. In fact, the first American cannon to fire a shot at the Battle of New Orleans was the latter gun. Quite likely this cannon, known simply as the "long eighteen," was especially lengthy like the Alamo's piece. They may well have been the same gun. The man who fired the first shot on January 8, 1815 was New Orleans-born Major Samuel Spotts, one of the few Americans in Jackson's army killed that day. But even more interesting, a good chance exists that General Pakenham was killed by grapeshot from the same 18-pounder that stood at the southwest corner of the Alamo.

Much like the defenders themselves, this large-caliber gun was at the Alamo quite by accident. The cannon had been brought to Texas by steamboat, the *Columbus*, in mid-October 1835 by the New Orleans Greys. But lacking cannonballs, the 18-pounder had been left behind at the port of Velasco, never having played a role in the 1835 campaign. In fact, the cannon had been nearly lost in a shipwreck, falling into the turbid waters of Matagorda Bay, but had been salvaged. Quite by chance, the narrowest of margins, and as if by a strange fate, the Alamo's largest gun that played a large role in Neill's and then Bowie's ill-fated decision to defend the fort almost never reached San Antonio in the first place, despite "every exertion to get her to Béxar."[79]

Once the gun finally arrived there was still the problem of ammunition, and a supply was not inherited from the surrender of General Cós, who had decided not to mount many pieces because of the lack of cannonballs. While Neill had some additional guns mounted for the first time, he yet lacked cannonballs; ironically, the decision to defend the Alamo had been based upon the large amount of artillery without considering the small amount of ammunition. The 18-pounder was placed by Jameson at the Alamo's southwest corner, facing San Antonio to command the town, where they knew an arriving Mexican army would come—a mock display of strength and largely an impotent symbol, because of the failure of logistics and planning by the Alamo's leadership.[80]

The Alamo's total of twenty-one cannon—all but two (possibly three) guns were mounted in time—were in reality not a great defensive asset as envisioned by the Alamo's garrison, and certainly not a sound military reason for the impromptu decision to defend the place. The fact that artillery pieces required six-man crews ensured that a large percentage of the Alamo garrison—nearly half—would not be using their rifles, shotguns, and muskets when an attack came. A relatively small band of defenders was left to serve as riflemen to defend the walls or to provide support fire for the gun crews. As prescribed by regulation, some 114 soldiers would be assigned to manning the nineteen guns. In reality, pieces could be served by fewer men if properly trained, but then the big 18-pounder was required by regulation to have a crew of up to 16, making a total of 124 required artillerymen. What seemed to be the Alamo's strongest asset—the large amount of artillery—actually comprised a Faustian bargain of sorts, because due to the high number of artillerymen, the advantage of small arms was taken out of the hands of garrison members who would be needed along the compound's 440-yard perimeter.[81]

Instead of holding the Alamo to the bitter end when no hope for a successful defense existed, the diminutive garrison should have defended—if San Antonio had to be held at all—a nearby compound that was far better for defensive purposes: the Mission Nuestra Senora De La Purisima Concepcion. With an architectural beauty all its own, this Spanish mission, with its elegant Moorish arches, located below the Alamo was simply known as Mission Concepcion. Of the five old Spanish missions established along the San Antonio River, the Alamo was the northernmost, while Mission Concepcion was next, located just to the south, the second in line of the row of missions that had converted so many Indians to Catholicism over the years. Below Mission Concepcion stood the other three old Spanish missions, reminders of the Spanish imperial missionary zeal that had won vast empires for Spain in the New World.[82]

One Texan who well understood the Alamo's unsuitability for defense was Reuben M. Potter, who wrote the first popular account of the battle, *The Fall of the Alamo, A Reminiscence of the Revolution of Texas*, published in San Antonio in 1860 just before the Civil War. Potter's account was especially important, because, in his own words: "As I was a resident of Matamoros [Mexico] when the event happened, and for several months after the invading army returned thither, I had opportunities for obtaining the kind of information referred to which few persons, if any, still living in Texas have possessed."[83]

The Spanish-speaking Potter ascertained from talking to Mexican officers and men how: "Santa Anna, when he marched for Texas had counted on finding a fortified position in the neighborhood of San Antonio, but not at the Alamo, for he supposed, with good reason, that the Mission of Concepcion would be selected [because] the small area of that strong building, which had room enough for Travis' force and not too much, and its compactness, which would have given better range to his cannon, would have made it a far better fortress than the Alamo."[84]

Potter's conclusion was right on the mark. As appeared in his December 7, 1835 orders to General Sesma, Santa Anna believed that the San Antonio garrison would naturally "entrench themselves at Missions Espade and Concepcion, the first a league from Bejar [sic] and the latter four" leagues away. Significantly, he made no mention of the Alamo, which had been Cós' fatal lure.[85]

But a possible decision to defend Mission Concepcion instead of the Alamo was not really important in the end. After all, in strategic terms, Goliad was a position of far more importance than remote San Antonio. Defending the east Texas settlements required a defensive stand at Goliad, which had been established as part of the defensive chain of presidios to protect New Spain's northern frontier. Goliad had been the easternmost, or coastal, presidio, located on the coastal plain of the Gulf of Mexico, blocking the strategic Atascosito Road that ran up the coast from Matamoros and straight into the heart of the Austin Colony.

Most important, Goliad's Presidio La Bahía, Fort Defiance, situated on high ground, was far more defensible than the Alamo, which even then was widely realized. Early in the Texas Revolution, a knowledge-able writer for the *New Orleans Bulletin* emphasized how "the fort of Goliad . . . with a garrison of three hundred and fifty patriots in the war of 1812–13, withstood a [lengthy] siege of an army of more than two thousand Spanish troops and forced them to retire [and] Goliad is of vastly more importance in a military point of view than Béxar," or San Antonio.[86]

And as revealed in the pages of the December 8, 1836 issue of the *Maryland Gazette*: "Goliad is of vastly more importance in a military point of view than Béxar, as the latter is in a valley upon the banks of the river and commanded by the hills on each side: it is therefore inde-fensible."[87]

Goliad was especially crucial strategically because it lay on the main route that linked San Antonio to the little gulf port town of Copano on the Aransas Bay that led to the Gulf. Much of U.S. manpower, supplies, and munitions for waging war were brought through Copano. While San Antonio was located too far inland to benefit from a quick resup-ply or reinforcements from east of the Sabine, Goliad was ideally situated for such timely assistance necessary for the revolution's survival.[88]

Even the editor of the *New Orleans True American* knew as much, writing, "the fort at Goliad [was] a very strong position, well supplied with munitions and provisions," in preparation for meeting an invasion from Mexico—unlike the Alamo.[89] Quite simply, therefore, Goliad was "the strongest fortification in the Mexican sub-province of Texas," even though Bowie and Neill overlooked that common, widespread view, even among non-military men.[90]

As Houston had advocated, the Alamo garrison should have evacuated San Antonio and the Alamo to combine with Fannin's troops at Goliad for a united stand. However, as throughout the 1836 campaign, Texas leaders got it exactly reversed: Fannin's forces attempted to march to San Antonio to assist in defending a place that was indefensible, while leaving behind the strongest fortress in Texas. The predictable result was a double disaster, with Texan forces at both Goliad and San Antonio fated to be wiped out with relative ease.

It should also be noted that the Alamo, as an advanced outpost on the southwestern frontier, would have made an ideal cavalry post. Every Texan owned a good horse, just like he carried a well-maintained rifle; both were necessary means of survival on a frontier vulnerable to sudden Indian strikes. However, both "Army of the People" volunteers who had captured San Antonio, and the Matamoros Expedition troops took almost all the horses in the town and surrounding area. This widespread pilfering of resources left the Alamo garrison stranded at a remote post located far from the populated areas of east Texas not only abandoned, but also far out on a limb by early 1836.

If horses had been available the Alamo garrison could have ridden east, bringing the guns with them as Houston had desired, perhaps leaving only a small mounted force of observation at the fort. Ironically, this simple solution was overlooked by Bowie and Neill, even though some defenders had served in Texas Ranger companies performing mounted service against the Indians, and knew the importance of mobility on Texas' prairies.

With a sense of urgency, a desperate Neill described how his small band of soldiers was stranded in the middle of nowhere in a pitiful letter to Houston: "We are in a torpid, defenseless condition and have not and cannot get from all the citizens here horses enough to send out a patrol or spy company [and if not reinforced] we will be over-run by the enemy" in the near future.[91]

William Barret Travis would certainly have preferred a mounted command. As it stood, he was not only an accidental but a reluctant officer at the Alamo. In fact, he hated the assignment on the southwestern frontier from the beginning. With romantic dreams of waging war like a chivalric knight of old, he had wrangled a lieutenant colonel's commission in the Texas regular army from Governor Smith. Travis was then appointed to command a cavalry unit, the Legion of Cavalry, though it existed mainly on paper. Plagued by his own failures and the general apathy among Texans to serve in the 1836 campaign, the young man's recruiting efforts fell far short. But as a strange fate would have it, he was destined to command the Alamo in time for the final showdown with the largest Mexican Army ever to march north of the Rio Grande.[92]

At the Alamo, Travis would find himself in the odd position of commanding infantry and artillerymen rather than cavalry, and more pieces of artillery than he had ever seen before. Like Johnson, Neill, and Bowie, he was simply not experienced enough to command the force he had been given, much less to defend a stationary position.

FATAL ACHILLES HEEL: TURBULENT TEXAS POLITICS

Yet another key factor that loomed large over the Alamo disaster was the tortured course of Texas politics. Mirroring the complex political, social, and class divisions in the United States, the Texas revolutionaries were widely divided along political lines with two opposing governments—the Consultation Convention and the General Council—struggling for power in the yet undeclared Republic of Texas. In striking contrast to early 1836, the successful revolt of 1835 was largely the fruit of a united effort.

President Jackson had been America's leader for eight years by 1836, leading a powerful political machine. In opposition to "Old Hickory," another national political party finally emerged in 1836 to challenge the Jacksonites for supremacy: the Whig Party. In general, the Whigs disagreed with the Jackson Democrats on almost all issues, but especially in regard to race relations, sectional rivalries, economic philosophies, and class. The Jackson Democrats strengthened economic ties—and hence dependency—on Europe to create a "negative, liberal state," while the more traditional, conservative Whigs stressed the importance of the common man. Reflecting the traditional beliefs of most Alamo defenders, the Whig Party represented the view that the common man deserved an equal opportunity to advance and rise ever higher in American society, supporting all citizens, especially the small farmer, small businessman, and even the menial laborer.[93]

This split grew so wide between the conservative Whig Party and the Jackson Democrats that transplanted Americans in Texas were essentially wagering a war among themselves for supremacy. Consequently, both the Texas government and the war effort against a resurgent Mexico found themselves divided by two political factions bitterly at odds, and unity had veritably collapsed by the time Santa Anna marched into Texas.

For the most part, the men of the Alamo were fundamentally of the Whig Party and supportive of the General Council, which was to form the provisional government, direct the revolt, and establish the Constitutional Convention. This governing body of Whig sentiment had risen to the fore in opposition to the previous authority, the Consultation Convention of Jackson Democrats, who had named Houston as commander-in-chief. Not surprisingly, then, the San Antonio garrison refused to accept Houston's authority and urged his replacement. A Jackson Democrat, Houston simply refused to relinquish command when the General Council, which had been appointed by the Consultation Convention, rose to power.

And as if this chaotic situation was not bad enough, the Texans were divided on overall strategic thinking. While the ever-radical Houston and Governor Smith sought to declare Texas independence, the conservative General Council was dominated by those, including the lieutenant governor, who desired to remain within the Republic of Mexico under the Constitution of 1824. They also wanted to ally themselves to like-minded Mexican liberals, convinced that a united front against Santa Anna was best for Texas. Fundamentally, the roots of this pervasive sentiment lay in the pre-revolution "Peace Party" consisting of the propertied, successful "Old Texians." These were the longtime citizens who had far more to lose than the opportunistic newcomers, like most Alamo garrison members, who had more to gain from a declaration of independence and a complete break with Mexico.

Consisting mostly of United States citizens, the Alamo garrison and its Whig leaders were in opposition to Houston, who was pro-Jackson, and supported Governor Henry Smith in opposition to the General Council. Therefore, while General Houston envisioned a defensive line east of San Antonio centered on the much more strategic points of Goliad and Refugio, the mostly volunteer Alamo garrison—in the time-honored, citizen-soldier tradition—decided for political reasons that San Antonio should be held.

Some historians have even speculated that because of self-destructive Texas politics, David Crockett, a Whig, "took a stand, not against Mexico, but once more against the Jacksonites," just as he had in the United States, though it had cost him his Congressional seat. In the beginning, this motivation served as a primary catalyst for the Tennessean's decision to go to San Antonio to join the garrison. Most likely, Crockett decided not to proceed on the ill-fated Matamoros Expedition because the San Antonio garrison was not only anti-Houston, but also anti-Jackson. The close link between Jackson and Houston went back to Horseshoe Bend, where Houston's courage garnered Jackson's not-easily-won respect, and forged a lifelong friendship between the two Scotch-Irish men. Evidently both Crockett and Houston, the two most popular Americans in Texas, were in the process of positioning themselves for the possibility of becoming the first president of the new Republic of Texas once independence was declared, which was only a matter of time, or so it seemed.[94]

Yet another reason—long overlooked by historians—why Crockett needed to be eliminated so as to never become Texas' president was because of his strong anti-slavery views. With the possibility of an anti-slavery and perhaps eventually even abolitionist Crockett elected to the head of the future Texas republic, he might well become a threat as ominous to slave-owners as Santa Anna. In this scenario, Houston was hardly the only one in Texas who wanted to see Crockett eliminated. Other of his politically-minded and more Machiavellian peers might have wished for the Alamo garrison's demise, especially if it included the ever-popular Crockett, a representative voice of the western frontier, who not only opposed slavery, but the wealthy planters and speculators who sought to get rich at the expense of the common man. Crockett remained true to his humble Scotch-Irish roots, and if he had become the first president of Texas, he would perhaps become a dangerous populist, one who had already condemned the hypocrisy of the United States by saying, "our boast land of liberty [was dominated by] the Yoke of Bondage," or the slave interests of the powerful Jackson political machine.[95]

It appears highly likely that Crockett indeed wanted to revive his sagging political fortunes in Texas. Along with his popularity, however, he also needed a distinguished war record and a defiant stance against his old enemies, the Jacksonites, both in Texas and the United States. Hence, Crockett joined the Texas army with high hopes, even if he was on a collision course while evidently aspiring to become the president of a new Texas republic—Houston's ambitious quest as well.[96]

The serious divisions that rent the infant Texas government, endless political maneuvering, pursuit of selfish interests, and deliberate attempts to sabotage both military and political careers of leading Texas officers might well explain why the Alamo garrison was eventually left on its own to be sacrificed. Before the rise of the legend of Houston as Texas' savior, it was widely believed that he "had deliberately allowed Bowie and the others to be destroyed" at the Alamo for selfish political reasons.[97] Indeed, not long after the Alamo's fall, Houston would be widely criticized for not taking serious efforts to relieve and reinforce the Alamo. But his negligence was nothing new. In regard to Austin's homespun "Army of the People" during the siege of Béxar in late 1835, the Council itself accused Houston of harboring "desires the defeat of our army that he may be appointed to the command of the next" army of Texas.[98]

Running true to his non-compliance form, Houston would believe that Travis' repeated, increasingly desperate appeals for assistance when besieged by Santa Anna's Army were simply "lies." The former Tennessee governor considered the pleas a mere ruse that was part of larger political "electioneering schemes" cleverly orchestrated by Travis to enhance his "own popularity" across Texas. Consequently, rumors circulated widely that Houston deliberately allowed the Alamo garrison to be sacrificed, especially his popular political rivals and future opponents for high office—Crockett, Bowie, and Travis—to ensure that his position as commander-in-chief remained secure, paving the way for the future presidency of the Republic of Texas.[99]

The deep divide between the regular and volunteer forces of Texas also proved grounds for Houston's apathy toward the Alamo's fate. After Houston was appointed by the Consultation Convention as commander-in-chief of the Texas regular army, which he believed was essential for success because of his past experience as a U.S. regular during the Creek War, he was fanatically pro-regular in sentiment. Unfortunately for the Alamo garrison consisting mostly of volunteers, only Travis and a handful of men were regulars. These volunteers, who had played the key role in San Antonio's capture, were not part of the regular army that Houston had been appointed to command. In this sense perhaps, as far as Houston was concerned, these independent-minded, unruly Alamo volunteers and their ambitious leaders, who also just happened to be political opponents—Whigs instead of Jackson Democrats like himself, and who openly defied, even mocked, his authority—were expendable to the Tennessean for fundamental military and political reasons. Ironically, the Mexican threat was underestimated and even ignored, in part because the Anglo-Celts were more focused on their own personal animosities and jealousies, waging a political war among themselves rather than uniting and adequately preparing to meet Santa Anna's Army.[100]

Not unlike Crockett, who knew the political value of military service, Travis also aspired to a politician's career. Ever ambitious, the Alabamian correctly believed that he could gain popularity as a successful soldier in the field. Travis had already been chosen as one of seven representatives to the Consultation from San Felipe de Austin, while Crockett planned to represent St. Augustine. Consequently, two members of the famed Alamo triumvirate were not only seeking their fortunes in Texas by way of land acquisition, but also by pursuing their personal political fortunes, which would soon be cut short by Santa Anna's own soaring ambitions and political priorities.[101]

In the art of war, nothing has been more guaranteed to pave the way to certain disaster than military decisions based not upon sound strategy, but upon political and personal factors. As much as Santa Anna's Army crossing the Rio Grande, Texas politics and political ambitions doomed the Alamo's common soldiers, who fell victim to the evils of personal intrigue long before Mexican bullets and bayonets. Not aspiring to lofty political and military positions like their inexperienced leaders, these young men and boys only wanted to survive the war to collect their rightful reward for Texas military service—all of those irresistible acres of fertile Texas land, to provide for themselves and their families.

THE CHOICE OF COMMAND

Another factor that undermined the chances of the men of the Alamo was the sudden departure of Lieutenant Colonel Neill. In modern times the holy trinity of Alamo heroes—Travis, Crockett, and Bowie—has overshadowed the leader who was most responsible not only for the decision to defend the Alamo, but also for keeping the garrison together during its darkest days during the gloomy winter of 1836. The departure of the ever-popular Lieutenant Colonel Neill, who had commanded the Alamo troops far longer than any other leader, comprised a psychological blow to the garrison. Neill's unexpected departure would leave the Alamo garrison "dejected," and morale would plummet to a new all-time low exactly when Santa Anna was pushing north toward San Antonio.[102]

But what the Alamo men had failed to realize was that it took more than mere popularity and the ability to make friends and tell jokes to win battles. Blessed with a sense of good timing, Neill would depart the Alamo in a hurry, even though he knew that Santa Anna was moving on San Antonio. Interestingly, this was not the first time in his military career that Neill had missed an important battle—during the siege of San Antonio in December 1835, Neill had fallen sick, or so it has been claimed. At that time, he relinquished command of the army's artillery to Captain Louis B. Franks, who owned a league of land on the Brazos River in Robertson's Colony, while Lieutenant William R. Carey continued to serve as his dependable top lieutenant.[103]

As a regular officer and according to military protocol in mid-February, Neill would hand over the Alamo's command to the next highest-ranking officer, Travis of the regular cavalry. This change would be unacceptable to the volunteers who made up the vast majority of the garrison. In the democratic tradition brought across the Sabine with volunteers from the United States, an election would be held at the Alamo. Detesting the thought of serving under a regular officer, the volunteers naturally elected to follow Bowie, while the regulars followed Travis. Therefore Travis and Bowie would agree to share joint command. Exhibiting rare western frontier diplomacy, especially in Texas, both leaders would thereafter share decision-making, even jointly signing correspondence. However, enough of a rift existed that Travis, in typical independent fashion, would establish his headquarters in San Antonio with the regulars, while Bowie and the volunteers occupied the Alamo. Then when Bowie collapsed with illness, falling victim to a respiratory ailment on the siege's second day, February 24, barely a month after arriving in San Antonio, Travis would suddenly be thrust into the position as the Alamo's sole commander by default, after having only reached San Antonio on February 3.[104]

As fate would have it, Travis, an inexperienced cavalryman, very experienced ladies man, and aspiring politician with an undeserved (he had not filled his cavalry legion) rank of lieutenant colonel that had been only bestowed for mostly political reasons a month earlier, and a young man who never wanted to serve at the Alamo in the first place, was destined to command the garrison.[105]

When given the choice, the Alamo garrison had clearly decided that of Neill, Bowie, and Travis, the young man from Alabama was the leader under whom they least desired to serve. Compared to Bowie and Neill, Travis was the Alamo's least popular commander, and the garrison's opinion was only confirmed when Travis would seal the fort's fate with a defiant cannon shot on the late afternoon of February 23, after Santa Anna's forces reached San Antonio. As much as Santa Anna, Travis ensured that there would be no quarter for the Alamo garrison. His firing of the 18-pounder—in response to Santa Anna's demand for an immediate surrender—was the type of flamboyant gesture right out of the popular historical fiction of the day that Travis so loved.[106]

But Travis' dramatic flair and sense of melodrama was serious business to Santa Anna. While Travis was only playing the part of a military leader, Santa Anna was a hardened veteran who knew how to crush an opponent. Taking Travis' defiance as a personal insult, Santa Anna would become more determined to destroy the Alamo garrison than before. Travis' rash behavior simply symbolized the all-too-common Anglo-Celtic arrogance in the eyes of the Mexican president, who unfortunately by then held the lives of garrison's members in his hands.

From beginning to end, Travis would be overmatched as the Alamo's commander. After all, he had arrived at the Alamo with only a handful of horse-soldiers of his "Legion of Cavalry." This command was one of the few integrated military units in Texas, with Tejanos, including Captain Juan Sequín, Lieutenant Placido Benavides, who had organized a band of local Tejano rancheros in October 1835 to join Austin's forces for the attack on San Antonio, and Lieutenant Manuel Carvajal, serving alongside young Southerners like Lieutenant James Butler Bonham.[107]

Besides Neill, Bowie, and Travis, the lack of qualified junior officers at the Alamo was pervasive. Even the few New Orleans Grays soldiers who remained at the Alamo by early 1836 were without their inspirational leader. Captain William Gordon Cooke, age twenty-seven, had arrived in Texas in late October 1835 as second in command of Captain Robert L. Morris' company of the Grays. He had led these New Orleans

Grays with distinction in overwhelming General Cós' garrison in December 1835, but he then departed the Alamo for more fertile military fields of opportunity, escaping the deathtrap. Cooke was destined to serve on General Houston's staff in the days ahead; however, even Cooke was more of a druggist than a soldier, learning the trade in Fredericksburg, Virginia before continuing his practice in New Orleans.[108]

Some good officers were either sick in the hospital or had been discharged for disability during the period before Santa Anna struck. Without facing Mexican soldiers in January and most of February 1836, and with so many social engagements and distractions in San Antonio, the remaining cohesion of the Alamo garrison dropped to new lows. When one low-ranking soldier was about to be arrested for disobeying an officer's order, he defiantly "resisted and swore with pistols in his hands that he would shoot down the first man that attempted his arrest."[109]

The ever-widening gulf between officers and enlisted men became a chasm just before Santa Anna's Army reached San Antonio. In the western frontier tradition, the Alamo's soldiers of all ranks cherished a distinct sense of individualism. From the beginning, they placed more faith in the individual than in the arbitrary dictates of government —either Anglo-Celtic or Mexican—wealthy elites, and especially blustering politicians of Texas. Therefore, not surprisingly, the Alamo's volunteers were almost as much anti-Texas regular army as they were anti-Santa Anna by early 1836. These outspoken volunteers were determined to do as they pleased, fight under the commander of their choice, and make their own decisions in both military and political matters.[110]

Aside from the shortage of good officers, the diminutive Alamo garrison also suffered from a shortage of simple essentials such as food and clothing. Paying a high price for a fractured Texas war effort in the dead of winter, the Alamo garrison had first fallen victim to three rampaging waves of scavengers: 1) San Antonio's victors who returned home to east Texas; 2) the Matamoros Expedition troops; and 3) even Cós' paroled men who took what they wanted or could hide on their persons before likewise marching south.[111] By January 12, 1836, in Captain Carey's embittered words, the Alamo's soldiers were "almost naked, destitute of funds[,] having expended all for food and munitions of war and not much to eat only some corn that we grind ourselves & poor beef [and] this constitutes our dayly [sic] food."[112]

But even more angry than Carey was Lieutenant Colonel Neill, especially after the Matamoros Expedition troops, under Francis White Johnson and Dr. James Grant, completed the process of stripping San Antonio and the Alamo garrison of provisions, horses, and supplies. As Neill complained in a January 6, 1836 letter to the government: "We have no provisions or clothing since Johnson and Grant left [and all the] clothing sent here . . . was taken from us by arbitrary measures of Johnson and Grant, taken from men who endured all the hardships of winter and who were not even sufficiently clad for summer, many of them having but one blanket and one shirt."[113]

In addition, the lengthy 1835 siege of San Antonio led to the consumption of provisions far and wide. What had not been earlier taken by General Cós' troops and later secured by Austin's besiegers that fall and winter was pilfered by the men of the Matamoros Expedition. In regard to the area around San Antonio, therefore, Fannin complained in a letter to Houston as early as mid-November 1835: "We have nearly consumed all the corn &c. near here." These words of desperation were an ominous portent for the young men and boys who remained in garrison at San Antonio more than three months later.[114] And food was not the only shortage. Precious little firewood to ward off the biting cold had been stockpiled in case of a lengthy siege. Many soldiers billeted themselves in Tejano homes, sharing their food, fires, and shelter, protecting them from January and February's coldness. The Alamo garrison had become not a cohesive military force but a group of undisciplined and discontented individuals.

BLACK POWDER

While the supply of small arms ammunition seemed sufficient for the Alamo garrison at first glance and on paper, the reserves of high-quality powder were actually quite low, and much of the finest powder had been taken by members of the Matamoros Expedition. In addition, a far-sighted General Cós had his paroled men pilfer the best powder from artillery reserves and place it in their cartridge boxes for the march south, along with artillery supplies. What was left behind at the Alamo was the worst of the powder reserves, reducing both artillery and small arms capabilities. Worst of all, the remaining supply of black powder captured from General Cós' troops in December 1835 was largely obsolete by early March 1836 because of its inferior quality, made worse by damp winter weather. Stored in two rooms of the church, the powder supply was adversely affected by the phenomena known as "rising damp," with moisture seeping up the four-foot-thick walls of limestone.

Mexican powder was "so badly damaged" and of such overall poor quality that the Texans who captured Mexican powder throughout the Texas Revolution wisely refused to use it."[115] In the words of one amazed Texan who examined captured Mexican black powder, "[I] found it little better than pounded charcoal and, after a trial, rejected it as all together useless [and] It was the worst powder I ever saw."[116]

Even young men in Texas service long used to dangerous lives on the western frontier, where ammunition was always in short supply, merely tore open Mexican paper cartridges to keep the lead ball, throwing away the black powder in contempt. No savvy riflemen or settler wanted their own lives, or those of family members, dependent on inferior powder that could cause a misfire.[117]

Therefore, not desiring to utilize Mexican black powder, which was all but "useless," unless nothing else was available, the Alamo's soldiers could only rely on the relatively limited supply of high-grade black powder (76% nitre, 14% charcoal, and 10% sulphur) from the Du Pont factory in Delaware. Established in 1802 by a French immigrant whose family had fled the terrors of the French Revolution, DuPont had supplied American troops during the War of 1812. Significant for events to come, Matamoros Expedition members left behind Mexican powder at the Alamo, while taking the Du Pont powder for themselves—after all, they were about to invade Mexico itself! Consequently, the lack of high-quality powder reserves was destined to become a serious liability for Alamo garrison members on the morning of March 6. On the night of March 5, ironically, the garrison might have assumed that the Mexican powder—already inferior since its creation—was yet good, when in fact it had failed to maintain integrity because of a combination of factors: the lengthy transport from Mexico, the high humidity of the central plains of Texas, lengthy storage in an area affected by "rising damp," and the cold, wet winter of 1835–36.

Even though the Alamo armory contained 816 British muskets, the 1809 India model Pattern Brown Bess musket (.75 caliber) that had been used by English troops during the later phase of the Napoleonic Wars, and 14,600 cartridges captured from General Cós in December 1835, this supply was of relatively little use to the garrison after the cold weather, rains, and ice storms of winter.[118]

Unlike the ill-equipped Alamo men, Napoleonic soldiers had long ensured that cartridges and black powder remained dry, because they possessed waterproof, leather cartridge boxes with metal regimental insignia on the flap to keep it down—something that the Alamo's soldiers did not have among their limited gear brought from home. Especially in Texas with the humid summers and the rainy winters, a lingering dampness wrecked havoc on the Alamo's black powder supply, making it of relatively little use by the time Santa Anna attacked.[119]

Indeed, the Alamo's defensive capabilities were considerably compromised, because the "weapons and ammunition were scarce [and] their ammunition was very low. That of many was entirely spent," wrote Enrique Esparza of the no-win situation that guaranteed a most feeble defense of the Alamo.[120]

Providence, Rhode Island-born Albert Martin, who galloped from the Alamo as a messenger but faithfully returned with the Gonzales Ranging Company to meet a tragic fate with his fellow citizens on March 6, wrote on February 25 how the Alamo garrison "was short of Ammunition when I left" on February 24, the siege's second day.[121]

And on March 3, Travis penned how "our supply of ammunition is limited. At least five hundred pounds of cannon powder [and] ten kegs of rifle powder . . . should be sent to this place without delay." Even bullets were in short supply. The cache of large-caliber Mexican bullets could not be used for rifles because the lead balls were too big. Travis also requested "a supply of lead" for the men to make bullets from molds.[122]

A persistent Alamo myth is that the defenders' firepower was greatly enhanced because each man possessed a number of captured muskets by his side. What has been overlooked by many is that there was not enough high-quality black powder on hand to ensure any reliable degree of firepower at the critical moment, even if every defender was at his assigned position. And with the Alamo located nearly 150 miles from the Gulf, ammunition resupply across the long coastal plain would never arrive in time.[123]

RAVAGES OF DISEASE

Another critical factor that has been overlooked in regard to the Alamo's defense may well have been the most important: the garrison's overall poor health. The fact that the garrison's declining health by

March 6 has been ignored is somewhat ironic, because a sickness or disease had even cut down the fort's co-commander, Bowie, by the time of the attack. Whatever Bowie had, he was assigned to an isolated room along the southern perimeter to keep it from spreading. In truth, the entire Alamo garrison had fought a long-running battle—one that it lost—with disease throughout the winter of 1835–36, long before Santa Anna's arrival.

By conducting his campaign in late winter and without staying in one place too long, Santa Anna's Army of Operations was in relatively good shape, and more healthy than the Alamo garrison, whose indiscipline, static position, and unsanitary ways led to the spread of disease. Like many of his men, especially the Vera Cruz lancers, Santa Anna, after having grown up in that city, was immune to yellow fever—one secret of his past success in campaigning against unacclimated Spanish troops in the lowlands in and around Tampico and Vera Cruz.[124]

Unfortunately, the Anglo-Celts had decided to make a defensive stand in what was the most unhealthy place in not only San Antonio, but possibly all of Texas. As strange fate would have it, many American settlers had initially poured into Texas from the United States, in part because of a smallpox epidemic. This fatal disease, brought to the New World by Europeans, had spread from the east to finally infect people in the southwest, including Texas, with especially devastating results for native people. For the newly arriving immigrants from the United States, Texas had remained unoccupied, in no small part because of smallpox's wrath. The disease had purged this land of much of its native population, allowing the opportunity for migrants east of the Sabine to take possession of a vast land with relative ease.[125]

By 1836 the once thriving Spanish mission in San Antonio represented a classic study of the ravages of disease. First and foremost, the Alamo compound was virtually sitting atop a vast, sprawling graveyard. The first burial sites at the Alamo consisted of Native Americans, who had lived along this stretch of the San Antonio River long before the Spanish arrived. Occupying a relatively small area along the watercourse, the heavy concentration of Indians, who were part of the mission system, made these people more vulnerable to epidemics. From 1736 to 1739, an unmerciful cholera outbreak drastically reduced the Mission Indian population housed at the Alamo compound. More than 1,000 Mission Indians were buried around the outside of the old chapel—the Alamo proper. These unfortunates were not only victims of cholera, but also epidemics of smallpox, pneumonia, and diphtheria.

For instance, in 1738 alone, 655 out of a total of 837 Mission Indians, mostly Tlaxcalans, died in an epidemic that resembled a holocaust. Waves of diseases had long ravaged the area along the San Antonio River, and the winter of 1835–36 was no different. By early 1836, the Alamo defenders were literally sleeping and walking atop an unseen cemetery of shallow, Native American graves. These contained hundreds of men, women, and children from tribes such as the Apache, Pasojo, Tucame, Charame, Mesquite, and Jumana, but without markers, of course.[126]

Some graves of smallpox victims were disturbed when the Alamo's defenses were strengthened by digging ground to bolster the weak north wall. Such a development would help to spread disease, which might well have been passed on to garrison members from contaminated corpses. Other diseases might well have infected the defenders; for instance, a cholera epidemic swept through not only Mexico but Texas, including San Antonio, between 1832 and 1834.[127]

A total of six physicians and other medical staff, led by Chief Surgeon Amos Pollard and his assistants, John Thomson, John Purdy Reynolds, Edward Mitchasson, and John Hubbard Forsyth served in the infirmary. Artilleryman Captain Almeron Dickinson also served as an unofficial physician to the garrison. However, the effectiveness of these men was largely negated because Matamoros Expedition members, aside from their other confiscations, had even stolen the post's supplies of medicine.

The small Alamo hospital could trace a lengthy military lineage, having been established more than three decades earlier. In fact, this little-known medical facility was not only the "First Hospital in Texas," but also the site of one of Texas' first dental shops. This "first serious attempt" to establish a general hospital at the Alamo for both the military and civilian populace of San Antonio began in 1805. However, the initial hospital served mostly as a military infirmary with the increase of the Spanish garrison to parry the growing American threat, after the United States acquired Louisiana, eliminating the historic French menace to the borderland. Only near the Spanish period's end, in 1814, was the Alamo hospital discontinued by the chaos of revolution. The infirmary had meanwhile treated a large number of patients with a variety of diseases and injuries for nearly a decade. Therefore, long before the Anglo-Celts garrisoned the place, the Alamo had served as the largest military hospital in all of Texas, which paradoxically contributed to making it an unhealthy place by the winter of 1835–36.[128]

In addition, the sizeable Mexican garrison of General Cós had occupied not only the Alamo in 1835 but the infirmary. Nothing spreads disease faster than a large number of soldiers trapped in a confined space for an extended period—one of the horrors of siege warfare, in which disease often killed more of the besieged than the opponent. Unfamiliar micro-organisms, bacteria, and germs from Mexico's tropical depths had thoroughly infested the Alamo compound, lingering through the winter of 1835–36, making the cramped place extremely unhealthy, both before and during the siege.

But the most deadly disease in Texas by early 1836 was a smallpox epidemic that very likely spread to the Alamo garrison. On his journey to the Alamo from which he would never return, Micajah Autry wrote in a December 13, 1835 letter from Natchitoches, Louisiana, on the Texas border, where zealous volunteers from the U.S. flowed into Texas like a stream: "The smallpox has recently broken out here very bad."[129]

Additionally, measles spread through the garrison, sending more soldiers to the infirmary. One such victim was twenty-six-year-old, Ohio-born Tapley Holland. He was a veteran of the 1835 campaign along with two brothers, whose father hailed from Canada. The Hollands were among the original settlers of the Austin Colony. Instead of taking a disability discharge and returning home like so many others, Tapley remained behind to recuperate at the Alamo hospital. A young artilleryman of Captain Carey's "Invincibles" from Grimes County, Texas, he planned to either eventually return home or remain with the garrison upon recovery.[130] Another Alamo garrison member stricken by measles was Lieutenant Sherwood Young Reams. This 24-year-old Tennessean had first fired at a Mexican soldier during the "Lexington of the Texas Revolution" at Gonzales, and he had also participated in San Antonio's capture. Reams' leadership skills were recognized, earning him a lieutenant's rank in Captain Dickinson's artillery company. However, this seasoned veteran was discharged from the Alamo garrison on December 28 because of measles, and sent off to Gonzales in the hope of preventing the disease's spread.[131]

The men from the United States who had never been so far south before had expected the subtropical-like weather of Texas to persist right on through the winter. Few young men, especially those from the Deep South, anticipated the severity of the bitter cold fronts of Arctic air that pushed south down the flat, rolling grasslands of the Great Plains. Quite unexpected to them, they discovered that San Antonio, swept by biting-cold air, sudden rapid drops in temperature, and the harsh winter winds sweeping over the prairies, was as cold as northern states. Such cold fronts were the infamous Texas "norther."

Initially believing that they had discovered another Spain-like climate in this region, Spanish explorers were stunned by the ferocity of the "norther's" wrath that descended upon them in the winter of 1528–29. These were the first Europeans to record this unique, climatic phenomena.[132] Even though snow was rare in south Texas, the biting cold was nearly as severe. As detailed in his diary during his inspection tour of the untamed frontier of New Spain, including San Antonio, in 1727, Pedro de Rivera described an undeniable reality of a brutal Texas winter that was unrealized by most Alamo soldiers recently from the United States: "The climate of this province is similar to that of Europe, because the cold is quite noticeable during the time of snows."[133]

Another factor that ensured the spread of disease was the atrocious state of sanitation among the Alamo garrison. Throughout the winter of 1835–36, sanitation was virtually nonexistent in a command that was more civilian than military. The indiscipline of amateurs at war, many of who were away from home for the first time, translated into poor personal hygiene and sanitation, ensuring a greater chance of spreading germs. By early 1836, the lack of a well at the Alamo further facilitated the contagions of disease. In a January 12, 1836 letter, Captain Carey complained how the garrison was "almost famished for water." And this serious situation was destined to worsen when Santa Anna's forces cut off the garrison's main water source—the irrigation ditch that led to the fresh waters of the San Antonio River.[134]

Garrison members of this multi-ethnic and multi-cultural command hailed from a wide variety of places and locales, coming from all across the United States—from Massachusetts to nearby Louisiana—and even western and central Europe, including Germany and Denmark. Because such a high percentage of garrison members hailed from rural areas and were mingling with a large group of individuals for the first time, they were more vulnerable to the spread of disease than their better-acclimated, urban peers. Now existing on poor rations in the Alamo's damp, cramped quarters, the cold winter weather of 1835–36 forced the garrison into even closer living conditions that only continued to serve as a greater breeding ground for illness.

THE GARRISON TRIES TO IMPROVISE

The decision to defend the Alamo was made mainly because of its large number of artillery pieces, since it possessed the guns left behind by General Cós. However, Cós had his men sabotage some of what remained, reducing capabilities. As he wrote in his report to Santa Anna: "Almost none of the part [of artillery supplies] did I leave in the power of the insurgents," while his men took powder reserves in violation of the surrender and parole terms when they marched out of San Antonio back to Mexico. Most significant, Cós reported that, "The rest of the armaments that I was not able to take was render[ed] useless."[135]

Other than the former militia artilleryman, Neill, no one among the garrison was more seduced by the Alamo's plentiful amount of artillery than Jameson. Beaming confidence, he was convinced that the garrison could literally "whip 10 to 1 with artillery."[136]

The best known company of Alamo artillerymen was led by the popular officer Captain Carey, who had long been Neill's trusted confidant. Near mid-January 1836 and with obvious pride, Captain Carey wrote in a letter how Lt. Colonel Neill "thinks a great deal of my judgment and consults me about a number of the proceedings before he issues an order."[137]

Neill and Carey had first formed tight bonds while serving together in the People's Army of Texas and during San Antonio's siege. Carey enlisted as a private but soon rose in rank with demonstrated leadership ability. Near the end of October 1835, he gained a second lieutenant's rank. During their siege of San Antonio, Carey displayed the ability that won him a promotion to first lieutenant from Neill, who commanded the artillery at the siege's beginning.

During the house-to-house fighting that swirled through San Antonio's streets, Carey had played a distinguished role. Reminiscent of General Washington's cannon firing at the Hessians down Trenton's snowy streets on December 26, 1776, he ordered a gun planted in the middle of one dusty street to suppress Mexican fire, including artillery, from defensive positions at close range. While fellow cannoneers fell around him in this exposed position and a hail of bullets cut through his clothes and hat, and even though blood dripped from a head wound, Lieutenant Carey directed fire that disabled a Mexican cannon. He and his gunners suppressed the incoming fire in a diversion that assisted the successful infantry attack.[138]

However, long before Santa Anna's arrival, the large amount of Alamo artillery was already largely negated because of the following factors: 1) the overall inexperience of the crews; 2) the relatively few proper firing positions because of lack of embrasures; 3) the lack of cannonballs of all types and sizes; 4) many of the artillery pieces set-up atop the walls were improperly placed, unable to be depressed sufficiently to hit attackers if they gained the wall's base; 5) the lack of both quality and quantity of black powder; 6) the unsuitability of small, former naval guns, which had been brought inland from the Spanish ships; and 7) the mostly small caliber of the guns, their antiquated age, and overall lack of maneuverability. These factors all combined to make the sizeable number of Alamo cannon largely moot. Travis was more prophetic than he knew when he wrote in a December 17, 1835 letter: "I could not be useful in the artillery," although the faulty decision to defend the fort was made in large part because of the artillery's presence.[139]

According to Jameson, the Alamo's chief engineer and Bowie's dependable aide-de-camp, only one solution existed to perhaps solve the vexing problem: much of the Alamo's artillery pieces were not placed in positions to be utilized effectively. Affectionately called Benito by Bowie, even though he hailed from the Bluegrass State, Jameson was blessed with a rare blend of both common sense and intelligence, which combined with a decidedly "mechanical bent" of mind to make him somewhat of a Renaissance man, especially in the context of the Texas frontier. His innovative defensive plan indicated that Jameson possessed considerable knowledge in the art of military science, gleaned from his intense study of the subject from any available military or engineering textbook that he could find. The former lawyer—part intellectual and part hands-on man—from San Felipe de Austin had transformed himself into a capable engineer, just as he had once taught himself to be a good attorney.

Supremely confident in the validity of his engineering views despite the lack of a formal military education, Jameson boldly proposed an imaginative defensive solution to the Alamo dilemma to Governor Smith: "The suggestion is to square the Alamo and erect a large redoubt at each corner supported by Bastions and have a ditch all around full of water. When squared in that way for cannon and fewer men would do more effective service than the twenty pieces of artillery do or can do in the way they are now mounted."[140]

For the most part, Jameson's defensive reasoning was sound. The

Alamo's most profound defensive liability was its sheer size of nearly three acres, and the reality that it was essentially "a fortified village" originally created only to protect people and livestock against Indian attack rather than a conventional opponent. Jameson's central dilemma was to somehow transform the Alamo's defensive liabilities into assets without sufficient time, manpower, or resources. Reducing the area of the Alamo to be defended was absolutely necessary, as Jameson realized. However, in the meantime, a strongpoint redoubt—well constructed and of adequate size—at each corner of the compound's plaza could give the artillery in each redoubt the ability to provide fire support for the adjacent one. With around twenty guns available, Jameson possessed ample cannon to place in each of the four proposed earthen redoubts, creating powerful bastions at each corner of the Alamo.

As he concluded his ambitious defensive vision in his informative letter: "If I were ordered to construct a new and effective Fortress on an economical plan, I would suggest a diamond [shape fortification] with two acute and two obtuse angles—with few men and Guns but with a sufficient entrenchment all around. Such a fortress with projecting redoubts and Bastions would command all points."[141]

But there was simply not enough time for Jameson's defensive vision to become reality. First, Governor Smith was officially disposed of power as the provisional government fell to pieces, leaving the Alamo garrison on its own. Such a massive construction project would have demanded a good deal of time before Jameson could even learn it had been approved. Consequently, work on the new defensive plan was never undertaken. In addition, a "scarcity of tools," complained Jameson, handicapped the type of wholesale reconstruction that the imaginative engineer envisioned with such clarity.

There was also the factor that the disposition of the Alamo garrison resulted in an ugly insubordination that made the average man in the ranks unwilling to do such heavy manual labor. To these volunteers mostly from slave-owning areas, especially Tennessee (30 men) and Kentucky (16 garrison members), the idea of such hard work usually delegated to slaves was not only distasteful, but unimaginable to aspiring Southern gentlemen. Many young soldiers, especially from Deep South states such as South Carolina (7 men) and Georgia (5 men), envisioned themselves as Southern gentlemen.

They were convinced that they would lose esteem befitting the elite planter class—even if it existed only in their minds—if they performed manual labor as required by Jameson, especially digging and hauling dirt and shovel-work. Therefore, Jamieson found himself not only without sufficient time, but also without the manpower to make the necessary improvements. The frustrated engineer penned to the governor: "The men I have will not labor and I cannot ask it of them until they are better clad and fed."[142]

Other factors also might well have sabotaged Jameson's ambitious plan to revamp the Alamo's defenses. For instance, he may have clashed with Travis, thwarting his defensive plans. Ironically, the overly emphasized animosity between Travis and Bowie was very likely less than that which existed between Travis and Jameson, who were rival lawyers before entering military service. After all, Travis had won a case against Jameson in a court of law. Travis' client came away winning a lawsuit against Jameson for which he was forced to pay $50.00, a good deal of money at the time. And Jameson was a close confidant and personal aide-de-camp to Bowie, placing him in opposition to Travis along the ever-widening volunteer versus regular divide.[143]

It was the cooperation of the men that was most crucial for enacting defensive improvements, however; yet they were increasingly unwilling or unable to provide it. As early as January 12, 1836, Captain Carey scribbled in a letter how, "The men in this place have sometimes been discouraged on account of the distressed situation we are in; for want of clothes and food [therefore] the Colo [Neill] and myself has twice called a general parade and addressed them in such a manner that they would get satisfied for a while, but we are now discouraged ourselves, and unless the provisional government of Texas do speedily send us assistance we will abandon this place."[144]

The fact that the Alamo garrison was on the verge of abandoning the place at this early date is a far cry from the mythology that these soldiers were determined to sell their lives as dearly as possible to win the salvation of Texas. That they decided to stand firm, moreover was largely due to misreading the situation they were in, both in regards to the Texas Revolution and Santa Anna. Like other Anglo-Celts throughout Texas, they were guilty of not only underestimating the Mexican soldado, but of not even taking the war seriously. Instead, from the beginning and despite ample warnings of the impending threat, "they acted as if they were on a lark, after which they would collect the land promised in payment for that service."[145]

Even before the infant Texas government fell apart, the garrison in

San Antonio was not only neglected by the people of Texas and the government, but treated almost as if it did not exist. For the most part, the Alamo garrison was an independent volunteer command, making decisions and acting beyond the jurisdiction of the government, the regular army, and General Houston, whose authority the defenders refused to recognize. Therefore, during the late winter of 1835–36, almost nothing by way of support—especially manpower and munitions—was forthcoming from the Texas government to San Antonio.

Much to Neill's and Bowie's dismay, the election officials and judges of San Antonio, who selected delegates for the Constitutional Convention, refused to either allow garrison members to vote or to accept representatives among them on the grounds that they "were merely occupying troops, citizens of neither Texas nor Mexico." This, of course, included Crockett. Ironically, he now served Texas to enhance his political prospects, but saw even his right to vote negated when he joined the Alamo garrison.[146] The men who would be the first in Texas to face Santa Anna's wrath had themselves been excluded from the democratic process.

SANTA ANNA'S MISPLACED DECISION TO ATTACK THE ALAMO

Perhaps Lieutenant Colonel de la Pena said it best. "In fact, we should have attacked the enemy at the heart [starting at Goliad] instead of weakening ourselves by going to Bejar, a garrison without any political or military importance [and] This was the unanimous opinion of all the military."[147]

Ironically, by early 1836, the only folly greater than the disastrous decision to defend the Alamo was Santa Anna's eventual decision to attack it at all. Quite simply, the Alamo was strategically unimportant. Santa Anna could have easily won his war had he simply marched his army past the Alamo to continue east to strike the settlements of east Texas. All Texas was ripe for the taking by early 1836.

Santa Anna's wiser subordinates advocated a far more sound strategy. They implored that wiping out the Texas rebellion called for a simple solution: a swift march past San Antonio to overrun the east Texas settlements and capture the unofficial capital of the Austin Colony at San Felipe de Austin, ending the Texas government in one stroke. But to Santa Anna, San Antonio, a place of some romance and nostalgia for him, became an enduring symbol of opposition and revolution that

needed to be eliminated. In this regard, political and personal consider-
ations, and even emotional and psychological factors, of Santa Anna far
outweighed sound strategic axioms when it came to his decision to capture San Antonio and the Alamo.[148]

Historian Stephen L. Hardin noted: "Given the strategic importance
of the coast, which was obvious to both sides, Santa Anna's earlier drive
against Béxar was a wasteful digression [and attacking the Alamo] made
little sense from a strategic viewpoint . . . an assault on the Alamo was
pointless."[149]

Mirroring Santa Anna's strategic error in targeting the Alamo, the
folly of attempting to defend the Alamo with an ill-clothed, powder-
and-cannonball-short, half-starved band of untrained and undisciplined
soldiers was only reinforced by the fact that tons of war supplies and
munitions—including invaluable United States muskets, flints, and
black powder—that had already poured into Texas ports such as
Matagorda and Brazoria, from New Orleans in January 1836, would
never reach the Alamo's doomed men, who were destined to die without the essentials to adequately defend themselves.[150]

Even citizens across the United States realized that the Alamo and
its small garrison were doomed. In the February 29, 1836 issue of the
New York Herald, Americans learned about the height of folly at San
Antonio in the latest segment, "Latest From Texas": "A letter received
at New Orleans from Texas, states that a force of 2,500 men had a short
time before at Laredo, and that 1,500 of them had advanced as far as
the Rio Fio, 80 miles from San Antonio. An attack on the city was daily
expected. In the Alamo there were but 75 men, and very little provisions," and an almost non-existent chance for a successful defense.[151]

THE FORGOTTEN MEXICAN SOLDADO

Meanwhile, Santa Anna and his army continued to march north at a
rapid pace toward a rendezvous with destiny at an old, crumbling
Spanish mission. Unlike Alamo garrison members, who stood to gain
their fortunes if they survived this war, the common Mexican soldier, or
soldado, possessed no such dreams of reaping vast rewards for his military service. This mostly Indian peasant in uniform was paid only
twelve and a half cents per day, and his future promised to be as bleak
as his past.

Some minor consolation for the hard life of the average fighting man in Santa Anna's army was the large number of soldaderas who accompanied the march northward. Continuing a tradition extending back centuries to the warrior societies of the Mesoamerican past and in the 1810 Wars of Independence, these female soldaderas functioned as an unofficial, logistical support system and quartermaster corps that supported the soldados by foraging, cooking, washing, and other services—an effective female logistical network. Some women had even fought as warriors during the struggle to liberate Mexico from Spanish rule. Playing key roles, other Mexican women administered to the sick and wounded in the absence of trained physicians and medical assistants in the Army of Operations during the 1836 Texas Campaign. Unlike the Alamo defenders, who were far from home and families, Santa Anna's soldiers benefited much from the women who followed the army north.

In this sense, Santa Anna's Army was not unlike a large traveling Mexican community, including the wives, lovers, and children of many soldados in the ranks. Indeed, more than 1,500 women and children followed Santa Anna's troops across the Rio Grande, but only around 300 would reach San Antonio because of the lengthy, punishing march.

This unofficial arm of the Mexican Army was needed not only for logistical and medical reasons. Such an emotional and psychological support system also helped to make harsh army life more tolerable for the common Mexican in the ranks. Not unlike the 19th-century British Army and Navy, Mexican army life was brutal, with severe punishments. Under harsh discipline, Mexican fighting men were often flogged for the slightest infractions. Reflecting the heritage of their Indian ancestors and the Spanish, some solados wore earrings, for which they were punished because aristocratic officers believed that such "feminine ornaments . . . lowered the military profession."[152]

Who were these young men and boys from the Republic of Mexico who fought at the Alamo, and what were their motivations? Were these soldados the so-called "convict" troops, so commonly disparaged in American accounts? Instead of convicts, a little more than half of Santa Anna's army consisted of active militia and presidio troops, while the rest were regular army, or "permanente" units.

Among the dependable officers of the San Luís Potosí Battalion were junior leaders like Lieutenant Irineo Guerrero. This promising young officer hailed from the small village of San Miguelito, Mexico. Lieutenant Guerrero was married to Hermengilda Vasques, but his wife would never see him again once he marched away from home with his finely uniformed unit. Lieutenant Guerrero was destined to meet his death at the Alamo. A brother officer of the San Luís Potosí Battalion, Second Lieutenant Antonio Carricante, would also be cut down on March 6, 1836.[153]

Much of Santa Anna's Army of Operations consisted of recruits who had been either impressed or drafted in Mexico along the army's route north, as ordered by the commander-in-chief. One of these men was Felix Nunez, who wrote: "I was forcibly conscripted in 1835 in the state of Guadalajara, Mexico [when] I was then 32 years of age."[154]

In the enlisted ranks of the San Luís Potosí Battalion were reliable, noncommissioned officers like Sergeant Anastacio Velaquer. Like Lieutenants Guerrero and Carricante, this tough sergeant inspired the battalion's enlisted men, including Francisco Ordas, Victoriano Tenerio, German Sánchez, Leonardo Ramos, Victoriano Perez, and Correlio Rosales. All of these men would meet their maker at the Alamo since, as fate would have it, the San Luís Potosí Battalion was destined to suffer more fatalities in the battle than any other Mexican unit.[155]

Also shattering the common Anglo stereotype of the "convict" soldado was Santiago Rabia, who served in the Tampico Cavalry Regiment of lancers. Unlike the Alamo defenders, the blond, blue-eyed Rabia was a professional soldier, well educated, and knowledgeable in the art of war. Looking as American as the Alamo's defenders, except for his resplendent Mexican uniform, Rabia was born in Spain in 1804. There, in the snow-capped Pyrenees of northern Spain, his Basque family had originally prepared him for the priesthood, but a far different destiny lay in store for the handsome young man of promise.

At age ten, his parents died. Rabia then migrated to the New World for a new start, just like so many Alamo men, after both personal and professional misfortune had changed their lives. Rabia gained entry into a military school in Mexico City, and upon graduation became an officer. Now his strange destiny took Rabia ever-farther north toward the Alamo and a greater distance from his home.[156]

More typically, soldiers in Santa Anna's Army had been impressed into service. Eager to secure cannon fodder for his war machine, Santa Anna's impressment gangs took single males over the age of fifteen from each family whenever possible, especially in large towns such as Saltillo. Like British naval impressment crews of the day, Mexican army recruiters grabbed whoever they could get their hands on.[157]

Convicts were not necessary to fight this war. Most of all, the revolt in Texas had united and rallied the Mexican nation like no other event in its recent turbulent history. In a December 30, 1835 notice, General Jose Antonio Fernandez implored that: "Everyone needs to cooperate for the support and integrity of the territory of the Republic that is being threaten[ed] by the ungrateful Colonists of Texas."[158]

However, Fernandez hardly needed to exaggerate the threat to the Mexican nation at this time. Many Mexican soldiers marched into Texas fueled by heady idealism. Mexican officers especially viewed service in Texas against the revolutionaries north of the Rio Grande as a noble crusade. With pride, Francisco Paredas y Arrillaga wrote to the Mexican Minister of War, Jose M. Tornel, how the Mexican troops that he now had "the honor to command, burn with desires to take some part in the glories of the Fatherland" during the Texas Campaign.[159]

Most important, contrary to Anglo-Celtic stereotypes of a mercenary, convict, and corrupt soldiery, the Mexican army, except perhaps some of those troops conscripted or impressed into service, was united solidly behind Santa Anna. Not only the republic's president, he was seen as Mexico's savior. Both enlisted men and officers believed that Santa Anna was just the man who could continue Mexico's winning tradition against foreigners. After all, he had first won fame as the governor of the Province of Vera Cruz, when he repulsed Spain's bid to reclaim her former possession by force. After Spanish forces landed near Tampico, Santa Anna had been at his best, acting instinctively and decisively in the manner of Napoleon. Santa Anna relied upon the axiom that the best defense was an aggressive offense, taking the initiative that the invaders had unwisely relinquished. Striking hard in August 1829, he unleashed "a master stroke of boldness," in one Mexican general's evaluation. Santa Anna attacked with vigor, forcing the surrender of the Spanish expeditionary force at Tampico in September. Combined with his recent Zacatecas victory, this smashing success made Santa Anna not only a national hero, but a seemingly invincible figure by the time of the Texas campaign. Most important, he had united the Mexican nation and people, while bestowing a sense of pride upon his newly formed Army of Operations not seen since the struggle for independence.[160]

And like Napoleon, Santa Anna led by personal example, demonstrating courage under fire. His tactical audacity inspired confidence among both his top lieutenants and the common soldiers in the ranks. Unlike so many other Mexican generals of the time, Santa Anna often rode ahead of his advancing army to conduct reconnaissance or direct tactical movements on his own, while escorted by only a handful of his favorite dragoons.[161]

Across the republic, therefore, Mexican political and civilian leaders were supremely confident of success by early 1836. Santa Anna was seen across the nation as the one man who could quickly quell the latest unrest to the north. Mexicans universally believed that Santa Anna's campaign to reclaim the "lost" province of Texas would result in an easy victory over the "northamericano" rabble, which would not stand a chance against Mexico's professional soldiers.[162]

Most of all, Santa Anna desired to "plant the eagle of the Mexican Empire" atop the Alamo and over the defenders' bodies. Just as the United States had adopted the eagle as its national symbol, so did Mexico, making it the central figure on its red, white, and green flag.[163] When Augustín de Iturbide declared the new nation's independence in 1821 with his Plan of Iguala, the Creole colonel proclaimed that he was guided by the divine hand of providence. Iturbide believed that God himself had inspired him to raise the banner of independence with "the Mexican eagle."[164]

Embracing a far more distinguished cultural and historical legacy than embodied in Houston's Cherokee nickname of the lowly, scavenging "raven," this majestic "imperial eagle" of Mexico had first flown "across the American heavens" to establish Mexican independence, and now it flew into Texas to accompany Santa Anna's avenging army to uphold the Catholic faith and Mexican nationhood.[165]

4

Lull Before the Storm: Fatal Overconfidence

Early and mid-February 1836 was a period of calm for the Alamo garrison. All the while, San Antonio—with its people, food, music, and Tejano culture—continued to be seductive to the young men who recently arrived from the United States. They thoroughly enjoyed this "season of almost utter abandon." But the most alluring intoxicant continued to be the land—its sheer size and majesty. Quite unlike anything they had seen before, this picturesque land seemed to have no end. The expansiveness and beauty of the rolling hills, fertile valleys, and sprawling prairies around San Antonio was yet an obsession for the Alamo garrison, even while Santa Anna's Army approached.

During the late winter, almost all of the "Old Texians" remained on their farmsteads of the east Texas piney lands and the fertile reddish soil of the "Redlands" around Nacogdoches. Here they enjoyed their Southern-style plantations, benefitting from the labor of their gangs of slaves, nestled in the river valleys of the Colorado and Brazos of east Texas. Winter in Texas, unlike in the north, was a busy time of year. Crops had to be planted in the spring, which arrived early in Texas, and were then harvested much earlier in the fall than in the United States. Beginning in late summer, the 1835 campaign had been won in no small part because so many farmers across Texas had left their ranches and plantations to win victories before harvest time in late fall. Unfortunately for the Alamo garrison, no such fortuitous sequence could be counted upon in early 1836.

Significantly, the most experienced fighters in Texas, mostly recent migrants themselves, were not at the Alamo. Now largely absent from this war, the "Old Texians" were as much fighters as farmers. Many years of wartime experiences in not only battling Native Americans, but also English regulars during the War of 1812, and even Spanish soldiers as filibusters, had given these men much pre-Texas Revolution military training. For instance, one such natural leader was Walter C. White, who had served with General Long during the filibuster expedition into Texas. And then he raised the "first crop of corn ever cultivated" along the Trinity River. Such experienced soldiers were needed at the Alamo instead of the mostly fresh-faced novices who had been left behind when the Matamoros Expedition left San Antonio.

In addition, a considerable cultural and ideological gap existed between these "Old Texians" which was a distinct "class" by early 1836, and the newcomers to Texas. While these "Old Texians" had been longtime Texas residents, who benefitted from their Spanish and Mexican land claims and had improved their considerable properties to amass assets to become "gentlemen" planters in the Deep South cultural tradition, the newcomers from the United States were on the make. They were mostly young risk-takers, gambling all on one throw of the dice. This resulted in a division between conservatives and radicals, which meant that while the "Old Texans" mainly supported the Constitution of 1824, the men of the Alamo, who were mostly opportunistic newcomers from east of the Sabine, were pro-independence.

Because these men were risk-takers out of necessity to get ahead because they were latecomers to Texas, they now found themselves virtually abandoned and forgotten at the Alamo. These young men and boys had yet to realize their Texas dream and reap the riches from this land of plenty, and this called for making at stand in San Antonio. Open resentment, if not outright hostility, from the "Old Texians" toward many of these new Texans was both natural and ironic. Indeed, these recent interlopers, compared to the long-settled "Old Texians," now defended the Alamo by early 1836.[1]

In addition to a generation and residential gap, another forgotten aspect divided the "Old Texians" and the newcomers to Texas as well. Ironically, this difference was based upon ethnicity—not unlike the cultural divide that separated Tejanos from Mexicans. Not only were the newcomers to Texas, including those at the Alamo, younger and of less means than the "Old Texians," but they were also more foreign, with many hailing from the Atlantic's other side.

For instance, the San Antonio victory in December 1835 resulted in a flood of European migrants to Texas. Recently from Ireland, England,

Germany, Wales, Scotland, and other European nations, these newcomers were now among a surprisingly high percentage of those who defended Texas by the late winter of 1835–36. And the Alamo garrison was a classic example of this phenomena. With a mixture of disbelief, even Fannin complained on February 7, 1836 to acting governor Robinson: "I doubt if twenty-five citizens of Texas can be mustered in [the] ranks," while United States citizens and Europeans, including at the Alamo, served instead of Texians.

Ensuring a continued prosperity begun decades before, these farmers and ranchers of east Texas were busy in the fields and in improving their ranches, while the Alamo's soldiers languished in idle complacency far on the remote southwestern frontier. To explain this unusual situation, it was almost as if because the "Old Texians" had settled this land, risked all, suffered for years against the dual ravages of the unforgiving wrath of nature and Native Americans, they felt that these newcomers—including the young men and boys of the Alamo—had to pay the inevitable high price to lay claim to this fertile land.

Already, the great prize of Texas had already doomed one man of promise, Don Miguel Mier y Teran, as if paying for the sin of having loved Texas with a passion. He had been obsessed with the fact that Texas had been transformed into a radical, festering bastion of Protestantism and Anglo-Saxon culture, thanks to the Mexican government's liberal immigrant policy and naive hope that frontiersmen, pious Protestants, and longtime Anglo-Celtic conquers of nature, land, and Native Americans, could become good, peaceful Mexican citizens and even Catholics—an absolutely impossible transformation of settlers of mostly Scotch-Irish antecedents.

After touring Texas in 1828–29, a distressed Teran had warned the president in Mexico City that Mexican influence had simply "disappeared" north of San Antonio, and that Texas was all but lost to the republic if drastic action was not soon taken. The undeniable reality that Texas was slipping more and more out of Mexico's grip forever, as he sensed, caused Teran to commit suicide in 1832.[2]

And now that same alluring, irresistible dream of Texas, and its seemingly boundless possibilities that had doomed the unfortunate Teran was about to be turned into a surreal nightmare—something vindictive that would destroy the tiny Alamo garrison with a vengeance. As historian Barbara Tuchman has emphasized, perhaps the most important factor contributing to the "march of folly" was overconfidence.

Indeed, as Tuchman maintained: "the most frequent and fatal of self-delusions [has long been] underestimating of the opponent."[3]

Perhaps the best example of the overconfidence of the Alamo garrison can be found in the words of the capable, if not brilliant, engineer Jamieson. Utterly blinded into believing that the Alamo was a defensive bastion that could keep all of Santa Anna's Army at bay, he boasted in a January 18, 1836 letter to Governor Smith that, "in case of an attack we will move into the Alamo and whip 10 to 1 with artillery."[4]

Yet another example of the fatal overconfidence of the Alamo defenders was seen with the irrepressible Captain Carey and his company of artillerymen, the Invincibles. Unable to even imagine war's horrors, Cary's naive fifty-six young gunners, like the captain himself, were cocky and supremely overconfident. Organized after San Antonio's capture, these artillerymen then elected the young Marylander, Carey, as their captain in the democratic tradition of the western frontier.

In his January 12, 1836 letter to his siblings, Captain Carey wrote with an unbridled confidence that was ill-founded, if not fool-hardy: "I cannot close without saying something about my invincibles, as I call them, about twenty of my company (although the whole [fifty-six men] has been tired and I know them all) that will (to use their words) wade through h-ll, when I am at their head if I should give the order."[5]

One of Captain Carey's Invincibles was thirty-seven-year-old Private Jacob Walker. He was married to a Latin-speaking lady from the French aristocracy of the Mississippi Territory, the former Sarah Ann Vauchere. Walker hailed from Nacogdoches, where he was a landowner before volunteering to serve Texas.[6]

Another Invincible was Corporal Gordon C. Jennings. He had arrived in Texas from Missouri in 1833. Jennings left behind a wife, Catherine, and four children in a little log cabin on the sprawling prairie outside Bastrop, Texas, along the upper bend of the picturesque Colorado River, when he enlisted. He fought in the siege of San Antonio in December 1835. At age fifty-seven, in good health and sprightly, the Missouri-native was the oldest member of Carey's Invincibles.[7]

But even more revealing in his letter was Captain Carey's boast, which was a representative attitude among the Alamo's soldiers, who possessed a highly inflated feeling of superiority over any number of Mexicans: " . . . when we go to fight the Enemy and then I think a small number of us can whip an army of Mexicans."[8] Jameson displayed a different aspect of contempt for his opponent, writing in a letter how:

"The mexicans have shown imbecility and want of skill in this Fortress as they have done in all things else."[9]

Such unrestrained ethnocentric and racial overconfidence among the Anglo-Celts was pervasive not only at the Alamo, but also across Texas. But, of course, because of racial, cultural, and religious differences, Mexicans possessed equally outlandish prejudices, but less so based purely upon color. In a January 3, 1836 letter, John Lamar described a prevailing attitude in Texas, including at the Alamo, that discounted Santa Anna's gather Army: "5,000 Americans are fully competent to fight and defeat 20,000 Mexicans."[10]

One especially contemptuous Texan, like most settlers who conveniently overlooked the importance of contributions from thousands of slaves, was so confident as to write: "We occupy a country which but for our presence would ever have remained a wilderness, because the Mexicans were afraid to occupy a country inhabited by so many Indians . . . The confidence which the Americans in Texas feel in their power over the Mexican troops gives them less uneasiness than they have from their more powerful neighbors the Indians, most of whom we consider equal warriors to ourselves, while we calculate to whip the Mexican troops with great facility."[11]

Another representative example of the fatal overconfidence and bloated sense of racial superiority that had so long dominated Anglo-Celtic thinking was the belief of some garrison members that, in the words of Micajah Autry, "Santa Anna has become intimidated" by the Texan victories of 1835. Therefore, according to this common attitude across Texas and the United States, Santa Anna would therefore never dare to return at the head of a Mexican Army.[12]

And even when it was realized that Santa Anna was preparing to push north, the Anglo-Celts seemed to care little about the impending threat. Confidence and a sense of racial superiority remained so pervasive, that nothing could deflate it. David P. Cummings penned from the Alamo, despite knowing that a large Mexican Army was about to descend upon San Antonio, how the defenders "are confident that Texas cannot only sustain what she now holds but [will] take Mexico itself [one day and] did She think [so] on conquest."[13]

This, of course, was not only outlandish bravado, but also fatal delusion. But the false illusion of the supremacy of American arms and the superiority of the Anglo-Celtic fighting man over the mixed-race and Indian-Mexican soldier was too deeply culturally ingrained to not be embraced by the Alamo's soldiers. Ironically, fueling this sense of Anglo-Celtic superiority based upon racism was the relatively easy 1835 victories, which had instilled a fatal overconfidence. During the campaign of 1835, a poorly motivated Mexican force—garrison troops—and overall poor leadership had made the task of driving all Mexican forces from Texas relatively easy.

The famed Long Rifle, known mostly as the Pennsylvania rifle, where most were made, or the Kentucky rifle where it was first extensively used, was a legendary weapon across America by the time of the Texas Revolution. One of the great myths of American history was that the range, deadliness, and accuracy of the Long Rifle—the best hunting rifle in America—was sufficient to defeat a conventional army. The Anglo-Celtic generation of the Texas Revolution had been raised in the stereotypical belief that the great American military successes—the American Revolution and the War of 1812—had been won largely by the superiority of the Long Rifle over the smoothbore musket. Neither of these commonly held beliefs were true, however. Relatively few of Washington's troops had been armed with Long Rifles, and these men had formed rifle companies and regiments, primarily from Maryland, Pennsylvania, and Virginia. And instead of the Long Rifle, the battle of New Orleans had been won chiefly by Jackson's well-placed and expertly manned artillery, including large-caliber cannon, fired both by United States regulars and Jean Lafitte's Baratarians.[14]

Nevertheless, the Long Rifle myth persisted among successive generations of Americans, and that enduring fable was alive and well by the time of the Texas Revolution. For example, one supremely confident "Texonian," with his usual utter contempt for the Mexican fighting man, wrote in a September 8, 1835 letter how: "We look upon our independence as absolutely certain . . . Some fifteen hundred troops have been sent against us, but they have (unexpectedly) returned; being afraid to move against our riflemen, to the amount of 300 or more."[15] These confident words revealed a widespread contempt toward Mexican troops, regardless of their numbers—a dangerous illusion, promising, if not inviting disaster at the Alamo.

Before the Alamo's fall provided yet another example of the folly of adhering to myths based upon race and alleged superiority, more proof of this serious underestimation of the Mexican Army's capabilities can be seen from the words that appeared in the *Red River Herald*: "Our riflemen are a deadly species of troops, as all the world knows."[16]

And even the editors of the *New Orleans Commercial Bulletin* emphasized with unbounded confidence how: "The great strength of the Texian forces consists of their riflemen; and these placed in the thickets upon the banks of the streams, will be more dangerous enemies than the Mexicans have ever yet met. It is these which will render the country unconquerable!!"[17]

But the unquestioned faith in the Long Rifle and the combat prowess of the Anglo-Celtic soldier, especially when it pertained to inexperienced, untrained garrison members of the Alamo, was a most dangerous myth. Two enduring myths combined to serve as the foundation of the popular version of the Alamo: that the Alamo garrison consisted largely of frontiersmen armed with the Long Rifle, providing a rationale for overly inflated Mexican casualty figures. But in truth, the young men and boys of the Alamo were neither frontiersmen nor veteran Indian fighters. Instead, they were almost exclusively farmers, ranchers, clerks, and merchants, with relatively little military experience and even less intimate knowledge of the Long Rifle. Better suited for a hunting trip on the grassy prairie rather than facing Mexican troops of a conventional army, the Alamo defenders, including Travis, carried mostly shotguns—both single and double-barrel—and smoothbore muskets, loaded with "buck and ball" for a shotgun-like effect, without rifled barrels like the Long Rifle.[18]

Especially after the brutal 1813 Texas campaign, Santa Anna and other contemptuous Mexican leaders mocked the Long Rifle's capabilities and the myth. As a life-long military man, the Creole president was never guilty of overestimating his opponent. Secretary of War Tornel openly derided the Long Rifle myth, proclaiming how the Mexican fighting man was far superior to the undisciplined "mountaineers of Kentucky and the hunters of Missouri."[19]

Tornel's opinion was not idle bravado based upon an over-active Mexican xenophobia. The most superior soldiers both north and south of the Rio Grande were not the Anglo-Celtic riflemen, but hard-riding Mexican cavalrymen. From beginning to end, the Mexican horse soldier repeatedly "hopelessly outclassed" the best fighting men that Texas could offer in both 1835 or 1836. This undeniable reality was common knowledge across Mexico, but yet had to be learned the hard way by the Alamo garrison. One of the few soldiers who realized as much and articulated this fact was B. H. Duval. With no illusions to cloud his thinking, he wrote how: "The greater portion of the Mexican troops are mounted, and of course have greatly the advantage over us."[20]

However, most everyone else in Texas, especially at the Alamo, clung to dangerous illusions to the bitter end. E.M. Pease explained the overconfidence, including among the Alamo garrison, by the late winter of 1836: "The people of Texas having been so fortunate thus far, imagined their Independence already achieved & trusted for security on the weaknesses and disorder of their enemy, to this apathy is to be attributed the [future] reverses of our arms last spring which came well nigh ruining the country."[21]

Indeed, never before had Texas and her people been more unvigilant or seemingly unconcerned about the possibility of danger, despite the fact that by early 1836 a serious threat existed just south of the Rio Grande. In a January 13 letter, an overconfident Autry wrote to his wife, Martha: "Some say that Santa Ana is in the field with an immense army and near the confines of Texas."[22] Autry was far more accurate than he realized. What the relative handful of garrison members at the Alamo failed to realize at this time was, it was reported, that the "motto to which the Mexican army were sworn, was 'extermination to the Sabine, or death'."[23]

Intoxicated by the romantic image of Napoleon, an increasingly ambitious Santa Anna possessed a grandiose vision for accomplishing fantastic military feats in the Texas campaign. In de la Pena's words, Santa Anna "wanted our soldiers to act brilliantly once the time came to salute the Sabine and plant our eagles on its banks."[24]

This was no exaggeration by the young lieutenant colonel. A concerned United States Council W.S. Parott dispatched a shocking December 14, 1835 report from Mexico City to Washington, D.C., warning that Santa Anna—remembering how British Napoleonic troops had easily captured and burned down Washington in August 1814— had bragged to both the British and French ambassadors that if he discovered that the United States government was supporting the Texas Revolution, he would lead his army to Washington D.C., and "place upon its Capital the Mexican Flag." Clearly, Santa Anna took his Napoleonic Era lessons quite seriously.[25]

FALSE SENSE OF SECURITY

Meanwhile, the men of the Alamo were not thinking about acting brilliantly or reaping glory. Because of their own xenophobia, ironically not unlike Santa Anna's own, the Anglo-Celts ignored one undeniable truth that would prove fatal for them in the end: "Few men have spent so much of their lives fomenting or crushing rebellions" than Santa Anna. He was the master of this deadly art, as demonstrated upon the hapless militia at Zacatecas.[26]

Throughout the winter, Alamo garrison members continued to enjoy life to the fullest, despite the shortage of provisions, lack of clothing, and support from across Texas. But with discipline at the Alamo almost nonexistent and officers not taking their responsibilities seriously, garrison members continued to bask in the soft Texas sunshine of winter and the relatively mild weather so unlike back home. Month after month, the young soldiers of San Antonio lived more like tourists in an exotic Tejano paradise than disciplined military men stationed at an outpost, which now served as the vulnerable first line of defense along the distant frontier.

Days spent drinking good old corn whiskey from Texas and the United States, Mexican mescal and tequila, eating spicy Tejano food—a mix of local dishes and those from deep in Mexico—dancing the night away at fandangos, and romancing the dark-eyed Tejano girls continued to leave little interest on enhancing the Alamo's defensive strength. For the Alamo's soldiers, both officers and enlisted men, no one seemed to be in a rush to improve the defenses. That could always wait until later, or so they believed. Meanwhile the Alamo's defenses languished, and its deplorable defensive liabilities were ignored until it was too late. It was almost as if everyone believed, and certainly hoped, that Santa Anna would not head for San Antonio: a fool's dream and an example of wishful thinking at a time when realistic military and strategic assessments were needed. Like the proverbial lesson of the ant and the grasshopper, the Alamo garrison members played the part of the grasshopper throughout early 1836.[27]

Meanwhile, both leaders and enlisted men took relatively little notice of the lowly Tejano peasants, who for some time had been quietly packing up their pitifully meager belongings and slipping out of San Antonio. They knew that Santa Anna was on his way with an army that far dwarfed the garrison's size. Held mostly in contempt by the Anglo-Celts and upper class Tejanos, especially those whose ancestors had come from the Canary Islands, an ever-increasing number of the mixed-race and Indian people of San Antonio's lower class had been departing their town since early January.[28]

Finally but belatedly, the commander at San Antonio began to understand why so many Tejano families were packing up and leaving town. As Colonel Neill, with a minuscule garrison of only 75 men, wrote in a January 14 letter to the governor and council: "There can exist but little doubt that the enemy is advancing on this post, from the number of [Tejano] families leaving town today . . . 1,000 [Mexican troops] are destined for this place."[29]

Then, after gaining some intelligence from Tejano scouts, Bowie wrote a desperate letter to the self-destructing Texas government amounting to a plea for assistance, after learning that 2,000 Mexican soldiers were preparing along the Rio Grande to invade Texas: "Very large forces are being gathered . . . with good officers, well-armed, and a plenty provisions."[30]

Actually the widely ignored expectation that Santa Anna would advance into Texas in the spring of 1836, and not in late winter, had also set the stage for the Alamo disaster. As written in a letter on December 13, 1835, revealing the truth that was common knowledge even as far away as Texas' eastern border, forty-two-year-old Private Micajah Autry, a member of twenty Tennessee men who had formed a small volunteer unit at Memphis, Tennessee, the Tennessee Mounted Volunteers under the command of Ohio-born Captain William B. Harrison, age twenty-five–and not Private Crockett—, " . . . it is thought that Santa Anna will make a descent with his whole forces in the Spring, but there will be soldiers enough of the real grit in Texas by that time to overrun all Mexico."[31]

And from the pages of the *New York Courier and Enquirer* not long after San Antonio was captured in December 1835, an editor revealed the widespread combination of blindness and arrogance so pervasive among the smug Texian victors across Texas: "No other [military] expedition can be fitted out by Mexico against Texas until spring; and then the army of the Patriots will be sufficiently strong to repel them."[32]

Also on December 13, 1835, North Carolina-born Autry, destined to die at the Alamo, penned in his letter from Nacogodoches to his wife Martha in Jackson, Tennessee: "Some say that Santa Anna is in the field with an immense army and near the confines of Texas, others say since the conquest of St. [San] Antonio by the Texians . . . Santa Anna has become intimidated for fear that the Texians will drive the war into his dominions and is now holding himself in readiness to fly to Europe."[33]

More rational and realistic was Jameson, the bright, imaginative former attorney from San Felipe de Austin, who seemed to possess more wisdom than Neill, Bowie, and Travis all together. On January 18, he wrote to Houston how: "Since we heard of 1000 to 1500 men of the enemy being on their march to this place."[34]

Such widespread, common knowledge of what Santa Anna was doing caused de la Pena to lament how "preparation for the campaign should have been secretly carried out" from the beginning. And Private David P. Cummings, age twenty-seven, wrote to his father, a friend of Houston, on January 20, 1836: "Letters have been intercepted to the Mexican citizens of Béxar informing them of the arrival of 2,000 troops on the Rio Grande, and now coming to retake that place, San Antonio."[35] This letter was written from Gonzales. Clearly, the news had already spread that a Mexican Army was about to invade Texas, but relatively few preparations were taken in San Antonio.

Only three days later, Neill was informed by José Antonio Navarro that the Tejano's brother, Eugene in San Luís Potosí, Mexico, had just sent him a message that Santa Anna and 3,000 Mexican troops had reached Saltillo, while another 1,000 men were in the community of Rio Grande, preparing to advance north. Nevertheless, despite the increasing number of warnings, in Sutherland's words, "little notice was paid to them."[36]

Then, in a letter from San Antonio on February 14, Cummings qualified his previous letter, writing with an assured confidence how, "under different views from what I stated [on January 20 from Gonzales] in as a sudden attack was expected on our garrison here [at San Antonio] and were called on for assistance. It is however fully ascertained that we have nothing of the kind to apprehend before a month or six weeks as the Enemy have not yet crossed the Rio Grande 180 mi[iles]. distant from this place nor are they expected to make any movement this way until the weather becomes warm or until the grass is sufficiently up to support their horses [and] we conceive it however important to be prepared as a heavy attack is expected from Santa Anna himself in the Spring as no doubt the despot will use every possible means and strain every nerve to conquer and exterminate us from the land."[37]

The only part of Cummings' analysis that was correct was his conviction that Santa Anna planned to "exterminate us" from Texas. And, as revealed in a February 12 letter, Travis also was convinced that Santa Anna "threatens to exterminate every white man" in Texas. But thorough, defensive preparations continued to be ignored at the Alamo. Harboring his doubts, Bowie, for instance, was yet uncertain if Santa Anna planned to march upon San Antonio. He could not ascertain if Santa Anna would target San Antonio or swing up the gulf coast by way of Matamoros. However, Santa Anna would keep Bowie and the entire Alamo garrison guessing until it was too late, choosing to divide his army in a classic Napoleon-like maneuver, embarking upon both strategic alternatives simultaneously.[38]

Meanwhile, the Alamo's defenders continued to remain supremely overconfident and complacent throughout early 1836. Incredibly, in the words of a New Orleans Greys member, the victors of the 1835 campaign, yet gloating over their success over Cós, which was thought to have intimidated Santa Anna, "considered ourselves almost invincible [which was] an opinion which later on brought us and our friends very near ruin."[39]

And Ireland-born Joseph M. Hawkins, more realistic than many United States citizens now under arms because of the Irish experience, wrote on January 24, 1836 with resignation how: " . . . we may in a short time expect stormy gales from Mexico [but Santa Anna] will be warmly received and nobly encountered, and find that to conquer Mexicans is one thing, but Americans another, if the latter will only do their duty in preparing with energy," which, ironically, would not be the case.[40]

While still below the Rio Grande, Santa Anna developed a well-conceived plan to catch the unprepared Anglo-Celtics of San Antonio and the east Texas settlements napping. In mid-February, Santa Anna and the main body of his forces crossed the Rio Grande at twin communities of Paso de Francia and Guerrero, the old Spanish town distinguished by stately colonial architecture and which contained Presidio de Rio Grande. Both towns along the Rio Grande were close to each other and southwest of San Antonio, about eighty miles upriver, or north of Laredo. This was a well-conceived crossing point. Thanks in part to an effective spy network and his own understanding of his complacent opponent, he knew full well that garrison members expected an advance upon San Antonio from the south along the Laredo Road from Laredo. Instead and most deceptively, he planned to sweep toward San Antonio from the west where least expected to appear.[41]

Crockett knew that if Santa Anna pushed toward San Antonio, then the place should be abandoned. And if the Mexican Army was not targeting San Antonio, which should have been the case because it was of no strategic importance, then perhaps the garrison could remain safely in place, because the war would then be waged near the east Texas settlements, if Santa Anna marched north from Matamoros and up the coast as expected. To the tactical reasoning of Crockett, a War of 1812 veteran, that revealed a measure of good sense: "If it is true that Santa Anna is coming to San Antonio, then our plans must be made one way. If he is not coming to San Antonio, they must be made another way."[42]

Indeed, Johnson, Neill or Bowie could, and should, have ordered San Antonio and the Alamo abandoned as Houston had suggested, because then its garrison could link up with the largest concentration troops in Texas at Goliad. Here, less than 100 miles southeast of the Alamo, Colonel James Walker Fannin, Jr., commanded newly arrived United States reinforcements and members of the aborted Matamoros Expedition. Not only a fine dirt road but also the easy-flowing San Antonio River led straight from San Antonio to Goliad and safety, almost beckoning the Alamo leadership to make the wise decision of abandoning their doomed position to save the tiny garrison.

However, the relative closeness of Colonel Fannin's force at Goliad—83 miles southeast of San Antonio—only bestowed upon the Alamo garrison a false sense of confidence. They naively believed that if Santa Anna's Army marched on San Antonio, then nearly 500 soldiers of Fannin's command could rush to the Alamo's relief. But despite his lofty rank in the Texas Army and unfortunately for the Alamo garrison, one of the highest-ranking officers in all Texas was in fact already a failed soldier. The illegitimate son of an influential Georgia physician and planter and raised on his grandfather's cotton plantation, he had followed in his father's footsteps, as Fannin himself was a Georgia planter, slave-owner, cotton planter, and physician. He had gained entry into the United States Military Academy at West Point, New York, in 1819, but only to discover that serious soldiering was not for him. In fact, he had already tired of the Texas Revolution by this time[43]

Nevertheless, thanks to the West Point experience that paid high dividends for him in a frontier land where few had received any kind of education, Fannin, not unlike Neill, possessed a lofty, if unfounded, reputation throughout Texas as "an able, decisive man" of action.[44]

From beginning to end, Alamo garrison members had made a big mistake in gambling that they could depend upon Fannin for timely support if Santa Anna descended upon San Antonio. After all, he had

gained sufficient West Point knowledge about strategy to know that he
would have to fight through Santa Anna's Army to reach the Alamo,
after leaving the coast undefended and Mexican Army's right wing an
open avenue to push north along the road to strike the east Texas settlements.[45]

Meanwhile, to celebrate Crockett's arrival in San Antonio on
February 8, as a member of Captain William Harrison's Mounted
Company, Travis and Bowie held a fandango on February 10. Most
important for the garrison's ladies' men, of which Travis was the leading candidate of the well-combed dandies of the Alamo garrison, "all of
the principal ladies of the City" were present. Around 1:00 a.m. on
February 11, and with the fandango in full swing, a Tejano messenger
arrived from Placido Bienavidas of Goliad, with a most timely report
from the little Mexican town of Camargo, where Bienavidas had been
watching for a crossing on the Rio Grande's south bank that indicated
the first troops of Santa Anna's Vanguard Division had crossed the Rio
Grande. Even more, the messenger warned that Santa Anna was closing
in "with the view of taking San Antonio" with an estimated 13,000
troops. Clearly, the "Napoleon of the West" and his large army would
arrive much sooner than anyone imagined or expected.

Shaken by the report, Bowie called Travis, who was dancing to the
music and no doubt feeling the effects of some potent liquid refresh-
ment, over to read the letter that contained such startling news. But
Travis merely retorted that "at the moment he could not stay to read letters, for he was dancing with the most beautiful lady in San Antonio."
Yet to be legally divorced after having departed Alabama for Texas in
1831—just another newcomer from the United States on the make—
Travis left behind his wife, Rosanna, who was five months pregnant
with their second child and already with a small son, and considered
himself a frontier ladies man at age twenty-four. Proud of himself and
what he could do in bed, despite violating traditional societal codes of
Southern gentlemanly conduct, he carefully recorded his growing number of nocturnal conquests—more than 50 including prostitutes and
slave women—in Spanish in his diary. Despite a "bad" case of venereal
disease stemming from his quite "active libido" that fueled his personal
downward spiral into moral "degradation," and regardless of an
engagement to Rebecca Cummings—which did little to end his ardent
pursuit of single, married, or working women—Travis had his sights set
on the Tejano beauty this night.

At more urging by Bowie, the distracted Travis finally relented. He read the letter, which was written in Spanish. Irritated that his seducement of one of San Antonio's fairest young maidens had been interrupted, Travis dismissed the stunning intelligence with the equally startling announcement that it would yet take Santa Anna 13–14 days to reach San Antonio from the Rio Grande more than 100 miles to the south, and that this was only the fourth day. Then, the young Alabama officer proclaimed in almost fatalistic fashion, "Let us dance to-night and to-morrow we will make provisions for our defense." Therefore, the fandango continued far into the night, not ending until around 7 a.m. Once again, the Alamo's soldiers were putting off tomorrow what they should of done today.[46]

With the almost casual dismissal of this recent intelligence, the folly of not only holding the Alamo, but also in doing relatively little to strengthen its defenses was raised to new heights. Clearly, in standing firm at the Alamo, Neill, Bowie, and Travis had made "a decision beyond their strategic abilities," wrote historian Mark Derr.[47]

As a native South Carolinian, evidently Travis, while loving the Tejano ladies, felt little esteem for Tejano men—even under the best circumstances. He routinely continued to dismiss the words and intelligence reports from Tejano males, both among the garrison and the San Antonio population, even though he had employed earlier reports from his Tejano "spies" of large numbers of Mexican troops concentrating on the Rio Grande to alarm the government in the hope of securing assistance. Even worse, Travis also ignored the sound advice of a Tejano priest of San Antonio, named Rodriguez, "to retreat from San Antonio before Santa Anna's forces overwhelmed him, but Travis did not believe that Santa Anna could mount so large an army within only three months after the Texas volunteers conquered San Antonio."[48]

Ironically, however, another priest had earlier informed Bowie that Santa Anna planned to invade to the east along the coast by way of Matamoros and would only "send a few hundred cavalry against this place at the same time." This advice came in January 1836 from Father Refugio de la Garza, who would later hold Mass for Santa Anna's troops. He had apparently played an insidious part in deliberately influencing Bowie's ill-fated decision to hold San Antonio.[49]

The Alamo's leaders held onto such delusions, even though one of Sequín's "spies"— his own cousin Balz Herrera—brought vital intelligence on February 20 that he had seen Santa Anna's mighty army crossing the Rio Grande to enter Texas four days before. Again, this timely information was simply dismissed because "it was only the report of a Mexican," even though Sequín begged the Anglo-Celts to listen and take the report seriously, but to no avail. Even more, Sequín also warned that Cós and hundreds of his men would not honor their paroles, and that they would have to be fought all over again. Captain Sequín was ignored.[50]

Regardless of what garrison members believed, Santa Anna was now in the process of demonstrating that he was very much the "Napoleon of the West," displaying the same energy, resourcefulness, and tactical ingenuity as he had in repulsing earlier Spanish bids to reclaim Mexico, or in crushing previous rebellions.[51]

He had already gained the element of surprise, employing a stealthy march north, while the garrison expected Santa Anna to advance by way of the Laredo Road from the south. As cleverly planned by Santa Anna, he was instead about to descend upon San Antonio from the west by way of the Camino Real.[52]

The overconfidence was so complete that it proved nearly fatal for the San Antonio garrison, almost negating a struggle altogether. General Santa Anna planned to overwhelm the Texans before they even knew what had hit them. Therefore, Mexican dragoons under Sesma, who led the army's advance north and his Vanguard Division, had been ordered to descend upon San Antonio in one swoop. It was a good plan based upon a combination of stealth and surprise, worthy of Napoleon's dashing premier cavalryman, General Joachim Murat, who became the most famous cavalry leader in Europe.[53]

This plan was based on timely intelligence gained from his effective Tejano spy network that he had ordered in early January to "report with certainty of the actual state of the City [San Antonio] and intentions of the rebels." In addition, Santa Anna picked the perfect time and opportunity to strike. He planned to capture the entire garrison when they were celebrating George Washington's birthday on the evening of February 22. Of course, the Anglo-Celts, cozy in San Antonio, had no idea that Santa Anna, with his 50-man, elite escort of the Dolores Cavalry Regiment, had crossed the Rio Grande on the cold afternoon of February 16 and reached the Texas-Coahuila border on February 21. But while Santa Anna prepared to strike with Sesma's 1,500-man Vanguard Division, with his Army of Operations yet far behind—ignoring the fact that February 21 was his forty-second birthday—the Alamo garrison members celebrated like their was no tomorrow. Rainy, cold weather had kept these young men idle and indoors most of the day, and now their pent-up energies erupted during the nighttime festivities.

As usual, tequila, mescal, and good old corn whiskey were drank to excess during the wild fandango, made memorable by those charming, dark-eyed Tejano senoritas on this Monday. After all, it was a customary practice for Americans to celebrate the birthday of the republic's founder, and Santa Anna knew as much. Therefore, he directed "a detachment of cavalry, part of the dragoons mounted on infantry officers' horses," which were relatively fresh, to push forward a good distance in army's advance.[54]

Envisioning a master stroke to scoop up the entire San Antonio garrison—still groggy and half-drunk from the night's partying—at the break of dawn before they could concentrate and defend themselves, Santa Anna planned to rush Sesma with a hand-picked detachment of cavalry mounted on fresh infantry officers' horses into San Antonio at dawn on February 23, catching his unwary opponents by surprise. The entire San Antonio garrison could be captured without a fight.

Ironically, this bold strategy was not unlike that of General Washington's brilliant crossing of the Delaware River at night to catch the German Hessians, the paid mercenaries of the British Crown, by surprise just after dawn on December 26, 1776, assuming that the night had been spent by the Germans in celebrating with too much Madiera wine and other spirits. Washington's early morning attack at Trenton, New Jersey, resulted in a complete success that helped to turn the tide of the American Revolution.[55]

After having dismissed intelligence reports of Santa Anna's approach on February 11, young Travis, ever the ladies man like his father before him, was not about to let these reports from ragtag Tejano scouts ruin his good time. He was more intent on consorting with the most beautiful Tejano women, to add yet another easy conquest on his ever-growing romantic resume, during the February 22 fandango than taking necessary precautions to defend San Antonio. He ignored both the timely Tejano warnings and the fact that Tejano families, including some that would be wiped out by Comanches, had been evacuating San Antonio in ever-increasing numbers.

Travis and the men of the Alamo, consequently, thoroughly enjoyed the drinks, good food, and dancing that enlivened the colorful establishment of Domingo Bustillo on Soledad Street in the heart of San

Antonio. Even Crockett added to the merriment with the strains of his fiddle, as if back in the hills of northeast Tennessee—where Indians killed his grandparents during the American Revolution—or like his Irish ancestors in the old country.[56]

Ironically, however, other Americans under arms in Texas—including those now far from San Antonio in east Texas—were more circumspect and concerned than Travis. For instance, on this same day, February 22, Virginian Jesse Benton wrote from Nacogdoches a letter that was as sobering as it was accurate: "Official information has just reached us that Santa Anna has crossed the Rio Grande and is marching against us with a large army for the purpose of exterminating us."[57]

But as in the past, Travis continued to refuse to believe these timely intelligence reports from Captain Juan Nepomuceno Sequín's Tejano scouts, because they were not white, and therefore could not be trusted. His racism and personal prejudices were already in the process of spelling the doom of the Alamo garrison.[58]

Fortunately for the tiny band of garrison members in San Antonio, the rain-swollen Medina River had slowed down the Mexican cavalry on the afternoon of February 21. Then, upon approaching San Antonio, Santa Anna failed to order Sesma to attempt to capture both the garrison and the town, but only to reconnoiter and cut off all avenues of withdrawal. Outsmarting himself, he could not fathom that these Americans were not fully aware of the threat. Or perhaps he only wanted to lure the overconfident garrison out into the open to face the Vanguard Division, or expected a quick surrender when he arrived with overwhelming might. But what Santa Anna did not know was that Travis would not become aware of the Mexican presence until nearly noon. Therefore, Santa Anna's ambitious plans for nabbing the garrison had vanished with the rising winter sun on February 23.

Nevertheless, the sudden approach of Mexican troops, both infantry and cavalry, relatively late in the day came as a surprise. After the Mexicans captured a handful of pickets, the Anglo-Celts just barely escaped the town to flee into the Alamo, racing down dusty Potrero Street like madmen. Ironically, no one seemed to note the irony that Cós and his men had also fled inside the Alamo when under attack—a place from which there was no escape. One of the last to flee to the Alamo was Captain Almeron Dickinson, who was staying with his wife and young daughter at the Tejano home of Don Ramón Múzquiz, where they were quartered.[59]

One of the foremost Mexican officers to lead the Vanguard Division men into town was the experienced Colonel José Vincente Miñon. With pride, he described how: "I was the first with a company of cazadores from the Matamoros Battalion that took possession of the Plaza de Bejar whose church was occupied by the enemy who deserted [the sacred place] at this moment, withdrawing themselves in self-defense and order to the nearby fortification of the Alamo."[60]

Santa Anna described how: "Our army's crossing into Texas was the cause of great surprise on the part of the filibusters, for they believed that Mexican soldiers would not cross again into Texas. Frightened by our invasion, they ran to a fortress called the Alamo [which had been] erected by the Spaniards." He also mocked "the celebrated Travis," who had become a source of contempt.[61]

Ironically, one of the great Alamo myths was that the legendary Long Rifle was destined to inflict a high toll on Santa Anna's troops. In truth, the Alamo garrison lacked a large number of Long Rifles in defending the Alamo, even before the Mexicans came. And this situation only became worse thanks to the Mexican cavalry's surprise arrival into San Antonio. So thorough was the lack of preparations that 50 invaluable rifles were left behind in San Antonio during the sprint to reach the Alamo's safety. Incredibly, no one had thought—not even Travis—to make sure that the rifles were relocated at the Alamo, even though they knew that Santa Anna was on his way: a mere continuation of a comedy of errors.

Therefore, with some disbelief, Santa Anna boasted in his report: "Fifty rifles, of the rebel traitors of the North, have fallen in our possession" when capturing San Antonio. Ironically, along with the chronic lack of ammunition, some of which was likewise evidently left behind in the town, this timely capture of a good many rifles helped to ensure that the Alamo's defense would sorely lack long-range firepower from the Long Rifle. Even more, evidence reveals that the weapon of choice, even for Travis and garrison members like Dr. John Sutherland, at the Alamo was in fact the shotgun and not the Long Rifle.[62]

But, in reality, this coup was small consolation. Santa Anna's failure to capture San Antonio and the Alamo left the generalissimo in a particularly bad mood only two days after his forty-first birthday. Ironically, this was a repeat performance for him. At only age 19 back in the hot summer of 1813, he had first seen San Antonio as a member of an invading Royal Spanish Army dispatched to crush rebels, including many Anglo-Celts. He now unfairly blamed Sesma, who had been only ordered to block the garrison's withdrawal rather than capture the town, and even the rainy weather—much like Napoleon had blamed winter weather for his failings in Russia in 1812. Offering an excuse, he wrote how this advance cavalry task force "should have fallen on Béxar in the early morning of February 23 [and] although the city was captured, the surprise that I ordered to be carried out would have saved the time consumed and the blood shed later in the taking of the Alamo."[63]

The garrison's existence now depended upon what Bowie, Travis, and Fannin would do in the next few days. All three men had already tired of the war, wanting to resign rather than fight to the bitter end. A thorough lack of preparation at the Alamo fueled Travis' plea, dispatched by courier, to Fannin at Goliad: "We have all our men into the Alamo. . . . We have one hundred and forty-six men [and] We have but little provisions, but enough to serve us till you and your men arrive."[64]

Ironically, almost no adequate defensive preparations had been made for withstanding a siege at the Alamo. Supplies, munitions, including even a good many rifles, and even firewood in the cold winter weather had not been brought into the compound in the past period of relative inactivity. Even worse, neither Travis nor Bowie had ensured open fields of fire around the Alamo by eliminating obstacles, such as jacales, that would prove advantageous to an attacker. Clearly, the garrison would have to pay a high price for its inexperience and untrained leaders to learn the art of war on the job. Ironically, this "surreal" situation was comparable to when Napoleon, then the complacent, overconfident master of Europe, had himself paved the way for one of the greatest disasters in military history by remaining in Moscow too long without preparing for either winter or a retreat from Russia.[65]

Because they had placed their faith in an indefensible position, the trapped Anglo-Celts could only cling to the fatal illusion in the faint hope of the arrival of reinforcements from Goliad: Fannin and his command, around three times the size of the Alamo garrison. Unfortunately, however, Texas lacked not only a unified overall military command, but was also deprived an acting provisional government—which had collapsed into chaos and seemingly endless in-fighting in February—to support it or hurry up aid and reinforcements to the Alamo. Even worse, the relatively few troops in Texas were hopelessly divided into two garrisons, San Antonio and Goliad—offering Santa Anna a perfect model for divide and conquer.

Texan leaders were divided not only about the best strategy—offensive or defensive—but the proper place to fight the war—Texas or Mexico—and even where to make a defensive stand if the location was ever agreed upon, which it was not. Some people in Texas wanted to declare independence, others did not. Therefore, by early 1836, the Alamo garrison was most of all expendable, representing the relatively few soldiers in Texas who supported the disposed Governor Smith, now facing possible impeachment. Making things worse, they aligned themselves against the commander-in-chief, Houston, who had wanted to evacuate San Antonio and the Alamo.[66]

Houston had predicted that "Dissension will destroy Texas," and, of course, the Alamo garrison. These young, inexperienced volunteers, or unruly members of "the ultra-democratic mob," were already expendable. For Houston, these independent-minded novices, who had rejected him as commander, had no permanent part in his long-range strategic plan of creating a professional, regular army of disciplined veterans. Many Texan politicians viewed the Alamo soldiers as "not only slackers but as inept and possibly corrupt." Houston wanted neither San Antonio as a strategic position nor its diminutive, always-troublesome garrison, and neither, or so it seemed, did the people of Texas.[67]

Unfortunately for Alamo garrison members, the personal quali ties—weakness, folly, blindness, doggedness, and overconfidence—of top civilian and military officers, such as Neill, Bowie, Houston, Fannin, and Travis, plus the feuding politicians, all contributed to sealing their fates in the end. Commanding the Texas Regular Army and not the volunteers at the Alamo, Houston saw the tiny garrison at that remote outpost as expendable, pawns to be sacrificed for the greater good, especially his own. Even their immediate commanders, Neill, Bowie, and Travis, had let the Alamo men down. Indeed, there would have been no Alamo to defend and no destruction of the garrison without the disastrous chain of miscalculations and erroneous decisions of leadership. The Alamo commander had failed to move sufficient supplies, including food, water, and ammunition, for an extended defensive stand at the Alamo, despite knowing that Santa Anna's Army was on his way north. Some provisions were collected, but most remained in the town, with Travis and Bowie believing they yet had plenty of time to move them into the Alamo. Garrison members had simply grabbed what they could during a wild dash for the Alamo before being cut off by Mexican cavalry upon Santa Anna's arrival on February 23.[68]

The garrison now paid a high price for Travis' belief, as expressed to Governor Smith only ten days before on February 13: "By the 15th of March I think Texas will be invaded," and not before.[69] He was wrong.

But in truth, Travis had actually believed that Santa Anna, if he marched upon San Antonio, would do so in the summer of 1836. He only emphasized the March 15 date to order to pressure the governor to send supplies and aid as soon as possible. John Sutherland described the true situation in which "no danger was apprehended [because so] Many had persuaded themselves, that Santa Anna would never attempt to conquer Texas [because] he was afraid to meet us." Incredibly, therefore, Travis and his men actually were convinced that Santa Anna, having learned his lesson with Cós' defeat, would "postpone his operations until the summer."[70]

Despite being in part responsible for the upcoming disaster, when it was already too late, a prophetic Governor Henry Smith implored the people of Texas to awake to the growing threat facing Texas and rush to aid them, so as "not to permit [the Alamo garrison] to be massacred by a mercenary foe."[71] And then, acting Governor James W. Robinson, designated by the Council to replace Smith— who had been dismissed by that ever-dysfunctional body of bickering statesmen and then promptly dissolved it—predicted "disastrous consequences" for not only the Alamo garrison, but also Texas.[72]

But such frantic pleas were not only too late, but also largely in vain across Texas. By this time, the Alamo garrison continued to be expendable to the established, longtime Texas leaders and residents, because the government had laid plans that had been more in line with remaining under Mexico's jurisdiction in the hope of preventing exactly what had happened: a large Mexican Army suddenly descended upon Texas like a howling "blue norther."

Therefore, the band of volunteers of the Alamo were largely expendable to not only the old Texian settlers, but also the government at San Felipe de Austin, which planned to establish a regular army for Texas and not a volunteer one. It was no wonder that the Alamo garrison now found itself abandoned, doomed by a combination of top-level political and military decisions by those both at the Alamo and at highest governmental levels. Consequently, especially because it had fallen apart, the Texas government never raised funds for the purchase of black powder, cannonballs, other munitions, or further reinforcement so vitally needed by the garrison.[73]

Launcelot Smither, who had been dispatched to Gonzales to secure reinforcements for San Antonio in February, was realistic about the stern challenges facing the Alamo garrison. From Gonzales, he sent a note to Nacogdoches with the unforgettable, prophetic words: "If every man cannot turn out to a man, every man in the Alamo will be murdered."[74]

Smither's sentiments only echoed earlier warnings by Tejano women, who lamented to the passing Anglo-Celts and handful of Tejanos as they dashed through San Antonio's streets on February 23, to take final refuge in the Alamo when Santa Anna's troops first appeared: "Poor fellows, you will all be killed."[75]

Nevertheless, the Alamo garrison was convinced otherwise. Incredibly, and indicating more their cultural bias rather than military experience, both Bowie and Travis yet believed that any number of Mexicans could be defeated, even though they only had around 150 men, approximately 850 soldiers short of what it would have taken to adequately man the sprawling perimeter. Based upon an overestimation in their own military prowess, and a gross underestimation of the Mexican fighting man of mostly Indian descent, this unbreakable, taken-for-granted faith—despite its delusional character—was based upon the belief that their weapons, such as Long Rifles, muskets, and cannon, could easily prevail over any Mexican Army, even if the odds were ten to one. And these men, from leading officers to the lowest private, were convinced that all Texas, both Fannin at Goliad and east Texas settlements, could quickly rally to their support. Such hopeful beliefs—although entirely illusionary and faulty—helped to ensure that the Alamo garrison would undertake no attempt to escape during the thirteen days of siege.[76]

What was unmistakable was the fact that Santa Anna's masterstroke in pushing so swiftly north was brilliant, catching an unwary, smug opponent completely by surprise. Perhaps B. H. Duval said in best in a late winter 1836 letter: "Contrary to the expectation of every one, he has invaded the Country when least expected."[77]

Most of all, by early 1836, Travis, Bowie, and their men had badly misjudged their opponent. They should have learned from the bloody lesson of what Santa Anna had done to fellow Mexican citizens at Zacatecas, crushing a huge, well-organized force of militiamen who were defending its own homeland with ease. But more important, so far in this late winter campaign deep in Texas, Santa Anna had indeed lived up to his reputation as the "Napoleon of the West." To the generalissi-mo's thinking, "Zacatecas was only the beginning," and the Alamo would be next.[78]

Caught by surprise of the Mexican onslaught like everyone else, Captain Carey very likely no longer believed his confident boast on January 12, 1836, of how: " . . . I think a small number of us can whip an army of Mexicans." Ironically, as the young artillery commander and bachelor of the "Invincibles," and from Washington-on-the-Brazos, Captain Carey now understood the ridiculousness of such words.[79]

The cocky Texian's confidence—mirroring that of the Alamo garri-son—was revealed in the pages of a newspaper: "Our enemies have a well appointed cavalry–raised by voluntary enlistment. We do not fear their infantry; it is composed of convicts, forced into the army as a pun-ishment for their crimes."[80] Bragging to an amused Little Rock, Arkansas, newspaperman back when the future looked so much brighter, Crockett had boasted that he would "have Santa Anna's head" before the war was over.[81]

Now at long last, a new sense of reality had come to the ill-prepared Alamo garrison. Meanwhile, Santa Anna had the Anglo-Celts exactly where he wanted them: trapped in an all but indefensible position. Therefore, he felt great relief to discover that his opponent had made the fatal mistake of attempting to defend the Alamo instead of retiring to the more formidable Mission Concepcion. And, unfortunately for the young men and boys of the Alamo garrison, Travis and Bowie followed Neill's folly of defending the Alamo "to the last" and deciding not to surrender, regardless of the circumstances to sound the death knell for the Alamo garrison.[82]

Indeed, no one was more responsible for the decision to both make a stand at the Alamo and never surrender than Colonel Neill, whose persuasive influence had proved decisive on others, including Bowie, Governor Smith, and other Council members. However, by this time, Neill was no longer the Alamo's commander. In fact, he was no longer at either the Alamo or San Antonio.

On February 11, the colonel, older than most of the men at the Alamo, had calmly mounted his beloved Tennessee Walker. He then rode away from his command, never to return or be seen by them again. He simply rode home, galloping away from the deathtrap that was in large part his own making. The excuse given was that family members were ill, stricken by some unknown aliment. The man most responsible for setting the stage for the Alamo disaster took himself out of harm's way. Before riding away from the Alamo and leaving the 26-year-old Travis in command, Neill told his men that he would return in twenty days. But by that time, garrison members would have only three days of life remaining in this world. In attempting to gather provisions for the garrison, Neill was delayed past his promised twenty days, until after the Alamo's fall. This former second in command of Fannin's First Regiment of Texas Artillery would be nowhere in sight, like his West Point-educated commander, when Santa Anna and his army reached San Antonio.[83]

Even more ironic, as artillery commander of the "Army of the People," Neill's guns had played a role in pounding the Alamo and Cós' garrison into submission in December 1835, inflicting the damage upon the walls that would later compromise the Alamo's defense on March 6. Therefore, the man largely responsible for damaging the Alamo's walls and demonstrating that the compound was a deathtrap, especially for a small garrison, was also the same individual who played the leading role in convincing influential others, both military men and politicians, that yet another defensive stand should be made at exactly the same place where the enemy had been so recently defeated. He left behind a new Alamo commander, who had begged the governor for a "recall" from the San Antonio assignment, and who knew so little about artillery that he had declined an appointment as the "first Major in the Artillery Regt." Ironically, as penned in a February 12 letter, William Barret Travis believed that Neill would be gone only "for a short time." Again, Travis was wrong.[84]

5

An Ineffective Siege

Ironically, in view of what was to come, an old Anglo proverb of early Texas that focused solely on the balmy weather, warm breezes, and healthy benefits—especially appropriate for the San Antonio area—proclaimed: "If a man wants to die there he must go somewhere else."[1]

In reality, nothing could be further from the truth in regard to the little Tejano town of Béxar. San Antonio was the graveyard of generations of Mexican, Tejano, and Texas revolutionaries and rebels, especially Anglo-Celts, who foolishly challenged Mexico City's authority. In fact, the very name Béxar had long been synonymous with revolution—and accompanying disaster—sparked by "foreigners" and outside agitators, especially from the United States.

Writing in 1848, General Filisola, Santa Anna's second in command during the 1836 campaign, was right on target when he summarized the grim reality for so many Anglo-Celtic revolutionaries, who had been seduced by the alluring dream of an independent Texas from Spanish and then Mexican control. The systematic crushing of each new revolt came with so much bloody ease, that it almost seemed to be "a sign perhaps that Providence destined for all the entrepreneurs in Texas a disastrous end, and that the occupation of Texas was to be the cause of the horrible and damaging bloody scenes that have occurred following the treaty of 1819."[2]

The harsh reality facing the revolutionaries in San Antonio was fully appreciated by a bemused Jon Whitefield Scott Dancy. In his March 27, 1837 diary entry he wrote an undeniable truth: "It is a little strange that San Antonio and its vicinity, one of the most beautiful places upon earth, a place where a man might so easily enjoy as many of the bless-

164

ings of life as this world can yield; it is strange that this place so lovely, should be the scene of more bloodshed, than any other perhaps on the American continent."[3]

But in fact, it had always been precisely this strange, irresistible appeal that had made San Antonio a bone of contention and one of the great killing grounds in all the southwest. In regard specifically to the Alamo garrison's eventual fate at Santa Anna's hands, a much more accurate, but grim, adage was offered from the pages of the *Troy Daily Whig*: "The course of Texas is plainly marked out. She shall drive every Mexican soldier beyond her limits, or the people of Texas will leave San Antonio the bones of their bodies."[4]

By February 23, everything had changed for the Alamo's soldiers with a blinding swiftness that had sent them reeling. With Santa Anna reaching San Antonio before the people of Texas expected, the surprise had been complete, changing the destinies of the Alamo men forever. Compared with only a few months ago, the war that these men had previously known—the intoxicating 1835 campaign that reaped easy victories and caused celebrations across Texas—had morphed under Santa Anna into a far more dangerous undertaking.

Unlike in the recent past, this war was now more serious, and a more deadly business than ever before. The war's character had changed completely from the time when the victors had naively allowed General Cós' vanquished Mexican troops to march out of San Antonio with the promise—a chivalric 18th-century gesture—that they would not return to Texas. Now, of course, General Cós and his soldiers filled Santa Anna's ranks: Seguin's warning had gone unheeded. Even worse for the Alamo garrison, Santa Anna and his troops were especially eager to avenge their humiliation at having lost San Antonio. One soldier, Jesse Benton at Nacogdoches, Texas, already sensed as much, writing in a February 22, 1836 letter how: "Colonel Cós and his troops we are informed have broken their parole and are returning against us [therefore] The country on the Rio Grande is given up to a brutal soldiery."

Bolstered with too much optimism and complacency, the Alamo's amateur soldiers had continued to play by the same old rules while garrisoning San Antonio until it was too late. Santa Anna had now brought a new type of warfare to Texas, involving ancient ways of dealing with revolutionaries, as the Alamo garrison would learn. The red flag of no quarter that Santa Anna raised from the bell tower of the San Fernando Church represented this brutal new reality. This banner proclaimed that there would be no mercy, no prisoners in this war. Travis and his soldiers had been caught off guard by the sudden transformation. This new reality was secured when Travis penned his famous February 24 dispatch to "The People of Texas and all Americans in the world," in which he stated: "I shall never surrender or retreat. . . . I am determined to sustain myself as long as possible & die like a soldier who never forgets what is due to his own honor & that of his country—Victory or Death." With such defiance, punctuated by a cannon shot on February 23, he had sealed the doom of both himself and the garrison.

For his part, Santa Anna's desire was to make an example of the Alamo men for political purposes, as a lesson to other Texians and Tejanos in arms. Therefore, he needed to reap a victory that was as thorough as it was swift. One example of how the Alamo defenders were caught amid a raging Mexican civil war was the fact that Mexican families were so divided by the conflict that sons served on opposing sides at the Alamo. What has been often overlooked about the Alamo's story was that the Tejano people had been revolutionaries long before the arrival of Houston, Travis, Bowie, and Crockett in Texas. Like America's own "brother's war" from 1861–65, the current civil war pitted Mexican family members against one another. A defender of the Alamo, for instance, was Tejano artilleryman Jose Gregorio Esparza, yet his brother, Francisco Esparza, sided with Santa Anna, serving under General Cós at the Alamo during the 1835 campaign. [5]

Not only Francisco, as a proud member of the unit, but also the entire Tejano militia company, Leal Presidios Company of Béxar, had been reactivated to join Santa Anna's army when it first reached San Antonio. As if Santa Anna did not already have sufficient numbers of troops, he gained additional soldiers from the militia company and from the Tejano population, making good his losses on the lengthy winter march to San Antonio.[6]

The young men of the Alamo knew nothing of the horrors of Mexico's civil war, and had forgotten, or never learned, of the nightmare of America's own civil war in the South during the American Revolution, which was "a fierce war of extermination." No one had told them of the rape of Zacatecas, the slaughter of unarmed militiamen, the killing of the wounded and the execution of survivors by Santa Anna. If the generalissimo treated Mexican rebels in such a savage manner, then he was certainly about to treat the Anglo-Celts worse, especially because he wanted to make a lasting example out of them.

For the band of defenders, the Alamo siege would be a race against time. Only one hope remained for the entrapped garrison: the possibility that sufficient Texan reinforcements might arrive in time. Santa Anna's vanguard had arrived in San Antonio with less than 1,500 men, many of whom were cavalry who could not assault fortress walls; but as the rest of the Mexican army and its artillery closed up, the odds would eventually be overwhelming. Only reinforcements from the rest of Texas could ensure that even at full strength Santa Anna's army would suffer a bloody repulse. As February neared its end there was still time for Texas to support the Alamo garrison, but that window of opportunity was quickly closing.

Instead of rallying support to reinforce the Alamo, however, the Virginia-born Houston did "nothing very constructive." Instead of rallying support, he made an Indian treaty with the Cherokee and their allies, that had no effect or strategic consequences in regard to stemming Santa Anna's invasion. At this time, many people across Texas already viewed Houston as an old soldier "who had lost the will to fight."

And in fact, Houston remained drunk much of the time in Washington-on-the-Brazos after his arrival on February 29, and during the constitutional convention sessions that would issue the Texas Declaration of Independence on March 2, which was also his 43rd birthday. He had already earned the nickname of "Big Drunk" from the Cherokee. At Washington-on-the-Brazos, instead of focusing on saving the Alamo garrison, Houston exhibited a strong penchant for a liquor-laced eggnog at the busy grog shops, getting considerably intoxicated, and probably also partook in opium. On one occasion, friends carried a passed out Houston to his bed. Then another time, after an all-night revelry, Houston stayed most of the next day in bed out of necessity. Instead of deserving renown as the "Father of Texas," as endlessly promoted by Texas and American historians, Houston should have been denounced as the "Father of the Alamo disaster," because of his apathy toward the Alamo's fate.[7]

Even when the March 2 *Brazoria Texas Republican* published Travis' stirring appeal for assistance, Houston still did nothing to rally reinforcements for the Alamo. Instead, with "his mind fogged by alcohol," he concluded that Mexicans troops were nowhere near San Antonio, and brushed off Travis' words as a crass political attempt to grandstand and gain popularity across Texas by way of "a damned lie."[8]

Since reading Travis' first missive, Houston saw nothing but sinister personal politics at work. He stated: "A fraud had been practiced upon the people by the officers of the frontier, for party purposes."[9]

Ever apathetic, Houston failed to assist the Alamo in part because he was concerned that "Travis might be just as ambitious [as Fannin, who coveted Houston's position as commander-in-chief], perhaps seeing holding on to Béxar as the means to become a hero in Texas and ride that to power. Thus, Houston dismissed both men's pleas [Travis and Fannin] for help at the Alamo." Even in the first days of March, when the convention met to vote on Texas' independence, Houston remained dismissive of the fate of Travis and his men. He even informed fellow delegates that "Travis exaggerated his position and only sought to aggrandize himself."[10]

Ironically, Fannin, who faced the advance of Santa Anna's right wing under General José Urrea, the pincer movement north into Texas that had moved up the coastal road from Matamoros, has taken the most blame from historians for losing the Alamo.[11] But in fact, it was the smug politicians and even the people of Texas who had turned their backs on the Alamo garrison during its hour of need. Then, on March 3, unknown to the Alamo's defenders, the Declaration of Independence was officially signed at Washington-on-the-Brazos, resulting in the birth of the Republic of Texas. On the following day, Houston, of all people, was named commander-in-chief: an ironic appointment for Texas, because he had done so little to gather support to reinforce San Antonio. It was almost as if Houston had been rewarded for allowing the Alamo garrison to be wiped off the face of the earth.[12] Clearly, it was already much too late for the Alamo men, who had become victims of a "pure and simple betrayal of the worst kind."[13]

This realization that they had been abandoned by the people of Texas had come relatively early to some Alamo garrison members. As Captain Carey penned in a January 12, 1836 letter to his brother and sister, the "Old Texians" only "came at the eleventh hour and remained in camps expecting us all to be killed and they men of property in this country and have their all in Texas did they come forward to protect the place. No. They pilfered us of our blankets and clothes and horses and went home [after capturing San Antonio] telling how they whipt the Spaniards reaping the laurels of a few."[14]

But not everyone in Texas had turned their back on the Alamo. At 3:00 a.m., in the cold darkness on March 1, the arrival of Pennsylvania-born Lieutenant George C. Kimbell, age 33, and his 32 men of the

Gonzales Ranging Company of Mounted Volunteers from Gonzales, the westernmost Anglo community in Texas and the only one west of the Colorado River, were the only reinforcement to the beleaguered Alamo garrison, only four days after Santa Anna reached San Antonio. Led by carpenter-turned-guide John W. Smith, who was nicknamed "El Colorado" by the Tejanos because of his flaming red hair, these Gonzales boys consisted of the town's "best citizens." With a determination to assist their comrades, Kimbell's men had ridden away from the Gonzales town square on February 27, never to see their families again.[15]

When Santa Anna was informed of the tiny reinforcement, he was more amused than anything else. To him, these Gonzales cavalrymen who had conveniently arrived at the Alamo would enable him to slaughter more rebels as part of his overall plan to purge Texas of colonists.[16]

Meanwhile, the siege of the Alamo progressed day after day. After inching forward to get within closer range, Mexican artillerymen in colorful uniforms blasted away with their light guns, hoping that a lucky shot might knock a hole in the walls for the unleashing of an infantry assault. But the Mexican cannons were not only antiquated, but much too light to knock down the strong limestone and abode walls. A notoriously impatient Santa Anna had begun the siege without waiting for the arrival of his heavier artillery, two 12-pounders. This dilemma was not unlike that faced by the ragtag "People's Army of Texas" in assaulting San Antonio before the arrival of their largest gun, the 18-pounder, which was now poised at the Alamo's southwest corner.[17]

On February 25, Santa Anna launched a probe against the Alamo's southern side, consisting of two or three hundred men. Launched in broad daylight, the defenders were waiting and sent the Mexicans reeling back with cannon and rifle fire, inflicting at least half a dozen dead and wounded. Afterward, garrison members sallied out to burn some huts where Mexicans were taking shelter, and also to bring in some of their materials for firewood. Meantime, as more Mexican artillery arrived, Santa Anna set up batteries on all sides of the Alamo.

Clearly not anticipating serious resistance, Santa Anna already knew that victory over the Alamo garrison was near. He was already thinking ahead, even bragging in a February 27 report to Mexico City: "After taking the fortress of the Alamo, I will continue my operations" in Texas.[18]

With the end drawing closer, and with the hope of reinforcements having faded away like the dropping late winter sun, the Alamo's defenders could only find solace in the heroic example of their own Anglo-Celtic ancestors of the American Revolution, not unlike how Santa Anna's soldiers looked with pride upon their forebears in Father Hildago's 1810 revolt against the Spanish. Ironically, both Americans and Mexicans shared an equally distinguished revolutionary heritage in throwing off the yoke of European and colonial powers.

Here, at the Alamo, Bowie took pride in his hardy ancestors, who first migrated from Scotland to the rich tobacco country along the Patuxent River country of southern Maryland during the first decade of the 1700s. Ancestor Captain Daniel Bowie had defended his piece of Prince George's County, Maryland, while serving with distinction in the spirited attack of Colonel William Smallwood's Maryland battalion during the campaign for New York in the Revolution. This headlong charge against impossible odds—both British and Hessian—helped to save hundreds of Washington's defeated troops at the height of the disastrous Battle of Brooklyn on August 27, 1776. Nearly every Marylander became a casualty, including Captain Bowie, who was captured.

But other Bowie family members moved south beyond the tobacco country of southern Maryland, migrating to South Carolina before the American Revolution. With a name denoting distinct Scottish roots, Rezin Bowie served in the command of Francis Marion, the famous "Swamp Fox," who repeatedly struck at British patrols and garrisons in the South Carolina lowlands.[19]

Like Bowie, who revered his American Revolutionary ancestors, Crockett admired his father's role at the unexpected patriot victory at Kings Mountain, South Carolina, in October 1780. He was especially proud of the fact that his father had served as a lowly private with the "over-mountain" men. Winning everlasting fame for the Long Rifle, these frontiersmen defeated Major Patrick Ferguson and his Loyalist troops—vanquishing an entire expeditionary force with one blow that began to turn the tide in the Southern theater. Indeed, while "his son David lost all recollection of anything else his father did in the Revolution, he never forgot John Crockett's role at King's Mountain."[20]

Here, trapped inside the Alamo's cold, dark confines without a prayer—even though he had yet to fully realize that bitter truth—Travis might well have recalled his family's role during the American Revolution. After migrating south from Virginia, Travis' ancestors lived in the largely Scotch-Irish community of Ninety-Six, South Carolina, which stood at the vortex of a vicious civil war among neighbors. In 1781, the Americans besieged the Tory garrison of Ninety-Six for 28 days without achieving victory. It is not known if Travis' ancestors in arms served as patriots or Tories, or remained neutral like so many Americans in the South.[21]

Perhaps some fatalistic Alamo defenders from Ireland identified with the last words of martyred revolutionary Robert Emmet, leader of the failed 1803 Irish revolt, before his September 20, 1803 execution by the British in Dublin: "I am going to my cold and silent grave; my lamp of life is nearly extinguished [and now] The grave opens to receive me . . . I am ready to die."[22]

By taking some inspiration in the military roles played by ancestors in America's struggle for independence, the Alamo defenders had no way of knowing how much they actually had in common with the Mexican troops, who had been sent north to "exterminate" them, sharing a proud revolutionary tradition. Instead, however, the Anglo-Celts only emphasized superficial differences in their opponents, especially a darker skin.

Indeed, the tortured course of the histories of both Mexico and the United States meant that Santa Anna's soldiers and the Alamo's defenders had very much in common, despite the considerable cultural and racial differences. Imbued with the identical republican ideals and enlightened revolutionary visions stemming from the 18th-century Enlightenment, the colonial people of both nations, Mexico and the United States, had broken away from their respective mother countries, Spain and Great Britain, in successful revolutions based upon the concept of egalitarianism for all men. But Mexico's enlightened vision applied to people of all colors, including those of African descent, unlike in the United States. And now, in early March 1836, a good many Americans and Mexicans were about to meet in mortal combat for supporting what were in essence the same principles, at least in theory. Therefore, in this sense, a strange fate and destiny had seemingly brought not only the Alamo defenders to wintry San Antonio in the first place, but also Santa Anna's soldiers.[23]

FEEBLE ARTILLERY BOMBARDMENT

Contrary to the traditional views of the Alamo, the siege was somewhat of a farce. The Mexican artillery arm that had completed the lengthy journey all the way from Mexico's depths under harsh winter conditions was even weaker, both in numbers and the diminutive size of the pieces, than the Alamo's "long arm" arsenal. Santa Anna's artillery arm was so weak that the mere idea of a siege reducing the Alamo's defenses was unrealistic. All that Santa Anna could rely upon to batter down the Alamo's walls was eight small artillery pieces: two 6-pounders, two 8-pounders, two 4-pounders, and two 7-inch howitzers—far too light to be effective. Even worse, these cannons were aging, nearly obsolete guns mounted on Gribeauval wooden carriages. By this time, the Mexican army's artillery arm was a hollow shell of its former self, having peaked more than a decade earlier in 1825. At that time, the power and accuracy of Mexican guns had forced the surrender of the Spanish garrison of the mighty fortress San Juan de Ulloa that protected Vera Cruz.

Cut off from Spain's cannon-making foundries after Mexico won its independence, Mexico's arsenal of artillery consisted of an odd assortment of antiquated Spanish and French artillery pieces from a bygone era. No cannon of Santa Anna's artillery arm came close to the size of the Alamo's 18-pounder. In addition, the overall inferior quality of Mexican black powder—extremely coarse, not fine like United States powder—bestowed relatively low propellant capabilities.[24]

Not surprisingly during such a feeble siege, no Alamo garrison members were killed during nearly two weeks of bombardment. Quite simply, Santa Anna's siege was little more than an imitation of a legitimate one. As Travis boasted in his March 3 letter: ". . . the walls are generally proof against cannon balls." Mocking Santa Anna's artillery fire throughout the bombardment, Travis added in the same letter: "At least two hundred shells have fallen inside of our works without having injured a single man."[25]

But as additional regiments and battalions of the Mexican army came marching into San Antonio, it became clear that, no matter how feeble the army's artillery, the sheer size of the besieging force would soon spell doom for the tiny Alamo garrison. And the no-quarter flag that began flying on the first day of the siege indicated Santa Anna's confidence. A writer for the *New Orleans True American* emphasized an undeniable reality that not only sealed the Alamo garrison's fate, but also was destined to send shock waves across the United States: "It is worthy of remark that the flag of Santa Anna's army at Béxar was a BLOOD RED ONE, in place of the constitutional tri-colored flag" of the Republic of Mexico.[26]

Such a development should not have surprised the Alamo garrison. The recent tragic fates of the 28 volunteers—mostly from the United States—after the mid-November 1835 attempt to capture Tampico should have served as a stern warning. A letter printed in the February 20, 1836 edition of the *Telegraph* and *Texas Register* explained the tragedy: "We the undersigned prisoners of war are condemned to be shot on Monday December 14, 1835 at Tampico."[27]

Some more realistic men in Texas had early warned in vain of the brutal brand of warfare that was about to sweep across Texas. As written by a history-minded Lieutenant Governor Robinson to the General Council on January 14: "The defenseless situation of our oppressed country calls for your prompt attention and speedy relief [because of the] glittering spears and ruthless sword of the descendants of Cortez, and his modern Goths and Vandals."[28]

The xenophobic Santa Anna possessed an almost identical low opinion of the Anglo-Celts of Texas, especially those recently from the United States. With undisguised contempt, he explained how the American "invaders were all men, who, moved by the desire of conquest, with rights less apparent and plausible than those of Cortes or Pizarro, wished to take possession of that vast territory extending from Béxar to the Sabine, belonging to Mexico."[29] Clearly, not only fighting to gain permanent possession of the same object—Texas—both sides in the Texas Revolution saw the other as immoral barbarians, a dark plague that had descended upon the land to threaten their respective civilizations. Such emotional and largely racial analogies of the Texas revolutionaries to ruthless Conquistadors had special appeal to the many Indians and Mestizos in Santa Anna's Army at the Alamo.

Ironically, the initial success of the United States and Tejano revolutionaries of the 1813–14 Gutierrez-Magee Expedition, who had captured Béxar and the Alamo during an earlier liberal revolt against the government in Mexico City, was hailed in sympathetic U.S. newspapers as a military expedition greater than that of Cortes.[30]

In historical terms, Mexico's extermination policy was not only a product of Moorish warfare, Cortes' conquest of the Aztecs, and the savage warfare between the Spanish and the Mexico people for the heart and soul of Mexico, but also a traditional feature of frontier warfare brought to Texas by the Anglo-Celts themselves. When Magee's American revolutionaries of the Gutierrez-Magee Expedition marched into San Antonio and took possession of the Alamo, which became their headquarters after the Spanish garrison surrendered, the head of one especially hated Spanish officer was cut off. The Spaniard's head was then placed on a pike at the Alamo's main gate to serve as a grim warning to liberal-minded Tejanos of San Antonio.

And while Santa Anna's greatest infamy stemmed from his no-quarter policy at the Alamo and Goliad, what has been conveniently overlooked is the fact that it had been the Texans themselves who had first entered the no-quarter concept into the equation of the Texas Revolution. Ironically, in a strange twist of fate, the Alamo's now disabled co-commander, Bowie, had in fact first threatened no quarter on Mexican troops in summer 1832. At that time, he declared that all Mexican troops of the Nacogdoches garrison who failed to surrender would be killed without mercy.

Then, in another irony, the second example of the Anglo-Celts threatening to unleash a no-quarter policy in the Texas Revolution came from Travis himself. He swore that he would "put every man to the sword," slaughtering the Mexican soldiers of the Anáhuac garrison if they refused to surrender. Therefore, a strange fate had seemingly come full circle for both Bowie and Travis, who by now no doubt regretted their earlier no-quarter pronouncements that helped to doom them and the Alamo garrison if captured, or if they surrendered to Santa Anna.[31]

Other examples of threatening no quarter by Texians can be found. In early October 1835, for instance, Captain Philip Dimmitt—who luckily departed the Alamo before it was overrun—and his Texians had threatened to vanquish the small Mexican garrison at Lipantitlan, Texas, by either "unconditional submission [surrender], or putting it to the sword."[32]

At an earlier date, even acting Texas Governor James Robinson got into the no-quarter act, fueling passions higher by imploring the people of Texas to give Santa Anna "war to the knife and knife to the hilt."[33]

Therefore, and for good reason, Santa Anna sincerely believed that it was not the Mexicans but the Texians who "have audaciously declared a war of extermination to the Mexicans and should be treated in the same manner."[34]

His message to wage no-quarter warfare was transferred to his top lieutenants early in the campaign. In his December 7, 1835 orders to General Sesma, Santa Anna emphasized how these "foreigners, who wage war against the Mexican Nation, have violated all laws and do not deserve any consideration, and for that reason, no quarter will be given them" to the garrison at San Antonio.[35]

Consequently, Alamo garrison members were about to pay a high price for all of the bravado, arrogance, and threats of their leaders— both military and civilian—since the Texas Revolution's beginning. As revealed in the pages of the *Tamaulipas Gazette*: "Don Santa Anna [plans] to wipe out the stain [to national honor] in the blood of those perfidious foreigners" who had rebelled against Mexico.

And as if ordained by the natural order of things, a seemingly high price had to be paid in full by the victorious Anglo-Celts of the Jackson generation for the destruction of the pro-British Creeks in Alabama, and the brazen confiscations of their ancestral homeland, the future Alabama. A veteran, Crockett was yet haunted by this brutal war, not to mention the slaughter of his own grandparents by Creeks in northeast Tennessee during the American Revolution. For both sides and for generations, this struggle between Native people and the Anglo-Celts for possession of the North America continent was a total war, often without compassion or mercy from either side.

As a ninety-day volunteer who enlisted in the Tennessee Mounted Militia when "my dander was up," after the Fort Mims massacre of nearly 300 whites and friendly Indians by the Red Sticks, Crockett would never forget the awful slaughter of men, women, and children by Jackson's revenge-seeking troops at the Creek village known as Tallusahatchee. With an odd mixture of pride and sympathy, he recalled how: "We shot them like dogs." Before the hell of Tallusahatchee ended, those yet resisting Creek warriors not shot were burned alive in their log lodges, bringing the final tally of Indian victims to nearly 200 killed.

From the beginning, Jackson and his soldiers sought revenge upon the Red Sticks. Jackson's strategy included a deliberate attempt to terrorize the Indian people to break their will and destroy their war-waging capabilities by burning villages and crops. Avenging Fort Mims, which was located just north of Mobile, Alabama—then the Mississippi Territory—and the August 30, 1813 massacre, Jackson proclaimed with satisfaction: "We have retaliated for the destruction of Fort Mims."[36]

But in fact, an even greater retaliation unleashed by Jackson that decisively broke the power of the Red Sticks came at Horseshoe Bend. After Jackson's men stormed the Creek breastwork of logs, they poured over the parapet to slaughter every Red Stick warrior they could find. Among the Creeks, "None asked for quarter," and none was given by the vengeful Anglo-Celts, ensuring that "the butchery was continued for hours." Perhaps as many as 800 Red Sticks were killed in a "terrible vengeance" during one of the bloodiest days in America's Indian Wars. But the American eagle of Manifest Destiny was soaring high. The slaughter opened up a vast land to settlement, including the cane break country of southwest Alabama that Travis called home.[37]

Quite simply, no quarter was a widely accepted brand of warfare on both the United States and Mexican frontiers. Americans practiced such utter ruthlessness for generations upon the enemies of their people—Indians, Spanish, Americans, and Mexicans—and vice-versa. In part, such slaughters evolved into the universal form of warfare practiced on the southwest frontier, partly because it was so remote from centers of government, big cities, societal restrictions, and cultural norms, allowing civilized rules to degenerate into barbarity.

Consequently, from the beginning of Texas' settlement, the colonists from the United States brought this no-quarter brand of warfare—Anglo-Celt cultural baggage—with them across the Sabine. When the Kickapoo attacked the Joseph Taylor family in the remote northern frontier of the Brazos River country in November 1835, tough Texas Rangers retaliated. The Rangers vented their wrath against two unfortunate Kickapoo warriors who they tracked down. Not satisfied with killing them, the Rangers—emulating the Spanish—then cut off their heads and mounted them on poles to serve as a warning to other Indians. In early 1836, other Indian fighters and hardened Rangers, like Noah Smith, decorated saddles with Indian scalps. Clearly, these frontier excesses indicated that nasty, ugly war was a common feature of life on the edges of civilization. Ironically, the cultured, privileged elites of Mexico City, who loved art, scholarly books, fine wine, Spanish architecture, and the refined niceties of Mexican society, likewise promoted the brutal policy of no quarter for the Texans and United States volunteers in arms.[38]

In overall terms, what had developed in America between the Anglo-Celts and the Indians was the racial war, pure and simple, and this racial animosity was given new life in Texas. Not unlike the seemingly endless, merciless religious wars—including the Crusades—between Islamic and Christian warriors for more than 1,000 years, this racial war between whites and Indians was noted for its savagery. The Red Stick Creeks had been inspired by Tecumseh's words of "Let the white race perish." Tecumseh had desired nothing less than the massacre of every white in America, driving them "back into the [Atlantic] water whose accursed waves brought them to our shores! [And] slay their wives and children, that the very breed may perish."[39]

And like the embattled Red Sticks before them, the Mexican people had now declared their own holy war of extermination upon the Anglo-Celts of Texas. The seemingly endless cycle of racial war had come full circle, continuing in yet another faraway land that had become just another savage racial frontier. As if in divine retribution for having encroached upon Texas lands at the expense of both the Native American and the Mexican people, and to mock the folly of the inexperienced leadership of Neill, Bowie, and Travis, who wanted to hold an indefensible position, a good many young men and boys were about to pay a stiff price for leadership mistakes. The Alamo defenders were about to be sacrificed to soldados committed to "saving" Mexico.[40]

Eerily, a past chapter of history was about to be repeated at the Alamo. During the First War for Texas' Independence, the mostly U.S. volunteers of the ill-fated Gutierrez-Magee Expedition of 1812–13 had captured Béxar. They then made an ill-advised defensive stand in the Alamo with a number of cannons, including the little "Come and Take It" gun that Neill had commanded after Gonzales had been given it by the Mexican government in 1831. Then, they raised a green flag with Irish revolutionary antecedents, which flew over the old Spanish mission that always seemed to draw revolutionaries like a magnet. Occupying both San Antonio and the Alamo with a blind overconfidence, this earlier group of largely Anglo-Celtic revolutionaries was doomed by indecision, lack of experience, underestimating their opponent, lack of discipline, and disunity of command—ironically, the same fatal formula now repeated by yet another generation of Anglo-Celts at the same place in early 1836. The twisting contours of history were once again about to repeat itself in San Antonio with the same bloody results.[41]

General Filisola explained the utter disaster for this earlier generation of Anglo-Celtic revolutionaries in Texas: "That was the fatal and inevitable consequence of the lack of a good system, unity, discipline and subordination to the leaders" of a revolutionary bid for independence.[42]

Ironically, during the siege, the Alamo's commander might have been the most delusional garrison member, having what was called "The Walter Scott disease." Unfortunately for his soldiers, Travis existed in the unrealistic world of romance and historical fiction. Like some chivalric knight of a bygone romantic age, Travis had wanted nothing

more than to have ridden off on a romantic Quixotic quest with the
Matamoros Expedition, instead of having been ordered to reinforce San
Antonio. Even so, the Alamo's leaders and their followers still expected
to vanquish any number of Mexicans hurled their way. Travis might
have gotten along better with Bowie had he known that a distant Bowie
relative was none other than the Scottish nationalist hero, Rob Roy
McGregor.[43]

John Sowers Brooks never realized how prophetic he had been when
he wrote: "I have resolved to stand by her [Texas] to the last, and in a
word, to sink or swim with her."[44]

And in a like manner, Travis also swore that he would follow the
Texas Revolution "right or wrong, sink or swim, live or die, survive or
perish."[45] The entire Alamo garrison, however, was not going to swim,
but sink from the weight of their own mistakes and miscalculations,
while being "sacrificed to the vengeance of a Gothic enemy," in Travis'
March 3 words.[46]

Drawing upon what little military experience he possessed, and
basically clueless in regard to the art of war, Travis was not prepared for
the role in which he now found himself. As many couriers as possible
had been dispatched by Travis to seek aid before it was too late. Little
more could be done. Without hesitation or second thoughts of the ugly
implications, Travis had risked all—especially his men's lives—on the
single hope that all of Texas would rise up to come to his assistance,
including from Fannin's force at Goliad.

But in fact, aside from the arrival of the tiny Ranger Company early
on March 1, no one else would be coming to the Alamo's succor.
Ironically, this reinforcement was not unlike the Morelos Battalion, that
had rushed all the way from Laredo to Cós' aid, only to be trapped and
captured inside the Alamo. And like Travis, these seasoned Mexican
troops had defiantly declared with pride to their besiegers how their
battalion "has never surrendered." Strangely, the Alamo deathtrap had
a way of causing so many defenders—filibusters, Tejanos, Mexican
troops, Texas rebels, U.S. volunteers—to stake their lives on an obscure,
indefensible place where they would most likely lose the bet.

Ironically, Fannin was in the process of becoming the convenient
scapegoat for the Alamo's fall rather than leaders like Neill, Travis,
Bowie, and Houston. Despite the fact that he needed to hold Goliad, as
it was more strategically important than San Antonio and the objective
of Santa Anna's right wing in his pincer movement across Texas, the

West Pointer would be blamed for not reinforcing the Alamo and saving the day, when in truth it was the fault of the people of Texas for staying home and not rushing to arms. As if already knowing that a cruel fate awaited the Alamo garrison, Fannin wrote to Lieutenant Governor Robinson and revealed what most of all doomed its defenders: "[W]ill not curses be heaped on the heads of the sluggards who remained at home?"[47]

Only one day before the Alamo's fall, an outraged editor of the *Telegraph and Texas Register* would lament an undeniable reality, because the poorer Texians remained out of military service since "they have already served longer [in the 1835 campaign] than some of their richer neighbors [and] we hear men say, they are ready to fight, but are not willing to turn out, while men possessed of lands and other property [slaves] are staying at home" while the forsaken Alamo garrison waited to die.[48]

Unfortunately for the Alamo's defenders, the all-important unity-first caused by General Cós' presence into Texas in 1835, which had so solidly united the old settlers and newcomers from the United States to serve as members of the "Army of the People," was no more.[49]

Clearly, by this time and with all hope gone, the Alamo's soldiers began to finally realize that their time on earth was short, save for a miracle. Only one reality remained: the haunting reminder of the grim fate that awaited them each time the no-quarter flag fluttered from the belfry of the San Fernando Church. As in the case of Custer's doomed men at Little Big Horn on the Great Plains, some suicide pacts were almost certainly made among garrison members. No one wanted to be captured alive by the Mexicans, who were known for their cruelty. If they surrendered or were captured, the no-quarter flag indicated that these Protestants might even be tortured by Catholics, like during the Spanish Inquisition.

During the siege, along with reading inspirational passages from the Torah, the handful of Jewish members might have contemplated the fate of the Jewish rebels of Masada, especially if they had read the work by renowned Jewish historian, Josephus. The Jewish rebels who fought against the powerful Roman legions looked upon suicide as a victory of sorts when success was unattainable, and especially when the Romans promised no-quarter, becoming almost a religious duty. As Josephus explained, some of the Jewish warriors "were driven to suicide [and] they made sure that at least they should not die at Roman hands."[50]

Jewish rebels who defied the imperial legions of Rome accepted the fatalistic concept that: "It is a brave act to kill onself."[51] Alamo garrison members were in a similar no-win situation like the Jewish rebels of Masada: surrounded and bottled up in a doomed, fortified position with no hope for survival or escape. In addition, the contrast between the Jewish rebels and the elite soldiers of the Roman Legions were similar to the wide differences between the Alamo defenders and Santa Anna's finest troops. Josephus explained that the difference was that the Jewish rebels who pitted themselves against Rome's imperial, centralized authority possessed "neither discipline nor experience in war, and are nothing but a rabble, not fit to be called an army."[52]

Like Santa Anna in facing the Texas rebels, so the Romans also benefited from the internal divisions among the rebellious Jews that made conquest easier. Nothing could stop the Roman Legions from conquering Masada, and the Hebrew warriors knew as much. During the lengthy siege, it seemed to the Hebrew defenders that "God was indeed on the side of the Romans," causing the Jewish rebels to become increasingly fatalistic.[53]

Besides Moses (or Louis) Rose, and Alabama-born teenager Gabia Fuqua of Gonzales, another Jewish defender of the Alamo was Private Anthony—or Avram or Abraham—Wolfe. At age 54, Wolfe was one of the oldest garrison members. A former Spanish subject of the Louisiana-Texas frontier before Jefferson's Louisiana Purchase from Napoleon, he possessed experience as an infantry lieutenant in the Louisiana militia in 1806. Wolfe was a unique, enlightened individual for the day, especially in dealing fairly with Native Americans while serving as an Indian agent by 1818 and into the early 1820s. As a member of Captain Carey's company, Wolfe now served as an artilleryman, operating one of Captain Dickinson's guns positioned on the elevated firing platform at the church's rear. In addition to this Jewish private from Washington County, Texas, were his two sons, age eleven and twelve. The three Wolfe males would find their own personal Masada on the remote Texas frontier, but not by way of suicide.[54]

On the night of March 5, at least two garrison members decided not to risk the fight at the Alamo. One might have been Moses (or Louis) Rose, another Jewish defender and a Napoleonic veteran who had been born in the Ardennes Forest region of France—a fact that might have gained Santa Anna's mercy if captured. Rose had taken a lesson from the tragic pages of Masada's story that had been overlooked by Wolfe:

get out while one was still able and before it was too late.[55]

Another garrison member leaving the Alamo was Captain Juan Nepomuceno Seguín, born in 1896 as the privileged son of a leading San Antonio Tejano, whose Tejano horse company had joined Austin's rustic "Army of the People" in the third week of October 1835, just in time for the siege of San Antonio. Chosen as a messenger, he evaded the Mexican forces by easing out under the cover of darkness along an irrigation ditch that concealed him from prying Mexican eyes and took him to the Gonzales Road.[56]

Regardless of what faith they held, some defenders now contemplated meeting their Maker due to their folly in remaining at the Alamo. They remembered Houston's inviting words to United States citizens on October 5, 1835, that had never left their minds: "If volunteers from the United States will join their brethren in [Texas], they will receive liberal bounties of land. We have millions of acres of our best lands unchosen, and unappropriated."[57]

On March 5, Houston's words now mocked the ugly reality that the Alamo's defenders, who were pent-up like animals in an old, crumbling Spanish mission, now came to realize. Instead of opening the door to a seemingly boundless future, Houston's alluring invitation to partake in all of those choice lands had only opened the door to the worst possible fate: dying at the hands of a merciless enemy, far from home and family in a strange land. For the young men and boys of the Alamo—including 15-year-old William Philip King, the youngest defender, and James Madison Rose, who was the nephew of former President James Madison, Houston's enticing words were indeed a fatal siren's song.[58]

Twenty-three-year-old Asa Walker, born in New York, had migrated to Texas in November 1835, and had then "hurried toward the Alamo with an almost haunting sense of urgency." Now a private in Captain Robert White's infantry company, the Bexar Guards, he summarized in a letter the winner-take-all attitude of the garrison, including his cousin, Tennessee-born Private Joseph R. (or Jacob) Walker, age 37, of Captain Carey's artillery company, ensuring his Tennessee family, who would never seen him again: "If I live to return, I will satisfy you for all. If I die I leave you my clothes to do the best you can with. . . . I will trust to change."[59]

Meanwhile, the cold winds of late winter swept over the south central Texas prairies, which were bare, dull, and colored a brownish hue, outside the old mission. The flat terrain was draped in winter's drabness, and the lack of tall timber—with exception of a few scrubby mesquite and bare cottonwoods—along the surrounding prairie presented a lifeless appearance. The overall bleakness of late winter contradicted the defenders' memories of the breathtaking beauty, fertility, and promise of this land during the spring and summer, along with their own earlier youthful idealism.

In the words of Alamo defender Daniel William Cloud—who had migrated to the Red River country in part because he so detested winter's harshness north of the Ohio River—in a December 26, 1835 letter: "If we succeed, the Country is ours. It is immense in extent, and fertile in its soil, and will amply reward all our toil. If we fail, death in the cause of liberty and humanity is not cause for shuddering. Our rifles are by our side, and choice guns they are, we know what awaits us, and are prepared to meet it."[60]

Captain Carey, commander of the self-styled Invincibles, penned in a final letter to his brothers and sisters, hoping against hope that "if I live, as soon as the war is over I will endeavor to see you all."[61]

Just like the soldiers trapped in the Alamo's squalor and rubble, the young soldados were also primarily focused on the same two things as the Anglo-Celts: praying for God to spare them in the upcoming battle, so that they may see their loved ones once again, and dreams of the fine Texas lands they had marched through to their rendezvous with destiny at San Antonio. Indeed, like the Alamo garrison members, the mere thought of possessing this fertile land, and thereby providing a better life for themselves and their families, lingered in the thoughts of Santa Anna's soldados, who saw lands far richer in comparison to arid and mountainous northern Mexico.[62]

Amid the windswept prairies surrounding the Alamo, a good many Mexican men must have wondered if they would ever return to their warm, sunny homeland. To these soldados of a strong Catholic faith, they must have felt an eerie uneasiness in besieging an old Catholic mission. Some soldados might have felt it was sacrilegious to bombard a fortified position that was dominated by an old Catholic church they could see in the distance. But even stranger for Santa Anna's troops was this unfamiliar land north of the Rio Grande. Few of Santa Anna's soldiers had ever been so far north before while, in de la Pena's words, fighting for the first time "men of a different language and a different religion, men whose character and habits were likewise different from theirs."

From small, remote villages in Mexico's isolated interior, some of these men had never even heard of Texas before. Typical soldados of Santa Anna's Army included young men, of Indian descent, from the Tres Villas Active Battalion. Members of this unit hailed from three villages in the state of Vera Cruz: Orizaba, amid the sugar cane and maize fields of central Mexico, located near the highest mountain peak in Mexico; Jalapa, which Santa Anna called home; and Cordoba, named after the fabled city held so long by the Moors in southern Spain.

What Santa Anna's soldiers saw around San Antonio was a land quite unlike anything that they had seen before. To these men, this was the far north, where cold weather and extremes in climate was second to none in Mexico. Few soldados from the heart of Mexico, including the semitropical central valley where oranges, limes, and other fruits now lay ripe on the trees, had experienced such a harsh winter before. These men had volunteered for eight years of service or had been conscripted and impressed for ten years.

Not only the weather extremes of Texas, but also the land itself, seemed eerie to these young soldados. This area around San Antonio consisted of a vast prairie region—the southern end of the central plains—that Santa Anna's troops had not seen before. And what was equally different, if not alarming, was the surprisingly widespread Anglo-Celtic cultural influence and imprint on the social fabric of San Antonio and its people. Even some Tejano men and women—especially those from wealthy families—wore American clothes, and even spoke the language with ease. This was the first time that most Mexican soldiers had encountered Tejanos. To many of Santa Anna's troops, Texas was very much a foreign land, and especially unforgiving during this late winter: cold, generally flat, and covered with a sea of grass and vegetation not previously seen. Also like the men of the Alamo, some of these young Mexican troops were now about to sacrifice their lives in defense of this strange land that they had never seen before.[63]

And, ironically, in much the same way, most Alamo men were also newcomers to this region, mere interlopers who now lusted for nature's richness like the Indians, Spanish, French, and Mexicans before them. This bountiful land was every bit as strange to the young soldiers from Pennsylvania, Kentucky, or North Carolina—and especially those men from Ireland, Germany, or France—as to Mexico's soldados now north of the Rio Grande for the first time: an unusual situation for men about to die for a land they had never previously seen and over the possession of a place of little strategic or military value.

Meanwhile, inside the Alamo, thoughts among garrison members were gloomy, while the cannon balls—though of small caliber—steadily rained down day after day. The dark, cloudy days and bare, wintry landscape added to the gloom and sense of hopelessness. No longer was Crockett boasting loudly that he would "have Santa Anna's head and wear it as a watch seal." All the confidence, braggadocio, and sense of cultural and racial superiority had long evaporated from the once-jaunty men of the Alamo. During the Mexican bombardment, with the prospects of reinforcements diminishing, spirits among the garrison sagged to new lows. During the siege of late February and early March, it became increasingly clear that no relief was coming.

Growing impatient for victory, General Santa Anna, as if emulating Napoleon, now contemplated unleashing a coup de main to overwhelm the Alamo. Displaying the typical aggressiveness upon which his reputation was founded, he knew that he had to overwhelm the pesky Alamo garrison, as it stood as a symbol of defiance that could no longer be tolerated. Santa Anna viewed the Alamo as representing Mexican failures both past and present, in two successive campaigns, including now having been unable to reduce it by a rather puny artillery bombardment during the past week and a half.

Deviating from Napoleon's usual style of one-man decisions, Santa Anna called a commander's conference on the chilly, late winter afternoon of Friday, March 4. But this time, the brisk cold winds of early morning had died down like the prospects of survival for the men in the Alamo. Agreeing with Santa Anna's arguments for launching a frontal assault, four Mexican commanders present at the conference advocated an attack. Not surprisingly and echoing his brother-in-law's views, one such aggressive leader wanting to strike was General Cós. As could be expected, he still wanted to redeem his reputation that had been stained at this same place only a short time before.

Those officers who opined against Santa Anna's viewpoint desired to await the arrival of their heavier guns—a couple of 12-pounders that were expected to reach the army on March 7—to blow a breach into the already badly damaged north wall before undertaking an all-out infantry attack. Santa Anna, along with General Joaquin Ramirez y Sesma and Colonel Juan Nepomuceno Almonte, were less prudent. Emboldened by the lack of accurate or sustained return fire from the Alamo, which indicated an ammunition shortage and insufficient artillery training among the gunners, Santa Anna now weighed options. Therefore, he thought about what his commanders had said during the "long conference" in which opinions were freely voiced.

Finally, around noon on March 5, Santa Anna made his final decision: an all-out assault on the Alamo would take place the next morning. His snap decision was based, in large part, on newly received intelligence that Travis and the garrison were planning to either surrender or make an escape attempt on March 6. But it also was the right choice because the past two weeks of artillery bombardment had proved so ineffective. After all, General Jackson had decided much the same at Horseshoe Bend, ordering a frontal assault when the sturdy log breastwork of green pine stood solid after an impotent artillery bombardment.[64]

With the Sapper Battalion, Lieutenant Colonel De la Pena described the true situation—deteriorating rapidly and near mutinous—inside the Alamo: "Travis's resistance was on the verge of being overcome; for several days his followers had been urging him to surrender [and] they had pressed him so hard that on the 5th he promised them that if no help arrived on that day they would surrender the next day or try to escape under cover of darkness."[65] Ironically, in view of what we now know of Houston's inactivity, another factor in Santa Anna's reasoning for deciding to launch an assault on the Alamo also exists. As revealed in a rare letter, Santa Anna felt that it was "necessary to storm the fortress before it was reinforced by General Houston who was coming to its relief."[66]

One of the Sapper Battalion's most promising officers, Lieutenant Colonel de la Pena, was amazed by the bold decision. Revealing the discontent among many high-ranking officers and enlisted men throughout the army, he believed that the Alamo garrison had been surprised because they "expected us to march on Goliad, the key position that would have opened the door to the principal theater of war [and] we should have attacked the enemy at the heart instead of weakening ourselves by going to Bejar, a garrison without any political or military importance."[67]

But by making this abrupt decision, Santa Anna faced a central military quandary that was as timeless for a commander as it was seemingly insoluble: the inevitable consequence of high losses in assaulting a fortified position. But an unbending faith in the wisdom of using the tactical offensive to reap victory had never been higher in military circles on both sides of the Atlantic at this time. After all, Napoleon's overwhelming battlefield successes had been won primarily by reliance upon the tactical offensive. From the military academy in Mexico City to West Point on the Hudson, it was emphasized as the key to success and preached as the gospel of victory. The most significant military theorist in the 1830s in America was West Point professor, Dennis Hart Mahan. To the young cadets at West Point, he advocated the wisdom of the tactical offensive, especially "the vigorous charge with the bayonet," influencing an entire generation of Civil War leaders on both sides.[68]

Contrary to popular misconceptions and negative stereotypes that continue to endure to this day, Santa Anna was in fact not more focused on gorging on fine foods, consuming quality liquors, the excitement of cock-fighting, whoring with peasant women, or making love to his make- believe Tejano "wife," than in developing a brilliant tactical plan to overwhelm the Alamo.

Santa Anna carefully positioned hundreds of his best troops around the old mission on the night of March 5, in preparation for striking the compound on each side with four columns: the old strategy of divide and conquer because the small garrison could not possibly defend every wall at once. He wisely ordered that "untrained recruits" remain in camp, placing his faith in reliable veterans who knew how to fight. The "First Column" was to be led by General Cós, while Colonel D. Francisco Dúque commanded the "Second Column." Meanwhile, the "Third Column" would be commanded by Colonel D. Jose Maria Romero. Colonel Don Juan Baptisto Morales would command a force so diminutive that it was not even officially designated as the "Fourth Column" in the March 5 orders issued at 5:00 p.m. His target was the main gate in the center of the south wall, if only to pin down the defenders in that sector.[69]

For this general attack to reclaim both national and family honor to avenge Cós' 1835 humiliation of losing San Antonio, Santa Anna possessed a special interest in restoring the image of his yet paroled brother-in-law, General Cós. In the Mexican Army's ranks, General Cós was popular and admired, even though he did had some critics—such as General Manuel Fernández Castrillón—for having lost San Antonio to a relatively small number of untrained Texians. A fine officer himself, Colonel Pedro Delgado described Cós as a "noble and young Mexican general" of promise.[70]

Despite the stain on his record, Cós' relative youth veiled the fact that, in the October 1835 words of George Fisher, "he is a man of experience" in the art of war. In leading Santa Anna's assault columns in striking the west wall, General Cós now possessed the opportunity to prove his worth as a commander on the offensive, instead of bottled-up in the Alamo.[71]

Santa Anna's burning desire to wipe out the garrison was also predicated on the fact that Travis had been pressured by his men, who naturally did not want to die for nothing, into either attempting an escape or making a desperate, last-minute offer to surrender all arms, artillery, and munitions "with the only condition of saving his life and that of all his comrades in arms," wrote General Filisola. Ironically, these were the same terms that Cós and his men had received, and it seemed possible that such an honorable surrender might yet be granted to the defenders—or so they hoped.[72]

In total, Santa Anna planned to unleash around 1,400 of his best, most experienced soldiers in a general assault. Santa Anna's finest soldiers had been trained in a set of military principles articulated by one of Napoleon's finest generals, the hard-hitting Marshal Nicholas-Jean de Dieu Soult, who led his crack IV Corps in the emperor's greatest "military masterpiece" at Austerlitz.[73]

Most important, however, was the plan to launch the attack under the cover of darkness. This tactic was a rarity in the annals of Napoleonic warfare. In military operations, then as today, nothing is more difficult than a night attack. Santa Anna displayed his strategic innovation by planning such an attack to overwhelm the Alamo as quickly as possible, before the garrison could rally or perhaps even awaken in time.

Santa Anna was not only familiar with night operations, but also excelled at this rare military art. A large part of his success in repulsing the Spanish from Mexican soil in summer 1829 was his relentless nighttime attacks around Tampico, near where the Spanish invasion force had landed in July. Santa Anna's offensive operations in darkness helped to convince stunned Spanish commanders to capitulate that September, ending Spain's ambitious invasion and reconquest attempt. Always unsuspected by his opponents, a well-honed secret weapon for Santa Anna and a key element of his tactical repertoire, the unexpected hard-hitting nighttime attack bestowed the "brilliance of Santa Anna's triumph [that] was so dazzling" to the Mexican nation.[74]

But Santa Anna had also learned a lesson in the steamy, coastal lowlands of Tampico when on Sepember 11, he hurled repeated attacks against a fortified position without his men even gaining the parapet.

Demonstrating his trademark impatience, he committed nearly a dozen assaults before the Spanish decided it was best to capitulate rather than be overwhelmed. Having learned those lessons well, Santa Anna had now adjusted his tactics, developing a masterful battle plan that was calculated to reap a swift victory, with only a single overpowering assault from multiple directions in the predawn darkness of March 6.[75]

Relying on what worked best, the old Zacatecas plan that brought an overwhelming victory against a powerful opponent in terms of sheer numbers and artillery, was also about to be repeated. On May 11, 1835, he had launched his attack at 2:00 a.m., catching thousands of militiamen completely by surprise, reaping an astounding victory.[76]

Even more, the cagey Santa Anna planned to attack on a Sunday. He knew that this was normally a day of rest and worship for the trapped Protestants, who needed to get closer to their God and desired a respite now more than ever before. Garrison members would almost certainly be even more ill-prepared on Sunday, resulting in more feeble resistance.

Additionally, Santa Anna took lessons from Cós' recent defeat at San Antonio, incorporating successful Texian tactics. Catching the Mexicans troops by surprise, Neill and his Texian artillerymen had moved into position under the cover of darkness to strike the first blow at 3:00 a.m., while Cós and his boys slept soundly. Neill had fired his first shot from a cannon at 5:00 a.m., when it was still dark, signaling two columns to launch their attack that had eventually forced Cós' surrender, after he had retired all of his forces into the Alamo's trap.

Even though four Mexican assault columns planned to strike the Alamo at different points along the perimeter, most of Santa Anna's strength would be directed at the battered north wall, despite largely ineffective attempts to batter it with artillery fire. For instance, a sizeable strategic reserve of 400 elite soldados was likewise poised before the north wall, behind the frontline troops of Colonel Dúque's column. Ironically, this weakness did not extend only along the commonly believed 40–60 foot section of the north wall, but in fact along its entire length. The entire perimeter had to be strengthened by an "elaborate wood outer-work cribbing," built up with earth and wood to support the crumbling north wall by reinforcing its front, thanks to the damage inflicted largely by the 1835 cannonade from some of the very artillerymen—Captain Carey's gunners of the New Orleans Greys—who had hammered the north wall during San Antonio's siege. Likewise this outer work, yet incomplete, stood along the entire north wall's length, unlike along the other three perimeters. And as opposed to elsewhere along the compound's perimeter, no buildings bolstered the length of the north wall, leaving it relatively weak and vulnerable.[77]

But while artillery had played a key role in reaping victory at the Alamo in December 1835, Santa Anna would not order his cannon to open fire to soften up the Alamo before unleashing his general assault. Indicating a well-conceived battle plan, this was not only a wise tactical decision, but also a calculated one, to play upon the garrison's greatest vulnerabilities: its overall exhausted state, inexperienced leadership, and the lack of training and discipline.

Seeming to have an intimate knowledge of Travis' weaknesses, Santa Anna also gambled that when his artillery stopped firing in the afternoon, leaving all quiet on the night of March 5, this unprecedented artillery pause would not signal Travis to heighten extra vigilance among the garrison. In this regard, Santa Anna had calculated correctly, revealing just how well he knew his opponent. Instead of questioning if the silence was a wily ploy to literally lull the garrison into a sense of false security, Travis would allow his boys to sleep during the early hours of March 6. After all, they had been worn down, not only by strengthening the north wall at night, but also by Santa Anna's waging of psychological warfare—continuous bombardment, Mexican bands playing music, and having his troops raise cheers—for nearly the past two weeks, which was effective in fraying the defenders' nerves. But throughout the siege, Santa Anna's most clever deception was to order cheering and musketry almost hourly during each nighttime bombardment, making the defenders believe that he was launching a night attack. The overall goal had been "to keep every American in position ready to repel the attack, thus through loss of sleep and increasing anxiety unfitting him for the final struggle."

While the defenders were fast asleep on the night of March 5, Mexican troops were preparing for battle. The chosen soldiers of the attack columns had received orders to "turn in after the night's prayer's as they will form their columns at midnight" for the assault. By this time, the worn Alamo garrison was in no shape or condition to adequately defend the old mission—especially the weak north wall. As Travis' slave, Joe, later recalled after the bombardment that had steadily pounded the Alamo: "The Garrison was much exhausted by hard labor [in strengthening the works] and incessant watching and fighting for thirteen days."[78]

While the Alamo garrison remained unvigilant in the early morning hours of March 6, Santa Anna was up early. He was busy, just like Napoleon in his prime, especially the night before Austerlitz when the French emperor had walked among the troops to inspire his soldiery. And like Napoleon, who wore a green tunic covered by a grey overcoat in Russia, he very likely now wore his trademark campaign coat—a green frock coat—to ward off the cold. Confidently, as if knowing the defenders could be swiftly overwhelmed on this chilly morning, Santa Anna had already boasted that he would "take his breakfast" in a fallen Alamo, once Mexican regimental and battalion battle flags and the national tricolor were flying proudly from its walls, after every man inside the compound had been put to death.[79]

Thanks to a well-conceived battle plan, meeting this tactical objective would be relatively easy, even if the garrison were not caught by surprise by the sudden attack out of the early morning blackness. Not only was the Alamo manned by far too few soldiers, but they lacked training, discipline, and munitions for a solid defense, even if everyone was ready, waiting, and in position for the attack. Because the Texas government had focused on buying tons of supplies, such as weaponry and munitions, for the future Regular Army of Texas, the Alamo volunteers—the revolution's stepchildren—continued to go without almost everything. While warm uniforms, shoes, and blankets were stockpiled, and new muskets were stacked in neat rows to fill storehouses for future regular troops, the Alamo's volunteers continued to lack proper clothing and went hungry, while wondering why both the Texas government and Texas people had abandoned them like sacrificial lambs.[80]

Finally, like a chess player, Santa Anna made his first move. Four columns of well-prepared Mexican troops moved stealthily forward over the bare landscape around 1:00 a.m. toward their assigned positions on the prairie, as designated by the commander-in-chief. With as little noise as possible, grim-faced soldados pushed quietly forward into the night, easing ever closer to the eerily silent walls of the Alamo now shrouded in darkness. An anonymous Mexican soldier of General Cós' column that had slipped unnoticed across the flat ground and toward the west wall, wrote how: "After a roundabout approach we stopped at 3:00 A.M. on the [west] side, about 300 paces" from the Alamo.[81]

Incredibly, in the cold blackness of the open prairie, 1,400 Mexican troops now lay down in attack positions on the open ground within easy striking distance of the Alamo—after some minor obstacles had been quietly removed—without detection. Here, they awaited the inevitable signal to charge forward. Especially out in the open, this winter night was cold and windy. Rolling, dark clouds hid the moonlight, but provided sufficient light for soldados to make necessary final preparations for the attack. The younger men, especially those with relatively little battle experience, tried to stay awake in the cold and remained more nervous than the hardened veterans in the ranks. Gusting prairie winds gently rustled the nearby clumps of grass in the pale moonlight. A Godsend, the winds had masked the relatively little noise rising from the advancing columns.[82]

Santa Anna had developed a plan to minimize his losses because he knew that his late winter Texas campaign had only barely begun. Envisioning a vigorous spring campaign, he was now planning to drive the Anglo-Celts and their heretical civilization all the way to the Sabine River and out of Texas before the spring rains descended upon the land. Like a good student of Napoleonic history, Santa Anna had learned of Napoleon's abundant mistakes in 1812 in marching across the steppes of Russia on the road to Moscow. Despite the summer season, Russian rains had played a role in slowing the advance, spreading sickness, and wearing out both men and horses. Santa Anna therefore demonstrated considerable wisdom in deciding not to invade Texas too late in the year, so as not to be slowed by spring rains. This decision also ensured that if the war against Texas developed into a lengthy conflict, or even a war of attrition, the Mexican troops would not face the worst winter weather in late 1836. Delaying too long in a foreign land, hundreds of miles from support systems, was a classic error that had led to Napoleon's defeat. In fact, some Anglo-Celtic soldiers in Texas now believed that the key to victory lay in utilizing the Russians' 1812 strategy, luring Santa Anna deeper into Texas.

While the Alamo's defenders rested blissfully in their first undisturbed sleep since the siege's beginning, dark masses of carefully chosen Mexican troops made final preparations to attack. In the cold darkness only "a short distance from the first trenches," the Mexican's dark blue uniforms helped them blend into the winter blackness that covered the silent prairie like a shroud. Demonstrating excellent discipline, hundreds of Mexican soldiers remained absolutely quiet amid the biting cold and breezes that cut to the bone in the damp air, while patiently awaiting the attack signal.

On the open prairie, no shelter existed for Santa Anna's troops from the harsh winter winds sweeping down the open river valley. Not a warming fire or even a pipe could be lit. The soldados suffered and shivered in disciplined silence, while embracing a grim fatalism that was a distinctive characteristic of the Mexican peasant—both Indian and Mestizo—who had been exploited for so long by autocratic military, church, and political leaders. Ensuring that they would be ready for the signal to attack, these foremost troops now possessed no blankets to ward off the biting cold, more frigid than anything they had felt in Mexico. The thin wool uniforms—made for summer campaigns in Mexico's heat and humidity—offered only meager protection from winter's harsh breath on this near-freezing night, though Santa Anna had taken the wise precaution to ensure that all assault troops now wore "shoes or sandals." Along with their Catholic God, ancient Mayan Gods, or Lady of Guadalupe, these young men from all parts of Mexico had placed their trust in their aristocratic commander and his tactical wisdom: a faith that would not be betrayed on March 6. But more important, Santa Anna had his young soldados highly motivated and ready for action. They now tightly gripped their heavy Brown Bess muskets—known as the *morena licha*—as Santa Anna had ordered, "All armaments [to be] in good shape—especially the bayonets."[83]

Meanwhile, the young men from Missouri, Tennessee, and Pennsylvania probably wished that they were far from the Alamo deathtrap and safe in their homes far away from San Antonio. While the Mexican soldados froze in the late winter night, garrison members slept in utter exhaustion. No longer deluded by unrealistic visions of reaping glory against Santa Anna's troops, these naive amateurs of war slept. It was almost as if the Alamo had become a warm, soothing place—or so it seemed—for garrison members, with sleeping quarters providing them shelter from both Santa Anna's wrath and the bitter cold. All of their previous dreams and ambitions of getting rich from suddenly gaining thousands of acres of Texas land and becoming wealthy gentlemen planters, owning gangs of slaves, and pursuing lucrative careers were no longer important to the men at the Alamo.

Thanks to the Army of Operation's arrival, their lives had been suddenly pushed to the edge of oblivion, mocking youthful ambitions of profiting by the quickest means. Indeed, this shortcut to acquiring land had meant that far greater risks had to be taken, and with stakes much higher than they had originally imagined. Like a wild gambler, so the Alamo's soldiers had gambled everything on one throw of the dice, just as Santa Anna had gambled on cornering them in the old Spanish mission and catching them by surprise

With sleep the top priority, both vigilance and defensive preparations were at an all-time low among the garrison this early morning. Therefore the muskets, Long Rifles, and other weapons and accouterments were either stacked in corners or by their owner's side. Except for several pickets stationed outside the walls in the trenches, seemingly everyone in the Alamo was asleep by the early hours of March 6. For the garrison members it would be their very last, as they were now on the verge of meeting their Maker. Travis made his final rounds of the silent, seemingly empty Spanish mission-turned-fort. He must have been relieved that the incessant artillery bombardment had halted the previous afternoon. But neither Travis nor his men—alike novices to the ways of conventional warfare—suspected that Santa Anna's clever stratagem of an orchestrated silence was actually the lull before the storm.

Hour after hour in the cold darkness, not a single garrison member detected any unusual activity or indications of an impending Mexican assault. The handful of ragtag pickets stationed outside the Alamo was also oblivious to what was happening around them. Now situated in the low-lying, cold trenches amid the slight valley of the San Antonio River, they lacked a good vantage point to not only see anything before them, but also to hear what was happening on the surrounding prairie. But just as important as the lack of vigilance among the defenders was the fact that the Mexican troops continued to display an iron discipline, keeping perfectly quiet hour after hour out in the open.

Meanwhile, seasoned Mexican officers moved silently down the lengthy assault formations poised in the silent prairie, preparing their men for the attack one last time. The upcoming attack before dawn posed a stiff challenge for these soldados. Nothing proved more difficult than unleashing a tactical offensive at nighttime with little—if any—visibility, as on this cloudy, winter night.

To maximize chances for success, Santa Anna had already made a number of well-calculated decisions: excluding recruits and selecting only his best troops from the Matamoros, San Luis Potosi, Jiménez, Toluca, Zapadores, and Aldama Battalions, and including a tactical reserve of crack troopsfor the attack. Each of these battle-ready battalions possessed six fusilier companies that served as the army's "solid backbone," and a company of cazadores, or light infantry, who were the army's best riflemen. All of these seasoned soldados now wore shoes or sandals so that they would utter no sound during the final sprint across the prairie. After all, advancing soldiers stepping on cactus, rocks, or on each other's feet would raise yelps of pain that might alert the garrison. Ladders had been distributed among the assault units of each column, instead of making the mistake of assigning a single unit with that important responsibility, which had played a role in sabotaging the British assault on Jackson's line at the battle of New Orleans.

Commanded by officers—both junior and senior—from upper-class Creole families, the best trained and drilled troops about to be unleashed were the permanentes, or the regulars, around which this largely conscript army had been created. However even the raw recruit, or the lowly peasant, was a tough, hardy fighting man, only too familiar with sacrifice, hardship, and suffering. And as in the past, these soldados were guaranteed to fight even harder than usual because they now faced invaders of a different race, culture, and religion on their own soil.

As the young men from Mexico continued to shiver from the biting cold of the open prairie, final orders from the officers to prepare for Santa Anna's signal to begin the attack made some soldados more apprehensive, yet all the while they continued to remain perfectly silently in neat formations from 3:00 a.m. to almost 5:00 a.m. Sneezes and coughs were muffled as much as possible by shirt and uniform coat sleeves in the biting cold of early morning.

Despite that the men were cold and with blistered feet from the rapid march north, with some soldados in various stages of sickness, Mexico's highly motivated fighting men maintained their composure. Knowing the importance of his troops reaching the Alamo's walls as quickly as possible, Santa Anna had ordered them not to wear either "overcoats or blankets, nor anything that may impede the rapidity of their motions." This was an adroit decision, which the British, despite being seasoned veterans of the Peninsular War, had failed to make at the battle of New Orleans, slowing their assault across the cold, January plain of Chalmette.

Troops of five companies of crack Mexican Grenadiers were yet dressed in summer uniforms of white cotton. Santa Anna had placed these men in reserve. Not a single Mexican had been detected by lookouts atop the roofs of the buildings, especially the Long Barracks. But more significant to facilitate Santa Anna's tactical plan were the winter winds, which blew away from the Alamo, masking the slightest sounds emitting from deployed soldiers ready to sprint forward upon cue. Seemingly, even nature herself had conspired against the Alamo garrison at this time.[84]

Equally prepared for the upcoming fight were General Sesma's cavalrymen and lancers, the finest soldiers of Santa Anna's Army. As quietly as possible, these troopers had saddled-up their horses around 3:00 a.m. With the veil of darkness concealing their movements and the wind blanketing their sounds, hundreds of Mexican cavalrymen rode slowly into the night to take up their new assigned positions. The horsemen began to fall into formation under and around the cottonwoods trees of the "Alameda." As directed by Santa Anna, General Sesma established his cavalry headquarters in the saddle. Here, southeast of the Alamo on elevated ground near Gonzales Road, he was in a good position to maneuver his cavalrymen once the sun rose.

Commanding the 280-man Permanente Regiment of the Dolores Cavalry, General Don Ventura Mora carefully aligned a section of Sesma's cavalry in the thick cover that bordered the river. Meanwhile, at the Alameda proper, Sesma deployed most of his horse soldiers in a lengthy line in the blackness. It was now the horse soldiers' mission, especially those of the elite lancers of the Dolores Cavalry regiment, "to prevent the possibility of an escape" from the Alamo.

Clearly, as Santa Anna envisioned, the most likely target of any escapees would be the Gonzales Road that led east to safety. Here, in Sergeant Manuel Lorcana's words, "a squadron of Lancers [of the Vera Cruz regiment], flanked by a ditch [the irrigation ditch that ran south, passing behind the church and leading to the Gonzales Road just below the west end of the Alameda], to cut off the retreat at the time of the assault." Sesma and his troopers knew that Santa Anna wanted no survivors. By making such well-placed cavalry deployments, Santa Anna revealed that he knew his opponents quite well, fully anticipating escape attempts from the indefensible Spanish mission, which was bound to be overwhelmed swiftly if everything went according to plan.[85]

And if any troops of Santa Anna's Army could fulfill the generalissimo's desire for no survivors, it was Sesma's veteran cavalrymen. These crack horsemen were well trained, highly disciplined, and natural killers, mirroring the qualities of their hard-bitten commander. Sesma and his cavalry division, especially the Vera Cruz Lancers, had been Santa Anna's iron fist in the Zacatecas victory, when they had eased around the militiamen's right flank and attacked an unwary opponent from the rear. This tactical envelopment led to the easy rout of hundreds of Zacatecas militiamen and their systematic slaughter. Above all, these Vera Cruz horsemen who took position near the Gonzales Road were proud of their favorite tool of destruction, the lance.[86]

Indeed, Santa Anna's cavalrymen, now mounted on relatively fresh horses requisitioned on the push north, could ride down a rabbit, deer, or man with relative ease, especially on the open prairie. Not even the finest Anglo-Celtic horseman in Texas could compare to an experienced Mexican or Tejano on horseback. Therefore, the worst nightmare for an Alamo garrison member would be to get caught out on the open prairie by Mexican horse soldiers—especially the elite lancers with their murderous weapons of death.

During the early morning hours of March 6, among the most vigilant Mexican soldiers were those who now stood beside a Congreve rocket battery that had been erected on the night of March 4, within musket range of the Alamo's north wall. But in keeping with Santa Anna's orders, alert Mexican artillerymen of the north battery would receive no orders this early morning to open fire from their commander-in-chief. To maximize surprise and to catch the slumbering garrison completely by surprise, Santa Anna wanted no artillery bombardment, as was customary, before a general attack.

But unlike the idle Mexican cannoneers who remained motionless in the darkness, the anxious rocket battery men awaited Santa Anna's word to fire a rocket to signal the attack. After all, Santa Anna wanted no bugle calls to echo through the night that would alert the Alamo garrison to the assault. The rocket, about to be fired in Texas for the first time in history, was now a Mexican secret weapon, even though they had been in use for sometime. (Not only were rockets used in the Napoleonic Wars, but also during the War of 1812 where they were immortalized in the words of America's national anthem: "By the rockets' red glare.")

All the while, Santa Anna, who received an adrenaline rush from battle, could hardly wait to unleash his multipronged assault calculated to strike each side of the Alamo compound at once. He wrote: "I took pride in being the first to strike in defense of independence, honor, and rights of my nation."[87]

While an enthusiastic Santa Anna embraced the battle cry of "On to the Alamo," the more practical common soldiers, mostly peasants in the ranks, like Felix Nunez, interpreted it in an entirely different light: "On to the Alamo was on to death." Thanks to officer's vigilance not to be observed, the moonlight shined off no earrings, rings or "other types of feminine ornaments that lowered the military profession" among the common soldiers in the silent, motionless ranks.[88]

One pureblood Aztec, who might have desired to wear such "ornaments," in the Army of Operations was Felix Rodriguez. Ironically, he would die in San Antonio not during the Texas Campaign, but in the early 20th century.[89]

At this time, the emotional and psychological symbolism and mystique of the legendary ancient Aztec warrior was yet alive and well in Santa Anna's ranks, serving as a powerful motivator. This was the legacy of the proud Anáhuacense soldier. Long before the Spanish Conquistadors arrived, Mexico was the "country of Anáhuac." One Mexican leader promised his troops vengeance upon the "horde of adventurers" who awaited a dismal fate at the hands of "the thousands of soldiers [of Mexico who] will make them bit[e] the dust. The foolish ones which in their delirium have provoke[d] the courage and mettle of the ANÁHUACENSE soldier." Therefore, future Mexican conquests in Texas, including at the Alamo, would be widely viewed as the "Eagle of Anáhuac hav[ing] extended its wings." Reaping a victory at the Alamo promised these fighting men the widespread reputation as the "Saviors of the Fatherland."[90]

Ironically, racial pride in the Indian past existed on both sides of the Alamo's walls. Father and son Gregorio and Enrique Esparza, of San Antonio, were equally proud of their own Indian heritage. Enrique explained how: "Many of my people are of mixed blood. I am of Indian and Spanish blood [and] We are proud of that ancestry."[91]

In time and after wiping out the Alamo garrison, Santa Anna himself would be viewed across Mexico as the invincible "father of Anáhuac," a title which appeared in the April 30, 1836 issue of Mexico City's *La Lima de Vulcano*.[92]

But not all Indians of Santa Anna's Army occupied the lowest ranks. Santa Anna's trusty aide-de-camp, Colonel Juan Almonte, was half Tlaxcala Indian. In a strange paradox, Santa Anna's Army of Operations consisted of a multiethnic and multicultural fighting force much like the Alamo garrison.[93]

Most important for the upcoming clash of arms, Santa Anna's four assault columns contained a good many reliable veterans, in both his Creole-dominated officer corps and in the enlisted ranks of peasant soldiery. These ranks had been culled in this increasingly brutal civil war, waged since 1832, leaving a hardened cadre of both officers and enlisted men of permanente and activo units alike. More so than the militia commands, the regular army units retained a large measure of pride, while embracing a stronger sense of national identity and nationalism. Some of Santa Anna's top lieutenants had even helped to defeat Napoleon's forces in Spain, waging both conventional and guerrilla war. Part of a fraternity, Santa Anna had served with many of these privileged Creoles of the upper class, such as Colonel José Juan Sánchez Navarro, as junior officers in the Royal Spanish Army and as a military school classmate before fighting together against the Spanish to help win Mexico's independence.

Second in command of Colonel Morales' column assigned to attacking the south wall was Colonel José Vicente Miñon, who had been born in the port city of Cadiz, Spain, in 1802. Miñon was already famous throughout the army for past battlefield exploits that defied the odds, especially in holding 400 Spanish soldiers at bay with only 30 men at the battle of Arroyo Hondo during the struggle for independence. Miñon also knew how to wage war unconventionally, battling for years against Indians, including the fast-moving Comanche. And he had played a key role in smashing the Zacatecas militiamen, where he had bloodied his saber on fellow countrymen who dared defy the republic. Commanding a force of handpicked mounted marksmen, Miñon led a cavalry charge that captured nearly fifty cannons at Zacatecas. Even though a member of Santa Anna's staff while serving as the commander's adjutant, he was eager for front line duty, lusting for action against Texas rebels.

Not surprisingly, he had been at the head of the initial company of Matamoros Battalion cazadores—the Spanish name for hunters or light infantry and riflemen—who stormed into San Antonio and chased Bowie's and Travis' men into the Alamo. Miñon's demonstrated initiative on February 23 caused an impressed Colonel Morales, who believed that this was the "most righteous of campaigns," to request his leadership as second-in-command for this attack column of chasseurs— the French name for hunters, or light infantry and riflemen—of the San Luís Potosí Activo Battalion.[94]

In addition to experienced officers like Miñon, a good many reliable, veteran soldados of the noncommissioned ranks were now posed before the Alamo. For instance, one of Santa Anna's trusted noncommissioned officers—who had drilled and molded their peasants into disciplined soldados—was Sergeant Santiago Rabia. Having served beside then lieutenant Santa Anna in Texas in 1813, Rabia's lost religious fervor was now rekindled in the cold darkness near the Alameda. As a member of the elite Tampico Lancers, he would shortly lose what little compassion remained in his heart for his fellow man, because these tough Mexican lancers would shortly perform the bloodiest work of any of Santa Anna's soldiers on the morning of March 6.[95]

Also among Santa Anna's infantry were soldados of pure African descent. Known as pardos, or Mexicans of African heritage, they would have been called mulattos in the United States. Continuing a distinguished legacy, blacks had fought in Mexico's war for independence against Spain as both officers and enlisted men, and even before then as well. For instance, during the American Revolution when Spain was allied with France and America against England, the Spanish Army included an African American militia company of free blacks, the Moreno Libres of Vera Cruz, and a battalion of blacks from Havana, Cuba, which served in North America.[96]

With Mexico's best military commander at their head, these soldados were supremely confident of success this early morning. Esprit de corps and a sense of righteousness had lifted motivation among the Mexican troops to new heights. The average American soldier, not to mention their Protestant religion and English and Irish cultural traditions, were held in utter contempt by Mexicans in part because of racial, cultural, and religious prejudices that were returned in kind. For instance, Secretary of War Tornel boasted how, "The superiority of the Mexican soldier" could not compare to the American citizen-soldiers, who were "ignorant of the art of war, incapable of discipline, and renowned for insubordination."[97]

However, in truth, Santa Anna's soldados now suffered from an inferiority complex of sorts. After Cós and his men had been humiliated and sent back to Mexico in disgrace, the early morning would finally present a long awaited opportunity to prove the falsehood of the Anglo-Celtic stereotype about the alleged inferiority of the Latino fighting man. A proud Sapper officer, De la Pena was incensed over the fiction that Mexican soldados "lacked the cool courage that is demanded by an assault." In a February 17 address to his troops, even Santa Anna mocked the overconfident Texians, because they considered "us incapable of defending our soil."[98]

Meanwhile, Travis and his men, including the pickets outside the Alamo, slept deeply in the darkness. These advanced pickets had been more concerned about staying warm and resting than anything else on this cold night. Within the relatively warm, thick abode walls, no one heard any noise from nearly 1,500 Mexican soldados almost within a stone's throw of the walls. Even more surprising, no one heard the hundreds of Mexican cavalrymen and lancers, or their horses.[99]

Compared to the handful of untrained regulars at the Alamo, a large percentage—a little less than half—of Santa Anna's Army consisted of regular units or permanentes. These regular infantry regiments were organized in 1833. Therefore, by the 1836 Texas Campaign, Santa Anna benefited from the fact that much of his army consisted of trained regular troops: a striking contrast to the mostly volunteer Alamo garrison. These regular troops were augmented by militia units, or activos: the Toluca, Tres Villa, San Luís Potosí, and Guadalajara Battalions. Of these, the Toluca Battalion, Colonel Dúque's own unit that he had long commanded, was the best activo command. However, neither the Mexican regular infantry nor militia could compare to Santa Anna's best, nonspecialized troops, the half dozen regular cavalry regiments. The savvy general, always an old cavalryman at heart, could count upon these horse commands without hesitation: the Vera Cruz, Dolores, Palmar, Iguala, Cuatla, and Tampico cavalry regiments. These units were not only the pride of Santa Anna and his army, but also of the Republic of Mexico.[100]

Santa Anna was eager to see what these fighting men of his 1836 Army of Operations—which had not yet fought a battle—could accomplish on the chilly early morning of March 6. As revealed in his February 1 report, for instance, a proud Santa Anna boasted with unbridled enthusiasm that "it has been years that I have not seen in the Republic a body of troops that are so brilliant in their discipline and equipment" as his newly formed Army of Operations.[101]

An 1886 depiction of the mythical storming of the Alamo. In this drawing
the Alamo church is the focal point of the battle and distinguished by its
trademark bell-shaped facade, built by the United States nearly a
decade and a half later.

An admirer of Napoleon, Antonio López de Santa Anna lamented the overall lack of resistance on March 6, describing the Alamo's capture as nothing more than a "small affair." *Daughters of the Republic of Texas Library at the Alamo*

An Italian with Napoleonic War experience, General Vincente Filisola was one of Santa Anna's most gifted top lieutenants. He possessed more sound military experience than all of the Alamo's commanders combined. *Amon Carter Museum, Fort Worth, Texas*

A member of the
Republic of Mexico's
most lethal warriors,
the Lancers, who
upheld their lofty rep-
utation outside the
walls of the Alamo on
the morning of
March 6. *Amon Carter
Museum, Fort Worth,
Texas*

Along with the Lancers,
the Mexican Dragoons also
played a leading role in
eliminating escapees from
the Alamo. *Amon Carter
Museum, Fort Worth, Texas*

This rare woodcut was the earliest depiction of the battle of the Alamo, though it more closely resembles a battle between French and English forces during the Peninsular War in Spain. *Author's collection*

The Alamo's largest cannon, the 18-pounder that stood at the compound's southwest corner. *Daughters of the Republic of Texas, the Alamo Museum, San Antonio*

Tejano Enrique Esparza who was the son of Alamo defender Gregorio Esparza. Enrique left vivid personal accounts of the battle for the Alamo, but these have been too often ignored. *Texas State Library and Archives Commission*

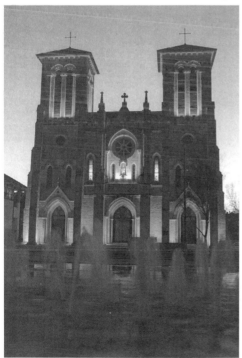

Santa Anna's flag of no quarter was raised from the bell tower of San Fernando Church, proclaiming that the Alamo garrison would be killed to the last man. *Photo by Jim Landers, courtesy of the City Centre Foundation, San Fernando Cathedral, and Executive Director Amelia Nieto-Duval*

Oil painting based on an image from the movie set of John Wayne's 1960 Alamo movie. *Author's collection*

A view of the Alamo from the rear, by the artist James Gilchrist Benton. The palisade had previously stood where the man in the sombrero is standing, connecting the church with the fort's south wall. Note the makeshift log footbridge spanning the irrigation canal in the foreground. *Amon Carter Museum, Fort Worth Texas*

Battle flag of the Permanente Matamoros Battalion which was part of Romero's assault column on March 6. This fine silk banner was captured at San Jacinto, where fortune no longer smiled upon Santa Anna.
Texas State Library and Archives Commission, Austin, Texas

William Barret Travis's ring. Toward the end of the 13-day siege, Travis removed this ring from his finger, placed it on a string, and hung it around the neck of Angelina Dickinson, the 15-month-old daughter of Captain Dickinson and his wife Susanna. Angelina became famous as the "Babe of the Alamo." The ring was donated to the Alamo Museum in 1955.

A depiction of the fighting outside the Alamo when fugitives from the fort encountered Santa Anna's cavalry, by the artist Gary Zaboly.
Author's collection

An early 20th-century view of the rear of the Alamo church.
Author's collection

An 1849 sketch of the crumbling, forgotten Alamo church by Edward Everett, before it was transformed into a shrine.

The initial goal of so many escapees, the western end of the Alameda, shown here in Herman Lungkwitz's 1857 painting, near where a large percentage of the Alamo garrison was killed. *San Antonio Public Library*

A depiction of the death of Lieutenant José María Torres, who was killed while attempting to take down the Alamo garrison's flag atop the Long Barracks. *Illustration by Ted Spring, courtesy Tim J. and Terry Todish*

A modern depiction of the first large flight of escapees from the Alamo, by the artist Gary Zaboly. These men have slipped through the sally port on the left of the stockade and crossed the irrigation ditch, only to meet Santa Anna's cavalry which had been positioned to intercept fugitives. Note the covering fire provided by Captain Dickinson's artillerymen atop the church. *Author's collection*

6

The Predawn Assault

In the hours before dawn on March 6, 1836, Santa Anna's men had little time for thinking about the future welfare of their lovers, wives, and children who remained with the army. Instead, shivering in the cold and contemplating their own fates, they had enough to worry about what would happen to them in the next hour or so. Since they had been ordered to rely upon "principally the bayonet," these soldados, especially the veterans, knew what lay in store. Tormented by their thoughts, Santa Anna's men more heavily weighed the legendary marksmanship of the Anglo-Celts, whose reputation in handling the Long Rifle had preceded them.

In the crack Zapadores Battalion, for instance, an uneasy Lieutenant Colonel de la Pena decided not to wear a white hat which might identify him as an officer, making him a target in the upcoming attack. An increasingly nervous de la Pena advised his friend, Lieutenant María Heredia, to do the same, because he believed "he and I would die" in the attack if such precautions were not taken. But the young lieutenant merely "laughed good-naturedly" and ignored the advice. In a fine dress uniform with shiny eagle buttons, the young lieutenant continued to wear his white hat: a decision he would soon come to regret.[1]

Eager to reaffirm his reputation as the "Napoleon of the West," and like the manic French emperor whose instincts had served him well until the brutal guerrilla war in Spain and the disastrous Russian invasion, Santa Anna's impatience and aggressive instincts had in fact gotten the better of him. Savvy veterans in the ranks, including leading officers, believed that an assault was unnecessary. For example, de la Pena lamented how "In fact, it was only necessary to wait the artillery's

201

arrival at Béxar for these [Alamo men] to surrender."[2]

Sensing that his own "Sun of Austerliz" was about to rise, Santa Anna now prepared to give the long-awaited order to attack at around 5:30 a.m., thereby avenging General Cós' December loss of San Antonio and redeeming the republic's honor in its first major blow to regain Texas.[3]

At the Mexicans' north battery, which stood "within musket range" of the Alamo's north wall, Santa Anna ordered a five-foot-long Congreve rocket to be fired into the black sky for all to see, except, of course, the sleeping Alamo garrison. The red and yellow rocket soared high into the black sky as a quiet signal to begin the assault. The black powder had been removed from the rocket so that the exploding charge would not alert the garrison.[4]

All the while, Alamo garrison members like Captain Carey and his "Invincibles" continued to sleep deeply on this cold night, unaware that all hell was about to break loose. In a lengthy letter written to his brother and sister, and as if possessing a portent of his own death, Carey had promised "that if I live, as soon as the war is over I will endeavor to see you all" once again.[5]

Perhaps no one in Santa Anna's army was now more motivated to redeem his reputation and honor today than young General Cós. And as Santa Anna's brother-in-law who was defeated in this same place only a few months before, he had much to prove both to himself and others. In his own February 1, 1836, words, he was "ready to vindicate myself [and restore] my vacillating reputation" for having lost San Antonio and the Alamo in the first place. To wash away that humiliation, Cós had been ordered to target the west wall as his column's objective. As a bachelor and unlike so many others in his assault column, General Cós had no concern about leaving a wife as a widow or children as orphans if killed this early morning. Amid the prone formation of Cós' troops, consisting of the three companies of the San Luís Potosí Activo Battalion and the 280-man Aldama Permanente Battalion, commanded by Lieutenant Colonel Gregorio Uruñuela, one soldado wrote of the dramatic moment when around 5:30 a.m. a rocket shot up through the air and suddenly "Cós yelled—on your feet! And placing himself at the head of the forces, we ran to the assault[;] the distance [to the Alamo] was short."[6]

In all four assault columns, scores of promising young officers in resplendent uniforms and from leading Creole families repeated the order to attack. In the early morning darkness, the Mexican ranks surged forward over the grassy prairie, covered in a low-lying mist, with discipline and determination. Composed of around 300 troops of the Matamoros Permanente and Jiménez Battalions, under Colonel Mariano Salas, Romero's column closed in on the east wall, while Dúque's column, consisting of around 400 soldados of the three "rifle" companies of the San Luís Potosí Battalion and all of the "Active" and the Toluca Battalions, advanced toward the north wall. Meanwhile, Morales' column, the little more than 100 cazadores of the Jimenez, Matamoros, and San Luís Potosí Activo Battalions, headed toward the low, wooden palisade along the south wall and their ultimate objective, the main gate. Every side of the Alamo was being attacked at once.

As they hurled themselves toward the undisturbed Alamo that lay silhouetted against the distant black skyline, the onrushing soldados felt confidence in the righteousness of their cause and numerical superiority. Providing solace and a certain peace of mind at this moment, the omnipresent spiritual presence of Lady of Guadalupe inspired the Mexican troops onward, providing inspiration to both officers of Castillian descent and pure-blood Indians to drive the interlopers from Mexico's sacred soil.

In the predawn darkness, the handful of Travis' soldiers posted outside the Alamo as pickets and sentries to give first warning of an attack never knew what hit them. Like a "blue norther," the sudden descent of the foremost Mexican light troops, or skirmishers, came swiftly out of the darkness. Death would come as quickly as unexpectedly for the pickets. Alamo garrison members were about to learn the hard way how Santa Anna's surprise attack that annihilated the Zacatacas militia had been launched in the night to catch opposing pickets asleep. Wrapped in thin blankets for warmth against the cold ground and winds sweeping over the prairie from west to east, the pickets remained perfectly still in the narrow confines of their trenches. Discipline at the Alamo had always been loose and these men simply lacked the training, experience, and discipline to obey orders to stay vigilant. Consequently, they continued to doze in a sleep from which they never awoke.

Death came quickly. With skirmishers descending upon them like ghosts in the night, they were easily overwhelmed and quickly dispatched by the first wave of fast-moving Mexicans skirmishers, who knew how to silently eliminate advanced sentries, especially when asleep, before they gave warning. No one knows if these pickets

attempted to sound an alarm before they met their Maker in the blackness that surrounded them. In part employing racial stereotypes that so
often demeaned the Mexican character, one popular author speculated
how a swift end came for those men stationed outside the Alamo's
walls: "One by one, it is known as certainly as if it was recorded, they
were dealt with by Mexican scouts crawling up on them in the dark. A
knife in the right spot and a hand on the throat to deny the sleeper even
the bark of death, and it was all over. None of them lived to give a peep
of warning."[7]

This popular version of the first Alamo deaths was almost certainly
not the case, however. After so carefully orchestrating the attack to
exploit the element of surprise, Santa Anna would not have risked that
coveted tactical advantage by overwhelming the pickets with only a few
scouts, needlessly running the risk that someone might fire a weapon to
alert the sleeping Alamo garrison.

But these pickets and sentries, their number unknown, were most
likely either bayoneted by enlisted men or sabered by officers from a
heavy line of skirmishers, who were especially proficient at bayonet
work. Clearly, these most advanced Mexican soldiers maintained excellent discipline in not only holding their fire but also in so quickly dis-
patching these advanced pickets, as directed by their officers. No one
knows the names of those first few men who died outside of the Alamo,
but they were probably all asleep and huddled together for body
warmth when their lives had ended so suddenly.

In a letter written not long after the Alamo's fall, E.M. Pease
described the ominous tactical development resulting from the complete
failure of the Alamo's advance warning: "It was supposed that our sentinels worn out with fatigue had fallen asleep & were killed at their
posts. [Before the sounding of] the first alarm within the fort, they were
on and within the Walls in large numbers . . . "[8]

Indeed, the lack of discipline of the Alamo's defenders outside the
walls now came to haunt the garrison, which remained unaware of
developments outside the walls at the most inopportune time. More
conscientious officers, who possessed ample experience with night duty,
were now fast asleep in the cozy warmth behind the closed doors of the
various rooms of the compound—especially the Long Barracks for the
enlisted men, a separate building for officers, and an artillery barracks—along the eastern perimeter. Clearly, from Travis, who was fast
asleep in his own quarters, to the pickets outside the Alamo, no one had

expected Santa Anna to attack at night.[9]

So far, Santa Anna's plan to catch the garrison by surprise was working to perfection. According to the traditional version of the Alamo's story, everything up to this point was going exactly as designed until some over-enthusiastic Mexican soldiers began shouting, or so claimed Santa Anna, who was a master at shifting blame. But the notoriously self-serving general had only employed this long-accepted explanation as a convenient excuse for what was considered an unnecessary assault when under increasing criticism from his countrymen for his San Jacinto defeat. Writing a largely fictional battle-report, Santa Anna explained how the Mexican troops "moved forward in the best order and with the greatest silence, but the imprudent huzzas of one of them awakened the sleeping vilgilance [sic] of the defenders of the fort [resulting in a] loss that was also later judged to be avoidable and charged, after the disaster of San Jacinto, to my incompetence and precipitation."[10]

However, if some ill-timed outbursts of shouts among the Mexican troops occurred, it was not widespread—and hence not sufficient to alert the sleeping garrison—and only occurred later after the first soldados reached the walls. Experienced Mexican officers made sure that silence was maintained while their troops rushed forward. With an anti-Santa Anna agenda, the ever-biased de la Pena described that a combination of wild shouting, the blaring of music from regimental bands, and the sounding of trumpets, and even premature volleys—allegedly fired at targets unseen—erupted simultaneously to alert the garrison, but this simply could not have been the case: Santa Anna would not have issued such orders to defeat his own plan for achieving complete surprise and to ensure that his troops would reach the walls before resistance was organized. De la Pena only used these examples to attempt to demonstrate Santa Anna's incompetence.

In truth, virtually all garrison members were still asleep when the first Mexicans reached the walls. This development meant that the foremost attackers, who were leading the way for Colonel Dúque's column pushing toward the north wall from the northwest, the skirmishers of the activo Toluca Battalion, initially met with no return fire during most of their dash to the wall. Moving rapidly forward in two lengthy lines, these skirmishers easily gained the north wall's base before any fire opened upon them. One dependable company commander of the light infantry skirmishers was young Captain José M. Herrera. He led his cazadores (the Spanish word for chassuers) to the north wall, reaching a position under the silent guns of the north battery draped in darkness and silence.

Behind these swiftly advancing twin lines of skirmishers that had gained the wall's base, the remainder of Dúque's troops continued to push forward. Through the darkness, these attackers headed toward the north wall's center, moving forward in column as fast as they could. The north wall, with its crumbling stone and abode bolstered by a timber and earth outwork, was the weakest link in the defensive perimeter, after the palisade. Consisting mostly of the activo Toluca Battalion, of around 365 men at top strength, Dúque's column was not yet encountering any fire from the north wall during its sprint forward. The unmanned cannons at the wall remained perfectly silent. Pushing forward from the east, Romero's column likewise met no initial fire in surging toward the Alamo from the rear, or east, revealing the extent of the total surprise. To the onrushing Mexican troops, the absence of defenders' fire seemed like a miracle, a special gift from a soldado-loving God and a special protective favor from the Lady of Guadalupe.[11]

After moving quickly over the open ground, unencumbered by knapsacks or accouterments, the skirmishers of the activo Toluca Battalion sighed breaths of relief after gaining the north wall in the pitch-blackness. Clearly, they had been fortunate in achieving a remarkable tactical success in gaining the north wall's base so quickly, reaping the benefits of Santa Anna's tactical plan. Catching their breath, these skirmishers now waited at the base of the wall for the arrival of Dúque's attack column that would shortly emerge out of the darkness. Meanwhile, selected soldiers of Dúque's column carried ten ladders forward for the scaling of the wall.

Joining its skirmishers, Dúque's column also reached the wall without taking fire. Here, they hurriedly began to set up their wooden ladders to scale the earth and timber outer work. Not only the dash across the open prairie but the placement of ladders against the north wall was a race against time, and Santa Anna's men won it. As planned, the Alamo's most vulnerable wall was now on the verge of being breached without the attackers having yet encountered any resistance.

With the advanced pickets wiped out so noiselessly, only one member of the entire garrison was now capable of performing the Alamo's most important mission at this critical moment. Thirty-five-year-old Captain John Joseph Baugh, the commander of the remaining handful of New Orleans Greys, had stayed in San Antonio after the departure of Captain William Gordon Cooke, the Fredericksburg druggist. Having arrived in Texas with the Greys as a lieutenant, he now served not only as the Alamo's dependable adjutant, but also second in command—both jobs in which he excelled. Although, like his commander, an aspiring gentleman planter of lofty ambitions, the capable Virginian did not get along with Travis. Like other volunteers, especially those feisty, independent-minded types from the crack New Orleans Greys, Captain Baugh had early clashed with Travis largely because the Alamo's commander was a regular officer. The young Virginian Baugh was now the sole representative of the late morning watch, after the relief of the late night and early morning watch. This earlier shift of bone-weary men had gone off duty sometime just before 3:00 a.m. when Travis, after he made his usual rounds, retired for the night, exhausted from supervising more shoring-up of the battered north wall.

Evidently stationed in an observatory position atop the roof of the high, two-storied Long Barracks, where some light, make-shift defenses had been constructed, Baugh was not at a good vantage point—too far from the north wall where the main attack would be directed—to serve as the Alamo's main lookout at this time. And on this night that was as dark as it was cold, therefore, he could see nothing out in the prairies to the east because Colonel Romero's attack column on the east had yet to strike. No sound of clattering accouterments, which were not worn by the attackers, could be heard in that direction.

At this time, of course, Baugh had no way of knowing that the pickets, who perhaps he himself had stationed outside the Alamo, were already dead. Baugh never knew that these blood-splattered soldiers, upon whom the garrison had placed so much faith to give early warning, were now lying lifeless at the bottom of cold, muddy ditches. Symbolically, the opening phase of the struggle had opened with a slaughter of garrison members outside the fort and would eventually end with a much greater slaughter on the same open plain.[12]

William Barret Travis, weighed down by command responsibilities, had retired more than two hours earlier to his headquarters, located in the building near the west wall's center, seeking relief from exhaustion and the winter weather. Captain Baugh, if not asleep by 5:30 a.m. when the assault began, after more than two hours on watch, was not sufficiently vigilant—like everyone else—to ascertain that a general assault was underway until it was already too late.

Clearly, indicating their inexperience, both Travis and Baugh had placed far too much confidence in the pickets and sentries–without officer supervision—outside the Alamo's walls. But with the noise emitting from pounding feet, ladders slapped up against the north wall, and Mexican officers now shouting orders to their men, Captain Baugh, very likely just awakened, at last finally recognized the onslaught against the north wall. He now heard the tumult of Mexican soldiers pouring forward by the hundreds. By this time, after reaching the north wall, Dúque's soldados were yelling and shouting, as if celebrating so easily gaining their objective.

Now alert to the threat's magnitude, a desperate Captain Baugh made a belated attempt to arouse the sleeping garrison in the practically sound-proof rooms of the Long Barracks. He very likely also tried to awake soldiers in the other sleeping quarters, especially the artillerymen who slept in the adobe building just to the north, and adjacent to, the Long Barracks. However, it was already too late to organize a solid defense along the Alamo's expansive perimeter, which spanned nearly a quarter of a mile, especially after the Mexicans had already gained the north wall. Not panicking but keeping his head, and in accordance to military protocol as he was the fort's executive officer, the Virginia captain dashed for Travis' sleeping quarters, located next to the artillery command headquarters situated near the center of the west wall. The assault was so stealthy and swift that the thoroughly exhausted Travis was still asleep at the decisive moment, since no attack had yet been directed at the nearby lunette.[13]

Unfortunately for the Alamo garrison, both artillerymen and infantrymen had been literally caught napping, while the Mexicans had already made significant tactical gains—especially in gaining the north wall without meeting serious resistance. By this time, dark, swirling masses of Dúque's troops "had their ladders against the [north] wall before the Garrison were aroused."[14]

An account taken from Joe, Travis' slave from Monroe County, Alabama, summarized on April 11, 1836 the totality of the success of Santa Anna's stealthy tactics that had gained a permanent tactical advantage that would never be relinquished: "It was dark, and the enemy were undiscovered until they were close to the walls, and before the sentinels had aroused the garrison, the enemy had gained possession of a part of the ramparts."[15]

In another account that appeared in the *Commonwealth* of Frankfort, Kentucky, on May 25, 1836, Joe revealed how the attackers were already "under the guns, and had their ladders against the wall before the Garrison were aroused to resistance."[16]

The slave's view was accurate, because it later became widely known that the garrison was only "roused from their sleep by the cry that, 'the enemy [is] on the walls'." Consequently, the son of Gregorio Esparza, who was a member of Captain Benavides' Tejano company of hardy rancheros, Enrique Esparza, a noncombatant because of his young age, explained how thoroughly Santa Anna's tactical surprise had gained irreversible dividends to seal the defender's fate: "The end came suddenly and almost unexpectedly and with a rush [and] It came at night and when all was dark . . . ."[17]

Consequently, the garrison members were suddenly "awakened to a nightmare" of almost unimaginable, surreal proportions in the blackness.[18] The Mexican plan based on stealth and surprise had worked to perfection. In the process, Santa Anna had overcome the major dilemma faced by military commanders assaulting a fortified position, solving a vexing tactical challenge that had existed for centuries: how to catch an opponent by surprise and overwhelm a defensive strongpoint and a garrison with a minimum loss of life. Santa Anna had already negated the Alamo's two principal defensive strengths in only a matter of minutes: its large number of artillery and the deadly Long Rifles.

The Alamo garrison had completely fallen for Santa Anna's trap, lulled not only into complacency, but also a deep sleep. Day after day during the siege, Santa Anna had simply worn the Alamo garrison out both physically and mentally by the nearly two-week siege, sapping their spirit and fighting resolve in the process. Therefore, they had been asleep at the exact moment when they should have been ready for action. And the deadly Long Rifles, now stacked or lying useless beside their owners, were silent as the Mexicans set up their ladders and began to scale the north wall.

To negate such an assault, Colonel Travis or Bowie should have developed a sensible defensive plan in which half of the garrison slept while the other half manned the defenses. The failure to develop such a rotating defensive plan to counter a surprise attack, especially at night, doomed any chance for effective resistance. Or they could have emulated Napoleonic troops who were not allowed to take off equipment or even clothes to sleep when in the enemy's presence and expecting an attack. But Travis was inexperienced in the art of war, and Bowie lacked knowledge in conventional warfare.

Clearly, such negligence was a fatal mistake that would ensure weak, almost token, resistance in defending the Alamo's lengthy perimeter. Based on racial and cultural stereotypes, this situation had in part resulted from the average psychology of the Alamo defenders, who underestimated the intelligence and military skill of their opponents, from Santa Anna down to the lowest soldado private. Indeed, as late as February 12 and barely ten days before Santa Anna's arrival outside San Antonio, Travis had assured Governor Smith "that with 200 men I believe this place can be maintained." From beginning to end, garrison members never believed that the Mexicans would be so shrewd or tactically innovative as to do anything so enterprising as to attack in the darkness and catch them by surprise. After all, not even Indian warriors attacked Anglo-Celtic settlers at night or fought in blackness. Negative racial stereotypes about the Mexican character lulled the defenders, especially the leadership, into a state of lax complacency.

Even worse, the Mexican cannonade during the siege had conditioned the men to enjoy the comforting shelter of the Long Barracks and other buildings to escape the shelling. When the bombardment ceased on the previous afternoon, Travis had failed to make the necessary tactical adjustments to adapt to the changed situation. Perhaps the more experienced Bowie, had he not been sick, might have been sufficiently savvy to take such defensive precautions. Santa Anna, thanks to Tejano collaborators who had seemed to know almost everything about what was transpiring inside the Alamo, was aware that the garrison's riflemen slept in the Long Barracks and other insulated—and hence quiet—quarters, with thick abode and limestone walls that made them nearly soundproof. And he knew that these quarters were located a good distance from the principal tactical target, the weakened north wall.

And few, if any, Alamo artillerymen rested at night beside their guns, while the riflemen slept in the barracks and other abode buildings, once so effective in stopping Apache and Comanche arrows. Therefore, when the Mexicans reached the north wall, began climbing their ladders, and even going over the top in the dark, they were not initially met by any massed or concentrated volleys of rifle-fire, because of the absence of both aroused defenders and the lack of firing positions— parapets, catwalks, portholes, or firing platforms—along the walls. For instance, even though a relatively short makeshift firing platform existed along the north wall, the lack of firing embrasures for riflemen meant that they would be exposed when rising up to fire. For the defenders, even if they reached their assigned places in time, the best firing positions were almost exclusively on building rooftops, a good distance from the north wall, at various points along the perimeter.

Almost before anyone among the comatose garrison realized it, the quickness of the Mexicans reaching the walls meant that almost all of the Alamo's artillery remained unmanned and silent for some time, because the gunners, if roused at all, had no time to race north from the artillery barracks and across the plaza. In addition, even if manned, the pieces could not be sufficiently depressed once the Mexicans had reached the north wall. After all, these guns had been mounted to meet daytime attacks with long-range fire. This disadvantageous situation made the majority of the Alamo's cannon almost useless when they were needed the most. Some historians have at least acknowledged that the Long Rifle had been largely negated, but not the majority of the Alamo's cannon at the attack's beginning.

Although the real battle had not yet actually begun, already it was too late for the diminutive band of garrison members to do anything but die. Travis' slave Joe described how the fight was already over once hundreds of Santa Anna's finest troops already gained the north wall, "before the Garrison [offered] resistance."[19]

Meanwhile, the 33-year-old Captain Baugh raced westward across the wide expanse of the pitch black plaza—in what must have seemed like an eternity for the Virginian—to reach Travis' small room in a building near the center of the west wall. In desperation, an out-of breath Baugh opened the wooden door of the Alamo commander's room and yelled, "Colonel Travis! The Mexicans are coming!"[20]

This startling pronouncement by the former New Orleans Greys' member, who had helped capture the Alamo only last December, might well have been one of the greatest understatements in Texas history.[21] Of course, the captain's frantic words gave no hint of the no-win tactical situation. Indeed, by this time, the Mexicans were not only "coming" in force, they had already arrived at the north wall in overpowering numbers. When Captain Baugh reached Travis' room, the foremost troops of Dúque's column might well have already been over the wall and inside the fort.[22]

Even Kentucky-born Drum Major Joseph G. Washington, age 28, did not have time to beat his drum in a belated attempt to awake and rally the yet comatose garrison.[23] Captain Baugh's frantic words that awoke Travis were yelled before a single blast from one of the Alamo's cannon that would have roused the Alamo's commander and his men. But worst of all in the confused chaos that was fast descending on the old Spanish mission compound, neither Captain Baugh nor anyone else in the Alamo realized that the greatest Mexican effort to scale the walls was concentrated on the north wall. Therefore, in part because his head-quarters room was located in an abode building at the center of the west wall and the Long Barracks was on the other side of the cavernous plaza yet draped in blackness, Travis would be unable to galvanize a solid defense at the most critical point, the north wall, because it was already too late to do so. Indeed, very likely few garrison members, including Travis, expected an attack on the north wall, which had been endlessly strengthened before Santa Anna's eyes, because the weakest sector—the palisade and the main gate—were located on the compound's opposite side, the south.

Long accepted by historians, traditional accounts of the battle have Travis gallantly rallying the Alamo garrison, with almost everyone rushing forth to defend the north wall to meet the attackers with fierce resistence, even repulsing not one but two attacks in that sector. But with the garrison fast asleep and with a high percentage of it either sick or injured in the hospital, this scenario of the mythical Alamo—where the garrison possessed plenty of time to rally and mount an organized defense along every wall—was simply not the case. Such a situation would have been impossible under the disadvantageous circumstance of being caught so completely by surprise. However, the mythology of the tenacious defense of the north wall provided the dramatic stage for the heroic death of Travis in defying the odds, while providing "evidence" of defenders inflicting a large number of casualties. But this traditional version is mere fantasy, as no Mexican attacks were repulsed because of defender fire, either from artillery or musketry that morning. General Filisola described, in regard to any defenders who might have reached the north wall, that they could not "use their rifles, thus because the parapet did not have a banquette on the inner-side."[24]

Joe's account was the first to have Travis meeting his death at the north wall, and this has been relied upon by many historians. Indicative of the attackers having penetrated farther than generally recognized, another version has it that "Travis fell on a stairway he was holding against a surging mob of Mexicans, shot through the head . . ." This well might have been the case, given the complete surprise of the attack and the Mexicans' rapid advance that had them penetrating the Alamo before the garrison was aroused. And Mexican Sergeant Francisco Becerra reported having found Travis inside a room of a building either at the low barracks or near the south wall. In another account, as a sharp rebuttal to what he considered the defamation of his Alamo heroes, Reuben M. Potter was perhaps the first, in 1860, to emphasize in his *The Fall of the Alamo* pamphlet—considered definitive by historians for generations—that Travis and Crockett were killed "early on the outworks," or north wall, expressly to dispel the circulating story and mounting evidence of Crockett's surrender and execution after the fight.[25]

In truth, it was not the defenders' tenacity along the north wall which held the Mexicans at bay according to the mythical Alamo, but ironically the attackers themselves. The first cannon shot of the day erupted from the alerted cannoneers at the elevated gun platform at the back of the church, sending Romero's column veering away toward the north wall, where no cannon roared. During the confused darkness in surging toward the Alamo's northwest corner, Cós' left flank had been hit by the fire of Toluca Battalion soldados of Dúque's column. Considerable disorder resulted when three separate assault formations suddenly collided in the darkness at the Alamo's northern perimeter. This accidental uniting of Dúque's, Cós', and Romero's columns formed a solid mass of hundreds of Mexican troops at the north wall's base. And additional Mexican troops in the rear crowded those in front, cramming and jamming the ranks together in a milling throng. At this point, separate unit organization was lost and the attacking columns became a mob in the dark.

Santa Anna had ordered too few ladders. This confused situation caused a delay among the attackers, though not from defenders' fire. Return fire was virtually non-existent, so swift had been the advance. Initially, the north wall cannon remained quiet, and would have been ineffective even if gunners had reached them, because the three cannon could not be depressed sufficiently to hit the Mexicans since they were at the wall's base.

All the while, hundreds of Dúque's, Romero's, and Cós' troops clamored under the walls, in relative safety, not only because most of the garrison was not yet aroused but because the cannon could not be depressed. Officers, like José Mariano Salas, born in 1797 and second in command of Romero's column, attempted to sort out the confusion and restore order, but in vain amid the tumult and darkness. And by now, though defenders' resistance remained disastrously weak, isolated shots fired into the throng by the first few Anglo-Celtic riflemen to reach the north wall couldn't help but find flesh.[26]

Disorder among the Mexican ranks resulted in a "confused mass," wrote de la Pena, from the merger of three columns of attackers smashing together from multiple directions. Making up for the lack of ladders, the outer work's ad hoc construction, unevenness, and incompleteness allowed for some soldados, using their own initiative, to climb up the wall. With muskets slung over shoulders, newly arriving Mexicans scaled the wall by grabbing holes in the outer-work or the end of protruding wooden beams that had not been sawed off.

"Misled by the difficulties encountered in the climbing of the walls" and the mashing together of multiple columns and from losses incurred by more friendly fire than defender fire, in de la Pena's words, Santa Anna, in the pitch darkness, could not ascertain what was really going on.[27]

Therefore, Santa Anna prepared to order in his crack reserves, the Sapper, or Zapadores, Battalion, which was attached to his personal headquarters. Today known as combat engineers who were among the army's most specialized, versatile troops, these were the army's crack reserves. And Santa Anna now utilized them as Napoleon employed his famed Old Guard, or the Imperial Guard, which served as a "shock reserve" to administer a coup-de-grace at the critical moment. But these troops were not as much engineers in the true sense as elite light infantrymen. With Napoleon's legacy in mind, Santa Anna had omitted nothing in his meticulous planning of the assault. Therefore, he had placed his reserves, both the Zapadores Battalion and nearly half a dozen companies of light troops, behind Dúque's column, facing the north wall. However, he was premature in now unleashing his reserve, under the command of Colonel Agustín Amat, before the battle had hardly begun.[28]

Nevertheless, these reliable sappers were among the army's best troops, earning Santa Anna's praise and confidence. They were men of character, who would later refuse to execute Alamo captives despite Santa Anna's personal command. One reliable young Creole officer of this hard-hitting force was Lieutenant Colonel de la Pena, who had been assigned to the Sapper Battalion on February 13. However, he now served in Dúque's column, having rushed forth with the first wave of attackers.

Indicating its high quality, another fine Sapper Battalion officer was Don José María Heredia. A "well-beloved" and "amiable youth," Lieutenant Heredia was haunted by the portent that he would meet his Maker in Texas, "never seeing his family again." He was correct in his apprehensions. Nevertheless, this young officer would lead his platoon during the assault. Ironically, Lieutenant Heredia was destined to receive a military funeral on his birthday, after suffering a mortal wound at the Alamo.

Like a gambler playing his highest hand, Santa Anna also had held five grenadier companies from the Matamoros, Toluca, Jimenez, San Luís Potosí, and Aldama Battalions in reserve with the Sapper Battalion, which was the real strategic reserve at the Alamo: a combined reserve force of around 400 soldiers, or more than one-fourth the size of the original attack force. The 200 men and officers of the Zapadores Battalion and the other 200 grenadiers prepared to attack. Both grenadiers and sappers of the reserves were determined to prove themselves this morning.

Born in 1790 in Spain and shielded by the darkness, Colonel Romulo Díaz de la Vega rode to the Sapper Battalion with Santa Anna's orders. Along with the five companies of Grenadiers, he then ordered it toward the north wall as directed by the commander-in-chief. Sapper Battalion buglers María Gonzáles and Tamayo blew their brass instruments, and the finely uniformed sappers snapped to attention. Then, on the double, these crack Zapadores rushed forward with high spirits and fixed bayonets.

Some inexperienced men, most likely untrained youths, faltered, but officers, like Lieutenant Heredia rose to the fore. "Urging on the platoon he commanded at times scolding with sword in hand the soldier who showed little courage as the Sapper Battalion advanced" upon the north wall. Soon thereafter, Santa Anna also dispatched his final reserve: his own 50-man general staff, which included well-educated, debonair officers like aide-de-camp Manuel Fernández Castrillón, who was fated to die not at the Alamo but at San Jacinto, Ricardo Dromundo as Purveyor, and José Reyes y Lopez as Commissary-General. Contrary to traditional accounts, these attacking reserves, high-spirited and overeager, made the most noise this morning, with bugle calls and shouts and cheering, as opposed to Dúque's attackers.[29]

But despite confusion and fratricide among the Mexicans at the north wall, it was already much too late for the Alamo garrison to mount any kind of organized, or solid defense of that sector. Large numbers of Mexican troops continued to reach the wall and surge up ladders or scale it by hand like a raging flood in the darkness, before the riflemen in the Long Barracks close to the southern perimeter could rally and rush forth to defend it with muskets and shotguns.[30]

Reacting on instinct, Colonel Travis grabbed his double-barreled shotgun, loaded with buckshot, and raced from his room into the plaza's darkness. This traditional hunting weapon, especially for winged game like quail or prairie chickens on the grassy prairie of Texas, could prove far more effective than the legendary, small-caliber Long Rifle. In the noisy confusion, it was impossible for Travis—half-asleep and very likely stunned beyond belief by how developments had so quickly swirled out of control—to gauge the exact tactical situation, or to get any real sense of what was occurring, especially on the far perimeter.

Numbed by the noise and the shock of having been caught so thoroughly by surprise, Travis sprinted across the wide, lonely expanse of the plaza, yet bathed in blackness, to reach the north battery. He attempted to rally some men who were nearby with a shout to encourage them, "Come on, Boys, the Mexicans are upon us and we'll give them hell."[31] But Travis' belated effort to rally a defense was largely ineffective except for a handful of solders—simply a case of too little, too late. Relatively few men followed Travis into the chaos swirling around the north wall. After all, while Travis raced toward the breakthrough, most men were yet arousing themselves from sleep and attempting to find gear and accouterments to strap on in the pitch-darkness of the Long Barracks and other nearly soundproof buildings.[32]

Some evidence has indicated that a number of soldiers, and evidently a larger group than previously thought—heresy to the mythical Alamo—deliberately remained in the Long Barracks and other buildings either out of fear or because of never receiving orders of any kind. Doing something that was entirely understandable under the circumstances, they apparently decided not to follow the lead of Travis' or other officers like Baugh, if they could at all be heard in the confusion, to defend the walls, as if they already knew it was too late to mount a successful defense.

Understandably shocked by the surprise attack, some defenders remained in bed or hid in a place of concealment, knowing an ugly ending for them was now inevitable. An exception was Gregorio Esparza, a Tejano artilleryman from San Antonio, who rushed from his sleeping quarters in the artillery barracks—indicating that cannoneers were not positioned beside their guns—and into the plaza's darkness never to return. But other garrison members resisted orders to go forward, as if knowing that they would soon meet a gruesome fate. Indeed, Travis' men were horrified to hear the panicked cry that the Mexican "soldiers [had already] jumped the wall." Two Alamo defenders near Esparza's young son, Enrique, were Brigidio Guerrero and an "American boy [who remained] wrapped in a blanket in one corner" of the room, simply refused to budge and participate in the Alamo's defense. Clearly, the shock of the surprise attack caused paralysis, which was entirely justified under such chaotic conditions.[33]

Just awakened to a surreal nightmare so far from his native Tennessee, Captain Dickinson also realized the end had come for the garrison even before it had a chance to fight back. Shell-shocked by the Mexican onslaught, he informed Susanna of the situation: "My dear wife, they are coming over the wall, we are all lost!"[34]

Of course, no one knows the exact number of soldiers who rushed forth into the darkened plaza with Travis. But almost certainly, relatively few garrison members, either artillerymen or riflemen, awoke from their deep sleep in time to rush forward to defend the north wall. Therefore, Travis very likely thought he was leading more men forward to defend the position than was actually the case. So belated was his attempt to rally a defense that Travis might have even unknowingly passed by the foremost Mexican soldiers, who had already surmounted the wall to penetrate into the sprawling plaza.

To many men it very likely made little sense to rush the lengthy distance of more than half the plaza's length in a futile attempt to reach the north wall. After all, by this time, nothing could stop the raging Mexican tide, and it was too late to rally the garrison into an organized defense, especially after word was passed that some of Santa Anna's troops had already come over the wall.[35]

And even if an adequate number of Travis' riflemen had reached the north wall before the Mexicans came over the top, the lack of firing platforms and catwalks hampered any chance of successful defense: reasons why Santa Anna had targeted the north wall with his heaviest attack. Fueling both fright and panic by this time, the escalating roar of hundreds of cheering and yelling Mexican troops only a short distance away was unnerving even for the most experienced soldiers, signaling to one and all that Santa Anna's surprise had been complete.

In addition, many soldiers may have either failed or refused to follow Travis to the north wall because he was simply not their leader. Naturally, Crockett's Volunteer State men stayed with the popular Tennessean, while Bowie's volunteers felt little loyalty to the upstart regular officer; the New Orleans Greys and even the Gonzáles volunteers almost certainly remained with their own leaders. Such a development further ensured a further division of command at the most critical moment was only natural in the confusion of a nocturnal surprise attack.

Drawing upon inaccurate sources, most historians have long believed that all the garrison's riflemen had spilled out of sleeping quarters and then rushed forth in time to calmly take firing positions along the north wall, from where they able to pick out targets and cut down great throngs of attackers with well-aimed shots, thanks to the illumination from cannon flashes. But this scenario is part of the mythical Alamo.[36]

This time-honored tactical scenario of the north wall's alleged tenacious defense was simply impossible for other reasons. First, and contrary to what imaginative writers and historians have speculated for so long, the north wall's main artillery bastion was largely negated, because gunners could not reach their three 9-pounders in time before the Mexicans gained the wall. Like the Alamo's infantry, the artillerymen had slept in their quarters for warm shelter instead of remaining at their posts on the perimeter.

After finally pouring forth from their sleeping quarters, therefore, it took some time for most cannoneers to dash across the wide plaza and to reach their guns. By the time gunners along the north wall reached their 9-pounders, it was already too late for any effective defense of an already weak position that had been completely compromised. And again, without embrasures along the north wall, cannon barrels could not be depressed sufficiently to fire upon the crowded throng of Mexican soldiers at the wall's base.

The ineffectiveness of the Alamo's artillery this early morning would not only be revealed by the relatively low Mexican casualties, but also by the words of the Kentucky-born colonel in Santa Anna's Army, Bradburn. He spoke exquisite Spanish and learned firsthand about what had actually happened—without romance or exaggeration—from Mexican soldiers, after reaching the Alamo only a few days after the struggle. What he learned from immediate Mexican oral sources was translated from Spanish to English by Colonel Francis White Johnson. One of the leading Texas officers in this war, Johnson had served as Colonel Edward Burleson's adjutant and inspector general. An old Indian fighter and War of 1812 veteran, he took charge of Texas forces in San Antonio, after Austin relinquished command during the siege of Béxar. Johnson had then commanded the Alamo, before turning over command to Neill. Colonel Johnson subsequently described the tactical situation that revealed the extent of the surprise that sealed the Alamo garrison's fate: "But a few and not very effective discharges of cannon from the works [on the east and south] could be made before the enemy were under them."[37]

Colonel Johnson's analysis of what had actually happened has been overlooked and discounted by historians, because it so directly countered the traditional romanticized, popularized versions of events, especially the heroic last stand of the mythical Alamo. A Kentuckian who had faithfully served Mexico during its bloody struggle for independence, Colonel Bradburn described to Johnson Santa Anna's easy victory—a rare oral communication about tactical events at the Alamo in English without translations from Spanish with its almost inevitable accompanying errors.[38]

And a reliable Mexican soldier's account by Sergeant Manuel Locanca supported Bradburn's view. Amazed by the attack's swiftness and the overall lack of resistance, he wrote how the assault "was so sudden that the fort had only time to discharge four of the eighteen cannon it had" mounted. And, of course, these guns could not have been fired effectively in the dark and swirling dust, without targets being ascertained and especially with the attackers having already gained the north wall's base.[39]

These Mexican views coincided with those inside the Alamo. For instance, Enrique Esparza recalled how: "We also had two cannon [evidently manned by Tejanos including his father, Gregorio], one at the main entrance and one at the northwest corner of the fort [but] the cannon were seldom fired."[40]

Providing solid collaborating evidence, a number of reliable American accounts also verify the truth of Johnson's words, and hence Bradburn's fact-finding mission about what really happened at the Alamo. Travis' slave, Joe, emphasized how the attackers gained the north wall *before* any artillery fire and safely got under the guns. In addition, E.M. Pease revealed in a January 8, 1837 letter how Mexican troops gained the walls before the garrison was rallied and before resistance. What was significant about all three accounts was that they were given and published in newspapers within a relatively short time after the Alamo's fall.[41]

Ironically, the first cannon shots from the Alamo—from the church's rear and at the main gate lunette—had a dramatic impact and unintended consequence on the overall course of the battle, explaining why the bulk of Santa Anna's attackers concentrated at the north wall, not by design but quite by accident. At least one, perhaps two, of Captain Dickinson's artillery pieces at the back of the church had blasted the left flank of Romero's column, causing it to veer away from the fire toward the compound's northeast corner. The other first-fired cannon, opening up on Morales' column, was located either at the palisade or the lunette—most likely the latter, protecting the main gate, which was Morales' target. At least one of the cannon at the main gate lunette fired at Morales' attackers, who then eased farther west along the southern perimeter to avoid additional fire from the lunette, which had no artillery piece facing west, because the long 18-pounder on the elevated platform at the compound's southwest corner fulfilled that role.

At the church's rear, Captain Dickinson's gun crews, who slept in the church rather than in the artillery barracks next to the Long Barracks, were able to get into place more quickly, long before artillerymen reached the north wall, which was a longer distance away. And initial cannon fire from the lunette was possible because gunners slept in the earthen stronghold before the main gate, which needed protection both day and night. These two initial artillery salvos—from the church's rear and from the front gate lunette before the firings of the north wall's 9-pounders—had a lasting, and ironically, a completely unexpected impact that altered the course of tactical developments.

One, perhaps, two guns at the church's rear that had raked the left flank of Romero's column forced it to veer away to the north to link with Dúque's troops in a concentrated tide. An accidental development likewise altered the attack on the west. The lack of an entry point along the west wall had forced Cós' column, without encountering much resistance, to shift north toward the compound's northwest corner. Ironically, in a case of more fratricide, Cós' soldados suffered more from an enfilade fire of Dúque's men on the right, who raked his left, than from defenders. Here, along the north wall, this accidental massing of strength—Dúque's, Romero's, and Cós' columns—also benefited from unforeseen tactical consequences that were transpiring along the south wall.

A longstanding myth of the Alamo's defense was that combined rifle-fire from Captain Harrison's Tennessee boys along the wooden palisade and a single cannon blast from the palisade's center caused Colonel Morales' column to veer past the palisade. But in fact, in the darkness, the defenders were very likely not yet aroused in time to take to their assigned positions along the palisade; after all, nothing could be seen in the cold blackness, even if they had been ready and in proper defensive placement. Instead, Morales led his men in an attack on the south wall, drawing defenders there and ensuring a weaker defense of the north wall.

But these initial bursts of combined artillery and infantry fire—the fort's first organized defiance—indicated that cannoneers and protecting riflemen slept in and were ready at the main gate lunette. Their fire caused Morales and his small column to veer southwest to take position around a stone house about 30 or 40 feet south of the Alamo's south west corner. Here, Colonel Morales' soldados remained in a stationary position, biding their time and not taking losses, mustering strength and wind for their next move. All in all, this was a significant tactical development, drawing the attention of what relatively few defenders—especially those in the lunette—along the south wall to focus on Santa Anna's weakest attack rather than the surging tide against the north wall. The situation evidently led these defenders, in a a fatal miscalculation, to believe that the main Mexican attack was occurring at the south wall instead of the north one, where cannon had yet to be fired.[42]

Overall, however, there were simply too few defenders, with such a high percentage of sick or injured, to adequately defend a perimeter that needed to be manned by at least 500 men, as E.M. Pease wrote in a January 1837 letter, and more likely as many as 1,000. Even if every garrison member was fully awake and in position in time to face the attack, there was still not enough soldiers to adequately man both the extensive walls and the artillery. Quite simply, it was impossible for so few garrison members to adequately defend the entire perimeter—480 yards—especially when caught asleep and by surprise in the darkness.

In consequence, many newly aroused defenders very likely remained on the Alamo's south side, either choosing not to rush forward to defend the north wall or taking positions along the south wall as planned, in a natural response to protect the main gate from the attack by Colonel Morales' column. Without hearing Colonel Travis' order, or any other, many defenders may not have realized in the chaotic tumult that the main attack was occurring on the north wall.

According to the commonly accepted (and most likely) scenario, among the relatively few defenders who reached the north wall was Travis and his slave, Joe, who allegedly was armed and serving as a garrison member. Carrying his shotgun, the Alabamian raced up the earthen embankment that led to the firing platform for the three guns. As if in disbelief that a major attack had been launched at night, Travis peered over the wall to ascertain what exactly was happening below him. What he saw must have taken his breath away. Dúque's troops already had their ladders in place against the wall, and were in the process of scaling it by both ladder and by hand. Most ominous of all, the darkened movements of the jumbled mass below indicated an immense attacking force. For the first time, Travis now realized that this was an all-out assault.[43]

Colonel Travis stood at the principal artillery position along the north wall, even though Mexicans were already scaling it, perhaps on both sides of him by this time, and very likely some of Santa Anna's foremost soldados might have gained the interior. This strongpoint, manned by three 9-pounders at the north wall's center, had been erected by General Cós' expert engineers. Fortin de Terán had been named after Don Manuel Mier y Terán; in fact, all of the Mexican-built firing platforms, or forts, were named after distinguished military men or politicians. Ironically, Terán had warned the Mexican president that Texas would be lost to the republic because of the ever-growing Anglo-Celtic influence, helping to set in motion the chain of events, including the clash at the Alamo, that made war inevitable.

In the darkness, Travis attempted to do the best he could in a tactical situation that indicated not only defeat but utter annihilation. In the noisy confusion, he joined the three gun battery of 9-pounders—very likely under the command of Captain Carey, because this weak defensive point needed to be manned by "Invincibles," who were considered the garrison's most reliable artillerymen.[44]

However, and even if manned in time, these guns were not only too few and too small to be effective, but their volunteer cannoneers were "unskilled in their use," a lack of ability that only further diminished during the surreal chaos of this night attack. In addition, because no embrasures existed for the three field pieces to fire through, the artillery-men who reached this position would be unprotected and exposed to musket-fire while serving their pieces.[45]

Unlike the riflemen yet stumbling out of the Long Barracks like drunken men, a handful of artillerymen had reached Fortin de Condelle (named in honor of Colonel Nicholas Condelle, who played a leading role in San Antonio's defense in December 1835 and served as com-mander of the Morelos Battalion), at the compound's northwest corner about the time of Travis' arrival. Here, unlike the Fort Terán artillery-men who manned the 9-pounders, the cannoneers at least possessed the benefit of embrasures so that barrels could be depressed to target attackers at the wall's base.

But yet some more precious time was wasted for the desperate artillerymen, who after having been abruptly aroused from their sleep in the artillery barracks and dashing across the plaza and up the earthen ramp to the Alamo's northwest corner, now labored in hurried despera-tion to load their guns as rapidly as possible in the noisy confusion. And this feat had to be accomplished in the dark and at a time when these gunners were in semi-shock from the attack's overpowering weight. With Dúque's, Cós', and Romero's soldiers scaling the north wall, they loaded their artillery pieces in frantic haste as best they could. At the two little forts along the wall, these artillerymen hoped at least to get off a single shot before they were completely overwhelmed by the raging tide of attackers, so close were the Mexicans by this time.[46]

In the early morning coldness and during the panic of the surprise attack, the largely untrained cannoneers along the north wall clumsily attempted to load their guns upon reaching them. This development resulted in more loss of time, while hundreds of Mexicans continued to charge closer across the blackened prairie, solidified their gains at the wall's base, and moved up their ladders. Amazed by the feeble resis-tance, General Filisola later told how the utter lack of "good artillery-men" and "trained men" to man the Alamo's guns made the job of reaching and going over the top of the walls relatively easy for the attackers.[47]

In addition, even the late-winter weather played a role in ensuring a feeble artillery defense. Just like muskets, shotguns, and Long Rifles, the powder charges of cannon were vulnerable to the winter elements, espe-cially dampness, dew, and condensation, if the pieces had been kept fully loaded. Therefore, the 9-pounders at the main north wall battery had remained unloaded and unable to fire for some time, since they were not fully manned because the cannoneers were not fully aroused, or were yet racing across the plaza to reach the north wall. Santa Anna's surprise attack had largely neutralized the garrison's most lethal weapon—the artillery arm—which had caused Neill and Bowie to make the fateful decision to defend the Alamo in the first place.

As Colonel Johnson explained in part from his own analysis but also from Colonel Bradburn's views taken from Mexican soldiers after the attack: "Thus the works were mounted with fourteen guns [actually around twenty] . . . The number, however, has little bearing on the merits of the final defense, with which cannon had very little to do. These guns were in the hands of men unskilled in their use, and owing to the construction of the works most of them had little width of range."[48]

Finally, the initial blast from a little 9-pounder from Fort Terán was belatedly unleashed. But in the words of Sergeant Nunez, born in 1802, who rushed forward in Dúque's ranks: "The first fire from a cannon of the Alamo passed over our heads and did no harm."[49]

Like other attackers, Nunez almost mocked the Alamo's initial blast from a cannon along the north wall. After the first shot sailed harmlessly over the heads of Dúque's rearward attackers, they continued onward unimpeded. Therefore, the only effective cannon fire from the north wall that morning finally erupted when the second gun, another 9-pounder, likewise opened up. This single blast of homemade canister struck the rear of the activo Toluca Battalion of Dúque's column, riddling a group of onrushing infantrymen.[50]

In attempting to magnify the folly of attacking the Alamo and the waste of Mexican lives to disparage Santa Anna's generalship, the ever-political de la Pena wrote that "a single cannon volley did away with half the company of chasseurs from Toluca," which was almost certainly an exaggeration. If de la Pena meant that these men were killed, then this would have represented a large percentage of the total Mexican dead at the Alamo. What he very likely meant to say was that these men were struck by the blast of improvised canister, as small as nails, that inflicted relatively minor wounds. This distinct possibility was verified by the words of an unidentified Mexican soldier, who described how this cannon blast "felled" forty attackers. He even mocked the ineffectiveness of the Alamo cannon, revealing in the April 5, 1836 issue of *El Mosquito Mexicano*: "It seemed that the bullets and grapeshot from the cannons and rifles were spent, bouncing harmlessly off the breasts of our soldiers."[51] These words also indicated that the garrison's limited powder supply was either damp or of poor quality, probably black powder left by General Cós, ensuring a lack of effective firepower, except of course at close range.

But what was not harmless was when Colonel Amat, unaware that Romero's and Cós' troops were now in front of him, ordered his reserves to halt and fire volleys, which cut down many soldados massed and milling together in a crowd at the north wall. If fired high, these volleys would have shot soldados off ladders and while scaling the wall by hand. In the darkness, Santa Anna, who also had no idea that Cós and Romero's columns had swung from their designated attack points to hit the north wall, had made a mistake in throwing in his reserves and at the wrong wall to make widespread fratricide all but inevitable.

The vast majority of Mexican attackers fell to friendly fire in the dark and confusion, and not fire from the Alamo's defenders. Indeed, in total less than half a dozen artillery pieces—perhaps only two from the church guns, one protecting the lunette at the main gate, and two at the north wall—were likely the only cannon fired in defense of the sprawling perimeter that surrounded the nearly three acres of the Alamo's vast interior space—a most feeble result from the garrison's greatest advantage and strength, its artillery arsenal. Indeed, Sergeant Nunez, of Dúque's column, was surprised how, "the cannonading from the Alamo was heard no more" and hardly before it had begun.

Along the southern perimeter, the cannon at the palisade and in the lunette only unleashed perhaps as few as two shots because it was yet dark and no targets existed to fire at, after Colonel Morales column veered away to the west to escape the wrath of the lunette's artillery pieces. This left the entire southern perimeter free of attackers in its immediate front. At the stone house located just outside the southwest corner of the Alamo, Morales' relative handful of men continued to remain behind cover to maintain a steady fire for some time, ensuring that the defenders' attention on the south remained on them, while Santa Anna's knock-out blow was delivered along the north wall.[52]

One of the strangest developments during the assault, unforeseen by either side, was that the Alamo's presumably strongest asset—its artillery—had an unintended detrimental effect on the defensive effort by causing two unplanned maneuvers: first, by driving Romero's column to the northeast corner of the weak north wall, which was the decisive point; and second, by forcing Colonel Morales' column to a new position, the stone house, from which it eventually assaulted and over-ran the Alamo's southwest corner.[53]

By focusing the defenders' attention on the south wall entrance, thanks to Morales' attack, prospects for the attackers' success were now only heightened at the north wall. Perhaps from the moment that he was awakened, therefore, Travis, like those soldiers who failed, either delib-erately or because they weren't ready, to rush to the walls, realized that all was lost. In fact, Travis had accepted the Alamo's fall for some time, and now it was happening ever so swiftly right before his eyes.

Even in the darkness, he might have seen how relatively few of his men had followed him in making the long, lonely sprint to the north wall. After having been caught by surprise, most of the Alamo garrison was yet consumed by a swirl of confusion, if not panic, after having awakened to a nightmare. Simply no time existed for officers to either rally the garrison or get them into their assigned defensive position to offer a solid resistance along the northern perimeter. More soldados gained the north wall's top with relative ease and without encountering serious resistance, rendering moot the limited artillery fire and Colonel Travis' best efforts. What relatively few riflemen reached the north wall could not sustain effective fire, and they were vulnerable targets to the massed throng below them, in having to expose themselves when firing over the wall.[54] The confusion among the newly awakened garrison members could not have been greater by this time. De la Pena recalled how all was pandemonium, "with desperate, terrible cries of alarm in a language we did not understand."[55]

With north wall resistance relatively light, meanwhile, Cuba-born General Juan Valentín Almador, a sprightly age 55, led his cheering sol-dados of the Toluca Battalion of Dúque's column over the top of the north wall, where the three light cannon of Fortin Terán were manned by only a few gunners. Most significant, he and his triumphant men then opened a "postern gate" to allow a flood of attackers to pour into the darkened plaza. Because of the weak defense and the relatively short duration of the fighting inside the compound this morning—perhaps as little as twenty minutes—this gate was opened much sooner than has been described or acknowledged by historians, who have embraced the traditional concepts of the mythical Alamo without question. The early opening of the gate allowed for a much quicker entry into the plaza for hundreds of Santa Anna's men, negating the disadvantage of the rela-tively few number of ladders. Therefore, more soldados gained entry into the Alamo through this gate rather than scaling the wall. Prior intelligence of the Alamo's interior would have bestowed knowledge of this gate and its exact location—almost certainly another reason why the north wall was the principal objective this morning.

Other key officers who played leading roles in overrunning the north wall were General Pedro Ampudia, Colonel Esteban Mora, and Lieutenant Colonel Marcial Aguirre. Surging forward with Almador's troops in overrunning the battery and the north wall, Colonel Romulo Diaz de la Vega led his Zapadores into the plaza. In part because fratricide had been so high and due to their discipline, these reserves of Sappers and Grenadiers, or granaderos, also led the way over the north wall and through the gate. Quite literally, the floodgates to the Alamo were opened for more than 1,000 troops of three columns. Now, according to Joe, the Mexicans came over the north wall and through the gate in a perfect herd "like sheep."[56]

For all practical purposes, the struggle for possession of the Alamo was over hardly before it had begun, primarily because the surprise had been so complete. For instance, the undeniable reality of this no-win situation was revealed by the words of Enrique Esparza, whose father, Gregorio, was one of the few Tejano defenders from San Antonio. The thorough surprise of the Alamo garrison was evident when Enrique's mother, who was awakened by shouting outside—she evidently had been sleeping in a building close to the north wall or near a window, and had to yell to her sleeping husband in the artillery barracks—that the Mexicans were already pouring over the walls: "Gregorio, the soldiers have jumped the wall. The fight's begun."[57]

A short time later, Enrique Esparza related the confused horror that faced the newly awoken garrison: "We could hear the Mexican officers shouting to the men to jump over [the north wall and] It was so dark that we couldn't see anything."[58] Thereafter, as Enrique continued, the bitter "end came suddenly and almost unexpectedly and with a rush. It came at night and when all was dark [and] Our men [had no chance because] Their ammunition was very low. That of many was entirely spent. Santa Anna must have known this, for his men had been able . . . to make several breeches in the walls [while] Many slept. Few there were who were awake. Even those on guard besides the breeches in the walls dozed."[59]

No disciplined volleys were forthcoming from the Alamo defenders, because they had been unable to wake up, organize in time, and reach assigned defensive positions to mass their already limited firepower. There was no real organized or united resistance of any duration along the north wall during the initial phase of the steamrolling Mexican attack. This development can explain why the reserves of the Sapper Battalion lost the lowest number of both officers and men—only 1 officer killed and 3 wounded—of any attacking unit despite leading the breakthrough over the wall. Since the Sappers helped to lead the way over the top and even into the plaza, fratricide might well have claimed these officers. This very likely was also the fate of many of Dúque's officers, such as Captain Don José María Macotela, who fell mortally wounded not long after he took over for Colonel Dúque who also was felled. Both Macotela and Dúque were wounded "in the vicinity of the enemy parapets" along the north wall, while Mexicans below them were firing upward and around them blindly in the night, resulting in what de la Pena lamented as the "destruction among ourselves" in the blackness.[60]

A man of considerable pride, vanity, and a strong sense of honor, Colonel Travis evidently already felt the shame of having failed as the Alamo's commander in terms of rallying the defenders and galvanizing a solid defense, which was now clearly doomed. In fact, he had been long consumed by a "certain fatalism," while possessing a strange sense of being about to be "sacrificed," as if having a portent of his own death.[61]

Not only was the Alamo already all but overrun, but relatively little resistance had been offered to the Mexican tide. For a man like the Byronic-minded Travis, who considered himself an honorable Southern soldier-gentleman, this prospect of an inglorious defeat was the ultimate humiliation, and quite unlike what he had ever read in Walter Scott's romantic novels. What was now happening at the Alamo had nothing to do with romance or the heroic. Santa Anna had brought a merciless reality to the young Alamo commander in the pitch-blackness. Now there were no knights on horseback, chivalric gestures between gentlemanly opponents, beautiful ladies in waiting, and heroism for the ages.

Instead, in the blinding darkness and gut-wrenching panic, there were now only hundreds of vengeful Mexicans swarming forward to exterminate every American and Texan soldier they could find. Like his dazed men who were overwhelmed as much as he was, Travis had realized for some time that his fondest images of a by-gone age had been mere illusionary fantasies. Instead, as revealed in his March 3, letter,

Travis had all but accepted that he and his men were about to be "sacrificed to the vengeance of a Gothic enemy" bent on the garrison's total annihilation.

Travis sensed that his good name and reputation—things that he cherished above all else—would now be stained forever, because he had failed to save his men or the Alamo, forever to be blamed for the failures of prior leadership. In the future, the Travis name would be linked to defeat, humiliation, and disaster. Most galling for him personally was that all of his frantic pleas for assistance had been ignored. Both the government and people of Texas, for which he was about to sacrifice himself, had let him down, abandoning him and his handful of soldiers to their tragic fates. Colonel Travis had earlier despaired of this thorough abandonment, understanding how he and his command were about to be killed for no strategic gain or reason. Therefore, at this time, he was angry, frustrated, and disillusioned by a garrison of mostly volunteers who had long wanted to surrender, the apathy of Fannin and Houston who had not come to their aid, the equally uncaring Tejanos of San Antonio, and the selfish people of Texas who failed to assist him in his darkest hour.

He also had to grapple with his own failure to come to terms—in fact, insulting Santa Anna—when there was still the possibility of an honorable capitulation. Travis was very likely haunted by his own leadership failings that doomed himself and the garrison. And he doubtless also felt abandoned by those men who failed to rush to the north wall with him. He had long been concerned that the disgruntled garrison would surrender instead of fighting to the end like heroes of yore, and now that bitter suspicion appeared evident.

In his mind's eye, Travis had most likely envisioned the climactic battle for the Alamo taking place in broad daylight, the Mexican army ponderously assembling in all its colorful splendor under the calm gazes of a garrison armed and ready at their posts along the walls. Then the fort's artillery would blast huge gaps in the approaching enemy's ranks while the garrison's Long Rifles would deal steady execution. He had probably never imagined a sneak attack in the dark that would breach the walls before the garrison hardly had a chance to fight. And now he found himself practically alone, with no one to command, and no one to witness his heroism save hundreds of swarming Mexican soldados bent on his destruction.

Therefore, by this time, with the searing notes of the Deguelló floating across the plain, and with the red no-quarter flag waving high on this night in hell, Travis evidently felt that he had only one recourse—suicide. As he stated in his March 3 letter, he was only too aware how Santa Anna's attackers were "fighting under a blood-red flag, threatening to murder all prisoners," eliminating any possibility of his survival.

In keeping with Travis' Byronic temperament, he almost naturally would have considered suicide, with Mexicans closing in and perhaps even surrounding him by this time, especially if he had fallen wounded and become helpless. It would have been a rational act under the circumstances. The last thing that Travis now desired was to experience the ultimate disgrace and humiliation, if he was taken alive by the Mexicans, who were now all around him. Capture, torture, and death were now all but inevitable for Travis, and he knew it, if taken alive. And like no other garrison member, Travis was a marked man to Santa Anna. Because of his early defiance to Mexican authority and with his reputation as one of the most militant "War Hawks" in Texas since the early 1830s—a fact known even in Mexico City—Travis was one of the most wanted men north of the Rio Grande. As revealed in his letter, a revengeful Santa Anna was yet enraged over Travis "insulting" replies to him and refusal to come to terms.

At the age of only 26 and despite his short military career, Travis was perhaps the most infamous man at the Alamo, and as a strange fate would have it, also its commander. Since the siege's beginning, in what became a duel of wills between two opposing leaders, Santa Anna was especially eager to do away with the troublesome young man from Alabama as much for personal as for political and military reasons. He had become "furious" with Travis's failure to surrender. Therefore, a stern example had to be made and an unforgettable message sent to other Texas revolutionaries in the form of Travis's death. As part of his overall plan to subjugate Texas, Santa Anna planned to execute all rebel leaders, and Travis would provide the initial example. An ugly death for young Travis would remind every rebel in Texas of the high price paid for those who stood in Santa Anna's way. Therefore, Travis quite correctly expected that "at the very least, he and Bowie would be executed if they surrendered" or were captured by this merciless "Gothic" foe from the heart of Mexico. And by now, it had become painfully clear to one and all that the Alamo was in the process of being completely overwhelmed before an adequate defense could even be attempted.[62]

Knowing that his fate was sealed as much by his own actions and decisions as anything else, Travis had already made his peace with God well before the Alamo's fall. He had already completed his will the previous year. And at the Alamo, as if obeying a dark portent and seemingly knowing his final fate was near, Travis had also taken off his beautiful black cat's eye ring, placed it on a string, and tied it in a loop to place around the neck of 15-month-old Angelina Arabella, the daughter of Pennsylvania-born Captain Dickinson and Susanna Wilkinson-Dickinson, both of whom had migrated to Texas in 1831. Travis seemed to know that he was about to meet his Maker.[63]

What could no longer be denied at the north wall was that nothing could now stop the raging tide of Mexican soldiers, nor now save the garrison or the Alamo. Consequently Travis very likely became convinced that only one option was left for him by this time, especially if surrounded and trapped on the gun platform of Fort Terán with most defenders either dead, wounded, or having abandoned the exposed position. With suicide, he would at least achieve a partial personal victory—like the defiant Jewish rebels at ancient Masada—in denying the victorious enemy his capture, with its consequent humiliation, torture, and inevitable execution. When about to be overwhelmed, and knowing that the Alamo was already doomed, Colonel Travis, ever-impulsive and melodramatic to the end, instead very likely committed suicide by pulling a flintlock pistol out of his belt and shooting himself in the head, "to escape the cruelties of the enemy," as shortly reported in the *Commercial Bulletin*.

This suicide scenario was affirmed by numerous contemporary accounts that Travis killed himself either with a shot to the head or by stabbing himself. However, according to the best evidence, Travis most likely shot himself in the manner of most firearm suicides of the 19th century, with a pistol shot to the forehead. Indeed, Francisco Antonio Ruiz, the alcade of San Antonio, would later personally view Travis' body, and wrote how he had been "shot only in the forehead." An account in the March 28, 1836 *New Orleans Post and Union*—one of the earliest primary documents to describe Travis' suicide—by Andrew Briscoe, a 24-year-old Mississippian and member of the War Party who owned a store in Anáhuac, Texas, held that "Travis, to prevent his falling into the hands of the enemy, shot himself."[64]

The most likely scenario that prompted Travis' suicide was that he fell wounded, lay virtually helpless in or around Fortin de Terán, and knew capture was inevitable with soldados now all around him.

Additionally, if wounded, Travis might well have believed the common rumor that the copper balls used by Mexican troops were poisonous, leading to a slow, agonizing death. In this scenario, Travis would have unknowingly followed the example of a respected German captain of Napoleon's Grande Armée, when a small rearguard force was making a stand against the pursuing Russian tide in a redoubt outside Vilna during the retreat from Moscow. When a Russian cannonball cut off both his legs, this capable young officer then calmly took out a pistol in front of his men and "blew his brains out." Other Napoleonic-era commanders likewise committed suicide by flintlock pistol shots in the head to avoid capture and to deny the enemy the triumph of killing them.[65]

What has been overlooked is the fact that Travis' suicide—if it indeed occurred—was completely understandable under the circumstances and fully accepted at the time. E.N. Grey wrote from Gonzáles on March 11, 1836 how "Travis killed himself."[66] Even General Houston more than once emphasized that Travis committed suicide. He had first learned as much from two Tejano rancheros—Anselmo Bergara and Andrés Barcenas—from present-day Floresville, Texas, who reached Gonzáles from San Antonio not long after the Alamo's fall. They had gathered as much intelligence in San Antonio as they possibly could from Mexican soldiers and civilians. At Goliad on March 11, as learned by Grey, Houston and others, what these two Tejanos presented was a "surprisingly accurate report" to Houston, in the words of historian Richard G. Santos. However, modern historians have casually dismissed this initial report of Travis' suicide, and all of those that followed, regardless of the source.

Having been in and around San Antonio at the time of the struggle for the Alamo, at least one of these men had learned of Travis' fate from a Mexican soldado, or civilian survivors, who had witnessed his suicide, and from viewing Travis' body which was later identified by Joe. Everyone, including Houston, fully believed without question, or even surprise for that matter, the report of Travis' suicide. Clearly, they evidently knew him and his general disposition and temperament well enough so that there existed relatively little surprise or skepticism when they learned of his suicide.[67] This final coup-de-grace was very likely a neat, clean shot, administered by a small-caliber pistol that Travis carried in his leather belt. No doubt like other doomed defenders, Travis had prepared for such a tragic eventuality, and had made his plans accordingly.

More romantic accounts of Travis' death, in the heroic last stand tradition, have maintained that he was shot in the head while firing his double-barreled shotgun over the north wall at Mexicans clustered at the wall's base, and that a volley erupting from below ended his life. This is not implausible, since despite the darkness and the poor marksmanship of the average Mexican soldado, there were certainly a lot of bullets flying around and one by chance could have caught Travis in the head. However, the type of wound caused by a Brown Bess musket at close range would have caused massive damage and been far more disfiguring than a pistol shot, and this sort of wound was not described by those who viewed Travis' body.

The first contemporary account that placed Travis at Fortin Terán was from Joe, who very likely had remained hidden in some building. After seeing Travis' body at the north wall, he and others merely assumed that Travis was killed by the enemy in combat. But Joe's testimony was embellished as he wanted to praise his former master and win favor from white interviewers. After all, he was a slave. For instance, barely a month after the battle, Joe even concocted a story of how after having been shot, Travis killed a Mexican general who was attempting to "behead him" with his saber. However, no general was killed at the Alamo. But most important, Joe indicated that Travis had been wounded, which adds plausibility to the scenario that the Alamo's commander, at the very end, lost all hope and decided to end his own life.

No single suggestion more disputes the Alamo's core mythology than that of suicides among the garrison, despite the fact that considerable primary evidence indicates that suicide was the fate of a number of defenders, including their commander. On March 11, 1836 less than a week after the Alamo's fall, and based upon the firsthand reports from Bergaras and Barcenas, Sam Houston wrote a letter from Gonzáles to his friend, Henry Raguet, which revealed a truth that seemed to surprise no one: "Our friend Bowie, as is now understood, unable to get out of bed, shot himself, as the soldiers approached [and 24-year old, Louisiana-born Charles] Despal[l]ier, [Christopher Adams] Parker [age 22], and others, when all hope was lossed [sic] followed his example," while "Travis, tis said, rather than fall into the hands of the enemy, stabbed himself."[68]

Then, on March 15, 1836, Benjamin B. Goodrich, a member of the Washington-on-the-Brazos Convention, wrote to his brother John Camp Goodrich from Washington-on-the-Brazos, reporting how, "Col.

Travis, the commander of the fortress, sooner than fall into the hands of the enemy, stabbed himself to the heart and instantly died."[69] Another early testament of Travis' suicide appeared in an April 16, 1836 issue of *The New Yorker* with the publication of a letter by Andrew Briscoe: "The brave and gallant Travis, to prevent his falling into the hands of the enemy, shot himself."[70] And the *Louisiana Advertiser* also told its readers of Travis' suicide, after he, and for good reason, decided that he would not suffer the dismal fate of "falling into the hands" of Santa Anna.[71]

On March 28, 1836, the *New Orleans Post and Union* likewise ran the story of the suicide of the Alamo's young commander, who, from all contemporary evidence, went down like a sea captain with his ship in a long-revered tradition, especially among military commanders.[72]

In addition, the April 16, 1836 issue of the *Western Courier and Piqua Enquirer* of Piqua, Ohio, reported the news that was far more believable to Americans at the time than today: "We stop the Press to announce the fall of Béxar, and the slaughter of 187 brave fellows, principally Americans . . . The gallant commander, Col. Travis, before he would suffer himself to be taken alive, drew a pistol from his belt and put an end to his existence by lodging its contents in his own head."[73]

What is especially interesting about this account and others is that they reveal none of today's negative social stigma, but a matter-of-fact acceptance, if not appreciation, of the concept of suicide under no-win circumstances that did nothing to damage the heroic reputation of the doomed yet gallant Alamo commander.

BREAKDOWN

With Colonel Travis dead, what little cohesion that remained among the confused, dazed, and half-asleep band of defenders, especially among the volunteers, now evaporated completely in the noise, panic, and darkness. After all, the garrison was never really a command in any sense of the word, with in-fighting as much among themselves as among Texas' notoriously quarrelsome politicians in San Felipe de Austin. Even more, the garrison—a truly multi-ethnic and multi-racial command in which barely half a dozen men were native Texians and even less were from San Antonio—was even not united by nationality, or state or community ties. Especially in such a disastrous situation, collapse of cohesion, and therefore organized resistance, was all but inevitable.

When Joe was horrified to see his Alabama-born master, who had purchased him almost two years earlier to the day, killed, he possessed the good sense to immediately take off on the run. At age 23, this African American now proceeded to do what most white soldiers at the north wall were now doing. The idea that Joe served as a soldier—after all he was a slave with no military experience—to defend the Alamo against those who would liberate him and bestow freedom upon him makes little sense. Instead, he headed back across the plaza on the double. Seeking survival, he found refuge in one of the buildings along the southern perimeter.

Young Captain Baugh, only an adjutant, now became "the de facto" commander of the Alamo after Travis' death. But like Travis, the captain could accomplish little, if anything. By this time, Baugh very likely realized that he would never see his Virginia family again. Without either the time or inclination to spring from the Long Barracks and other sleeping quarters to dash across the plaza's lengthy stretch to defend the walls, an unknown number of soldiers remained behind in the temporary shelter of the Long Barracks or other buildings out of fear and shock. Therefore, some garrison members failed to make the dash to assigned defensive posts, because with the surprise so complete, they seemed to instinctively know that resistance would make little difference in the end.[74]

Such factors also explain why the vast majority of the Alamo's cannon remained silent so long. Knowing the end was now near, a shocked 26-year-old Captain Dickinson, who commanded the cannon at the church's rear, had only been awake for a few minutes when he revealed to his horrified bride Susanna, who was in the ill-lit sacristy, the truth of the situation: "Great God, Sue, the Mexicans are inside our walls!"[75] The shock could not have been more complete. In the artillery barracks with his father, Enrique Esparza never forgot the moment when "We could hear the Mexican officers shouting to the men to jump over."[76]

Incredibly, the foremost Mexican troops were inside the Alamo before most garrison members were fully awake, aroused, and on their way to defensive positions. Indeed, overrunning the north wall had been so relatively easy—ironically thanks in part to the artillery damage inflicted in this sector by Neill's artillery during the 1835 siege of Santa Antonio—that Lieutenant Colonel José Juan Sánchez-Navarro described with some astonishment how, "Our jefes, officers, and troops, at the same time as if by magic, reached the top of the north wall [and] jumped within."[77] Revealing some relief that the task had not been more difficult, he said, "The four columns and the reserves as if by a charm at the same time climbed the enemy's wall and threw themselves inside his enclosure."[78]

Ironically, the attackers' own numbers proved to be a greater impediment than defenders' fire. After all, the soldados "had their ladders against the wall before the Garrison were aroused," and had been scaling the north wall without encountering serious opposition. Young Lieutenant José María Torres of the Zapadores Battalion had already planted the Mexican tricolor on the north wall, proclaiming victory.[79]

All the while, larger numbers of Mexicans continued to pour over the walls and through the gate like a raging tide of humanity. Such a tactical achievement was one of Santa Anna's proudest moments as a military commander. Even long after the Alamo's capture, and as revealed in a previously unpublished letter, Santa Anna still glowed at the memory of when so many "Mexican soldiers scaled those stone walls climbing them with courage."[80] And it had all happened so quickly, less than fifteen minutes since the attack's opening, giving garrison members a very narrow window of opportunity to wake up, strap on gear, and dash to assigned positions to mount a defense.

At this time, the plaza's north end was filled with swarming soldados. Mexican targets, dark-skinned enlisted men of Indian and mixed heritage, and lighter-colored Creole officers, both wearing dark-blue colored uniforms, could not yet be seen clearly by the defenders in the night. Therefore, targets were not yet clear for Travis's men, adding to the confusion and overall lack of resistance. What little, if any, hope of galvanizing a solid defense only continued to evaporate further in the confusion, the blackness, and the noise. As if this situation was insufficiently unnerving for the numbed garrison, soldiers yet emerging groggily from sleeping quarters to enter the plaza's expanse now heard the spontaneous chant of the onrushing soldados, "Muerte a los Americanos," or "Death to the Americans!"[81]

Even if the men of the Alamo did not speak Spanish, they could guess the meaning of the war-cry, while Tejano defenders could already understand the frantic commands of shouting Mexican officers. Most of all, no defender could forget the sight of that red flag waving over the church, and what it signified. Like so many garrison members, romantic-minded Micajah Autry, a crusty War of 1812 veteran compared to the beardless youths around him, who was yet an idealistic dreamer at over forty, was about to fulfill his promise, or death wish at the Alamo. In one of his final letters to his wife, Martha, he wrote, "I am determined to provide for you a home or perish."[82]

From beginning to end, relatively feeble resistance in the face of the overpowering onslaught was all but inevitable. The lack of effective leadership, careful coordination of the defense, and command incohesiveness that had been evident for so long now rose to the fore. Inexperienced novices in the ways of war, Alamo garrison members were also divided by race (Tejano verus Anglo-Celts); nationality (Americans verus Europeans); regional difference (North versus South); the direction of Texas' future, (pro-Constitution of 1824 verus pro-independence); regulars and volunteers; native Texians versus United States volunteers; leadership (Travis versus Bowie); and even along political party lines (Whigs verus Jacksonian Democrats). These considerable differences helped to ensure that the garrison would act anything like a cohesive force—after all they were citizen-soldiers and volunteers—rather than as disciplined soldiers.

Along with Santa Anna's hard-hitting, stealthy tactics, a host of factors, including Travis' death, plagued the garrison to prevent a unified defense, paving the way for panic and a complete rout. As in any such divided military organization, especially one caught unprepared during a nocturnal surprise attack, such internal differences and divisions were only magnified under the stress of battle, rising to the fore at the moment of crisis. One of the great Alamo myths was that the garrison—which never previously faced a combat situation—fought and died as one in a well-coordinated, tenacious defensive effort.

Instead, what relatively little resistance offered to the Mexican attackers easily broke down under the shock of an onrushing enemy who so quickly descended upon them in overwhelming numbers. What few tentative, belated defensive efforts that existed, therefore, fragmented even further in the noise, fear and panic—a natural, if not inevitable, development under the circumstances. In fact, a majority of the Alamo garrison offered little, if any, resistance—the antithesis of the fabled last stand.

This undeniable reality of a lack of a unified and organized defensive effort was explained in the first official account of the Alamo's fall. Significantly, in his report written for the Mexican Minister of War and Navy, Santa Anna himself explained how "there was a large number [of defenders] that still had not been able to engage" the attackers, because they had not gone to the north wall, but fled toward the compound's south side, now free of attackers.[83]

Like other officers, Captain Baugh, could not organize effective resistance now that he was the acting senior commander.[84] In desperation, this former New Orleans Grey continued to attempt to rally riflemen beyond the relative handful of soldiers who had attempted to take defensive positions. But in the dark and confusion, like his predecessor, there was little that he could do.

Nevertheless, Captain Baugh and others continued frantic efforts to arouse and organize the riflemen from their isolated sleeping quarters in various buildings of the Alamo compound, after Baugh had already alerted those in the two-story Long Barracks. Indeed, for too long this morning when time was of the essence, the captain had urgently attempted to arouse some "of the defenders out of their sleep immediately, but others, in their fatigue-induced slumber, awoke slowly and were confused" under the shock of the surprise attack.[85]

By this time additional dazed soldiers had emerged from the darkness of their warm barracks and sleeping rooms only to encounter the chaos, tumult, and confusion that was swirling around the Alamo's plaza like a tornado. Enrique Esparza later recalled, "I ran out to the [church] courtyard from a deep sleep."[86]

Indeed, there simply was no time to rally the men, so complete was the Mexican success in overrunning the north wall before the garrison could be aroused.[87] It had now become a desperate situation of every man for himself. In the midst of the Mexicans surging over the wall in the darkness, a wave of panic naturally swept through the defenders, who deserted firing positions along the perimeter and fled back into the plaza.[88]

After Travis died, the few defenders, mostly artillerymen who had been so easily overpowered at the north wall, fled through the plaza and toward the Long Barracks to escape the onslaught. As if the convergence of three attack columns before the north wall was not enough to overpower the resistance there, the few defenders there had also been flanked on their left when Cós' troops overran the Alamo's northwest corner. This position had been bolstered by an artillery platform and two cannon—dubbed Fortin de Condelle—but had been easily overwhelmed.[89]

Therefore, what few men who continued to race from the Long Barracks and other sleeping quarters to go to the north wall, if that was the case, were now met in the Alamo plaza by onrushing Mexicans, who had already scaled the wall or entered its postern gate. Ironically, more actual fighting now took place not on the wall but in the open plaza, where even less chance for the garrison's survival existed. Amid wreaths of sulphurous smoke that hung heavy over the plaza, further obscuring visibility, these close-range encounters were nightmarish, with Mexican troops using their bayonets with brutal effectiveness.[90]

Stunned garrison members who continued to emerge from their sleeping quarters were shocked to suddenly see a good many swarthy men—in general smaller than the Anglo-Celts—in dark blue uniforms. To the startled defenders now caught in the plaza, these fighting men from Mexico emerged like phantoms out of the blackness, charging across the plaza toward the south wall. Equally unnerving was the fact that the onrushing Mexicans were yelling like banshees and flashing bayonets, while officers shouted orders in a language they could not understand. Sensing a victory had already been won, these soldados now fought far more aggressively than the overconfident garrison members had ever believed possible.

Therefore, besides that of the surprise attack and the Mexicans already swarming through the plaza, yet another shock further stunned the Alamo defenders by this time: the warrior-like qualities and the courage exhibited by the attacking soldados. Now inside the plaza, these fighting men from Mexico defied so many ugly racial stereotypes about their lack of combat prowess and courage. Consequently, the sense of terror among the Alamo defenders only rose to new heights. These developments were indicated by the words of de la Pena, who wrote how thoroughly the dazed defenders were "terrified," when swiftly overpowered by the Mexican onslaught in the plaza. As among the relatively few defenders who had initially rallied in time to attempt to fight back, this ever-escalating shock and panic was contagious to the newly-aroused troops yet spilling forth and into the plaza's dark expanse, after emerging from buildings along the perimeter.[91]

Besides the surprise, the absolute swiftness of the Mexican advance in getting over the north wall stunned the Alamo men, sending them reeling. Indeed, as explained by Johnson who had learned the truth first-hand of the Mexican's rapid success from the victors not long after the fighting, "This all passed within a few minutes after the garrison [was] driven from the thin manned outer defences, whose early loss was inevitable."[92]

Indeed, thanks to having set up ladders along the north wall "before the Garrison were aroused to resistance" and with the Alamo's walls virtually defenseless, the vigorous rush of the Mexican troops up and over the barrier and then through the plaza was most of all distinguished by its swiftness. Survivor Susanna Dickinson, reinforcing the prevalent racial image of an onrushing tide of barbarians, later spoke of "the Aztec horde [which] came on like the swoop of a whirlwind."[93]

The fact that some Americans were armed with Kentucky Long Rifles now worked to their disadvantage during the clash in the plaza. Historians have long assumed that these legendary rifles were the defenders' best assets. But in the confused darkness of the open plaza, these feared weapons of the western frontier were all but useless at the critical moment. Especially, now in the dark-shrouded plaza, the Long Rifle—the range of which Santa Anna had already thoroughly negated by his surprise attack at night—proved largely ineffective because of its small caliber. Feared since the American Revolution, this frontier weapon was more ideally suited for hunting game no larger than a white-tailed deer, while proving totally unsuitable to resist swarming attackers practically atop the defenders in the darkness. Travis and some other garrison members knew as much, carrying double-barrel shotguns.

With the Mexicans rushing upon the startled garrison members in the open plaza, what was now needed for any chance of hurling back this initial wave of attackers was a close-range volley from shotguns loaded with deadly "buck and ball." Shotguns were the only weapon that would have been effective at close range. A deliberately aimed shot from a Kentucky or Pennsylvania Long Rifle at an attacking Mexican, especially in the blackness when visibility was yet almost zero, was of little value.

Worst of all, these weapons could not be enhanced with what the defenders now needed most—bayonets—to fend off the foremost attackers pouring through the plaza. In addition, and unlike the much sturdier British Brown Bess muskets carried by Santa Anna's men, the Kentucky Long Rifle was even unworthy as a club in close quarter fighting. Indeed, compared to the heavier Napoleonic muskets, this slight hunters' rifle "was more fragile and [therefore] it could not be used as effectively in extremity as a club."[94]

When defenders met attackers headlong in the plaza's blackness, the Long Rifle only helped to ensure an additional lack of firm resistance, because it took so long to reload, especially during the heat of battle. After the first shot from a Long Rifle, Travis' men would have to spend nearly a minute loading the weapon, elegant in its craftsmanship and design, even under ideal conditions. In the darkness, panic, and clamor of the steamrolling Mexican attack, nervous fingers took even longer to reload their weapons. Dazed garrison members caught in the open plaza were quickly dispatched, either bayoneted, shot, or knocked down by a musket-butt by the fast-moving Mexican soldados racing from north to south toward the Long Barracks and church. Some of Travis' soldiers died grisly deaths from jabbing bayonets, while attempting to defend themselves with the day's finest long-range weapon, when it was most likely empty, either never having been fired in the first place or after getting off only one shot.[95]

In contrast to the Long Rifle, the durable, smooth-bore musket of the Mexican soldier, was a heavy weapon of large caliber and much more reliable in close combat. The large .75 caliber round shot of this musket, that the British government obtained from the East India Company to confront Napoleon's then seemingly invincible legions, could inflict terrible damage on its victims, unlike the Long Rifle's small caliber ball.[96]

So in regard to the close-quarter fighting inside the Alamo's walls, it was *not* those Americans armed with the Long Rifle but the Mexicans who possessed a distinct advantage, because of their use of "buck and ball" cartridges in muskets. The buckshot-plus-bullet ammunition made the discharge from the Brown Bess almost like a mini-shotgun. Along with the well accepted fact of the general inaccuracy of the Napoleonic musket, this shotgun effect negated the lack of marksmanship training of the Mexican fighting men in Santa Anna's ranks.[97]

Besides shortages of ammunition, one previously unexplored issue in regard to explaining why it took so long for Travis' men to get ready for action and why the defenders' resistance was so weak was because of the time that it took to get their firearms ready for action. If garrison members—mostly rookies without military experience—had kept their weapons loaded during the night in case of a surprise attack, their powder charges would have been of little use by early morning. For instance, when General Houston's army learned of Santa Anna's approach toward San Jacinto in April 1836, hundreds of soldiers would be forced out of necessity, even on a warm day, to fire their weapons in the air "to clear their barrels by blowing away the wetness," so that they could reload their weapons with fresh powder charges.[98]

However, under immediate attack and surprised from a deep sleep, the Alamo men possessed little, if any, time this morning to fire off their old rounds in order to reload. Consequently, a good many defenders' weapons, if they had kept them loaded through the cold night, could not be fired by the time of the attack. In addition, the firing mechanisms of flintlock muskets—unlike new model British muskets with waterproof flash pans—were not moisture-proof, preventing the flints causing sparks to ignite the firing pan and thus the powder charge in the barrel. In contrast, Santa Anna's troops had possessed ample time to make sure their weapons were in proper working order before the attack was ordered. Naturally, a host of misfired weapons would have created even more panic among the defenders.

In the dark still shrouding the Alamo like a funeral pall, many garrison members were likely caught without loaded weapons and were defenseless when the swiftly advancing Mexicans descended upon them. These unfortunate men were either shot down, sabered, or bayoneted while either racing across the parade ground toward the north wall or in retiring south in an attempt to find shelter or a semblance of organized resistance. One account has claimed that Crockett was killed when "he crossed the fort's parade ground."[99] Indeed, Andrea Castanon de Vallanueva described how Crockett "advanced from the Church building towards the wall or rampart running from the end of the stockade . . . when suddenly a volley was fired by the Mexicans [who had scaled the north wall] causing him to fall forward on his face, dead."[100]

In addition, the overall lack of resistance very likely could also be attributed to not only damp ammunition from winter conditions, but also because the defenders used the vastly inferior Mexican reserves of powder left behind by Cós' troops, who took the best Mexican powder with them, thanks to Cós' covert directive to circumvent the capitulation agreement. As if that was not bad enough, Matamoros Expedition members, acting on Johnson's and Grant's "arbitrary measures," had later taken most of the best powder for themselves, the fine-grained, double DuPont Powder from the Brandywine Powder Mills, which was far superior to the coarse Mexican power. After all, on March 3, Travis had requested black powder from the government, citing only ten kegs remaining. If the defenders attempted to use the powder from the paper cartridges of the thousands of rounds left behind by Cós, they then very likely discovered that it was "damaged" and "useless" at this critical moment. Poor quality Mexican powder was so impotent that Texians had earlier in the revolution discovered that they were entirely safe "from any injury by their guns." Therefore, the Alamo's defenders had been left with the worst powder, after the best had been taken not only by paroled Mexican troops but also Matamoros Expedition members, leaving them ill-prepared to meet the attackers.[101]

Ironically, after the north wall was overrun by the tide of Dúque's, Cós, and Romero's attackers, the second penetration of Mexican troops surging into the compound came at what was considered one of its strongest points, the southwest corner. Traditional historians have over-looked the importance of the role of the well-trained cazadores of Colonel Morales' column, viewing this attack as merely a feint because it struck the Alamo's south side and failed in its central objective of overrunning the main gate. In fact, this was not a diversion or feint, because Morales and his soldados had been given a key assignment—to capture the very entrance to the Alamo. And Colonel Morales' column consisted of elite troops. Indeed, in a rare compliment from a seasoned cavalryman, Sergeant Loranca, bestowed an honorary name upon the men of the San Luís Potosí Battalion. He described them as the "Firmas," because of their reliability and combat prowess, almost a crack Grenadier Guard.

In the end, Santa Anna's faith in these troops was rewarded not at the main gate, as he had planned, but at one of the Alamo's strongest defensive points. This position at the compound's southwest corner was guarded by the garrison's largest cannon, the 18-pounder. It had been set in place to fire over the wall because no embrasures existed at this wood and earthen firing platform accessed by a lengthy ramp. Morales understood the advantages of overrunning the Alamo's southwest cor-ner and the garrison's largest artillery piece: a guarantee to further unhinge the belated, floundering defensive effort.

Here, at the Alamo's southwest corner, resistance was almost non-existent because of tactical developments elsewhere, especially the over-running of the north wall. By this time, most of the artillerymen and defending infantry in this sector had evidently retired back toward the Long Barracks and the church area, after ascertaining that the north wall had been overwhelmed and Mexicans were now charging through the plaza to gain their rear. Even if the gunners had remained in posi-tion, the 18-pounder was faced in the wrong direction, west toward San Antonio and not toward Morales' attackers.

Morales' men had earlier eased within short striking distance of the southwest corner, after having moved west along the protective cover of the irrigation ditch to take cover behind the stone house, out-flanking this elevated defensive position and the Alamo's largest cannon from the south. And in the darkness, the mere handful of artillerymen at the 18-pounder, if yet manned, very likely never saw Morales' small column shifting west and moving along the irrigation ditch, taking cover behind the house, and eventually targeting the southwest corner's flank until it was too late. Such a stealthy approach in the dark doomed this artillery position. To justify the epic resistance effort of the mythical Alamo, some historians have speculated that defenders at the south and west walls left their positions to bolster the north wall's defense, but this was almost certainly not the case, because that sector, known for lack of good firing positions for riflemen, had already been overrun in short order. Being too little and too late, any reinforcements rushing to the north wall would have been subsumed into the oncoming mass of soldados. Instead, these defenders headed toward the Long Barracks and church rather than waste their lives defending another wall that could not be held.[102]

Taking the initiative on their own, like so many other attackers this early morning and in a "daring move," in General Filisola's words, Colonel Morales' men emerged from around the stone house, only a short distance from the fort's southwest corner. They then advanced straight north against the Alamo. Encouraged by the lack of resistance along the south wall, Colonel Morales capitalized on his bold move. These light troops scaled the wall from both the south and west, over-running the elevated artillery position with a cheer that could be heard above the crackling gunfire.

Leading the way and inspiring his troops onward, Colonel Miñon, second in command of Morales' column, was the first man to jump inside this elevated strongpoint, after climbing the shaky ladder planted against the stone wall. Resplendent in a fine uniform like Santa Anna's other high-ranking officers, Miñon was not hit by a bullet, musket-butt, or Bowie knife, because resistance was almost totally lacking by this time. Incredibly, this key bastion was all but undefended at the critical moment.

Surprised by the absence of defenders, Miñon, a veteran officer who knew how to lead men in combat, described with pride—as he could not see what was transpiring at the north wall—how "I managed to achieve, along with his force, that it was the first one that was successful in victory inside of the enemy perimeter." The example of a full ranking colonel having been the first inside the compound in this key sector indicated one secret of Santa Anna's success on this day: reliable, hardened high-ranking officers who led the way rather than commanding from the rear. The same was true in the performance of high-ranking officers in the attack on the north wall.

As directed by Morales and Miñon, these victors of the San Luis Potosi Battalion at the compound's southwest corner took firing positions at high points along the perimeter. Perhaps they planted the Mexican tricolor, with its majestic golden eagle perched atop a cactus with a snake in its beak, beside the captured 18-pounder, symbolizing their success. Then, well-trained for this close-range business of killing even in the dark, these reliable light troops, or chasseurs, blasted away from elevated perches atop the walls and the cannon's firing platform. What relatively few surviving defenders who had been at or near the compound's southwest corner now headed east across the plaza and toward the Long Barracks and church.[103]

New Englander Colonel R.L. Crompton was the only Anglo who witnessed what had happened at the Alamo's southwest corner. He was surprised to see how easily "the Mexicans effected a lodgment on an undefended part of the wall."[104]

He viewed the action, illuminated by flashes of gunfire, from the vantage point of the window of a mud-and-thatch jacale (Tejano house) in Pueblo de Valero, which was located south of the Alamo, just outside the main gate and along the Gonzáles Road just west of the Alameda. From here, this young man from Massachusetts could easily view events swirling around the Alamo's southwest corner. Crompton was a solitary volunteer reinforcement who had never reached the Alamo. In riding down the Gonzáles Road in pitch blackness previous to March 5, he had been hit by gunfire from Sesma's cavalrymen, who guarded the road to keep reinforcements from entering the fort. Fortunately, as a veteran of San Antonio's capture in December 1835, he knew of a Tejano friend who gave him shelter at his home in Pueblo de Valero.[105]

Such evidence has revealed that resistance might have been non-existent because the 18-pounder gunners might have never even reached their positions. Quite likely, with the artillery barracks on the compound's opposite side, these artillerymen might have not been awakened in time, or had been cut-off from reaching the southwest corner artillery platform by Mexican troops swarming from the north wall. Now, after seizing the 18-pounder and the compound's southwest corner, Colonel Morales' men, from good firing positions atop the walls and rooftops, poured a hot fire from their elevated perches, blasting down into the dark plaza at the whiteness—face and necks—of Travis' men. Some time later, San Luís Potosí Battalion soldados would advance to take possession of the main gate and the lunette from the rear.[106]

In overall tactical terms, the relatively easy overrunning of the compound's southwest corner also partly explains why the Mexican advance once inside the walls was so swift and overpowering, meeting light resistance. Nothing could now stop the attacker's momentum, especially when facing only a relative handful of dazed, half-asleep defenders, who hardly knew what had hit them. But with large numbers of Mexicans inside the Alamo's walls and descending into the plaza from the north, some dazed Anglo-Celts elected not to flee into the Long Barracks, but instead retired back toward the main gate, which was free from attack by Colonel Morales' soldiers, who had concentrated at the Alamo's southwest corner. In the darkened tumult, neither Captain Baugh nor any other officer could stop or fully comprehend the fast-moving tactical events now swirling out of control around them.[107]

Even worse, the defenders' position along the southern perimeter—at the lunette guarding the main gate, along the palisade, and along the rooftops—was destined to be compromised from behind, after Colonel Morales' chasseur troops overran the Alamo's southwest corner. Ironically, the most formidable weapon in the Alamo's artillery arsenal, already facing the wrong direction and far too heavy to turn, might well have not fired a single shot. As a partial testament to the overall feeble defensive effort was the fact that Santa Anna's smallest attack column—the San Luís Potosí Battalion chasseurs—had made a significant tactical gain.

Consequently, when Morales' troops overwhelmed the Alamo's vulnerable southwest corner, they also flanked the defenders along the west wall on the left. This tactical development resulted in some of the remaining west wall defenders fleeing back into the plaza, heading north for the Long Barracks' relative safety, or south toward the palisade's sally port, hoping to escape the deathtrap. Some of these retiring soldiers were almost certainly wiped out in the plaza by Mexicans, who had poured over the north wall on the left. Overall, and especially only with a relative handful of men, Colonel Morales' success was impressive, and small wonder that he later described this struggle as "the glorious battle of the Alamo."[108]

Overwhelmed by debilitating "combat shock," no organized lines of defense, concentrated volleys, or standing fire took place among the stunned Anglo-Celts, who had been so thoroughly worn down both physically, emotionally, and psychologically by the nearly two-week siege, the lack of sleep, and their hopeless plight. Especially with the Mexicans pouring over the walls, the flight or fight impulse had been triggered among the remaining survivors. And now flight was not only instantaneous but also automatic—an unthinking, natural response to survive—under dire circumstances. A panic triggered by the surprise attack in darkness became more widespread, enhanced by the sights and sounds of vengeful soldados giving no quarter. All the while, the "screams of the crazy, exultant Mexicans increased every moment [with] the yell [compared to] the yell of a mountain panther or lynx."

By this time, almost every surviving defender had bolted away from the north wall, west wall, and southwest corner, heading either toward the south wall and church or the Long Barracks. De la Peña described the rout of the stunned band of Anglo-Celts, caught in the open in the pitch-blackness of the nearly three acres of the open plaza, writing how the "terrified defenders withdrew at once into quarters placed to the right and to the left of the small area that constituted their second line of defense. . . . Not all of them took refuge, for some remained in the open, looking at us before firing, as if dumbfounded at our daring."[109]

What was transpiring in the plaza and buildings little resembled a battle. With so many Mexicans now swarming through the plaza with wild shouts of victory and revenge, the Anglo-Celtic defenders were so easily overwhelmed that the contest now began to resemble more of a massacre than anything else. Quite naturally among the survivors, escape from such a no-win situation became paramount. Relatively few defenders, therefore, now retired into the relative safety of the Long Barracks, as traditional accounts have claimed. One of the great Alamo myths was that after the north wall was overrun, the survivors acted upon prearranged plans that if the Mexicans came over the walls, they would retire to make a last stand in the Long Barracks.

Some historians have even described the Long Barracks, or the old convent building, as the Alamo's previously designated "second" defensive line; but almost certainly neither Travis nor any other officer gave such a command in the confusion. After all, such a decision to retire into the Long Barracks' confines was not a tactical solution but suicide. At best, shelter in the two-story building could provide a few more moments of life; meantime, entire sectors of the perimeter remained attack-free at this time, offering inviting avenues of escape. The Alamo's south side—especially the palisade and the main gate—had been clear since Morales' men had veered toward the compound's southwest corner. Therefore, both the main gate and the low palisade of wooden stakes, just a short distance from the Long Barracks, now became ideal escape routes.

Consequently, only a relatively handful of men took refuge in the Long Barracks—including those who never left it that morning in the first place. In part because of the confusion, smoke of battle, and darkness, those who entered the Long Barracks, never to leave it, evidently failed to see so many of the surviving garrison members now making for the Alamo's opposite side, the south, to escape from the heavier Mexican attack pouring across the plaza from the north wall. Very likely these soldiers did not know that so many comrades were now fleeing past them in the blackness, heading toward the palisade.

But in truth, the stiffest resistance this morning came not from a previously designated "second" line of defense in the Long Barracks but from the large number of sick and wounded confined to the hospital on the building's second story. These defenders included not only the sick and injured—or walking wounded—but also those men who served as nurses and attendants. Meanwhile, healthy and able men fired from the Long Barracks' rooftop, blasting away from this 18-foot-high perch.

More wounded and sick garrison members were located in the second story of the Long Barracks than previously recognized by historians. The siege had resulted in a number of relatively minor casualties, despite the ineffective bombardment. Consequently, soldiers who had only been slightly injured during the siege helped to defend the hospital. Also men who had been wounded during San Antonio's capture in December 1835 remained in recuperation on the second floor. Quite likely, one of these convalescents was Ireland-born Private James Magee, a former member of the New Orleans Greys who now served in Captain Blazeby's infantry company. The Irishman had been severely wounded in the attack on Béxar. Magee should have learned from the tragic death of fellow Irish revolutionary, Augustus Magee of an earlier generation, who succumbed in San Antonio far from his native Ireland for an earlier, premature vision of Texas independence.

By the time of Santa Anna's attack on the Alamo—three months after the Texans had captured San Antonio—recuperating wounded and sick men were able to defend themselves to some degree. On the other hand, the number of diseased garrison members—like Bowie—increased as the siege lengthened, with rations, sanitation, and overall health and living conditions deteriorating to new lows. Altogether, perhaps as many as 75 sick and wounded men were now located in the hospital. For instance, Susanna Dickinson estimated that "50 or 60" wounded men, who had fallen in the December attack, were there. Such soldiers wounded during the siege of Béxar included England-born Private James Nowlan, age 27, and quite likely 31-year-old Sergeant William Daniel Hersee, who had also been born in Great Britain and was one of Captain Carey's "Invincibles."

A fairly high number of wounded and sick men was also verified by the fact that a number of Tejano and Indian women attended them. A low figure of only 60 wounded and sick at the infirmary represented more than a third of the entire Alamo garrison at the time of the siege's beginning. Such a high overall percentage also ensured that any adequate defensive effort was all but impossible.

Meticulous with such details, engineer Jameson had counted only 34 men—out of a total of 114, including officers—in the Alamo's hospital on January 18, 1836, but the garrison's health quickly worsened. More than two months later, ravages of disease and sickness had stricken a much larger number of men, like Bowie, and the lengthy siege had only made the situation worse, with additional garrison members falling ill. Even without those inflicted by a serious disease and illnesses, the rigors of the siege, the cold weather, ragged clothing to ward off the elements, no medical supplies, and lack of wood for fires guaranteed that a good many garrison members were sick by the time of the attack, and more than previously realized. Indeed, just before the Alamo's fall, Dr. Sutherland wrote how "when I left the Alamo [as a courier on February 23] there was 143 men, 110 of which was on the sick list." How many of these attempted to rouse themselves and go outside to either fight or escape is not known.

What is clear is that quite possibly more men—albeit mainly sick or injured ones—defended the hospital than had attempted to defend the northern and western perimeters, and even the lower floor of the Long Barracks. But the struggle at the second-story hospital was more intense than that of the better-publicized defense of the lower floor of the Long Barracks, the armory. These soldiers occupied the Long Barracks not because of a previously agreed upon tactical plan for a second line of defense, but because so many sick, wounded, and attendants had been caught at this location and were unable to escape. In contrast, most able-bodied men had fled toward the southern perimeter, which was not under attack, seeking to escape the slaughter.

The second story hospital atop the armory of the old convent building was the scene of the hardest-fought struggle inside the Alamo. Thanks to Mexican soldier accounts, Johnson revealed as much when he described how "it was not until then, when they became more concentrated and covered within, that the main struggle began. They were more concentrated as to space, not as to unity of command . . . "[110]

Ironically, the principal "battle"—the real last stand—within the Alamo compound's confines was not fought along the walls and perimeter, but in and around the hospital. It was there that a large percentage of the garrison was concentrated, and even if infirm, now fought for its last chance of survival. This new view of a higher percentage of defenders who were unable to defend the walls corresponds with the words of Susanna Dickinson, who said that on March 6 "about seventy-five men who had been wounded in the fight with Cós" were present with the garrison, ironically after receiving treatment from paroled Mexican surgeons.[111]

According to this number, the percentage of sick and wounded Alamo soldiers at the infirmary was higher than 40 percent. This estimation coincided in part with the opinion of a Mexican soldier born in Guanajuato, Mexico, in 1810 during the dramatic year of Hidalgo's revolution, who described particularly stiff resistance. Sergeant Francisco Becerra described the hardest fighting he faced on his day: "There was a long room [and]—it was darkened. Here the fight was bloody. It proved to be the hospital. The sick and the wounded fired from their beds and pallets."[112]

But any defense of the Long Barracks, the hospital, and other buildings was a guaranteed death sentence. Those men who entered these abode and stone structures in the hope of survival would never leave them alive. Other quick-thinking, or more fortunate soldiers realized as much, and had wisely forsaken the shelter of the Long Barracks and other structures. A large number of Alamo defenders now headed toward the palisade under the veil of darkness, unseen by the attackers. In the context of the exodus from the Alamo about to take place, it is all but certain that an unknown number of able-bodied men and walking wounded slipped out of the hospital to join them, rather than join the hopeless, confused fight at the north wall and in the plaza. Instead they rushed in the opposite direction, toward the palisade.[113]

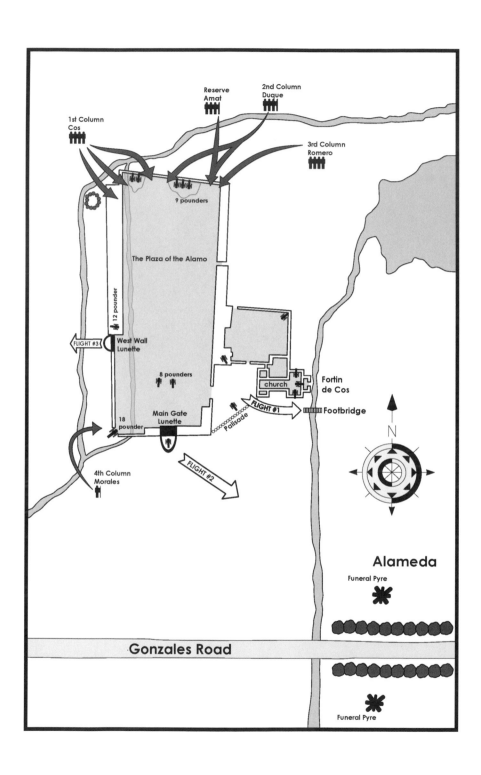

1st Column
Cos

Reserve
Amat

2nd Column
Duque

3rd Column
Romero

9 pounders

The Plaza of the Alamo

12 pounder

FLIGHT #3

West Wall
Lunette

8 pounders

church

Fortin
de Cos

FLIGHT #1

Footbridge

Palisade

Main Gate
Lunette

18
pounder

N

FLIGHT #2

4th Column
Morales

Alameda

Funeral Pyre

Gonzales Road

Funeral Pyre

7

Flight Rather than Fight

As Mexicans continued to pour into the Alamo in the dark early morning hours of March 6, most garrison members who withdrew from the north and west wall or fled the Long Barracks before entrapment understood that seeking refuge in the fort's buildings was suicidal. Therefore, a large number of men chose life over death by retiring past the Long Barracks toward the southern perimeter, away from the main Mexican attack on the north. By this time, with Morales' troops still remaining in and around the southwest corner, this sector continued to offer a relatively open avenue of withdrawal.

Ironically, by not understanding the upcoming exodus from the Alamo, historians have gotten the exact scenario reversed, with defenders dashing north across the plaza to defend the north wall instead of moving south. They have assumed that south wall defenders, especially those stationed at the palisade, raced across the plaza's great length to assist in the north wall's defense. But this traditional scenario was virtually an impossibility given the time sequences and the fact that the Mexicans had already come over the north wall and entered the plaza practically before the garrison was fully aroused.

All the while, the vast majority of the Alamo's artillery continued to be silent. Instead of cannon blasts erupting from the defenders, the loudest roar inside the Alamo came from the firing of Brown Bess muskets from the attackers, developments made possible not only by the surprise attack but also by tactical developments which made the Alamo's cannon largely useless. General Filisola explained another reason for the cannon's silence: ". . . the instinct of the [Mexican] troops as they attack, moving to the right and to the left on the North side and the movement made by Miñon and Morales with their column on the West corner of the South side which they attacked, left without a target all the guns that the enemy had located on the other three sides."[1]

In addition, because the tops of the walls were so narrow, most Alamo artillery pieces had not been placed at elevated points to defend the perimeter except at the timber and earth artillery platforms. As throughout this morning, the Alamo's considerable defensive liabilities continued to negate an abundance of artillery, even while the Mexicans surged through the plaza. There was simply no time for the vast majority of cannon along the perimeter to be turned inward to wreak havoc on the attackers in the plaza's darkness. [2]

Clearly, the considerable amount of time it took for the gunners to rush from their artillery barracks to reach their assigned positions, and then to load their cannon—combined with an inability to depress most pieces sufficiently to fire—made the Alamo's artillery all but obsolete from the beginning to the end of the struggle. Amazed by the lack of artillery fire, General Filisola concluded: "The way their cannon were positioned they were not alongside the wall, nor could they aim their fire against our men once they were surrounded by the wall itself." Therefore, perhaps only one cannon—that which had raked the Toluca Battalion—was truly effective that morning. As indicated by Filisola, the traditional story that artillery pieces were turned inward to fire inside the wide plaza swarming with Mexican troops was a myth to justify allegedly high attacker losses.

Indeed, contrary to the mythological Alamo, neither sufficient time nor manpower existed for cannon to be turned inward. For instance, the barrel alone of the 18-pounder weighed more than a ton, and, like other guns, especially those mounted on naval carriages, could not be turned inward. Most important, the relatively easy overwhelming of the key artillery positions along the perimeter—Forts Teran and Condelle and the southwest corner—was simply too swift for cannoneers to turn their guns around, which would have meant exposing their backs to the attackers.[3]

To support the myth of the defenders' combat prowess, the time-honored view that the Alamo's cannon, all loaded with homemade canister and firing effectively at close range, wreaked terrible havoc in the Mexican ranks—both inside and outside the Alamo—was a fiction to justify defensive heroics and grossly inflated Mexican losses. But General Filisola told the truth of the artillery's impotence this early

morning because of poor positioning and the lack of trained cannoneers, which ensured that even if gunners reached their pieces in time,
these artillery pieces would still have been largely ineffective.[4]

Ironically, most Mexican soldiers who became casualties from
defenders' fire—rifle, not artillery—very likely fell not outside the
Alamo's walls but on the inside, having been cut down by return fire
from the Long Barracks, the hospital, and the rooftop. Compared to the
open plaza that had become a killing field, the Long Barracks had
offered an inviting refuge, or so it seemed, to panicked survivors yet
reeling from the shock of a surprise attack at night. Therefore, for the
first time all morning, a substantial number of Alamo defenders had
come together, not by design but quite by accident.[5]

With resistance having shifted ever higher, "a lively rifle fire," in de
la Pena's words, came from the Long Barracks' rooftop at a height of
nearly twenty feet, a commanding perch. This was the most galling,
concentrated rifle and shotgun fire unleashed by the defenders that
morning. Given the hundreds of soldados massed together in the plaza,
each bullet fired could hardly miss, sometimes passing through the flesh
of more than one attacker. For the first time, Alamo riflemen finally had
a decent firing position, making a stand around the garrison's flag,
which could not yet be seen by the attackers in the darkness.[6]

Meanwhile, a large number of garrison members continued to dash
toward the southern perimeter, heading for the palisade and main gate,
which were free of attackers. Combined with the shock, surprise, and
sheer terror of the Mexican onslaught, the thought of hundreds of
attacking Mexican soldiers wielding bayonets—15 to 18 inches of cold
steel—against defenders with little ammunition, few leaders remaining,
and no bayonets of their own, hastened the flight of those men who had
not taken shelter in the Long Barracks.

Indeed, the most powerful impact of the bayonet was purely psychological, a fact well understood by Napoleon. He had found that the
mere threat of employing the bayonet was often more effective than the
weapon itself. Even the best trained soldiers of Napoleonic-era armies
often broke and ran when faced with hand-held steel, or as one British
veteran put it: "One side turns and runs away as soon as the other
comes close enough to do mischief."[7] And the Alamo defenders were
the antithesis of such veterans, without training, experience, or discipline, and therefore far more vulnerable to that fear.[8] Once they had
fired their muskets and rifles, they possessed no weapons of sufficient

length to fend off the attackers' lethal bayonets. As Santa Anna had foreseen, the panic among the reeling Anglo-Celts who were now streaming south stemmed in part from the grim prospect of facing Mexican bayonets and a miserable death.[9]

What developed, therefore, had been a merely natural response from the defenders that morning. Instead of rushing forth in a futile attempt to man the undefendable north wall, a large number of garrison members, after emerging from their sleeping quarters, remained either in the area south of the Long Barracks or the plaza. After all, in the dark, confusion, noise, and chaos, no one could tell exactly where the main attack was coming from. Consequently, other newly awakened men had rushed not to the north wall, but south to defend both the palisade and the main gate, whose defenders had been firing at Morales' column.

While the north wall had been overwhelmed, therefore, the south wall defenders along the so-called low barracks, facing the wrong way, had played no role in attempting to stop the Mexicans from pouring into the plaza. Ironically, these defenders along the south wall remained largely out of action, even after Colonel Morales' column overran the elevated 18-pounder firing platform and then joined in the attack on the Long Barracks.

With no Mexican attack striking the southern perimeter and with Santa Anna's troops swarming into their rear from the north wall, the defensive role of the men in position along the south wall, including the main gate lunette with its artillery, was negated in swift, effective fashion. If they remained in position along the south wall, then these soldiers would soon be struck from behind by the Mexicans now surging through the plaza from the north. By this time, even though the fighting in and around the Long Barracks continued unabated, groups of soldados poured farther south, advancing toward the palisade's rear. However, and fortunately for them, darkness yet protected garrison members who fled to the southern perimeter.

At this time, consequently, a large number of garrison members, primarily those defending the southern perimeter and those who had fled the north wall and bypassed the Long Barracks, now began to come together near the palisade. They either acted on their own, or at the urging of officers who had kept their heads in the chaos, like Captains Baugh or Missouri-born William Charles M. Baker, or twenty-nine-year-old Samuel Blair from McGloin's Irish Colony, if not yet killed by this time, or reliable noncommissioned officers, like English-born Sergeant James R. Dimpkins, a former member of the New Orleans Greys.

Not surprisingly, much of the Alamo garrison's strength was naturally concentrated along the southern perimeter for two primary reasons: first, to protect the wooden palisade which was the weakest sector; and second, because the Alamo's main gate was located at the south wall's center. If garrison members had acted instinctively to leave their defensive positions along the southern perimeter on their own, then a capable officer might have attempted to take charge of the chaotic situation just south of the Long Barracks, perhaps in the Alamo courtyard. With Mexicans yet scaling the north wall, charging through the plaza, or focusing on reducing the Long Barracks, some time remained for men along the southern perimeter to organize themselves. Acting out of natural impulse, these soldiers came together in the day's second ad hoc concentration of defenders, after the Long Barracks concentration.

If Sutherland was correct in his estimate that some two-thirds of garrison members were on the sick list at the siege's beginning, then some sick and walking wounded had escaped the hospital and slipped out through the darkness unseen by the attackers, traversing the relatively short distance across the courtyard to the palisade.

In the darkness and wreaths of battle-smoke that yet shielded them from the attackers' eyes, this concentration of garrison members near the palisade at the church's southwest corner was completely understandable under the circumstances. For the most part, and before an enduring legend transformed them into mythical killing machines like Thermopylae's Spartans, the Alamo men were in general more conservative and sensible compared to their more reckless comrades who had embarked upon the Matamoros expedition with relatively few troops only to meet with disaster from Santa Anna's right wing. These young men and boys at the Alamo had only wanted to survive the war—after having decided to remain in remote San Antonio which was far safer than attacking Mexico—collect land for their military service, and settle down to live the rest of their lives in peace. No one wanted to needlessly sacrifice themselves and die a noble death for an apathetic Texas, which had yet to declare its independence, as far as they knew. And now these young soldiers so far from home suddenly found themselves facing a grisly death at the hands of an enraged soldiery bent on their destruction.

Meanwhile, additional Mexicans surged toward them, and with

time running out, these refugees from the west, north, and south walls and any escapees from the Long Barracks who managed to get out in time, continued to unite as one near the palisade. Amid the relative safety of darkness, these survivors gathered together in the open ground at the southern end of the plaza, either in front of the church or in the palisade's rear. A thin window of opportunity existed for this massing of survivors because the main struggle still raged at the Long Barracks, whose doomed defenders had unwittingly bought precious time for this concentration, drawing most of the Mexicans' attention. Unobserved by Santa Anna's troops in the blackness, this tactical situation allowed time for scores of garrison members to assemble near the low, wooden palisade. Clearly, now was the time to make a break for it before it was too late, and these desperate men, fortunate in having survived in the death trap so far, knew as much.

As Santa Anna later explained without exaggeration, one of the long-overlooked realities of this bloody morning was how "a large number" of the garrison attempted to get out of the Alamo alive, "hoping to escape the bayonets of the infantry . . ."[10]

In fact, a large-scale flight from the Alamo had been fully expected by Santa Anna and was an all but inevitable result of not only the disastrous situation within the compound but due to earlier decisions. For instance, de la Pena described how Travis had informed his men on March 5 that if no help arrived, then "they would surrender the next day or would try to escape under cover of darkness." Quite simply, since the surprise attack negated any chance of the garrison's surrender as a body, only one logical alternative remained: an opportunity which, ironically, Santa Anna's nighttime assault—providing a shield of darkness—had provided.[11]

So far the overrunning of the Alamo had been surprisingly brief, perhaps only fifteen minutes had passed since the unleashing of the 5:30 a.m. assault. However, 6 a.m. was approaching, and around that time, the first faint light of day.[12]

Therefore, the natural primal instinct of flight, rather than fight, was now the only alternative for the survivors gathered at the palisade. However, the tragic fate of those men now planning to flee the indefensible Alamo was already preordained, just like the slaughtered Mexican militiamen at Zacatecas, where Sesma's lancers and dragoons had demonstrated their efficiency and ruthlessness in slaughtering opponents, including the wounded, especially after they broke and fled. And now Mexico's most apt killers of rebels, who were also the most resplendently uniformed soldiers in Santa Anna's Army, were positioned on commanding ground around the Alameda. Sesma's proud lancers looked like the famed French and Polish lancers at Napoleon's zenith of power. The colorful, elegant uniforms of Sesma's men disguised the fact that they were merciless killers. As in the past, these lancers were again inspired by the bugles blaring the Deguello, which was commanding them to kill without pity.

And now on March 6's early morning, the situation would be much worse for far fewer rebels of a different race, culture, and religion. Long before reaching San Antonio, Santa Anna had desired to get the Alamo garrison out in the open, an ideal scenario in which it could be easily destroyed: American riflemen without cover matched up against the "superior equestrian skills" of tough cavalrymen and well-trained lancers for whom even Texas cavalrymen were no match. As early as November 1835, an American in Texas wrote of an ugly reality that was about to be enacted on the early morning of March 6 outside the Alamo's walls: "But in our open prairies, riflemen cannot withstand a vigorous charge of cavalry," especially on this cold morning.[13]

As directed by the melodramatic Santa Anna, the brass regimental band of the Dolores Cavalry continued to play the Deguello's haunting strains, inspiring the soldados to kill without mercy. Little more than a funeral dirge for those about to attempt to escape the Alamo, this surreal-sounding tune spoke of a bloody past of bitter warfare—an 800-year holy crusade—between Spaniards and Islamic warriors, before the Christians finally swept the Moors out of Spain during the Reconquesta. No quarter had long distinguished this brutal religious conflict that raged across the plains and mountains of Spain for what seemed like an eternity. Inspired by the Koran's harsh justice to "infidels," the Moors had long perfected the brutal art of no quarter by way of beheading unfortunate captured Christians.

Now on this increasingly violent morning, the unforgettable tune from a haunted, vindictive past represented a brutal killing time thousands of miles from Spain. Instead of disdaining the dark-skinned fighting men of Santa Anna's Army, the color-conscious Anglo-Celts would have been far less overconfident had they realized that the conquering Islamic armies had included large numbers of fighting men of African descent. And contrary to the mythical Alamo, the playing of the eerie-sounding Deguello would set the mood for the killing of more northamericano rebels outside the Alamo than inside.[14]

Like a well-oiled machine, Santa Anna's cavalrymen and lancers were well prepared—both in terms of experience and in position placement at the Alameda—for the bloody work that lay ahead. Santa Anna's horsemen—"a well appointed cavalry" in one American's words—had brutally "finished the job" of exterminating hundreds of the hapless Zacatecas Mexican militiamen: an ugly, but highly effective, performance, which was about to be repeated by these hardened cavalrymen from far-away Mexico.[15]

Ever since he had taken command, the politically minded Travis, over-zealous to make a name for himself, although the Alamo's command had been thrust upon him almost by accident, had been the chief obstacle for the many garrison members—the majority in fact—who had long wanted to either attempt a surrender, or to make a break for safety rather than be killed to the last man as proclaimed by Santa Anna's red flag. This considerable divergence of opinion in no small part explained the overall feeble defensive effort, because a good many soldiers—choose not to rush to the walls to die with Travis to attempt to do the impossible. With Travis, along with other officers, now dead at the north wall, in the plaza, and in the Long Barracks, the way was now clear for common soldiers to make a break for it.

As ever-independent minded volunteers, Alamo defenders had earlier refused to take orders from Travis and other officers they deemed unsuitable, ensuring that they would act largely on their own during the moment of crisis such as this. Inexperienced and with little discipline, surviving garrison members now readily agreed with the wise sentiments of Crockett—a common sense soldier and "high private"—who had earlier voiced a widespread opinion that especially applied at this moment: "I think we had better march out and die in the open air [as] I don't like to be hemmed up" like the doomed Creeks at the gruesome killing fields at Tullusahatchee and Horseshoe Bend.[16]

Contrary to the mythical Alamo, Travis had held the Alamo "against the will of his subordinates," in the words of de la Pena, who later learned as much from Travis' own slave, Joe. But now the Alamo's commander was dead, and the men could make decisions entirely on their own, especially about living or dying in a worthless old mission.[17]

One modern historian, W.H. Brands, recently surmised that: "Quite conceivably, Travis was considering a fighting retreat [east down the Gonzales Road]. After all, by now the chances of surviving a Mexican attack appeared negligible; the Alamo simply could not be held. The men could either die where they were or die trying to get out—and in the latter case some might survive. There would be no dishonor in trying to save his force now that it had become clear—as a result of the refusal of the provisional government, of the rest of the army, and of the citizens of Texas to relieve the garrison—that the Alamo could not be saved [therefore] once the shooting started [there would be] little control over what the men did. Would they fight harder in the Alamo, with no hope of surviving, or on the road to Gonzales, with some hope?"[18]

Amid such chaos, noise, and confusion, what made this ad hoc group of around 62 Alamo defenders near the palisade possible was the fact that the gathering was very likely based upon a pre-determined plan of escape made by the common soldiers and not officers. But if officers were part of this decision, then they most likely would have been volunteers rather than regulars. Instead of facing a night attack, the men had only shortly before expected to reach terms with the enemy, and "being allowed to march out with their arms and go join their government," wrote Sergeant Manuel Loranca of Sesma's cavalry.[19]

Indeed, Travis' slave Joe stated that the Alamo's commander had made the decision that if no reinforcements arrived on March 5, then they would attempt one last negotiation with Santa Anna the next morning, and if that effort failed then they would "try to escape" from the Alamo on the night of March 6. This desperate scheme would in part explain why these men formed up at the palisade as if according to a prearranged plan. The development even raises the interesting, if remote, possibility that Travis might have formed these men and led them out of the Alamo himself. After all, as far as anyone really knows, because of the problems with the testimony of Joe, who very likely never went to the north wall (especially as a soldier like he claimed), Travis could have fallen at any stage of the fight.[20] While the contemporary evidence points to his death early in the battle at the north wall—quite likely by suicide—it must also be acknowledged that in the darkness and confusion of that morning, other scenarios may have occurred.

Historian William C. Davis has speculated that Travis "may even have suggested that if the enemy breached their defenses, the men should resist as long as possible, then go over the east wall and try to get away as best they could toward Goliad."[21]

But most likely, this plan to escape was a common soldiers' arrangement. The men of the garrison had to think and act for themselves in the heat of combat, especially after the walls were breached. And this apparently also meant ignoring whatever the upstart Travis had ordered them to do that morning, including rushing forward to defend the north wall that could not be held. This last-ditch plan for flight evidently had been established for some time, and by the common soldiers in the ranks who wanted neither glory nor higher rank, but to live on for their wives and children.[22]

While Travis' eloquent letters and defiant cannon shot on February 23 had proclaimed his fiery determination to hold the Alamo to the bitter end, the common soldiers in the ranks felt differently about such a needless sacrifice for no tactical or strategic sense. Unlike Travis and other, the average man in the ranks—especially the volunteers whose dependability was questioned by their Alabama commander—were not seeking glory or immortality, or pursuing personal ambition at any cost. Most of all, these soldiers wanted to survive and fight another day, and this was not possible if they remained inside the Alamo by either fighting or surrendering. To better understand the real Alamo that so thoroughly contradicts the mythical Alamo, this struggle must be analyzed from the bottom up—or from the view of the common soldiers—and not from that of the Alamo's leadership, which traditional historians have glorified for so long. Most significant, Travis' own "insulting" replies to Santa Anna had sealed the Alamo garrison's fate long before the final attack, and this death-sentence—organized not by the enemy but by their commander—had not sat well with garrison members.[23]

Therefore, most likely, this daring plan of escape had been developed by the men in the ranks for some time, thanks to the growing sense of abandonment, ever-dwindling supplies of ammunition, futility of resistance against impossible odds, and the prospect of no reinforcements arriving in time during the siege. And the best chance for escape had been a break-out at night to gain the Gonzales Road for a flight east to safety. In a strange twist of fate, moreover, Santa Anna's pre-dawn attack now provided an opportunity for escape after all.

Knowledge of the planned escape attempt was well known both inside and outside the Alamo before March 6. After all, Santa Anna had decided to launch his attack in the predawn hours partly because he had received reliable intelligence about a nighttime escape attempt. That daring plan had been postponed by Travis from March 5 until the next night, perhaps so that garrison members could finally get some rest to maximize their chances for a successful escape.

In addition, the plan might have been not only worked out in detail, but also even rehearsed to some extent, which would explain how the attempt was formed in the near-darkness with the battle raging around them. Word of Travis' death, as well as knowledge of Bowie's incapacitation, would have given survivors more cause to decide to attempt to get out of the death trap as soon as possible.

Once again, rather than a manifestation of cowardice in such a no-win situation, such a perfectly logical decision was fully understandable under the circumstances. What has been so often overlooked in explaining what exactly happened in regard to the exodus from the Alamo was the fact that the Alamo's defenders were not soldiers in the conventional sense—and even some of the best trained troops would have broken in such a situation. Therefore, even de la Pena felt some sympathy for these men "inexperienced and untried in the science of war." Contrary to the enduring Alamo myth, the defenders were anything but hardy frontiersmen who knew had to handle a Long Rifle—now in short supply—with expert skill, swing a tomahawk, and slash with a knife. In fact, five defenders were city boys from Philadelphia, and many others hailed from large urban areas, where a rifle's use was hardly a requirement of daily life. Instead, these amateurs under arms were mostly clerks, merchants, farmers, craftsmen, teachers, and lawyers instead of well-trained fighting men. The large number of immigrants, especially the Irish, also indicated the lack of military backgrounds. The fact that so many defenders chose to flee rather than fight at this point was perfectly in keeping with their civilian backgrounds, natural proclivities, little military experience, and citizen-soldier inclinations. Contrary to the traditional Alamo mythology, possessing a death-wish or desiring to die as a martyr for Texas were the lowest of all priorities at this time.

But perhaps best explaining the flight rather than flight impulse was the fact that the Alamo garrison had been on the verge of surrender. After lawyer-turned-courier Lieutenant James Butler Bonham, of South Carolina, and a twenty-nine-year-old former member of the Mobile Greys, brought the news on March 3 that Fannin would not reinforce the Alamo from Goliad, plans for both a surrender and an attempt to escape were formulated by garrison members. However, such decisions played a role in sabotaging the possibility of a solid defense. Not only was the Alamo garrison divided in regard to the very leaders they supported, but also by multiple strategies: 1) stand-and-fight at the Alamo to buy time for Texas; 2) surrender to Santa Anna before he attacked;

or 3) make an attempt to escape the Alamo at night. Volunteers, like their leader Bowie and including Crockett and his Tennesseeans, were most inclined to make a last-minute attempt to negotiate with Santa Anna, while the regulars, Travis followers, were more resolute.

Continuing to fight inside the fort, of course, ensured that it was only a matter of time before the entire garrison was overwhelmed. Since the defenders knew of the no-quarter policy, remaining inside the compound meant risking capture, especially if wounded. Then, the worst of all fates was expected: torture, before being killed by the victors. For these men, the common frontier analogy between the Mexicans and Native Americans early existed. So pervasive was this conviction that even Crockett's death would later be attributed by American newspapermen in part to a tomahawk wound! The fear of torture had been a regular feature of warfare with Native Americans, ever since the Anglo-Celtic people had migrated west from the eastern seaboard. Unfamiliar with either Tejano or Mexican culture or ways of war, the naive Alamo men, therefore, had long viewed the Mexican soldado like the Native American warrior in this regard.

Very likely among these 62 men assembling at the palisade and forming into line were a large percentage, if not all, of the 32 volunteers from Gonzales. More than any other garrison members, they possessed more good reason to attempt this desperate bid to escape and reach the Gonzales Road, which, after all, led straight to their homes and families some 70 miles to the east, unlike other Alamo defenders far from home.

Since their March 1 arrival, the Gonzales volunteers had been almost certainly appalled by the deplorable conditions inside the Alamo: the lack of ammunition; the relatively few defenders; the fort's overwhelming size; the Mexican Army's might; sinking morale among the garrison with each passing day; the considerable deep divisions among leaders and men; the lack of thorough defensive preparations; no reinforcements from Goliad; and prospect of torture before execution if captured or wounded, as proclaimed by the no quarter flag.

The Gonzales volunteers were very likely early to realize that their presence made absolutely no difference at the Alamo, and that they would only lengthen the list of dead. Worst of all, dying a soldier's death in San Antonio might well seal the fate of families at home, for everyone knew that Santa Anna would next march to Gonzales, the westernmost Anglo-Celtic community in Texas, after the Alamo fell. Long vulnerable and isolated, Gonzales already had been burned to the ground by Indians, and now it was sure to happen again when a vengeful Santa Anna arrived.

Consequently, the 32 soldiers from Gonzales would have been especially eager to make the attempt to bolt from the Alamo to gain the Gonzales Road to eventually reach their homes and families. Given these factors, instead of having raised the garrison's morale, the distinct possibility exists that these Gonzales volunteers might have been among the most vocal advocates of breaking out of the Alamo. Therefore, at the timbered palisade, 32 Gonzales men may well have made up the first group of escapees who prepared to move out in an organized, disciplined manner, as if by deliberate, premeditated design. Gonzales soldiers like George Kimbell and teenager John Benjamin Kellogg, who had married only the year before the former wife of Alamo defender Thomas R. Miller, possessed double reasons to flee since both their wives were now pregnant. (More than twice Kellogg's age and the wealthiest man in Gonzales, Miller might well have delighted in having seen his upstart rival, evidently handsome and robust, already killed this morning in hell.)

Also perhaps with this group of 62 men at the palisade's rear were the three Tennessee-born Taylor brothers of Liberty, Texas, 22-year-old James, George, age 20, and Edward Taylor, age 24. Since kids back in the Volunteer State, they had always stuck together, especially in a crisis. They certainly now realized what an impact the devastating news of the loss of three sons would have on their parents, Anson and Elizabeth, bestowing them with another strong motivation to escape.

With a no-quarter flag flying high in the morning's fading darkness and the Deguello blaring from bugles and regimental bands, the plan of escape called for an initial break-out through the small sally port, where the wooden palisade met the southwest corner of the church, in an attempt to gain the Gonzales Road. Sandwiched between the church and the low barracks, this weakest point along the entire Alamo perimeter offered an ideal escape route. Then a swift march eastward could reach safety and meet Houston's reinforcements now gathering in the east to come to the Alamo's relief, or so they believed.

Consequently, 62 men began to form in an ad hoc but organized formation that seemed to indicate some prior planning, because such discipline under stress was a characteristic lacking in such untrained, inexperienced troops when in the process of being overrun. Despite the utter shock of the surprise attack, deafening noise, and chaotic confusion, the first organized formation of garrison members now took shape at the palisade. An escalating sense of desperation and fast-fleeting hopes for survival guaranteed that these unruly volunteers, who could hardly form a straight line or take an officer's order without endless questions prior to the attack, fell into a neat formation that would have impressed even Travis.

Many of these men—a large percentage of the entire Alamo garrison—perhaps never fired a shot from either the walls or the plaza area, since they had hastened to the palisade in such short order. Even Santa Anna, an experienced commander who had fought against Spanish, Mexicans, and Indians, was incredulous at the garrison's relatively feeble resistance. He wrote how "a large number" of the Alamo garrison never fought in the conflict.[24]

Assembled in tight ranks in an organized manner that perhaps indicated not only previous planning but also that some discipline had been instilled by Lieutenant Tony Finch, a regular United States Army veteran who had served as the garrison's drill master earlier that winter, the formation of 62 soldiers prepared to move out. These men were about to march away from the struggle continuing to roar in the Long Barracks, slipping away from their doomed comrades, including the relative handful of artillerymen yet working their guns at the church's rear. On command, these men now marched rapidly through the Alamo's sally port, a relatively small opening at the left end of the low wooden palisade. A perfect opportunity for escape now existed, because it was still dark and no Mexicans stood before the southern perimeter at the time. As important, the eastern edge of the timbered palisade offered the second best point—after the main gate near the south wall's center—for a large number of garrison members to escape the compound.

At this especially weak point between the church and the southern perimeter of walls and buildings, the wooden palisade covered a front of around 100 feet. It extended from the church's southwest corner to the east end of the south wall, a narrow building like so much of the perimeter. This palisade was a relatively low barrier consisting of two parallel rows—about six feet apart and with earth packed in between—of upright cedar logs that stood about six to seven feet high. Outside this timbered palisade, defended by at least one gun, perhaps two, of relatively small caliber in the center, was a ditch with an abatis of felled trees before it. This obstacle for advancing infantry had been set in place by Cós' troops the previous year.[25]

Very likely every man of this sizeable escape column knew what lay just beyond on higher ground to the southeast: the Alameda. The Alameda's western end was about 300 yards distant, while its eastern end was around 400 yards. It was named for a double row of tall, majestic Rio Grande cottonwood trees, now bare of leaves and wearing their dull, brown winter appearance but with light gray bark, that lined both sides of the Gonzales Road. Perched on relatively high ground with the Alamo nestled in the lowest point of the shallow river valley below, the Alameda overlooked the compound now wreathed in battle-smoke and echoing with sounds of fury. Most important for the escapees, the Gonzales Road led to the even higher ground of Powder House Hill, located on the distant eastern horizon, rising above the grassy, wind-swept prairie like a beacon to soldiers desperate to escape a living night-mare. And, of course, these men fully realized that the town of Gonzales and safety lay down this dusty road to the east.

One central Alamo myth holds that the compound was surround-ed and attacked by Mexican troops on all sides, making any escape of defenders impossible. But in reality, this was not the case: in fact, because three of the four assault columns had concentrated at the north wall, this left most of the Alamo's perimeter wide open, on the east, south, and west. This erroneous assumption—not seriously questioned before—lies at the heart of the last stand myth, serving as a primary rea-son why the escape of so many garrison members has seemed like an unimaginable, unrealistic possibility to both historians and buffs for so long.

Another assumption that bolstered the last stand mythology was that defenders at the palisade and the south wall abandoned their posi-tion to assist in the north wall's defense. But very likely many of these men at the palisade and other south wall sectors did not race north across the plaza to defend Fortin Teran, but in fact remained in place. In addition, other newly aroused soldiers assigned to the north wall might have gone in the other direction, or south, after emerging from their sleeping quarters in the Long Barracks. When Cós' troops swarmed over the north end of the west wall, or the northwest corner at Fortin Condelle, they also entered the compound through buildings at the northern end of the west wall with the aid of tools, like axes, because resistance was so "surprisingly light." This development would seem to indicate that these west wall defenders had likewise fled across the plaza to join the first group of escapees, avoiding the risk of getting cut off from attackers pouring over the north wall and through the plaza.

Fast-moving tactical developments provided several opportunities for Alamo men to escape but none more than at the palisade and the south wall. And Santa Anna had realized as much from the beginning, employing his cavalry in an attempt to eliminate escapes at these points by placing his cavalry at the Alameda. After all, Colonel Morales' column was too small to achieve any gains along the southern perimeter. Instead, Morales' troops had pushed along the perimeter and then attacked west to strike the Alamo's southwest corner, opening up a lengthy avenue and gaping hole for potential escape for defenders not only from the palisade's sally port, but also eventually from the lunette protecting the main gate.

After overrunning the southwest corner, Morales' troops joined in the attack on the Long Barracks, leaving these two exit points wide open. Escape was now possible for the 62 men, because of all points along the Alamo's extensive perimeter, the palisade was the most accessible entry-exist point, thanks to the sally port, or gate, by the corner of the church.

Ironically, Santa Anna's forces had not attacked the low palisade, which was the Alamo's weakest link. Such a seemingly incomprehensible tactical error might have caused a perplexed de la Pena to complain how his aristocratic Creole commander-in-chief was simply not "a wise general."[26]

Instead of having targeted the palisade with a heavy column, three of Santa Anna's columns had converged on the north wall, which was a strongpoint in comparison. From a strictly tactical viewpoint, therefore, Santa Anna's plan of assault seemed to make little sense. After all, why would the main focus of Santa Anna's attack be on the north wall, where the guns of both Forts Teran and Condelle stood defending a position that had been repeatedly strengthened, when the Alamo's opposite side, the southern, was the weakest point along the entire perimeter? In the past, historians have merely dismissed Santa Anna's tactical errors and miscalculations during the attack as simply yet another example, like at San Jacinto, of inferior generalship. But was this really the case?

Many have assumed that because Crockett and his Tennessee riflemen—once again the magical aura of the Long Rifle dominated—were stationed at the palisade, Santa Anna had been afraid to attack this point. Consequently, the mythology grew that the palisade provided the

Alamo's most staunch defense that morning, when in fact it saw little initial action, because Morales' column did not target the palisade but the main gate, simply bypassing the position.

But has this casual denunciation of Santa Anna's tactical abilities really been well founded? Would an imaginative, audacious general who had achieved so much success in the past now so seriously blunder in his plan to storm the Alamo? Perhaps in the end, it had been no tactical error committed by Santa Anna in sending his smallest group of attackers—a mere 100 to 125 men of his "Scouting Companies" under Colonel Morales—against the southern perimeter.[27]

First, thanks to leaked solid and timely information, Santa Anna was already aware of the garrison's desperate plan to attempt to flee the next night. This was one primary reason why he had attacked that early morning instead of starving out the garrison with a more lengthy siege, or waiting for the arrival of his larger caliber artillery to simply batter down the Alamo's walls. In fact, the distinct possibly exists that Santa Anna committed no tactical blunder at all, and that his apparently glaring omission may have been part of the generalissimo's calculated, deliberate plan. It may have been no coincidence that the palisade was left open as a tempting avenue of escape, since Santa Anna had placed his lancers in the exact position, around the Alameda, for exactly the eventuality that occurred—the initial exodus from the Alamo from a palisade free of attackers.[28]

Santa Anna, therefore, quite likely laid a clever trap for the demoralized garrison to either die in the Alamo or attempt an escape: a choice that was simple under the circumstances. The best avenue—the little gate at the low palisade—by which a large number of survivors could escape was left largely open. Most likely, the cagey Santa Anna, who yet thought like the cavalryman that at heart he was, desired most of all to get a large percentage of his enemy out in the open, where they could easily be cut to pieces by his horse-soldiers, who he had set in place for such an eventuality. By a large percentage of the garrison choosing flight to fight, the Mexican commander could negate not only the Alamo's defensive arrangements and the garrison's Long Rifles, but also the largest concentration of artillery between New Orleans and Mexico City. If this was indeed the case as evidence suggests, then such a clever scheme worked to perfection that morning.

Such a well-conceived tactical plan is attested in the diary of Josiah Gregg, who recorded his conversations with Don Jose Antonio

Navarro, who told him that Santa Anna had deliberately "left the eastern side of the fortification free, in hopes the Texans would escape." Either Gregg misunderstood, or perhaps the translation was erroneous, because Navarro most likely meant the southeastern side, because Colonel Romero's column—much larger than Morales' column—had been selected to strike the eastern perimeter. But because of the exodus from the Alamo, what Navarro almost certainly meant to confer was that the southwest corner of the church at the palisade had been deliberately left open.[29]

As dawn was about to break on that hellish March 6, an organized group of 62 men prepared to march out of the Alamo under the shroud of darkness. They began to file swiftly through the sally port, while the vast majority of Santa Anna's troops remained busy, rooting out defenders in the Long Barracks, the hospital, and other dark, dank buildings that had become death-traps for their defenders. In an orgy of killing, the Mexicans now "went from room to room looking for an American to kill." But their sacrifice was not wasted. The struggle swirling around the Long Barracks and hospital allowed a large percentage of the garrison to assemble and take the inviting bait of an escape route left open by Santa Anna, if that was the case, while those still fighting tied up Santa Anna's attackers and bought additional time—though unwittingly—for the evacuation through the palisade.

Santa Anna, however, was determined that there would be no escape from the Alamo. The Mexican cavalry had therefore been placed in and around the Alameda to ensure that no garrison members reached the Gonzales Road. Then he had ordered his elite cavalry troops to form in an expansive ring around the Alamo to guard against any breakouts.[30]

More important in tactical terms, Santa Anna had cleverly kept the highest concentration of General Sesma's cavalry out-of-sight of the garrison, perhaps so that defenders would be more likely to attempt their escape. As a young, impressionable cavalryman who had chosen the utterly-ruthless General Arredondo as his mentor, Santa Anna had been part of the hard-riding Mexican horsemen who played a key role in slaughtering American and Tejano revolutionaries at the 1813 battle of Medina, after their battle-lines were smashed and flight resulted: an earlier Zacatecas formula for success. In many ways, the essence of Santa Anna as a military commander had been forged on that day. Especially now on this early morning, Santa Anna never forgot the Medina's bloody lessons, which called for the same brutality to destroy the current dream of a Texas Republic and its believers.[31]

Unfortunately for the Alamo's would-be escapees, it was already too late for the 62 men who by this time had slipped out of the palisade. Ironically, as de la Pena emphasized, "Travis could have managed to escape during the first few nights [of the siege], when vigilance was much less," but now it was much too late but to die lonely deaths far from home and families.[32]

Santa Anna had deliberately kept his cavalry out-of-sight at the Alameda so that anyone fleeing the Alamo would continue to believe that a chance of escape existed. And because it was yet half-dark, the desperate young men and boys who fled through the palisade sally port never realized that some of Santa Anna's finest combat troops were before them, awaiting their arrival with what they feared the most: the cavalrymen's long lances.

Contrary to the time-honored tradition of the mythical Alamo, it was not so much the Alamo's walls that were the real trap for the defenders, but in fact the clever tactical trap laid by Santa Anna *outside* the fort. Along with the concentration of cavalry in and around the Alameda, the ring of Mexican horse-soldiers around the Alamo to eliminate escape had been formed in the darkness, so that garrison members did not know of their deployment.

With high hopes for survival, the 62 soldiers continued to emerge through the sally port of the palisade at the church's southwest corner. So eager were these men to depart that they left behind not only an ever-dwindling band of comrades but the flag of the New Orleans Greys. In a hurry to escape detection by any soldados who had advanced into the Alamo courtyard, the escapees then jumped over the ditch and struggled through the abatis of felled timber—that pointed the other way—in the first faint light of day that began to illuminate the scene of massacre. Once over the abatis of felled mesquite and larger cottonwood trees and limbs, the escapees reformed into line on the open ground opposite the church's southeast corner. These men now wisely remained close together for protection, knowing that a concentrated volley might deter any pursuers. Then, in a sprint for life, they dashed forward on the double into the open beyond the Alamo's immediate confines with discipline that would soon astound awaiting Mexican cavalrymen.

After all, these detested northamericano "rebels" were long considered nothing but an unruly rabble by Mexico's military elite. Therefore, from the Alameda's relatively high ground, General Sesma could hardly believe his eyes in the first faint glimmer of morning light, which now revealed the escape attempt. A faint glow on the horizon indicated that they had lost their gamble to reach the Gonzales Road under cover of darkness. As General Sesma wrote in his March 11 report to Santa Anna: "Many of them believed their retreat was secure as they left the fort from the right [the southeast], and so many came out that they marched organized on the plains . . . ."[33]

In another missive, Sesma summarized the exact tactical sequence that caused this sizeable flight of defenders: "When the fire began and the enemy was dislodged from their first line of fortifications [the north wall] many of them had believed that they could find a place of safety by leaving the fort on the right [and] Indeed, a sufficient number of them came forth that [they] ran in an organized manner towards the unobstructed flatland . . . " Hardly believing his eyes, Sergeant Manuel Loranca, of the Dolores Cavalry Regiment, stationed around the Alameda, never forgot the sight with the dawn's first light that revealed from the environs around the Alamo, now shrouded in a rising cloud of sulphurous battle smoke, how some "Sixty-two Texians [had] sallied from the east side of the fort . . . ."[34]

Moving quickly to save themselves in the half-light before the sun inched higher over the eastern horizon to more fully reveal their desperate flight, the immediate objective of this "organized" escape attempt was the relatively high, open ground of the Alameda and the Gonzales Road. Simple survival now depended upon the men reaching the Alameda to the southeast. Here, the alluring sight of the picturesque twin rows of cottonwood trees—like an oasis on the prairie in the half-light—was now barely illuminated.[35]

These Texas men and United States volunteers very likely were also making an attempt to reach the high ground to make a defensive stand on this natural perch that dominated the lower-lying Alamo. Here, from good cover provided by the cottonwood trees, they could at least defend themselves and fight Indian-style. After all, throughout the siege, some Alamo defenders had wanted to escape the Alamo to fight in the open. The diminutive, red-haired jockey, Henry Warnell, a 24-year-old artilleryman of Captain Carey's "Invincibles," who either deserted his cannon or never reached it in the first place that morning, was very likely one of these escapees. A sharp horse trader from Arkansas who had settled in Bastrop, Texas, he had earlier expressed a common sentiment among garrison members by saying, "I'd much rather be out in that open prairie [as] I don't like to be penned in like this."[36]

Well known as much for his love of chewing tobacco as riding horses, Warnell was one of the few fortunate defenders destined to survive not only the fighting, but also the flight from the Alamo. It is not known which group of escapees he departed with on this bloody morning. Or perhaps he went out individually on his own without being seen, slipping by Mexican cavalrymen. But the best chance for him to have escaped the death-trap was with the first group that dashed from the palisade, because the Mexicans would be better prepared for later escape attempts in more daylight. In addition, and contrary to the mythical story that he "deserted" the garrison before the assault, Rose also very likely "would have been among those that ran," especially the 62 soldiers who had suddenly emerged from the palisade's sally port.[37]

The flight of this largest group of garrison members—more than a third of the garrison—was very likely as much a maneuver to reposition themselves to gain some slight tactical advantage to defend themselves as it was a bid for eventual freedom to escape down the Gonzales Road. This possibility was indicated by the relative discipline of those marching out from the palisade. Amazingly, from the beginning and thereafter, this escape attempt was not a wild flight but the departure of an "organized" force of garrison members, who were fully prepared to do more fighting but in a new place, preferably high ground, of their own choosing. And because a Mexican encampment, now vacated with the general attack well underway, was nearby, perhaps this large group of men, now low of ammunition, desired to capture the Matamoros Battalion's camp in the Alameda area to secure black powder.[38]

Of course, no one knows how much, if any, ammunition the soldiers of this formation yet possessed. Throughout the siege, black powder supplies were low, and by March 6 the amount was far lower, resulting in a "scarcity of ammunition." To secure additional ammunition, therefore, black powder rather than shot, was a top priority by this time. Even killing Mexican soldiers met along the way would have meant gaining black powder from their cartridge boxes.

Additionally a Mexican artillery emplacement had been seen earlier in the Alameda area. This position might have been targeted for capture because these men, especially if nearly out of ammunition, knew that black powder would have been available for the guns. Hence, this artillery emplacement might have been deliberately targeted by this first group of escapees, who "ran in an organized manner," and seemingly with purpose beyond that of escape, from the Alamo.[39]

In addition, freshly dug trenches were now located in the area in and around the Alameda. These had been dug by the Matamoros Battalion's soldados to protect their encampment during the siege, and in case the Alamo garrison attempted to reach the Gonzales Road. For thirteen days of siege, the defenders had viewed these earthworks being dug by Mexican troops, who were just out of lethal killing range of even the Long Rifle. These light works up ahead were now empty, with the Matamoros Battalion in action. However, even as the morning's first light descended upon the land and with visibility yet low, especially on the lower ground near the church's rear, the escapees failed to realize that Santa Anna's cavalrymen were in position up ahead. Not even the brightly colored banderolas, or the pennons, of the Vera Cruz lancers could yet be seen.

With either Captain Baugh or another leading officer, perhaps even Crockett or Travis himself, leading the way, these 62 men not only escaped a death-trap but also now gained an opportunity—denied those inside the Alamo—to fight a defensive battle from cottonwood trees and trenches on ground, if gained, that commanded a wide area. Open prairie land below the Alameda offered attackers little, if any, cover, and was part of "the unobstructed flatland," in General Sesma's words.

Perhaps if a defensive stand could be made at the Alameda, and they could hold out on the high ground along the Gonzales Road, then they could buy time to eventually escape that night across the rolling prairie lands leading from San Antonio to Gonzales. But before reaching the Alameda to the southeast, the 62 men first had to cross around 300 yards of mostly open terrain to gain the western edge of the Alameda, its closest point. The only natural vegetation was underbrush and little, snarled mesquite trees and small cottonwood saplings that thrived in low-lying areas near water, in this case the deeply gorged aqueduct, or irrigation ditch, that ran roughly north-south along the Alamo's eastern perimeter and perpendicular to its southern perimeter. This lengthy ditch—ironically part of the same irrigation network by which Colonel Morales' column had advanced westward undetected to strike the Alamo's southwest corner—flowed from the Alamo church's rear to nearly the Alameda's western end before crossing the Gonzales Road. General Sesma described the area around the irrigation ditch as "bushy and craggy ground" that was distinctive because the other surroundings were either open prairie or old cornfields without trees or underbrush.

Previous Alamo messengers, such as Missourian John W. Smith, age 44 and from the river town of Hannibal (birthplace of Mark Twain) on the Mississippi, and 28-year-old, Rhode Island-born Captain Albert Martin of Gonzales, had only escaped Santa Anna's vigilant cavalry by first taking shelter in this irrigation ditch, slipping away undetected to reach the Alameda and the Gonzales Road. Since the siege's beginning, the entire garrison was well aware of the Alamo's best and most reliable escape route, which now could serve as shelter if the men were suddenly attacked on the open prairie. Indeed, this convenient ditch had served as the Alamo's primary entry and exit point throughout the siege. Both then and now, only one simple formula for escape remained, and it was simply to generally follow "the irrigation ditch [and] then left, onto the Gonzales road."[40]

Even many years later but blessed with a keen memory, Tejano Enrique Esparza recalled, "There was a ditch of running water back of the church."[41]Generating a steady flow of brackish water from the San Antonio River, these old aqueducts had been dug by the Spanish as early as 1718, when the mission was founded, and irrigated the fields sufficiently to provide food in this dry region.[42]

Perhaps the shelter of the irrigation ditch had been part of the original plan of escape. However, this ditch had definitely become an ideal escape avenue because of two developments that occurred almost simultaneously: first, the sun had risen higher, and second, more important, now was positioned "on the east, a squadron of lancers, flanked by a ditch, to cut off the retreat at the time of the assault," in the words of Sergeant Manuel Loranca of the Dolores Cavalry Regiment, who was stationed at the Alameda. Alerted to the lengthy line of lancers up ahead after the foremost soldiers of the escape column had crossed the little log foot-bridge over the irrigation ditch, these men naturally took full advantage of the position. The irrigation ditch provided good cover, thanks to the natural vegetation growing thickly alongside and because it was deeply gorged at a level of several feet or more. Best of all for the 62 men who had slipped out of the Alamo, this ditch led straight south toward the Alameda. Here, only a relatively short distance southeast of the timbered palisade, this sheltered avenue and natural ingress point, half-hidden by tangles of underbrush, offered the only shelter and place of concealment on the open prairie.

But this stealthy maneuver of pushing through the screen of brush by way of the aqueduct in an attempt to eventually gain the Alameda's high ground did not go unnoticed by Santa Anna's leading cavalryman. Thanks to his vantage point at the Alameda, General Sesma viewed the fast-moving drama being played out below him. He wrote how these 62 men, after having marched out of the compound and into the open now sought concealment in the saplings and underbrush lining the irrigation ditch, attempting "to take advantage of the nearby branal [sic]" in the half-light.[43] (As used by General Sesma in this context, the Spanish word "brenal" meant ground that was overgrown with weeds, saplings, and underbrush.)

Pushing ever farther south and away from the palisade under the cover of the brushy, muddy aqueduct after nearly two weeks of siege, these 62 men must have initially felt a new lease on life. After all, they had escaped a death-trap and an inevitable massacre. Even now, those comrades left behind in the Alamo's dark recesses, the Long Barracks, hospital, church, and other buildings, were in the process of being slaughtered to the last man.

With the first rays of dawn lightening the eastern horizon that allowed them to be seen by General Sesma, the escapees hoped that by moving away—south instead of southeast—from the squadron of Vera Cruz Lancers with whom they had first exchanged shots, they could yet escape. In and around the aqueduct's shelter they moved steadily south in the hazy half-light, hoping to reach the Alameda. Even more in their desperate situation, any officers with this party would have attempted to keep everyone together in a tight group. After all, an organized formation would be needed to reach the Alameda in strength, because a clash was all but inevitable, after they had earlier sparred with the foremost members of the veteran lancer squadron.

At this time, these men might have planned to emerge from the aqueduct's cover at some point just below the western end of the Alameda, around 300 yards from the Alamo. But it was already too late for a successful escape. At some point and for whatever reason, perhaps encountering either deeper water in the irrigation ditch or no longer concealed by its natural vegetation, the 62 men emerged from the area of the ditch and made a dash across open ground. In response, the ever-vigilant General Sesma now took decisive action after sighting the escapees emerge out in "the plains." The luck of these Alamo defenders had now come to an abrupt end.[44]

With their quarry flushed from the Alamo's dark confines as if a

Godsend from a smiling, all-knowing Lady of Guadalupe, General Sesma and his elite cavalrymen were ready and waiting—as Santa Anna had foreseen—for the first group of escapees when they suddenly burst into the open like a covey of quail. General Sesma was a hardened professional and a martinet. Always wanting to improve his soldier's effectiveness, this serious-minded cavalry commander had petitioned authorities in Mexico City to eliminate the time-honored practice of allowing women camp followers, who reduced the army's mobility and speed. With little compassion for either these women or children, and far less for the northamericano rebels, Sesma wanted to uphold the service's professionalism. This natural cavalryman, like Santa Anna, was now presented with a golden opportunity to wipe out a large percentage of the Alamo garrison on the open ground outside the walls.

Leaping at the opportunity, General Sesma could hardly wait to give the fateful order for his most trusty cavalrymen to advance to entrap the escapees, who continued to push farther from the Alamo's walls. Indeed, after first catching sight of the daring escape attempt when they emerged from the aqueduct area into the open, General Sesma took immediate action. In his words: "As soon as I observed this, I sent a company from the [Cavalry] Regiment of Dolores with my assistants like lieutenant colonel Don Juan Herrera, captain Cayetano Montero, the Superior Lieutenant from Dolores the lieutenant colonel Don Juan Palacios, the second lieutenant Don Jose Maria Medrano so that they would harass the enemy from the sides of the branal [sic]."[45]

Here, as General Sesma realized, was a rare opportunity for the elite Mexican cavalry and lancers to win laurels before Santa Anna's very eyes. Now the Mexican infantrymen, who were busy slaughtering the defenders inside the compound, would not be the only ones to cover themselves with glory on March 6. The intense, but natural, inter-service rivalry between the regular infantry and cavalry only further motivated the horsemen of the Dolores Cavalry and the Tampico Lancers and Cavalry Regiment of Vera Cruz, all crack permanente units. They were determined to uphold not only individual but unit and national pride at the expense of those who had escaped.

Like the rest of Santa Anna's Army of Operations, vengeance was very much on the minds of these elite Vera Cruz lancers on this late winter morning, in part because five of their lancer comrades, good men like Juan Manuel Maldonado and Juan Nepomuceno Tello, had been killed in the late 1835 siege of San Antonio. Because the Vera Cruz lancers were Santa Anna's favorite horsemen, the Dolores Cavalry Regiment, even though its members served as his personal guard and escort, and the Tampico Lancers would rise to the occasion this morning. Indeed, born and raised in the gulf port city, Santa Anna yet considered himself more of a Veracruzano than a member of Mexico City's aristocracy, and identified with these hard-fighting lancers from his own hometown.

Especially after having just missed the opportunity to capture the entire Alamo garrison in the late February strike foiled by a combination of the Medina River's swollen waters and later by Santa Anna's own miscalculations, these battle-hardened Mexican cavalrymen lusted for this opportunity to demonstrate their worth, especially before their commander-in-chief. Consequently, they were now most enthusiastic about a chance to steal away the laurels now being garnered by the Mexican infantrymen in exterminating the last holed-up survivors inside the Alamo's embattled buildings.

Long considered Mexico's most elite troops, General Sesma's men of the Dolores Cavalry Regiment were highly motivated. Here was an opportunity for them to live up to the inspirational legacy of Father Hidalgo, striking a blow as the Mexican Revolution's protectors and inheritors of the revolutionary warcry, "Viva Mexico," and "Viva la Virgen de Guadalupe." Now consisting of 290 horsemen in shiny helmets and ornate breastplates, the Dolores Cavalry had been named in honor of the birthplace of Father Hidalgo's September 1810 revolt, the tiny village of Dolores, where the bells of the parish church had first rallied Indian and mestizo revolutionaries. Here, this fiery parish priest first raised the call for equality and freedom for the downtrodden peasants to rise up against their Spanish masters. Hidalgo's revolutionary spark began the resistance movement that culminated in Mexico's independence from Spain.[46]

Ironically, because it was not yet full light and visibility was low, escaping garrison members had not initially realized that they were heading toward the teeth of the dragoon. Unknown to the 62 escapees, the Alameda's high ground now served as the mobile command post of General Sesma and his cavalry and lancers. As a cruel fate would have it, the escapees now pushed not toward safety and freedom, as they believed, but toward a cavalry strongpoint and a rendezvous with disaster. Unfortunately, these fleeing men were about to encounter the finest troops in all Mexico.

Santa Anna, fully exploiting his best asset, had circled the entire Alamo with a screen of cavalrymen, including the much-feared lancers. Dressed in blue riding pants with red stripes and wearing black leather helmets decorated with lengthy, dark-colored horse-hair plumes that hung down their backs, the lancers at the Alameda were ready for action. What most distinguished them as a lethal killing machine, especially on the open ground, was the seven-foot-long lance. A deadly instrument of war, the lengthy wooden shaft carried by the crack Vera Cruz, Tampico, and Dolores lancers was topped by an iron, arrow-shaped spear point. Even more, the escaping garrison members never imagined that the number of Santa Anna's lancers, around 400 well-trained men, was more than double the entire Alamo garrison. Therefore, the flight that these escapees believed would take them to safety was about to lead them into a living nightmare instead.

General Sesma had chosen the perfect moment to unleash his lancers, who now moved in for the kill, sweeping ever closer to their victims. He had allowed the escapees to advance sufficiently far from the Alamo's walls to preclude any possibility of a flight back to the compound. Like Santa Anna, Sesma wanted to destroy these men in the open, eliminating every revolutionary who had defied Mexico.[47]

But at this critical moment and almost as if by a miracle, the 62 men who had fled the Alamo were not without assistance during their life-or-death bid to escape. In one of the most spirited, selfless actions among the Alamo defenders on this morning, about a dozen cannoneers of both Captain Dickinson's and Carey's artillery companies rose to the fore. Swept by chilly winds whistling across the prairie and especially at the top of the church, these ill-clothed gunners, who were stationed on the elevated wooden gun platform at the church's rear, spied the attempt of so many men to save themselves. Or perhaps an officer or enlisted man with foresight had had the presence of mind to have previously informed them of the escape attempt and requested protective fire before the breakout. After Romero's troops had earlier shifted to strike the north wall, these gunners had no targets for most of the morning. Now they saw a good many finely uniformed targets on the open prairie before them.

From their elevated perch, the gunners, including cannoneers like thirty-seven-year-old Jacob Walker from Nacogodoches, a member of Captain Carey's artillery and the brother of the famed mountain man Joseph R. Walker, went into action to aid their fleeing comrades, old friends, and perhaps relatives. They therefore hurriedly man-handled their 12-pounder guns, that had been facing east, at an angle to the right, or more southeast. In the early morning half-light, they now sighted their guns, loaded with cannon balls for long-range shots rather than short-range canister, on the Mexican cavalry that had suddenly appeared on the horizon and was now descending on the 62 men, now vulnerable, after having left the area of the ditch.

Commanding the Alamo's most elevated battery, Captain Dickinson, and even perhaps Captain Carey if present, very likely helped to serve the 12-pounders at the top of the gradually-sloping elevated ramp that led to the wood and earth artillery platform at the church's rear. Raised on the busy, cobblestone streets of Philadelphia, Captain Dickinson, no longer serving as the garrison's unofficial physician, was now attempting to save more men in a combat situation than he ever could as a man of medicine. After all, the effort to provide protective fire for the escapees was an act of salvation on this early Sunday morning in hell. Here, at Fortin de Cós, the former Gonzales blacksmith was about to forge one of the most heroic actions at the Alamo.

Acting with haste while Mexican bullets from the plaza and nearby walls whistled around their heads, this handful of feisty artillerymen sighted their guns upon the lengthy line of brightly colored Dolores, Vera Cruz, and Tampico lancers, who were swiftly approaching the escapees. Santa Anna's cavalry was yet far enough from the fleeing soldiers that these gunners now prepared to fire over the escapee's heads to send projectiles toward the surging Mexican cavalry formations.

At least one, perhaps two, 12-pounders now blasted away at the cavalrymen in the vain hope of preventing the inevitable slaughter on the prairie. With a sense of admiration rather than pity, Sergeant Francisco Becerra of the Activo San Luís Potosí Battalion, never forgot the sight of the valiant attempts of the artillerymen, even though they knew that they were hastening their own doom by assisting their fleeing comrades instead of defending themselves: "On the top of the church building I saw eleven Texians [and] They had some small pieces of artillery, and were firing on the cavalry. . . ."[48]

But of course this gallant action of the few artillerymen, who willing sacrificed themselves to save their comrades, came at a high price. Ironically, in now firing more times at the fight's end than perhaps all the Alamo's other cannon this morning, these hard-working gunners from a commanding height loaded and fired their guns as fast as they could and as long as possible in attempting to save their comrades, even while they knew that they had only a short time to live. Here, at the church's rear and in close conjunction with the exodus from the compound, was what could be described as Captain Dickinson's last stand, the Alamo's authentic Thermopylae in miniature. As long as ammunition remained, these few artillerymen of Fortin de Cós continued to fire even while the Mexicans entered the church and gained the ramp's base, and then shot down the gunners, now sitting ducks, one by one. Additionally, some of Santa Anna's men outside the walls, evidently Mexican troopers who had advanced close to the wall to cut off more escape attempts from this point, also opened up to eliminate this booming threat to their own horse-soldier comrades, who continued to descend upon the 62 escapees.

Inside the embattled church now surrounded by Mexican infantry and cavalry, Enrique Esparza described how: "The roof of the Alamo [church] had been taken off and the south side filled up with dirt almost to the roof on that side so that there was a slanting embankment up which the Americans could run and take positions [and now] I saw numbers [of artillerymen] who were shot in the head as soon as they exposed themselves from the roof."[49]

One of these last-stand gunners was Captain Dickinson, who commanded the three-gun battery of 12-pounders at the church's rear. But at least one, maybe two cannon, had expended their rounds by this time and, combined with the number of gunners shot down, now became useless. Therefore, and perhaps even hoping yet to escape to the outside after having seen so many of their comrades fleeing, three unarmed gunners had left the firing platform and entered the rooms on the church's first floor, where they were dispatched by bullets from a tide of Mexicans swarming into the building. One of these unfortunate victims was Jacob Walker, who attempted to escape the elevated gun platform but too late. He was shot and then killed with a flurry of bayonets in a dirty, dank corner of a darkened room before he could escape from the chapel now engulfed by screaming soldados. Like his fellow cannoneers of Fortin de Cós, he had bravely given his life in part to save his fleeing comrades.[50]

Ironically, this dramatic episode and one of the most heroic actions of that March 6 has been overlooked by historians in part because of a stubborn refusal to accept reliable Mexican accounts that reveal, or even hint of, an exodus from the Alamo.

Meanwhile, as more light of day illuminated the plain outside the fort, the sight of a large number of Mexican cavalry surging toward them presented a nasty surprise to the escapees. After all, during the twelve days of siege, garrison members had seen no such sizeable cavalry deployment, or even the repositioning of Mexican horsemen in the early hours of March 6.

Not only had young men of dissimilar cultures, religions, and races clashed at the Alamo, but the battle also involved dissimilar means of waging warfare. And this wide difference in battle tactics was forcefully demonstrated outside the Alamo's walls. What was now about to transpire outside the Alamo was a confrontation between two means of waging war that had been transferred to the New World. While most garrison members had learned how to fight as a foot soldier, Mexican superiority was manifested in its rich cavalry traditions and heritage. Even more than natives from the South, where horse culture dominated, the Mexicans, like the Spanish before them, were masters of horsemanship: a lengthy tradition brought from the dry plains and mountainous regions of Spain.

Unlike the Anglo-Celtic riflemen primarily from the Deep and Upper South, the Mexican cavalry was ideally suited for waging war amid the dry, open prairies around San Antonio, which so closely resembled Spain's interior. More then any other aspect of the struggle, therefore, the fighting outside the walls would represent the clash of two distinct traditional means of waging war. Contrary to the mythical Alamo last stand, meanwhile, only a relatively handful of men now attempted to defend themselves inside a compound now overflowing with the soldado tide. Eulalia Yorba described the final contest swirling in and around the Long Barracks, including the church: "It did not seem as if a mouse could live in a building so shot at and riddled as the Alamo was that morning."[51]

However, the men who had stayed inside the Alamo were destined to die mercifully compared to the grisly fates awaiting those who fled outside the walls. Vacating the open prairie to seek some meager shelter after seeing the onrushing Mexican cavalry, they had retired back into the brushy shelter of the irrigation ditch to make a stand. Dispatched by General Sesma, a lancer company of the Dolores Regiment swept down to smash into the 62 men from the flank after they took defensive positions in the "bushy and craggy ground," while other Mexican lancers attacked them in front. While those garrison members who remained behind trapped in the Alamo faced ugly demises from muskets shots and bayonets, the escapees—who now made the forgotten last stand not inside but outside the Alamo—would have to face Mexico's most highly skilled killers.

As best they could, these men now had to fend off blows delivered with heavy dragoon sabers that could split skulls open and sever and arms held up in vain for protection. But worst of all, they confronted the most feared of all opponents, the deadly Mexican lancers, who charged them in front. As revealed by Sergeant Loranca of the Dolores Cavalry, in a revealing 1878 article that appeared in the *San Antonio Daily Express*, the "Sixty-two Texans who sallied forth . . . were received by the Lancers," the pride of Mexico.[52]

But almost as shocking as facing lancers was the fact that the escapees now confronted some black soldiers for the first time in their lives. With the port city's heavily mixed population, people of African descent had long served in Vera Cruz's military units, including the elite Vera Cruz Lancers: an integrated military unit since the time of the American Revolution. And by 1798, the majority of the Vera Cruz lancers consisted of pardos—lighter skinned descendants of blacks and Spaniards—and morenos, who were darker-complected offspring of Spanish and African parents. These dark-skinned Jarochos (citizens of "Puerto de Veracruz") were proud of their beautiful port city and their African heritage. Ironically, for the doomed white soldiers, even the lengthy lances that were now employed with such business-like efficiency had been inherited from Islamic Moors of African descent.[53]

The unfortunates outside the Alamo's walls were all but defenseless at this time. With little, if any, powder remaining, they were also without bayonets, the standard weapon with which infantrymen defended themselves against cavalry throughout the Napoleonic Wars. Without bayonets to fend off charging Mexican horsemen, mounted on fast mustangs that were smaller than American horses, these escapees were at the mercy of the seven-foot-long deadly lances.[54]

Before Santa Anna began his march on San Antonio, at least one insightful evaluation from the *Red River Herald* had offered a grim warning for any unlucky Texas riflemen caught in the open, and that now proved most prophetic for the 62 escapees: " . . . they will be powerless against cavalry. . . . Bayonets and lances are what are, therefore, needed by American volunteers" fighting in Texas.[55]

The struggle outside the walls began as a conventional fight: an organized defense that was remarkable under the circumstances. While hit in front by the lancers, the dragoons of the Dolores Cavalry Regiment smashed into their flank, flushing some survivors from the irrigation ditch. Now out in the open and far from the Alamo's walls, those men who sought to escape met a grisly end during a brutal mismatch that was little more than a bloody game of predator pursuing its doomed quarry. They could neither escape nor survive out in the open for long. Meanwhile, other men continued to defend themselves from the ditch's cover.

Contrary to traditional accounts and newer, more controversial assertions, including the de la Pena memoir, Crockett very likely was killed at this time far from the Alamo's walls and not far from the Alameda. One of the most persistent Alamo myths has been the alleged tenacious defense at the wooden palisade by Crockett and his Tennessee volunteers. Armed with Long Rifles, they have been viewed as the Alamo's most deadly defenders. But very likely the Tennessee men were among the 62 who escaped through the palisade. It would have been almost beyond human endurance, not to mention common sense, for a handful of Tennessee men to stand by to die for no gain, after so many garrison members had left by way of the palisade.

If the Tennesseans had been part of this exodus, which was likely the case, then might Crockett have joined them instead of remaining in the church area? The former Tennessee Congressman possessed perhaps more reasons than anyone to depart with more than 60 comrades: a bright political future in a new Texas revolutionary government that he would "consider . . . a paradise," as he wrote in a letter; the Alamo's defense was already compromised by this time; and, of course, he had a wife and family yet dependent upon him. Therefore, he quite likely joined the first escape attempt out of the compound. He might even have led it.

Earlier, Crockett had informed Susanna Dickinson that "we had better march out" of the Alamo death-trap. If he had led the escape effort, this would also explain why so many garrison members departed from the palisade. A natural leader, any decisions made by this popular Volunteer State frontiersman-turned-politician would have been followed by many garrison members. For his part, the Tennessean faced two distinct choices once the Mexicans had poured into the fort: either withdraw to the "safety" of the Long Barracks or the Alamo chapel, or go out through the palisade not only with his Tennessee boys, if that is the case, but with the day's largest concentration of defenders on that nightmarish morning.

A number of Mexican officers and soldados viewed this large-scale escape from the Alamo, because it was not only the first but also the most concentrated attempt of a large number of garrison members to reach safety. Mapmakers José Sánchez-Navarro and Estado De Parras both noted this desperate flight from out of the palisade. On his 1836 map and quite correctly, Navarro described the wooden palisade as "the weakest part of the fort. It is defined only by a stockade and a bad tree fall [abatis]; from this post, in vain, when all was lost some colonists attempted to escape."[56]

And in his 1840 map, Parras also indicated that the wooded palisade was the "point [where] some colonist[s] attempted to escape" the slaughter inside the Alamo's walls. Evidently, not knowing the location of the little gate, or sally port, at the church's southwest corner at the palisade's edge, he indicated, as in the 1836 map, that the exact point of escape was located at the cannon embrasure, or opening at the center of the wooden palisade. But most significant, both early Alamo mapmakers considered the flight of garrison members from the palisade to be of some historical significance, when they instead could have omitted it to glorify the victory won by embracing the core tenants of the mythical Alamo last stand.[57]

But there was little to glorify in the struggle so far outside the walls. In General Sesma's words that described the attack on the 62 escapees, including perhaps Crockett himself, around the aqueduct: "The gallant lancer officers charged them, and in the same manner the troop [of the Dolores Cavalry] that they had commanded also charged" the defenders in a one-two punch.[58]

All the while, the lively, almost festive "music of the regiment of Dolores" inspired hundreds of lancers and dragoons to make their killing as efficient as possible. After initial resistance was broken, the slaughter of so many garrison members took on an almost a carnival-like atmosphere far from the Alamo's walls in a vicious, life-and-death struggle that has long been overlooked by historians.[59]

Meantime, either shortly before or while while the 62 escapees were under attack outside the walls, the panic among the few survivors along the south wall—in the low barracks and at the main gate—became more widespread, with every man for himself. The mounting shock and terror caused primeval instincts to rise to the fore, and it was now a matter of simple survival, which called for one final act—flight—to escape the massacre. Unlike the first escape attempt out the palisade, therefore, the two subsequent flights of Alamo men would not be as organized, resulting more out of panic to escape a slaughter than a prearranged design. However, one Anglo emphasized not only the first escape attempt but also those that followed, concluding that nearly the entire garrison had fled. William C. Murphy, who evidently learned what had really happened from Mexican prisoners taken at San Jacinto or from Tejano eyewitnesses, spoke to a reporter and described how resistance inside the Alamo had continued until "finally [the garrison] was compelled to abandon the fort."[60]

Appearing in his obituary in the February 23, 1895 issue of the *New York Times* (appropriately on the 59th anniversary of the arrival of Santa Anna's army in San Antonio), Murphy's rare account of what actually happened on the morning of March 6 is most significant, because it is the only known Texian version in existence today that has described the exodus from the Alamo, coinciding with Mexican accounts before the latter were known or seen by him.[61]

But besides the ample number of Mexican accounts, perhaps the best evidence of these multiple flights of escapees was the fact that overall resistance had been so feeble from beginning to end. As revealed by the journal of Juan Nepomuceno Almonte (both the aristocratic general and his journal were captured at San Jacinto) less than 300 Mexican soldiers would fall on this day, including a large percentage from friendly fire. The illegitimate son of Mexican revolutionary leader Jose Maria Morales, he served as Santa Anna's Chief of Staff, and knew the truth of what actually occurred on March 6th. He therefore penned in his journal how, less than a half hour after the attack's opening, "the enemy attempted to fly" from the Alamo. Most important, both Murphy and Colonel Almonte indicated a widespread collapse of resistance and how a large percentage of the garrison attempted to flee.[62]

As a proud member of the Dolores Cavalry Regiment, however, Sergeant Loranca had only witnessed the first flight of 62 men from the palisade, and he spent sometime that morning fighting and slaughtering escapees on the open prairie. Consequently, he failed to bear witness to subsequent flights from the Alamo.[63]

But the account of Colonel Almonte, a highly respected officer esteemed on both sides, was especially reliable. No wonder the surprised editors of the *New York Herald* who published Almonte's journal, which had been picked up on the San Jacinto battlefield by Private Anson Jones, a future president of the Texas Republic, could only write with some dismay: "The assault on the Alamo is very briefly given. It will be observed that Almonte's account differs very essentially from what we received at the time through the Texas papers."[64]

SECOND FLIGHT FROM THE ALAMO

Additional escape attempts by desperate soldiers in such a no-win situation as the Alamo garrison faced were not only to be expected but inevitable. Even the most disciplined veterans of the French and English armies of the Napoleonic Wars ran for their lives when defensive lines broke, no hope existed for either success or survival, or when facing bayonets and a policy of no mercy.[65]

And even the most battle-hardened Germans troops, often considered invincible, of the Second World War often gave way "to the primal terror and the urge to flee" the battlefield, if hard-hit or caught by surprise. Despite separated by more than a century, both situations and examples applied to the Alamo defenders.[66]

To insist that the Alamo's men, who were neither seasoned nor well-trained soldiers in the conventional sense, died to the last man in going down fighting in a heroic final stand actually borders on the far-fetched, given the circumstances From beginning to end, the heroic last stand of myth was all but an impossibility for undisciplined citizen-soldiers in a no-win situation, under a no-quarter threat, with little ammunition, and few leaders left alive, especially after the Alamo's walls had been breached. To believe otherwise indicates a lack of understanding of the basic nature of not only combat but that of the fighting man, human behavior, psychology, and the history of warfare through the ages.

Therefore, it was all but inevitable that the flight of the first 62 members from the little sally port of the log palisade would be followed by other escape attempts—except more desperate by this time—especially on the Alamo's south side, or the low barracks, where Colonel Morales' attacker's were invitingly absent and no Mexican cavalry could yet be seen in the distance thanks to the dim light of early morning. Indeed, while the close-quarter combat yet swirled in the claustrophobic darkness of the Long Barracks and the church area, additional fighting outside the Alamo was about to erupt on the open ground.

General Sesma felt some satisfaction now with his assault on the 62

men near the Alameda, until another unexpected challenge suddenly
arose. From the vantage point of the Alameda's relatively high ground,
Sesma was astounded to see yet another flight of soldiers streaming
from the Alamo. In disbelief, the general described how all of a sudden,
yet "Another group of around fifty men then came from the center of
the fort . . . ."[67]

From General Sesma's elevated viewpoint from the southeast
around the Alameda, the right of the fort was the Alamo chapel—or
more specifically Fortin de Cós—and the palisade area at the southwest
corner, while the center of the fort was the half-moon-shaped earthen
lunette that jutted forward from the south wall before the main gate,
which it protected. Constructed by General Cós' engineers, the crescent-
shaped earthwork adjoined the low barracks near the center of the
southern perimeter.

Protecting the main entry point into the Alamo, seemingly the most
likely objective of any attackers, this well-constructed lunette, surrounded by a deep ditch for extra security, projected south from the
arched main gate. A solid, practical structure created during the fall
1835 defensive enhancement, this lunette of dark prairie sod and sand
was known by Cós' soldados as Porte Cochere. To Sesma, this appeared
to be the center of the fort. This finely crafted lunette was buttressed by
double rows of cedar logs with dirt packed in between, and contained a
sally port for entry and exist.

What made the protruding U-shaped lunette, about 75 feet in length
and 65 feet in width, especially formidable was that it contained
artillery. The veteran cavalryman Sergeant Loranca also appreciated
how "the Fort Alamo had only one entrance . . . and the approach was
made winding to impede the entrance of the cavalry." In an ideal scenario, both cannon-fire and riflemen positioned in the lunette could
rake attackers from the flank to both the north and south.

This strong defensive feature, fully realized by Santa Anna and, of
course, General Cós, might explain in part why only a relative handful
of attackers—Colonel Morales' diminutive column—had been sent by
Santa Anna toward the south wall, and also why Morales' column had
moved farther west to attack the compound's southwest corner and then
the Long Barracks. Conversely, this tactical situation along the Alamo's
southern perimeter now allowed an ideal opportunity to escape by way
of the main gate. Also, the belated advance of Morales' men into the
plaza had applied additional pressure to force survivors out the main

gate. Unknown to the escapees, this main gate—now a Godsend for an escape attempt—possessed an ominous history. In 1813, when the Anglo-Celt filibusters captured the Alamo, they had placed the severed head of an unfortunate Spanish officer on a pike at the gate as a grim warning for all to see.[68]

Quite likely, this second escape attempt of around 50 soldiers out of the main gate was also sparked by the sight or knowledge, or both, of so many defenders—62 men—slipping out through the palisade's sally port. If so, then this second large group of men would have only felt a sense of abandonment, fueling and hastening their own flight for safety. These soldiers could also have believed that the Alamo's abandonment had been ordered by whichever highest ranking officer remained alive—and perhaps it had been.

Once again as for the men who fled through the palisade's sally port, the inviting sight of the Alameda's double rows of cottonwood trees to the southeast and the high ground of the Alameda and Powder House Hill, farther east down the Gonzales Road, was the immediate goal for these escapees, who followed in the same general direction as the first group but further to the west. For all of these reasons, around 50 defenders spilled out of the main gate and through the lunette, scrambling over the earthen parapet or through the cannon embrasures in the half-light.

It is likely that one escapee of this second contingent was Ireland-born Sergeant William B. Ward, age 30. Fond of fun, Irish gigs, and strong drink, this capable Son of Erin, who had adopted New Orleans, distinguished by its large Irish immigrant community since before the War of 1812, as his home, had been assigned to the artillery in the plaza. These two guns were positioned in rear of the main gate, just in case Mexican attackers overran the lunette and burst through the gate, which of course never happened. Almost certainly, the lunette's 10 gunners joined the flight out of the main gate in an attempt to live and fight another day.

But as before, with the ill-fated band of 62 defenders who had fled from the palisade, General Sesma, from his vantage point around the Alameda, again made immediate tactical decisions to wipe out the second group of escapees. After all, Santa Anna's orders were that there would be no survivors on this day. Therefore, Sesma "ordered the company of Lancers from the Regiment of Dolores under the orders of Superior Lieutenant Colonel Don Ramon Valera, Lieutenant Don

Tomas Castillo, and Second Lieutenants Don Leandro Ramirez and Don Tomas Viveros to charge them."[69]

In total by this time, at least 112 garrison members, perhaps more, had taken themselves outside the Alamo walls, with large-scale escape attempts occurring within minutes of each other and both initially shielded by half-darkness.[70] These two sizeable escape attempts resulted in two different clashes between foot-soldiers and Mexican cavalry and lancers, which occurred within a relatively short time and not far from the west end of the Alameda. Both of these dual clashes were the most cruel—no small distinction compared to the massacre yet occurring inside the Alamo walls—fought by the majority of the garrison outside the walls, with Mexican cavalry, not infantry, playing the larger role in the morning's killing.

All the while, Mexican equestrian skill with the saber and the lance rose to the fore in the chasing down of fugitives, when the eastern horizon was now more illuminated with the pale dawn. Few contests were so one-sided or unmerciful as these clashes outside the walls. Nothing now could save those who had fled the Alamo and believed initially that they had escaped a no-quarter policy inside, only to discover to their horror that an even worse fate awaited them on the prairie. Completely exposed out on the open plain and chased down by pursuing lancers, the Long Rifles were now of little use. For a garrison member now caught in the open after firing an initial shot, there simply was no time to reload as galloping horsemen closed in.[71]

With the sun inching higher, thus eliminating the escapees' protective cloak of darkness, resistance became more feeble among the survivors of the first group of escapees. An elite lancer, Manuel Loranca, was astounded by the swift destruction of the last of the 62 men. In his own words: "Only one of these made resistance; a very active man, armed with a double-barrel gun and a single-barrel pistol, with which he killed a corporal of the Lancers named Eugenio."[72]

Colonel Almonte recorded in his journal how a large number of escapees "were overtaken and put to the sword" in systematic fashion by veteran lancers and cavalrymen, who had refined the art of killing.[73] General Sesma, watching his dragoons and lancers, described the "Texians" as offering a "desperate resistance,"[74] even as the low casualty rate among the Mexican cavalry indicated, at best, that the escapees were low on ammunition. De la Pena concurred with General Sesma's assessment of resistance, writing how: "Those of the enemy who tried to escape fell victims to the sabers of the cavalry, which had been drawn up for this purpose, but even as they fled they defended themselves."[75]

Clearly, the accounts of Mexican cavalrymen such as Sergeant Locanca of the Dolores Cavalry Regiment and especially General Sesma, were more specific and accurate in regard to exact numbers and placements of escapees and their routes of flight, while infantry officers, like de la Pena, and Almonte, both of whom assaulted the north wall on the Alamo's other side, would not have seen all three separate flights of men.

No single aspect of the Alamo's story has been more overlooked or neglected by historians than the duration and amount of fighting outside the walls, largely because that would be an admission of widespread flight—the antithesis of a last stand. However, these dual clashes outside the Alamo comprised more of a slaughter than inside its walls, and resulted in more victims. The horror of what happened on the open ground outside the Alamo's walls was nightmarishly surreal: spirited resistance and then panic sweeping through the survivors; young men and boys swiftly cut down by saber blows or pistol and carbine shots; lances thrust through victims' bodies with high impact generated from a horse's speed; frightened men running in vain for their lives across the open prairie; Mexican lancers making grim sport of demonstrating their horsemanship and killing prowess to comrades and commanding officers; frightened garrison members pleading for mercy or offering signs of submission, after tiring in running and halting to confront their tormentors, only to be slaughtered by the cavalrymen and lancers in methodical fashion; expert riders directing horses to trample men to the ground, where they were quickly dispatched.[76]

If an escapee was lucky, then death came swiftly but this unfortunately was not the case in many instances for those who had fled the Alamo. Wounds inflicted by saber blows and even glancing lancer thrusts were simply not likely to cause immediate death. Therefore, for those unlucky men caught out in the open, it was hell on earth, dying an agonizing death on the prairie, in the irrigation ditch, or behind slight cover near the Alameda. Here, a good many young men and boys died in the open. The last thing that some of these soldiers saw was the sight of the nearby stately cottonwoods of the Alameda, looking like trees that must have reminded them of home, a more innocent time, and a peaceful existence without war's horrors.

In the ranks of Sesma's cavalrymen who saw exactly what was transpiring in this sector beyond the wooden palisade and near the Alameda, Manuel Loranca described the horror when the first group of 62 escapees were "all killed [and] These were all killed by the lance, except one, who ensconced himself under a bush and it was necessary to shoot him."[77]

General Sesma also described the slaughter of the garrison members who were swiftly cut down on the open ground near the Alameda "with valiant officers' short lances/spears, and in this way the troop that they [Lieutenant Colonel Herrera, Captain Montero, Lieutenant Colonel Palacios, and Second Lieutenant Medrano] commanded charged and knifed them in moments, without letting the desperate resistance of [the doomed Anglo-Celts] make them vacillate for a moment."[78]

In another translation of his battle report, Sesma emphasized how his "gallant lancer officers charged them, and in the same manner the [Dolores Cavalry Regment] troop that they had commanded also charged and put them to the sword in moments . . . ."[79]

As written in the rare journal of a member of the Activo San Luís Potosí Battalion, an unidentified Mexican officer described the grisly fate of the first group of escapees, and indicated six more than Sesma's count of 62: "The Dolores Regiment, presidiales and piquetes of the Tampico and Veracruz Regiments were commanded by General [Sesma] and were deployed . . . to pursue those who were routed, sixty-eight of which they killed."[80]

Not long after the final destruction of the first band of more than 60 men, the second group of 50 Alamo garrison members suffered a comparable fate, but only after putting more formidable resistance. Ironically, this less organized band of soldiers fought back with more spirit—perhaps because they had more ammunition—than the larger group of escapees also because they were not caught as much out in the open like the first group, and took shelter for a longer period in the aqueduct after evidently forming a more lengthy defensive line. These men might well have witnessed the slaughter of the 62 escapees, because they had left the Alamo only a short time later, and additional daylight existed to ascertain the Mexican cavalry maneuvers. Unlike the first group, therefore, this second party of escapees possessed more time and more daylight to prepare to meet the Mexican cavalry that descended upon them. This second band of men fired upon the attacking Mexican lancers and cavalry from the shelter of the irrigation ditch, after taking good cover. Here, they possessed a better chance to defend themselves, unlike their more unfortunate comrades who had earlier been caught mostly out in the open.

In the words of General Sesma: "Upon seeing this movement [of Mexican horsemen], the enemy availed themselves of a trench/ditch and made such a vigorous defense that I had to send [a] Lieutenant . . . with twenty Lancers from Tampico and twelve from Veracruz to help this force which, although it never vacillated, I feared would be repulsed, and [therefore I then sent] the Captain of the Rio Grande, Don Manuel Barrigan, and the Lieutenant of the same company, Don Pedro Rodriguez, with fifteen men of the same company, in order to defeat the [men in the cover of the aqueduct]. All of these officers executed the movement with such decision and exactitude that some men truly barricaded in that position and resolved to lose their skins only at great expense, were run over in just a few minutes and knifed" to death.[81]

But this bloody work of elimination by the gaily uniformed lancers was not easy. With the "possession of a ditch," these men fought back as best they could before being overwhelmed. At least one Mexican soldier was killed in this struggle that swirled in and around the irrigation ditch, where brush, cottonwood saplings, and scrubby mesquite trees provided some cover. Feeling sympathy for a young cavalryman's mother who lived in the little adobe village of Santiago Tlaguinterco, Mexico, General Sesma referred to a "corporal of the Regiment of Dolores, Jose Hernández, who was killed in the charge upon those who had availed themselves of the trench."[82]

Cavalry Brigade commander General Juan de Andrade reported how the Dolores Cavalry Regiment lost one killed and three wounded in this second contest far from the Alamo's walls. Indeed, the fighting grew so intense in wiping out the second group of escapees that General Sesma described in his March 11 report how, "I feared that they might be driven back [and therefore] I sent in a captain of the Rio Grande unit [because] some men were really protected as by a parapet in that position and therefore were determined to sell very dear their lives."[83]

By this time, the systematic, but quite messy, elimination of the first two escape groups—more than half of the Alamo garrison—was all but complete. Small, isolated pockets of resistance had yet to be wiped out, however. Besides the first two large groups of men who attempted to escape from a living hell, some Alamo defenders, caught in the confusing chaos of the nightmarish fighting, made their own individual attempts. With noise and rising layers of battle smoke providing a screen, individual garrison members slipped beyond the Alamo's walls in futile bids to escape. For instance, one account described four defenders who "bolted over one of the compound walls" to escape the slaughter. All but one were killed by the lethal Mexican cavalry, which pounced on these hapless soldiers like a hawk after a dying rabbit.[84]

One of the desperate soldiers who tried to reach safety was the Alamo's quartermaster, Eliel Melton, age 38. The Georgia-born merchant from the community named Nashville-on-the-Brazos (because so many Tennesseans called it home) was a successful merchant before making the fatal decision to become a Texas soldier. He had survived the 1835 assault that resulted in San Antonio's capture, but this time he would not be so fortunate. Refusing to die inside the Alamo and knowing that the only chance for survival meant flight rather than fight, Melton belatedly sprang from the compound's confines. He went out by way of the timbered palisade, after the organized group of 62 had already departed and while the Mexicans were yet focused on reducing stubborn resistance in the Long Barracks. He hoped against hope to evade the omnipresent Mexican dragoons and lancers to be reunited with his pretty, aristocratic Tejano wife, Juana. And, not far behind the fast-moving lieutenant, who bolted for his life, a "few others followed, and together they raced pell-mell into the graying dawn."[85]

Never forgetting the quartermaster's desperate bid for freedom, Susanna Dickinson, who saw relatively little, described how "During the engagement, one Milton, jumped over the ramparts & was killed."[86]

Another defender jumped to his death from the top of the church, falling around 22 feet to the ground below. This well-publicized incident has made relatively little sense to historians because it resulted in not one but two deaths. The most accepted theory has been that the act was suicide. But suicide was highly improbable because the man—long thought to have been Captain Dickinson— had a child in his arms. Consequently, this incident has been described as the "most bizarre story of the Alamo," remaining one of the battle's mysteries. However, a rather simple, but logical, explanation exists.

The most sensible explanation was that Captain Dickinson, if this was the jumper as so long believed, was attempting to follow those men who had streamed out of the palisade by way of the gate at the church's southwest corner. After all, he had stayed at his position at Fortin de Cós as long as possible helping to protect the escapees with his artillery fire from the church's rear. And he had leaped down near the chapel's southwest corner, where stood the palisade's sally port, in full view of many Mexicans now in the plaza and courtyard. By this time the Mexicans, with bayonets flashing and vengeance in their eyes, had gained entry into the church, driving him to his desperate escape attempt. Since he had his "young son in his arms," in de la Pena's words, this incident only makes sense if he was attempting to save not only himself but his son, and this meant following those who had dashed out through the palisade.[87]

But all later escapees, following upon the heels of the first 62 men and second group of 50 soldiers who fled, had even less chance for survival, with the cavalry now fully alerted and waiting. In some amazement, Santa Anna described how "a large number" of garrison members met their deaths from his cavalry "in the immediate areas" outside the Alamo's walls.

These words reveal that a fair number of other garrison members were killed as individual escapees and were not part of the two largest groups to flee the Alamo. Santa Anna's words also indicate that the ever-tightening ring of Mexican cavalry and lancers had moved closer to the Alamo's walls by this time, after witnessing the first two escape attempts, as preventive measures to ensure no more defensive stands from the irrigation ditch or any other cover. After all, for General Sesma's cavalrymen and lancers, it proved far easier to kill escapees close to the walls as opposed to chasing them across the prairie, or in attempting to drive them out of the irrigation ditch and its surrounding vegetation.[88]

FINAL FLIGHT OF DEFENDERS

The final sizeable flight of Alamo defenders never got as far as the first two groups, because the Mexican cavalry and lancers had advanced so close to the Alamo's walls, while awaiting more panic-stricken men to attempt to make a break for it. All the while, more than 100 musicians, including Fifer Apolinario Saldigna, but mostly drummers and "Horn players," continued to play lively airs to mock an ugly slaughter of those remaining inside the compound and those yet alive on the open prairie.[89]

Meanwhile, one of the most heroic acts at the Alamo took place inside the doomed fort. Rather than the mythical heroics which have been endlessly embellished as part of the romanticized last stand mythology, Ireland-born Major Evans, though wounded, rose to the challenge. Like so many Irish revolutionaries before him, Evans was not running or giving up this morning, demonstrating a feisty Celtic-Gaelic fighting spirit. In fact, he was determined to take as many Mexican soldiers with him as possible. With his last thoughts perhaps on his beloved Ireland and with a flaming torch in hand, Evans made a dash for the powder magazine. With the black powder reserves located at the southwest and northwest corners of the church, the Green Islander attempted to blow-up the remaining supply. But the 36-year-old was shot down before he fulfilled his mission. Ironically, a soldier not born in either Texas or America, but across the sea, gave his life in one of the most heroic actions on that March 6 morning.[90]

While the two fights were dying down by this time between the groups of escapees and the Mexican cavalry and lancers on the open prairie, yet another clash—the third, smallest, and last outside the Alamo this morning—was about to begin. General Sesma, from his vantage point from the high ground of the Alameda, now saw yet more defenders attempting to escape, "who were coming off the fort from the left . . . "[91]

This semicircular "fort" on the left was an earthen lunette or a "Semicircular palisade and narrow trench," that was positioned near the west wall's center. Here, on the wall that faced San Antonio, around 400 yards away across the San Antonio River, this lunette—smaller than the one protecting the main gate on the south wall—hugged the outer fort as the only entry and exit point of pickets along the sprawling west wall, not far from Travis' headquarters.[92]

As along the southern perimeter for the first two groups of escapes, the western perimeter had been devoid of attackers for some time, allowing an opportunity for a handful of survivors to make a dash for safety. Indeed, from the assault's beginning, General Cós' column had veered away from the west wall in overrunning Fort Condelle at the Alamo's northwest corner and then pushed into the plaza to attack the Long Barracks and church. With the main attack on the north wall and with Morales' belated strike at the Alamo's southwest corner, almost the entire length of the west wall had remained wide open, especially the lunette, which became a natural exit point. With Cós and Morales having struck at opposite corners of the western wall—the Alamo's longest walled side—most of its length had been attack-free longer than any perimeter. This tactical development resulted in some defenders, who had not retired back into the plaza, remaining in place in buildings along the western perimeter until forced to flee out the lunette when Mexicans gained the plaza behind them or after the Long Barracks was finally overpowered. Men fleeing the western lunette naturally made for the brush, trees, and cover along the nearby San Antonio River, which offered a better chance for survival than the open prairie around the Alameda.

Some evidence, from San Antonio's mayor in 1836, Francisco Antonio Ruiz, indicated that Crockett might have been killed at the lunette located at the west wall's midpoint. If so, this might well indicate that Crockett was shot and killed by Mexican cavalry, who were close to the wall by this time, while attempting to escape. Following the Mexican soldier's practice of calling isolated strongpoints "forts," Ruiz later claimed he saw Crockett's body in "the small fort opposite the city," which would have been the lunette at the west wall's center. He also reported that Crockett's body "was found in the west battery," which indicated that at least one artillery piece was located in the lunette.[93]

But because the sun had risen higher to reveal a fuller view of the surrounding area, including the Alamo compound, the last flight of garrison members was the most ill-timed of the three sizeable attempts. By this time, the first two groups of Alamo escapees were either wiped out or in the process of being eliminated; consequently, an even larger percentage of Santa Anna's cavalry was poised nearby, sabers drawn and lances at the ready, and closer to the walls after their bloody work in completing the destruction of the first groups of escapees. In General Sesma's words: "Then the Superior Captains of Lieutenant Colonels of the Regiment of Dolores, Don Manuel Montellano, Don Jose Fato, and second lieutenant Don Jose Guijarro, were detained with another company in order to charge those who were coming off the fort from the left [the west wall lunette], and who were also killed by these officers and troops upon showing themselves, and whose companions had not exceeded them in anything."[94]

In his March 11 report to Santa Anna, General Sesma complimented those who had escaped the Alamo only to meet a tragic fate outside of its walls: "It is in vain to show Your Excellency the desperate resistance of these men because you were in the middle of the risk dictating my orders and you were a witness who [saw] better than any other the deeds of each man."[95] Therefore, Sesma saw no need to exaggerate or embellish the cavalry's role today if Santa Anna was also a witness. The general's statement also indicated that Santa Anna was in the Alameda area. Most significant, therefore, Sesma had only described not only what he had seen in regard to the exodus from the Alamo, but also what Santa Anna had seen. This, of course, meant that the number of men he saw escaping was not an embellishment to make either himself or his men look like they accomplished more than was actually the case. (And unlike the de la Pena memoir, Sesma's words came from an official battle report written only days after the Alamo's capture, and not a politically inspired or biased document.)

Besides the factor of sheer panic, such a wide discrepancy between the number of escapees and Mexican cavalry losses has provided some evidence that a good many of the men—more than half the entire Alamo garrison—were out of ammunition by this time, which also might partly explain why they departed the Alamo in the first place. This scenario seems more likely with the last two groups of men who fled the Alamo rather than the first group, because of the tactical situation and time sequences.

When Mexican troops converged and struggled to kill the last defenders in the Long Barracks, hospital, and church, their attention became more focused on the Alamo's eastern side. Combined with the confusion, deafening noise, and thick smoke of battle, this tactical development allowed a slight opportunity for the last group of survivors, probably mostly west wall defenders, to dash for safety by way of the lunette, and perhaps even the elevated position of the 18-pounder at the southwest corner, after Morales' troops had descended upon the Long Barracks and the church. Of course, these three distinct flights of defenders only hastened the end of those who remained inside. So many men had fled the Alamo that many attacking Mexicans could not fathom what happened to all the defenders. A perplexed Lieutenant Colonel José Juan Sánchez-Navarro, not only a respected member of Cós' staff but also a promising poet, wrote how "By six-thirty in the morning not a single enemy existed" in the Alamo. And Sergeant Felix Nunez of Dúque's column, gained the distinct impression that "all the Americans had taken refuge in the church" by this time, because they could be seen nowhere else.[96] It seemed to those Mexican soldiers now inside the Alamo that many garrison members had simply disappeared off the face of the earth—a mystery best explained by the mass exodus from the Alamo.

Knowing the bitter end was fast approaching, some survivors inside the buildings tried in vain to surrender to the swarm of Mexican soldiers. Some cornered defenders in the Long Barracks waved white cotton socks in futile attempts to surrender. Trapped inside the church from which there was no escape, Anthony Wolfe and one of his sons—the other had already been killed by bayonets or bullets, or both—attempted to escape, but in vain. Out of desperation, both leaped from the church's top, very likely in a last-ditch attempt to join the exodus. But both young men of the Jewish faith were killed in a hail of bullets.[97]

Combined with having gained the element of surprise over the garrison even though it had long expected an assault, Santa Anna had effectively orchestrated the combined use of infantry and cavalry to reap success in what was essentially a night battle. Shortly after the fighting ended on March 6, therefore, Santa Anna boasted to the Mexican Minister of War and Navy how perhaps the majority of the Alamo garrison "fell under the sabers of the cavalry that was placed in that position just for this purpose [and] I am then able to guarantee that very few will have gone to notify their companions of the outcome."[98]

Not surprisingly, the flurries of isolated fighting outside of the Alamo continued for some time. But, of course, it was a one-sided contest outside the walls from beginning to end. It took time for the Mexican cavalrymen and lancers to locate survivors in gullies and aqueducts and amid underbrush, and to kill all of those who fled outside the walls. The slaughter was accelerated by the fact that the cavalrymen's horses were in good shape and relatively fresh, having been confiscated from haciendas on the long push north to replace their broken down animals that had carried their riders hundreds of miles.

Ironically, the slaughter outside the Alamo's walls lasted for hours, while the fighting inside the Alamo lasted less than a half hour. Moreover, those dying outside were the only garrison members killed in broad daylight. Alamo nurse Juana Navarro de Alsbury, the daughter of a Mexican officer who had married Dr. Horace Alsbury, an Alamo garrison member luckily dispatched on a scouting mission when Santa Anna laid siege (though destined to be killed in the Mexican-American War of 1846), recalled that scattered firing continued till mid-day.[99]

In his first March 6 battle report, written at 8:00 a.m. and before the slaughter had ended, a smug Santa Anna merely summarized how: "Victory goes with the Mexican Army [and] a great many who had escaped the bayonet of the infantry fell in the vicinity under the sabres

of the cavalry." What was most revealing was the fact that he emphasized how "a great many" Alamo defenders escaped to die outside the
Alamo's walls and "in the vicinity," which meant the Alameda area
along the Gonzales Road.[100]

Another translation of Santa Anna's first report was also illuminat-
ing: "And in the immediate areas [outside of the Alamo compound]
there was a large number that still has not been able to engage and hoping to escape the bayonets of the infantry, fell under the sabers of the
cavalry that was placed in that position just for this purpose."[101] Along
with General Sesma, Santa Anna had viewed the three flights from a
good vantage point on the Alameda, taking satisfaction in his well-conceived plan. However, Santa Anna's most revealing words have been
both overlooked and dismissed by historians who have so strongly
embraced the mythical Alamo.

And in a most revealing March 23, 1836 circular to the people of
Vera Cruz by Department Governor Joaquín de Muñoz y Muñoz, he
expressed pride in the chasing down and slaughter of so many Alamo
escapees, including by lancers from his own proud city: "The invincible
eagles of the Republic have been placed once again in the fortress of the
Alamo. And the glorious national colors wave triumphant on the wall
which was the hope of some rebel colonists [who were] pursued and
destroyed in all directions" on the bloody morning of March 6.[102]

Alamo historian and premier artist Gary S. Zaboly summarized
how: "A substantial number of Alamo defenders—perhaps as many as
one hundred—attempted to escape [and the] skirmishes that followed
between the fleeing Texans and the Mexican cavalry comprised an
entirely separate phase of the Alamo battle, but one no less vicious than
the action taking place within the compound."[103]

Again, the soldiers who fled the Alamo for their lives were anything
but cowards. Most of all, they were ordinary men—more farmers,
clerks, and merchants than either frontiersmen or trained soldiers. They
had died for their adopted homeland, Texas, serving to the bitter end,
when they could have, and probably should have, earlier deserted and
just gone home. But they did not go. Instead these men who participated in the desperate breakouts died just like their comrades inside the
Alamo. By fleeing from the Alamo, these escapees had only vacated a
doomed position in the hope of surviving to fight another day on better
terms.

Finally, the last outbursts of fighting outside the Alamo sputtered to an end long after the slaughter inside had concluded. And the fondest wishes of countless Mexican officials and military leaders had been realized with Santa Anna's resounding victory. They had long prayed "that these perverse [revolutionaries] will be destroyed" to the last man.[104]

All Mexico would celebrate Santa Anna and his Alamo success. For instance, an editor in the March 22 issue of *El Mosquito Mexicano* boasted: "We congratulate the world for the bandits Mexico has forever laid to rest" on the cold, misty morning of March 6.[105] And in the March 22, 1836 issue of the *La Lima de Vulcano*, Mexico City, the editor trumpeted the Alamo victory, proclaiming, "The rebel standard [the New Orleans Greys' flag] lies prostrate before our national flag; they have bitten the earth they profaned [and thanks to] the fire and steel of our valiant men, their black souls have expired."[106]

Santa Anna never felt more confident of future success. Another victory had been reaped over the Anglo-Celts at San Antonio, as when he had been a teenage soldier under Arredondo. A land he loved, all of Texas now loomed before him, seemingly for the taking. Texas resistance had been wiped out at the Alamo, and any place where these ill-starred revolutionaries could be found. Basking in his victory, Santa Anna now perhaps thought of "the beauty of this country," which "surpasses all description," that had been all but regained for Mexico—or so it seemed, after the last rebel defender of the Alamo had been killed not inside but outside the Alamo's walls.[107]

8

The Alamo's Most Bitter Legacies

From the beginning, no Alamo myth has been more time-honored than the belief that all the Alamo defenders willingly sacrificed themselves for the greater good, ensuring the birth of a new Texas republic, and buying time for Houston to create an army. But in the insightful words of historian Bill Groneman, "The traditional and incorrect view of the Alamo battle is that every man there made a conscious choice to die gloriously in its defense. Any scenario which deviated from that preconceived notion, such as the willing surrender of any of its defenders, has hardly been tolerated over the years."[1]

Groneman also argued against an enduring controversy of the Alamo story, Crockett's supposed execution, which the author refuted in his 1994 book, *Defense of a Legend: Crockett and the de la Pena Diary*. But in fact, the most groundbreaking aspect of the Alamo's story should never have been the manner of Crockett's death—in itself unimportant—but the fact that such a large percentage of the garrison attempted to escape the Alamo only to meet their deaths outside the walls. Indeed, historians, scholars, and the public have missed the point in regard to the real importance of the de la Pena account, focusing mostly on how a single garrison member died instead of the more important story, about so many "of the enemy who attempted to escape."

The escape attempts by a majority of the Alamo garrison—more than 100 and perhaps as many as 120 men—has been revealed by more than half a dozen reliable Mexican sources, especially General Sesma's March 11, 1836 report, and the San Luis Battalion logbook. While the mythological Alamo has long romanticized that these men all died willingly in a heroic example of self-sacrifice so that Texas would live, the historical reality of what actually happened on March 6 was the exact opposite. Indeed, Texas had a better chance to live if the Alamo garrison had escaped and survived to fight another day, when the odds were better and the tactical situation was more favorable.

At the Alamo, therefore, it perhaps took more real courage—and certainly more sense—to escape from a deathtrap than to die for no gain, advantage, or purpose. Attempting to escape the Alamo instead of dying in vain for abstract, rhetorical principles of "a borrowed cause," since so few garrison members were native Texians, was only a natural response for these unfortunate men, who had been abandoned by Texas and her people. In addition, the flight of Alamo defenders might well be explained by the fact that ammunition was low or largely unusable. Toward the battle's end, some men fought until ammunition had been expended before bolting from the Alamo. Such factors would further demonstrate the wisdom of flight rather than fight. After all, the Alamo garrison lacked adequate amounts of both powder and bullets from the beginning, and especially after thirteen days of siege.[2]

Along with other accounts and Travis' own words, Enrique Esparza recorded that the ammunition "of many was entirely spent" by the time the Mexicans poured over the walls, indicating that solid resistance was all but impossible, and that flight rather than fight presented a sound alternative.[3]

Given such realities, perhaps the most lofty example of defender heroism on March 6 was the fact that most Alamo garrison members waited until almost the final moment before attempting to break out of a deathtrap instead of days before. Indeed, the greatest heroism was not in struggling in vain to the death, but that fact that these men of such diverse backgrounds had united at all in a common decision to defend the Alamo in the first place. In this regard, the defenders were truly heroic, living up to the idealized and romantic image of the mythical Alamo, and leaving an inspiring moral example.

In the words of historian Wallace O. Chariton, "The truth is, it's a miracle the men stayed as long as they did. They were tired, hungry, frustrated over the poor conditions and the lack of promised pay, and bewildered because the people of Texas did not turn out in mass to come to their aid. . . . There was little to do but watch and wait for the end. For the besieged Texans there was no longer any doubt about what the end would be; the only question was when would it come, today, tomorrow, or the day after. The fact that the men did not run until the final assault was underway and all hope was literally gone is testimony to their grit and gallantry."[4]

Ironically, the truth of what really happened on March 6 can be seen in a fact that has been most often overlooked by historians. Like in regard to so many other traditional aspects of the Alamo's story, historians have never questioned or investigated why the bodies of Alamo garrison members were burned so far away from the Alamo. Why would Santa Anna's men have taken so much trouble and effort in hauling so many bodies some 300–400 yards up the gradual slope to the relative high ground of the Alameda, when battlefield dead were almost always buried where they were slain? Quite simply, the long-overlooked answer to this Alamo mystery was the fact that Santa Anna's men never dragged the vast majority of bodies from the Alamo compound as so long assumed.

When the fighting ended, the bodies of most Alamo garrison members were lying not inside the Alamo's walls, but around and near the Alameda, because of the multiple escape attempts. For health reasons, the bodies of the relatively few men killed inside the Alamo were hauled out of the fort by Santa Anna's cavalrymen to the Alameda—an unpleasant, but relatively easy exercise because they represented the minority of defenders.

Indeed, perhaps the best physical evidence of the mass exodus that streamed out of the Alamo was the fact that most bodies lay so far beyond the Alamo's walls. Such placement of the slain can explain why Santa Anna ordered the bodies gathered and placed into three funeral pyres on either side of the double rows of cottonwood trees along the Alameda.[5]

Other solid evidence—equally ignored—of the large-scale flights of so many defenders from the Alamo, was that more men than previously believed actually escaped the slaughter of the Mexican lancers and cavalrymen. Collaborating what Sesma recorded in his March 11 report and other Mexican accounts, even Santa Anna alluded as much when he described how among the "large number" of men who escaped the Alamo compound in making a dash for life, "I am, then able to guarantee that very few will have gone to notify their companions of the outcome" of the Alamo.[6]

An unknown number of escapees hid under cover on the prairie or in the irrigation ditch, praying for darkness when they could slip away undetected. Some of these men were discovered. We have already seen how Sergeant Loranca of the Dolores Cavalry described one soldier who had "ensconced himself under a bush" and nearly escaped detection, until finally discovered and dispatched without mercy.[7]

Another account has revealed that six garrison members who escaped the Alamo were discovered hiding under the small wooden bridge where the Gonzales Road crossed the San Antonio River, southwest of the Alamo. These escapees—most likely from the west wall lunette—had run around 220 yards undetected to find shelter under the bridge, located just west of the Alameda on the road to Gonzales. In keeping with Santa Anna's orders, these men were all killed out-of-hand by the first soldados who spied them.[8]

The Alamo's most famous escapee was the French Napoleonic veteran, Louis (or Moses) Rose. Like the mythical line supposedly drawn in the sand by Travis, so the story of Rose's departure from the Alamo has been shrouded in legend. Alamo mythology, which unfairly branded him as a coward and even a turncoat for not dying in the mythical last stand, strongly hints of anti-Semitism. The legend has been long espoused that Rose left the Alamo and deserted his more heroic non-Jewish comrades—who willingly chose to die in an example of heroic self-sacrifice—on the night before the attack. In this sense, Rose served as a convenient scapegoat—a Frenchman and a Jew, a double handicap, who were so often lampooned and hated in this period—so as to diminish any idea that true-blooded Anglo-Celts might have tried to escape the Alamo. In truth, Rose was most likely a member of the three groups of escapees who fled the Alamo, and survived to tell the tale.

In the view of historian Bill Groneman, Rose "probably escaped during the predawn battle itself, rather than after a solemn line drawing ceremony. . . . However, men escaping from the Alamo just because they did not want to be shot and stabbed to pieces did not exactly fit the story, so it is possible that [William P.] Zuber may have jumped into the breach and invented the [Travis] line drawing scene."[9]

Another lucky soul who escaped the Alamo massacre was Henry Warnell, a rather slick horse trader, a bit of a con artist, and somewhat of a "rouge and an outlaw"—ideal characteristics for a survivor of one of the most infamous slaughters in American history. Warnell was a wheeler-dealer, who made a living outsmarting less worldly customers, including selling stolen horses. In and around the little Texas town of Bastrop, where he migrated in 1835, he was called "jockey," as he was

also known among garrison members, not only because of his small size
but also because of his easy way with temperamental horses.

Warnell manned one of the two or three cannon inside the oval-
shaped lunette that protected the main gate near the south wall's center.
One of the self-styled "Invincibles" of Captain Carey's artillery company, Warnell was almost certainly among the second group of escapees
from the "center" lunette who survived the infamous "massacre at the
Alamo." The hope of seeing his wife, Ludie Ragsdale, and their infant
son, born in November 1834, and his beloved Red River country fueled
the race for his life outside the Alamo's walls. Warnell barely made it,
but succeeded in getting away. He was wounded by Mexican cavalrymen, who killed so many garrison members around the Alameda area.
Defying the odds, he eventually reached the safety of the low-lying gulf
coast. But this spunky soldier died of his wounds at Port Lavaca on the
gulf less than three months after the Alamo's capture.[10]

On March 8, 1869, Susanna Dickinson, now remarried after her
husband's death, gave a disposition on behalf of Warnell's heirs. She
recalled a statement from Warnell that reflected the sentiment of so
many garrison members, and which he fulfilled by somehow managing
to escape the Alamo and survive the onslaught of hundreds of Mexican
lancers and cavalry: "I recollect having heard him remark that he had
much rather be out in the open prairie, than to be pent up in that manner" inside the Alamo.[11]

Later, as revealed in the March 29, 1836 edition of Little Rock's
Arkansas Gazette, two other fortunate survivors, who had also escaped
General Sesma's vengeful horsemen, reached the town of Nacogdoches,
Texas, northeast of San Antonio. One of the men was seriously wounded and likely soon died of his injuries. Here, to the horrified town folk,
they brought the first news of the "massacre" at the Alamo. Indeed, the
two dirty, ragged survivors "said San Antonio had been retaken by the
Mexicans, the garrison put to the sword—that if any others escaped the
general massacre besides themselves, they was not aware of it."[12]

But because so many garrison members had fled the Alamo in what
could only be described as a mass exodus, the odds of escaping the
Mexican cavalry poised outside the Alamo was much greater than previously realized by those who had embraced the romance of the mythical last stand. A veteran of San Antonio's 1835 capture and the battle
of San Jacinto, William C. Murphy, who presented an amazingly accurate version of both the exodus and a higher number of survivors than

previously believed, stated to a reporter that when the garrison was "compelled to abandon [the Alamo] only eight men escaped alive."[13] Most likely, these fortunate survivors were among those who fled from the main gate, having the best chance for survival because Sesma's men had been focused on chasing down and slaughtering the first group of 62 escapees before turning on the second group. Murphy's revealing statement coincided with the first battle report written by Santa Anna at 8:00 a.m., when his cavalry was yet engaged in hunting down and slaughtering escapees on the open prairie, revealing that these men continued to fight back, hide, and evade their pursuers. Disgusted by the slaughter and Santa Anna's no-quarter order, or just tired of killing, some compassionate Mexican cavalrymen might even have allowed hiding or fleeing men to survive.[14]

Another long-overlooked lucky escapee who somehow dodged Mexican sabers, bullets, and lances this bloody morning was young William James Cannon. Indeed, "There was a survivor [at the Alamo and he was] A boy [who] by some miracle escaped the universal slaughter. It was William James Cannon, 'the child of the Alamo'." Perhaps his fluency in Spanish and familiarity with Tejano ways and culture had assisted Cannon, one of the youngest garrison members, in escaping the bloodbath.[15]

But despite the many collaborating primary Mexican sources, the truth of what really happened at the Alamo—the exodus—has been overlooked by historians, scholars, and writers since 1836. One of the few American historians who has even dared to hint—and even then ever so carefully—at the scale of the exodus from the Alamo was the respected author of *Blood of Noble Men: The Alamo, Siege and Battle* (1999), Alan C. Huffines, who later served with distinction as a U.S. Army colonel in Iraq. However, he only dealt with this most controversial aspect of the Alamo's story in a footnote, reasoning like a detective in attempting to uncover a central mystery of the Alamo's story: "It appears that near the end of the battle a large group of Texian defenders attempted a withdrawal. This is absolutely contrary to current Alamo interpretation, but [more than half a dozen Mexican, both officers and enlisted men] witnessed it. . . . How would the cavalry have taken casualties several hundred yards away from the battle? Why did the Texian gunners [under Captain Dickinson] on the church fire on the cavalry. . . . The answer is simple: A large body of Texians made a break for it, going in the only direction they knew, toward Gonzales."[16]

Alamo authority Gary S. Zaboly wrote with honesty in early April 2008, revealing the truth of the exodus from the Alamo: "But a sober reflection will allow that, if all seems lost, fighting men aren't always so disposed to stand in place and just let themselves be killed. For what purpose?The Alamo defenders weren't all as heroically Byronic as Travis: an escape route seemed open, and there was the chance to live and fight another day. So, many of them took it. A similar thing occurred at Little Big Horn."[17]

Roger Borroel, historian and translator of many rare Mexican documents pertaining to the Alamo and the Texas Revolution, concluded in no uncertain terms: "Well over 100 Alamo defenders sought to escape the battle by fleeing for their lives at the height of the struggle . . . they left their buddies [all] alone to die in the Alamo fort [therefore] Sesma's Dolores Cavalry Regiment [and other horse units] played a major role in the struggle, killing at least 50% of the Alamo garrison as they tried to escape" the Alamo.[18]

Even the leading role played by the Mexican lancers and dragoons on March 6 has been largely distorted by historians, who assigned Santa Anna's horsemen solely with the mission of driving the "cowardly" Mexican peasants forward to the attack and "to shoot every man that turned back."[19] Of course this convenient explanation not only reveals cultural and racial arrogance, but has also masked the real and more important role played by Sesma's cavalry, obscuring the truth about the mass exodus from the Alamo.

In the end, therefore, considerable evidence has revealed that very likely the majority of the Alamo garrison was killed not inside but outside the Alamo's walls, not by infantrymen but by cavalrymen, not in darkness but in broad daylight, and not only far from the Alamo but even farther from the romance and glory of the mythical last stand. Still haunted by the horrors he had witnessed, an unidentified soldado described the ugly truth of the Alamo in *El Mosquito Mexicano* on April 5, 1836, when he described the battle as "a pitiful but deserved slaughter of the ungrateful colonists, who threw down their weapons and thought to find safety in escape . . . Miserable souls! They no longer exist."[20]

Unfortunately, the most popular book yet written about the Alamo—Walter Lord's *A Time to Stand*, and other respected works on this ever-fascinating topic of heroism and sacrifice have failed to tell the Alamo's true story, because that chapter simply did not fit neatly into the mythical Alamo, or conform to simplistic American notions of the meaning of heroism. But in truth, a more appropriately descriptive title of what really happened at the Alamo on the morning of March 6 should have been, *A Time to Withdraw.*

LIGHT MEXICAN CASUALTIES TELL THE TRUE STORY

From the beginning, Mexican reports and firsthand personal accounts presented a story far different than the one later told by legions of American writers, historians, journalists, and filmmakers, who possessed a vested interest, including cultural, emotional, and racial, in creating and then romanticizing the last stand legend. The greatest distortion—a direct corollary of the tenacious last stand with every man selling his life as dearly as possible against an avalanche of attackers—was the gross inflation of Mexican casualties to demonstrate last stand heroics. But the truth of what really happened was far different.

The process of distortion began almost immediately after the battle—and has continued unabated to this day—with newspaper journalists across the United States dramatically inflating both the number of Mexican attackers, and especially their losses. For instance, the editor of the prestigious *New York Herald* on April 12, 1836 wrote: "The loss of the Mexicans in storming the [Alamo] was not less than 1000 killed and mortally wounded, and as many wounded, making their loss in the first assault between 2 and 3000 men." And two days later, the same newspaper reported how the Alamo garrison of 187 men had been overwhelmed with great difficulty by 40 times their number, or more than 7,000 troops.[21]

And in the May 12, 1836 issue of the same newspaper, the editor emphatically maintained to his news-starved east coast readers how: "It is also a matter of history that [Santa Anna's] loss in killed and wounded exceeded one thousand" on March 6.[22]

One reason why the allegedly high number of Mexican casualties had not been seriously challenged by historians before was because a host of films and Alamo books, and utterly fictionalized paintings only continued the process of creating the myth of a great epic battle and a heroic last stand to the bitter end. The myth of the last stand was born out of the fiction that only a tenacious defense—fortified by "superior" Anglo-Celtic culture, fighting spirit, and character—could have possibly accounted for the supposed high casualties among Santa Anna's troops.

What was also fabricated was the fiction that Alamo garrison members all willingly choose to die rather than surrender to a dictator because of their egalitarian, republican convictions, or American values, that were worth dying for regardless of the odds and no matter how hopeless the situation: the mythical Alamo that automatically ruled out the mere suggestion or thought of any garrison member—except of course the much maligned Rose—escaping the Alamo.

For such reasons, other Texas revolutionary battles—besides the Alamo—also provide evidence of over-exaggeration of Mexican numbers. A recent scholarly study by Allwyn Barr, *Texans in Revolt: The Battle for San Antonio, 1835*, has challenged the battle's mythology in regard to the exaggeration of Mexican numbers: "The popular view has been that three hundred Texans captured Béxar [San Antonio] from twelve hundred Mexicans. Instead, a reconstruction of the armies shows the Texans to have been slightly more numerous than the Mexicans until late in the fighting.[23]

However, the example of the Alamo provides, by far, the greatest distortion and exaggeration of both Mexican numbers and casualties. First published not long after the Second World War, *The Alamo*, written by John Myers, represented a classic example of depicting the mythical Alamo. After elaborating on the traditional interpretation of the defender's heroic self-sacrifice to ensure that Texas would live forever, Myers maintained that "there were about sixteen hundred [Mexican] dead, and there must have been a good few wounded, many of them seriously."[24] The figure was based on evidence from more than a century earlier, as it is the total given by Travis' slave Joe, who could neither read nor write, and as published in the April 12, 1836 issue of the *Memphis Enquirer*. Joe boasted how "SIXTEEN HUNDRED of the Mexicans [were] killed" at the Alamo.[25]

Thereafter, this ludicrous figure of 1,600 Mexican killed has been accepted as fact to this day. This distortion began before the battle of San Jacinto, not afterward, as commonly believed by historians. For instance, author Thomas Ricks Lindley speculated that the number of Mexican dead was deliberately exaggerated by Mexican prisoners captured at San Jacinto to patronize the victors and save themselves. Lindley emphasized: "Because the Texians were consumed with the belief that they were far superior soldiers to the soldiers of Mexico, they seem to have accepted the unbelievable figures."[26]

However, modern historians have only perpetuated the fairy tale of astoundingly high Mexican casualties. In 1968, an almost pleading T.R. Fehrenbach retold the traditional Alamo story in *Lone Star: A History of Texas and Texans*, saying how the battle lasted more than four and a half hours and grossly overstated Mexican losses. He described how during "The five-hour engagement . . . The Battalion of Toluca, the assault shock force of 800 men, had lost 670 killed. The other battalions had lost in each case approximately 25 percent. In all, there were nearly 1,600 Mexican dead. These figures are reliable."[27]

And even the notoriously precise and conservative Walter Lord more than doubled the actual number of Mexican casualties in *A Time to Stand*, writing that the "best estimate seems about 600 killed and wounded."[28]

But the inflation of Mexican casualties was hardly a feature of 20th century Alamo historiography. The root of such outlandish distortions developed almost immediately after the battle, in part to bestow upon the Alamo defenders—especially Crockett and Bowie—heroic, glorious deaths against all odds. In Smith's 1836 *Col. Crockett's Exploits and Adventures in Texas*, he emphasized not only multiple assaults but also frightful Mexican losses: "The loss of the Mexicans in storming the place was not less than 800 killed and mortally wounded, making their losses since the first assault more than fifteen hundred."[29]

Much of the myth of high Mexican casualties developed in part from the traditional interpretation that the defender's firepower was maximized because each garrison member had many loaded muskets by his side. As Historian William C. Davis explained in his fine book, *Three Roads to the Alamo*: " . . . every man on the parapets had several loaded rifles, muskets, or pistols at his side, for that was one commodity of which Travis suffered no shortage [because of the] number of captured long arms taken in the surrender of Béxar in December came into his hands [and] As a result, there were 816 rifles, shotguns, pistols and English brown Bess muskets on hand and with his garrison now numbering more than two hundred men, that meant that four apiece."[30]

But such a defensive plan to unleash massive volumes of firepower would have been impossible. First, ammunition was of poor quality and in short supply. Indeed, a rare Mexican account from an unidentified officer of the Activo San Luís Potosí Battalion revealed the truth. He scribbled in his journal how the garrison not only "lack[ed] sufficient cannon balls," but also Mexican troops were only greeted with little more than "pistol fire from the parapets" when they first neared the

Alamo's walls on February 25, before even more ammunition was expended during the next nearly ten days of siege.[31]

Generations of authors had merely emphasized this traditional story of piles of weapons beside each defender to explain the allegedly high Mexican losses. In truth, and even before the struggle began, two distinct developments had already negated this alleged overabundance of weaponry: the damp and cold winter weather and the complete surprise of Santa Anna's attack, which made such a scheme unworkable.

By the time of Santa Anna's attack, many, if not most, defenders' weapons had been rendered all but useless by the cold, wet weather of late winter. A wide discrepancy between the amount of powder in the church's two powder rooms—extracted from an estimated 36,000 to 20,000 cartridges, containing inferior Mexican powder, left by Cós—and the actual amount of available good powder explains the mystery of Travis' seemingly contradictory statements about the lack of ammunition and the large amount of powder found after the Alamo's fall. On the early morning of March 6, in part due to the phenomena of "rising damp" that compromised powder reserves inside the church, the fragile black powder in muskets, rifles, shotguns, and the flintlock flash pans would have become damp, and thereby ineffective under such conditions. What historians have overlooked is the simple fact that for these weapons to have been operable to meet Santa Anna's attack, they would of had to have been fired first, or "cleared."

Defying logic, the enduring image of Texas defenders firing one loaded musket after another, inflicting terrible damage, became one of the long-accepted, time-honored tenants of the mythical last stand. Another myth was that more than twenty Alamo cannon, loaded with homemade canister, inflicted serious damage, cutting down hundreds of attackers, which was simply not true. The vast majority of the Alamo's artillery was negated by the surprise assault, with most gunners unable to get into position and load their guns in time. Instead of homemade canister, artillery fire from the Alamo did not include canister but cannonballs. For instance, one cannonball took off the arm of an unfortunate Lieutenant Colonel José María Mendoza.

One of the most overlooked aspects of the Alamo's story, the real truth of exactly how and who really inflicted the most damage upon Mexican troops on the morning of March 6, came not from the defenders, but ironically from the attackers themselves. In fact, according to a number of reliable Mexican accounts, the majority of Santa Anna's casualties resulted from a widespread fratricide, or friendly fire, in the darkness. Foremost of these accounts was that of General Filisola, who described how "most of our dead and wounded" were caused by fratricide. In perhaps the Alamo's most haunting irony, Mexican bullets from the English Brown Bess actually caused greater damage than all of the Texas Long Rifles, Bowie knives, shotguns, pistols, sabers, and cannon combined. Such a paradoxical development was all but inevitable in the collision of multiple assault columns, the attack in the darkness, and the fact that the Army of Operations was fighting its first battle.

In his classic work, *Sacrificed at the Alamo*, Richard Bruce Winders, the Alamo's official historian, wrote of the widespread fratricide when "in the compound [the attackers] soon found themselves in grave danger from their own comrades. Fellow soldiers firing out of the darkness began to kill and wound those who had rushed ahead [and Mexican] officers later attributed the majority of their casualties to friendly fire rather than from the defenders."[32]

In his book *Duel of Eagles*, Jeff Long went further, coming even closer to the truth. He reasoned that "fully three-quarters of the Mexican casualties . . . were caused by Mexican bullets" and not defender fire. Even this high estimate can be explained by General Filisola, who wrote how during the attack on the north wall: "Our own men . . . had to suffer all that [fratricide fire] from our men themselves from the opposite sides. Since they attacked in a closed column, all the shots, the direction of which was turned somewhat downward, aimed the bullets towards the backs of those ahead of them. Thus it was that most of our dead and wounded that we suffered were caused by his misfortune."[33]

Conscripted into Santa Anna's Army in 1835, Sergeant Felix Nunez, of Dúque's assault column, described the frightful rate of fratricide, which existed from the beginning to the end of the attack, including inside the compound: "The soldiers in the moments of victory became entirely uncontrollable, and, owing to the darkness of the building [church] and the smoke of battle, fell to killing one another, not being able to distinguish friend from foe."[34]

As much as the clash of multiple assault columns converging on the north wall at different angles, this high rate of fratricide resulted from the confused assault in the darkness and fragmentation of commands, which began outside and then continued unabated inside the Alamo. Enrique Esparza, for instance, described the utter confusion among the

Mexican ranks inside the Alamo amid the blackness, when Santa Anna's infantrymen "kept firing on the men who had defended the Alamo. For fully a quarter of an hour they kept firing upon them after all of the defenders had been slain."[35]

Not only had three separate assault columns collided, and even fired into each other on hit flanks, but also rearward troops fired to take "a fearful toll of those in front." In fact, the high rate of fratricide revealed that Mexican troops were more deadly to themselves than from the fire of all the defenders' Long Rifles and cannon combined. With a gift for understatement, Sergeant Manuel Loranca described: "In the act of assault a confusion occurred, in which the Mexican troops opened fire on each other."[36]

Widespread fratricide was so extensive that it had even determined the struggle's outcome. Historian Alan C. Huffines emphasized how such intense friendly hit Colonel Cós' column, that his men were forced to surge closer toward the west wall for protection before veering northward, to eventually unite with Dúque's and later Romero's columns at the north wall. In striking the lightly manned northwest corner, Cós' redirected attack "almost certainly made the difference in the overall assault on the Alamo."[37]

Overall, this massive "crush" from three assault columns at the north wall was considerable, because hundreds of attackers possessed relatively few scaling ladders. Both General Cós' and Colonel Dúque's attack columns possessed only ten ladders each, while Colonel Romero's column had only six, and Colonel Morales' column brought along only two ladders. Clearly, all four Mexican columns had attacked with far too few ladders, and even these were of a "poor" quality. Besides the accidental merger of three assault columns, this lack of foresight also ensured a pile up of a great mass of soldados at the north wall's base: an ideal scenario for fratricide, with attackers from behind firing blindly ahead and into the mass in the confused darkness.[38]

Fratricide occurred almost as much inside the Alamo as outside. De la Pena described how even after the Mexicans swarmed inside the Alamo compound, "Behind these [foremost attackers] came others, who [now] fired their shots against friends and enemies alike, and in this way our losses were most grievous [indeed] one was as likely to die by a friendly hand as by an enemy's [and this] confusion . . . was increasing the number of our victims [and in total] around fifty thousand cartridges had been used up."[39]

However, generations of American and Texas historians have under-estimated this high level of fratricide at the Alamo, assuming that the Mexican losses came from the combat prowess of fully alerted defenders in the fabled last stand. But in truth, garrison members were either asleep or in the process of being aroused when the Mexican struck and gained the north wall. And the exodus from the Alamo also meant that far fewer defenders were firing back in attempting to repel the attack.

Perhaps as much as tactical mishaps, the highest level of fratricide occurred because the average Mexican soldier was a poor marksman. Poverty ensured the lack of firearms and the absence of a firearm cultural and hunting tradition among most of Mexico's civilian populace. Marksmanship training in the Mexican army was rare, especially for the new recruits and conscripts that made up such a large percentage of Santa Anna's forces. Therefore, Mexican soldiers generally fired their muskets, which packed a tremendous kick, from the hip rather than the shoulder, ensuring not only inaccuracy but also a high rate of fratricide, especially in a night attack during their first engagement. Recent archeological findings of soldado remains from a south Texas battlefield during the Mexican-American War—by that time not much had changed in this regard—revealed bruising on the hips of Mexican troops, who fired the Brown Bess musket without aiming: an indication that this common, popular perception in 1836 Texas was not an unjustified stereotype.[40]

Indicating the lofty rate of fratricide, casualties were highest in Dúque's column, which received the brunt of friendly fire losses. Huffines emphasized how: "Of all the Mexican units taking part in the assault on the Alamo, the activo Toluca Battalion chalked up the highest casualty rate of all" in the attack of the Alamo.[41] According to General Filisola, the activo Toluca Battalion of Colonel Dúque's column lost a total of 20 killed, and another 79 who fell wounded.[42]

Rather than the fire from defender firearms and artillery, most of Dúque's column were shot down by their own comrades, because it had been their unit that led the assault, paying a high price for charging ahead of everyone else in the darkness. The former Toluca Battalion commander, Colonel Dúque, was very likely the victim of fratricide instead of artillery fire as alleged by de la Pena, when cut down in the "vicinity of the enemy parapets," which indicated that he was too close to be hit by cannon fire. In the darkness, the Mexican troops, including Santa Anna's 400-man reserve, failed to realize that Cós' and Romero's troops were before them. Therefore, in the confusion of combat, they fired toward the wall in the night, striking the backs of the foremost attackers. Perhaps like Houston, who very likely was hit by friendly fire in leading his attackers across the grassy meadow at San Jacinto, Colonel Dúque went down from a large-caliber musket ball from a Brown Bess and not a canister ball from an Alamo cannon. Walter Lord was indeed correct in his analysis of how the three attack "columns— merging from different directions—continued to fire blindly ahead, more often hitting friend than foe. And the men in the rear, unable to see, took a fearful toll of those in front."[43]

Correctly reasoning how Santa Anna's reserves committed more slaughter among the soldados than Texan bullets or cannonballs, Long wrote how the Zapadores and five reserve companies of light troops, to the sound of bugles blaring in the night, "ran toward the Alamo, the four hundred reserves blindly fired off their weapons [and] bullets raked the shoulders and heads of [Dúque's] troops in front of them, mowing down more Mexican soldiers," who never knew what hit them.[44]

Additionally, Mexican Army reports have revealed that the second largest number of casualties suffered on March 6 was in the San Luís Potosí Battalion. In this fine unit, two officers—First Lieutenant Irineo Guerrero and Second Lieutenant Antonio Carricante—and seven enlisted men were killed. Among the slain enlisted men were Sergeant Anastacio Velaquer, Grenadier Victoriano Perez, and two cazadores, Privates German Sánchez and Victoriano Tenerio. Charging forward behind the activo Toluca Battalion in Dúque's attack column, the San Luís Potosí Battalion suffered a total of 37 wounded and nine killed.[45]

Especially for the activo Toluca Battalion, which was initially massed against the north wall, these high losses came primarily from friendly fire from rearward soldiers, especially Amat's 400 reserves, who could not see anyone before them in the dark. Fatally stricken officers, like Captain José M. Macotela, might well have been hit from the rear. Indeed, most of the San Luís Potosí and the Toluca Battalion's losses came from the fire of hundreds of Santa Anna's reserves.[46]

But in truth, the relatively low number of Mexican casualties revealed a most feeble defense of the Alamo. As printed in the pages of the newspaper El Mosquito Mexicano, a Mexican Army surgeon, Jose Faustino Moro, wrote a letter to the publication that revealed the relatively few losses. He described how "an assault was given and there was more than two hundred wounded men as a result of that battle" on March 6, 1836.[47]

Additionally, an unsigned pamphlet written by a Mexican soldier who fought at the Alamo was reprinted in Mexico City's leading newspaper, *El Mosquito Mexicano* on April 5, 1836. In this rare, anonymous account, the author emphasized how Mexican losses were surprisingly low, especially given the garrison's relative strength in holding a fortified position defended by so much artillery. Most significant, he also wrote that Santa Anna's Army had in fact suffered a loss of only two hundred men and officers wounded in the assault.[48]

Santa Anna estimated that the Alamo's capture resulted in "costing us seventy dead and about three hundred wounded," but this was a hasty conclusion.[49] The general had merely estimated both the number of killed and wounded soldados in the first official report of the battle that was written at 8 a.m. on March 6. Therefore, a later, more careful tally of the wounded Mexican troops was not made by the time Santa Anna estimated that he had suffered about 300 wounded, which was too high of a figure.[50]

Santa Anna also overestimated the number of fatalities in his hasty morning report. In reality, and after a more precise count after more time passed, General Filisola counted a total of only 60 Mexican fatalities suffered at the Alamo.[51]

The overall lack of resistance from the fort can be seen in the case of the elite Sapper Battalion. Historian John B. Lundstrom noted, with a sense of ironic contradiction, a major mystery of the Alamo, writing with some dismay how "the Zapadores only took 27 casualties, in spite of the fact that the unit was the first over the wall and led the assault down the east walls and barracks." This surprising development can be best explained by the fact that these rearmost attackers upon the north wall suffered less from fratricide than those command in front.[52]

Overall, the fact that around 2,000 attackers suffered only 60 fatalities—many of which were caused by fratricide—indicated what weak resistance was offered that early morning, adding additional evidence that a large percentage of the Alamo garrison chose flight instead of fighting to the bitter end. While Santa Anna reported 70 killed and around 300 wounded, General Andrade, of the cavalry, listed a total of only 311 killed and wounded during the assault. In the first and earliest detailed summary of Mexican casualties, Andrade counted 60 dead and 251 wounded.

And Colonel Almonte described a comparably low casualty figure of 65 killed and 223 wounded for a total of 288.[53] In his March 6 journal entry, he wrote: "Our loss was 60 soldiers and 5 officers killed, and 198 soldiers and 25 officers wounded—2 of the latter General officers. The battalion of Toluca lost 98 men between the wounded and killed."[54]

Offering a more accurate tabulation and testimonial in the battalion's journal, the adjutant of the San Luís Potosí Battalion revealed that 316 total casualties were suffered by Santa Anna's attackers, which corresponded with other equally low totals of around 300. For instance, General Bradburn stated that "300 men were lost," including killed and wounded.[55]

In his 2002 biography of Santa Anna, Robert L. Scheina came close to the truth by writing how: "Santa Anna lost 78 dead (which included 26 officers) and 251 wounded (including 18 officers)."[56] Providing evidence in his diary, Colonel José Juan Sánchez-Navarro wrote how: "two hundred forty-seven of our troops were wounded and one hundred killed"—a total of 347 men.[57]

Therefore, Mexican losses were not only well below 400, but possibly under 300. Therefore, Santa Anna was indeed correct in later deriding the politically inspired criticism for his relatively light Alamo losses that were "later judged to be avoidable and charge, after the disaster of San Jacinto, to my incompetence and precipitation."[58]

Combined with other collaborating evidence, the final casualty figure from Colonel Almonte, who was the best educated member of Santa Anna's staff, serving as the generalissimo's trusty "chief" and "special advisor," was in fact the more correct figure. Indeed, as Santa Anna's chief of staff, he would have known better than anyone the exact number of losses for the Army of Operations on this day. Therefore, on March 6 he wrote in his detailed Order Book the correct total of the Army of Operation's losses: 65 killed and 223 wounded, for a total of 288.[59]

One of the most heroic Mexican deaths was that of Lieutenant José María Torres of the Zapadores Battalion, who was killed while tearing down the garrison's flag flying from the roof of the Long Barracks. Of course, equally heroic was the unknown Alamo defender who shot him down while while briefly able to protect the garrison's banner.

The relatively low number of Mexican casualties is in line with the realities of the surprisingly brief—around 20 minutes—struggle for the Alamo's possession. And if around half of the Mexican losses resulted from fratricide, as numerous Mexican accounts indicated, then all resistance from the Alamo's defenders might well have accounted for less than 150 Mexican casualties.

It is also important to consider that there may have been more men present at the Alamo than previously recognized. De la Pena disputed the standard, long-accepted number of 182 Alamo defenders. As he wrote: "According to documents found among these men [and] subsequent information, the force within the Alamo consisted of 182 men; but according to the number [of dead bodies] counted by us it was 253."[60] It can be remembered that prior to the reinforcement of the 32 men of the Gonzalez Ranging Company, Travis had reported 150 men at his disposal, which corresponds with other primary evidence; however, he may have been referring only to able-bodied defenders, not those who were sick or disabled, some of whom may have been able to handle weapons, if not serve on active duty. After the tough fight in the Alamo's hospital, there may indeed have been more bodies for the Mexicans to count than commonly recognized.

In conclusion, based on Colonel Almonte's casualty figure of 288, from his highly precise journal, and de la Pena's figure of 252 defender's bodies, the ratio of defenders to killed or wounded attackers has increased considerably. Even more, if approximately half of the Mexican losses were inflicted by fratricide, which was very likely according to Mexican sources, then less than 150 Mexican casualties resulted from defender's fire. These facts and figures all additionally verify the exodus from the Alamo relatively early in the battle, as opposed to the last stand mythology of fighting to the bitter end.[61]

NEW VIEW OF CROCKETT'S DEMISE

Ironically, the attempt to explore what really happened on March 6, 1836 has resulted in discovering a good many revelations not originally intended or even expected, including a new perspective about what has been the most controversial aspect of the Alamo story: that Crockett indeed died a hero's death, though not in the conventional sense according the traditional legend of the mythical Alamo. Not a single eyewitness account exists of the traditional view of Crockett's death, with the forty-nine-year-old Tennessean swinging his musket and slaying great numbers of the enemy.

Therefore, author James Atkins Shackford, who wrote the definitive account of Crockett's life, was quite correct in his final analysis of the historical record: "According to the evidence, David was not among the five who surrendered. Nor was he one of the last to die, inside the fortress, in the [church] doorway, fighting off a whole regiment. Instead, he died on the outside, one of the earliest to fall, with no gun on him, going on some mission which apparently made him oblivious to danger." This view seems to partly coincide with Ruiz's account of having seen Crockett's body at the main exit point in the west wall's center at the lunette. If this was the case, then Crockett was killed early in his mission.[62]

Indeed, in attempting to separate fact from fantasy about the most romanticized death at the Alamo, Shackford emphasized in no uncertain terms how: "What evidence remains suggest that, in fact, David's death was quite undramatic, that he was one of the first to fall, and that he died unarmed."[63]

Since this 1956 analysis, a considerable amount of new information and documentation has come to light, especially about the flight of so many Alamo defenders. Shackford, however, was incorrect about where Crockett died. Ironically, Crockett's death was most likely not inside the Alamo but on the outside, and not while engaged in some unknown daring "mission," but when fleeing with so many others to escape certain death inside the old Spanish mission.

But if Crockett did not flee the Alamo with so many other escapees, then even this distinct possibility would be most revealing, because that would place the Tennessean's decision to remain in an entirely new perspective. The fact that such a large percentage of the Alamo garrison fled in a desperate bid to escape has transformed Crockett's alleged capture and execution in a much more heroic light, which, ironically, would be in keeping with the romantic image and legend, if that was the case. Indeed, perhaps unlike a majority of the Alamo garrison, Crockett, despite being stationed in the most vulnerable defensive position—the low palisade—and with more opportunity to escape than anywhere else along the perimeter, did not flee the doomed Alamo like so many others. Even more, because the largest body of men departing the Alamo passed through the edge of the palisade, which was defended by Crockett and the Tennessee volunteers, he might have watched these men leave, after deciding not to join them. Crockett had faced a quandary. After all, his political career was at stake, and perhaps his dream of becoming the future president of the Republic of Texas. If he fled with the other 62 escapees, then Crockett realized he risked earning a coward's label, which would have ruined a future political career in Texas.[64]

Crockett, therefore, might have made his fatal decision to remain behind, sealing his fate inside the Alamo compound for political reasons. Nevertheless, he remained true to his contrarian nature in defying convention: one reason why he had come to Texas in the first place. In this sense, Crockett did what he thought was the right thing to do under the circumstances: remain behind in the Alamo and defend it to the very end. Instead of fleeing, which certainly would have been the natural impulse with a no-quarter fate awaiting him, Crockett might well have stayed behind to die with a minority of the garrison. In such a situation, Crockett would have certainly proved to be one of the most courageous Alamo defenders. With perhaps the majority of the garrison having fled the Alamo, there was nothing else to do for remaining defenders but to seek safety in the church and other buildings. From such shelter, according to the de la Pena diary and other Mexican accounts, Crockett later emerged in a futile attempt to surrender but was executed.

Yet other evidence—a significantly lesser amount, and more circumstantial, than exists about his possible execution—indicated that Crockett might well have joined the flight of the 62 men who went out through the wooden palisade, where he and his Tennessee boys were stationed. After all, this was the ideal place to exit the Alamo. Such a possibility coincides with existing "evidence that indicates that Crockett was not among the five who surrendered."[65]

Ironically, perhaps some indirect evidence of Crockett's flight might indirectly be gleamed from the controversial de la Pena memoir. De la Pena became Santa Anna's sworn enemy who had a heavy political axe to grind—seemingly the overall purpose of writing his postwar memoir based upon a diary and then embellished—and because of the lingering doubts about the diary's authenticity and provenance and because he also incorporated other Mexican soldier accounts and even American 1836 newspaper articles that described Crockett's execution after surrender, he evidently only rewrote an old tale of Crockett's surrender and execution scene to raise even more hatred against Santa Anna after the Alamo's fall.[66]

Actually, the distinct possibility also existed that Crockett actually died a death even more heroic than imaged or previously known. If Crockett indeed went down fighting around his assigned position at the palisade, as tradition has it, then his last stand was in fact far more heroic than simply slaying as many Mexicans as possible for no gain: Crockett may well have stayed in position at the palisade to buy time and protect the flight of his comrades. If so, then such a heroic scenario was reminiscent of what Captain Dickinson and his gunners accomplished in providing timely protective fire for the escapees, during one of the most valiant acts on the bloody morning of March 6.

Ironically, while the Alamo defenders became heroes across Texas and the United States, the young soldados, who won a one-sided victory, continued to be yet denounced as inferior fighting men during this campaign. In a strange paradox, the overall character and quality of the Mexican fighting man continued to be held in utter contempt by the Anglo-Celts. For instance, the *Louisville Journal* ran an Alamo story under the headline, "Convicts Used to Storm Béxar!!!"

What was occurring was an attempt by Texans and Americans—both in Texas and the United States—to retain the moral high ground by yet demonstrating the inferiority of Mexican people, represented by their fighting men, in order to provide a guilt-free, righteous basis for a claim to bountiful Tejano and Mexican land that was not their own. Not long after the Alamo's fall, the editor attempted to solve the mystery of how allegedly inferior Mexican soldiers could possibly have defeated even a relative handful of Anglo-Celts at the Alamo: "The tyrant [Santa Anna] brought with him 1,508 convicts from the Mexican prisons [and] he placed the whole body of them as a forelorn [sic] hope in advance of the rest of the army [and] each convict who attempt to escape or retreat, should be instantly shot or cut down" by those troops in the rear. Even in reaping a one-sided success, the courage of the average soldado was yet derided by Americans.

This Kentucky editor also described how Santa Anna "then ordered the convicts to storm the fortress, setting before them liberty and promotion if they succeeded, and immediate death in the event of their failure. They rushed forward with the fury of devils, and, in less than an hour, every man in the garrison was massacred. Out of the fifteen hundred [attackers], all but three or four hundred were either killed or mortally wounded."[67]

Even de la Pena was confused about "convict" troops. Santa Anna had ordered his commanders to secure "useful men familiar with firearms" from the towns along the army's path toward Texas. Therefore, what had been incorporated into the army were border men, frontiersmen from northern Mexico, especially along the Rio Grande.

Because of their rough manner and looks, de la Pena, an aristocratic, inexperienced young officer with a naval background, believed them to be convict soldiers, which was not the case. Nevertheless, he was complimentary of their military skills in unconventional warfare, which far exceeded those of the regulars.[68]

Popular negative stereotypes—of freedom-loving Alamo garrison members having been overrun by a mindless, barbarian "Aztec horde" that had been prodded forward by officers and rearward troops—not only robbed the average Mexican soldado of a well-deserved valor in storming the Alamo, but also overlooked the success of Santa Anna's tactical plan.[69]

While the Alamo's legacy has been glorified and romanticized by generations of American historians and writers to create a heroic epic based upon the last stand, what has been overlooked were the forgotten victims—the real long-term casualties—resulting from the Texas Revolution's success, the Mexican and Tejano people of Texas. The mythical Alamo played a role in setting the cultural, racial, and political foundation for the establishment of modern Texas. This mythology provided a moral, righteous justification for discrimination and the acquisition of Tejano and Mexican lands, because it was based upon an alleged Latino inferiority, which was exemplified by a relative handful of Anglo-Celts bravely standing up to multitudes of allegedly inferior soldiers: the mythical last stand With the silencing of the truth of massive flight rather than fight, the Alamo's story was transformed into a moral triumph and the legendary "Cradle of Texas Liberty," symbolizing the birth of a new republic, or the domination of Anglo-Celtic Texas over Tejano and Mexican Texas.

Therefore, the Alamo's story—based upon the mythical last stand—evolved into a holy resurrection, a defeat that only paved the way for decisive victory by Houston's ragtag army at San Jacinto, justifying a sense of cultural and racial superiority and a "racial enmity" that continues to exist to this day. In this way, the slaughter of the Alamo garrison was transformed into a great moral victory, a regenerative act of God's will, a necessary sacrifice for the establishment of a dominant Anglo-Celtic civilization.[70]

Therefore, the Alamo's story was really, in essence, one of the first battles of a war of politics, culture, economics, race, and power in a larger, ongoing struggle that continues well into the 21st century. As emphasized by Richard R. Flores in his classic work, *Remembering the*

Alamo: Memory, Modernity and the Master Symbol, the Alamo myth, especially the heroic last stand, served as an essential foundation for the creation of a modern Texas and the establishment of the new social, political, and racial order, justifying a sense of cultural, moral, and racial superiority during both the 19th and 20th centuries.[71]

Consequently, even respected Tejano Texas Revolutionary heroes eventually became villains, while Anglo-Celtic real-life tyrants became heroes. Ironically, despite his own distinguished service in leading his hard-riding Tejano cavalry company during the Texas Revolution, Juan Nepomuceno Seguín, a Castilian as fair-skinned as those who now targeted him, became an early victim when his former Texian allies turned against him. Officially denounced in Mexico during the summer 1836 as "Seguín and his henchmen," which consisted of 65 Tejano rancheros and vaqueros, he would eventually be forced from Texas—his own homeland that he had fought to defend—just "for being Mexican," after his ranchero was burned down by vengeful Texans.

A revival of a lust for land, a "Texas fever," once again consumed white Texans, who now held all the political power in the antebellum period. The legacy of the Alamo's dark shadow loomed over long-time Tejano rancheros around San Antonio, especially along the San Antonio River. More than one hundred Tejano families were forced to leave their well-developed, ancestral lands. But the land grabbing was especially prevalent in the ranching country of south Texas. Existing for hundreds of years, legitimate ancient Spanish land grants were routinely dismissed by white judges. Additionally, state and local government raised taxes to force foreclosure of Tejano properties, which were then eagerly gobbled up by large white ranchers. Unlike in the early 1830s, stealing vast amounts of lands from the Tejano people was now systematically accomplished legally, and with the blessings of power brokers.[72]

Like Captain Seguín, another Tejano victim was Placido Benavides. In commanding a band of rancheros during the 1835 Texas Campaign, he was second only to Seguín as a leading Tejano patriot. Not long after the war began, he had organized local Tejano rancheros from the Goliad area to fight against Mexico. This young Tejano captain served at the battle of Concepcion, then in San Antonio's capture, and later at the Alamo as part of Travis' "Legion of Cavalry." Benavides was denied a well-deserved pension for his Texas military services as late as 1875, even though he and other Tejanos had risked all by having taken "up arms against our own kindred and country, believing we were right."[73]

Segregation of Tejanos in Texas, along with its accompanying discrimination, became regular features of daily life in Texas for generations. Justification for this widespread discrimination and disenfranchisement was partly founded upon the righteous Anglo-Celtic versus evil Hispanic stereotype rooted in an Alamo story that had evolved into an idiological and racial symbol for the state.[74]

But the most tragic legacies of both the Alamo and San Jacinto ensured the enslavement of tens of thousands of African-American men, women, and children for the next nearly thirty years. New Texas laws and constitutions protected slavery when Texas became part of the vast slave empire of the Deep South. Human rights were defined in purely racial terms, ensuring that Texas slaves of the new Republic of Texas remained in bondage for life. And because the victorious Texans described freedom for whites only, even the liberties of the free black population were stripped away. Not surprisingly, some free blacks had departed with the retiring Army of Operations after San Jacinto. After all, for generations of African-Americans, the Republic of Mexico was viewed quite correctly as the true land of the free.[75]

Starting after the American Revolution's end in 1783, Jefferson's utopian vision of a "land of liberty" that spread into the Deep South, thanks in part to General Jackson's crushing of the Creek Nation, had evolved into one of the greatest slave empires on earth. This process only continued unabated after San Jacinto, thrusting southwestward into the former lands of Mexico. In this sense, what happened at the Alamo could be seen as only part of the overall American expansionist push into the southwest that spread slavery by violent means, including by way of revolution. After all, though separated by more than half a century, both the American Revolution and the Texas Revolution were major victories for the continuation of slavery.

As part of the triumphant march "of Jacksonian nationalism and its inseparable ingredient of slavery"—that Crockett had hated so passionately—which resulted in the relentless advance of a slavery frontier, Texas would become as Southern as Mississippi, and San Antonio as Southern as Montgomery, Alabama, by the time of the antebellum period. As envisioned by Austin so long ago, much of Texas had evolved into a vast plantation and cotton empire, thanks in no small part to what happened at the Alamo. The attacking Texans and Americans, inspired by the cry "Remember the Alamo" in their victory at San Jacinto, unleashed an uncontrollable flood of human misery that brought the "demographic, economic, and political weight of plantation slavery" across Texas.[76]

Texas thrived as part of the Cotton Kingdom of the United States. Symbolically, in the same late winter and spring of 1836, when the dead bodies of the Alamo defenders were unceremoniously burned by the victors, African-Americans in the United States were burned alive by angry mobs of white Americans. But while Santa Anna's final act of burning the remains of the Alamo defenders solidified his place as the stereotypical arch-villain, white Americans who committed the same act against blacks—even though they were alive and not dead—were treated as local heroes in their white communities.[77]

Despite having fought in the Texas Revolution against Santa Anna, free blacks were banished from Texas because they were seen as dangerous, inspirational examples for slaves. Instead of promising opportunity and liberty to free blacks, the Texas Constitution that created a new republic proclaimed: "No free person of African descent either in whole or in part, shall be permitted to reside permanently in the republic, without the consent of Congress."[78]

And thus the additional entry of free blacks into Texas was limited. Such harsh legal discrimination based upon race was ironic, because a black presence in Texas dated back hundreds of years and to the beginning of Spanish settlement in Texas. African-Americans living, fighting, and dying in Texas was a longer-established tradition than in any other section of the United States, existing centuries before the first Anglo-Celtic settlement in Texas.[79]

But the Texans themselves could hardly be blamed for this pervasive racism that differed so markedly from more enlightened Tejano attitudes around them. Clearly, like their music, food, architecture, and cultural beliefs, the Anglo-Celts had brought their own racial stereotypes and hatreds—the accepted norm of the day—with them when they migrated across the Sabine. In striking contrast, Tejano culture, including in San Antonio, readily accepted African-Americans, especially those of mixed race. By 1777, at the time of the American Revolution, for instance, more than 150 African-Americans lived in San Antonio.[80]

Beyond the simple romantic mythology and hero-worship, Alamo garrison members had been sacrificed in the name of the relentless tide of Anglo-Saxon progress and westward expansion across the North American continent. In the end, what happened at the Alamo played a key role in transforming a vast expanse of Mexican lands into one of the great land grabs in American history, while also setting the stage for an even larger national land grab, the Mexican-American War. In this sense, the "battle" of the Alamo was only one chapter of the ongoing clash between race, culture, value systems, politics, economics, and class that yet continues to this day.

Placing the Alamo in a proper historical perspective, the enlightened editor of the *Patriot* in Woonsocket, Rhode Island, praised Santa Anna's march of liberation across Texas and the commander-in-chief himself: "How can we style him a tyrant . . . who opposed the efforts of rebels and used them with deserved severity [in part because they desired to] substantiate the horrible system of slavery."[81]

Ironically, by overlooking such contradictions to the myth, the Alamo was transformed into a great moral victory, based upon racial and cultural superiority, to justify not only the stealing of this fertile Mexican province, but also to justify the enslavement of thousands of African-Americans. An Englishman early understood as much before San Jacinto, writing how in contrast to the Texans, "the Mexicans stand at a proud moral distance from them in regard to slavery, which is abolished in the republic [and] in defiance of human freedom [the Anglo-Celts proceed] to people the country with slaves."[82]

Consequently, the Alamo's defenders stood in the path of the march of human progress and enlightenment in regard to slavery. After all, Santa Anna himself wrote on February 16, 1836, only a week before trapping the tiny garrison inside the Alamo: "There exists in Texas a considerable number of slaves . . . who, according to our laws, should be free."[83]

When Santa Anna was taken to Washington, D.C. after his capture at San Jacinto, he was greeted wildly by anti-slavery American citizens across the upper South, who viewed the Texas Revolution as a Southern conspiracy to extend slavery. Therefore, the commander was hailed in the United States as a great "hero of human liberty" by enlightened, race-blind Americans. Clearly, what had happened at the Alamo was already forgotten by many Americans, paling in significance to larger, more important moral issues of the day.[84]

A MORE HONEST PERSPECTIVE

For the young men and boys who were massacred at the Alamo, there was neither glory nor romance, but only ugly, miserable deaths both inside and outside of the compound. Mirabeau B. Lamar, who commanded the Texas cavalry at San Jacinto, perhaps best summarized the "battle" of the Alamo in a letter to his brother on April 10, 1836: "San Antonio has been retaken by and every man in the fort murdered."[85] Only the ceaseless efforts of generations of imaginative historians, writers, journalists, screenplay writers, and filmmakers have transformed this massacre into an epic battle, especially the defiant last stand, that the struggle for the Alamo never was.

It is most paradoxical that perhaps the most glorified battle in American history was in truth merely a brief slaughter. A veil of darkness mercifully shrouded a brutal massacre from the sight of many participants. There was nothing glorious in Santa Anna's no-quarter policy and its bloody results: scared young men far from home attempting to surrender in vain, and scores of escapees running for their lives out on the open prairie, only to be cut down by the sabers and lances of Mexican cavalrymen outside the Alamo.

Perhaps a United States major named John P. Gaines, best summarized the real truth of the battle of the Alamo, when he scribbled in his diary on October 13, 1846, after visiting the site: "The town [of San Antonio and the Alamo] is here called a slaughter pen, many battles having been fought in it, and a vast number of lives lost [and] I might call it 'the dark and bloody ground'."[86]

Ironically, had not a minor military miracle occurred at San Jacinto on April 21, 1836, what happened at the Alamo would have been all but forgotten by Americans, not unlike the massacre at Goliad, which has only recently received its due notice from historians. But thanks to the myth makers, the Alamo slaughter was transformed into something that it was not: a climactic, epic clash of arms. Perhaps no better example of the time-honored axiom that history was written by the winner can be found than in the Alamo's case.

In addition, if the primary triumvirate of Alamo heroes—the "holy trinity" of Crockett, Bowie, and Travis—had not died at the Alamo, the brief struggle at a remote frontier outpost would have been largely forgotten by history. But the death of these three Alamo leaders helped to elevate a massacre into an enduring, romantic legend.

Historians have failed to tell the Alamo's true story in regard to its most important aspect, the exodus, preferring a time-honored, socially-constructed, racially-inspired, and idiologically-based mythical narrative. More than any other aspect of Alamo historiography, the exodus from the Alamo challenges the most sacred of all traditional views: the heroic last stand. Soldiers in all wars, in all times, and of all nations have responded the same—flight rather than fight—under such disadvantageous circumstances—a natural response that is part of the human condition, and one that rose to the fore at the Alamo.

To think that Americans, especially those of the Alamo, were incapable of such an instinctive response to a no-win situation blinds us not only to the truth of the past, but also to present and future realities. What Americans must accept about the past is our nation's real history, and not a romantic mythology. In this way, we can better understand ourselves, other people, and our present and future military operations in a seemingly incomprehensible world that continues to become increasingly complex. Here, perhaps lies the Alamo's real, but forgotten, importance and meaning for today.

The real truth of what doomed the Alamo can in part be seen in the words of William Fairfax Gray. He complained how "the vile rabble here [the politicians at San Felipe de Austin] cannot be moved" to assist the men of the Alamo. After learning of the Alamo's fall, Gray prophesied about what would happen in the future, which would come true with the creation of the mythical Alamo: "Texas will take honor to herself for the defense of the Alamo and will call it a second Thermopylae, but it will be an everlasting monument of national disgrace."[87]

Perhaps this is yet another forgotten reason why the Alamo has been endlessly glorified and romanticized: to hide ugly truths. Almost as much as Santa Anna and the Mexican Army, it after all had been Texas and its people who had actually sealed the fate of the Alamo defenders, who had been betrayed and sacrificed in the end for no gain. No historical event in American history has been shrouded in more layers of myth, romance, emotion, and fantasy, while hiding the truth of racial, cultural, and political agendas, than the Alamo. In this way, a sad, tragic historical narrative of disaster was transformed into a heroic epic centered around the last stand myth.[88]

9

Flames Rising High

With the sulphurous smoke of battle yet hovering over the conquered Alamo on the early morning of March 6, and with the Mexican tricolor, planted by Lieutenant Torres, waving in triumph from its north wall, Sergeant Manuel Loranca of the Dolores Cavalry Regiment never forgot the scene of carnage. Loranca had seen the sheer brutality demonstrated "by the lance" when so effectively utilized by Tampico, Dolores, and Vera Cruz lancers on the unfortunate escapees. He described that last pitiful act on this tragic day: "There in front of the [fort, near the west end of the Alameda] were gathered the bodies of all those who died by the lance."[1]

Backing up his earlier promise that "he would burn the last one of them," Santa Anna ordered that all bodies of the Alamo defenders be burned. Perhaps this gesture was calculated to be a special insult to the memory of these mostly Protestant soldiers, because the act of cremation had been outlawed by the churches of Europe in centuries past. Cremation denied these citizen-soldiers from so far away the Christian burial enjoyed by generations of their ancestors on both sides of the Atlantic.

Since so many young men and boys had been killed outside of the Alamo, perhaps lying as far as several hundred yards away, two main funeral pyres were built by Santa Anna's soldados on either side of the leafless cottonwoods of the Alameda. A distinctive landmark on the open prairie, the Alameda had been named for the stately Mexico City boulevard so beloved by upper class Creoles.[2] Ironically, perhaps no place in all San Antonio was more picturesque than the tree-lined Alameda, which meant a shaded public thoroughfare in Spanish. A

330

Tejano of the town, Don Pablo, whose brother served in Santa Anna's ranks during the attack, described the Alameda as "a broad and spacious place used as a promenade and also as a highway of ingress to and egress from the city on the east side of the [San Antonio] river [and] On each side of the Alameda was a row of large cottonwood trees." These trees had been planted around 1804 by Spanish soldiers as part of a beautification effort.[3]

But marring the Alameda's beauty on March 6 was that its vicinity had been transformed into a place of slaughter. Because so many Alamo defenders had died near the thoroughfare, Santa Anna reasoned that it would be far easier for his men to drag the fewer number of dead from the Alamo to the Alameda. Here, around 5:00 p.m on March 6, as Pablo explained, the bodies of the Alamo men "were burned on two different pyres[.] These two separate pyres were located about 250 yards apart and one was on each side of the Alameda."[4] If this estimation of distance is correct, it would indicate that some escapees might have managed to reach a point beyond the south side of the Alameda. The funeral pyre south of the road was about ten feet wide and sixty feet in length. The other pyre was larger, at around ten feet wide and some eighty feet long.[5] A smaller third pyre was later created to burn more bodies as they were found.

In the late afternoon of March 6 the yellow flames, fueled by additional offerings of dry mesquite and cottonwood "from the neighboring forest"—interspersed with layers of defenders' bodies—leaped ever-higher into the late winter sky. Perhaps some abatis limbs from in front of the fort's palisade were used to fuel the flames. Here, the bodies of garrison members burned for some time. Santa Anna desired that no traces of his vanquished enemy should remain to be mourned. He hoped that this final act in the Alamo's drama would serve as an unforgettable lesson to the other revolutionaries—Texan, Tejano, or Mexican—who dared to oppose him and his Army of Operations.

As the sun lowered over San Antonio and temperatures grew colder during this relatively short day, red and yellow flames continued to leap higher, as the fire was fed by more fuel for an intense heat. Even the bones of the Alamo men were incinerated by Santa Anna to eliminate all traces of the defiant rebels who had dared to oppose him.

Eventually, the flames died away, like this horrific day for so many young men from the United States, Texas, Europe, and Mexico. Then, the soft, swirling palls of smoke ceased rising through the lonely, twin rows of stately cottonwood trees that made the Alameda such a picturesque setting even in late winter. Finally, the last bodily remains of the Alamo men were no more. They had been reduced to ashes and shattered fragments of charred bone. Strangely, these piles of ash remained in place in forgotten piles unburied by soldiers or civilians, Tejanos, Mexicans, or Anglo-Celts, for months to come.

Some family members learned of the sad fate of relatives at the Alamo not long after the slaughter. One wife especially shaken by the news was Elizabeth Crockett. She learned of both her husband's death and his enlistment in the Texas military at the same time, from a letter received two weeks after the Alamo's fall.[6]

In an emotional June 5, 1836 letter to her sister in Tennessee, a grief-stricken Frances "Menefee" Sutherland lamented the tragic fate of her son, William DePriest Sutherland, a seventeen-year-old medical student who had served with the garrison for less than two months. "I have lost my William. O, yes he is gone, my poor boy is gone, gone from me. The sixth day of March in the morning, he was slain in the Alamo in San Antonio. Then his poor body [was] committed to the flames."[7]

As in earlier failing to provide assistance during the siege, Texas and her people almost immediately forgot about those who were sacrificed at the Alamo, despite an emotional March 24, 1836 appeal from the concerned editors of *The Telegraph and Texas Register*: "Our dead were denied the right of Christian burial, being stripped and thrown into a pile and burned. Would that we could gather up their ashes and place in urns!"[8]

A final resting place on either side of the Alameda signified not only the physical deaths of Alamo garrison members, but also the deaths of their once-soaring personal dreams of Texas that had caused so many young men to cross the Sabine with such high hopes. After all, the Alamo defenders had gambled all and lost all in their bid to make their dreams come true. What they lost were thousands of acres of an earthly "paradise" second to none. One soldier who survived the Texas Revolution estimated that the lands that he gained for his military service equated to a monetary value of nearly $2,000—a fortune in that time.[9]

Meanwhile, in the days, weeks, and months ahead, the majority of the families of the Alamo men, especially those from the United States, either never learned or were informed belatedly of what happened to their fathers, sons, cousins, brothers, or uncles. For instance, Cornelia

Vancleve Barnes of New Haven, Connecticut, who feared the worst, wrote in an August 2, 1836 letter that was published in *The Telegraph and Texas Register* on August 2, 1836: "I had a brother by the name of Wm. D. LEWIS, who was in San Antonio on the 2d of last May, nearly a year ago, since which time I have not had a line or heard any thing from him. . . . Yesterday, we beheld the name of LEWIS among the murdered ones at San Antonio [and] My brother was [from] Philadelphia, but his father was from Wales."[10]

A distraught Cornelia was searching for news about Virginia-born Private William Irvine Lewis, age 29. The pampered son of a prominent physician in Philadelphia, he had been visiting a friend in North Carolina when he suddenly decided to head for Texas and what he thought would be an adventurous life in the distant southwest. William's grieving mother never recovered from her son's tragic loss at the Alamo. As late as October 1840, the poor woman even placed an appeal that was published in *The Telegraph and Texas Register* begging for a small memento of her long-lost son, who never returned home from his trip to North Carolina. Therefore, a "small monument carved from a stone from the Alamo ruins was sent to her."[11]

In the end, and like Mexican dead at both the Alamo and San Jacinto, the Alamo's forgotten victims were the hundreds of loved ones and family members these young men had left behind not only in Texas but all across the United States and Europe. In this sense, the Alamo's saddest legacy lived on for generations, including seemingly endless legal complications. An example was when a grieving Elizabeth Rowe petitioned "Probate Court of Gonzales Co. . . . for letters of adm. in 2 cases [regarding the estate] of her late former husband James GEORGE, who died at the Alamo, and also in [the] case of her bro[ther] William DEARDUFF, who also died in same battle."[12]

Private James George, age 34, was one of the ill-fated Gonzales Rangers reinforcements who had voluntarily ridden into the death-trap on March 1. He had married pretty Elizabeth Dearduff on February 29, 1821. George's team of oxen had transported the little "Come and Take It" cannon of Gonzales that had helped to spark a war when Neill fired the first shot of the Texas Revolution in early October 1835. George's brother-in-law was Tennessee-born William Dearduff, who had settled in the DeWitt Colony. Both men had served in the Gonzales Ranging Company before meeting their Maker at the Alamo.[13]

Even from faraway Germany came a property claim for a family member who had died at the Alamo. In December 1838, "John Jacob MATHERN of Frankfort, Germany, seeks succ[essor] of [the] est[ate] of Peter MATTERN, who was killed at the Alamo in March 1836."[14]

Meanwhile, in a strange, perplexing irony, the young men and boys who had been needlessly sacrificed at the Alamo continued to be forgotten by a victorious Texas for decades after San Jacinto. Life had seemingly moved on for everyone, as Texas and her people enjoyed a boom period of growth, development, and prosperity. Land speculation, unrestricted immigration from the United States, and securing the most fertile lands for development took precedence in Texas after San Jacinto. No one had much time to contemplate the Alamo's meaning or the lost defenders who had so easily slipped from memory. After all, this was now a time to look ahead, not backward. As appearing in the November 16, 1836 issue of *The Telegraph and Texas Register*, a special committee voted down a resolution for a $500 donation for the "relief for Mrs. Susannah DICKINSON and her child by late Lt. DICKINSON who fell at the Alamo."[15]

Even Travis' slave, Joe, who had survived the Alamo, became a hunted fugitive after he escaped from a new master in the less racially tolerant environment of post-San Jacinto Texas. As revealed in the May 26, 1837 issue of *The Telegraph and Texas Register:* a "$50 reward will be given for delivering to me on Bailey's Prairie, 7 miles from Columbia, a Negro man named JOE, belonging to . . . the late Wm. Barret TRAVIS, who ranaway [sic] and took with him a Mexican, two horses, saddles and Bridles. This Negro was in the Alamo with his master when it was taken, and was the only man from the colonies not put to death."[16] Only later, with the beginning of the rise of the mythical Alamo that captured the national imagination, would Susannah Dickinson and Joe become revered as Alamo survivors. But clearly such was not the case immediately after the Alamo's fall.

While Alamo garrison members would eventually be transformed into honored heroes, the average Mexican soldados who gave their lives for their republic on March 6, 1836 were largely forgotten by their own nation. In 1836, Lieutenant Colonel José Juan Sánchez-Navarro, an aspiring poet who served on General Cós' staff, proposed the erection of a stately monument to honor the Mexicans who gave their lives to reclaim part of the national homeland. He not only sketched the monument's design but also wrote, on March 6, a poem that contained inspiring words in a tribute to be chiseled in stone:

The bodies lying here were inspired
by souls, since ascended to heaven,
to savor the glory they'd gained by the
deeds they'd done on earth.

Their last human tribute they paid,
with no fear of death at the end,
for the patriots death, far from death,
is transition to far greater life."[17]

However, the proposed monument would never be erected in memory of the Mexican soldados who fought and died at the Alamo in order to preserve their country's integrity and to save the fragile Mexican union of states. Therefore, only the memory of what these young men of the Republic of Mexico had accomplished at the Alamo remained vivid in the minds of those who fought there. Ironically, like the defenders who they had so systematically slaughtered on March 6, the final resting place of Republic of Mexico soldados lies not in their native homeland to be honored but in obscurity in San Antonio.

Under the care of Father Refugio de la Garza, the Mexican dead were buried by Santa Anna's soldiers—and not by Tejanos of San Antonio as often assumed—in the Catholic burial ground known as Campo Santo, or the town cemetery on San Antonio's western edge. In addition, some fallen local Tejano soldiers from Santa Anna's permanent "battalion of the Alamo" were buried by wives and family members in this cemetery. For instance, the name of one deceased local Mexican soldier—Lieutenant José Maria Alcala—was faithfully recorded and documented by Father Garza of San Fernando Cathedral.[18]

But not all Mexican dead received a decent burial in the town's cemetery. According to Francisco Antonio Ruiz, whose father signed the Texas Declaration of Independence at Washington-on-the-Brazos on March 2, 1836: "The dead Mexicans of Santa Anna were taken to the graveyard but, not having sufficient room for them, I ordered some of them to be thrown in the river."[19] In corroboration, de la Pena recorded how only the "greater part of our dead were buried by their comrades" in the Catholic cemetery of San Antonio.[20]

For some time, few Texans looked to the Alameda site with any sense of reverence. John Sutherland described the irony of how "the bones of the Texians, as remained, lay for nearly a year upon the ground, while the ashes floated upon the breeze [because] There was no friend to collect or preserve" the remains. More than a year after the Alamo's fall, Colonel Juan Sequín, as reported in the *The Telegraph and Texas Register*, "paid final honors of war to the remains of the Alamo heroes; ashes were found in three separate places."[21]

Long before the fabrication of Alamo mythology to create an enduring romantic legend, Colonel Sequín reported that at "each of the three spots . . . ashes were found," including two located on either side of the Alameda to mark the places near where perhaps the majority of the Alamo garrison had died.[22] Unfortunately, today the exact locations of the funeral pyres and what little may remain of the Alamo defenders have been lost to historians, preservationists, and archeologists. The final resting place of these men are known only to God.[23]

After reaping an easy victory at relatively little cost, the slaughter of the Alamo garrison only fueled Santa Anna's confidence to new heights. Nothing else was left to do but mop-up resistance, if any remained, across Texas—or so it seemed to Santa Anna. Crushing revolution in Texas was going to be Zacatecas all over again. However, Santa Anna's overconfidence and disdain for the Anglo-Celtic fighting man, including the legendary rifleman, was destined to prove to be his undoing. Even before scoring one victory after another in Texas during this campaign, he had boasted to the French ambassador in Mexico City: "If the Americans do not behave themselves I will march across their country and plant the Mexican flag in Washington."[24]

Not only Santa Anna, but also the civil and military officials in Mexico City believed that the Texas campaign of 1836 had already been won with the Alamo's fall. From Mexico City and with the Alamo's capture in mind, Lucas Alaman penned with delight how: "Senor Santa Anna has so prevailed over the Anglo-American colonists who have rebelled in Texas that we may consider the matter over and done with."[25]

People across the Mexican republic basked in the belief that the conquest of all Texas was now inevitable. In a cathartic scene that symbolized the emotionalism surrounding the issue of Texas, Secretary of War Tornel and Mexican Congressional members symbolically stomped upon the trophy—the blue, silk flag of the New Orleans Greys that Santa Anna had sent back to Mexico City to demonstrate that the Texas insurrection was not only fueled primarily from the United States but also could be easily crushed by his Army of Operations.[26]

With the Alamo's fall and the Goliad disaster occurring hardly before the 1836 Texas campaign had begun, a wave of panic swept Texas, and shock waves reverberated throughout the United States. Written by a citizen of New Orleans, a letter published in the *Troy Daily Whig* from Texas predicted a grim future for Texas arms: "The garrisons of La Bahia, or Goliad, as well as that of San Antonio, have been cut off almost to a man. Houston, with a small force, much exaggerated I imagine, is falling back behind the Colorado [River]. My opinion is, they will be nearly exterminated! It has become a war of fanaticism."[27]

And the *National Intelligencer* lamented the fates of the remaining settlers in Texas: "It is a war of extermination. I am afraid, unless Uncle Sam gives them a helping hand, the Texians will be in a bad situation."[28] And with some understatement, the stunned editor of the *New Orleans True American* could only write: "We learn by [river boat] passengers . . . that the war in Texas has at length assumed a serious character. Many of those who left this city, determined to lay down their lives in the cause of Texas, have bravely yielded them up at Béxar. Three young men from our office, we learn, are among the slain; the names of Captain William Blazeby and Private Robert [B.] Moore [of Blazeby's infantry company] have been mentioned to us; that of the other we could not ascertain."[29]

The initial reports of the Alamo disaster and the ruthless character of the war were hardly exaggerations. In Santa Anna's own words, "In this war there are no prisoners." Santa Anna had embraced the concept of ethnic cleansing as the ultimate solution for the long-existing Texas problem. Therefore, he was determined to sweep away every Anglo-Celtic man, woman, and child, both squatters and those of the colonies, from Texas soil. Quite simply, Santa Anna, and the Mexican Republic, "wanted a brown Texas, not a white one."[30]

In early January 1836, a far-sighted Colonel Neill, who had wisely departed the Alamo before it was too late, had accurately predicted the harsh nature of this struggle for the heart and soul of Texas. He penned how Santa Anna and his invading army sought "to reduce the State [to what] it originally was in 1820," before Anglo-Celtic colonization in Texas.[31]

But the heady optimism that surged through Mexico City over a successful 1836 campaign to win back Texas was short-lived, ending even before the spring rains had ceased. After General Houston's impossible victory on the gulf coast plain at San Jacinto on April 21, 1836, and in regard to the citizens of Texas and the United States who now claimed Texas as their own, Colonel Pedro Delgado lamented Texas's loss with a cynical, but honest, final evaluation: "Now they could, without danger, squabble over the league of land, or for the ownership of the land of plenty."[32]

REQUIEM

After Santa Anna's vanguard force was crushed in a twenty-minute battle by Houston's ad hoc army of volunteers, hundreds of families across Mexico, from Vera Cruz on the Gulf of Mexico to Acapulco on the Pacific, mourned for the sons, brothers, fathers, and husbands, who had been slaughtered along the San Jacinto River and Buffalo Bayou. Mexican and Indian peasant families from the Yucatan Peninsula and northern and central Mexico mourned for more than 600 fallen common soldiers, just like the aristocratic families of Mexico City and other leading Mexican cities who lamented lost officers who never returned home. Victims of a massacre that dwarfed that of March 6, Mexican dead at San Jacinto were more than three times as numerous as the dead of the Alamo garrison.

Unlike the Alamo defenders who were cremated, the Mexican slain—all except the proud, chivalrous General Castrillon—were left unburied on San Jacinto's killing field, rotting where they had fallen and picked apart by wild hogs, dogs, and turkey vultures. But even ugly battlefield deaths were a more dignified fate than that which befell some survivors of the decisive battle. Some African infantrymen of Santa Anna's Army who survived the San Jacinto slaughter were sold into slavery by the victors.[33]

Meanwhile, despite never having been held accountable for the Alamo's abandonment because of his belated foot-dragging when he was commander-in-chief of the Texas Regular Army, the surprising victory at San Jacinto vaulted Houston to the presidency of the Republic of Texas. He became a hero across the United States, reaping laurels and fame, while the sacrificed martyrs of the Alamo were forgotten. What was conveniently overlooked by Americans—both then and today—was the fact that Houston had played a major role in the Alamo fiasco from beginning to end.[34]

For the young Republic of Mexico—even though she had yet to either fully realize or acknowledge the fact—Texas was lost forever and her national trauma would continue for generations in consequence. As if fearing as much, an angry Colonel Pedro Delgado, yet haunted by the San Jacinto slaughter, never forgot the sickening sight of the wild celebration among Texans on the first anniversary of the San Jacinto victory at Liberty, Texas, on April 21, 1837: "The ball was intended to commemorate the bloody 21st of April, 1836, on which day so many illustrious Mexicans were immolated."[35]

CONCLUSION

Like other nations around the world, many of America's most revered historical episodes are in fact little more than myths such as the Alamo last stand. Indeed, in this regard, the mythology of the Alamo last stand has been no aberration or exception to the rule. In his classic work, *Founding Myths: Stories that Hide Our Patriotic Past*, Ray Raphael ably demonstrated how much of what Americans cherish most about the American Revolution and their nation's founding are simply untrue. He emphasized how mythology rather than fact has dominated the historical memory of the American Revolution, thanks to a highly imaginative "invention of history" without the need for documentation or accuracy. Like the Alamo for the people of Texas, the young American nation had needed not only to invent itself but also to morally justify and explain its birth in violent revolution.

In much the same way, the romanticized story of the Alamo's last stand was created in a process of historical invention to produce a popular mythology. Consequently, instead of the true story of relatively weak resistance and flight among such a large percentage of the Alamo garrison, the epic last stand—with every man standing his ground to the bitter end—was created. According to the mythical Alamo, no defenders, save perhaps a craven individual or two, could have possibly attempted to escape, because it ran contrary to romantic notions of manhood, racial, and cultural superiority, and the alleged willing self-sacrifice of the garrison so that Texas would live.

Most significant, such an extensive whitewashing of the Alamo's darker side came almost immediately, regardless of the abundance of facts that indicated otherwise. When Santa Anna's first battle report, written at 8:00 a.m. on March 6, became known across the United States and to the American press, no part of it triggered greater disbelief and outrage than the information that a good many Alamo garrison members had attempted to flee the Alamo and were cut down by Mexican cavalry outside its walls. For instance, in the May 12, 1836 issue of the *Maryland Gazette*, the outraged editor wrote: "The *Gazette* of the 23d March contains the official report of Santa Anna of the capture of the Alamo [and] He reports that after storming the Alamo . . . General Sesma followed the fugitives, who attempted to escape, few if any of whom, remain to tell the tale of their disaster! Was there ever exhibited on the part of a commander of an army such wanton and disgraceful misrepresentation! It is a matter of history that the whole garrison of the Alamo . . . was inhumanly put to the sword within its walls, instead of flying and being pursued by Sesma."[36] Even at this time, barely two months after the Alamo's capture, the myth of the heroic last stand had already grown larger than the facts.

Clearly, in the same month that the Alamo fell a controversy had been born, though it has laid dormant for more than 170 years, while the less significant Crockett execution controversy has continued to dominate the attention of American historians, buffs, and scholars. But in truth no controversy should have existed at all in regard to the well-documented exodus from the Alamo, because more than half a dozen reliable and collaborating Mexican accounts of officers and enlisted men and others tell the truth of what really happened that morning.

The relatively light Mexican losses, the high level of fratricide, and the fact that the soldados so easily and quickly overwhelmed a fortified position manned by a large number of cannon all indicated that resistance was surprisingly weak. In addition, the short amount of time—from around 5:30 a.m. to about 5:50—that it took for Mexican troops to overrun the Alamo can best be explained by the flight of so many garrison members.

Therefore, the time-honored story of the last stand—the core of the mythical Alamo—has been the greatest of all Alamo legends, even as ample primary and secondary evidence have verified that it never happened as we have been led to believe. As embellished by generations of writers, journalists, painters, and historians, the traditional Alamo last stand was constructed for self-serving purposes beyond that of simply a good story—it was deliberately manufactured as a testament to an alleged Anglo-Celtic cultural and racial superiority, while obscuring the crucial roles played by slavery, land acquisition and speculation, and the fact that the conflict was only part of a much larger Mexican civil war. Indeed, the Alamo last stand was transformed into a historical "icon within an icon," which has become a "sacred national myth."[37]

Most contemporary newspapers across the United States actually got the story right in the beginning. What happened at the Alamo was nothing more than a "massacre" that not even remotely resembled the last stand of legend that has long dominated popular culture and the national consciousness. However, the creation myth of the Alamo last stand was necessary, stemming from the omnipresent process of transforming the American past into a saga of heroism, while absolving America of guilt from the ugliest legacies of Manifest Destiny, slavery, Indian removal, and massacres such as Horseshoe Bend and San Jacinto. And no part of America's story has been more romanticized than its expansion to the west. At the heart of this myth was that white Americans fought against inferior peoples of color, Indian, Mexican, and Mestizo, in the name of progress, civilization, and the highest Christian virtues. Almost seamlessly in yet another chapter of western expansion, the myth of the heroic Alamo last stand fulfilled these same vital cultural, historical, and racial requirements for both Texas and the American nation: in a willing self-sacrifice for a greater good, a band of heroic white men bravely stood up for righteousness and liberty against barbarous hordes from an alien and inferior culture.

Therefore, for the creation of the mythical Alamo and especially the heroic last stand, the most reliable Mexican accounts, despite their validity, accuracy and number, were either ignored or purged from the history in a thorough silencing of nonconforming views and facts that challenged the romantic legend. The collaborating truths of these multiple Mexican accounts became a victim of the mythology which proved far stronger than the facts. Because the Battle of the Alamo was such a largely self-induced fiasco, the creation of a heroic last stand resulting in at least a moral triumph was necessary to maintain a posture of cultural and racial superiority. Therefore, what was required for not only Texas but also the U.S. was the fabrication of an heroic fable of how a small band of defenders willingly sacrificed themselves while slaughtering hordes of attackers to achieve a great "moral and spiritual victory."

Perhaps an indicator of what was really most relevant for the contemporary U.S. public was expressed in an emotional letter to Mrs. David Crockett not long after the Alamo's fall. In his letter, Isaac N. Jones, who had met Crockett on the Tennessean's way to meet his cruel fate at the Alamo, paid a final tribute to the former Congressman, who hated slavery and how it had corrupted the American republic's most idealistic values: "His military career was short. But though I deeply lament his death, I cannot restrain my American smile at the recollection of the fact that he died as a United States soldier should die, covered with his slain enemy."[38]

Clearly, and like so many others, both then and today, Jones had allowed his imagination to take flight, because he believed that a popular personality of Crockett's stature should have easily killed a horde of allegedly inferior opponents. Indeed, in the analysis of historian Mark Derr, who explained in part how the last stand myth—by way of a national obsession with Crockett's demise—became so firmly entrenched in the national consciousness: "By the 1950s, American filmmakers and writers were fixated on the notion that Crockett had died while killing Mexicans, in no small measure because, fresh from the Second World War and the conflict in Korea, they were obsessed with the hero's death in battle. The growing myth of the Alamo demanded too that all the brave defenders died fighting."[39]

Ironically, the story of the Alamo last stand began to grow to mythological proportions only in the later years of the 19th century. Even a principal leader of the Texas Revolution, realistic-thinking Colonel Francis White Johnson, was bemused by the power of the growing myth: "The old popular tale of Texas that the Alamo was stormed by ten thousand men, of whom a thousand or more were killed, shows how rapidly legend may grow up even in their age."[40] And though without directly challenging the last stand mythology, respected historian David J. Weber concluded how: "A number of the cherished stories about the Alamo have no basis in historical fact, but have moved out of the earthly realm of reality into the stratosphere of myth."[41]

And in his recent book, *Sleuthing the Alamo*, James E. Crisp emphasized how in regard to the battle, "Myths offer the false comfort of simplicity, and this simplicity is accomplished by the selective silencing of the past."[42] This is precisely why the truth of the mass exodus of defenders from the Alamo has been silenced for so long: because it runs so directly contrary to the iconic and romantic version of events.

This work about what really happened at the Alamo was written in the hope of presenting a more honest and realistic version of the events of March 6, 1836 than has ever been presented before. Based upon fact rather than fiction, truth rather than mythology, and an unbiased, open-minded approach rather than embracing prejudicial stereotypes and an out-dated legend, this new perspective of the Alamo has also been presented in the hope of uniting many Americans who yet have radically opposing views of the Alamo's meaning today. Perhaps the old, time-honored perceptions of the mythical Alamo, rooted in the complex dynamics of politics, economics, and race, should be erased from the national memory, especially given the new realities of American society and culture. Hopefully, a new and more honest understanding of what really happened at the Alamo will make it a story—of heroics on both sides—not from the biased perspective of a single group but of lasting importance for all Americans today. Horace Greeley's famous words, "When the legend is better than the fact, print the legend," should no longer apply to the Alamo.

In this sense, therefore, the Alamo should be a monument not to a mythical last stand, but as an enduring monument to folly and the inevitable high price paid by common soldiers for leadership mistakes. Ironically, the area around the Alamo church and in the compound itself very likely saw less fighting and killing than outside the fort's walls, because of mass exodus from the Alamo. Today, now covered by parking lots, office buildings, and traffic moving along the busy, downtown streets of San Antonio, the area where most Alamo garrison members were killed has no marker or monument to memorialize the forgotten fights and last stands in and around a long-forgotten irrigation ditch outside the walls.[43]

Instead of the mythical "line in the sand" story in which every defender crossed Travis' line, in reality the majority of Alamo garrison members unhesitatingly chose life when they attempted to save themselves by escaping a certain deathtrap in the cold, late winter darkness. It had been a bloody early Sunday morning that would live on as both history and legend. Even though most garrison members died outside the Alamo's walls, romantic myth not only had these young men and boys of the Alamo garrison dying in the wrong location, but also under the wrong circumstances: the mythical last stand.

Notes

Chapter I: THE GREAT PRIZES: LAND AND SLAVES
1. Randolph B. Campbell, *An Empire for Slavery: The Peculiar Institution in Texas* (Baton Rouge: Louisiana State University Press, 1989), pp. 1–3.
2. Campbell, *An Empire for Slavery*, p. 3; *Connecticut Herald*, New Haven, Connecticut, September 22, 1829.
3. Paul Horgan, *Great River: The Rio Grande in North American History* (Hanover: Wesleyan University Press, 1984), p. 485; Patrick J. Carroll, *Blacks in Colonial Veracruz: Race Ethnicity, and Regional Development* (Austin, Texas: University of Texas Press, 2001), pp. 130–131.
4. Horgan, *Great River*, p. 485.
5. Horgan, *Great River*, p. 486.
6. Campbell, *An Empire for Slavery*, p. 25; Editors of Time-Life Books, *The Texans* (Alexandria, Texas: Time-Life Books, 1975), p. 225.
7. Robert H. Thonhoff, *The Texas Connection with the American Revolution* (Austin, Texas: Eakin Press, 1981), p. 7; Jack Jackson, *Imaginary Kingdom: Texas as Seen by the Rivera and Rubi Military Expeditions, 1727 and 1767* (Austin, Texas: Texas State Historical Association, 1995), pp. 20–22, 25; *Connecticut Herald*, September 22, 1829.
8. Donald E. Chipman, *Spanish Texas, 1519–1821* (Austin, Texas: University of Texas Press, 1992), pp. 200, 206–207, 250.
9. Cecil Robinson, editor and translator, *The View from Chapultepec, Mexican Writers on the Mexican-American War* (Tucson: University of Arizona Press, 1989), pp. 36–37, 44.
10. Campbell, *An Empire for Slavery*, pp. 2–4, 48.
11. Campbell, *An Empire for Slavery*; John Frances Bannon, *The Spanish Borderlands Frontier, 1513–1821* (New York: Holt, Rhinehart and Winston, 1970), pp. 206–231.
12. Campbell, *An Empire for Slavery*, p. 18; Time-Life Editors, *The Texans*, p. 16.
13. Eugene Barker and Amelia W. Williams, editors, *The Writings of Sam Houston, 1813–1863* (8 vols., Austin: University of Texas Press, 1938), vol. 1, p. 304; James Webb, *Born Fighting, How the Scots-Irish Shaped America* (New York: Broadway Books, 2004), pp. 9–184; Jeff Long, *Duel of Eagles: The Mexican and U.S. Fight for the Alamo* (New York: William Morrow, 1990). p. 12.
14. Susanne Starling, *Land, Is the Cry!* (Austin, Texas: Texas State Historical Association, 1998), pp. 42–44, 52.
15. Stephen B. Oates, ed., *Rip Ford's Texas* (Austin, Texas: University of Texas Press, 1998), p. 9.
16. John A. Garraty, *The American Nation: A History of the United States to 1877* (New York: Harper Collins, 1971), pp. 327–329; Fayette Copeland, *Kendall of the Picayune* (Norman: University of Oklahoma Press, 1997), p. 17; Long, *Duel of Eagles*, pp. 12–84.
17. Copeland, *Kendall of the Picayune*, pp. 17, 29, 31, 36–37.
18. Barker and Williams, eds., *The Writings of Sam Houston*, vol. 1, pp. 302, 304.
19. *New York Herald*, New York, June 18, 1836.
20. *New York Herald*, New York, March 21, 1836.
21. Glenn Tucker, *Poltroons and Patriots: A Popular Account of the War of 1812* (New York: Bobbs-Merrill Company, Inc., 1954), p. 68; Walter Lord, *A Time to Stand: A Chronicle of the Valiant Battle at the Alamo* (New York: Bonanza Books, 1987), p. 86.
22. *New York Herald*, March 21, 1836; September 10, 1836.

23. Phillip Thomas Tucker, "Motivations of United States Volunteers During the Texas Revolution," *East Texas Historical Journal*, vol. 29, no. 1 (1991), p. 29.

24. *New York Herald*, June 20, 1836.

25. Todd Hansen, ed., *The Alamo Reader: A Study in History* (Mechanicsburg, Pennsylvania: Stackpole Books, 2003), p. 113.

26. *New York Times*, New York, December 15, 1907; Richard Boyd Hauck, *Davy Crockett: A Handbook* (Lincoln: University of Nebraska Press, 1982), pp. 28–29, 36–48; Buddy Levy, *American Legend: The Real-Life Adventures of David Crockett* (New York: Berkley Books, 2005), pp. 56, 235; Kim Robertson, *Buffalo Bill's Bridge*, "Woman born in Arnold captured Cody's heart," *Arnold-Imperial Leader*, Arnold, Missouri, August 17, 2006.

27. *New York Times*, December 15, 1907; Levy, *American Legend*, p. 241.

28. *New York Times*, December 15, 1907; Hauck, *David Crockett*, p. 39; Levy, *American Legend*, pp. 233–235, 141; James Atkins Shackford: *David Crockett, The Man and the Legend*, (Lincoln: University of Nebraska Press, 1986), p. 211.

29. Levy, *American Legend*, p. 244.

30. John H. Jenkins, ed., *Papers of the Texas Revolution* (10 vols., Austin: Presidial Press, 1973), vol. 3, p. 453; Levy, *American Legend*, p. 247.

31. Jenkins, ed., *Papers of the Texas Revolution*, vol. 3, p. 453; Hauck, *Davy Crockett*, p. 50.

32. Ron Jackson, *Alamo Legacy: Alamo Descendants Remember the Alamo* (Austin: Eakin Press, 1997), pp. 34–35; Lord, *A Time to Stand*, p. 46; Bill Groneman, *Alamo Defenders, A Genealogy: The People and Their Words* (Austin: Eakin Press, 1990), p. 30.

33. Oates, ed., *Rip Ford's Texas*, p. 16.

34. Jackson, *Alamo Legacy*, p. 36.

35. Jackson, *Alamo Legacy*, p. 80; Marshall De Bruhl, *A Life of Sam Houston* (New York: Random House, 1993), p. 173.

36. Copeland, *Kendall of the Picayune*, p. 55.

37. *Connecticut Herald*, September 22, 1829.

38. Ibid., pp. 17–21; Bob Priddy, *Across Our Wide Missouri*, (3 vols., Jefferson City: Bob Priddy, 1984), vol. 1, p. 143; Lord, *A Time to Stand*, p. 24; Groneman, *Alamo Defenders*, pp. 7–8.

39. William C. Binkley, *The Texas Revolution* (Austin, Texas: The Texas State Historical Association, 1979), p. 21.

40. Jackson, *Alamo Legacy*, pp. 21–25; Groneman, *Alamo Defenders*, p. 24.

41. James E. Winston, "Kentucky and the Texas Revolution," *Southwestern Historical Quarterly*, vol. 16 (1912), p. 53.

42. Tucker, "Motivations," pp. 25–33.

43. H. W. Brands, *Andrew Jackson* (New York: Anchor Books, 2006), pp. 342–343.

44. James Alexander Gardner, *Lead King: Moses Austin* (St. Louis: Sunrise Publishing Company, 1980), pp. 156–158, 160, 167; Horgan, *Great River*, pp. 485–486.

45. Horgan, *Great River*, pp. vii–440; Chipman, *Spanish Texas*, 1519–1821, pp. 3–4; H. W. Brands, *Lone Star Nation: How a Ragged Army of Volunteers Won the Battle for Texas Independence—And Changed America* (New York: Doubleday, 2004), pp. 3–4; William C. Davis, *Lone Star Rising: The Revolutionary Birth of the Texas Republic* (New York: The Free Press, 2004), p. 2.

46. Binkley, *The Texas Revolution*, p. 20.

47. Davis, *Lone Star Rising*, p. 59.

48. *Connecticut Herald*, September 22, 1829.

49. William Trout Chambers and Lorrin Kennamer, Jr., *Texans and Their Land* (Austin: Steck-Vaughn Company, 1963), pp. 1–23, 33, 35, 39, 103–104; Chipman, *Spanish Texas*, p. 4; Davis, *Lone Star Rising*, p. 2.

50. Stephen L. Moore, *Eighteen Minutes: The Battle of San Jacinto and the Texas Independence Campaign* (Lanham: Republic of Texas Press, 2002), p. 56.

51. Horgan, *Great River*, p. 456; Jackson, *Alamo Legacy*, p. 156.

52. Lozano, *Viva Teja, The Story of the Tejanos, The Mexican-born Patriots of the Texas Revolution* (San Antonio, Texas: The Alamo Press, 1985), pp. 13–14.

53. Ruben Rendon Lozano, *Viva Tejas*, pp. 13–14; Donald R. Hickey, *Don't Give Up the Ship: Myths of the War of 1812* (Chicago: University of Illinois Press, 2006), p. 191.

54. Fehrenbach, *Fire & Blood*, pp. 377–378; Webb, *Born Fighting*, pp. 135–139; Long, *Duel of Eagles*, p. 50; Billy Kennedy, *The Scots-Irish in the Hills of Tennessee* (Londonderry, Ireland: Causeway Press, 1995), pp. 19–25.
55. Lozano, *Vivia Tejas*, p. ii–iii.
56. Horgan, *Great River*, pp. 459, 485–486; Don M. Coerver and Linda B. Hall, *Tangled Destinies: Latin America and the United States* (Albuquerque: University of New Mexico Press, 1999), p. 16.
57. Fehrenbach, *Lone Star*, p. 100.
58. Fehrenbach, *Fire & Blood*, p. 378.
59. Hugh G. J. Aitken, *Did Slavery Pay?* (Boston: Houghton Mifflin Company, 1971), p. 212; Hardin, *Texas Iliad* (Austin: University of Texas Press, 1994), p. 6.
60. Fehrenbach, *Fire & Blood*, p. 378.
61. *New York Times*, December 15, 1907; Brands, *Lone Star Nation*, pp. 164–167; Archie P. McDonald, *William Barret Travis* (Austin, Texas: Eakin Press, 1976), pp. 22–62, 69–70, 75–83, 92; William C. Davis, *Three Roads to the Alamo: The Lives and Fortunes of David Crocket, James Bowie, and William Barret Travis* (New York: Harper Collins Publishers, 1998), pp. 202, 282–283, 262–266; Trevor Burnard, *Mastery, Tyranny, and Desire: Thomas Thistlewood and his Slaves in the Anglo-Jamaican World* (Chapel Hill, North Carolina: University of North Carolina Press, 2004), pp. 39, 90–92; C. Richard King, *James Clinton Neill: The Shadow Commander of the Alamo* (Austin, Texas: Eakin Press 2002), pp. 7–8, 29, 37; Richard Penn Smith, *On to the Alamo: Colonel Crockett's Exploits and Adventures in Texas* (New York: Penguin Group, 2003), p. xxxix; Randy Roberts and James S. Olson, *A Line in the Sand, The Alamo in Blood and Memory* (New York: The Free Press, 2001), p. 35; Ray Raphael, *Founding Myths: Stories that Hide Our Patriots* (New York: MJF Books, 2004), pp. 185–191.
62. Davis, *Three Roads to the Alamo*, pp. 379, 384, 447.
63. Brands, *Lone Star Nation*, pp174–175; Hopewell, *James Bowie*, pp. 3–5, 11, 18–21, 23–24, 61, 63–67; Long, *Duel of Eagles*, pp. 29–30.
64. James A. Michener, *The Eagle and the Raven* (Austin, Texas: State House Press, 1990), pp. 36–37.
65. Alwyn Barr, *Black Texans: A History of African Americans in Texas, 1528–1995* (Norman: University of Oklahoma Press, 1996), p. 16; William O. Chariton, *Exploring the Alamo Legends* (Plano: Wordware Publishing, Inc., 1990), p. 136; Michener, *The Eagle and the Raven*, p. 134; Roberts and Olson, *A Line in the Sand*, pp. 132–133; Long, *Duel of Eagles*, pp. 29–30.
66. Jackson, *Alamo Legacy*, pp. 155–158; Steven M. Wise, *Though the Heavens May Fall: The Landmark Trial That Led to the End of Human Slavery* (New York: Da Capo Press, 2005), p. 13; John Hope Franklin, *From Slavery to Freedom: A History of Negro Americans* (New York: Alfred A. Knopf, 1974), pp. 138–163; Raphael, *Founding Myths*, 189–191.
67. Long, *Duel of Eagles*, pp. 225–226, 252; Jackson, *Alamo Legacy*, pp. 52–53.
68. William C. Binkley, editor, *Official Correspondence of the Texas Revolution, 1835–1836* (New York: D. Appleton-Century Company, 1936), pp. 60–61, note 1.
69. Bob Boyd, *The Texas Revolution, A Day-by-Day Account* (San Angelo: Standard Times, 1986), pp. 27–28.
70. *New York Herald*, May 8 and May 19, 1836; Paul D. Lack, *The Texas Revolutionary Experience: A Political and Social History 1835–1836* (College Station, Texas: Texas A & M University Press, 1992), p. 239.
71. Campbell, *An Empire for Slavery*, pp. 1–4, 18, 48; Roberts and Olson, *A Line in the Sand*, p. 35.
72. Campbell, *An Empire for Slavery*, pp. 13–14, 19, 26; Davis, *Lone Star Rising*, p. 60.
73. Davis, *Lone Star Rising*, pp. 66–67; Roberts and Olson, *A Line in the Sand*, p. 35.
74. Davis, *Lone Star Rising*, pp. 20–21; Roberts and Olson, *A Line in the Sand*, p. 35.
75. *The Telegraph and Texas Register*, Columbia, Texas, December 13, 1836; Editors of Time-Life Books, *The Texans*, pp. 28–29, 34, 36; Brands, *Lone Star Nation*, p. 149; Editors of Time-Life, *The Texans*, p. 28.
76. *The Telegraph and Texas Register*, August 23 and December 13, 1836; Nevin, *The Texans*, pp. 28–29, 36; Brands, *Lone Star Nation*, p. 149; Davis, *Lone Star Rising*, p. 138; Lack, *The Texas Revolutionary Experience*, p. 218; Editors of Time-Life, *The Texans*, pp. 32, 225; *Connecticut*

Herald, September 22, 1829; Stephen L. Hardin, *Texian Iliad*, pp. 11–12; *New York Times*, August 18, 1869.

77. Franklin, *The Militant South*, p. 102; Davis, *Lone Star Rising*, pp. 74–77; Editors of Time-Life, *The Texans*, p. 34.

78. Alfred N. Hunt, *Haiti's Influence on Antebellum America: Slumbering Volcano in the Caribbean* (Baton Rouge, La: Louisiana State University Press, 1988), p. 127.

79. Richard Bruce Winders, *Sacrificed at the Alamo: Tragedy and Triumph in the Texas Revolution* (Abilene: State House Press, 2004), pp. 18–19.

80. Horgan, *Great River*, p. 486; Roberts and Olson, *A Line in the Sand*, p. 35.

81. Horgan, *Great River*, p. 486; Hardin, Texas Iliad, p. 6.

82. Horgan, *Great River*, pp. 486–487.

83. Campbell, *An Empire for Slavery*, pp. 22–24; Horgan, *Great River*, pp. 487–488.

84. Nathaniel W. Stephenson, *Texas and the Mexican War* (New York: United States Publishers Association, Inc., 1978), pp. 24–25, 30.

85. William H. Goetzmann, *When the Eagle Screamed: The Romantic Horizon in American Diplomacy, 1800–1860* (New York: John Wiley & Sons, Inc., 1966), p. 27; Horgan, *Great River*, pp. 488–489; William Chemerka, *Alamo Anthology* (Austin, Texas: Eakin Press, 2005), p. 3.

86. Campbell, *An Empire for Slavery*, pp. 29, 33–34; Will Fowler, *Santa Anna of Mexico* (Lincoln, Nebraska: University of Nebraska Press, 2007), p. 163.

87. Campbell, *An Empire for Slavery*, p. 34; Hardin, *Texas Iliad*, p. 6; Connecticut Herald, September 22, 1829.

88. Campbell, *An Empire for Slavery*, pp. 29–31; Horgan, *Great River*, p. 472.

89. Campbell, *An Empire for Slavery*, p. 35.

90. Campbell, *An Empire for Slavery*, p. 35.

91. Campbell, *An Empire for Slavery*, pp. 36–39, 48; Frank W. Johnson to W. A. McArdle, November 27, 1837, *The McArdle Notebooks* (Archives and Information Services Division, Texas State Library and Archives Commission, Austin, Texas); Fowler, *Santa Anna of Mexico*, p. 163.

92. Johnson to McArdle, November 27, 1837, TSL and AC.

93. Campbell, *An Empire for Slavery*, p. 18; Robinson, trans. and ed., *The View from Chapultepec*, p. 37; Fowler, *Santa Anna of Mexico*, p. 163.

94. Fowler, *Santa Anna of Mexico*, p. 163.

95. Fowler, *Santa Anna of Mexico*, p. 163; Lack, *The Texas Revolutionary Experience*, pp. 4, 13, 20–23, 36–37.

96. Lack, *The Texas Revolutionary Experience*, p. 241.

97. Lack, *The Texas Revolutionary Experience*, p. 241.

98. Roberts and Olson, *A Line in the Sand*, p. 43.

99. Lack, *The Texas Revolutionary Experience*, pp. 239–244.

100. Hunt, *Haiti's Influence on Antebellum America*, pp. 1–192.

101. Hunt, *Haiti's Influence on Antebellum America*, pp. 1–192; Campbell, *An Empire for Slavery*, p. 28; William C. Davis, *The Pirates Laffite: The Treacherous World of the Corsairs of the Gulf* (New York: Harcourt, Inc., 2005), pp. 72–74; Laurent Dubois, *Avengers of the New World: The Story of the Haitian Revolution*, (Cambridge, Mass: Harvard University Press, 2004), pp. 3–305.

102. Horgan, *Great River*, pp. 490–491.

103. Horgan, *Great River*, p. 490.

104. Franklin, *The Militant South*, p. 76.

105. Hunt, *Haiti's Influence on Antebellum America*, p. 100.

106. Gardner, *Lead King*, pp. 160, 167.

107. *The Telegraph and Texas Register*, August 5, and September 16, 1837 and April 18, 1838; *Enquirer*, August 30, 1831; Hunt, *Haiti's Influence on Antebellum America*, pp. 1–100; John B. Duff and Peter M. Mitchell, eds., *The Nat Turner Rebellion: The Historical Event and the Modern Controversy* (New York: Harper & Row Publishers, Inc., 1971), pp. 92–112.

108. Franklin, *The Militant South*, pp. 80–81, 96–97.

109. Franklin, *The Militant South*, pp. 96–97, 101–104; Hunt, *Haiti's Influence on Antebellum America*, pp. 1–36, 107–146; Lack, *The Texas Revolutionary Experience*, pp. 239–244.

110. Lack, *The Texas Revolutionary Experience*, pp. 239–240.

111. Lack, *The Texas Revolutionary Experience*, pp. 239–244.

112. Barr, *Black Texans*, p. 32; Brands, *Lone Star Nation*, p. 255

113. Campbell, *An Empire for Slavery*, p. 40; Carlos E. Castaneda, *The Mexican Side of the Texan Revolution* (Dallas: P. L. Turner Company, 1928), p. 330; Lord, *A Time to Stand*, p. 86.

114. Campbell, *An Empire for Slavery*, p. 42; Herbert G. Uecker, *The Archaeology of the Alamo* (Bulverde: Monte Comal Publications, 2001), pp. 29, 84; Jeff Milan to H. A. McArdle, January 2, 1901, *The McArdle Notebooks*.

115. *Maryland Gazette*, Annapolis, Maryland, February 2, 1837; John Mahon, *History of the Second Seminole War* (Gainesville: University of Florida Press, 1967), pp. 87–327; George Buker, "Introduction," *Notices of East Florida* (Gainesville, Florida: University of Florida Press, 1973), pp. 41, 44–45, 48, 84–85; Frank Laumer, *Massacre!* (Gainesville, Florida: University of Florida Press, 1968), pp. 1–165.

116. Castaneda, *The Mexican Side of the Texan Revolution*, p. 383.

117. Castaneda, *The Mexican Side of the Texan Revolution*, p. 383; Bisson, *Nat Turner*, pp. 41–97.

118. Campbell, *An Empire for Slavery*, p. 41.

119. *New York Herald*, April 28, 1836.

120. Lack, *The Texas Revolutionary Experience*, p. 242.

121. Campbell, *An Empire for Slavery*, p. 42.

122. Gustave de Beaumont, *Ireland* (Cambridge, Massachusetts: The Belknap Press of Harvard University Press, 2006), pp. vi–xii; Fowler, *Santa Anna of Mexico*, pp. 174–175.

123. *New York Herald*, April 23, 1836.

124. *New York Herald*, April 30, 1836; *The Telegraph and Texas Register*, November 21, 1835.

125. Jerry J. Gaddy, *Texas in Revolt: Contemporary Newspaper Accounts of the Texas Revolution* (Fort Collins: The Old Army Press, 1973), p. 15.

126. Gaddy, *Texas in Revolt*, p. 15.

127. Joel W. Martin, *Sacred Revolt: The Muskogees' Struggle For a New World* (Boston: Beacon Press, 1991), pp. ix–167; Alexander Walker, *The Life of Andrew Jackson* (Philadelphia, Pa: G. G. Evans Publisher, 1860), p. lxxiii.

128. *The Telegraph and Texas Register*, November 14, 1835; Stephen L. Moore, *Savage Frontier: Rangers, Riflemen, and Indian Wars in Texas, Volume I, 1835–1837,* (Plano, Texas: Republic of Texas Press, 2002), pp. vii, 14, 29–30.

129. *The Telegraph and Texas Register*, June 2, 1838; *Maryland Gazette*, February 2, 1837; Groneman, *Alamo Defenders*, p. 82; Lord, *A Time to Stand*, pp. 46, 48.

130. Campbell, *An Empire for Slavery*, p. 48–49.

131. Alwyn Barr, Texans in Revolt, The Battle for San Antonio, 1835, (Austin: University of Texas Press, 1990), pp. 13–14, 56; Samuel Carter, III, *Blaze of Glory, The Fight for New Orleans, 1814–1815* (New York: MacMillan London Ltd., 1971), pp. 69–86, 349–263, 320; Christopher Leslie Brown and Philip D. Morgan, *Arming Slaves: From Classical Times to the Modern Age* (New Haven: Yale University Press, 2006), pp. 4, 6–9, 120–179, 209–270.

132. George Nelson, *The Alamo: An Illustrated History* (Uvalde, Texas: Aldine Books, 1998), p. 32; Carter III, *Blaze of Glory*, 1814–1815, pp. 69–86, 249–263.

133. Jackson, *Alamo Legacy*, pp. 148–149; Herman L. Bennett, *Africans in Colonial Mexico: Absolutism, Christianity, and Afro-Creole Consciousness, 1570–1640 (Blacks in the Diaspora)* (Bloomington, Indiana: Indiana University Press, 2003), pp. 1–125; Fehrenbach, *Lone Star*, p. 65; Long, *Duel of Eagles*, pp. 16, 18–19.

134. Winders, *Sacrificed at the Alamo*, pp. 21–22; Chipman, *Spanish Texas*, pp. 188–189; Hansen, ed., *The Alamo Reader*, pp. 112–113.

135. Starling, *Land Is the Cry!*, p. 71; Chipman, *Spanish Texas*, p. 250.

136. Lack, *The Texas Revolutionary Experience*, p. 14.

137. Winders, *Sacrificed at the Alamo*, pp. 18–19.

138. Bennett, *Africans in Colonial Mexico*, pp. 1–125.

139. Chipman, *Spanish Texas*, p. 212.

140. Ivan Van Sertima, *Golden Age of the Moor* (London: Transaction Publishers, 2004), pp. 1–2, 7, 161–162.

141. Alwyn, *Black Texans*, pp. 5–6.

142. Alwyn, *Black Texans*, p. 15; Fowler, *Santa Anna of Mexico*, p. 163.

143. Reginald Horsman, *Race and Manifest Destiny: The Origins of American Racial Anglo-Saxonism* (Cambridge: Harvard University Press, 1981), pp. 213–215.

144. Vincent, *The Legacy of Vincente Guerrero*, pp. 1–338; Carmen Perry, ed. and trans., *With Santa Anna in Texas: A Personal Narrative of the Revolution by Jose Enrique de la Pena*, (College Station: Texas A & M Press, 1975), pp. 24, 32.

145. Tucker, *Poltroons and Patriots*, p. 59.

146. Jackson, *Alamo Legacy*, pp. 155–158.

147. Davis, *Three Roads to the Alamo*, p. 584; Hardin, *Texas Iliad*, p. 6.

148. Shackford, *David Crockett*, pp. 238–239.

149. Davis, *Lone Star Rising*, pp. 207–208.

150. Lack, *The Texas Revolutionary Experience*, p. 154.

151. Lack, *The Texas Revolutionary Experience*, pp. 211–221.

152. Gaddy, *Texas in Revolt*, pp. 20–21; Fowler, *Santa Anna of Mexico*, pp. 162, 174.

153. Fowler, *Santa Anna of Mexico*, p. 174.

154. Brands, *Andrew Jackson*, pp. 343–345; Brands, *Lone Star Nation*, p. 63.

155. Hardin, *Texas Iliad*, p. 6.

156. Pedro Sanchez, March 4, 1836 letter, Box 2Q174, vol. 334 (Center of American History, University of Texas, Austin, Texas).

157. King, *James Clinton Neill*, pp. vii, 78, 85–86, 89.

158. Fehrenbach, *Lone Star*, pp. 81–109; Kennedy, *The Scots-Irish in the Hills of Tennessee*, pp. 19–41, 99–100; Max Dixon, *The Wataugans, First "free and independent community on the continent"* (Johnson City, Tennessee: Overmountain Press, 1976), pp. 4–37, 73–75.

159. Graham Davis, *Land! Irish Pioneers in Mexican and Revolutionary Texas* (College Station: Texas A & M Press, 2002), pp. 9, 11, 39–153, Chipman, *Spanish Texas*, pp. 182, 184–187, 190.

160. Davis, *Land!*, pp. 9–10, 147–148; Moore, Eighteen Minutes, p. 53.

161. Moore, *Eighteen Minutes*, pp. 15, 49.

162. Mary Ann Noonan Guerra, *Heroes of the Alamo and Goliad: Revolutionaries on the Road to San Jacinto and Texan Independence* (San Antonio: The Alamo Press, 1987), pp. 5, 24–25; David T. Gleeson, *The Irish in the South, 1815–1877* (Chapel Hill: University of North Carolina Press, 2001), pp. 31–32; Gary Brown, *The New Orleans Greys: Volunteers in the Texas Revolution* (Plano: Republic of Texas Press, 1999), pp. 302–306, 308; *St. Louis Republican*, St. Louis, Missouri, April 28, 1836; *The Telegraph and Texas Register*, March 24, 1836; Groneman, *Alamo Defenders*, pp. 21, 34, 42, 47–48, 58, 63, 77–78, 113–114, 117–118; Lord, *A Time to Stand*, pp. 47–48.

163. Groneman, *Alamo Defenders*, pp. 47–48.

164. Groneman, *Alamo Defenders*, pp. 88–89.

165. King, *James Clinton Neill*, pp. 1, 3–4.

166. Guerra, *Heroes of the Alamo*, n.p.

167. Gleeson, *The Irish in the South*, pp. 31–32; Editors of American Heritage, *Andrew Jackson, Soldier and Statesman* (New York: Harper and Row, 1963), pp. 11–14.

168. Gleeson, *The Irish in the South*, p. 32; Craig H. Roell, *Remember Goliad!*, (Austin: Texas State Historical Association, 1994), pp. 24–27, 31.

169. Gleeson, *The Irish in the South, 1815–1877*, pp. 26–28; 31–32.

170. Brown, *The New Orleans Greys*, pp. 18, 37, 299, 302–304, 306, 308.

171. Mary Frances Cusack, *An Illustrated History of Ireland, from AD 400 to 1800* (London: Bracken Books, 1995), pp. 257–634.

172. Roberts and Olson, *A Line in the Sand*, p. 56.

173. Jackson, *Alamo Legacy*, pp. 47–51.

174. *New York Times*, January 27, 1895.

175. *St. Louis Republican*, April 28, 1836; Brown, *The New Orleans Greys*, pp. 36–37, 81; King, *James Clinton Neill*, pp. 79–80; Nelson, *The Alamo*, p. 111; Hansen, ed., *The Alamo Reader*, pp. 712–713; Winders, *Sacrificed at the Alamo*, pp. 89–95.

Chapter 2: NAPOLEONIC INFLUENCES

1. Fowler, *Santa Anna of Mexico*, pp. ix–xi, xviii–xix; Scheina, *Santa Anna*, p. vii.

2. Robinson, ed. and trans., *The View From Chapultepec*, p. xv; Fowler, *Santa Anna of Mexico*, pp. ix, xviii–xix, xxiii.

3. *New York Herald*, June 10, 1836; Adam Zamoyski, *Moscow 1812: Napoleon's Fatal March*, (New York: Harper Collins Publishers, 2004), pp. 294–295; Richard K. Riehn, *1812: Napoleon's Russian Campaign*, (New York: John Wiley and Sons, 1991), pp. 265–407; Roberts and Olson, *A Line in the Sand*, p. 10; Fowler, Santa Anna of Mexico, ix, xviii–xix, xxiii, 170, 179.

4. Robert L. Scheina, *Latin America's Wars: The Age of the Caudillo, 1791–1899*, (Washington, D.C.: Brassey's, Inc., 2003), p. 157; Roberts and Olson, *A Line in the Sand*, pp. 6, 9; Fowler, *Santa Anna of Mexico*, p. 163.

5. Fowler, *Santa Anna of Mexico*, pp. xi, xxi, xxii, 6–7, 12–13, 15; Edwin Williamson, *The Penguin History of Latin America*, (New York: Penguin Books, 1992), pp. 258–261; John Charles Chasteen, *Born in Blood and Fire: A Concise History of Latin America*, (New York: W.W. Norton and Company, 2001), pp. 126–127, 152–153; Scheina, *Santa Anna*, pp. 4–5; Brands, *Lone Star Nation*, pp. 41–42; Roger Borroel, editor and translator, *Field Reports of the Mexican Army During the Texan War of 1836*, (East Chicago: "La Villita Publications," 2001), vol. iii, p. 51.

6. Weems and Weems, *Dream of Empire*, p. 8; Perry, ed. and trans., *With Santa Anna in Texas*, p. 60.

7. *The Portable Gibbon: The Decline and Fall of the Roman Empire*, (New York: The Viking Press, 1952), pp. 515–630.

8. Winders, *Sacrificed at the Alamo*, pp. 15–19; Perry, ed. and trans., *With Santa Anna in Texas*, pp. 60; Groneman, *Alamo Defenders*, p. 81.

9. De Brahl, *Sword of San Jacinto*, p. 206; Hardin, *Texian Iliad*, pp. 209–210.

10. De Brahl, *Sword of San Jacinto*, pp. 199–213; James W. Pohl, *The Battle of San Jacinto*, (Austin: Texas State Historical Association, 1989), pp. 22–48; Hardin, *Texian Iliad*, pp. 188–217; James Marshall-Cornwall, *Napoleon*, (Princeton, N.J.: D. Van Nostrand, 1967), pp. 127, 142–145; Roger Borroel, ed. and trans., *Field Reports of the Mexican Army During the Texan War of 1836*, (East Chicago: "La Villita Publications," 2001), vol. iv, p. 16; F. G. Hourtoulle, Austerlitz, *The Eagle's Sun*, (Paris, France: Histoire & Collections, 2003), pp. 4–127.

11. *New York Herald*, June 15, 1836; Hardin, *Texian Iliad*, pp. 216–217; De Brahl, *Sword of San Jacinto*, p. 206.

12. Fowler, *Santa Anna of Mexico*, pp. ix, xviii–xix, xxiii; Scheina, *Santa Anna*, p. 3.

13. Scheina, *Santa Anna*, pp. 18–21; Leonard Cooper, *Many Roads to Moscow: Three Historic Invasions*, (New York: Coward-McCann, Inc., 1968), pp. 3, 71–177; Vincent Cronin, *Napoleon*, (New York: Harper Collins Publishers, 1994), pp. 302–335.

14. Richard G. Santos, *Santa Anna's Campaign Against Texas, 1835-1836*, (Waco, Texas: Texian Press, 1968), p. 10.

15. Scheina, *Santa Anna*, pp. 18–21; Philip G. Dwyer, *Napoleon and Europe*, (London: Pearson Education Limited, 2001), pp. 128–135; Cronin, *Napoleon*, pp. 302–334; Roberts and Olson, *A Line in the Sand*, pp. 6–7.

16. Fowler, *Santa Anna of Mexico*, xi, 17; Brands, *Lone Star Nation*, pp. 140–141.

17. De Bruhl, *Sword of San Jacinto*, p. 174; Hourtoulle, *Austerlitz*, pp. 4–127.

18. R. F. Delderfield, *Napoleon's Marshals*, (New York: Cooper Square Press, 2002), p. 34; Scheina, *Santa Anna*, p. 6; Cronin, *Napoleon*, pp. 111–165.

19. Fowler, *Santa Anna of Mexico*, pp. 7, 19, 89; Scheina, *Santa Anna*, pp. 6, 24; Roberts and Oslon, *A Line in the Sand*, pp. 5–6, 66–67, 72; Perry, ed. and trans., *With Santa Anna in Texas*, p. 21; Cronin, *Napoleon*, pp. 43. 205–206.

20. Hardin, *Texian Iliad*, p. 102; Roberts and Olson, *A Line in the Sand*, p. 7.

21. Scheina, *Santa Anna*, pp. 7–8,14, 16; Cronin, *Napoleon*, p. 279.

22. "The Last Testament of Santa Anna," Vera Cruz, Mexico, September 26, 1867, Roger Borroel, translator, Collection, East Chicago, Indiana: Scheina, *Santa Anna*, pp. 7–8, 14, 16; Julia Kathryn Garrett, *Green Flag over Texas: The Story of the First War of Independence in Texas*, (New York: Jenkins Publishing Company, 1939), pp. 32–235; Brands, *Lone Star Nation*, pp. 41–42; Michener, *The Eagle and the Raven*, pp. 43, 45, 46–73; Roberts and Olson, *A Line in the Sand*, pp. 6–9; Perry, ed. and trans., *With Santa Anna in Texas*, p. 18; Fowler, *Santa Anna of Mexico*, pp. 11–12, 17–29, 89.

23. Robert L. Tarin, Jr., Papers, Southwest Collection, Texas Tech University, Lubbock, Texas; Horgan, *Great River*, pp. 476–477; Davis, *Lone Star Rising*, pp. 116–117, 163–164; Fehrenbach, *Lone Star*, pp. 128–130

24. Jasper Ridley, *Maximilian and Juarez*, (London, England: Phoenix Press,1992), pp. 10–11.

25. Stephenson, *Texas and the Mexican War*, pp. 27–28; *The Telegraph and Texas Register*, February 20, 1836; Miller, *New Orleans and the Texas Revolution*, pp. xi–209.

26. Binkley, *The Texas Revolution*, pp. 21–22

27. William G. Cooke Papers, Daughters of the Republic of Texas Library at the Alamo, San Antonio, Texas; Brown, *The New Orleans Greys*, pp. 11–289.

28. Miller, *New Orleans and the Texas Revolution*, pp. 51, 122; Hopewell, *James Bowie*, pp. 95–96.

29. Scheina, *Santa Anna*, pp. 23–26; Michener, *The Eagle and the Raven*, pp. 112–113; Roberts and Olson, *A Line in the Sand*, pp. 14–26; Winders, *Sacrificed at the Alamo*, pp. 44–47; William A. DePalo, Jr., *The Mexican National Army, 1822–1852*, (College Station: Texas A & M Press, 1997), p. 33.

30. Scheina, *Santa Anna*, p. 26; *The Telegraph and Texas Register*, September 13, 1836; Michener, *The Eagle and the Raven*, p. 113; Roberts and Olson, *A Line in the Sand*, p. 26.

31. Michener, *The Eagle and the Raven*, p. 113; Roberts and Olson, *A Line in the Sand*, p. 27.

32. Scheina, *Santa Anna*, pp. 25–26; Perry, ed. and trans., *With Santa Anna in Texas*, p. 18.

33. Scheina, *Santa Anna*, p. 27; Lozano, *Viva Tejas*, pp. 10–11; Hardin, *Texian Iliad*, p. 102; Perry, ed. and trans., *With Santa Anna in Texas*, pp. 8, 9, 11; Long, *Duel of Eagles*, pp. 109–110; Fowler, *Santa Anna of Mexico*, pp. 15–16. 161,179.

34. Santos, *Santa Anna's Campaign Against Texas*, p. 1; Roger Borroel, editor and translator, *Field Reports of the Mexican Army During the Texan War of 1836*, (East Chicago, Indiana: "La Villita Publications," 2006), vol vi, p. 42; Perry, ed. and trans., *With Santa Anna in Texas*, pp. 11, 16, 29; Roger Borroel, editor and translator, *Field Reports of the Mexican Army During the Texan War of 1836*, vol. ii, (East Chicago, Indiana: "La Villita Publications," 2001), pp. 7, 9, 25; DePalo, *The Mexican National Army*, pp. 30–31; Lord, *A Time to Stand*, p. 69.

35. *New York Herald*, March 23, 1836; Borroel, ed. and trans., *Field Reports of the Mexican Army During the Texan War of 1836*, vol. ii, pp. 29-30; DePalo, *The Mexican National Army*, p. 48.

36. Borroel, ed. and trans., *Field Reports of the Mexican Army During the Texan War of 1836*, vol. ii, p. 31.

37. Barr, *Texans in Revolt*, p. 63.

38. "The Last Testament of Santa Anna," RBC; McDonald, *William Barret Travis*, p. 86; Scheina, *Santa Anna*, p. 14, 29; Brands, *Lone Star Nation*, p. 238; Huffines, *Blood of Noble Men*, p. 57; Hopewell, *James Bowie*, p.68; Perry, ed. and trans., *With Santa Anna in Texas*, p. 18; Hansen, ed., *The Alamo Reader*, p. 20; Fowler, *Santa Anna of Mexico*, pp. 166–167.

Chapter 3: THE ULTIMATE FOLLY: THE DEFENSE OF THE ALAMO

1. Winders, *Sacrificed at the Alamo*, pp. 78–110; Brands, pp. 160, 338–339; King, *James Clinton Neill*, pp. 80–81.

2. George Fisher to Stephen Austin, October 20, 1836, Center for American History, University of Texas, Austin, Texas; Editors of Time-Life, *The Texans*, pp. 71, 74.

3. Jackson, *Alamo Legacy*, p. 30.

4. Ibid., pp. 31–32; John Sutherland Manuscript, "Fall of the Alamo," Amelia W. Williams Papers, Center for American History, University of Texas, Austin, Texas; Hardin, *Texian Iliad*, pp. 111, 117; Mark Derr, *The Frontiersman, The Real Life and the Many Legends of Davy Crockett*, (New York: William Morrow and Company, Inc., 1993), pp. 240–241; Shackford, *David Crockett*, pp. 224–227; Brands, *Lone Star Nation*, pp. 160, 338–391; Winders, *Sacrificed at the Alamo*, pp. 88–89, 93–94; King, *James Clinton Neill*, pp. 77–78, 80; Long, *Duel of Eagles*, pp. 30–32, 70; Hansen, ed., The Alamo Reader, pp. 15–29; Lord, *A Time to Stand*, p. 56.

5. Winders, *Sacrificed at the Alamo*, p. 94; Hardin, *Texian Iliad*, pp. 111, 117; Roberts and Oslon, *A Line in the Sand*, p. 98; Lord, *A Time to Stand*, p. 83.

6. Joseph Wheelan, *Invading Mexico, America's Continental Dream and the Mexican War, 1846-1848*, (New York: Carroll and Graf Publishers, 2007), p. 46; Borroel, ed. and trans., *Field Reports of the Mexican Army During the Texan War of 1836*, vol. iii, p. 31.

7. Shackford, *David Crockett*, p. 225; Borroel, ed. and trans., *Field Reports of the Mexican Army During the Texan War of 1836*, vol. iii, p. 23.

8. Editors of Time-Life, *The Texans*, p. 70.

9. Gaddy, *Texas in Revolt*, p. 36; Uecker, *The Archaeology of the Alamo*, pp. 9, 17, 49, 52–54 78–79, 87, 90; Hardin, *Texian Iliad*, pp. 128, 130–131; Hansen, ed., *The Alamo Reader*, pp. 43–44.

10. *Maryland Gazette*, December 3, 1835.

11. Brands, *Lone Star Nation*, p. 288.

12. King, *James Clinton Neill*, pp. vii, 11, 21, 33, 37, 44, 78, 81–82, 85–87; Santos, *Santa Anna's Campaign Against Texas*, pp. 44–45; Jackson, *Alamo Legacy*, p. 28.

13. Thonhoff, *The Texas Connection*, pp. 4–6; Jackson, *Imaginary Kingdoms*, pp. 4–5; Chipman, *Spanish Texas*, pp. 117, 135–136; James Lockhart and Stuart B. Schwartz, *Early Latin America, A History of colonial Spanish America and Brazil*, (New York: Cambridge University Press, 1983), pp. 290–293; Brands, *Lone Star Nation*, p. 143.

14. Jackson, *Imaginary Kingdom*, pp. 27, note 29; Chipman, *Spanish Texas*, p. 117; Mary Ann Noonan Guerra, *The Missions of San Antonio*, (San Antonio, Texas: The Alamo Press, 1982), pp. 1–37.

15. Nelson, *The Alamo*, pp. 39–40.

16. Perry, ed. and trans., *With Santa Anna in Texas*, p. 43; Jackson, *Imaginary Kingdom*, pp. 4–7.

17. Jackson, *Imaginary Kingdom*, pp. 79–80, 209–210; Chipman, *Spanish Texas*, pp. 4, 133.

18. Nelson, *The Alamo*, p. 111; Jackson, *Alamo Legacy*, p. 30.

19. Alamo Vertical Files, Barker Texas History Center, University of Texas, Austin, Texas; Starling, *Land Is The Cry!* p. 71; Lack, *The Texas Revolutionary Experience*, 211; Jackson, *Alamo Legacy*, p. 30.

20. Gaddy, *Texas in Revolt*, p. 43.

21. Starling, *Land Is the Cry!*, p. 71.

22. Brown, *The New Orleans Greys*, pp. 46, 88.

23. Lack, *The Texas Revolutionary Experience*, pp. 47–48; Nelson, *The Alamo*, p. 111.

24. Brown, *The New Orleans Greys*, p. 94.

25. Lack, *The Texas Revolutionary Experience*, p. 51; Nelson, *The Alamo*, p. 111.

26. Lack, *The Texas Revolutionary Experience*, p. 152.

27. Chariton, *Exploring the Alamo Legends*, pp. 95–98; Nelson, *The Alamo*, p. 111.

28. Gaddy, *Texas in Revolt*, p. 44.

29. Lack, *The Texas Revolutionary Experience*, p. 212.

30. Ibid., pp. 213–214.

31. De Bruhl, *Sword of San Jacinto*, 189.

32. Scheina, *Latin America's Wars*, p. 159.

33. Jackson, *Alamo Legacy*, p. 32.

34. Fehrenbach, *Lone Star*, pp. 30–33, 57–58.

35. Fehrenbach, *Lone Star*, pp. 30–36, 57–58; Brands, *Lone Star Nation*, p. 46, 49; Hardin, *Texan Iliad*, p. 5; Wheelan, *Invading Mexico*, p. 51.

36. Chipman, *Spanish Texas*, pp. 133–135, 138–139, 145, 200.

37. Stephen L. Moore, *Savage Frontier, Rangers, Riflemen, and Indian Wars in Texas, 1835–1837*, (3 vols., Plano: Republic of Texas Press, 2002), pp. vii–8, 14, 16–24, 30–32, 90; Groneman, *Alamo Defenders*, pp. 31–32, 36–37.

38. Nelson, *The Alamo*, p. 46; Borroel, ed. and trans., *Field Reports of the Mexican Army During the Texan War of 1836*, vol. iii, p. 31.

39. Jackson, *Alamo Legacy*, p. 28; Fehrenbach, *Lone Star*, pp. 58–59.

40. Lord, *A Time to Stand*, p. 59.

41. Ibid., p. 60; Editors of Time-Life, *The Texans*, p. 79; Huffines, *Blood of Noble Men*, pp. 122–127; Hardin, *Texian Iliad*, p. 131.

42. Hansen, ed., *The Alamo Reader*, p. 115.

43. Uecker, *The Archaeology of the Alamo*, p. 32; Nelson, *The Alamo*, pp. 4–40, 46–48.

44. Jackson, *Alamo Legacy*, p. 31.

45. Winders, *Sacrificed at the Alamo*, p. 12; Huffines, *Blood of Noble Men*, p. 27.

46. Hardin, *Texian Iliad*, p. 128; Chipman, *Spanish Texas, 1519–1821*, pp. 130, 136–37, 246–247.

47. Chipman, *Spanish Texas*, p. 4; Winders, *Sacrificed at the Alamo*, p. 85; Hardin, *Texian Iliad*, p. 128.

48. Jackson, *Alamo Legacy*, pp. 29–32; E. A. Brininstool, *Troopers with Custer, Historic Incidents of the Battle of Little Big Horn*, (Lincoln, Neb: University of Nebraska Press, 1989),   pp. 14, 16–18; Hopewell, *James Bowie*, p. 113; Nelson, *The Alamo*, pp. 111, 263; need more.

49. Lack, *The Texas Revolutionary Experience*, pp. 196–197.

50. Jackson, *Alamo Legacy*, pp.99–101.

51. Nelson, *The Alamo*, p. 46; Lack, *The Texas Revolutionary Experience*, pp. 196–197; Lord, *A Time to Stand*, pp. 31, 57.

52. Levy, *American Legend*, p. 257; Lack, *The Texas Revolutionary Experience*, p. 200; Hansen, ed., *The Alamo Reader*, p. 462.

53. Clifford Hopewell, *James Bowie, Texas Fighting Man*, (Austin: Eakin Press, 1994), pp. 64–69; Lord, *A Time to Stand*, 27.

54. Jackson, *Alamo Legacy*, pp. 138, 140; Lord, *A Time to Stand*, pp. 21,125.

55. Jackson, *Alamo Legacy*, p. 31; Roberts and Olson, *A Line in the Sand*, pp. 118–119; Hansen, ed., *The Alamo Reader*, p. 462; Lord, *A Time to Stand*, pp. 23, 27, 86; Groneman, *Alamo Defenders*, p. 75.

56. Huffines, *Blood of Noble Men*, pp. 107–108; Jackson, *Alamo Legacy*, p. 99–100.

57. Nelson, *The Alamo*, pp. 46, 49.

58. Davis, *Lone Star Rising*, pp. 215–216; Lack, *The Texas Revolutionary Experience*, pp. 166–167, 182; Winders, *Sacrificed at the Alamo*, p. 86.

59. Lack, *The Texas Revolutionary Experience*, pp. 167, 182.

60. Hopewell, *James Bowie*, p. 65; Levy, *American Legend*, pp. 157, 161, 241–242; Winders, *Sacrificed at the Alamo*, pp. 86–87; Hansen, ed., *The Alamo Reader*, p. 113; Groneman, *Alamo Defenders*, p. 102.

61. Nelson, *The Alamo*, p. 46.

62. Castaneda, *The Mexican Side of the Texan Revolution*, p. 195; Chemerka, *Alamo Analogy*, p. 68; Hardin, *Texian Iliad*, pp. 128, 131; Alan C. Huffines, *Blood of Noble Men, The Alamo, Siege & Battle* (Austin: Eakin Press, 1999), pp. 2, 15; Fowler, *Santa Anna of Mexico*, p. 179.

63. Castaneda, *The Mexican Side of the Texan Revolution*, p. 208; Wallace Woolsey, translator, *Memoirs For The History of the War in Texas, Don Vicente Filisola*, (Austin, Texas: Eakin Press, 1985), pp. xvii–xix; Hansen, ed., *The Alamo Reader*, pp. 113–115.

64. Guerra, *The Missions of San Antonio*, p. 24; Borroel, ed. and trans., *Field Reports of the Mexican Army During the Texan War of 1836*, vol. iii, p. 23; Santos, *Santa Anna's Campaign Against Texas*, pp. 34, 56, Roger Borroel, *The Texan Revolution of 1836*, (East Chicago: "La Villita Publications," 1989), p. 46.

65. Lockhart and Schwartz, *Early Latin America*, p. 294.

66. Uecker, *The Archaeology of the Alamo*, pp. 40–44; Hardin, *Texian Iliad*, pp. 128–130.

67. Hansen, *The Alamo Reader*, p. 393; *Maryland Gazette, November 26, 1835.*

68. Hardin, *Texian Iliad*, p. 131; John Myers Myers, *The Alamo*, (New York: Bantam Books, 1966), p. 134.

69. DeBruhl, *Sword of San Jacinto*, pp. 187–188.

70. Sutherland Manuscript, CAH; Fowler, *Santa Anna of Mexico*, p. 164; Hardin, *Texian Iliad*, pp. xii–xiii, 30–35, 63–66, 73, 128–131; Derr, *The Frontiersman*, pp. 237, 240–241; *Maryland Gazette*, November 26, 1835; King, *James Clinton Neill*, pp. 78, 81, 86–88; Dee Brown, *Andrew Jackson and the Battle of New Orleans*, (New York: G. P. Putnam's Sons, 1972), p.10

71. Hardin, *Texian Iliad*, pp. 10, 130; DeBruhl, *Sword of San Jacinto*, pp. 41–44, 186; Hopewell, *James Bowie*, pp. 6–7; *New Orleans Advertiser*, July 13, 1832; Groneman, *Alamo Defenders*, p. 57–58, 105; Jon Latimer, *1812: War With America*, (Cambridge, Massachusetts: Harvard University Press, 2007), pp. 369–386; Walker, *The Life of Andrew Jackson*, pp. 194–195, 222–248, 260–261.

72. Walker, *The Life of Andrew Jackson*, pp. Lxx–lxxii; King, *James Clinton Neill*, pp. 78, 81, 86–87.

73. Jackson, *Alamo Legacy*, pp. 133–134; Winston Groom, *Patriotic Fire: Andrew Jackson and Jean Laffite and the Battle of New Orleans*, (New York: Alfred A. Knopf, 2006), p. 51; King, *James Clinton Neill*, pp. 78, 81, 86–87.

74. Jackson, *Alamo Legacy*, pp. 126, 131–132; Gordon C. Jennings, Biographical Sketch from the Jennings Heritage Project, Washington, D.C.

75. Hardin, *Texan Iliad*, pp. xii–xiii, 83, 98–101, 130; Walker, *The Life of Andrew Jackson*, pp. 135, 194–195; Hopewell, *James Bowie*, pp. 113–119.

76. Hardin, *Texan Iliad*, p. 111; Lord, *A Time to Stand*, p. 76; John B. Lundstrom, *Assault at Dawn: The Mexican Army at the Alamo, Campaign, no. 1*, (Summer 1973), p. 8; King, *James Clinton Neill*, pp. vii, 78, 81, 84, 86–87; Hansen, ed., *The Alamo Reader*, p. 330.

77. King, *James Clinton Neill*, pp. 78, 81.

78. Frank W. Johnson, *A History of Texas and Texans*, (Chicago: American Historical Association, 1914), pp. 412; Roberts and Olson, *A Line in the Sand*, p. 127; Hardin, *Texian Iliad*, p. 131.

79. Brown, *The New Orleans Greys*, pp. 35–36; Walker, *The Life of Andrew Jackson*, pp. 241, 312–313, 325; Major Samuel Spotts Monument File, Chalmette National Military Park, St. Bernard Parish, Louisiana; Borroel, *The Texan Revolution of 1836*, p. 38; Bradfield, *Rx Take One Cannon*, p. 99.

80. King, *James Clinton Neill*, p. 78; Lord, *A Time to Stand*, pp. 76–77; Huffines, *Blood of Noble Men*, pp. 15, 107.

81. Chemerka, *Alamo Anthology*, pp. 65–66; Hardin, *Texian Iliad*, pp. 130–131; National Park Service historians, "18-pounder Revolutionary War Cannon," Fort Moultrie, National Park Service File, Fort Sumter National Monument, Charleston, South Carolina.

82. Guerra, *The Missions of San Antonio*, pp. 23–24.

83. Potter, *The Fall of the Alamo*, p. 3.

84. Ibid., p. 14.

85. Santos, *Santa Anna's Campaign Against Texas*, p. 10; King, *James Clinton Neill*, pp. 78, 81, 85, 87.

86. Gaddy, *Texas in Revolt*, pp. 35–36; Garrett, *Green Flag over Texas*, pp. 6, 9–10, 42.

87. *Maryland Gazette*, December 8, 1836.

88. Moore, *Savage Frontier*, p. 33.

89. Gaddy, *Texas in Revolt*, p. 50; Boyd, *The Texas Revolution*, p. 9.

90. Boyd, *The Texas Revolution*, p. 9.

91. Derr, *The Frontiersman*, p. 237.

92. Ibid., p. 241.

93. Roger D. Launius, *Alexander William Doniphan: Portrait of a Missouri Moderate*, (Columbia: University of Missouri Press, 1997), pp. 32–34; Weems and Weems, *Dream of Empire*, p. 43; Dan Kilgore, *How Did Davy Die?*, (College Station, Texas: Texas A & M Press, 1978), p. 12.

94. Hauch, *Davy Crockett*, pp. 49–50; Shackford, *David Crockett*, pp. 219–221; Starling, *Land Is The Cry!*, p. 45; Levy, *American Legend*, p. 148; Kilgore, *How Did Davy Die?*, p. 12; Lord, *A Time to Stand*, pp. 134–135.

95. *New York Times*, December 15, 1907.

96. Shackford, *David Crockett*, pp. 175–194, 219–221; Hauck, *Davy Crockett*, pp. 48–50.

97. Shackford, *David Crockett*, pp. 233–234.

98. Hardin, *Texas Iliad*, p. 63.

99. Moore, *Eighteen Minutes*, p. 41; Shackford, *David Crockett*, pp. 220–227, 233–234.

100. Shackford, *David Crockett*, pp. 220–227, 233–234.

101. McDonald, *William Barret Travis*, pp. 129–130; Brands, *Lone Star Nation*, p. 332; Levy, *American Legend*, p. 246, 248.

102. Moore, *Eighteen Minutes*, pp. 2–3.

103. Moore, *Savage Frontier*, pp. 82–83.

104. Hardin, *Texian Iliad*, p. 129; Moore, *Eighteen Minutes*, pp. 2–3; Levy, *American Legend*, pp. 159–160; Stuart Reid, *The Texan Army, 1835–46*, (Oxford, Osprey Publishing Limited, 2003), p. 15.

105. *The Telegraph and Texas Register*, January 9, 1836; McDonald, *William Barret Travis*, pp. 94–95, 129–130; Hansen, ed., *The Alamo Reader*, pp. 15–19.

106. McDonald, *William Barret Travis*, p. 86; Huffines, *The Blood of Noble Men*, pp. 29–31, 35.

107. *The Telegraph and Texas Register*, January 9, 1836; Lorano, *Viva Tejas*, pp. v, 47, 72–73; Perry, ed. and trans, *With Santa Anna in Texas*, p. 50.

108. William G. Cooke Papers, DRT Library; Moore, *Eighteen Minutes*, p. 16; *The Telegraph and Texas Register*, November 7, 1835.
109. Jackson, *Alamo Legacy*, pp. 32–33.
110. Ibid., Winders, *Sacrificed at the Alamo*, pp. 77–78.
111. Jackson, *Alamo Legacy*, pp. 30–31; Borroel, trans. and ed., *Field Reports of the Mexican Army in the Texan War of 1836*, vol. iii, p. 31.
112. Jackson, *Alamo Legacy*, pp. 30–31.
113. Chariton, *Exploring the Alamo Legends*, p. 110.
114. Lack, *The Texas Revolutionary Experience*, p. 189.
115. Sutherland Manuscript, CAH; Nofi, *The Alamo*, pp. 105–106; Roberts and Olson, *A Line in the Sand*, p. 104; Borroel, ed. and trans., *Field Reports of the Mexican Army During the Texan War of 1836*, vol. iii, p. 31; Bill and Marjorie K. Walraven, *The Magnificent Barbarians, Little Told Tales of the Texas Revolution*, (Austin, Texas: Eakin Press, 1993), p. 52; Hansen, ed., *The Alamo Reader*, p. 59; *American-Statesman*, Austin, Texas, April 15, 2004.
116. Hardin, *Texan Iliad*, p. 34.
117. Davis, *Lone Star Rising*, p. 176.
118. Ibid; Sutherland Manuscript, CAH; Lindley, *Alamo Traces*, p. 88; Hardin, *Texan Iliad*, p. 34; Huffines, *Blood of Noble Men*, p. 95; Borroel, ed. and trans., *Field Reports of the Mexican Army During the Texan War of 1836*, vol. iii, pp. 31, 36; John K. Borchardt, "DuPont Marks Its Bicentennial," *Chemistry Chronicles*, vol. 11, no. 6, (June 2002), pp. 43–46; Hansen, ed., *The Alamo Reader*, p. 59; *American-Statesman*, April 15, 2004.
119. Gunter E. Rothenberg, *The Art of Warfare in the Age of Napoleon*, (Bloomington: Indiana University Press, 2005), p. 67; *American Statesman*, April 15, 2004.
120. Jackson, *Alamo Legacy*, pp. 92–93.
121. Groneman, *Eyewitness to the Alamo*, p. 6.
122. Huffines, *Blood of Noble Men*, p. 107.
123. Sutherland Manuscript, CAH; Davis, *Lone Star Rising*, p. 3.
124. Fowler, *Santa Anna of Mexico*, p. 9.
125. *San Antonio Daily Express*, April 28, 1881; Sutherland Manuscript, CAH; Brands, *Lone Star Nation*, p. 45.
126. Sutherland Manuscript CAH; *San Antonio Daily Express*, April 28, 1881; Uecker, *The Archaeology of the Alamo*, pp. 4, 11–12, 14, 36, 44; Winders, *Sacrificed at the Alamo*, pp. 21–22; Nelson, *The Alamo*, p. 112.
127. Long, *Duel of Eagles*, p. 32; Elizabeth A. Fenn, to author, April 8, 2004.
128. *San Antonio Express*, February 24, 1929; Sutherland Manuscript, CAH; Chipman, *Spanish Texas*, pp. 258–259; Nelson, *The Alamo*, p. 40.
129. Groneman, *Alamo Defenders*, p. 130.
130. Sutherland Manuscript, CAH; *San Antonio Daily Express*, April 28, 1881; Jackson, *Alamo Legacy*, p. 73–76; Groneman, *Alamo Defenders*, pp. 61–62.
131. Moore, *Eighteen Minutes*, p. 29; Nelson, *The Alamo*, p. 111.
132. Chipman, *Spanish Texas*, p. 9; Lord, *A Time to Stand*, p. 111.
133. Jackson, *Imaginary Kingdom*, p. 42.
134. Uecker, *The Archaeology of the Alamo*, pp. 24, 32; need more
135. Jackson, *Alamo Legacy*, pp. 31–32; Borroel, ed. and trans., *Field Reports of the Mexican Army During the Texan War of 1836*, vol. iii, pp. 31, 35.
136. Nelson, *The Alamo*, p. 46; King, *James Clinton Neill*, pp. 18–19.
137. Jackson, *The Alamo*, p. 31.
138. Jackson, *Alamo Legacy*, p. 30.
139. Uecker, *The Archaeology of the Alamo*, p. 38; Johnson, *The History of Texas and Texans*, pp. 412–413; Hansen, ed., *The Alamo Reader*, pp. 15, 392–394, 416–417, 712–713.
140. Nelson, *The Alamo*, p. 48; Guerra, *Heroes of the Alamo and Goliad*, p. 15.
141. Nelson, *The Alamo*, p. 48; Lord, *A Time to Stand*, p. 23; Winders, *Sacrificed at the Alamo*, p. 115.
142. Nelson, *The Alamo*, pp. 46–48; Groneman, *Eyewitness to the Alamo*, p. 3; Nelson, *The Alamo*, p. 111.

143. Chariton, *Exploring the Alamo Myths*, p. 82; Groneman, *Eyewitness to the Alamo*, p. 3; Robert K. Wright, *The Continental Army*, (Washington, D.C.: Center of Military History, 1983), pp. 3–90.
144. Jackson, *Alamo Legacy*, pp. 31–32.
145. Derr, *The Frontiersman*, p. 238.
146. Ibid., p. 242; Winders, *Sacrificed at the Alamo*, pp. 77–78; Kilgore, *How Did Davy Die?*, p. 10.
147. Perry, ed. and trans., *With Santa Anna in Texas*, p. 18.
148. Barr, *Texans in Revolt*, p. 64; Wheelan, *Invading Mexico*, p. 46; Fowler, *Santa Anna of Mexico*, pp. 160, 163, 165.
149. Hardin, *Texian Iliad*, p. 185.
150. Miller, *New Orleans and the Texas Revolution*, pp. 129–143; Huffines, *Blood of Noble Men*, p. 107.
151. *New York Herald*, February 29, 1836.
152. Elizabeth Salas, *Soldaderas in the Mexican Military, Myth and History*, (Austin, Texas: University of Texas Press, 2006), pp. xi, 1–30; Kevin R. Young, "Finding a Face: El Soldado Mexicano, 1835–1848," Palo Alto Battlefield Archive, Brownsville, Texas.
153. San Luis Battalion Logbook, Jose Enrique de la Pena Papers, Center for American History, University of Texas, Austin, Texas; DePalo, *The Mexican National Army*, p. 50.
154. *San Antonio Daily Express*, June 30, 1889; Santos, *Santa Anna's Campaign Against Texas*, p. 9.
155. San Luis Battalion Logbook, De la Pena Papers, UT; Perry, ed. and trans., *With Santa Anna in Texas*, p. 8.
156. Jackson, *Alamo Legacy*, pp. 144–145.
157. Ibid., pp. 135–137.
158. General Jose Antonio Fernandez, December 30, 1835 notice, Center for American History, University of Texas, Austin Texas, The Matamoros Archives, Box 2 Q266, Vol. IV.
159. Francisco Paredas y Arrillaga to Minister of War Jose M. Tornell, June 10, 1836, CAH, Box 2Q174, vol. 334.
160. Scheina, *Santa Anna*, pp. 18–20; Brands, *Lone Star Nation*, pp. 77, 140–141; DePalo, *The Mexican National Army*, pp. 37–38.
161. Scheina, *Santa Anna*, pp. 87–88.
162. *El Mosquito Mexicano*, Mexico City, Mexico, March 1 and March 11, 1836; *El Censor*, Vera Cruz, Mexico, March 2, 1836; *La Lima de Vulcano*, Mexico City, March 5, 1836.
163. Scheina, *Santa Anna*, pp 87–88; Brands, *Lone Star Nation*, p. 77.
164. Brading, *Mexican Phoenix*, p. 237.
165. Ibid., pp. 237, 239; De Bruhl, *Sword of San Jacinto*, p. 32.

Chapter 4: LULL BEFORE THE STORM: FATAL OVERCONFIDENCE
1. Hardin, *Texian Iliad*, pp. 53, 106, 135; Ford, *Rip Ford's Texas*, pp. 13–15; *The Telegraph and Texas Register*, November 18, 1837; Winders, *Sacrificed at the Alamo*, 95–100; Long, *Duel of Eagles*, pp. 114–116; Nelson, *The Alamo*, p. 111.
2. Fehrenbach, *Lone Star*, pp. 164–166, 178; Hardin, *Texian Iliad*, p. 158; Nelson, *The Alamo*, p. 111.
3. Tuchman, *The March of Folly*, p. 25,
4. Nelson, *The Alamo*, p. 46.
5. Jackson, *Alamo Legacy*, pp. 31–32.
6. Ibid., pp. 85–88.
7. Ibid., pp. 123–126.
8. Ibid., p. 31.
9. Roberts and Olson, *A Line in the Sand*, p. 107.
10. Chariton, *Exploring the Alamo Legends*, p. 156; Roberts and Olson, *A Line in the Sand*, pp. 26, 51.
11. Gaddy, *Texas in Revolt*, pp. 12–13.
12. Jackson, *Alamo Legacy*, p. 20.
13. Ibid., p. 35.

14. Hardin, *Texian Iliad*, pp. xii–xiii, 10; Boatner, *Encyclopedia of the American Revolution*, pp. 934–936; Heidler and Heidler, eds., *Encyclopedia of the War of 1812*, p. 20; Wright, Jr., *The Continental Army*, pp. 25, 49, 67–70, 78–82; Latimer, *1812*, pp. 380–386; Robert Lagermann and Albert C. Manucy, *The Long Rifle*, (Washington, D.C.: Eastern Acorn Press, 1980), pp. 5–32.

15. Gaddy, *Texas in Revolt*, pp. 10,14.

16. Ibid., p. 26.

17. Ibid., p. 46.

18. Chemerka, *Alamo Anthology*, p. 66; Huffines, *Blood of Noble Men*, p. 75; Hansen, ed., *The Alamo Reader*, pp. 71, 163; Nelson, *The Alamo*, p. 111; Groneman, *Alamo Defenders*, pp. 4–125.

19. Hardin, *Texian Iliad*, p. 110.

20. Ibid., p. 248; Anthony J. Scotti, Jr., *Brutal Virtue: The Myth and Reality of Banastre Tarleton*, (Bowie, Maryland: Heritage Books, Inc., 2002), pp. 13–217.

21. Hansen, ed., *The Alamo Reader*, p. 611.

22. Jackson, *Alamo Legacy*, p. 20.

23. *Army and Navy Chronicle*, New York, New York, vol. iii, no. 4, July 28, 1836.

24. Perry, ed., and trans., *With Santa Anna in Texas*, p. 19.

25. Fowler, *Santa Anna of Mexico*, p. 163; Walter R. Borneman, *1812: The War That Forged A Nation*, (New York: Harper Perennial, 2004), pp. 216–235.

26. Roberts and Olson, *A Line in the Sand*, pp. 8, 14–26.

27. Levy, *American Legend*, pp. 257–258, 261–262; Derr, *The Frontiersmen*, pp. 242–243; Lord, *A Time to Stand*, p. 86.

28. Lack, *The Texas Revolutionary Experience*, pp. 196–197.

29. Winders, *Sacrificed at the Alamo*, pp. 92–93.

30. Ibid., pp. 99–100.

31. Jackson, *Alamo Legacy*, pp. 17–18; Groneman, *Alamo Defenders*, pp. 7, 58.

32. Gaddy, *Texas in Revolt*, p. 38.

33. Jackson, *Alamo Legacy*, p. 20; Groneman, *Alamo Defenders*, p. 7.

34. Roberts and Olson, *A Line in the Sand*, p. 109; Lord, *A Time to Stand*, p. 59.

35. Perry, ed. and trans., *With Santa Anna in Texas*, p. 6; Jackson, *Alamo Legacy*, p. 37; Groneman, *Alamo Defenders*, p. 30.

36. Sutherland Manuscript, CAH; King, *James Clinton Neill*, p. 90.

37. Jackson, *Alamo Legacy*, p. 35.

38. Winders, *Sacrificed at the Alamo*, p. 100; Hansen, ed., *The Alamo Reader*, pp. 20–21.

39. Sutherland Manuscript, CAH; Hardin, *Texas Iliad*, p. 91.

40. Groneman, *Alamo Defenders*, p. 144.

41. Levy, *American Legend*, p. 260; Santos, *Santa Anna's Campaign Against Texas*, pp. 29–30, 34, 43, 53; Perry, ed. and trans., *With Santa Anna in Texas*, pp. 24, 32; Lord, *A Time to Stand*, p. 73.

42. Jackson, *Alamo Legacy*, pp. 106–107.

43. Nofi, *The Alamo*, p. 49; Boyd, *The Texas Revolution*, p. 27; Roberts and Olson, *A Line in the Sand*, pp. 132–134; Lord, *A Time to Stand*, p. 91; Long, *Duel of Eagles*, pp. 199–203.

44. Roberts and Olson, *A Line in the Sand*, pp. 134–135; Nofi, *The Alamo*, pp. 87, 89.

45. Roberts and Olson, *A Line in the Sand*, pp. 134–135.

46. Hardin, *Texian Iliad*, pp. xiii–xiv; Levy, *American Legend*, pp. 257–258; Matovina, *The Alamo Remembered*, pp. 118–119; Brands, *Lone Star Nation*, pp. 238–239; Long, *Duel of Eagles*, pp. 33–35.

47. Derr, *The Frontiersman*, p. 240.

48. Sutherland Mauscript, CAH; Matovina, *The Alamo Remembered*, p. 7; Hansen, ed., *The Alamo Reader*, p. 23.

49. Death Records, San Fernando Church, San Antonio, Texas, Catholic Archives of Texas, Austin, Texas; King, *James Clinton Neill*, p. 90; Perry, ed. and trans., *With Santa Anna in Texas*, 188; Hansen, ed., *The Alamo Reader*, p. 20.

50. Sutherland Manuscript, CAH.

51. Brands, *Lone Star Nation*, pp. 140–141.

52. Hardin, *Texas Iliad*, pp. 120–121; Santos, *Santa Anna's Campaign Against Texas*, p. 34.

53. Delderfield, *Napoleon's Marshals*, pp. 12–13, 48; Roberts and Olson, *A Line in the Sand*, p. 118.

54. Groneman, *Eyewitness to the Alamo*, p. 43; Santos, *Santa Anna's Campaign Against Texas*, pp. 29–30, 43; Santos, *Santa Anna's Campaign Against Texas*, pp. 45, 53–54, 60.
55. William M. Dwyer, *The Day is Ours! November 1776-January 1777: An Inside View of the Battles of Trenton and Princeton*, (New York: Viking Press, 1983), pp. 227–276; Groneman, *Eyewitness to the Alamo*, p. 37.
56. Levy, *American Legend*, pp. 7, 257, 261–262; Santos, *Santa Anna's Campaign Against Texas,* p. 51; Long, *Duel of Eagles*, pp. 34–35; Walraven and Walraven, *The Magnificent Barbarians*, p. 59.
57. *Richmond Whig*, Richmond, Virginia, April 15, 1836.
58. James E. Crisp, *Sleuthing the Alamo: Davy Crockett's Last Stand and Other Mysteries of the Texas Revolution*, (Oxford: Oxford University Press, 2005), pp. 62–63; Lord, *A Time to Stand*, pp. 87–88.
59. Moore, *Savage Frontier*, p. 88; Groneman, *Eyewitness to the Alamo*, pp. 43–44; Huffines, *The Blood of Noble Men*, pp. 5, 8, 11; Santos, *Santa Anna's Campaign Against Texas*, pp. 60–63; Barr, *Texans in Revolt*, p. 55; Hansen, ed., *The Alamo Reader*, p. 45; Lord, *A Time to Stand*, p. 95.
60. Roger Borroel, editor and translator, *Field Reports of the Mexican Army During the Texan War of 1836*, vol. vi, (East Chicago, Indiana: "La Villita Publications," 2006), p. 27.
61. Crawford, ed., *The Eagle*, pp. 26, 50–51.
62. *San Antonio Express*, May 18, 1907; *Memphis Enquirer*, April 12, 1836, Groneman, *Eyewitness to the Alamo*, p. 8; Santos, *Santa Anna's Campaign Against Texas*, p. 67; Hansen, ed., *The Alamo Reader*, p. 163.
63. Groneman, *Eyewitness to the Alamo*, pp. 43–44; Roberts and Olson, *A Line in the Sand*, p. 61; Santos, *Santa Anna's Campaign Against Texas*, pp. 60–63, 67; Zamoyski, *Moscow 1812*, pp. 522–523.
64. Levy, *American Legend*, pp. 264; Lord, *A Time to Stand*, pp. 56, 91; Hansen, ed., *The Alamo Reader*, pp. 18–19.
65. Eric Niderost, *"No Mercy!," Military Heritage*, (February 2004), pp. 60–61; Digby Smith, *Napoleon Against Russia: A Concise History of 1812*, (Barnsley, England: Pen & Sword Military, 2004), p. 156; Lord, *A Time to Stand*, p. 111.
66. Lack, *The Texas Revolutionary Experience*, pp. xiii–ix, xvi–xxiii, 53–237.
67. Ibid., pp. 117–118, 120, 126–132, 147, 173.
68. Roberts and Olson, *A Line in the Sand*, p. 127; Davis, *Three Roads to the Alamo*, pp. 547–548, 568; Hansen, ed., *The Alamo Reader*, pp. 19–20, 22; Huffines, *Blood of Noble Men*, p. 5.
69. Hansen, ed., *The Alamo Reader*, p. 23.
70. John Sutherland Manuscript, CAH.
71. Roberts and Olson, *A Line in the Sand*, p. 139.
72. Ibid., p. 100; King, *James Clinton Neill*, pp. 91–92.
73. Winders, *Sacrificed at the Alamo*, p. 134; Hardin, *Texas Iliad*, pp. 53, 59; Wheelan, *Invading Mexico*, p. 46.
74. Moore, *Savage Frontier*, p. 88.
75. Matovina, *The Alamo Remembered*, p. 50; Roberts and Olson, *A Line in the Sand*, p. 127.
76. Sutherland Manuscript, CAH; Brands, *Lone Star Nation*, p. 349; Hansen, ed., *The Alamo Reader*, pp. 20, 22.
77. Chariton, *Exploring the Alamo Legends*, p. 240.
78. Michener, *The Eagle and Raven*, pp. 112–113, 141–142; Hansen, *The Alamo Reader*, pp. 20, 22.
79. Jackson, *Alamo Legacy*, p. 31; Groneman, *Alamo Defenders*, p. 22.
80. *Maryland Gazette*, November 5, 1835.
81. Roberts and Olson, *A Line in the Sand*, pp. 92, 126–126.
82. Huffines, *Blood of Noble Men*, p. 16; King, *James Clinton Neill*, pp. 78, 85–86.
83. Hardin, *Texian Iliad*, pp. 12, 119; King, *James Clinton Neill*, pp. 76, 78, 85–86, 97–100; Roberts and Olson, *A Line in the Stand*, p. 114; Winders, *Sacrificed at the Alamo*, 88.
84. Barr, *Texans in Revolt*, pp. 45–56; Hansen, ed., *The Alamo Reader*, pp. 15, 18, 22.

Chapter 5: AN INEFFECTIVE SIEGE
1. Copeland, *Kendall of the Picayune*, p. 56.

2. Woolsey, trans., *Memoirs For the History of the War in Texas*, p. 42.

3. Lindley, *Alamo Traces*, pp. 330–331.

4. Gaddy, *Texas in Revolt*, p. 22.

5. Sutherland Manuscript, CAH; Jackson, *Alamo Legacy*, pp. 99–101; Lozano, *Viva Tejas*, pp. i–ii; Santos, *Santa Anna's Campaign in Texas*, p. 34.

6. Jackson, *Alamo Legacy*, pp. 99–101; Tim J. and Terry S. Todish, *Alamo Sourebook 1836: A Comprehensive Guide to the Alamo and the Texas Revolution* (Austin: Eakin Press, 1998), pp. 42, 65.

7. Derr, *The Frontiersman*, p. 246; Levy, *American Legend*, p. 271; De Bruhl, *Sword of San Jacinto*, pp. 108, 119; Shackford, *David Crockett*, pp. 223–226; Brands, *Lone Star Nation*, pp. 355–356; Davis, *Lone Star Rising*, p. 229; Davis, *Three Roads to the Alamo*, p. 547; Lindley, *Alamo Traces*, pp. 1–25; Walker, *The Life of Andrew Jackson*, p. xv; Lyman C. Draper, *King's Mountain and Its Heroes*, (Johnson City, Tennessee: The Overmountain Press, 1996), pp. 139–141, 157–159, 200; Bruce Marshall, *Uniforms of the Alamo and the Texas Revolution*, (Atglen, Pennsylvania: Schiffer Military History, 2003), pp. 6–7, 14; Perry, ed. and trans, *With Santa Anna in Texas*, pp. 7–8; Huffines, *Blood of Noble Men*, pp. 107–108.

8. Levy, *American Legend*, pp. 271; Roberts and Olson, *A Line in the Sand*, p. 148.

9. Davis, *Lone Star Rising*, pp. 229–230.

10. Ibid., pp. 229–230; Lindley, *Alamo Traces*, pp. 1–25.

11. Ibid., p. 135.

12. Levy, *American Legend*, p. 275; Davis, *Three Roads to the Alamo*, pp. 548–551; Lindley, *Alamo Traces*, pp. 1–25.

13. Lindley, *Alamo Traces*, pp. 1–25.

14. Jackson, *Alamo Legacy*, p. 30.

15. Sutherland Manuscript, CAH; Morris, *Savage Frontier*, pp. 91–92, 97–98; Bradfield, *Rx Take One Cannon*, p. 23; Groneman, *Alamo Defenders*, p. 70; Huffines, *Blood of Noble Men*, p. 13.

16. Motovina, *The Alamo Remembered*, p. 51.

17. Scheina, *Santa Anna*, pp. 28–29; Brown, *The New Orleans Greys*, p. 74; Robert Forczyk, *Toulon 1793: Napoleon's first Great Victory*, (Oxford, United Kingdom: Osprey Publishing Limited, 2005), pp. 7–85; Robert Harvey, *The War of Wars: The Great European Conflict, 1793–1815*, (New York: Carroll and Graf Publishers, 2006), pp. 63–67; Santos, *Santa Anna's Campaign Against Texas*, pp. 34, 68; Fowler, *Santa Anna of Mexico*, p. 170.

18. Santos, *Santa Anna's Campaign Against Texas*, pp. 67–68.

19. *Maryland Gazette*, September 5, 1776; Davis, *Three Roads to the Alamo*, pp. 35–36; Hopewell, *James Bowie*, pp. 1–2; *Maryland Gazette*, September 12, 1776; Smith, *New York 1776*, pp. 42–46; Fowler, *Santa Anna of Mexico*, p. 21.

20. Davis, *Three Roads to the Alamo*, p. 12; *The Royal Gazette*, New York, February 24, 1781.

21. McDonald, *William Barret Travis*, pp. 22–24; Boatner, *Encyclopedia of the American Revolution*, pp. 804–808.

22. Helen Litton, *Irish Rebellions, 1798–1916*, (Niwot: Colorado: The Irish American Book Company, 1998), pp. 7–51, 122; Thomas Pakenham, *The Year of Liberty: The Great Irish Rebellion of 1789*, (London: Weidenfeld and Nicolson, 1997), pp. 40–81; Thomas Bartlett, Kevin Dawson, and Daire Keogh, *The 1798 Rebellion: An Illustrated History*, (Niwot, Colorado: Roberts Rhinehart Publishers, 1998), pp. 128–134; Bernard A. Cook, *Women and War: A Historical Encyclopedia from Antiquity to the Present, Volume Two*, (2 vols., Oxford, England: ABC CLIO, Inc., 2006), pp. 644–645; Michael Kenny, *The 1798 Rebellion: Photographs and Memorabilia from the National Museum of Ireland*, (Dublin, Ireland: Country House, 1996), pp. 25, 38–39; Charles Murphy, *The Irish in the American Revolution*, (Groveland, Massachusetts: Charles Murphy Publications, 1975), pp. 1–99; Groneman, *Alamo Defenders*, pp. 88–89.

23. Fowler, *Santa Anna of Mexico*, pp. 21, 174–175; Huffines, *Blood of Noble Men*, p. 35.

24. Nofi, *The Alamo*, pp. 103–106; Winders, *Sacrificed at the Alamo*, p. 115; Santos, *Santa Anna's Campaign Against Texas*, pp. 69–70; Rene Chartrand, *Santa Anna's Mexican Army 1821–48*, (Oxford, England: Osprey Publishing Limited, 2004), pp. 64–65; DePalo, *The Mexican National Army*, p. 51.

25. Levy, *American Legend*, p. 173; Groneman, *Eyewitness to the Alamo*, p. 10.

26. *New York Herald*, April 12, 1836; Gaddy, *Texas in Revolt*, p. 49.

27. *The Telegraph and Texas Register*, February 20, 1836.
28. Moore, *Savage Frontier*, pp. 69–70.
29. Brands, *Lone Star Nation*, p. 309.
30. Garrett, *Green Flag over Texas*, p. 181.
31. Davis, *Lone Star Rising*, pp. 88–89, 126–127.
32. Sutherland Manuscript, CAH; Hardin, *Texian Iliad*, p. 42; Hansen, ed, *The Alamo Reader*, p. 157.
33. Roberts and Olson, *A Line in the Sand*, p. 109.
34. Santos, *Santa Anna's Campaign Against Texas*, pp. i 11.
35. Ibid., p.11
36. Levy, *American Legend*, pp. 38–41, 43, 49–52; Brands, *Lone Star Nation*, pp. 115–116.
37. Walker, *The Life of Andrew Jackson*, pp. Lxxiii–lxxv.
38. Boyd, *The Texas Revolution*, pp. 29, 59.
39. Levy, *American Legend*, pp. 39–40.
40. Stephenson, *Texas and the Mexican War*, p. 29; Groneman, *Alamo Defenders*, pp. 9, 50, 89, 120; Lord, *A Time to Stand*, p. 125.
41. Garrett, *Green Flag over Texas*, pp. 178–237; Woolsey, trans, *Memoirs For the History of the War in Texas*, pp. 21–33; Bradfield, *Rx Take One Cannon*, 99–100, 103.
42. Woolsey, trans., *Memoirs For the History of the War in Texas*, p. 33.
43. Brands, *Lone Star Nation*, p.349; McDonald, *William Barret Travis*, p. 86; Hopewell, *James Bowie*, p. 1; Hansen, ed., *The Alamo Reader*, pp. 15, 22. Robert E. Morsberger and Katharine M. Morsberger, *Lew Wallace: Military Romantic* (New York: McGrw-Hill, 1980), p. 23.
44. Lord, *A Time to Stand*, p. 49.
45. Davis, *Three Roads to the Alamo*, p. 445; Hardin, *Texian Iliad*, p. 117.
46. Huffines, *Blood of Noble Men*, p. 107.
47. Hardin, *Texian Iliad*, p. 135; Derr, *The Frontiersman*, p. 246; Davis, *Three Roads to the Alamo*, pp. 568–569; Santos, *Santa Anna's Campaign Against Texas*, p. 6; Barr, *Texans in Revolt*, p. 56.
48. *Telegraph and Texas Register*, March 5, 1836.
49. Winders, *Sacrificed at the Alamo*, pp. 14, 25.
50. Josephus, *The Jewish War* (Baltimore, Md: Penguin Books, 1959), p. 197; Thomas B. Marquis, Keep the Last Bullet for Yourself: The True Story of Custer's Last Stand, (Algonac: Reference Publications, 1985), pp. 172–179.
51. Josephus, *The Jewish War*, p. 200.
52. Ibid., p. 208.
53. Ibid., pp. 242, 358–361.
54. Nofi, *The Alamo*, p. 131; Josephus, *The Jewish War*, pp. 197–361; Groneman, *Alamo Defenders*, pp. 51, 122–123; l; Donald H. Harrison, *Louis Rose: San Diego's First Jewish Settler and Entrepreneur*, (San Diego: Sunbelt Publications, Inc., 2005), p. 25.
55. Nofi, *The Alamo*, p. 131; Harrison, *Louis Rose*, pp. 24–25.
56. Matovina, *The Alamo Remembered*, p. 27; Santos, *Santa Anna's Campaign Against Texas*, p. 4; Huffines, *Blood of Noble Men*, pp. 1–2.
57. Gaddy, *Revolt in Texas*, p. 16.
58. Levy, *American Legend*, p. 234; Groneman, *Alamo Defenders*, pp. 70, 94.
59. Lord, *A Time to Stand*, pp. 82–83; Groneman, *Alamo Defenders*, pp. 116–117, 120.
60. Jackson, *Alamo Legacy*, p. 24; Lord, *A Time to Stand*, pp. 21–23.
61. Jackson, *Alamo Legacy*, p. 33.
62. Winders, *Sacrificed at the Alamo*, pp. 43–44; Perry, ed. and trans., *With Santa Anna in Texas*, p. 99, note; Todish and Todish, *Alamo Sourcebook*, p. 139.
63. Perry, ed. and trans., *With Santa Anna in Texas*, pp. xvi, xx, 6; Winders, *Sacrificed at the Alamo*, p. 39; Hardin, *Texan Iliad*, p. 95.
64. Groneman, *Eyewitness to the Alamo*, p. 33; Huffines, *Blood of Noble Men*, p. 109; Winders, *Sacrificed at the Alamo*, p. 122; Perry, ed. and trans, *With Santa Anna in Texas*, p. 44–45; Brown, *Andrew Jackson and the Battle of New Orleans*, pp. 10–11; Lord, *A Time to Stand*, p. 139.
65. Perry, ed. and trans., *With Santa Anna in Texas*, pp. 44–45.
66. Santa Anna to McArdle, March 19, 1874, TSL and AC.

67. Perry, ed. and trans., *With Santa Anna in Texas*, p. 18.
68. Grady McWhiney and Perry Jameson, *Attack and Die: Civil War Military Tactics and the Southern Heritage*, (University, Alabama: University of Alabama Press, 1982), pp. 41–42.
69. *San Antonio Express*, June 23, 1878; Groneman, *Eyewitness to the Alamo*, pp. 13–14; Winders, *Sacrificed at the Alamo*, p. 126; Crawford, ed., *The Eagle*, pp. ix–xii; Huffines, *Blood of Noble Men*, p. 57; Perry, ed. and trans., *With Santa Anna in Texas*, p. 46.
70. *The Battle of San Jacinto* by Pedro Delgado, The McArdle Notebooks, Archives and Information Services Division, Texas State Library and Archives Commission, Austin, Texas; Borroel, ed. and trans., *Field Reports of the Mexican Army During the Texan War of 1836*, vol. iii, p. 21; Michel-Rolph Trouillot, *Silencing the Past: Power and the Production of History*, (Boston: Beacon Press, 1995), pp. 38–39.
71. Fisher to Austin, October 20, 1835, Center for American History, University of Texas, Austin, Texas; Perry, ed. and trans., *With Santa Anna in Texas*, p. 45.
72. Hardin, *Texian Iliad*, pp. 90–91, 136–137; Borroel, ed. and trans., *Field Reports of the Mexican Army in the Texan War of 1836*, vol. iii, pp. 31, 35–37; Perry, trans. and ed., *With Santa Anna in Texas*, pp. 44–45.
73. Winders, *Sacrificed at the Alamo*, p. 28; Borroel, *The Texan Revolution of 1836*, p. 54; Marshall-Cornwall, *Napoleon*, pp. 139–145.
74. Brands, *Lone Star Nation*, p. 141; Scheina, *Santa Anna*, pp 19–20; DePalo, *The Mexican National Army*, p. 36; Fowler, *Santa Anna of Mexico*, p. 9.
75. DePalo, *The Mexican National Army*, p. 38.
76. Fowler, *Santa Anna of Mexico*, pp. 159–160.
77. Sutherland Manuscript, CAH; Lundstrom, "Assault at Dawn," *Campaign*, p. 9; Roberts and Oslon, *A Line in the Sand*, p. 106; Brown, *The New Orleans Greys*, pp 75, 122–123; Hardin, *Texian Iliad*, p. xviii; Barr, *Texans in Revolt*, pp. 45–59; Perry, ed. and trans., *With Santa Anna in Texas*, p. 46; Lord, *A Time to Stand*, p. 159.
78. Sutherland Manuscript, CAH; Groneman, *Eyewitness to the Alamo*, p. 25.
79. Groneman, *Eyewitness to the Alamo*, p. 57; Fowler, *Santa Anna of Mexico*, p. 163; Smith, *Napoleon Against Russia*, p. 112.
80. Sutherland Manuscript, CAH; Winders, *Sacrificed at the Alamo*, p. 134; Hardin, *Texas Iliad*, p. 59.
81. Groneman, *Eyewitness to the Alamo*, p. 19; Perry, ed. and trans., *With Santa Anna in Texas*, p. 46.
82. Borroel, ed. and trans., *Field Reports of the Mexican Army During the Texan War of 1836*, vol. iv, p. 59; Huffines, *Blood of Noble Men*, p. 134; Perry, ed. and trans., *With Santa Anna in Texas*, pp. 46–47; Roberts and Olson, *A Line in the Sand*, p. 161.
83. Sutherland Manuscript, CAH; *Richmond Whig*, April 15, 1836; Groneman, *Eyewitness to the Alamo*, pp. 13–14; Roberts and Olson, *A Line in the Sand*, p. 161; Chartrand, *Santa Anna's Mexican Army*, p. 7; DePalo, *The Mexican National Army*, p. 50; Perry, ed. and trans., *With Santa Anna in Texas*, pp. 18, 46–47.
84. Kevin Young, editor, "The Siege of the Alamo: A Mexican Army Journal," *Journal of the Alamo Battlefield Association*, vol. iii, no. 1, (Fall 1998), p. 33; Levy, *American Legend*, pp. 177–178; Brands, *Lone Star Nation*, p. 366; Groneman, *Eyewitness to the Alamo*, pp. 13–14; Roger Borroel, editor and translator, *Field Reports of the Mexican Army During the Texan War of 1836*, (East Chicago, Indiana; "La Villita Publications," 2001), vol. iv, p. 59; Santos, *Santa Anna's Campaign Against Texas*, pp. 45–46; Chartrand, *Santa Anna's Mexican Army*, pp. 7–8, 12, 61; Perry, ed. and trans., *With Santa Anna in Texas*, pp. 8–9, 46; DePablo, *The Mexican National Army*, p. 24; Huffines, *Blood of Noble Men*, pp. 82–83.
85. *San Antonio Express*, June 23, 1878; Groneman, *Eyewitness to the Alamo*, pp. 14–15; Roberts and Olson, *A Line in the Sand*, pp. 67, 159; Winders, *Sacrificed at the Alamo*, p. 125; Hardin, *Texian Iliad*, p. 97; Borroel, ed. and trans., *Field Reports of the Mexican Army During the Texan War of 1836*, vol. vii, p. 52; Santos, *Santa Anna's Campaign Against Texas*, pp. 14, 74.
86. *San Antonio Daily Express*, June 23, 1878 and June 30, 1889; Winders, *Sacrificed at the Alamo*, pp. 46–47; Lundstrom, "Assault at Dawn," *Campaign*, p. 7; Chartrand, *Santa Anna's Mexican Army*, p. 18.

87. Crawford, ed., *The Eagle*, p. 50; Fowler, *Santa Anna of Mexico*, p. 160.
88. *San Antonio Daily Express*, June 30, 1889, Roberts and Olson, *A Line in the Sand*, p. 160; Hardin, *Texian Iliad*, p. 104; Salas, *Soldaderas*, pp. 29–30; Perry, ed. and trans, With Santa Anna in Texas, p. 68; DePalo, *The Mexican National Army*, p. 51.
89. *Washington Post*, Washington, D.C., May 5, 1907.
90. Borroel, ed. and trans., *Field Reports of the Mexican Army During the Texan War of 1836*, vol. iii, pp. 51, 53; Branding, *Mexican Phoenix*, 41, 74, 239.
91. Hansen, ed., *The Alamo Reader*, pp. 112–113.
92. *La Lima de Vulcano*, Mexico City, Mexico, April 30, 1836; Perry, ed. and trans., *With Santa Anna in Texas*, pp. xix, xx, 8, 44–45.
93. Huffines, *Blood of Noble Men*, p. 31.
94. Santos, *Santa Anna's Campaign Against Texas*, pp. 41, 44–45; Borroel, ed. and trans., *Field Reports of the Mexican Army During the Texan War of 1836*, vol. vi, pp. 22, 25–27, 34–35, 42; DePalo, *The Mexican National Army*, pp. 23–24, 41, 48; Kevin R. Young, "Understanding the Mexican Army," Kevin R. Young Papers, Rossville, Illinois.
95. General Joaquin Ramirez Sesma Report, March 11, 1836, Secretaria de la Defensa Nacional, Archivo Historico Militar Mexicano, Mexico City, Mexico; Jackson, *Alamo Legacy*, pp. 144–145; Lindley, *Alamo Traces*, p. 265.
96. *New York Times*, February 22, 1891; Lack, *The Texas Revolutionary Experience*, p. 244; Nelson, *The Alamo*, p. 32; Uniformology Research File, Weatherford, Texas; DePalo, *The Mexican National Army*, p. 31.
97. Hardin, *Texan Iliad*, p. 98.
98. Perry, ed. and trans, *With Santa Anna in Texas*, pp. 40, 45.
99. Sutherland Manuscript, CAH; Davis, *Three Roads to the Alamo*, p. 559.
100. Winders, *Sacrificed at the Alamo*, pp. 38–39; DePalo, *The Mexican National Army*, p. 50.
101. Hardin, *Texian Iliad*, pp. 137–138; Borroel, ed. and trans., *Field Reports of the Mexican Army During the Texan War of 1836*, vol. ii, 31.

Chapter 6: THE PREDAWN ASSAULT
1. Perry, ed. and trans., *With Santa Anna in Texas*, pp. 62–63; Hardin, *Texian Iliad*, p. 138; Smith, *Napoleon Against Russia*, p. 115.
2. Ibid., p. 42; Hart, *Strategy*, pp. 114–139.
3. Pedro Sanchez, March 4, 1836 letter, Box 2Q174, vol. 334, Center for American History, University of Texas, Austin, Texas; Levy, *American Legend*, p. 178; Borrell, ed. and trans., *Field Reports of the Mexican Army During the Texan War of 1836*, vol. iv, p. 60; Miguel A. Sanchez Lamego, *The Siege & Taking of the Alamo* (Santa Fe: The Press of the Territorian, 1968), pp. 35, 37.
4. Huffines, *Blood of Noble Men*, pp. 95, 137, 139; Groneman, *Eyewitness to the Alamo*, p. 19; Hansen, ed., *The Alamo Reader*, p. 47.
5. Jackson, *Alamo Legacy*, p. 33.
6. *San Antonio Express*, June 23, 1878; Groneman, *Eyewitness to the Alamo*, p. 20; Jackson, *Alamo Legacy*, p. 82; Borroel, ed. and trans., *Field Reports of the Mexican Army During the Texan War of 1836*, vol. iii, p. 33; Hardin, *Texian Iliad*, p. 138; Roberts and Olson, *A Line in the Sand*, 158; DePalo, *The Mexican National Army*, 24; Chartrand, *Santa Anna's Mexican Army*, p. 12; Santos, *Santa Anna's Campaign Against Texas*, p. 15; Perry, ed. and trans., *With Santa Anna in Texas*, p. 45; Borroel, *The Texan War of 1836*, p. 37; Huffines, *Blood of Noble Men*, p.130; Lamego, *The Siege & Taking of the Alamo*, p. 32.
7. *San Antonio Express*, June 23, 1878; *Frankfort Commonwealth*, Frankfort, Kentucky, May 25, 1836; Myers, The *Alamo*, p. 146; Roberts and Olson, *A Line in the Sand*, pp. 23–25, 158–159; Salas, *Soldaderas*, p. 25; Hardin, *Texian Iliad*, pp. 138–139; Perry, ed. and trans., *With Santa Anna in Texas*, pp. 45–46; Santos, *Santa Anna's Campaign Against Texas*, pp. 14–15; *Commercial Bulletin*, New Orleans, Louisiana, April 11, 1836; Lamego, *The Siege & Taking of the Alamo*, pp. 32–33, 35.
8. *Frankfort Commonwealth*, May 25, 1836; *Commercial Bulletin*, April 11, 1836; Hansen, ed., *The Alamo Reader*, p. 611; Winders, *Sacrificed at the Alamo*, p. 82.
9. Huffines, *Blood of Noble Men*, pp. 124, 127; Nelson, *The Alamo*, p. 46.

10. Borroel, ed. and trans., *Field Reports of the Mexican Army During the Texan War in 1836*, vol. iv, p. 56.

11. *Frankfort Commonwealth*, May 25, 1836; *Commercial Bulletin*, April 11, 1836; Perry, ed. and trans, *With Santa Anna* in Texas, p. 47; Huffines, *Blood of Noble Men*, pp. 125, 147; Borroel, ed. and trans., *Field Reports of the Mexican Army During the Texan War of 1836*, vol. iv, p. 55; Groneman, *Eyewitness to the Alamo*, pp. 21, 25; Hardin, *Texian Iliad*, pp. xviii,138–139; Rene Chartrand and Bill Younghusband, *The Portugese Army of the Napoleonic Wars*, vol. 2, (Oxford, England: Osprey Publishing Limited, 2000), p. 5; Hansen, ed., *The Alamo Reader*, p. 61.

12. *Commercial Bulletin*, April 11, 1836; *Frankfort Commonwealth*, May 25, 1836; Hansen, ed, *The Alamo Reader*, pp. 22–23, 611; Brown, *The New Orleans Greys*, pp. 173, 186, 188; William R. Chemerka, Director of The Alamo Society, to author, November 14, 2003; Lord, *A Time to Stand*, p. 159; Myers, *The Alamo*, p. 146; Groneman, *Eyewitness to the Alamo*, pp. 14, 21, 25; Davis, *Three Roads to the Alamo*, p. 558; Hardin, *Texian Iliad*, pp. xviii, 138–139, 147; Cooke Papers, DRT Library.

13. Sunderland Manuscript, CAH; Brown, *The New Orleans Greys*, p. 186; Lord, *A Time to Stand*, pp. 154–155; *Frankfort Commonwealth*, May 25, 1836; Goneman, *Alamo Defenders*, p. 11; Chemerka, *Alamo Anthology*, pp. 71–73; Groneman, *Eyewitness to the Alamo*, pp. 21, 25; Winders, *Sacrificed at the Alamo*, p. 125; Huffines, *Blood of Noble Men*, pp. 75, 122, 125–126; Hansen, ed., *The Alamo Reader*, p. 611; *Commercial Bulletin*, April 11, 1836.

14. *Frankfort Commonwealth*, May 25, 1836; Huffines, *Blood of Noble Men*, 147; Groneman, *Eyewitness to the Alamo*, pp. 21, 25; Hansen, ed., *The Alamo Reader*, p. 611; *Commercial Bulletin*, April 11, 1836.

15. Groneman, *Eyewitness to the Alamo*, p. 21.

16. *Frankfort Commonwealth*, May 25, 1836.

17. Jackson, *Alamo Legacy*, p. 93; Hansen, *The Alamo Reader*, pp. 97, 684.

18. Levy, *American Legend*, p. 279.

19. Groneman, *Eyewitness to the Alamo*, p. 25.

20. *Commercial Bulletin*, April 11, 1836; Lord, *A Time to Stand*, p. 155; *Memphis Enquirer*, April 14, 1836; *Frankfort Commonwealth*, May 25, 1836; Goneman, *Alamo Defenders*, p. 11; Chemerka, *Alamo Anthology*, p. 71; Groneman, *Eyewitness to the Alamo*, p. 25; Hardin, *Texian Iliad*, p. 143, 146–147; Hansen, ed. *The Alamo Read*, p. 611.

21. Lord, *A Time to Stand*, p. 155; Goneman, *Alamo Defenders*, p. 11.

22. *Frankfort Commonwealth*, May 25, 1836; *Commercial Bulletin*, April 11, 1836; Matovina, *The Alamo Remembered*, pp. 70–71, 82; Johnson, *A History of Texas and Texans*, pp. 412–413; Groneman, *Eyewitness to the Alamo*, pp. 21, 25.

23. Groneman, *Alamo Defenders*, p. 119; Hansen, ed., *The Alamo Reader*, p. 78.

24. *Frankfort Commonwealth*, May 25, 1836; *Commercial Bulletin*, April 11, 1836; Sutherland Manuscript, CAH; *San Antonio Daily Express*, April 28, 1881; Johnson, *A History of Texas and Texans*, pp. 412–413; Groneman, *Eyewitness to the Alamo*, pp. 21, 25; Hardin, *Texian Iliad*, pp. 1143, 146–147; Hansen, ed., *The Alamo Reader*, pp. 392–393, 611.

25. *Washington Post*, Washington, D.C., April 9, 1916; *Frankfort Commonwealth*, May 25, 1836; Hansen, ed., *The Alamo Reader*, p. 611; Kilgore, *How Did Davy Die?*, pp. 24–31.

26. *Commercial Bulletin*, April 11, 1836; Matovina, *The Alamo Remembered*, pp. 70–71, 82; Hardin, *The Alamo 1836*, pp. 40–41; Groneman, *Eyewitness to the Alamo*, pp. 14, 21, 25; Perry, ed. and trans., *With Santa Anna in Texas*, pp. 48–49; Borroel, ed. and trans., *Field Reports, of the Mexican Army During the Texan War of 1836*, vol. vi, p. 47; Hansen, ed., *The Alamo Reader*, pp. 392, 611; Huffines, *Blood of Noble Men*, p. 145.

27. Perry, ed., and trans., *With Santa Anna in Texas*, pp. 48–49; Lord, *A Time to Stand*, pp. 158–159

28. Perry, ed. and trans., *With Santa Anna in Texas*, pp. 13, 48–49, 96; Stephen Pope, *Dictionary of the Napoleonic Wars*, (New York: Facts on File, Inc., n.d.), pp. 264–265; Christopher Duffy, *Borodino and the War of 1812*, (London: Cassell and Company, 1972), p. 131; F. G. Hourtoulle, *Borodino-The Moskova*, The Battle for the Redoubts, (Paris, France: Histoire and Collections, 2000), p. 66; Groneman, *Alamo Defenders*, p. 63.

29. Jose Enrique de la Pena Papers, Center for American History, University of Texas, Austin, Texas; Perry, ed. and trans., *With Santa Anna in Texas*, pp. 9, 14, 26, 44, 46–49, 51, 53, 62–63, 148;

Borroel, ed. and trans, *Field Reports of the Mexican Army During the Texan War of 1836*, vol. vi, p. 47; Lundstrom, *"Assault at Dawn," Campaign*, p. 9; Roberts and Olson, *A Line in the Sand*, pp. 159, 164; Santos, *Santa Anna's Campaign Against Texas*, p. 14; Borroel, *The Texan War of 1836*, p. 77, note; Lord, *A Time to Stand*, p. 158.

30. *Frankfort Commonwealth*, May 25, 1836; Matovina, The Alamo Remembered, pp. 70-71, 82; Groneman, Eyewitness to the Alamo, pp. 14,21, 25; Lord, A Time to Stand, p. 159.

31. *Frankfort Commonwealth*, May 25, 1836; *Memphis Enquirer*, Memphis, Tennessee, April 12, 1836; Levy, American Legend, p. 279.

32. Levy, *American Legend*, p. 279; Groneman, *Eyewitness to the Alamo*, pp. 21, 25; Long, *Duel of Eagles*, pp. 34–35; Hansen, ed., *The Alamo Reader*, pp. 22–23.

33. Matovina, *The Alamo Remembered*, pp. 70–71, 83; Groneman, *Eyewitness to the Alamo*, pp. 21, 25; Perry, ed. and trans., *With Santa Anna in Texas*, pp. 44–45; Lord, *A Time to Stand*, p. 105.

34. *San Antonio Express*, February 24, 1929.

35. *Frankfort Commonwealth*, May 25, 1836; *Commercial Bulletin*, April 11, 1836; Matovina, *The Alamo Remembered*, pp. 70–71, 83; Hansen, ed., *The Alamo Reader*, pp. 22–23, 611.

36. *San Antonio Express*, April 28, 1881; *San Antonio Light*, November 26, 1911; Paul Andrew Hutton, "'It was but a Small Affair,' The Battle of the Alamo," *Wild West*, (February 2004), p. 47; Matovina, *The Alamo Remembered*, pp. 70–71; Groneman, *Eyewitness to the Alamo*, pp. 21, 25l; Roberts and Olson, *A Line in the Sand*, p. 157; Perry, ed. and trans., *With Santa Anna in Texas*, p. 49; Hansen, ed., *The Alamo Reader*, pp. 392–393.

37. *Frankfort Commonwealth*, May 25, 1836; Johnson, *A History of Texas and Texans*, pp. 412–413, 418; Boyd, *The Texas Revolution*, p. 36; Reid, *The Texan Army, 1835–46*, p. 13; Groneman, *Eyewitness to the Alamo*, pp. 21, 25; Lindstrom, *"Assault at Dawn," Campaign*, p. 17; Hansen, ed., *The Alamo Reader*, pp. 392–393.

38. Johnson, *A History of Texas and Texans*, pp. 412–413, 418; Lundstrom, *"Assault at Dawn," Campaign*, p. 17.

39. Groneman, *Eyewitness to the Alamo*, p. 75.

40. *San Antonio Express-News*, November 22, 1902.

41. *Commercial Bulletin*, April 11, 1836; *Frankfort Commonwealth*, May 25, 1836; Hansen, ed., *The Alamo Reader*, p. 611.

42. Chemerka, *Alamo Analogy*, pp. 66-67; Winders, *Sacrificed at the Alamo*, p. 126; Huffines, *Blood of Noble Men*, pp. 37, 143,165; Perry, ed. and trans, *With Santa Anna in Texas*, pp. 48, 50; Roberts and Olson, *A Line in the Sand*, pp. 127, 157; Borroel, *The Texas Revolution of 1836*, p. 49.

43. *Memphis Enquirer*, April 12, 1836; *San Antonio Light*, November 26, 1911; *San Antonio Express*, April 28, 1881; Sutherland Manuscript, CAH; Perry, ed. and trans., *With Santa Anna in Texas*, pp. 48, 50; Levy, *American Legend*, p. 279; Hardin, *Texian Iliad*, p. 139; Huffines, *Blood of Noble Men*, pp. 143, 145; Lord, *A Time to Stand*, p. 159.

44. Jackson, *Alamo Legacy*, pp. 30–32; Fehrenbach, *Lone Star*, pp. 164–165, 178; Hardin, *Texian Iliad*, p. 146; *Frankfort Commonwealth*, May 25, 1836; *Memphis Enquirer*, April 12, 1836; Hansen, ed., *The Alamo Reader*, p. 611; Borroel, *The Texan War of 1836*, p. 49.

45. *Frankfort Commonwealth*, May 25, 1836; Johnson, *A History of Texas and Texans*, p. 412.

46. Lundstrom, *"Assault at Dawn, The Mexican Army at the Alamo," Campaign*, p. 8; *Memphis Enquirer*, April 14, 1835; Craig H. Roell, *Remember Goliad!*, (Austin: Texas State Historical Association, 1994), p. 36; Barr, *Texans in Revolt*, pp. 13, 33, 54–56, 63; Nelson, *The Alamo*, p. 12; Perry, ed. and trans., *With Santa Anna in Texas*, p. 48.

47. Young, ed., *"The Siege of the Alamo: A Mexican Army Journal," JABA*, p. 32; Hansen, ed., *The Alamo Reader*, p. 393; Johnson, *A History of Texas and Texans*, p. 412; Huffines, *Blood of Noble Men*, p. 125.

48. Johnson, *A History of Texas and Texans*, pp. 412, 418; Chermerka, *Alamo Anthology*, pp. 65–66; Lundstrom, *"Assault at Dawn," Campaign*, p. 14.

49. *San Antonio Daily Express*, June 30, 1889; Groneman, *Eyewitness to the Alamo*, pp. 101–104.

50. *San Antonio Daily Express*, June 30, 1889; Huffines, *Blood of Noble Men*, p. 147; Perry, ed. and trans., *With Santa Anna in Texas*, p. 47.

51. *El Mosquito Mexicano*, April 5, 1836; Perry, ed. and trans., *With Santa Anna in Texas*, pp. 45, 47, 55–57, 59, 72, 95.

52. *San Antonio Daily Express*, June 30, 1889; Chemerka, *Alamo Anthology*, p. 67; Johnson, *A History of Texas and Texans*, p. 413; Winders, *Sacrificed at the Alamo*, p. 126; Perry, ed. and trans., *With Santa Anna in Texas*, pp. 48, 50; Huffines, *Blood of Noble Men*, pp. 37, 143, 147; Lord, *A Time to Stand*, p. 158; Long, *Duel of Eagles*, p. 246.

53. Perry, ed. and trans., *With Santa Anna in Texas*, pp. 48, 50; Huffines, *Blood of Noble Men*, pp. 37, 143.

54. *Memphis Enquirer*, April 14, 1836; Johnson, *A History of Texas and Texans*, pp. 412–413; Hardin, *Texian Iliad*, pp. 134, 146; Hansen, ed., *The Alamo Reader*, pp. 392–393.

55. Perry, ed. and trans., *With Santa Anna in Texas*, p. 49.

56. Ibid. pp. 44–45, 49–50; Huffines, *Men of Noble Blood*, pp. 130, 134, 141 152, 159; Niderost, "No Mercy!," *Military Heritage*, p. 65; Lindstrom, "Assault at Dawn," *Campaign*, p. 14; Sutherland Manuscript, CAH.

57. Matovina, *The Alamo Remembered*, pp. 68–71, 82; Johnson, *A History of Texas and Texans*, pp. 412–413; Winders, *Sacrificed at the Alamo*, p. 126.

58. Matovina, *The Alamo Remembered*, pp. 70–71, 82; Winders, *Sacrificed at the Alamo*, p. 126.

59. Matovina, *The Alamo Remembered*, p. 82.

60. Brininstool, *Troopers with Custer*, p. 81; Winders, *Sacrificed at the Alamo*, p. 127; Hardin, *Texian Iliad*, pp. 134–135; Borroel, *The Texan Revolution of 1836*, pp. 63, 92; Huffines, *Blood of Noble Men*, p. 134; Perry, ed. and trans., *With Santa Anna in Texas*, pp. 47, 49–50.

61. Hansen, ed., *The Alamo Reader*, pp. 17–19, 21–23, 29, 35–38.

62. Santos, *Santa Anna's Campaign Against Texas*, pp. 36, 72–73; Levy, *American Legend*, p. 265; Johnson, *A History of Texas and Texans*, pp. 412–413; Chariton, *Exploring the Alamo Legends*, p. 65; McDonald, *William Barret Travis*, p. 86; Santa Anna to McArdle, March 19, 1874, TSL and AC; Wheelan, *Invading Mexico*, p. 46; Perry, ed. and trans, *With Santa Anna in Texas*, p. 42; Hardin, *Texian Iliad*, pp. 134–135.

63. McDonald, *William Barret Travis*, pp. 93, 175–176; Santa Anna to McArdle, March 19, 1874, TSL and AC; Hardin, *Texian Iliad*, pp. 134–135; Hansen, ed., *The Alamo Reader*, p. 630.

64. *New Orleans Post and Union*, New Orleans, Louisiana, March 28, 1836; *The New Yorker*, New York, New York, April 16, 1836; *Western Courier and Piqua Enquirer*, Piqua, Ohio, April 16, 1836; Groneman, *Defense of a Legend*, pp. 79–80; Derr, *The Frontiersman*, p. 248; Gaddy, *Texas in Revolt*, p. 47; Johnson, *A History of Texas and Texans*, pp. 412–413; *Columbia Observer*, Columbia, Tennessee, April 14, 1836; Chariton, *Exploring the Alamo Legends*, p. 65; Lindley, *Alamo Traces*, pp. 42–44; Hardin, *Texan Iliad*, p. 29; Santa Anna to McArdle, March 19, 1874, TSL and AC; Matovina, *The Alamo Remember*, p. 44; *Morning Commercial and New York Enquirer*, July 18, 1836; Paul Fregosi, *Dreams of Empire: Napoleon and the first world war, 1792–1815*, (New York: Carol Publishing Group, 1990), p. 211.

65. *Morning Courier and New York Enquirer*, New York, July 18, 1836; Smith, *Napoleon Against Russia*, pp. 224–225; *Western Courier and Pique Enquirer*, April 16, 1836; Gregg J. Dimmick, *Sea of Mud, The Retreat of the Mexican Army After San Jacinto: An Archeological Investigation*, (Austin, Texas: Texas State Historical Association, 2004), pp. 235–236; Fregosi, *Dreams of Empire*, p. 211.

66. Groneman, Defense of a Legend, p. 79.

67. Moore, Eighteen Minutes, pp. 45-46; Hansen, ed., The Alamo Reader, pp. 499, 512-518; Santos, Santa Anna's Campaign Against Texas, p. 87; Roberts and Olson, A Line in the Sand, pp. 169-170; Kilgore, How Did Davy Die?, p. 17.

68. General Sam Houston to Henry Raguet, March 13, 1836, Madge W. Hearne Collection, Texas State Library, Archives Division, Austin, Texas; Santos, *Santa Anna's Campaign Against Texas*, p. 87; Roberts and Olson, *A Line in the Sand*, pp. 169-171; Groneman, *Alamo Defenders*, pp. 35, 88–89; Kilgore, *How Did Davy Die?*, p. 17.

69. Ibid; Roberts and Olson, *A Line in the Sand*, p. 171.

70. *The New Yorker*, April 16, 1836.

71. Gaddy, *Texas in Revolt*, p. 47.

72. *New Orleans Post and Union*, March 28, 1836.

73. *Western Courier and Piqua Enquirer*, April 16, 1836.

74. *San Antonio Daily Express*, June 23, 1878; *Frankfort Commonwealth*, May 25, 1836;

Matovina, *The Alamo Remembered*, pp. 70–71, 82; Brown, *The New Orleans Greys*, p. 292; Santos, *Santa Anna's Campaign Against Texas*, p. 72; Perry, ed. and trans., *With Santa Anna in Texas*, pp. 44–45, 50-51; Hardin, *Texian Iliad*, p. 146; Hansen, ed., *The Alamo Reader*, pp. 82, 147; Roberts and Olson, *A Line in the Sand*, p. 156; Nelson, *The Alamo*, p. 111; Lord, *A Time to Stand*, p. 162.

75. *Frankfort Commonwealth*, May 25, 1836; *Commercial Bulletin*, April 11, 1836; Huffines, *Blood of Noble Men*, p. 175.

76. *San Antonio Express-News*, November 22, 1902; Lord, A Time to Stand, p. 105.

77. *San Antonio Daily Express*, June 23, 1878; Nelson, *The Alamo*, p. 49; Long, *Duel of Eagles*, p. 75; Lord, *A Time to Stand*, p. 105.

78. Groneman, *Eyewitness to the Alamo*, p. 20.

79. *Frankfort Commonwealth*, May 25, 1836; *San Antonio Daily Express*, June 23, 1878; Groneman, *Eyewitness to the Alamo*, p. 25; *Commercial Bulletin*, April 11, 1836; Hansen, ed., *The Alamo Reader*, p. 439; Lord, *A Time to Stand*, p. 163; Perry, ed. and trans., *With Santa Anna in Texas*, p. 49; Long, *Duel of Eagles*, p. 244.

80. Santa Anna to McArdle, March 19, 1874, TSL and AC.

81. *San Antonio Express-News*, San Antonio, Texas, November 22, 1902; Levy, *American Legend*, p. 279; Johnson, *A History of Texas and Texans*, pp. 412–413.

82. *San Antonio Express-News*, November 22, 1902; Lord, *A Time to Stand*, p. 24; Groneman, *Alamo Defenders*, p. 7.

83. *San Antonio Daily Express*, June 23, 1878; *San Antonio Express-News*, November 22, 1902; Perry, ed. and trans., *With Santa Anna in Texas*, p. 51; Borroel, ed. and trans., *Field Reports of the Mexican Army During the Texan War of 1836*, vol. iv, p. 60; Johnson, *A History of Texas and Texans*, pp. 412–413; Matovina, *The Alamo Remembered*, pp. 70–71, 82; Hardin, *Texian Iliad*, p. 147; Sesma Report, March 11, 1836, Secretaria de la Defensa Nacional, Archivo Historico Militar Mexicano.

84. Groneman, *Alamo Defenders*, p. 11.

85. *San Antonio Express-News*, November 22, 1902; Brown, *The New Orleans Greys*, p.186; Johnson, *A History of Texas and Texans*, pp. 412–413; Matovina, *The Alamo Remembered*, pp. 70–71, 82.

86. *San Antonio Express-News*, November 22, 1902; Howard R. Driggs and Sarah S. King, *Rise of the Lone Star: A Story of Texas Told by its Pioneers*, (New York: Frederick A. Stokes Company, 1936), p. 225; Matovina, *The Alamo Remembered*, pp. 70–71, 82.

87. *Frankfort Commonwealth*, May 25, 1836; *San Antonio Express-News*, November 22, 1902; Johnson, *A History of Texas and Texans*, pp. 412–413; Matovina, *The Alamo Remembered*, pp. 70–71, 82; *Commonwealth Bulletin*, April 11, 1836.

88. Borroel, ed. and trans., *Field Reports of the Mexican Army During the Texan War of 1836*, vol. iv, p. 60; Johnson, *A History of Texas and Texans*, pp. 412–413; Matovina, *The Alamo Remembered*, pp. 70–71, 82.

89. Perry, ed. and trans., *With Santa Anna in Texas*, pp. 49–50; Huffines, *Blood of Noble Men*, p. 145; Chemerka, *Alamo Anthology*, p. 72.

90. Perry, ed. and trans., *With Santa Anna in Texas*, pp. 49–50; Levy, *American Legend*, p. 281; Johnson, *A History of Texas and Texans*, pp. 412–413; Matovina, *The Alamo Remembered*, pp. 70–71, 82.

91. *San Antonio Express-News*, November 22, 1902; Perry, ed. and trans., *With Santa Anna in Texas*, pp. 49–50, 52.

92. Sesma Report, March 11, 1836, Secretaria de la Defensa Nacional, Archivo Historico Militar Mexicano; Perry, ed. and trans., *With Santa Anna in Texas*, p. 45; Johnson, *A History of Texas and Texans*, p. 413.

93. *San Antonio Express-News*, November 22, 1902; Groneman, *Eyewitness to the Alamo*, pp. 25, 80–81.

94. *Memphis Enquirer*, April 12, 1836; Perry, ed. and trans., *With Santa Anna in Texas*, p. 50; Sutherland Manuscript, CAH; Buchanan, *The Road to Guilford Courthouse*, p. 214; Matovina, *The Alamo Remembered*, pp, 70–71, 82.

95. *Memphis Enquirer*, April 12, 1836; Perry, ed. and trans, *With Santa Anna in Texas*, p. 50; Buchanan, *The Road to Guilford Courthouse*, p. 214.

96. Buchanan, *The Road to Guilford Courthouse*, p. 214; Rothenberg, *The Art of Warfare in the Age of Napoleon*, p. 63

97. Perry, ed. and trans., *With Santa Anna in Texas*, p. 45; Lindley, *Alamo Traces*, p. 45; Rothenberg, *The Art of Warfare in the Age of Napoleon*, pp. 64–65; Nelson, *The Alamo*, p. 111; Lord, *A Time to Stand*, p. 67.

98. Perry, ed. and trans., *With Santa Anna in Texas*, p. 45; Pohl, *The Battle of San Jacinto*, p. 27; Matovina, *The Alamo Remembered*, p. 82; Johnson, *A History of Texas and Texans*, p. 413; *Maryland Gazette*, November 5, 1835; Nelson, *The Alamo*, p. 111; Frederick Cook, *Journals of the Military Expedition of Major General John Sullivan* (Ann Arbor: University Microfilms, 1967), pp. 10, 29, 203.

99. Perry, ed. and trans., *With Santa Anna in Texas*, p. 45; Smith, *On to the Alamo*, p. vii; Johnson, *A History of Texas and Texans*, p. 413; Jean-Roch Coignet, *Captain Coignet: A Soldier of Napoleon and the Imperial Guard from the Italian Campaign to Waterloo* (London: Leonaur Ltd., 2007), p. 123; Ed Gilbert, *Frontier Militiamen in the War of 1812: Southwestern Frontier* (Oxford: Osprey Publishing, 2008), p. 54.

100. Groneman, *Eyewitness to the Alamo*, p. 109.

101. Sutherland Manuscript, CAH; *American-Statesman*, April 15, 2004; Perry, ed. and trans., *With Santa Anna in Texas*, p. 182; Huffines, *Blood of Noble Men*, pp. 88, 107; M. L. Crimmins, "American Powder's Part in Winning Texas Independence," *Southern Historical Quarterly*, vol. 52, no. 1, (July 1948) pp. 109–111; Borchardt, *"DuPont Marks Its Bicentennial,"* Chemistry Chronicles, pp. 43–46; Winders, *Sacrificed at the Alamo*, p. 94; Hardin, *Texian Iliad*, pp. 107–108; King, *James Clinton Neill*, pp. 81–82; Borroel, ed. and trans., *Field Reports of the Mexican Army During the Texan War of 1836*, vol. iii, p. 31-36; DePalo, *The Mexican National Army*, p. 34; Walraven and Walraven, *The Magnificent Barbarians*, p. 52; Hansen, ed., *The Alamo Reader*, p. 59.

102. *San Antonio Express*, June 23, 1878; Roberts and Olson, *A Line in the Sand*, pp. 165–166; Sesma Report, March 11, 1836, Secretaria de la Defensa Nacional, Archivo Historico Militar Mexicano; *Washington Post*, July 30, 1887; Huffines, *Blood of Noble Men*, pp. 37, 143, 165; Perry, ed. and trans., *With Santa Anna in Texas*, p. 46; Lindstrom, *"Assault at Dawn," Campaign*, pp. 14–15; *Washington Post*, July 30, 1887.

103. Jose Vincent Miñon Service Record, Latin American Library, Tulane University, New Orleans, Louisiana; Borroel, ed. and trans., *Field Reports of the Mexican Army During the Texan War of 1836*, vol. vi, 25–27, 34, 46, 50; Huffines, *Blood of Noble Men*, pp. 143, 152, 165; Niderost, *"No Mercy!," Military Heritage*, p. 65; Lindstrom, *"Assault at Dawn," Campaign*, pp. 14–15.

104. *Washington Post*, July 30, 1887; Roberts and Olson, *A Line in the Sand*, p. 130; Hansen, ed., *The Alamo Reader*, p. 522.

105. *Washington Post*, July 30, 1887; Hansen, ed., *The Alamo Reader*, p. 522.

106. Perry, ed. and trans., *With Santa Anna in Texas*, pp. 50, 52; Huffines, *Blood of Noble Men*, pp. 125, 165.

107. *San Antonio Express-News*, November 22, 1902; Brown, *The New Orleans Greys*, pp. 186–188; Johnson, *A History of Texas and Texans*, p. 413.

108. Sesma Report, March 11, 1836, Secretaria de la Defensa Nacional, Archivo Historico Militar Mexicano; Chemerka, *Alamo Anthology*, pp. 69, 71; Johnson, *A History of Texas and Texans*, p. 413; Groneman, *Eyewitness at the Alamo*, p. 30; Winders, *Sacrificed at the Alamo*, p. 126; Borroel, ed. and trans., *Field Reports of the Mexican Army During the Texan War of 1836*, vol. vi, pp. 43, 50; NPS historians, "18-pounder Revolutionary War Cannon," FSNM.

109. De la Pena, *With Santa Anna in Texas*, p. 50.

110. Sesma Report, March 11, 1836, Secretaria de la Defensa Nacional, Archivo Historico Militar Mexicano; Johnson, *A History of Texas and Texans*, pp. 413–414; Matovina, *The Alamo Remembered*, pp. 70–71, 82; Groneman, *Eyewitness to the Alamo*, p. 82.

111. Groneman, *Eyewitness to the Alamo*, p. 82; Borroel, ed. and trans., *Field Reports of the Mexican Army During the Texan War of 1836*, vol. iii, p. 36.

112. Groneman, *Eyewitness to the Alamo*, pp. 82, 90, 93.

113. Ibid., p. 82; Sesma Report, March 11, 1836, Secretaria de la Defensa Nacional, Achivo Historico Militar Mexicano; Huffines, *Blood of Noble Men*, pp. 176–179; Hansen, ed., *The Alamo Reader*, p. 163.

Chapter 7: FLIGHT RATHER THAN FIGHT
1. *Commercial Bulletin*, April 11, 1836; *Frankfort Commonwealth*, May 25, 1836; Hansen, ed., *The Alamo Reader*, p. 393; Roberts and Olson, *A Line in the Sand*, pp. 162, 165; Sesma Report, March 11, 1836, Secretaria de la Defensa Nacional, Archivo Historico Militar Mexicano.
2. Chemerka, Director of the Alamo Society, to author, November 14, 2003.
3. Johnson, *A History of Texas and Texans*, pp. 412–413; Perry, ed. and trans., *With Santa Anna in Texas*, p. 47; NPS historians, "18-pounder Revolutionary War Cannon," FSNM; Hansen, ed., *The Alamo Reader*, p. 392.
4. Hansen, ed., *The Alamo Reader*, pp. 392–394; Lord, *A Time to Stand*, pp. 85, 159–160.
5. *San Antonio Daily Express*, June 30, 1889; Chemerka, Director of The Alamo Society, to author, November 14, 2003; Hardin, *Texian Iliad*, p. 131; Hansen, ed., *The Alamo Reader*, pp. 392–393; Perry, ed. and trans., *With Santa Anna in Texas*, pp. 48, 50.
6. Sesma Report, March 11, 1836, Secretaria de la Defensa Nacional, Archivo Historico Militar Mexicano; Perry, ed. and trans., *With Santa Anna in Texas*, pp. 47–48; Hansen, ed., *The Alamo Reader*, pp. 392–393; Lord, *A Time to Stand*, 163.
7. Rothenberg, *The Art of Warfare in the Age of Napoleon*, p. 69.
8. Sesma Report, March 11, 1836, Secretaria de la Defensa Nacional, Archivo Historico Militar Mexicano, Rothenberg, *The Art of Warfare in the Age of Napoleon*, pp. 68–69; Perry, ed. and trans., *With Santa Anna in Texas*, p. 21.
9. Ibid; Borroel, ed. and trans., *Field Reports of the Mexican Army During the Texan War of 1836*, vol. iv, p. 60.
10. *San Antonio Express-News*, November 22, 1902; Sesma Report, March 11, 1836, Secretaria de la Defensa Nacional, Archivo Historico Militar Mexicano; Groneman, *Alamo Defenders*, pp. 9–10, 14–15, 41–42; Borroel, ed. and trans., *Field Reports of the Mexican Army During the Texan War of 1836*, vol. iv, p. 60.
11. *San Antonio Express*, June 23, 1878; Perry, ed., and trans., *With Santa Anna in Texas*, pp. 44–45.
12. Sutherland Manuscript, CAH; Groneman, *Eyewitness to the Alamo*, p. 34.
13. *San Antonio Express*, June 23, 1878; *Maryland Gazette*, November 5, 1835; Hardin, *Texian Iliad*, pp. xii, xiii, 6–7, 39; Sesma Report, March 11, 1836, Secretaria de la Defensa Nacional, Archivo Historico Militar Mexicano; Santos, *Santa Anna's Campaign Against Texas*, p. 60; Roberts and Olson, *A Line in the Sand*, pp. 24–25.
14. Sesma Report, March 11, 1836, Secretaria de la Defensa Nacional, Archivo Historico Militar Mexicano; Roberts and Olson, *A Line in the Sand*, p. 10; Groneman, *Eyewitness to the Alamo*, p. 76; Innes, *The Conquistadors*, pp. 12–21; Christopher Leslie Brown and Philip D. Morgan, *Arming Slaves: From Classical Times to the Modern Age*, (New Haven: Yale University Press, 2006), pp. 5–6; *Maryland Gazette*, November 5, 1835.
15. Sesma Report, March 11, 1836, Secretaria de la Defensa Nacional, Archivo Historico Militar Mexicano; *San Antonio Express*, June 23, 1878; Roberts and Olson, *A Line in the Sand*, pp. 23–25.
16. Levy, *American Legend*, pp. 51–52, 256, 276; Winders, *Sacrificed at the Alamo*, pp. 108–110.
17. Perry, ed. and trans., *With Santa Anna in Texas*, pp. 44–45, 50.
18. Brands, *Lone Star Nation*, pp. 367–368.
19. *San Antonio Daily Express*, June 23, 1878; Sesma Report, March 11, 1836, Secretaria de la Defensa Nacional, Archivo Historico Militar Mexicano; Groneman, *Eyewitness to the Alamo*, p. 75; Perry, ed. and trans., *With Santa Anna in Texas*, pp. 44–45.
20. Sesma Report, March 11, 1836, Secretaria de la Defensa Nacional, Archivo Historico Militar Mexicano; Davis, *Lone Star Rising*, p. 220.
21. Davis, *Three Roads to the Alamo*, p. 554.
22. *San Antonio Express-News*, November 22, 1902; Hansen, ed., *The Alamo Reader*, p. 370; *San Antonio Express*, San Antonio, Texas, June 23, 1878.
23. Huffines, *Blood of Noble Men*, p. 35; Santa Anna to McArdle, March 19, 1874, TSL and AC; Raphael, Founding Myths, pp. 1–7, 247–277; Perry, ed. and trans., *With Santa Anna in Texas*, pp. 44–45, 50; Lord, *A Time to Stand*, p. 80.
24. Sesma Report, March 11, 1836, Secretaria de la Defensa Nacional, Archivo Historico Militar Mexicano; *San Antonio Daily Express*, June 23, 1878; *San Antonio Express-News*, November 22,

1902; Borroel, ed. and trans., *Field Reports of the Mexican Army During the Texan War of 1836*, vol. Iv, p. 60: Perry, ed. and trans, *With Santa Anna in Texas*, pp. xix, xx, 21, 44–45; Roberts and Olson, *A Line in the Sand*, p. 162; Bradfield, *Rx Take One Cannon*, pp 23, 101; Groneman, *Alamo Defenders*, pp. 15, 68, 79; Lord, *A Time to Stand*, pp. 82, 153, 171.

25. *San Antonio Daily Express*, June 23, 1878; Sesma Report, March 11, 1836, Secretaria de la Defensa Nacional, Archivo Historico Militar Mexicano; Uecker, *The Archaeology of the Alamo*, pp. 40–41; Huffines, *Blood of Noble Men*, p. 126; *Maryland Gazette*, November 26, 1835; King, *James Clinton Neill*, p. 79.

26. *San Antonio Daily Express*, June 23, 1878; Sesma Report, March 11, 1836, Secretaria de la Defensa Nacional, Archivo Historico Militar Mexicano; De la Pena, *With Santa Anna in Texas*, p. 45; Roberts and Olson, *A Line in the Sand*, pp. 165–166; Hardin, *Texian Iliad*, p. 148.

27. Lundstrom, *"Assault at Dawn," Campaign*, pp. 12–14; Hutton, *"It was but a Small Affair," WW*, p. 46; Perry, ed. and trans., *With Santa Anna in Texas*, pp. 46–48; Lamego, *The Siege & Taking of the Alamo*, p. 33.

28. *San Antonio Daily Express*, June 23, 1878; Lundstrom, *"Assault at Dawn," Campaign*, p. 14; Perry, ed. and trans., *With Santa Anna in Texas*, pp. xix, xx, 21, 44–46.

29. *San Antonio Daily Express*, June 23, 1878; Sesma Report, March 11, 1836, Secretaria de la Defensa Nacional, Archivo Historico,Militar Mexicano; Matovina, *The Alamo Remembered*, p. 27; Perry, ed. and trans., *With Santa Anna in Texas*, pp. 44–45, 48; Hansen, ed., *The Alamo Reader*, p. 521.

30. *San Antonio Daily Express*, June 23, 1878; Sesma Report, March 11, 1836, Secretaria de la Defensa Nacional, Archivo Historico Militar Mexicano; *San Antonio Express-News*, November 22, 1902; Santos, *Santa Anna's Campaign Against Texas*, p. 74; Borrell, ed. and trans., *Field Reports of the Mexican Army During the Texan War of 1836*, vol. iv, p. 60; Perry, ed. and trans., *With Santa Anna in Texas*, pp 44–45.

31. *San Antonio Daily Express*, June 23, 1878; Garrett, *Green Flag over Texas*, pp. 223–229; Winders, *Sacrificed at the Alamo*, p. 125.

32. Perry, ed. and trans., *With Santa Anna in Texas*, p. 41.

33. Sesma Report, March 11, 1836, Secretaria de la Defensa, Archivo Militar Mexicano; *San Antonio Daily Express*, June 23, 1878; Hansen, ed., *The Alamo Reader*, p. 370; *San Antonio Daily Express*, June 23, 1878; Winders, *Sacrificed at the Alamo*, pp. xii, 57; *Maryland Gazette*, November 26, 1835; Hardin, *Texian Iliad*, p. 224; Huffines, *Blood of Noble Men*, p. 177 note.

34. *San Antonio Daily Express*, June 23, 1878; Huffines, *Blood of Noble Men*, p. 177 note; Borroel, *The Texan Revolution of 1836*, pp. 80–81.

35. *San Antonio Daily Express*, June 23, 1878; Sesma Report, March 11, 1836, Secretaria de la Defensa Nacional, Archivo Historico Militar Mexicano; Nelson, *The Alamo*, p. 54.

36. Sesma Report, March 11, 1836, Secretaria de la Defensa Nacional, Archivo Historico Militar Mexicano; *San Antonio Daily Express*, June 23, 1878; Lord, *A Time to Stand*, p. 118; Jackson, *Alamo Legacy*, pp. 88–90; Hansen, ed., *The Alamo Reader*, pp. 44–45, 313, 324; Perry, ed. and trans., *With Santa Anna in Texas*, pp. 44–45, 50; Groneman, *Alamo Defenders*, p. 118.

37. Chariton, *Exploring the Alamo Legends*, pp. 29, 32.

38. Sesma Report, March 11, 1836, Secretaria de la Defensa Nacional, Archivo Historico Militar Mexicano; *San Antonio Daily Express*, June 23, 1878; Nelson, *The Alamo*, p. 53; Huffines, *Blood of Noble Men*, p. 66.

39. Sesma Report, March 11, 1836, Secretaria de la Defensa Nacional, Archivo Historico Militar Mexicano; *San Antonio Daily Express*, June 23, 1878; Nelson, *The Alamo*, p. 53; Huffines, *Blood of Noble Men*, p. 66; Borroel, *The Texan Revolution of 1836*, p. 59.

40. Sesma Report, March 11, 1836, Secretaria de la Defensa Nacional, Archivo Historico Militar Mexicano; *San Antonio Daily Express*, June 23, 1878; *Maryland Gazette*, November 26, 1836; Priddy, *Across Our Wide Missouri*, vol. 1, p. 142; Nelson, *The Alamo*, pp. 8–9, 54; Borroel, *The Texan Revolution of 1836*, pp. 68, 70, 81; Matovina, *The Alamo Remembered*, pp. 106, 113; Lindstrom, *"Assault at Dawn," Campaign*, p. 14; Chartrand, *Santa Anna's Mexican Army*, p. 23; Huffines, *Blood of Noble Men*, p. 177 note; Engineer Green B. Jameson map, The Daughters of the Republic of Texas Library at the Alamo, San Antonio, Texas; Groneman, *Alamo Defenders*, pp. 76, 101–102; Lord, *A Time to Stand*, p. 15.

41. *San Antonio Express-News*, November 22, 1902.

42. Guerra, *The Missions of San Antonio*, p. 30; Nelson, *The Alamo*, pp. 31–32; Huffines, *Blood of Noble Men*, p. 5; Young, ed., *"The Siege of the Alamo: A Mexican Army Journal,"* *JABA*, p. 33; Matovina, *The Alamo Remembered*, p. 113.

43. Sesma Report, March 11, 1836, Secretaria de la Defensa Nacional, Archivo Historio Militar Mexicano; *San Antonio Daily Express*, June 23, 1878; Hansen, ed., *The Alamo Reader*, p. 370 and note 2; Nelson, *The Alamo*, pp. 4–5, 8–9; Borroel, *The Texan Revolution of 1836*, pp. 68, 70; James Gilchrist Benton sketch, "A view of the Alamo from the rear," Amos Carter Museum, Fort Worth, Texas; Matovina, *The Alamo Remembered*, p. 113; Lord, *A Time to Stand*, p. 15.

44. Sesma Report, March 11, 1836, Secretaria de la Defensa Nacional, Archivo Historico Militar Mexicano; *San Antonio Daily Express*, June 23, 1878; Hansen, ed., *The Alamo Reader*, p. 370; Huffines, *Blood of Noble Men*, p. 177 note; Borroel, *The Texan Revolution of 1836*, pp. 68, 70; Matovina, *The Alamo Remembered*, p. 113.

45. Sesma Report, March 11, 1836, Secretaria de la Defensa Nacional, Archivo Historico Militar Mexicano; *San Antonio Daily Express*, June 23, 1878; Hansen, ed., *The Alamo Reader*, p. 370; Salas, *Soldaderas*, pp. 29–30; Borroel, *The Texan Revolution of 1836*, pp. 68, 70, 81; Huffines, *Blood of Noble Men*, p. 177 note; Matovina, *The Alamo Remembered*, p. 113.

46. Sesma Report, March 11, 1836, Secretaria de la Defensa Nacional, Archivo Historico Militar Mexicano; *San Antonio Daily Express*, June 23, 1878; Winders, *Sacrificed at the Alamo*, pp. 16–18; Roberts and Olson, *A Line in the Sand*, p. 18; Borroel, *The Texan Revolution of 1836*, p. 35; Huffines, *Blood of Noble Men*, pp. 5–16 and 177 note; Dimmick, *Sea of Mud*, p. 7; Borroel, ed. and trans., *Field Reports of the Mexican Army During the Texan War of 1836*, vol. iii, p. 26; Santos, *Santa Anna's Campaign Against Texas*, p. 45; "Caminos de Guanajuanto," *American Airlines Mexo*, p. 40; Fowler, *Santa Anna of Mexico*, pp. xi, xxii, 9, 13, 20.

47. Sesma Report, March 11, 1836, Secretaria de la Defensa Nacional, Archivo Historico Militar Mexicano; Huffines, *Blood of Noble Men*, p. 177 note.

48. *San Antonio Daily Express*, June 23, 1878; *Maryland Gazette*, November 26, 1835; *San Antonio Daily Express*, February 24, 1929; Hansen, ed., *The Alamo Reader*, pp. 56, 457; Jackson, *Alamo Legacy*, pp. 85–88; Groneman, *Alamo Defenders*, p. 117; Huffines, *Blood of Noble Men*, pp. 2, 173, 175; Lord, *A Time to Stand*, p. 165; Winders, *Sacrificed at the Alamo*, p. 57; Hardin, *Texian Iliad*, p. 113; Hansen, ed., *The Alamo Reader*, p. 60.

49. *San Antonio Express-News*, November 22, 1902; *San Antonio Daily Express*, June 23, 1878; Huffines, *Blood of Noble Men*, p. 173

50. Huffines, *Blood of Noble Men*, pp. 173, 175; Lord, *A Time to Stand*, p. 166.

51. *San Antonio Express*, June 23, 1878; Matovina, *The Alamo Remembered*, pp. 55–56; *Maryland Gazette*, November 5, 1835.

52. *San Antonio Daily Express*, January 5, 1878; Sesma Report, March 11, 1836, Secretaria de la Defensa Nacional, Archivo Historico Militar Mexicano; Borroel, *The Texan Revolution of 1836*, p. 81; Matovina, *The Alamo Remembered*, p. 113.

53. Jackie R. Booker, *"Needed but Unwanted: Black Militiamen in Vera Cruz, 1760–1810,"* *The Historian*, vol. 55, issue 2, (1993) p. 259–277.

54. *San Antonio Daily Express*, June 23, 1878; Rothenberg, *The Art of Warfare in the Age of Napoleon*, p. 69; Joseph E. Chance, *Jefferson Davis's Mexican Regiment* (Jackson: University Press of Mississippi, 1991), p. 97.

55. *San Antonio Daily Express*, June 23, 1878; Gaddy, *Texas in Revolt*, p. 26.

56. *San Antonio Daily Express*, June 23, 1878; Sesma Report, March 11, 1836, Secretaria de la Defensa Nacional, Archivo Historico Mexicano; Secretaria de la Defensa, Archivo Historico Militar Mexicano; Nelson, *The Alamo*, p. 50; Borroel, *The Texan Revolution of 1836*, p. 81.

57. Nelson, *The Alamo*, pp. 50-51.

58. *San Antonio Daily Express*, June 23, 1878; DePalo, *The Mexican National Army*, p. 24; Borroel, *The Texan Revolution of 1836*, p. 81.

59. *San Antonio Daily Express*, June 23, 1878.

60. *San Antonio Daily Express*, June 23, 1878; *New York Times*, February 23, 1895; Fox, *Archaeology, History, and Custer's Last Battle*, pp. 49–60, 260–262, 267–269; Perry, ed. and trans., *With Santa Anna in Texas*, pp. 50–52; Fox, *Archaeology, History, and Custer's Last Battle*, pp.

46–50, 337.
61. *New York Times*, February 23, 1895.
62. Ibid; Huffines, *Blood of Noble Men*, pp. 2, 176–179; *New York Herald*, June 27, 1836; Long, *Duel of Eagles*, p. 244.
63. *San Antonio Express*, June 23, 1878.
64. *New York Herald*, June 27, 1836.
65. Rothenberg, *The Art of Warfare in the Age of Napoleon*, pp. 68–70; Matovina, *The Alamo Remembered*, p. 106; Perry, ed. and trans., *With Santa Anna in Texas*, p. xvi; Georges Blond, *La Grande Armée* (London: Arms and Armour, 1997), p. 279.
66. Stephen G. Fritz, *Frontsoldaten, The German Soldier in World War II* (Lexington, Ky: University Press of Kentucky, 1997), p. 70.
67. *San Antonio Express*, June 23, 1878; Hansen, ed., *The Alamo Reader*, p. 457; Uecker, *The Archaeology of the Alamo*, p. 41; Winders, *Sacrificed at the Alamo*, p. 117.
68. *San Antonio Express*, June 23, 1878; Hansen, ed., *The Alamo Reader*, p. 457; Lundstrom, "Assault at Dawn," *Campaign*, p. 10; Nelson, *The Alamo*, pp. 48, 107; Uecker, *The Archaeology of the Alamo*, pp. 25–28, 31–32, 34; Hardin, *Texian Iliad*, p. 148.
69. *San Antonio Daily Express*, June 23, 1878; Sesma Report, March 11, 1836, Secretaria de la Defensa Nacional, Archivo Historico Military Mexicano; Hansen, ed., *The Alamo Reader*, pp. 370, 477; Chemerka, *Alamo Anthology*, pp. 69–70; Groneman, *Alamo Defenders*, pp. 117–118; Walker, *The Life of Andrew Jackson*, p. 72.
70. Sesma Report, March 11, 1836, Secretaria de la Defensa Nacional, Archivo Historico Militar Mexicano; Borroel, ed., *The Texan Revolution of 1836*, pp. 68, 81.
71. Hansen, ed., *The Alamo Reader*, p. 477.
72. Ibid; *San Antonio Daily Express*, June 23, 1878.
73. *New York Herald*, June 27, 1836.
74. Borroel, *The Texan Revolution of 1836*, p. 81.
75. Sesma Report, March 11, 1836, Secretaria de la Defensa Nacional, Achivo Historico Militar Mexicano; Perry, eds and trans., *With Santa Anna in Texas*, p. 52.
76. Hansen, ed., *The Alamo Reader*, p. 477.
77. Hansen, ed., *The Alamo Reader*, p. 477; *San Antonio Daily Express*, June 23, 1878.
78. Ibid., p. 370.
79. Borroel, ed., *The Texan Revolution of 1836*, p. 81.
80. Sesma Report, March 11, 1836. Secretaria de la Defensa Nacional, Archivo Historico Militar Mexicano; Young, ed., "The Siege of the Alamo: A Mexican Army Journal," *JABA*, p. 34.
81. *San Antonio Express*, June 23, 1878; Hansen, ed., *The Alamo Reader*, p. 370.
82. Hansen, ed, *The Alamo Reader*, p. 371; Borroel, *The Texan Revolution of 1836*, pp. 81, 83.
83. Lundstorm, "Assault at Dawn," *Campaign*, n.p.; Borroel, *The Texan Revolution of 1836*, pp. 81–82.
84. Jackson, *Alamo Legend*, pp. 89–90.
85. *San Antonio Daily Express*, June 23, 1878; *San Antonio Express-News*, November 22, 1902; Lord, *A Time to Stand*, p. 161; Groneman, *Alamo Defenders*, pp. 74, 78–79; Huffines, *Blood of Noble Men*, p. 33, note.
86. Hansen, ed., *The Alamo Reader*, p. 48.
87. Perry, ed. and trans., *With Santa Anna in Texas*, p. 52; Hansen, ed., *The Alamo Reader*, p. 65; Huffines, *Blood of Noble Men*, pp. 173, 176.
88. *San Antonio Daily Express*, June 23, 1878; Borroel, *The Texan Revolution of 1836*, p. 69; Sesma Report, March 11, 1836, Secretaria de la Defensa Nacional, Archivo Historico Militar Mexicano.
89. Borroel, *The Texan Revolution of 1836*, p. 69; Hansen, ed., *The Alamo Reader*, p. 330.
90. Groneman, *Alamo Defenders*, pp. 47–48; Huffines, *Blood of Noble Men*, p. 23.
91. Hansen, ed., *The Alamo Reader*, p. 370.
92. Ibid; Hardin, *Texian Iliad*, pp. 112, 114.
93. Chemerka, *Alamo Anthology*, pp. 107–110; Perry, ed. and trans., *With Santa Anna in Texas*, pp. 48; Kilgore, *How Did Davy Die?*, p. 30; Utley, *Custer and the Great Controversy*, p. 112.
94. Hansen, *The Alamo Reader*, p. 371.
95. Ibid.

96. Groneman, *Eyewitness to the Alamo*, p. 100; Borroel, *The Texan Revolution of 1836*, pp. 47, 80–81, 83–85, 223; Kilgore, *How Did Davy Die?*, p. 38; Huffines, *Blood of Noble Men*, p. 3.

97. Perry, ed. and trans., *With Santa Anna in Texas*, p. 51; Long, *Duel of Eagles*, pp. 250, 252.

98. Borroel, *Field Reports of the Mexican Army During the Texan War of 1836*, Vol. IV, p. 60.

99. *San Antonio Daily Express*, June 23, 1878; Sesma Report, March 11, 1836, Secretaria de la Defensa Nacional, Archivo Historico Militar Mexicano; Matovina, *The Alamo Remembered*, pp. 48, 106; Groneman, *The Alamo Defenders*, pp. 5–6; Santos, *Santa Anna's Campaign Against Texas*, pp. 27–28, 32–33; Sutherland Manuscript, CAH.

100. Groneman, *Eyewitness to the Alamo*, p. 17.

101. Borroel, ed. and trans., *Field Reports of the Mexican Army During the Texan War of 1836*, vol. iv, p. 60.

102. Governor Joaquin de Munoz y Munoz circular to Vera Cruz's citizens, Box 2Q174, vol. 334, March 23, 1836, Center for American History, University of Texas, Austin, Texas.

103. Huffines, *Blood of Noble Men*, p. 179.

104. General Francisco Vital Fernandez to Secretary of War, February 15, 1836, Box 2Q174, vol. 334, Center for American History, University of Texas, Austin, Texas.

105. *El Mosquito Mexicano*, March 22, 1836.

106. *La Lima de Vulcano*, March 22, 1836.

107. Fowler, *Santa Anna of Mexico*, pp. 28–29.

Chapter 8: THE ALAMO'S MOST BITTER LEGACIES

1. Groneman, *Defense of a Legend*, p. 88; Hardin, *Texian Iliad*, p. 156.

2. Young, ed., "The Siege of the Alamo: A Mexican Army Journal," *JABA*, 33; Levy, *American Legend*, p. 273; Groneman, *Eyewitness to the Alamo*, p. 6; Hardin, *Texian Iliad*, p. 156; Nelson, *The Alamo*, p. 111.

3. Jackson, *Alamo Legacy*, p. 93.

4. Young, ed., "The Siege of the Alamo: A Mexican Army Journal," *JABA*, 32; Chariton, *Exploring the Alamo Legends*, p. 33; Nelson, *The Alamo*, p. 111.

5. Nelson, *The Alamo*, p. 54; Matovina, *The Alamo Remembered*, p. 106.

6. Sesma Report, March 11, 1836, Secretaria de la Defensa Nacional, Archivo Historico Militar Mexicano; Borroel, ed. and trans., *Field Reports of the Mexican Army During the Texan War of 1836*, vol. iv, p. 60; Huffines, *Blood of Noble Men*, pp 176–177; Murray Montgomery, "Eyewitness to the Battle of the Alamo, an Unidentified Mexican Soldier's Personal Account of the Historic Struggle," TexasEscapes.com; *San Antonio Daily Express*, June 23, 1878.

7. Hansen, ed., *The Alamo Reader*, p. 477.

8. Huffines, *Blood of Noble Men*, p. 31; Groneman, *Defense of a Legend*, p. 68.

9. Groneman, *Defense of a Legend*, p. 74.

10. Chariton, *Exploring the Alamo Legends*, pp. 30, 32; Bob Bowman, "The Alamo's Red River Connection," December 17, 2000, TexasEscapes.com.; Henry Warnell biography, Handbook of Texas Online; Hansen, ed., *The Alamo Reader*, p. 44–45, 313, 324.

11. Hansen, ed., *The Alamo Reader*, pp. 44–45.

12. *Arkansas Gazette*, March 29, 1836.

13. *New York Times*, February 23, 1895.

14. Borroel, ed. and trans., *Field Reports of the Mexican Army During the Texan War of 1836*, vol. iv, p. 60.

15. *Washington Post*, October 1, 1888; *San Antonio Daily Express*, June 23, 1878; Sesma Report, March 11, 1836, Secretaria de la Defensa Nacional, Archivo Historico Militar Mexicano.

16. Sesma Report, March 11, 1836, Secretaria de la Defensa Nacional, Archivo Historico Militar Mexicano; Huffines, *Blood of Noble Men*, pp. 176–177; *San Antonio Daily Express*, June 23, 1878.

17. Gary S. Zaboly, New York City, to author, April 4, 2008.

18. Borroel, *The Texan Revolution of 1836*, pp. 83–85.

19. Hansen, ed., *The Alamo Reader*, p. 64.

20. *El Mosquito Mexicano*, April 5, 1836; DePalo, *The Mexican National Army*, pp. 52, 64–65; Roberts and Olson, *A Line in the Sand*, p. 25.

21. *New York Herald*, April 12 and 14, 1836; Smith, *New York 1776*, p. 20; Fox, *Archaeology,*

History, and Custer's Last Battle, pp. 230, 255; McWhiney and Jameson, *Attack and Die*, p. 34.

22. *Maryland Gazette*, May 12, 1836.

23. Barr, *Texans in Revolt*, p. ix; Lindstrom, "Assault at Dawn," *Campaign*, p. 17.

24. Myers, *The Alamo*, p. 157.

25. *Memphis Enquirer*, Memphis, Tennessee, April 12, 1836.

26. Lindley, *Alamo Traces*, pp. 277–278.

27. Fehrenbach, *Lone Star*, p. 214.; Moore, *Eighteen Minutes*, p. 339.

28. *New York Herald*, June 27, 1836; Lord, *A Time to Stand*, p. 209.

29. Smith, *On to the Alamo*, p. 120.

30. Davis, *Three Roads to the Alamo*, p. 557.

31. Young, ed., "The Siege of the Alamo: A Mexican Army Journal," *JABA*, pp. 32–33; Walker, *The Life of Andrew Jackson*, p. 327.

32. Winders, *Sacrificed at the Alamo*, p. 127; Long, *Duel of Eagles*, pp. 244, 246; DePalo, *The Mexican National Army*, p. 52; Hansen, ed., *The Alamo Reader*, p. 392.

33. Long, *Duel of Eagles*, pp. 244, 246; Hansen, ed., *The Alamo Reader*, p. 392.

34. *San Antonio Daily Express*, June 30, 1889.

35. Jackson, *Alamo Legacy*, pp. 94–95; Hansen, ed., *The Alamo Reader*, p. 392.

36. Groneman, *Eyewitness to the Alamo*, p. 76; Hansen, ed., *The Alamo Reader*, p. 392; Huffines, *Blood of Noble Men*, p. 145; Lord, *A Time to Stand*, p. 158; Long, *Duel of Eagles*, p. 246.

37. Huffines, *Blood of Noble Men*, pp. 145, 155; William Ayers, "Fratricide: Can it be Stopped?," Global Security Library, Alexandria, Virginia; Hansen, ed., *The Alamo Reader*, p. 392

38. Groneman, *Eyewitness to the Alamo*, p. 14; Perry, ed. and trans., *With Santa Anna in Texas*, p. 48; Walker, The Life of Andrew Jackson, pp. 329, 367–368; Hansen, ed., The Alamo Reader, p. 392; Huffines, *Blood of Noble Men*, p. 155; Lord, *A Time to Stand*, p. 67.

39. Perry, eds., *With Santa Anna in Texas*, pp. 80–81.

40. D. Clark Wernecke, Texas Archeological Research Laboratory, University of Texas at Austin, Texas, paper and presentation "Forgotten Heroes of the Republic,"; Sesma Report, March 11, 1836, Secretaria de la Defensa Nacional, Archivo Historico Militar Mexicano.

41. Huffines, *Blood of Noble Men*, p. 147.

42. Nofi, *The Alamo*, pp. 135; Perry, ed. and trans., *With Santa Anna in Texas*, p. 47.

43. Perry, ed. and trans., *With Santa Anna in Texas*, p. 47; Lord, *A Time to Stand*, p. 158; Borroel, *The Texan War of 1836*, p. 63.

44. Long, *Duel of Eagles*, p. 146; Perry, ed. and trans., *With Santa Anna in Texas*, p. 46, 49.

45. San Luis Battalion Logbook, Jose Enrique De la Pena Papers, UT; Nofi, *The Alamo*, p. 135; Hansen, ed., *The Alamo Reader*, p. 392.

46. Perry, ed. and trans., *With Santa Anna in Texas*, p. xxii; Borroel, ed. and trans., *Field Reports of the Mexican War During the Texan War of 1836*, vol. p. 55; Long, *Duel of Eagles*, pp. 146, 244; Hansen, ed., *The Alamo Reader*, pp. 392–393.

47. Sutherland Manuscript, CAH; Roger Borroel, editor and translator, *Papers of Lt. Col. Jose Enrique de la Pena* (East Chicago, Indiana: "La Villita Publications," 2001), vol. ii, p. 33.

48. *El Mosquito Mexicano*, April 5, 1836.

49. R. Borroel, ed. and trans., *Field Reports of the Mexican Army during the Texan War of 1836*, vol. iv, (East Chicago, In.: "La Villita Publications," 2001), pp. 53, 56, 60.

50. *New York Herald*, June 27, 1836; Borroel, ed. and trans., *Field Reports of the Mexican Army during the Texan War of 1836*, vol. iv, pp. 53, 56, 60.

51. Nofi, *The Alamo*, pp. 135–136; Borroel, ed. and trans., *Field Reports of the Mexican Army during the Texan War of 1836*, vol. iv, pp. 53, 56, 60.

52. Lindstrom, "Assault at Dawn," *Campaign*, p. 17.

53. Chariton, *Exploring the Alamo Legends*, p. 224; Lindley, *Alamo Traces*, p. 265; Hansen, ed., *The Alamo Reader*, p. 341.

54. Groneman, *Eyewitness to the Alamo*, p. 34.

55. Lindley, *Alamo Traces*, p. 265; Hansen, ed., *The Alamo Reader*, p. 511.

56. Scheina, *Santa Anna*, p. 28.

57. Nelson, *The Alamo*, p. 49.

58. Borroel, ed. and trans., *Field Reports of the Mexican Army during the Texan War of 1836*, vol.

iv, p. 56; Borroel, ed. and trans., *Papers of Lt. Col. Jose Enrique de la Pena*, vol. ii, p. 33; Nofi, *The Alamo*, pp. 135–136; Chariton, *Exploring the Alamo Legends*, p. 224.

59. *New York Herald*, June 27, 1836; Chariton, *Exploring the Alamo Legends*, p. 224; Groneman, *Eyewitness to the Alamo*, p. 34; Jackson, "Santa Anna's 1836 Campaign," *Journal of South Texas*, p. 12; Todish and Todish, *Alamo Sourcebook*, pp. 113, 165; Lamego, *The Siege & Taking of the Alamo*, p. 39.

60. Perry, ed., and trans, *With Santa Anna in Texas*, p. 54.

61. Ibid., pp. 47–51, 55; *New York Herald*, June 27, 1836; Hansen, ed., *The Alamo Reader*, p. 392; Jakie L. Pruett and Everett B. Cole, Sr., *Goliad Massacre: A Tragedy of the Texas Revolution* (Austin: Eakin Press, 1985), p. 143.

62. Shackford, *David Crockett*, p. 235; Kilgore, *How Did Davy Die?*, pp. 30, 39.

63. Shackford, *David Crockett.*, p. 229.

64. Sesma Report, March 11, 1836, Secretaria de la Defensa Nacional, Archivo Historico Militar Mexicano; *New York Times*, December 15, 1907; Levy, *American Legend*, pp. 146–149, 164, 181–182; Sutherland Manuscript, CAH.

65. Sesma Report, March 11, 1836, Secretaria de la Defensa Nacional, Archivo Historico Militar Mexicano; *New York Times*, December 15, 1907; Shackford, *David Crockett*, p. 235.

66. Groneman, *Defense of a Legend*, pp. 1–153.

67. Gaddy, *Texas in Revolt*, p. 51.

68. Santos, *Santa Anna's Campaign Against Texas*, p. 9; Perry, ed. and trans., *With Santa Anna in Texas*, pp. xii, 21.

69. Groneman, *Eyewitness to the Alamo*, p. 80; Jackson, "Santa Anna's 1836 Campaign," *Journal of South Texas*, p. 28; Hardin, *Texian Iliad*, p. 250.

70. Brear, *Inherit the Alamo: Myth and Ritual at an American Shrine*, pp. ix–4; Hardin, *Texian Iliad*, p. 250.

71. Richard R. Flores, *Remembering the Alamo: Memory, Modernity, and the Master Symbol* (Austin, Texas: University of Texas Press, 2002), pp. xvi–xvii, 3–12, 33–34, 60, 70–82. 95; Hardin, *Texian Iliad*, p. 250.

72. *Clarksville Standard*, Clarksville, Texas, March 4, 1887; Hardin, *Texian Iliad*, pp. 28, 83; Santos, *Santa Anna's Campaign Against Texas*, p. 4; Borroel, ed. and trans., *Field Reports of the Mexican Army During the Texan War of 1836*, vol. iii, pp. 71–72; Flores, *Remembering the Alamo*, p. 32; Lozano, *Viva Tejas*, pp. 71–75; Roberts and Olson, *A Line in the Sand*, pp. 215–216.

73. *The Telegraph and Texas Register*, January 9, 1836; Flores, *Remembering the Alamo*, pp. xvi–xvii, 3–12, 33–34, 47, 60, 70–82, 95.

74. Brear, *Inherit the Alamo*, pp. 8–17; Hardin, *Texian Iliad*, p. 250

75. Lack, *The Texas Revolutionary Experience*, pp. 250–252, 263–265; Hardin, *Texian Iliad*, p. 250.

76. *New York Times*, December 15, 1907; Larry P. Knight, "Defending the Unnecessary: Slavery in San Antonio in the 1850s," *Journal of South Texas*, vol. 15, no. 1 (Spring 2002) p. 57; Adam Robinson, *Slave Country, American Expansion and the Origins of the Deep South* (Cambridge, Mass: Harvard University Press, 2005), pp. ix–35, 188–224.

77. Charles Ball, *Fifty Years in Chains* (New York: Dover Publications, Inc., 1970), pp. vii–viii.

78. Alwyn Barr and Robert A. Calvert, editors, *Black Leaders, Texans For Their Times* (Austin: Texas State Historical Association, 1981), pp. 30–31; Barr, *Black Texans*, pp. 6–7.

79. Barr, *Black Texans*, pp. v, 3, 11–12.

80. Ibid., pp. 3, 5–8.

81. Long, *Duel of Eagles*, p. 272.

82. Robin G. Osterweis, *Romanticism and Nationalism in the Old South* (New Haven: Yale University Press, 1949), p. 50.

83. Fowler, *Santa Anna of Mexico*, pp. 174–175.

84. Ibid., p. 182.

85. Mirabeau B. Lamar to Jefferson Lamar, April 10, 1836, Mirabeau B. Lamar Papers, No. 351, Archives and Information Services Division, Texas State Library and Archives Commission, Austin, Texas; Sutherland Manuscript, CAH; Sutherland Manuscript, CAH; Perry, ed., and trans., *With Santa Anna in Texas*, p. 53.

86. Typescript Diary of Major John P. Gaines, Journals and Diaries Folder, 1846, Missouri Historical Society, St. Louis, Missouri; Sutherland Manuscript, CAH.
87. Weems and Weems, *Dream of Empire*, pp. 67–75
88. Trouillot, *Silencing the Past*, pp. 1–2.

Chapter 9: FLAMES RISING HIGH
1. Groneman, *Eyewitness to the Alamo*, p. 76; Sesma Report, March 11, 1836, Secretaria de la Defensa Nacional, Archivo Historico Militar Mexicano; Huffines, *Blood of Noble Men*, pp. 176–179; *San Antonio Daily Express*, June 23, 1878.
2. Parish Death Records, January–March 1836, San Fernando Church, CAT; Ridley, Maximilian and Juarez, p. 8; Uecker, *The Archaeology of the Alamo*, p. 73; *San Antonio Daily Express*, June 30, 1889; Nelson, *The Alamo*, pp. 4–5; Sesma Report, March 11, 1836, Secretaria de la Defensa Nacional, Achivo Historico Militar Mexicano
3. Borroel, ed. and trans., *Field Reports of the Mexican Army in the Texan War of 1836*, vol. vii, p. 52; Matovina, *The Alamo Remembered*, p. 104; Nelson, *The Alamo*, p. 54; Valerie Menard, "Remember the Cottonwood?," *Texas Park and Wildlife Magazine*, (March 2006).
4. Matovina, *The Alamo Remembered*, pp. 104–105.
5. Nelson, *The Alamo*, pp. 5, 54; Santos, *Santa Anna's Campaign Against Texas*, p. 77; *The Telegraph and Texas Register*, March 28, 1837.
6. Derr, *The Frontiersman*, p. 252; Uecker, *The Archaeology of the Alamo*, p. 9; Nelson, *The Alamo*, 55; Hansen, ed., *The Alamo Reader*, p. 47.
7. Jackson, *Alamo Legacy*, pp. 151–152; Groneman, *Alamo Defenders*, p. 109.
8. *The Telegraph and Texas Register*, March 24, 1836.
9. Davis, *Land!*, p. 130.
10. *The Telegraph and Texas Register*, August 2, 1836.
11. The Groneman, *Alamo Defenders*, p. 71.
12. *The Telegraph and Texas Register*, July 7, 1838; Nelson, *The Alamo*, p. 111.
13. Groneman, *Alamo Defenders*, pp. 33, 53–54.
14. *The Telegraph and Texas Register*, December 8, 1838.
15. *The Telegraph and Texas Register*, November 16, 1836.
16. Ibid., May 26, 1837; *Frankfort Commonwealth*, May 25, 1836.
17. Nelson, *The Alamo*, p. 57; Santos, *Santa Anna's Campaign Against Texas*, p. 78; Huffines, *Blood of Noble Men*, p. 3.
18. Parish Burial Documents, Campo Santo, Catholic Archives, San Antonio, Texas; Perry, ed. and trans, *With Santa Anna in Texas*, pp. 55, 63; Parish Death Records, January–March 1836, San Fernando Church, CA.
19. Matovina, *The Alamo Remembered*, p. 40.
20. Perry, ed. and trans, *With Santa Anna in Texas*, p. 55.
21. *The Telegraph and Texas Register*, March 28, 1837; Sutherland Manuscript, CAH.
22. *The Telegraph and Texas Register*, March 28, 1837.
23. Uecker, *The Archaeology of the Alamo*, p. 9.
24. Scheina, *Santa Anna*, pp. 25–26; Hardin, *Texian Iliad*, pp. 188,191, 248.
25. Scheina, *Santa Anna*, p. 29.
26. Jackson, "Santa Anna's 1836 Campaign," *Journal of South Texas*, p. 32; Lord, *A Time to Stand*, p. 163; Perry, ed. and trans., *With Santa Anna in Texas*, p. 49.
27. Gaddy, *Texas in Revolt*, p. 75.
28. Ibid., p. 78.
29. Ibid., p. 49.
30. Jackson, "Santa Anna's 1836 Campaign," *The Journal of South Texas*, pp. 11–33.
31. Winders, *Sacrificed at the Alamo*, pp. 94–95.
32. "The Battle of San Jacinto," by Colonel Pedro Delgado, TSL and AC.
33. Lack, *The Texas Revolutionary Experience*, pp. 244, 246; Moore, *Eighteen Minutes*, pp. 389–390, 392.
34. Chariton, *Exploring the Alamo*, pp. 1–3, 6–17.
35. "The Battle of San Jacinto" by Colonel Pedro Delgado, TSL and AC.

36. *Maryland Gazette*, May 12, 1836; Huffines, *Blood of Noble Men*, pp. 176–179; Sesma Report, March 11, 1836, Secretaria de la Defensa Nacional, Archivo Historico Militar Mexicano.
37. Sutherland Manuscript, CAH; Crisp, *Sleuthing the Alamo*, pp. 140–141, 144; Sesma Report, March 11, 1836, Secretaria de la Defensa Nacional, Archivo Historico Militar Mexicano; Huffines, *Blood of Noble Men*, pp. 176–179; Allen Brown, "Trying for the Truth about the Alamo," *American Heritage*, (November/December 2003), AmericanHeritage.com.
38. *New York Times*, December 15, 1907; Gaddy, *Texas in Revolt*, p. 53.
39. Derr, *The Frontiersman*, pp. 267–268; Nelson, *The Alamo*, p. 111.
40. Johnson, *A History of Texas and Texans*, pp. 416–417.
41. Flores, *Remembering the Alamo*, p. xv.
42. Crisp, *Sleuthing the Alamo*, 178.
43. Sesma Report, March 11, 1836, Secretaria de la Defensa Nacional, Archivo Historico Militar Mexicano; Huffines, *Blood of Noble Men*, pp. 176–177, 179.

Bibliography

Manuscript Sources

Alamo Vertical Files, Texas State Library and Archives, Austin, Texas.

Alamo Vertical Files, Barker Texas History Center, University of Texas, Austin, Texas.

Archivo Historico Militar Mexicano, Secretaria de la Defensa Nacional, Mexico City, Mexico. Expediente XI, 481.3, 1149; Expediente XI, 481.3, 1151; Expediente XI, 481.3, 1655; Expediente XI, 481.3, 1900.

Army and Navy Chronicle, New York, New York.

Francisco Paredas y Arrillaga to Minister of War Jose M. Tornell, June 10, 1836, Center for American History, Box 2Q174, vol. 334.

William Ayers. "Fratricide: Can it be Stopped?" Global Security Library, Alexandria, Virginia.

Roger Borroel, trans. "The Last Testament of Santa Anna," Verz Cruz, Mexico, September 26, 1867, Roger Borroel Collection, East Chicago, Indiana.

William R. Chemerka, Director of the Alamo Society, to author, November 14, 2003.

William G. Cooke Papers, Daughters of the Republic of Texas Library at the Alamo, San Antonio, Texas.

Typescript Diary of Major John P. Gaines, Journals and Diaries Folder, 1846, Missouri State Historical Society, St. Louis, Missouri.

General Sam Houston to Henry Raguet, March 13, 1836, Madge W. Hearne Collection, Texas State Library, Archives Division, Austin, Texas.

Mirabeau B.Lamar to Jefferson Lamar, April 10, 1836, Mirabeau B. Lamar Papers, no. 351, Archives and Information Services Division, Texas State Library and Archives Commission, Austin, Texas.

Parish Death Records, January to March 1836, San Fernando Church, San

Antonio, Texas, Catholic Archives of Texas, Austin, Texas.

Pedro Delgado, "The Battle of San Jacinto," The McArdle Notebooks, Archives and Information Services Division, Texas State Library and Archives Commission, Austin, Texas.

Elizabeth A. Fenn, to author, April 8, 2004.

General Francisco Vital Fernandez to Secretary of War, February 15, 1836, Box 2Q174, vol. 334, Center for American History, University of Texas, Austin, Texas.

General Jose Antonio Fernandez, December 30, 1835 notice, Matamoros Archives, Box 2Q266, vol. iv, Center for American History, University of Texas, Austin, Texas.

George Fisher to Stephen Austin, October 20, 1836, Center for American History, University of Texas, Austin, Texas.

Gordon C. Jennings Biographical Sketch, Jennings Heritage Project, Washington, D.C.

Frank W. Johnson to W. A. McArdle, November 27, 1837, *The McArdle Notebooks*, Archives and Information Services Division, Texas State Library and Archives Commission, Austin, Texas.

Jeff Milan to H. A. McArdle, January 2, 1991, *The McArdle Notebooks*, Archives and Information Services Division, Texas State Library and Archives Commission, Austin, Texas.

Santa Anna to Harry Arthur McArdle, March 19, 1874, *The McArdle Notebooks,* Archives and Information Services Division, Texas State Library and Archives Commission, Austin, Texas.

Jose Vincent Minon Service Record, Latin American Library, Tulane University, New Orleans, Louisiana.

National Park Historians, "18-pounder Revolutionary War Cannon," Fort Moultrie, National Park Service File, Fort Sumter National Monument, Charleston, South Carolina.

Governor Jaoquin de Munoz y Munoz circular to Vera Cruz's citizens, Box 2Q174, vol. 334, March 23, 1836, Center for American History, University of Texas, Austin, Texas.

José Juan Sanchez Navarro, Daughters of the Republic of the Texas Library at San Antonio, Texas.

Parish Burial Documents, Campo Santo, Catholic Archives, San Fernando Church, San Antonio, Texas.

Parish Death Records, January to March 1836, San Fernando Church, San Antonio, Texas, Catholic Archives, Austin, Texas.

Jose Enrique de la Pena Papers, Center for American History, University of Texas, Austin, Texas.

R. R. Royall to Stephen Austin, October 16, 1835, The Moses and Stephen

F. Austin Papers, 1765-1889, Center for American History, University of Texas, Austin Texas.

Pedro Sanchez, March 4, 1836 letter, Box 2Q174, vol. 334, Center for American History

Major Samuel Spotts Monument File, Chalmette National Military Park, Chalmette, Louisiana.

San Luis Battalion Logbook, Jose Enrique de la Pena Papers, Center for American History, University of Texas, Austin, Texas.

General Joaquin Ramirez Sesma Report, March 11, 1836, Secretaria de la Defensa Nacional, Archivo Historico Militar Mexicano, Mexico City, Mexico.

"St. Valentine's Day; or, The Fair Maid of Perth," Edinburgh University Library, Edinburgh University, Edinburgh, Scotland.

John Sutherland Manuscript, "Fall of the Alamo," Amelia W. Williams Papers, Center for American History, University of Texas, Austin, Texas.

Robert L. Tarin, Jr., Papers, Southwest Collection, Texas Tech University, Lubbock, Texas.

Uniformology Research Files, Weatherford, Texas.

D. Clark Wernecke, Texas Archeological Research Laboratory, University of Texas at Austin, Texas, paper and presentation "Forgotten Heroes of the Republic."

Kevin R. Young, "Understanding the Mexican Army," Kevin R. Young Papers, Rossville, Illinois.

Kevin R. Young, "Finding a Face: El Soldado Mexicano, 1835–1848," Palo Alto Battlefield Park Archives, Brownsville, Texas.

Gary S. Zaboly, New York City, to author, April 4, 2008.

Newspapers

American Statesman, Austin, Texas.
Arnold-Imperial Leader, Arnold, Missouri.
Clarksville Standard, Clarksville, Texas.
Columbia Observer, Columbia, Tennessee.
Commercial Bulletin, New Orleans, Louisiana.
Connecticut Herald, New Haven, Connecticut.
Edmonton Sun, Edmonton, Canada.
El Censor, Vera Cruz, Mexico.
El Cosmopolita, Mexico City, Mexico.
El Mosquito Mexicano, Mexico City, Mexico.
El Nacional, Mexico City, Mexico.
Enquirer, Richmond, Virginia.

Frankfort Commonwealth, Frankfort, Kentucky.
Imprenta Del Mercurio de Matamoros, Matamoros, Mexico.
La Lima de Vulcano, Mexico City, Mexico
Maryland Gazette, Annapolis, Maryland.
Memphis Enquirer, Memphis, Tennessee.
Missouri Gazette, St. Louis, Missouri.
Morning Courier and *New York Enquirer*.
New Orleans Advertiser, New Orleans, Louisiana.
New Orleans Post and *Union, New Orleans, Louisiana*.
New York Herald, New York, New York.
New York Times, New York, New York.
Niles' National Weekly Register, Baltimore, Maryland.
Richmond Whig, Richmond, Virginia.
San Antonio Daily Express, San Antonio, Texas.
San Antonio Express, San Antonio, Texas.
San Antonio Express News, San Antonio, Texas.
San Antonio Ledger, San Antonio, Texas.
San Antonio Light, San Antonio, Texas.
St. Louis Republican, St. Louis, Missouri.
The Catholic Telegraph, Cincinnati, Ohio.
The New Yorker, New York, New York.
The Royal Gazette, New York, New York.
The Telegraph and Texas Register, Columbia, Texas.
The Texas Republican, Brazoria, Texas.
Toledo Blade, Toledo, Ohio.
Washington Post, Washington, D.C.
Western Courier and Piqua Enquirer, New York New York.

Published Sources

Aitken, Hugh G. J. *Did Slavery Pay?* Boston: Houghton Mifflin Company, 1971.

Alden, John R. *A History of the American Revolution*. New York: Da Capo Press, 1969.

Bannon, John Frances. *The Spanish Borderlands Frontier, 1513–1821*. New York: Holt, Rhinehart and Winston, 1970.

Barker, Eugene and Williams, Amelia W., eds. 8 vols. *The Writings of Sam Houston, 1813–1863*.

Barr, Alwyn. *Black Leaders, Texans For Their Times*. Austin: Texas State Historical Association, 1981.

Barr, Alwyn. *Black Texans, A History of African Americans in Texas, 1528–1995*. Norman: University of Oklahoma Press, 1996.

Barr, Alwyn, *Texans in Revolt, The Battle for San Antonio, 1835.* Austin: University of Texas Press, 1990.

Bartlett, Thomas; Dawson, Kevin; Keogh, Daire. *The 1798 Rebellion, An Illustrated History.* Niwot: Roberts Rhinehart Publishers, 1998.

Bennett, Herman L., *Africans in Colonial Mexico, Absolutism, Christianity, and Afro-Creole.* Bloomington: Indiana University Press, 2003.

Binkley, William C. ed. *Official Correspondence of the Texas Revolution, 1835-1836.* New York: D. Appleton-Century Company, 1936.

Bisson, Terry. *Nat Turner.* New York: Chelsa House Publishers, 1988.

Boatner, Mark McKay, III. *Encyclopedia of the American Revolution.* New York: David McKay Company, Inc., 1966.

Bobrick, Benson. *Angel in the Whirlwind, The Triumph of the American Revolution.* New York: Penguin Books, 1997.

Borchardt, John K. "DuPont Marks Its Bicentennial." Chemistry Chronicles, vol. 11, no. 6, (June 2002).

Booker, Jackie R. "Needed but Unwanted: Black Militiamen in Vera Cruz, 1760–1810." The Historian, vol. 55, issue 2 (1993)

Borroel, Roger, trans. and ed. *Field Reports of the Mexican Army During the Texan War of 1836.* East Chicago: "LaVillita Publications," Vols. II–IV, 2001; Vols. VI–VII, 2006.

Borroel, Roger. *The Texan Revolution of 1836.* East Chicago: "La Villita Publications," 1989.

Bowman, Bob. "The Alamo's Red River Connection." December 17, 2000, TexasEscapes.com.

Boyd, Bob. *The Texas Revolution, A Day-by-Day Account.* San Angelo: Standard Times, 1986.

Bradford, Jane. *Rx Take One Cannon, The Gonzales Come & Take It Cannon of October 1835.* Shiner: Patrick J. Wagner Research and Publishing Company, 1981.

Brands, H. W. *Andrew Jackson.* New York: Anchor Books, 2006.

Brands, H. W. *Lone Star Nation, How a Ragged Army of Volunteers Won the Battle for Texas Independence–and Changed America.* New York: Doubleday, 2004.

Brear, Holly Beachley, *Inherit the Alamo, Myth and Ritual at an American Shrine.* Austin: University of Texas Press, 1995.

Brinkley, William C. *The Texas Revolution.* Austin: The Texas State Historical Association, 1979.

Brown, Allen. "Trying for the Truth about the Alamo." *American Heritage,* (November/December 2003), AmericanHeritage.com

Brown, Christopher Leslie and Morgan, Philip D. *Arming Slaves, From Classical Times to the Modern Age.* New Haven: Yale University Press,

2006.

Brown, Dee. *Andrew Jackson and the Battle of New Orleans*. New York: G. P. Putnam's Sons, 1972.

Brown, Gary. *The New Orleans Greys, Volunteers in the Texas Revolution*. Plano: Republic of Texas Press, 1999.

Buchanan, John. *The Road to Guilford Courthouse, The American Revolution in the Carolinas*. New York: John Wiley & Sons, Inc., 1997.

Campbell, Randolph B. *An Empire For Slavery, The Peculiar Institution in Texas*. Baton Rouge: Louisiana State University Press, 1989.

Carroll, Patrick J. *Blacks in Colonial Veracruz: Race, Ethnicity, and Regional Development*. Austin: University of Texas Press, 2001.

Carter, Samuel, III. *Blaze of Glory, The Fight for New Orleans, 1814–1815*. New York: MacMillan London Ltd., 1971.

Cartledge, Paul. *Thermopylae, The Battle that Changed the World*. Woodstock: The Overlook Press, 2006.

Castaneda, Carlos E. *The Mexican Side of the Texas Revolution*. Dallas: P.L. Turner Company, 1928.

Chambers, William Trout, and Kennamer, Lorrin, Jr. *Texans and Their Land*. Austin: Steck-Vaughn Company, 1963.

Chariton, Wallace O. *Exploring the Alamo Legends*. Plano: Wordware Publishing, Inc.,1990.

Chartrand, Rene. *Santa Anna's Mexican Army 1821–48*. Oxford: Osprey Publishing Limited, 2004.

Chasteen, John Charles. *Born in Blood and Fire, A Concise History of Latin America*. New York: W. W. Norton and Company, 2001.

Chemerka, William. *Alamo Anthology*. Austin: Eakin Press, 2005.

Chipman, Donald E. *Spanish Texas, 1519–1821*. Austin: University of Texas Press, 1992.

Coerver, Don M. and Hall, Linda B. *Tangled Destinies: Latin America and the United States*. Albuquerque: The University of New Mexico Press, 1999.

Cook, Bernard A. 2 vols. *Women and War, An Historical Encyclopedia from Antiquity to the Present, vol. 2*. Oxford: ABC CLIO, Inc., 2006.

Cooper, Leonard. *Many Roads to Moscow, Three Historic Invasions*. New York: Coward-McCann, Inc., 1968.

Copeland, Fayette. *Kendall of the Picayune*. Norman: University of Oklahoma Press, 1997.

Cornwall, James Marshall-, *Napoleon*. Princeton: D. Van Nostrand, 1967.

Crawford, Ann Fears, ed. *The Eagle, The Autobiography of Santa Anna*. Austin: State House Press, 1988.

Crimmins, M.L. "American Powder's Part in Winning Texas Independence." Southern Historical Quarterly, vol. 52, no. 1 (July 1948).

Crisp, James E. *Sleuthing the Alamo, Davy Crockett's Last Stand and Other Mysteries of the Texas Revolution*. Oxford: Oxford University Press, 2005.

Cronin, Vincent. *Napoleon*. New York: Harper Collins Publishers, 1994.

Cunliffe, Barry. *The Ancient Celts*. Oxford: Oxford University Press, 1997.

Curry, Andrew. "Custer's bluster, His courageous last stand may be a figment," *US News*, July 24, 2000.

Cusack, Mary Frances. *An Illustrated History of Ireland, From AD 400 to 1800*. London: Bracken Books, 1995.

Davis, Graham. *Land! Pioneers in Mexican and Revolutionary Texas*. College Station: Texas A & M Press, 2002.

Davis, William C. *Lone Star Rising, The Revolutionary Birth of the Texas Republic*. New York: The Free Pres, 2004.

Davis, William C. *The Pirates Laffite, The Treacherous World of the Corsairs of the Gulf*. New York: Harcourt, Inc., 2005.

Davis, William C. *Three Roads to the Alamo, The Lives and Fortunes of David Crockett, James Bowie, and William Barret Travis*. New York: Harper Collins Publishers, 1998.

De Bruhl, Marshall. *Sword of San Jacinto, A Life of Sam Houston*. New York: Random House. 1993.

Delderfield, R. F. *Napoleon's Marshals*. New York: Cooper Square Press, 2002.

DePalo, William A., Jr. *The Mexican National Army, 1822–1852*. College Station: Texas A & M Press, 1997.

Derr, Mark. *The Frontiersman, The Real Life and the Many Legends of Davy Crockett*. New York: William Morrow and Company, Inc., 1993.

Dimmick, Greg J. *Sea of Mud, The Retreat of the Mexican Army After San Jacinto, An Archeological Investigation*. Austin: Texas State Historical Association, 2004.

Dippie, Brian W. *Custer's Last Stand, The Anatomy of an American Myth*. Lincoln: University of Nebraska Press, 1994.

Dixon, Max. *The Wataugans, First "free and independent community on the continent."* Johnson City: Overmountain Press, 1976.

Draper, Lyman C. *King's Mountain and Its Heroes*. Johnson City: The Overmountain Press, 1996.

Driggs, Howard R. and King, Sarah S. *Rise of the Lone Star: A Story of Texas Told by its Pioneers*. New York: Frederick A. Stokes Company, 1936.

Dubois, Laurent. *Avengers of the New World, The Story of the Haitian Revolution*. Cambridge: Harvard University Press, 2004.

Duff, John B. And Mitchell, Peter M., eds. *The Nat Turner Rebellion, The Historical Event and the Modern Controversy*. New York: Harper & Row Publishers, Inc., 1971.

Dwyer, William M. *The Day is Ours! November 1776–January 1777: An Inside View of the Battles of Trenton and Princeton*. New York: Viking Press, 1983.

Editors of Life-Time Books. *The Texans, The Old West*. New York: Time-Life Books, 1975.

Editors of American Heritage, *Andrew Jackson, Soldier and Statesman*. New York: Harper and Row, 1963.

Fenn, Elizabeth A. *Pox Americana*. New York: Hill and Wang, 2001.

Fergusson, Erna. *Our South West*. New York: Knopf, 1946.

Flores, Richard R. *Remembering the Alamo, Memory, Modernity, and the Master Symbol*. Austin: University of Texas Press, 2002.

Forczyk, Robert. *Toulon 1793, Napoleon's first Great Victory*. Oxford: Osprey Publishing Limited, 2005.

Fowler, Will. *Santa Anna of Mexico*. Lincoln: Univ. of Nebraska Press, 2007.

Franklin, John Hope. *The Militant South, 1800–1861*. Chicago: University of Illinois Press, 1984.

Franklin, John Hope. *From Slavery to Freedom, A History of Negro Americans*. New York: Alfred A. Knopf, 1974.

Fehrenbach, T. R. *Lone Star, A History of Texas and Texans*. New York: Da Capo Press, 1968.

Fergusson, Erna. *Our South West*. New York: Knopf, 1946.

Fleming, Thomas. *Liberty! The American Revolution*. New York: Viking Press, 1997.

Fox, Richard Allen, Jr. *Archaeology, History, and Custer's Last Battle*. Norman: University of Oklahoma Press, 1993.

Gaddy, Jerry J. *Texas in Revolt, Contemporary Newspaper Account of the Texas Revolution*. Fort Collins: The Old Army Press, 1973.

Gardner, James Alexander. *Lead King: Moses Austin*. St. Louis: Sunrise Publishing Company 1980.

Garraty, John A. *The American Nation: A History of the United States to 1877*. New York: Harper Collins, 1971.

Garrett, Julia Kathryn. *Green Flag over Texas, The Story of the First War of Independence in Texas*. New York: Jenkins Publishing Company, 1939.

Gilbert, Ed. *Frontier Militiaman in the War of 1812: Southwestern Frontier*. Oord: Osprey Publishing, 2008.

Gleeson, David T. *The Irish of the South, 1815–1877*. Chapel Hill: University of North Carolina Press, 2001.

Goetzmann, William H. *When the Eagle Screamed, The Romantic Horizon in American Diplomacy, 1800–1860.* New York: John Wiley & Sons, Inc., 1966.

Graham, Richard. *Independence in Latin America, A Comparative Approach.* New York: McGraw-Hill Inc., 1994.

Groom, Winston. *Patriotic Fire, Andrew Jackson and Jean Laffite and the Battle of New Orleans.* New York: Alfred A. Knopf, 2006.

Groneman, Bill. *Alamo Defenders, A Genealogy: The People and Their Words.* Austin: Eakin Press, 1990.

Groneman, Bill. *Eyewitness to the Alamo.* Plano: Republic of Texas Press, 1996.

Guerra, Mary Ann Noonan. *Heroes of the Alamo and Goliad, Revolutionaries on the Road to San Jacinto and Texan Independence.* San Antonio: The Alamo Press, 1987.

Guerra, Mary Ann Noonan. *The Missions of San Antonio.* San Antonio: The Alamo Press, 1982.

Hanley, Thomas O'Brien. *The American Revolution and Religion.* Washington, D.C.: The Catholic University of America Press, 1971.

Hansen, Todd, ed. *The Alamo Reader, A Study in History.* Mechanicsburg: Stackpole Books, 2003.

Hardin, Stephen L. *Texian Illiad.* Austin: University of Texas Press, 1994.

Hardin, Stephen L, ed. "The Feliz Nunez Account and the Siege of the Alamo: A Critical Appraisal." *Southwestern Historical Quarterly*, vol. 94, no. 1. (July 1990).

Hart, B. H. Liddell. *Strategy.* New York: Alfred A. Knopf, 1984.

Hauck, Richard Boyd. *Davy Crockett, A Handbook.* Lincoln: University of Nebraska Press, 1982.

Harvey, Robert. *The War of Wars, The Great European Conflict, 1793–1815.* New York: Basic Books, 2006.

Heidler, David S. And Heidler, Jeanne T. eds. *Encyclopedia of the War of 1812.* Annapolis: Naval Institute Press, 2007.

Hickey, Donald R. *Don't Give Up the Ship, Myths of the War of 1812.* Chicago: University of Illinois Press, 2006.

Hopewell, Clifford. *James Bowie, Texas Fighting Man.* Austin: Eakin Press, 1994.

Horgan, Paul. *Great River, The Rio Grande in North American History.* Hanover: Wesleyan University Press, 1984.

Horsman, Reginald, *Race and Manifest Destiny, The Origins of American Racial Anglo-Saxonism.* Cambridge: Harvard University Press, 1981.

Huffines, Alan C. *Blood of Noble Men, The Alamo, Siege & Battle.* Austin: Eakin Press, 1999.

Hunt, Alfred N. *Haiti's Influence on Antebellum America, Slumbering Volcano in the Caribbean.* Baton Rouge: Louisiana State University Press, 1988.

Hutton, Paul Andrew. "'It was but a Small Affair,' The Battle of the Alamo," *Wild West*, (February 2004).

Innes, Hammond. *The Conquistadors.* New York: Alfred A. Knopf, 1969.

Jackson, Jack. *Imaginary Kingdom, Texas as Seen by the Rivera and Rubi Military Expeditions, 1727 and 1767.* Austin: University of Texas Press, 1992.

Jackson, Jack. "Santa Anna's 1836 Campaign: Was It Directed Toward Ethnic Cleanings!," *The Journal of South Texas*, vol. 15, no. 1, (Spring 2002).

Jackson, Ron. *Alamo Legacy, Alamo Descendants, Remember the Alamo.* Austin: Eakin Press, 1997.

Jelinek, Pauline. "War Stress Pushing Army Suicide Higher." Associated Press, August 16, 2007.

Jenkins, John H., ed. 10 vols. *Papers of the Texas Revolution.* Austin: Presidial, 1973.

Johnson, Frank W., *A History of Texas and Texans.* Chicago: 1914.

Josephus. *The Jewish War.* Baltimore: Penguin Books, 1959.

Kennedy, Billy. *The Scots-Irish in the Hills of Tennessee.* Londonderry: Causeway Press, 1995).

Kenny, Michael. *The 1798 Rebellion, Photographs and Memorabilia from the National Museum of Ireland.* Dublin: Country House, 1996.

Kilgore, Dan. *How Did Davy Die?* College Station: Texas A & M Press, 1978.

King, C. Richard. James Clinton Neill, *The Shadow Commander of the Alamo.* Austin: Eakin Press, 2002.

Knight, Larry P. "Defending the Unnecessary: Slavery in San Antonio in the 1850s," *Journal of South Texas*, vol. 15, no. 1, (Spring 2002).

Lack, Paul D. *The Texas Revolutionary Experience, A Political and Social History, 1835–1836.* College Station: Texas A & M University Press, 1992.

Lagermann, Robert and Manucy, Albert C. *The Long Rifle.* Washington, D.C.: Eastern Acorn Press, 1980.

Lamego, Miguel A. Sanchez. *The Siege & Taking of the Alamo.* Santa Fe: The Press of the Territorian, 1968.

Langguth, A. J., *Union 1812, The Americans Who Fought the Second War of Independence.* New York: Simon and Schuster, 2006.

Launius, Roger D. *Alexander William Doniphan, Portrait of a Missouri Moderate.* Columbia: University of Missouri Press, 1997.

Levy, Buddy. *American Legend, The Real-Life Adventures of David Crockett*. New York: Berkley Books, 2005.

Lindley, Thomas Ricks. *Alamo Traces, New Evidence and New Conclusions*. Lanham: Republic of Texas Press, 2003.

Linn, Joseph John. *Reminiscences of Fifty Years in Texas*. New York: D&J Sadler Company, 1883.

Litton, Helen. *Irish Rebellions, 1798–1916*. Niwot: The Irish American Book Company, 1998.

Lockhart, James and Schwartz, Stuart B. *Early Latin America, A History of Colonial America and Brazil*. New York: Cambridge University Press, 1983.

Long, Jeff. *Duel of Eagles, The Mexican and U.S. Fight for the Alamo*. New York: William Morrow, 1990.

Lorano, Ruben Rendon. *Viva Tejas, The Story of the Tejanos, The Mexican-born Patriots of the Texas Revolution*. San Antonio: The Alamo Press, 1985.

Lord, Walter. *A Time to Stand, A Chronicle of the Valiant Battle at the Alamo*. New York: Bonanza Books, 1987.

Lundstrom, John B. "Assault at Dawn: The Mexican Army at the Alamo." Campaign, no. 1, (Summer 1973).

MacDonald, Archie. *William Barret Travis*. Austin: Eakin Press, 1976.

Mahon, John. *History of the Second Seminole War*. Gainesville: University of Florida Press, 1973.

Marshall, Bruce. *Uniforms of the Alamo and the Texas Revolution*. Atglen: Schiffer Military History, 2003.

Martin, Joel W. *Sacred Revolt, The Muskogees' Struggle For a New World*. Boston: Beacon Press, 1991.

Marquis, Thomas B. *Keep the Last Bullet for Yourself, The True Story of Custer's Last Stand*. Algonac: Reference Publications, 1985.

McCardell, John. *The Idea of a Southern Nation*. New York: W. W. Norton and Company, inc., 1979.

McGuire, Thomas. *Battle of Paoli*. Mechanicsburg: Stackpole Books, 2000.

McWhiney, Grady and Jameson, Perry. *Attack and Die, Civil War Military Tactics and the Southern Heritage*. University: University of Alabama Press, 1982.

Menard, Valerie. "Remember the Cottonwood?" *Texas Park and Wildlife Magazine*, (March 2006).

Michener, James A. *The Eagle and the Raven*. Austin: State House Press, 1990.

Miller, Edward L., *New Orleans and the Texas Revolution*. College Station: Texas A & M University Press, 2004.

Miller, Kerby A; Schrier, Arnold, Boling, Bruce D, and Doyle, David N. *Irish Immigrants in the Land of Canaan, Letters and Memoirs from Colonial and Revolutionary America, 1675–1815.* Oxford: Oxford University Press, 2003.

Moore, Stephen L. *Eighteen Minutes, The Battle of San Jacinto and the Texas Independence Campaign.* Lanham: Republic of Texas Press, 2004.

Moore, Stephen L., *Savage Frontier, Rangers, Riflemen, and Indian Wars in Texas, vol. 1, 1835–1837.* Plano: Republic of Texas Press, 2002.

Montgomery, Murray. "Eyewitness to the Battle of the Alamo, An Unidentified Mexican Soldier's Personal Account of the Historic Struggle." TexasEscapes.com, September 5, 2001.

Motivina, Timothy M. *The Alamo Remembered, Tejano Accounts and Perspectives.* Austin: University of Texas Press, 1995.

Myers, John Myers. *The Alamo.* New York: Bantam Books, 1966.

Nelson, George. *The Alamo, An Illustrated History.* Uvalde: Aldine Books, 1998.

Niderost, Eric. "No Mercy!," *Military Heritage,* (February 2004).

Nofi, Albert A., *The Alamo and the Texas War for Independence,* September 30, 1835-April 21, 1836. Conshohocken: Combined Books, 1992.

Oates, Stephen B., ed. *Rip Ford's Texas.* Austin: University of Texas Press, 1998.

Osterweis, Robin G. *Romanticism and Nationalism in the Old South.* New Haven: Yale University Press, 1949.

Pakenham, Thomas. *The Year of Liberty, The Great Irish Rebellion of 1789.* London: Weidenfeld and Nicolson, 1997.

Patton, Charles. *Chalmette, The Battle of New Orleans, and How the British Nearly Stole the Louisiana Territory.* Bowling Green: Hickory Tales Publishing, 2001.

Perry, Carmen, trans. and ed., *With Santa Anna in Texas, A Personal Narrative of the Revolution by Jose Enrique de la Pena.* College Station: Texas A & M Press, 1975.

Pohl, James W. *The Battle of San Jacinto.* Austin: Texas State Historical Association, 1989.

Poole, Stanley Lane-. *The Story of the Moors of Spain.* Baltimore: Black Classics Press, 1990.

Pope, Stephen. Dictionary *of the Napoleonic Wars.* New York: Facts on File, Inc., 1991.

Popkin, Jeremy D. *Facing Racial Revolution, Eyewitness Accounts of the Haitian Revolution.* Chicago: University of Chicago Press, 2007.

Potter, Reuben M. *The Fall of the Alamo.* n. p. 1860.

Potter, Woodburne. *The War in Florida*. Baltimore: Lewis and Coleman, 1836.

Priddy, Bob. 3 vols. *Across Our Wide Missouri*. Jefferson City: Private printing, 1984.

Pruett, Jakie L. and Cole, Everett B., Sr. *Goliad Massacre: A Tragedy of the Texas Revolution*. Austin: Eakin Press, 1985.

Raphael, Founding *Myths, Stories That Hide Our Patriots*. New York: MJF Books, 2004.

Reid, Stuart. *The Texan Army, 1835–46*. Oxford: Osprey Publishing Limited, 2003.

Richardson, Robert. *Larrey, Surgeon to Napoleon's Imperial Guard*. London: Quiller Press, 1974.

Ridley, Jasper. *Maximilian and Juarez*. London: Phoenix Press, 1992.

Riehn, Richard K. *1812, Napoleon's Russian Campaign*. New York: John Wiley and Sons, 1991.

Roberts, Randy, and Olson, James S. *A Line in the Sand, The Alamo in Blood and Memory*. New York: The Free Press, 2001.

Robinson, Adam. *Slave Country, American Expansion and the Origins of the Deep South*. Cambridge: Harvard University Press, 2005.

Robinson, Cecil, ed. and trans. *The View from Chapultepec, Mexican Writes on the Mexican-American War*. Tucson: University of Arizona Press, 1989.

Roell, Craig H. *Remember Goliad!* Austin: Texas State Historical Association, 1994.

Rothenberg, Gunter E. *The Art of Warfare in the Age of Napoleon*. Bloomington: Indiana University Press, 1980..

Rothman, Adam. *Slave Country, American Expansion and the Origins of the Deep South*. Cambridge: Harvard University Press, 2005.

Rrading, D. A. *Mexican Phoenix, Our Lady of Guadalupe: Image and Tradition Across Five Centuries*. New York: Cambridge University press, 2002.

Salas, Elizabeth. *Soldaderas in the Mexican Military, Myth and History*. Austin: University of Texas Press, 2006.

Santos, Richard G. *Santa Anna's Campaign Against Texas, 1835–1836*. Waco: Texian Press, 1968.

Scheina, Robert L. *Latin America's Wars, The Age of the Caudillo, 1791–1899*. Washington, D.C.: Brassey's, Inc., 2003.

Scheina, Robert L. *Santa Anna, A Curse upon Mexico*. Washington, D.C. Brassey's Inc., 2002.

Schwoerer, Lois G. "No Standing Armies!," *The Antiarmy Ideology in Seventeenth Century England*. Baltimore: The John Hopkins University

Press, 1974.

Scotti, Anthony J. *Brutal Virtue, The Myth and Reality of Banastre Tarleton.* Bowie: Heritage Books, Inc. 2002.

Shackford, James Atkins. *David Crockett, The Man and the Legend.* Lincoln: University of Nebraska Press, 1986.

Smith, Digby. *Napoleon Against Russia. A Concise History of 1812.* Barnsley: Pen & Sword Military, 2004.

Smith, Richard Penn. *On to the Alamo, Colonel Crockett's Exploits and Adventures in Texas.* New York: Penguin Group, 2003.

Starling, Susanne. *Land, Is the Cry!.* Austin: Texas State Historical Association, 1998.

Stephenson, Nathaniel W. *Texas and the Mexican War.* New York: United States Publishers Association, Inc. 1978.

Tanner, Marcus. *Ireland's Holy Wars, The Struggle For a Nation's Soul, 1500–2000.* New Haven: Yale University Press, 2001.

Thonhoff, Robert H., *The Texas Connection with the American Revolution.* Austin: Eakin Press, 1981.

Todish, Tim J. and Todish, Terry S. *Alamo Sourcebook, 1836: A Comprehensive Guide to the Alamo and the Texas Revolution.* Austin: Eakin Press, 1998.

Tragle, Henry Irving. *The Southampton Slave Revolt of 1831.* New York: Vintage Books, 1973.

Tranie, J., Lachouque, Henry, and Carmigniani, J-C, *Napoleon's War in Spain, The French Peninsular Campaigns, 1807-1814.* London: Arms and Armour Press, 1982.

Trouillot, Michel-Rolph. *Silencing the Past, Power and the Production of History.* Boston: Beacon Press, 1995.

Tucker, Phillip Thomas. "Motivations of United States Volunteers During the Texas Revolution." *East Texas Historical Journal*, vol. 29, no. 1, (1991).

Tuchman, Barbara W. *The March of Folly, From Troy to Vietnam.* New York: Alfred A. Knopf, 1984.

Uecker, Herbert G. *The Archaeology of the Alamo.* Bulverde; Monte Comal Publications, 2001.

Utley, Robert M. and Washburn, Wilcomb E. *The American Heritage History of the Indian Wars.* New York: American Heritage Publishing Company, Inc., 1977.

Vincent, Theodore, G. *The Legacy of Vincent Guerrero, Mexico's First Black President.* Gainesville: University of Florida Press, 2001.

Walker, Alexander. *The Life of Andrew Jackson.* Philadephia: G. G. Evans Publisher, 1860.

Walraven, Bill, and Walraven, Marjorie K. *The Magnificent Barbarians, Little Told Tales of the Texas Revolution.* Austin: Eakin Press, 1993.

Webb, James. *Born Fighting, How the Scots-Irish Shaped America.* New York: Broadway Books, 2004.

Weems, John Edward and Weems, Jane. *Dream of Empire, A History of the Republic of Texas, 1836–1846.* New York: Barnes & Nobles, 1995.

Wheelan, Joseph. *Invading Mexico, America's Continental Dream and the Mexican War, 1846–1848.* New York: Carroll and Graf Publishers, 2007.

Winders, Richard Bruce. *Sacrificed at the Alamo. Tragedy and Triumph in the Texas Revolution.* Abilene: State House Press, 2004.

Winston, James E. "Kentucky and the Texas Revolution." *Southwestern Historical Quarterly,* vol 16, (1912).

Woolsey, Wallace, trans. *Memoirs for the History of the War in Texas, Don Vincente Filisola.* Austin: Eakin Press, 1985.

Young, Kevin. ed. "The Siege of the Alamo: A Mexican Army Journal." *Journal of the Alamo Battlefield Association,* vol. iii, no. 1, (Fall 1998).

Index

White, Walter C., 140
Williams, Amelia W., 4
Williams, Ezekiel, 83
Williamson, Robert McAlpin, 40
Wilson, David L., 59
Winders, Richard Bruce, 313
Wolfe, Abraham, 34
Wolfe, Anthony, 180, 299
Wolfe, Benjamin, 34

Wolfe, Michael, 34

Yorba, Eulalia, 282

Zaboly, Gary S., 300, 308
Zacatecas, Mexico, 71-74, 137, 147,
    161-162, 166, 188, 195-196, 198,
    258, 260, 270, 336
Zuber, William P., 2-3, 305